Drugs in America

Drugs in America

A Documentary History

EDITED BY

David F. Musto, M.D.

New York University Press

NEW YORK AND LONDON

NEW YORK UNIVERSITY PRESS
New York and London

Library of Congress Cataloging-in-Publication Data
Drugs in America : a historical reader / [compiled by] David F.
Musto.
p.cm.
Includes bibliographical references and index.
ISBN 0-8147-5662-X (alk. paper) — ISBN 0-8147-5663-8 (pbk. : alk.
paper)
1. Substance abuse—United States—History. 2. Substance
abuse—United States—History—Sources. 3. Alcoholism—
United States—History. 4. Alcoholism—United States—History—Sources. 5. Drug abuse—United States—History. 6. Drug abuse—United States—History—Sources.
I. Musto,David F., 1936–
HV4999.2 .D78 2002
362.29'0973—dc21   2001059192

New York University Press books are printed on acid-free paper,
and their binding materials are chosen for strength and durability.

Manufactured in the United States of America

10 9 8 7 6 5 4 3 2 1

This book is dedicated to John B. McDiarmid, Edward C. Roosen-Runge,
Erling J. Ordal, Theodore C. Ruch, and James W. Haviland

Contents

      Marihuana: A Psychiatric Study   441
      Walter Bromberg

70   The La Guardia Report   452
      The Marihuana Problem in the City of New York   452
      Mayor's Committee on Marihuana
      The *Journal of the American Medical Association*
          Attacks the La Guardia Report   458

71   Recommending a "Discouragement Policy"   460
      Marijuana: A Signal of Misunderstanding   460
      National Commission on Marihuana and Drug Abuse

72   Long-Term Effects Uncertain   478
      Report on the Health-Related Effects of Marijuana   478
      Institute of Medicine

73   The Legalization of Marijuana: Hearings   484
      Opinion and Recommended Ruling on the Marijuana
          Rescheduling Petition   484
      U.S. Department of Justice, Drug Enforcement
          Administration
      Denial of Marijuana Scheduling Petition   494
      U.S. Department of Justice, Drug Enforcement
          Administration

74   Medical Legalization of Marijuana   534
      Statement by the Director of the Office of National Drug
          Control Policy   534
      Barry R. McCaffrey

75   Therapeutic Benefits and Health Risks of Marijuana   542
      Marijuana and Medicine: Assessing the Science Base   542
      Janet E. Joy, Stanley J. Watson, and John A. Benson

76   Scientific Research on Marijuana   552
      White House Drug Policy Office Issues Statement
          on Institute of Medicine's Report on Marijuana and
          Medicine   552

      Sources and Permissions   555
      Index   561
      About the Editor   575

Acknowledgments

After teaching the history of drugs and alcohol for more than three decades, I think it is appropriate to publish documents that trace the changing attitudes toward these substances. The idea for this book, however, came not from me but from Stephen Magro, editor at New York University Press. He has been a most helpful advisor and guide in compiling these readings.

I also am indebted to Cynthia Wells, formerly of Yale University Press, who has been my research associate during the preparation of the book. Her expertise at editing, as well as the precise care she has given to the texts, introductions, and details such as obtaining permissions for republication, has been deeply appreciated. Ms. Wells was aided by both Gretchen Krueger and, for a shorter period, Kari Theobald, energetic and reliable graduate students in the history of medicine. Ms. Krueger also served as an outstanding teaching fellow for several years in the course from which these readings arise. My work on the volume was aided by a Senior Scientist award, grant K05 DA00219, from the National Institute on Drug Abuse.

The mentors to whom this book is dedicated have had a profound influence on my life and career, for which I am grateful.

David F. Musto, M.D.

Editor's Note

In the documents presented here I have omitted all footnotes or parenthetical citations that were not relevant to the excerpts. Where necessary I have added clarifications in square brackets. For those who are interested in consulting the original, complete texts, full citations are listed in the "Sources and Permissions" section.

Part I

Alcohol

Introduction

The purpose of this anthology is to illustrate the changing assumptions and attitudes that have dramatically shifted control of alcohol and other drugs from use to abstinence and back again to use. Recurrent anti-alcohol/drug movements in the United States exhibit a remarkable similarity; through careful reading of documents from the past one can gain an insight into the nature of these powerful movements. Such an understanding is particularly useful now because since about 1980 we have been entering the third such movement in our nation's history. Will it end with some extreme position that evokes a backlash, as did Prohibition, or will it end with a sustainable attitude toward drugs and alcohol?

Throughout the history of the United States, popular attitudes and legal responses regarding the consumption of mood-altering substances have oscillated from toleration to disapproval and back again in cycles roughly the length of a lifetime. Few contemporary Americans, today so concerned about the abuse of illegal drugs, are aware that opiate use, for example, was also a burning issue for their grandparents or great-grandparents in the first decades of the twentieth century. Similarly, popular attitudes toward alcohol have moved gradually from periods in which it is regarded as a beverage with a safe upper limit of use to the point where it is seen as a poison. In the case of alcohol, in the period immediately following the American Revolution, a generally favorable view of the health benefits and food value of alcoholic beverages coincided with levels of consumption that far exceeded anything registered in modern times. But even as consumption of alcohol was reaching unprecedented levels, an awareness of the damage done to individuals and society by drink emerged, and a countermovement was born. This first temperance movement culminated in 1855, by which date thirteen states and territories had prohibited the sale and manufacture of alcoholic beverages.

Soon, however, the anti-alcohol movement lost ground and, due to popular resentment and the absorption of reforming energies in the Civil War, state prohibition laws were almost all ignored, found unconstitutional, or repealed. Though in eclipse, the movement never completely disappeared. It emerged again at the end of the nineteenth century, when the conditions that created the Progressive Era again favored health and reform movements, including a new appraisal of alcohol as a source of social and personal deterioration. The great accomplishment of that second temperance movement was the Eighteenth Amendment to the Constitution and the Volstead Act of 1919, excerpts of which are included in the anthology.

It now appears that we are experiencing the third temperance era. About 1980 we started to drink less alcohol, a drop of 15 percent by the early 1990s. The biggest drop has been in distilled spirits, especially the darker beverages like scotch and bourbon. Wine use also waned, and in 1990 per capita wine consumption fell even in California. Beer has fallen less, but nonalcoholic brews—an echo of licit beer during Prohibition—have been rising in popularity.

Alcohol, Driving, and Youth: How the Modern Temperance Era Began

Our shifting attitude is apparent in a glance at the changes in drinking age. In 1971 the Twenty-sixth Amendment to the Constitution—the most rapidly ratified amendment in the nation's history—lowered the voting age to eighteen. Soon many state legislatures were lowering the drinking age to conform with the voting age, but then, beginning about 1980, a countermovement started rolling back the drinking age to twenty-one. Taking away drinking rights from voters might seem an unlikely venture, but the movement was popular, even among many in the eighteen-to-twenty-one-year-old target group.

Finally in June 1984 the federal government, which cannot itself set the drinking age, enacted a law that would deduct part of the federal highway funds from any state that did not raise its drinking age to twenty-one. Within a short time every state and the District of Columbia were in compliance: Puerto Rico was the only holdout.

The issue that initially galvanized public activism against alcohol abuse was drunk driving. In 1978 the East Coast saw the genesis of a grassroots organization, Remove Intoxicated Drivers (RID), devoted to reducing the incidence of drunken driving. The next year, in Sacramento, California, Mothers Against Drunk Drivers (MADD) was established with a similar goal. Both groups attacked weak drunk-driving laws and judicial laxness, especially the general absence of severe and predictable punishment for drivers who may have been repeatedly arrested for drunk driving (some even having been responsible for fatalities in the crashes they caused) but never imprisoned. These groups also targeted drinking age laws that allowed teenagers easy access to alcohol. In 1981 Students Against Driving Drunk (SADD) was established to improve the safety of high school students by promoting a contract between parents and children. The agreement stipulates that transportation be provided for children who have been drinking, and that a cooling-off period be observed by parents before they demand explanations. RID and MADD accuse SADD of sanctioning, rather than trying to reduce, youthful drinking.

Across the nation RID and MADD have strengthened the drunk-driving laws. Although at times at odds with each other, they both have successfully lobbied for per se laws (lifting a driver's license without a hearing if a Breathalyzer reads above a legal limit), reducing the legal threshold of intoxication, and increasing the likelihood of incarceration.

The Fetal Alcohol Syndrome

Another early concern was that of alcohol's effects on fetal development. This problem became a subject of widespread attention in the 1970s when researchers at the University of Washington described what they called the Fetal Alcohol Syndrome (FAS). At first, only consumption of large amounts of alcohol by a pregnant woman appeared to be the prerequisite of a definable syndrome that extended from morphological to mental and emotional expression in the infant. As these researchers have continued their studies, the level of alcohol they believe worthy of concern has declined. They now argue that alcohol consumed at the earliest stage of embryonic development, when there may be no awareness of pregnancy, is a particularly potent teratogen. Popular understanding of this warning is caught in a *New York Times* headline declaring in 1989, "Lasting Costs for Child Are Found from a Few Early Drinks."

The findings of these scientists were the primary impetus behind a unique provision contained in the Anti–Drug Abuse Act of 1988. The act, excerpted in this anthology, requires that every container of beverage alcohol manufactured after November 18, 1989, for sale in the United States include the following warning label: "Government Warning: (1) According to the Surgeon General, women should not drink alcoholic beverages during pregnancy because of the risk of birth defects. (2) Consumption of alcoholic beverages impairs your ability to drive a car or operate machinery, and may cause health problems."

Anti-Alcohol Guidelines

The Anti–Drug Abuse Act of 1988 also set up the Office of Substance Abuse Prevention (now the Center for Substance Abuse Prevention) in the Department of Health and Human Services. OSAP took on as one of its duties the approval of information on alcohol and drugs—or, in the language of the field, "prevention messages"—whenever federal aid is being sought from OSAP for publication and distribution to schools and the public. In April 1989 OSAP established guidelines for prevention material, excerpted here. These criteria are surprisingly thorough in their opposition to alcohol. The idea of a threshold, a safe upper limit of consumption, is rejected, as it was by anti-alcohol reformers in both previous temperance movements. For example, the guidelines require that

> material [give] a clear message that risk is associated with using any form or amount of alcohol or other drugs. . . . Even small amounts of alcohol and other drugs can increase risk of injury or to health. . . . Materials recommending a designated driver should be rated unacceptable. They encourage heavy alcohol use by implying it is okay to drink to intoxication as long as you don't drive.

The guidelines are equally clear-cut about drinking while pregnant:

> Material that merely warns about the dangers of drinking during pregnancy without stating an abstinence message should be rated as unacceptable. . . . Materials stating

that "research is inconclusive" or "not enough is known to make a judgment" or "some believe this ... while others believe that" are waffling. In fact, since not enough is known about how much alcohol is acceptable, for whom, and during which stages of pregnancy, the safest choice is not to drink during pregnancy.

OSAP also provides "editorial guidelines" that encourage media to change current language when describing drug and alcohol issues. For example, rather than use the phrase "responsible use," writers are urged to say just "use (since there is a risk associated with all use)." Similarly, "recreational use of drugs" should be replaced by "use (since no drug use is recreational)." These federal guidelines are in close harmony with the American Temperance Society in the 1830s and the Anti-Saloon League early in the twentieth century.

The OSAP guidelines restrict what FAS information can be released to the public in "approved" documents—for the public's own good. The experience of a Seattle woman prompts the question, When health science cannot clearly resolve an issue, should that doubt be withheld and a categorical statement made in the interest of public welfare? And who is to decide what is in fact the public welfare? The woman, who was nine months and a couple of weeks pregnant (and had abstained from alcohol during her pregnancy), decided to have a drink with her meal in a Seattle restaurant. The waiters warned her against it and gave her a copy of the warning label. She became angry; the waiters lost their jobs. The issue went public and was widely discussed in the media. All this happened because some people thought that one drink even at the end of pregnancy could cause fetal damage. One University of Washington embryology expert, in response to the incident, suggested that pregnant women should no longer be served alcohol in public.

A Contrary View of Alcohol

Our current worry over the effect of small amounts of alcohol is so striking because in the decades before the 1970s, physicians and scientists held a very different view of alcohol during pregnancy. In the 1930s and 1940s, as Americans reeled from Prohibition, experts announced that even large amounts of alcohol could not affect the fetus. Scientific studies published in the early 1930s by a leading authority on embryological development, Professor Charles Stockard of Cornell, concluded that "if comparisons with human embryos are possible they indicate that the content of alcohol in human blood is fortunately never sufficiently high to present a danger to the developing embryo." In 1932 Stockard summarized alcohol's effects on genetics: "We may assume from the experiments on the effects of alcohol in development and inheritance that it is highly improbable that the quality of human stock has been at all injured or adversely modified by the long use of alcohol."[1] At the same time, Professor Harold T. Hyman of Columbia University College of Physicians and Surgeons reviewed human experiments and found that "the habitual use of alcohol in moderate amounts by the normal human adult appears to be without any permanent organic effect deleterious in character."[2]

In 1942 two of the nation's leading experts on alcohol, E. M. Jellinek and Howard Haggard of the Yale Center of Alcohol Studies, wrote in their popular book *Alcohol Explored* (excerpted in this anthology),

> The fact is that no acceptable evidence has ever been offered to show that acute alcoholic intoxication has any effect whatsoever on the human germ, or has any influence in altering heredity, or is the cause of any abnormality in the child. All facts point to the contrary. This is a question to which much study has been given.

Understandably, in the face of such confidence in the harmlessness of alcohol to the fetus, the announcement that even a small amount could cause great damage came as an astounding reversal of how one ought to view alcohol. But what is particularly curious about the 1970s FAS discovery is that this belief about alcohol's ability to damage the fetus was not really new: it has been a theme in America's two previous temperance movements dating back to the eighteenth century.

The public, however, is cut off from this history. A phenomenon similar to the one currently known as "political correctness" seems to take control of the discourse on alcohol with the end result that, when one extreme view is dominant, any accurate account of the preceding and contrary image of alcohol stands little chance of a hearing. In an era of increasing alcohol use and of general conviction that it poses little risk to life and health, temperance movements are derided as ignorant and puritanical. In the end stage of a temperance movement, the makers, sellers, and drinkers of alcohol fare no better. Eras of anti- and pro-alcohol sentiment alternate at intervals of about a lifetime.

The Gin Epidemic

In England an anti-spirits crusade of the eighteenth century predated what would be the first temperance crusade in America. There condemnation of distilled spirits—which for centuries had been praised by physicians as aqua vitae, the "water of life"—occurred in response to the "gin epidemic," the rapidly growing production and consumption of cheap spirits that swamped London over the first half of the eighteenth century. Gin's burgeoning use was blamed for a dramatic rise in deaths and a falling birthrate.

In 1725, with an insight that foreshadows the modern alarm over FAS, the College of Physicians of London issued a formal warning, reprinted here, that parents drinking spirits were committing a "great and growing evil" that was "too often the cause of weak, feeble, and distemper'd children, who must be, instead of an advantage and strength, a charge to their country." Religious reformers such as John Wesley as well as physicians directed their attacks at spirits. The eminent physiologist. Stephen Hales (excerpted here) summarized newly revised scientific opinion when he warned that distilled spirits, far from being a boon to imbibers, are a "direct poison to human bodies." That is, there was no safe upper limit of use. Yet distilled spirits' change of image was not simply an anti-alcohol crusade; Hogarth's powerful prints *Gin Lane* and *Beer Street* were designed to contrast the desolation caused by gin with the healthy prosperity enjoyed by beer drinkers. The logical extension of concern from spirits to all alcoholic beverages, which has recurrently led to legal prohibition in the United States, never achieved political supremacy in Britain.

The First Temperance Movement

Dr. Benjamin Rush of Philadelphia, celebrated physician and inveterate reformer, was America's most prominent advocate of limited alcohol use at the start of the first temperance movement. Rush's *Inquiry into the Effects of Ardent Spirits upon the Human Body and Mind* (1785), excerpted here, was eventually distributed by the tens of thousands across the United States. He drew on themes familiar from the British gin epidemic. Rush observed that "ardent" or distilled spirits caused many social and bodily ills. His "moral thermometer" introduced a powerful visual tool to illustrate the graduated effects of beer and wine (health and wealth), and spirits (intemperance, vice, and disease). Rush urged the abandonment of spirits except for a few medical purposes.

Rush's censure of spirits but acceptance of the beneficent effects of beverages with lower alcohol content characterizes the early stage of American temperance movements. When reformers "took the pledge" in the early years of the nineteenth century, it was a pledge to abstain from distilled spirits, not all alcoholic beverages. Yet even as concern grew, so did the drinking of spirits made from grain. Consumption peaked around 1830, when, it is estimated, the average American drank three times as much alcohol as today, primarily in the form of whiskey.

Until the 1830s, most Americans believed that strong alcoholic drinks gave strength and health: they were thought to be necessities for hard work, to ward off fevers along with other illnesses, and to relieve colds and snakebite. Rum was included in the daily rations of the army and navy, and whiskey had a ceremonial role for marking any social event from a family gathering or visit to an ordination. Eventually the consequences of this binge became apparent, as had the excessive use of cheap gin in Britain a century earlier. In the United States, however, this change of attitude went farther. The complete development of anti-alcohol trends in this country had begun, a shift to total abstention from any form of alcohol.

Rush's work presaged the temperance era, and the creation of the Massachusetts Society for the Suppression of Intemperance in 1812 marked the organized establishment of the campaign at the state level. But the tide began to turn in earnest in the 1820s, inspired by one of the most dynamic writers and speakers of the nineteenth century, the Reverend Lyman Beecher.

Lyman Beecher and Total Abstention

In 1824 the annual meeting of the Connecticut Congregational Church received a report on the enormous rise in drinking and concluded, regretfully, that nothing could be done about it. An outraged Beecher thoroughly rejected the pessimists and appeasers within the church. He demanded that a new report be written and then produced one himself overnight. In the face of still rising alcohol consumption, he struck out against drinking and foresaw the kind of organization and effort that would turn back the scourge afflicting America. Two years later he limned the specifics of his argument in his epochal *Six Sermons* on *the Nature, Occasions, Signs, Evils and Remedy of Intemperance* (1826), reprinted here.

One has to read this slim book with its multitude of arguments, vivid metaphors, and moving appeals to physiology, religion, self-interest, family, and nation to understand how Beecher's words swept hundreds of thousands into the logical culmination of America's first temperance movement. One of Beecher's signal contributions to the anti-alcohol movement was to extend the condemnation of spirits to the total range of alcohol-containing beverages. He threw out compromise—how can you compromise with a poison?—and denounced "moderation" as well. "It is not enough," Beecher declaimed, "to erect the flag ahead, to mark the spot where the drunkard dies. It must be planted at the entrance of his course, proclaiming in waving capitals—THIS IS THE WAY TO DEATH!! Over the whole territory of 'prudent use,' it must wave and warn." For Beecher (as well as OSAP), any amount of alcohol in any of its forms constituted risk.

Beecher's argument that total abstinence is the inevitable final stage of temperance gradually achieved dominance. In 1836 the American Temperance Society (founded in 1826) officially changed its definition of temperance to abstinence. The logic of the situation impelled followers to rally for prohibition of a substance finally revealed as having no redeeming qualities, but rather posing a risk even to the most moderate of imbibers. Fifteen more years would pass before passage of the Maine prohibition law (1851). Within only five years more, our first temperance movement reached its peak of state prohibition. Taking about four decades, the change of attitude was slow and suffered some setbacks but nevertheless followed a discernible trajectory to its culmination.

Abraham Lincoln encapsulated the altered perception of beverage alcohol in an 1842 address before the Washingtonians (a national temperance organization of reformed drinkers) of Springfield, Illinois. Lincoln recalled that before the temperance era, damage done by alcohol was thought to result from "abuse of a very good thing," whereas now Americans understood that it was "from the use of a bad thing."[3] By 1855 about a third of Americans lived under democratically achieved laws that prohibited the sale of alcohol. Coincidentally with this changed attitude and restriction of sale, alcohol consumption fell by about two-thirds in the 1830s and has never again reached the level of the early republic.

The Woman's Crusade and the WCTU

In the decades after the Civil War, abstinence forces lacked the power that they had wielded in the 1850s, but important anti-alcohol events continued. The most dramatic was the "Woman's Crusade," which began in Ohio in 1873 and spread extensively, with group demonstrations employing hymn-singing and prayers against saloons. Out of this expression against alcohol evolved the Woman's Christian Temperance Union, a group now associated only with prohibition but in its prime an expression of reform on the behalf of women far broader than alcohol. The WCTU platform included equal legal rights for women, the right to vote, kindergartens, and an attack on tobacco.

The WCTU's multiple political interests clustered around alcohol because alcohol, as an unquestioned enemy of the home and family, legitimized women's participation in national political life. Women had been relegated to defense of the home. Therefore, they could reasonably argue that they had a duty to oppose alcohol and saloons, which were efficiently separating men from their paychecks and turning them into drunken menaces to their wives and children.

The battle over alcohol is, in the main, a battle of perceptions. Just as OSAP is endeavoring to inculcate the "correct" view of alcohol to the public, so did the WCTU form a Department of Scientific Temperance Instruction. It successfully fought for mandatory temperance instruction in the public schools. The WCTU also oversaw the writing of approved texts. Extreme statements peppered the descriptions of alcohol so that pupils would learn, among other information, that "The majority of beer drinkers die of dropsy. When alcohol passes down the throat it burns off the skin leaving it bare and burning. Alcohol clogs the brain and turns the liver quickly from yellow to green to black. Alcohol is a colorless liquid poison." This kind of childhood instruction may have had a second impact when students became voters.

The Second Temperance Movement and the ASL

In 1880 the Prohibition Party was founded but was soon torn between the "narrow gaugers," who wanted the party to hew to a strict anti-alcohol program, and the "broad gaugers," advocates of a comprehensive reform platform including, among other controversial proposals, an income tax. The party gradually faded under these controversies; fifteen years after its birth, leadership of the anti-alcohol movement was seized by a new organization that, at the beginning, had as its goal not prohibition of alcohol but abolition of an outlet for alcohol, the saloon, a social cesspool that had already elicited broad public condemnation.

In 1895 the national Anti-Saloon League was formed in Washington, D.C. The ASL went on to become the most successful single-issue organization in American history. Based on congregations as the organizational unit, the league attracted leadership that could slug out political battles with an energy, strategy, and deal making that matched, and often outmatched, professional politicians.

At first the league sought local option, that is, a decision at the local level whether to allow or forbid saloons and the sale of liquor. As sentiment against alcohol escalated, however, so did the league's anti-alcohol agenda. It finally aimed at national prohibition through a constitutional amendment. In December 1914, the same month in which the Harrison Antinarcotic Act was passed, a majority although not the required two-thirds of the House of Representatives voted for such a change in the Constitution. Part of that debate is excerpted here:

In 1917 what would become the Eighteenth Amendment did pass both houses by the two-thirds majority and two years later, three-quarters of the states having approved, became part of the Constitution. Constitutional Prohibition took effect in one year, that is, January 1920. Four decades earlier the WCTU had been founded. Two and a half decades had passed since the Anti-Saloon League had assumed leadership of the U.S. temperance movement. In the time span of a generation, campaigns against alcohol had reached a point where prohibition seemed to a political majority of Americans to be a reasonable response to alcohol.

The first temperance movement had rallied a broad segment of society alarmed at excessive spirits drinking, and only later moved to alcohol in general. Similarly, this second temperance movement focused on that widely condemned feature of urban life, the saloon, and later extended condemnation to all alcohol. The beer companies hoped to escape the onslaught on the distillers; they ran advertisements about the Constitution's guarantees featuring founding fathers such as Alexander Hamilton who drank beer without any deleterious effects. Beer, its makers argued, was the "drink of moderation." It was to no avail: beer contained alcohol and the prohibition movement eventually caught up with it. Such loss of meaningful distinctions among various types of alcoholic beverages also characterized the earlier temperance movement. Just as Lyman Beecher proclaimed that beer and wine were as evil as whiskey because all three contained alcohol, so in the second movement that common thread inevitably submerged all distinctions various beverages had acquired. As the Canadian economist and wit Stephen Leacock wrote in 1918, "There were days when we called it Bourbon whiskey and Tom Gin, and when the very name of it breathed romance. That time is past. The poor stuff is now called alcohol. . . . I wish somehow we could prohibit the use of alcohol and merely drink beer and whiskey and gin as we used to."[4]

Constitutional Prohibition lasted almost thirteen years. On its positive side, deaths from liver cirrhosis declined steadily as state after state went dry, and reached an all-time low during federal Prohibition. The death rate from liver cirrhosis was cut in half from its peak in 1907 and did not start to rise again until repeal. Prohibition's other characteristics—the blatant inability to control alcohol distribution, the failure to convince a large majority of Americans that alcohol is intrinsically destructive, and, after 1929, the specious hope that revival of the alcoholic beverage industry would help lift the nation out of the Great Depression—all led to the overwhelming rejection of Prohibition in 1933.

The American Way?

As we look at the ways alcohol has been addressed in the United States we might ask, Is prohibition the ultimate and unavoidable outcome—even if briefly—of temperance movements? Is our Puritan heritage of uncompromising moral imperatives still supplying righteous energy to the battle against alcohol? During the 1920s, when many nations of the Western world turned against alcohol, a sustained and powerful campaign against alcohol in the Netherlands led by the workers' movement and religious groups reduced alcohol consumption by 1930 to a very low level, but without legal prohibition. Likewise in Britain prohibition was not an end point of an anti-alcohol movement. In America, prohibition had an appeal as the final and necessary statement of disapproval.

Underlying our travail with alcohol is the persistence of a sharp dichotomy in the way we perceive it: it is either very good or very bad. Any exception to this viewpoint is fiercely resisted by adherents. Any value of alcohol in the diet is resisted by one side; any positive effect of Prohibition denounced by the other. One problem with painting alcohol in so unrelievedly negative a light is that compromise then seems immoral, particularly when you have achieved the political power to outlaw alcohol. How can you compromise with a poison?

Current deeply held attitudes can redesign history, as happened in the case of the Currier and Ives print of Washington saying farewell to his officers. In the 1876 print the wine glasses and bottle were removed; if teetotalism is the only moral lifestyle, how could the Father of His Country be a drinker? Late in the first temperance movement Rush's *Inquiry* was "reprinted" with the text abruptly ending before he praises the value of wine and beer. On the other side, how many can comfortably associate progressive and sophisticated Eleanor Roosevelt with ardent support of Prohibition? Our beliefs about alcohol and other drugs are so fundamental to our sense of right and wrong that we are pressured to edit our heroes and heroines to conform with current beliefs on drugs and alcohol.

Struggling to deal on a practical level with alcohol while trying to maintain either a totally favorable or totally condemnatory attitude is fraught with problems. The backlash to repeal made discussion of the alcohol problem extremely difficult because those worried about alcohol would often be labeled bluenoses or prohibitionists. Prohibition deeply undermined confidence in the rule of law to control alcohol use. Not until fifty years passed and new generations emerged did grassroots movements like RID and MADD arise and without apology attack drunk driving and promote new laws. Drunk driving is the issue that initially draws concerned and outraged citizens together for this latest temperance movement, just as distilled spirits was for the first and the saloon was for the second. The question before us is, Are we capable of reaching a politically viable role for alcohol that can be indefinitely internalized as part of our culture? Or will we again achieve an extreme but unsustainable position that will create a lengthy, destructive backlash?

NOTES

1. Charles R. Stockard. "The Effects of Alcohol in Development and Heredity," in *Alcohol and Man: The Effects of Alcohol on Man in Health and Disease*, ed. Haven Emerson, M.D. (New York: Macmillan, 1932; reprint ed., New York: Arno, 1981), 711, 119.

2. Harold T. Hyman, "The Effect of Moderate Amounts of Alcohol on the Normal Human Individual," in *Alcohol and Man: The Effects of Alcohol on Man in Health and Disease*, ed. Haven Emerson, M.D. (New York: Macmillan, 1932; reprinted ed., New York: Arno, 1981), 77.

3. Abraham Lincoln, "Address to the Washingtonian Temperance Society of Springfield, Illinois," in *Speeches and Writings, 1832–58* (New York: Library of America, 1989), 84.

4. Stephen Leacock, *Frenzied Fiction* (New York: John Lane, 1918), 200, 201.

Chapter 1

Alcohol in the British Colonies in America

The Puritans often are thought of as abstemious and anti-alcohol. That this is not the case may be gleaned from the reference to the manifest of the ship Arabella. *(Note that a tun was equal to about 250 gallons and a hogshead to about 125 gallons.) From the other excerpts in this selection, however, it is clear that the Puritans, as well as others in colonial America, were concerned about excessive drinking that led to drunkenness.*

THE EVOLUTION OF PROHIBITION IN THE UNITED STATES

E. H. Cherrington

1619

The Colony of Virginia enacts a law against playing dice, cards, drunkenness, idleness and excess in apparel. This law also requires that drunkards shall be publicly reproved by ministers.

1620

Massasoit visits the settlement at Plymouth and is treated by the Governor to a military salute with music and "a pot of strong water."

1623

The Dutch Reformed Church is established on the Island of Manhattan and takes strong grounds against "the excessive use of intoxicating drinks."

1629

The office of the Massachusetts Colony in London directs Governor Endicott as follows:

"We pray you endeavor, though there be much strong water for sale, yet so to order it that the savage may not, for our lucre sake, be induced to the excessive use or rather abuse of it; and at any time take care our people give no ill example; and if any shall exceed in the inordinate kind of drinking as to become drunk, we hope you will take care his punishment be made exemplary for all others."

The ship "Arabella" bringing Governor Winthrop to Massachusetts Bay has among its supplies the following: "42 tuns of beer, 14 tuns of water, 1 hogshead of vinegar, 2 hogsheads of cider and 4 pumps for water and beer."

The Virginia Colonial Assembly enacts a law providing that "ministers shall not give themselves to excess in drinkinge, or riott, or spending their tyme idellye by day or night."

1630

Governor Winthrop of Massachusetts discontinues the practice of drinking healths one to another and "wishes others to do the like."

1632

Massachusetts Bay Company gives to John Winthrop Governor's Island on condition that he shall plant an orchard upon it.

Virginia enacts the provisions of the law of England against drunkenness.

1633

Massachusetts Bay Colony stipulates that the Governor's permit is necessary to sell liquor, and it is declared that already many are "distempering themselves with drinke."

Robert Cole of Massachusetts Colony having been frequently punished for drunkenness is ordered to wear a red D about his neck for a year.

Chapter 2

A British Argument against Distilled Alcohol

In this remarkable essay from about 1730, Stephen Hales (1677–1761) sets forth a counterattack against the centuries-old belief that consuming distilled alcohol helps to fight disease and preserve life. Hales, an Anglican priest, studied alcohol, as well as such other scientific issues as plant physiology, blood pressure, and artificial ventilation. The arguments against alcohol that Hales discusses here have been cited again in every temperance movement since his time. Curiously, many of his points, though they are always valid, seem to receive widespread attention and credibility only during anti-alcohol movements. Can you think of any attack on drinking that he has not mentioned?

Note, however, that Hales disparages distilled spirits such as rum and gin, not alcohol per se. This approach is characteristic of the early stages of temperance movements. In Britain these movements never progressed to the prohibition of all alcohol, as happened in the United States.

A FRIENDLY ADMONITION TO THE DRINKERS OF BRANDY AND OTHER DISTILLED SPIRITUOUS LIQUORS

Stephen Hales

Man, not contented with what his bountiful and munificent Creator intending for his comfort, has wisely tempered with such a due proportion of strength, as that, taken in moderation, would make his heart glad, has unhappily found means to extract, from what God intended for his refreshment, a most pernicious and intoxicating liquor, to which, in a great measure, is owing, the remarkable increase of *drunkenness* of late years. This vice reigns to a most enormous degree among the habitual drinkers of *brandy* and other *distilled liquors* which are found to be most pernicious and destructive: for at the same time that they *coagulate and thicken the blood, they also contract and narrow the blood-vessels. This has, in fact, been found to be true by experiments purposely made with brandy on the blood and blood-vessels of animals.*

Whence we may evidently see the reason why those liquors do so frequently cause obstructions and stoppages in the *liver*; whence the *jaundice, dropsy,* and many other fatal diseases. It is in like manner also that they destroy and burn up the *lungs* too. Hence also it is, that by frequently contracting and shriveling, and then soon after relaxing, they weaken and wear out the substance and coats of the stomach on which they more immediately prey every time they are drank. Hence, I say, it is, that these spirituous liquors rarely fail to destroy the appetite and digestion of those who habituate themselves to them; for by drying up and spoiling the nerves, they make them insensible; they destroy also many of the very fine blood-vessels, especially where their fibers are most tender, as in the brain; whereby they spoil the memory and intellectual faculties, and by thus inflaming the blood and disordering the blood vessels and nerves, they vitiate and deprave the *natural temper*.

When first drank, they seem to comfort the stomach by contracting its too relaxed and flabby fibers, and also to warm the blood; but as the warmth which they give, on mixing with the blood, soon goes off, as it is in fact found to do when we mix brandy with blood, so also the spirituous part of the brandy being soon dissolved, and soaking into the watery humors of the body, it can no longer contract and warm the substance and coats of the stomach and other parts. Therefore as soon relaxing, the unhappy persons are thereby in a little time reduced to a cold, relaxed, languid, and dispirited state, which gives them so much uneasiness that they are impatient to get out of it by fresh supplies of the same deadly liquor which, instead of curing, daily increases their disease more and more. Hence it is, that their soul fainting within them, these unhappy wretches are ever thirsting after it, and with the *horse-leech* [an insatiable person], *cry, give, give*, but alas! never are, nor can be satisfied. For these strong liquors, tho' called spirituous, are so far from refreshing and recruiting the spirits that, on the contrary, they do in reality depress and sink them; and extinguish the natural warmth of the blood to such a degree that, as physicians have observed, *their prescriptions or medicines are found to have little or no effect, toward restoring these unhappy persons, when sick, to their health*.

The spirituous liquors soon intoxicate and fuddle, which intoxication soon goes off again and leaves them faint and languishing. Immediately put into the veins of an animal, they cause sudden death; so when drank in a large quantity at once, they coagulate and thicken the blood to such a degree as to kill instantly, many instances of which we frequently hear of. When they are not drank in such quantities as to kill immediately but are daily used, then, besides many diseases, they are apt to breed *polypuses* [polyps], or fleshy substances in the heart by thickening the blood there. *Polypuses*, as they grow larger and larger, do, by hindering and retarding the motion of the blood through the heart, thereby further contribute to the faintness and dispiritedness of those unhappy persons and at length, by totally stopping the course of the blood, do as effectually kill, as if a dart had been struck through the liver.

These distilled liquors, which, by reason of their great strength are found to be so destructive to our bodies, are observed by Chymists to be all of them composed and to consist of *water*, a *spirit*, and an *acid oil*. They find also upon the nicest scrutiny and enquiry *that all distilled fermented spirits are the same* whether distilled from the fermented juice of grapes, as is done in *France*, and some other countries, or from corn, grain, or other fermented fruits.

The truth of this any one may easily be convinced of by putting small pieces of flesh in any distilled spirituous liquors whatsoever, whether brandy alone or any compositions mixed with it, such as *orange-brandy, ratefea* [ratafia], *cinnamon-water, citron-water, plague* or *surfeit-water*; for it has been found by repeated trials that these all harden any raw flesh that has lain in them for some time. A plain and obvious proof [is] that since they all have the same effect on flesh, the *spirit* of them all is the same: which is agreeable to what the chemists find in all imaginable trials and attempts which they have made to discover if there were any sensible difference in any of them. And accordingly the pernicious effects of all these *distilled spirituous liquors* upon human bodies, are found to be the same. For 'tis well known, that multitudes are, in and near *sea-port-towns*, as effectually destroyed by the habitual drinking of *French-brandies* as are those who habituate themselves to drink other *distilled spirituous liquors*. And the same holds true of *rum* which destroys such multitudes in *America*, as even in a manner to depopulate whole countries of the native *Indians* who buy it of the neighboring *Christian planters*. Yet notwithstanding this, 'tis common to hear men plead in behalf of *rum* as a very wholesome liquor, being ready to catch at any slight argument in favor of what they love tho' at the manifest hazard of what is most valuable and dear to them, viz. their health and lives. They flatter themselves that *rum* is very wholesome because they have heard that if raw flesh be put into it, it will preserve it in a plump, fresh, supple and soft state, whereas *brandy* hardens it; and so does *rum* too, when it has continued in it for some time, but sooner or later in proportion to the strength of the *rum*. This holds good of all other *distilled spirituous liquors*. Some may indeed be more palatable than others, *but they are all in a manner equally pernicious and dangerous that are of an equal strength; and those most destructive and deadly which are the strongest, that is, which have the most spirit in them*. Which *spirit* being of a very harsh, fiery and acrimonious nature, as it is found to seize on and harden raw flesh put into it, so does it greatly injure the stomach, bowels, liver, and all other parts of human bodies, especially the nerves, the immediate and principal instruments of life and action. Hence it is, that it so remarkably enfeebles the habitual drinkers of it and also depraves the memory, by hardening and spoiling the substance of the brain, which is the seat of life. This is an inconvenience which the great drinkers of *punch* often find, as well as the *dram* drinkers.

But notwithstanding men find by daily experience both in themselves and others the destructive effects of these liquors. Tho' they yearly see *a thousand fall at their side, and ten thousand at their right hand*, yet will they not be warned so as to avoid them. There is that predominant *bewitching of naughtiness* in these fiery liquors, as strongly and impetuously carries men on to their certain destruction, in spite of the contrary natural strong desire they have *to live long, and see good days*; so effectually does this insatiable *wandering of concupiscence* after them, *undermine the simple*. As the wise man observes, *Wisdom* [of Solomon] IV. 12. 'Tis the peculiar misfortune of these unhappy wretches, that they seldom have so much as a heart to be set free. Now when a man's will and affections are thus depraved, and he is delighted with this worst of slavery, there is little hopes of him. To recover him from this condition, he must be, as it were, forced into his liberty and rescued in some measure from his own depraved desires: he must be dealt with like a madman and be bound down to keep him from destroying himself.

We find the strong and almost invincible propensity of habitual sinners to continue on in their evil courses most emphatically expressed in scripture. *Can the Ethiopian change his skin*, says God to the rebellious Israelites, *or the leopard his spots? Then may ye also do good that are accustomed to do evil*: Jeremiah XIII, 23. Which melancholy truth may with greater certainty be said of the unhappy *habitual* drinkers of brandy, and the like distilled spirituous liquors, than of those who labor under any other vices whatsoever. For how rarely, how very rarely do we see any of these unhappy persons reclaimed; they are absolutely deaf to all admonition, *neither will they hear the voice of the charmer, charm he never so wisely* [Psalms LVIII.5]. No considerations whatsoever, neither of this world nor the next, have any weight with them; they will forgo all that is most desirable here and endure the utmost miseries in life for the sake of it. How many does it reduce to suffer the hardships of the extremest poverty, not only by wasting their substance by a continual drain to satisfy a false, vitiated appetite, but also by so enfeebling and disabling them that they have neither will nor power to labor for an honest livelihood; *which is a principal reason of the great increase of the poor in this nation, as also of the much greater number of robberies that are committed of late years than were in former ages.* And as to the health of these miserable people, the most desirable because the foundation of all other enjoyments, it is greatly depraved and sottishly given in exchange for a false, unnatural sensation of it, which each fresh dram seems to give for the present while it is at the same time really undermining and destroying their healths. Nay, so bewitching is this infatuation, tho' they cannot, most of them, but be sensible that they are manifestly shortening their days, and just plunging themselves into their graves, yet will they not refrain.

This an eminent physician was so sensible of from his own unhappy experience that he said, when men had got a habit of it, they would go on tho' they saw hell-fire burning before them. Hence we see what little hopes there is of reclaiming by any arguments whatever these miserable wretches who are thus enslaved. For these reasons men ought to be extremely cautious how on any pretense whatsoever they indulge the beginnings of so pernicious a custom. *But if they are unhappily entangled in it, I have heard physicians say that bath waters drank on the spot, or, when that cannot be done with convenience, then a course of warm bitters will restore such to their health, provided nature is not too far worn out.* So that these unhappy persons have great encouragement to hope for a recovery would they but so far get the mastery of their greatest enemy (that is, themselves) as resolutely to forbear the indulging in what they cannot but be conscious is certain poison to them. Sure, the strong desire that all men have to enjoy health and length of days, together with the powerful arguments of religion, should be sufficient inducements to prevail with rational creatures to abstain from what is so destructive of their healths, and instantly apply for a cure.

Would God! that at least those who have not yet engaged in these unhappy courses might thereby be effectually deterred from such destructive ways. It is most easy at first to avoid, but very difficult to refrain from for those who are once habituated to such liquors.

But alas! the infection is spread so far and wide that if it continues its destructive conquests in the same manner and to the same degree that we have unhappily lived to see it advance within these thirty or forty years, it must needs, in a few generations, infect all mankind with its baneful influence. For it makes its way into the world as a friend to mankind, and insinuates itself under the disguise of grateful flavors. Under the notion of helping digestion, comforting the spirits, and cheering the heart, it produces the direct contrary effects. And tho' these deceitful *Hydras* are found, by daily experience, to destroy multitudes of mankind, yet they are received and entertained with so general applause that they boldly lift up their envenomed heads in every street to such a degree as looks as if it were the business of a considerable part of mankind to destroy the other. And tho' thousands and ten thousands, nay, millions over the whole earth perish yearly thereby, *yet no man layeth it to heart*, excepting the heads of the poor wild *Indians* in *New-England, Carolina*, and the other parts of *North America*, who being sensible of the great destruction distilled spirituous liquors have made among them, have frequently and earnestly desired that no such liquors might be sold to their people as they have made great havoc among them. So it is observed to do the same among those Christians who both taught them that beastly and destructive vice and are continually furnishing them with materials to continue in it. And what more just and reasonable than that those who reach forth the envenomed cup to others should themselves also perish by it.

'Tis a matter of wonder that the indignation of all mankind is not raised against so destructive a *pest*, is it possible for men that have any sense of humanity, any bowels of pity, but especially for those who profess themselves to be Christians, to stand by and see unconcerned so universal a destruction rage uncontrolled among their fellow-creatures? 'Tis sure the duty of every man to set to his helping hand and oppose it to the utmost, but more especially of those who have it in their power to keep up the fences against the encroachments of this terrible destroyer. For of all the miseries and plagues that unhappy man has been incident to none was ever so effectually destructive as this, not even those three sore judgments of war, pestilence, or famine—all which, after having raged for some time, cease. But this evil *spirit* is an unrelenting merciless destroyer that threatens endless destruction from generation to generation. This is indeed a master-piece of the Devil's, whereby he makes men their own executioners, which consigns them over not only to present but eternal death also.

Yet notwithstanding these, its most pernicious and destructive effects, where is that Christian country that desires with the abovementioned poor ignorant Indians, their people to be restrained from it? So far from that, that they seem rather to establish it by law insomuch that there is little hopes of any attempts being made towards suppressing it, till the spreading evil is grown more and more flagrant as to become at last so enormously destructive that it will be in a manner impossible for human species to subsist under it.

And this time seems to be coming on apace; for the infection, as it has for these thirty or forty years made a surprising advance, so it continues to spread far and wide. Nay, the unhappy influence of these liquors reaches much farther than to the destruction of those who indulge in the use of them, even to their posterity, to the children that are yet unborn. Of this we have too frequent instances, where the unhappy mothers habituate themselves to these distilled liquors, whose children, when first born, are often either of a diminutive, pigmy size, or look withered and old, as if they had numbered many years, when they have not, as yet, alas! attained to the evening of the first day. How many more instances are there of children, who, tho' born with good constitutions have unhappily sucked in the deadly spirituous poison with their nurses' milk. And how many other children are effectually destroyed thro' the indifference of their parents, by teaching them in their younger years to drink of these destructive and pernicious liquors.

For nature is then under a necessity of drawing out very slender threads of life when the nourishment of either unborn, or born children, is hardened and spoiled by such pernicious liquors. Whence it is evident that in proportion as the contagion spreads farther and farther among mankind, so must the breed of human species be proportionably more and more depraved, and will accordingly degenerate more and more from the more manly and robust constitution of preceding generations.

As sobriety and temperance are the best means we can possibly make use of in order to preserve our health and strength so drunkenness and excess are the ready means to destroy them, and the surest way to make a man's days few and evil upon the earth. By intemperance the body is over-charged with redundant and superfluous humors whereby the natural heat is extinguished and the constitution destroyed by grievous diseases as *dropsy, jaundice, palsy, apoplexy*, and the like.

Physicians observe that these distilled spirituous liquors which are inflamed by repeated distillations are in a manner direct *poison to human bodies*, which [bodies] are—most of them—of too delicate a make long to bear being corroded by such burning actual *cauteries* [hot irons]. For they observe that not only the constitution of the blood is thereby spoiled, its red part being consumed and burnt, whereby the blood is impoverished to such a degree as to have ten times more *serum* in it than red parts; but also that the fine tender blood vessels of the liver, or lungs, or some other important bowel, are thereby destroyed. Whence *Hectick Fevers*, consumptions, and the like diseases. Whence also sometimes great loss of blood by the blood vessels being corroded and torn asunder; or else by being too much weakened, relaxed, and broken the thin sharp *serum*, easily oozing through their substances, throws those unhappy persons into fatal dropsies. How many have drank to that excess as to die instantly, with the destructive weapon, as it were, in their body; whose deaths charity itself must needs judge most miserable since they die in their sins and are taken away in God's just wrath, even whilst they are sacrificing their souls to the devil. But tho' the number of this sort be many, yet it is but small in comparison of those multitudes whom it sweeps away by a gentle and unperceived decay. For it does, by little and little, quench the natural heat and extinguish the lamp of life and so lead men, tho' not by so direct a passage, yet but a little about, to their graves, as certainly tho' not so speedily. If then we think it a fearful sin for a man to murder himself and by laying violent hands on his own person to shorten his life, then let us not esteem drunkenness as a small sin since it produces the same effects, though by other means, and brings us to an untimely death, though it be by a different method. The plain reason why so vastly greater numbers are taken off by untimely deaths in this than in former ages is evidently this, that drunkenness and intemperance are in an extraordinary manner increased among us, especially by the detestable use of brandy and other distill'd spirituous liquors which are most pernicious to our constitutions. There are, indeed, some few of so strong a constitution that they can lead an intemperate life for a good number of years without feeling any sensible decay in themselves. Yet at length they usually pay dear for their former excesses when the effects of their strong liquors vent themselves in sickness and diseases, and make the unhappy wretches a miserable monument of the sad effects of the beastly sin of drunkenness. Thus we see that this sin, by an almost necessary and fatal consequence, brings death along with it.

But let us consider the spiritual as well as temporal evils that men bring upon themselves by the sin of drunkenness. They who live in a constant habitual course of debauchery are dead in their sins. It commonly brings them to a state of final impenitence. All sense of religion is apt to wear off from those who give themselves up to this vice; they in effect say unto God, depart from us, for we will have no knowledge of thy laws. And though they may sometimes have good dispositions, yet they very rarely put them into execution: their heads are so shattered and discomposed that they cannot have any settled serious thoughts. But God knows, 'tis very seldom that the drunkard entertains the least thoughts of repentance; for he is rather for encouraging himself and others to go on in sinning than to break them off by repentance; *Isa. LVI.12. Come ye, say they, I will fetch wine, and we will fill ourselves with strong drink; and to morrow shall be as this day, and much more abundant.* Daily experience convinces us how hard it is to reclaim drunkenness which should, in reason, make men dread, abhor, and detest this vice, which leads them to a state of impenitence, the greatest evil that is incident to us in this life since it is the sure forerunner of eternal misery in the next.

In order therefore to have a just hatred and detestation of this sin, it behooves men seriously to consider the heinousness of it and the manifold evils and mischiefs that accompany it. It being a vice that is condemned both by God and man, by infidels, as well as Christians and is withal most injurious to our selves by weakening and destroying our bodies and thereby shortening our lives: *How oft is the candle of the wicked put out? and how frequently cometh their destruction upon them? God distributeth sorrows in his anger*, Job XXI.17. *Job* calls it *their destruction* for themselves are the authors of it.

The prophet *Jeremiah*, XXXV.14. tells us, that *the words of Jonadab, the son of Rechab, that he commanded his sons not to drink wine, are observed*: but our bountiful God has permitted the use thereof only with this charge, *Be ye [And be] not drunk with wine, wherein is excess*, Ephes. V.18. Yet men do not obey his voice, therefore the *Rechabites* will be their judges, and it will be more tolerable in the day of judgment for Mahometans and idolaters than for sottish Christians.

The habitual drinkers of brandy, and other distilled spirituous liquors especially are grown to that height of impiety that they even glory in their shame; they that are now drunk are not drunk in the night only; they do not desire that the darkness should cover their shameful wickedness for they commit the sin openly and at noon-day, in the face of the sun: *They add drunkenness to thirst*, Deut. XXIX.19.

When we reflect on the unhappy course and life of these miserable, infatuated wretches, how ought it to affect us with concern to consider that it is destructive of their happiness both here and hereafter. Could we peep into the chambers of death and see those unhappy souls who were once indulging in excessive drinking here on earth, on whom the pit has shut her mouth; who are full of anguish and indignation for their former folly when it is too late. It much imports us therefore to remember that there remains still the same threatening to the drunkards of this generation which was formerly denounced by the prophet against the drunkards of *Ephraim; [They] shall be trodden under feet*, Isa. XXVIII.3.

It is commonly pleaded by those who are under a habit of drunkenness that they cannot forsake it; so they flatter and deceive their own souls that either God will not require them to do an impossible thing and therefore they shall be excused; or they say he is a hard master to shut a man out of heaven and cast him into hell for doing a thing which he could not help. But O wicked servant! Wherefore dost thou, to keep thy own wickedness, accuse God foolishly and falsely? *For he will not lay upon man more than right, that he should enter into judgment with God*, Job XXXIV.23. The son of *Sirach* justly observes, that *God hath commanded no man to do wickedly, neither has he given any man a license to sin*, Ecclesiasticus. XV.20. If those who are diseased with a dropsy will, when they are advised by a physician, restrain their appetite and refrain from much drink, though, by reason of their distemper they are continually tormented with an insatiable thirst, and this for the sake of recovering their health and to preserve for a while their temporal life: then how much more should those who have been addicted to drunkenness bridle their appetite and abstain from intemperance, not withstanding they have thereby brought upon themselves such an unnatural depraved thirst as gives them great uneasiness to forbear drinking. So many and great are the evils that do necessarily accompany this vice, both in this life and in the life to come, that are much more earnestly to be avoided than many deaths.

No habit, however long in contracting, is impossible to be removed. It may be done, though, with some difficulty. There is no one so far gone in the disease of drunkenness, or any other sin whatever, but there is room for a cure; which would certainly be obtained, if seriously and in earnest sought after; for God affords his grace to all that ask it; 'tis only to the obstinate and impenitent, that he shuts up his bowels of mercy and compassion. It greatly behooves men therefore not to forfeit the divine grace and assistance by their obstinate perseverance in this beastly sin, but to repent and reform, that this and all their other sins should be forgiven them.

They who would not be led away, nor enslaved by this vile vice of excessive drinking must carefully avoid of the company of drunkards, pursuant to the advice of the wise man, Prov. XXIII.20 *Keep not company with drunkards*. It much imports us therefore to avoid drunk company and to shun their conversation; for if once we give ground and comply, we are lost; the sin will, by little and little, prevail upon us. Thus many who have purposed to lead temperate lives by venturing into the company of tipplers, where they have been gradually drawn in, to be partakers of their bestiality, have at length arrived to that pitch of excess as to drown all their serious and pious resolutions in a continual flow of drunkenness.

If men did, in the sincerity of their hearts, use such proper means there is no doubt but they would be able to overcome this vice, how long soever they may have been accustomed to it. They therefore who continue under the power of it can never excuse themselves by the impossibility of amendment; but should rather accuse the falseness of their own hearts, that have still such a love for this sin, that they will not, in good earnest, make use of the proper means to avoid it.

In a word, if all these considerations will not deter men from this odious vice, they must wallow in their vomit and continue in this sottish, senseless condition till the flames of hell rouse them, when they will, by sad experience, find what they will not now believe, that *the end of these things*, as the apostle says, (Rom. VI.21) *is death*.

I shall conclude with the words of St. *Paul*, and St. *Peter, I Thess. V.5, 6 [7, 8], I Pet. V.8. I Pet. I.13* [last citation not printed]. *Ye are all the children of light, and the children of the day; we are not of the night, nor of darkness; therefore let us not sleep as do others, but let us watch and be sober. For they that sleep, sleep in the night; and they that are drunken, are drunken in the night; but let us who are of the day be sober. Be sober, be vigilant, because your adversary the devil, as a roaring lion, walketh about seeking whom he may devour.*

Chapter 3

British and U.S. Physicians on the Dangers of Alcohol

Two eighteenth-century petitions reveal the early role of the organized medical profession in attacking distilled spirits. The first, from London physicians in 1725, states one of the oldest themes in the argument against spirits: that mothers who drink concentrated alcoholic beverages can damage their unborn children. Today this phenomenon is called Fetal Alcohol Syndrome. This petition also attacked the effects of heavy alcohol use on health and productivity.

Similarly, the petition from Philadelphia's College of Physicians sixty-five years later refuted the common claim that drinking distilled spirits improved health. Of particular interest is the physicians' expressed disappointment in the powers of reason and religion to change American drinking habits and their consequent appeal for governmental action to curb drinking.

PETITION TO THE HOUSE OF COMMONS

College of Physicians, London

We, the President and College or Commonality of the Faculty of Physick in London who are appointed by the laws of the kingdom to take care of his Majestie's subjects in London and within seven miles circuit of the same, do think it our duty most humbly to represent that we have with concern observed, for some years past, the fatal effects of the frequent use of several sorts of distilled spirituous liquors upon great numbers of both sexes, rendering them diseas'd, not fit for business, poor, a burthen to themselves and neighbours, and too often the cause of weak, feeble, and distemper'd children, who must be, instead of an advantage and strength, a charge to their country.

We crave leave further most humbly to represent that this custom doth every year increase, notwithstanding our repeated advices to the contrary. We therefore most humbly submit to the consideration of Parliament, so great and growing evil. In testimony thereof, we have this nineteenth day of January, 1725, caus'd our common seal to be affixed to this our representation.

DELETERIOUS EFFECTS OF DISTILLED SPIRITS ON THE HUMAN SYSTEM

College of Physicians, Philadelphia

To the Senate and House of Representatives of the United States in Congress assembled: the memorial of the College of Physicians of the City of Philadelphia respectfully showeth:

That they have seen with great pleasure, the operation of a National Government, which has established order in the United States.

They rejoice to find, amongst the powers which belong to this government that of restraining, by certain duties, the consumption of distilled spirits in our country.

It belongs more peculiarly to men of other professions to enumerate the pernicious effects of these liquors upon morals and manners. Your memorialists will only remark that a great proportion of the most obstinate, painful, and mortal disorders which affect the human body are produced by distilled spirits; that they are not only destructive to health and life, but that they impair the faculties of the mind, and thereby tend equally to dishonor our character as a nation, and to degrade our species as intelligent beings.

Your memorialists have no doubt that the rumor of a plague or any other pestilential disorder, which might sweep away thousands of our fellow citizens, would produce the most vigorous and effectual measures in our government to prevent or subdue it.

Your memorialists can see no just cause why the more certain and extensive ravages of distilled spirits upon human life should not be guarded against with corresponding vigilance and exertions by the present rulers of the United States.

Your memorialists beg leave to add further, that the habitual use of distilled spirits, in any case whatever, is wholly unnecessary; that they neither fortify the body against the morbid effects of heat or cold, nor render labor more easy nor more productive; and that there are many articles of diet and drink, which are not only safe and perfectly salutary, but preferable to distilled spirits, for the above-mentioned purposes.

Your memorialists have beheld with regret the feeble influence of reason and religion in restraining the evils which they have enumerated. They centre their hopes, therefore, of an efficient remedy for them, in the wisdom and power of the Legislature of the United States; and in behalf of the interests of humanity, to which their profession is closely allied, they thus publically entreat the Congress, by their obligations to protect the lives of their constituents, and by their regard to the character of our nation, and to the rank of our species in the scale of beings, to impose such heavy duties upon all distilled spirits as shall be effectual to restrain their intemperate use in our country.

Chapter 4

An Esteemed Physician Encourages First Temperance Movement

Like Stephen Hales, Benjamin Rush (1745–1813) represents the early stage of temperance advocacy. A signer of the Declaration of Independence, Rush published the first edition of his Inquiry *in 1785. The position he took in this tract, reprinted below, seemed quite exceptional then, and for several decades thereafter, because it contravened the common assertion in the young nation that distilled, or "ardent," spirits improved health and made possible hard work, such as harvesting.*

Rush's argument was common, however, among Quaker physicians in Britain, where he had studied medicine. In later editions Rush added to his essay a "moral thermometer," which promised health to those who drank wine or beer in moderate amounts but increasing problems to anyone who extended their drinking to rum or other ardent spirits. As the temperance movement that Rush had a large role in stimulating expanded its targets, new editions of the Inquiry *retained only the first part, which condemned ardent spirits, and omitted the section arguing that wine and beer were acceptable.*

Many remedies Rush proposed for alcoholism are still current, though no one treatment is effective for all. The mystery of addiction — self-destructive behavior that is resistant to self-control — puzzled Rush, as it continues to puzzle us today.

AN INQUIRY INTO THE EFFECTS OF ARDENT SPIRITS UPON THE HUMAN BODY AND MIND

Benjamin Rush

By ardent spirits, I mean those liquors only which are obtained by distillation from fermented substances of any kind. To their effects upon the bodies and minds of men, the following inquiry shall be exclusively confined. Fermented liquors contain so little spirit, and that so intimately combined with other matters, that they can seldom be drunken in sufficient quantities to produce intoxication, and its subsequent effects, without exciting a disrelish to their taste, or pain, from their distending the stomach. They are moreover, when taken in a moderate quantity, generally innocent, and often have a friendly influence upon health and life.

The effects of ardent spirits divide themselves into such as are of a prompt, and such as are of a chronic nature. The former discover themselves in drunkenness, and the latter, in a numerous train of diseases and vices of the body and mind.

I. I shall begin by briefly describing their prompt, or immediate effects, in a fit of drunkenness.

This odious disease (for by that name it should be called) appears with more or less of the following symptoms, and most commonly in the order in which I shall enumerate them.

1. Unusual garrulity.
2. Unusual silence.
3. Captiousness, and a disposition to quarrel.
4. Uncommon good humour, and an insipid simpering, or laugh.
5. Profane swearing, and cursing.
6. A disclosure of their own, or other people's secrets.
7. A rude disposition to tell those persons in company, whom they know, their faults.
8. Certain immodest actions. I am sorry to say, this sign of the first stage of drunkenness sometimes appears in women, who, when sober, are uniformly remarkable for chaste and decent manners.
9. A clipping of words.
10. Fighting; a black eye, or a swelled nose, often mark this grade of drunkenness.
11. Certain extravagant acts, which indicate a temporary fit of madness. These are singing, hallooing, roaring, imitating the noises of brute animals, jumping, tearing off clothes, dancing naked, breaking glasses and china, and dashing other articles of household furniture upon the ground, or floor. After a while the paroxysm of drunkenness is completely formed. The face now becomes flushed; the eyes project, and are somewhat watery; winking is less frequent than is natural; the under lip is protruded; the head inclines a little to one shoulder; the jaw falls; belchings and hiccup take place; the limbs totter; the whole body staggers. The unfortunate subject of this history next falls on his seat; he looks around him with a vacant countenance, and mutters inarticulate sounds to himself. He attempts to rise and walk; in this attempt, he falls upon his side, from which he gradually turns upon his back. He now closes his eyes, and falls into a profound sleep, frequently attended with snoring, and profuse sweats, and sometimes with such a relaxation of the muscles which confine the bladder and the lower bowels, as to produce a symptom which delicacy forbids me to mention. In this condition, he often lies from ten, twelve, and twenty-four hours, to two, three, four, and five days, an object of pity and disgust to his family and friends. His recovery from this fit of intoxication is marked with several peculiar appearances. He opens his eyes, and closes them again; he gapes, and stretches his limbs; he then coughs and pukes; his voice is hoarse; he rises with difficulty, and staggers to a chair; his eyes resemble balls of fire; his hands tremble; he loathes the sight of food; he calls for a glass of spirits to compose his stomach; now and

then he emits a deep-fetched sigh, or groan, from a transient twinge of con-science, but he more frequently scolds, and curses every thing around him.

In this state of langour and stupidity he remains for two or three days, before he is able to resume his former habits of business and conversation.

Pythagoras we are told maintained that the souls of men, after death, expiated the crimes committed by them in this world, by animating certain brute animals; and that the souls of those animals, in their turns, entered into men, and carried with them all their peculiar qualities and vices. This doctrine of one of the wisest and best of the Greek philosophers, was probably intended only to convey a lively idea of the changes which are induced in the body and mind of man by a fit of drunkenness. In folly, it causes him to resemble a calf; in stupidity, an ass; in roaring, a mad bull; in quarrelling, and fighting, a dog; in cruelty, a tiger; in fetor, a skunk; in filthiness, a hog; and in obscenity, a he-goat.

It belongs to the history of drunkenness to remark, that its paroxysms occur, like the paroxysms of many diseases, at certain periods, and after longer or shorter intervals. They often begin with annual, and gradually increase in their frequency, until they appear in quarterly, monthly, weekly, and quotidian or daily periods. Finally, they afford scarcely any marks of remission, either during the day or the night. There was a citizen of Philadelphia, many years ago, in whom drunkenness appeared in this protracted form. In speaking of him to one of his neighbours, I said, "does he not *sometimes* get drunk?" "You mean," said his neighbour, "is he not *sometimes* sober?"

It is further remarkable, that drunkenness resembles certain hereditary, family, and contagious diseases. I have once known it to descend from a father to four out of five of his children. I have seen three, and once four brothers, who were born of sober ancestors, affected by it, and I have heard of its spreading through a whole family composed of members not originally related to each other. These facts are important, and should not be overlooked by parents, in deciding upon the matrimonial connections of their children.

Let us next attend to the chronic effects of ardent spirits upon the body and mind. In the body, they dispose to every form of acute disease; they moreover *excite* fevers in persons predisposed to them, from other causes. This has been remarked in all the yellow fevers which have visited the cities of the United States. Hard drinkers seldom escape, and rarely recover from them. The follow-ing diseases are the usual consequences of the habitual use of ardent spirits, viz.

1. A decay of appetite, sickness at stomach, and a puking of bile, or a dis-charge of a frothy and viscid phlegm by hawking, in the morning.

2. Obstructions of the liver. The fable of Prometheus, on whose liver a vulture was said to prey constantly, as a punishment for his stealing fire from heaven, was intended to illustrate the painful effects of ardent spirits upon that organ of the body.

3. Jaundice and dropsy of the belly and limbs, and finally of every cavity in the body. A swelling in the feet and legs is so characteristic a mark of habits of intemperance, that the merchants in Charleston, I have been told, cease to trust the planters of South Carolina, as soon as they perceive it. They very naturally

conclude industry and virtue to be extinct in that man, in whom that symptom of disease has been produced by the intemperate use of distilled spirits.

4. Hoarseness, and a husky cough, which often terminate in consumption, and sometimes in an acute and fatal disease of the lungs.

5. Diabetes, that is, a frequent and weakening discharge of pale, or sweetish urine.

6. Redness and eruptions on different parts of the body. They generally begin on the nose, and after gradually extending all over the face, sometimes descend to the limbs in the form of leprosy. They have been called "rumbuds," when they appear in the face. In persons who have occasionally survived these effects of ardent spirits on the skin, the face after a while becomes bloated, and its redness is succeeded by a death-like paleness. Thus the same fire which produces a red colour in iron, when urged to a more intense degree, produces what has been called a white heat.

7. A fetid breath, composed of every thing that is offensive in putrid animal matter.

8. Frequent and disgusting belchings. Dr. Haller relates the case of a notorious drunkard having been suddenly destroyed, in consequence of a vapour discharged from his stomach by belching accidentally taking fire, by coming in contact with the flame of a candle.

9. Epilepsy.

10. Gout, in all its various forms of swelled limbs, colic, palsy, and apoplexy.

Lastly, 11. Madness. The late Dr. Waters, while he acted as house pupil and apothecary of the Pennsylvania hospital, assured me, that in one third of the patients confined by this terrible disease it had been induced by ardent spirits.

Most of the diseases which have been enumerated are of a mortal nature. They are more certainly induced, and terminate more speedily in death, when spirits are taken in such quantities, and at such times, as to produce frequent intoxication: but it may serve to remove an error with which some intemperate people console themselves, to remark, that ardent spirits often bring on fatal diseases without producing drunkenness. I have known many persons destroyed by them, who were never completely intoxicated during the whole course of their lives. The solitary instances of longevity which are now and then met with in hard drinkers, no more disprove the deadly effects of ardent spirits, than the solitary instances of recoveries from apparent death by drowning, prove that there is no danger to life from a human body lying an hour or two under water.

The body after its death, from the use of distilled spirits, exhibits by dissection certain appearances which are of a peculiar nature. The fibres of the stomach and bowels are contracted; abscesses, gangrene, and schiri, are found in the viscera; the bronchial vessels are contracted; the blood-vessels and tendons, in many parts of the body, are more or less ossified; and even the hair of the head possesses a crispness, which renders it less valuable to wig-makers than the hair of sober people.

Not less destructive are the effects of ardent spirits upon the human mind. They impair the memory, debilitate the understanding, and pervert the moral faculties. It was probably from observing these effects of intemperance in drinking upon the mind, that a law was formerly passed in Spain, which excluded drunkards from being witnesses in a court of justice. But the demoralizing effects of distilled spirits do not stop here. They produce not only falsehood, but fraud, theft, uncleanliness, and murder. Like the demoniac mentioned in the New Testament, their name is "legion," for they convey into the soul a host of vices and crimes.

A more affecting spectacle cannot be exhibited, than a person into whom this infernal spirit, generated by habits of intemperance, has entered. It is more or less affecting, according to the station the person fills in a family, or in society, who is possessed by it. Is he a husband? How deep the anguish which rends the bosom of his wife! Is she a wife? Who can measure the shame and aversion which she excites in her husband! Is he the father, or is she the mother of a family of children? See their averted faces from their parent, and their blushing looks at each other! Is he a magistrate? or has he been chosen to fill a high and respectable station in the councils of his country? What humiliating fears of corruption in the administration of the laws, and of the subversion of public order and happiness, appear in the countenances of all who see him! Is he a minister of the gospel? Here language fails me.—If angels weep,—it is at such a sight.

In pointing out the evils produced by ardent spirits, let us not pass by their effects upon the estates of the persons who are addicted to them. Are they inhabitants of cities? Behold their houses stripped gradually of their furniture, and pawned, or sold by a constable, to pay tavern debts! See their names upon record in the dockets of every court, and whole pages of newspapers filled with advertisements of their estates for public sale! Are they inhabitants of country places? Behold their houses with shattered windows! their barns with leaky roofs! their gardens over-run with weeds! their fields with broken fences! their hogs without yokes! their sheep without wool! their cattle and horses without fat! and their children filthy, and half clad, without manners, principles, and morals! This picture of agricultural wretchedness is seldom of long duration. The farms and property thus neglected, and depreciated, are seized and sold for the benefit of a group of creditors. The children that were born with the prospect of inheriting them are bound out to service in the neighbourhood; while their parents, the unworthy authors of their misfortunes, ramble into new and distant settlements, alternately fed on their way by the hand of charity, or a little casual labour.

Thus we see poverty and misery, crimes and infamy, diseases and death, are all the natural and usual consequences of the intemperate use of ardent spirits.

I have classed death among the consequences of hard drinking. But it is not death from the immediate hand of the Deity, nor from any of the instruments of it which were created by him. It is death from SUICIDE. Yes! thou poor degraded creature, who art daily lifting the poisoned bowl to thy lips, cease to avoid the unhallowed ground in which the self-murderer is interred, and wonder no longer that the sun should shine, and the rain fall, and the grass look green, upon his grave. Thou art perpetrating gradually, by the use of ardent spirits, what he has effected suddenly, by opium or a halter. Considering how many circumstances, from a sudden gust of passion, or from derangement, may palliate his guilt, or that (unlike yours) it was not preceded and accompanied by any other crime, it is probable his condemnation will be less than yours at the day of judgment.

I shall now take notice of the occasions and circumstances which are supposed to render the use of ardent spirits necessary, and endeavour to show that the arguments in favour of their use in such cases are founded in error, and that in each of them, ardent spirits, instead of affording strength to the body, increase the evils they are intended to relieve.

1. They are said to be necessary in very cold weather. This is far from being true; for the temporary warmth they produce is always succeeded by a greater disposition in the body to be affected by cold. Warm dresses, a plentiful meal just before exposure to the cold, and eating occasionally a little gingerbread, or any other cordial food, is a much more durable method of preserving the heat of the body in cold weather.

2. They are said to be necessary in very warm weather. Experience proves that they increase instead of lessening the effects of heat upon the body, and thereby dispose to diseases of all kinds. Even in the warm climate of the West Indies, Dr. Bell asserts this to be true. "Rum (says this author) whether used habitually, moderately, or in excessive quantities, in the West Indies, always diminishes the strength of the body, and renders men more susceptible of disease, and unfit for any service in which vigour or activity is required." As well might we throw oil into a house, the roof of which was on fire, in order to prevent the flames from extending to its inside, as pour ardent spirits into the stomach, to lessen the effects of a hot sun upon the skin.

3. Nor do ardent spirits lessen the effects of hard labour upon the body. Look at the horse: with every muscle of his body swelled from morning till night in the plough, or a team, does he make signs for a draught of toddy or a glass of spirits, to enable him to cleave the ground, or to climb a hill? No; he requires nothing but cool water, and substantial food. There is no nourishment in ardent spirits. The strength they produce in labour is of a transient nature, and is always followed by a sense of weakness and fatigue.

But are there no conditions of the human body in which ardent spirits may be given? I answer there are. 1st. When the body has been suddenly exhausted of its strength, and a disposition to faintness has been induced. Here a few spoonsful, or a wine-glassfull of spirits, with or without water, may be administered with safety and advantage. In this case we comply strictly with the advice of Solomon, who restricts the use of "strong drink" only "to him who is ready to perish." 2dly. When the body has been exposed for a long time to wet weather, more especially if it be combined with cold. Here a moderate quantity of spirits is not only safe, but highly proper to obviate debility, and to prevent a fever. They will more certainly have those salutary effects, if the feet are at the same time bathed with them, or a half pint of them poured into the shoes or boots.

These I believe are the only two cases, in which distilled spirits are useful or necessary to persons in health.

But it may be said, if we reject spirits from being a part of our drinks, what liquors shall we substitute in their room? I answer, in the first place,

1. Simple water. I have known many instances of persons, who have followed the most laborious employments for many years in the open air, and in warm and cold weather, who never drank any thing but water, and enjoyed uninterrupted good health. Dr. Moseley, who resided many years in the West Indies, confirms this remark. "I aver (says the Doctor) from my own knowledge and custom, as well as the custom and observations of many other people, that those who drink nothing but water, or make it their principal drink, are but little affected by the climate, and can undergo the greatest fatigue without inconvenience, and are never subject to troublesome or dangerous diseases."

Persons who are unable to relish this simple beverage of nature, may drink some one, or of all the following liquors, in preference to ardent spirits.

2. Cyder. This excellent liquor contains a small quantity of spirit, but so diluted, and blunted, by being combined with a large quantity of saccharine matter, and water, as to be perfectly wholesome. It sometimes disagrees with persons subject to the rheumatism, but it may be made inoffensive to such people, by extinguishing a red hot iron in it, or by mixing it with water. It is to be lamented, that the late frosts in the spring so often deprive us of the fruit which affords this liquor. The effects of these frosts have been in some measure obviated by giving an orchard a north-west exposure, so as to check too early vegetation, and by kindling two or three large fires of brush or straw, to the windward of the orchard, the evening before we expect a night of frost. This last expedient has in many instances preserved the fruit of an orchard, to the great joy and emolument of the ingenious husbandmen.

3. Malt liquors. The grain from which these liquors are obtained is not liable, like the apple, to be affected by frost, and therefore they can be procured at all times, and at a moderate price. They contain a good deal of nourishment; hence we find many of the poor people in Great Britain endure hard labour with no other food than a quart or three pints of beer, with a few pounds of bread in a day. As it will be difficult to prevent small beer from becoming sour in warm weather, an excellent substitute may be made for it by mixing bottled porter, ale, or strong beer, with an equal quantity of water; or a pleasant beer may be made by adding to a bottle of porter, ten quarts of water, and a pound of brown sugar, or a pint of molasses. After they have been well mixed, pour the liquor into bottles, and place them, loosely corked, in a cool cellar. In two or three days, it will be fit for use. A spoonful of ginger added to the mixture renders it more lively, and agreeable to the taste.

4. Wines. These fermented liquors are composed of the same ingredients as cyder, and are both cordial and nourishing. The peasants of France, who drink them in large quantities, are a sober and healthy body of people. Unlike ardent spirits, which render the temper irritable, wines generally inspire cheerfulness

and good humour. It is to be lamented that the grape has not as yet been sufficiently cultivated in our country, to afford wine to our citizens; but many excellent substitutes may be made for it, from the native fruits of all the states. If two barrels of cyder, fresh from the press, are boiled into one, and afterwards fermented, and kept for two or three years in a dry cellar, it affords a liquor, which, according to the quality of the apple from which the cyder is made, has the taste of Malaga, or Rhenish wine. It affords, when mixed with water, a most agreeable drink in summer. I have taken the liberty of calling it Pomona wine. There is another method of making a pleasant wine from the apple, by adding four and twenty gallons of new cyder to three gallons of syrup made from the expressed juice of sweet apples. When thoroughly fermented, and kept for a few years, it becomes fit for use. The blackberry of our fields, and the raspberry and currant of our gardens, afford likewise an agreeable and wholesome wine, when pressed and mixed with certain proportions of sugar and water, and a little spirit, to counteract their disposition to an excessive fermentation. It is no objection to these cheap and homemade wines, that they are unfit for use until they are two or three years old. The foreign wines in common use in our country require not only a much longer time to bring them to perfection, but to prevent their being disagreeable, even to the taste.

5. Molasses and water, also vinegar and water, sweetened with sugar or molasses, form an agreeable drink in warm weather. It is pleasant and cooling, and tends to keep up those gentle and uniform sweats, on which health and life often depend. Vinegar and water constituted the only drink of the soldiers of the Roman republic, and it is well known they marched and fought in a warm climate, and beneath a load of arms which weighed sixty pounds. Boaz, a wealthy farmer in Palestine, we find treated his reapers with nothing but bread dipped in vinegar. To such persons as object to the taste of vinegar, sour milk, or butter-milk, or sweet milk diluted with water, may be given in its stead. I have known the labour of the longest and hottest days in summer supported, by means of these pleasant and wholesome drinks, with great firmness, and ended, with scarcely a complaint of fatigue.

6. The sugar maple affords a thin juice, which has long been used by the farmers in Connecticut as a cool and refreshing drink, in the time of harvest. The settlers in the western counties of the middle states will do well to let a few of the trees which yield this pleasant juice remain in all their fields. They may prove the means, not only of saving their children and grand-children many hundred pounds, but of saving their bodies from disease and death, and their souls from misery beyond the grave.

7. Coffee possesses agreeable and exhilarating qualities, and might be used with great advantage to obviate the painful effects of heat, cold, and fatigue upon the body. I once knew a country physician, who made it a practice to drink a pint of strong coffee previously to his taking a long or cold ride. It was more cordial to him than spirits, in any of the forms in which they are commonly used.

The use of the cold bath in the morning, and of the warm bath in the evening, are happily calculated to strengthen the body in the former part of the day, and to restore it in the latter, from the languor and fatigue which are induced by heat and labour.

Let it not be said, ardent spirits have become necessary from habit in harvest, and in other seasons of uncommon and arduous labour. The habit is a bad one, and may be easily broken. Let but half a dozen farmers in a neighbourhood combine to allow higher wages to their labourers than are common, and a sufficient quantity of *any* of the pleasant and wholesome liquors I have recommended, and they may soon, by their example, abolish the practice of giving them spirits. In a little while they will be delighted with the good effects of their association. Their grain and hay will be gathered into their barns in less time, and in a better condition, than formerly, and of course at a less expense, and a hundred disagreeable scenes from sickness, contention, and accidents, will be avoided, all of which follow in a greater or less degree the use of ardent spirits.

Nearly all diseases have their predisposing causes. The same thing may be said of the intemperate use of distilled spirits. It will, therefore, be useful to point out the different employments, situations, and conditions of the body and mind, which predispose to the love of those liquors, and to accompany them with directions to prevent persons being ignorantly and undesignedly seduced into the habitual and destructive use of them.

1. Labourers bear with great difficulty long intervals between their meals. To enable them to support the waste of their strength, their stomachs should be constantly, but moderately, stimulated by aliment, and this is best done by their eating four or five times in a day during the seasons of great bodily exertion. The food at this time should be *solid*, consisting chiefly of salted meat. The vegetables used with it should possess some activity, or they should be made savoury by a mixture of spices. Onions and garlic are of a most cordial nature. They composed a part of the diet which enabled the Israelites to endure, in a warm climate, the heavy tasks imposed upon them by their Egyptian masters; and they were eaten, Horace and Virgil tell us, by the Roman farmers, to repair the waste of their strength by the toils of harvest. There are likewise certain sweet substances, which support the body under the pressure of labour. The negroes in the West Indies become strong, and even fat, by drinking the juice of the sugar cane, in the season of grinding it. The Jewish soldiers were invigorated by occasionally eating raisins and figs. A bread composed of wheat flour, molasses, and ginger (commonly called gingerbread) taken in small quantities during the day, is happily calculated to obviate the debility induced upon the body by constant labour. All these substances, whether of an animal or vegetable nature, lessen the desire, as well as the necessity, for cordial drinks, and impart equable and durable strength to every part of the system.

2. Valetudinarians, especially those who are afflicted with diseases of the stomach and bowels, are very apt to seek relief from ardent spirits. Let such people be cautious how they make use of this dangerous remedy. I have known many men and women of excellent characters and principles, who have been betrayed, by occasional doses of gin and brandy, into a love of those liquors, and have afterwards fallen sacrifices to their fatal effects. The different preparations

of opium are much more safe and efficacious than distilled cordials of any kind, in flatulent or spasmodic affections of the stomach and bowels. So great is the danger of contracting a love for distilled liquors, by accustoming the stomach to their stimulus, that as few medicines as possible should be given in spirituous vehicles, in chronic diseases. A physician, of great eminence and uncommon worth, who died towards the close of the last century, in London, in taking leave of a young physician of this city, who had finished his studies under his patronage, impressed this caution with peculiar force upon him, and lamented at the same time, in pathetic terms, that he had innocently made many sots, by prescribing brandy and water in stomach complaints. It is difficult to tell how many persons have been destroyed by those physicians who have adopted Dr. Brown's indiscriminate practice in the use of stimulating remedies, the most popular of which is ardent spirits, but, it is well known, several of them have died of intemperance in this city since the year 1790. They were probably led to it, by drinking brandy and water, to relieve themselves from the frequent attacks of debility and indisposition, to which the labours of a physician expose him, and for which rest, fasting, a gentle purge, or weak diluting drinks, would have been safe and more certain cures.

None of these remarks are intended to preclude the use of spirits in the low state of short, or what are called acute diseases, for, in such cases, they produce their effects too soon to create a habitual desire for them.

3. Some people, from living in countries subject to intermitting fevers, endeavour to fortify themselves against them, by taking two or three wine-glasses of bitters, made with spirits, every day. There is great danger of contracting habits of intemperance from this practice. Besides, this mode of preventing intermittents is far from being a certain one. A much better security against them, is a tea-spoonful of the jesuits bark, taken every morning during a sickly season. If this safe and excellent medicine cannot be had, a gill or half a pint of a strong watery infusion of centaury, camomile, wormwood, or rue, mixed with a little of the calamus of our meadows, may be taken every morning, with nearly the same advantage as the jesuits bark. Those persons who live in a sickly country, and cannot procure any of the preventives of autumnal fevers which have been mentioned, should avoid the morning and evening air; should kindle fires in their houses, on damp days, and in cool evenings, throughout the whole summer; and put on winter clothes about the first week in September. The last part of these directions applies only to the inhabitants of the middle states.

4. Men who follow professions, which require constant exercise of the faculties of their minds, are very apt to seek relief, by the use of ardent spirits, from the fatigue which succeeds great mental exertions. To such persons, it may be a discovery to know, that tea is a much better remedy for that purpose. By its grateful and gentle stimulus, it removes fatigue, restores the excitement of the mind, and invigorates the whole system. I am no advocate for the excessive use of tea. When taken too strong, it is hurtful, especially to the female constitution; but when taken of a moderate degree of strength, and in moderate quantities with sugar and cream, or milk, I believe it is, in general, innoxious, and at all

times to be preferred to ardent spirits, as a cordial for studious men. The late Anthony Benezet, one of the most laborious schoolmasters I ever knew, informed me, he had been prevented from the love of spirituous liquors by acquiring a love for tea in early life. Three or four cups, taken in an afternoon, carried off the fatigue of a whole day's labour in his school. This worthy man lived to be seventy-one years of age, and died of an acute disease, with the full exercise of all the faculties of his mind. But the use of tea counteracts a desire for distilled spirits, during great *bodily*, as well as mental exertions. Of this, captain Forest has furnished us with a recent and remarkable proof, in his History of a Voyage from Calcutta to the Marqui Archipelago. "I have always observed (says this ingenious mariner) when sailors drink tea, it weans them from the thoughts of drinking strong liquors, and pernicious grog; and with this they are soon contented. Not so with whatever will intoxicate, be it what it will. This has always been my remark. I therefore always encourage it, without their knowing why."

5. Women have sometimes been led to seek relief from what is called breeding sickness, by the use of ardent spirits. A little gingerbread, or biscuit, taken occasionally, so as to prevent the stomach being empty, is a much better remedy for that disease.

6. Persons under the pressure of debt, disappointments in worldly pursuits, and guilt, have sometimes sought to drown their sorrows in strong drink. The only radical cure for those evils is to be found in religion; but where its support is not restored to, wine and opium should always be preferred to ardent spirits. They are far less injurious to the body and mind than spirits, and the habits of attachment to them are easily broken, after time and repentance have removed the evils they were taken to relieve.

7. The sociable and imitative nature of man often disposes him to adopt the most odious and destructive practices from his companions. The French soldiers who conquered Holland, in the year 1794, brought back with them the love and use of brandy, and thereby corrupted the inhabitants of several of the departments of France, who had been previously distinguished for their temperate and sober manners. Many other facts might be mentioned, to show how important it is to avoid the company of persons addicted to the use of ardent spirits.

8. Smoking and chewing tobacco, by rendering water and simple liquors insipid to the state, dispose very much to the stronger stimulus of ardent spirits. The practice of smoking segars has, in every part of our country, been more followed by a general use of brandy and water as a common drink, more especially by that class of citizens who have not been in the habit of drinking wine, or malt liquors. The less, therefore, tobacco is used in the above ways, the better.

9. No man ever became suddenly a drunkard. It is by gradually accustoming the taste and stomach to ardent spirits, in the forms of grog and toddy, that men have been led to love them in their more destructive mixtures, and in their simple state. Under the impression of this truth, were it possible for me to speak with a voice so loud as to be heard from the river St. Croix to the remotest shores of the Mississippi, which bound the territory of the United States, I would say, Friends and fellow-citizens, avoid the habitual use of those two seducing liquors,

whether they be made with brandy, rum, gin, Jamaica spirits, whiskey, or what is called cherry bounce. It is true, some men, by limiting the strength of those drinks by measuring the spirit and water, have drunken them for many years, and even during a long life, without acquiring habits of intemperance or intoxication, but many more have been insensibly led, by drinking weak toddy and grog first at their meals, to take them for their constant drink, in the intervals of their meals; afterwards to take them, of an increased strength, before breakfast in the morning; and finally to destroy themselves by drinking undiluted spirits, during every hour of the day and night. I am not singular in this remark. "The consequences of drinking rum and water, or *grog*, as it is called (says Dr. Moseley) is, that habit increases the desire of more spirits, and decreases its effects; and there are very few grog-drinkers who long survive the practice of debauching with it, without acquiring the odious nuisance of dram-drinkers breath, and down right stupidity and impotence." To enforce the caution against the use of those two apparently innocent and popular liquors still further, I shall select one instance, from among many, to show the ordinary manner in which they beguile and destroy their votaries. A citizen of Philadelphia, once of a fair and sober character, drank toddy for many years, as his constant drink. From this he proceeded to drink grog. After a while nothing would satisfy him but slings made of equal parts of rum and water, with a little sugar. From slings he advanced to raw rum, and from common rum to Jamaica spirits. Here he rested for a few months, but at length, finding even Jamaica spirits were not strong enough to warm his stomach, he made it a constant practice to throw a table-spoonful of ground pepper in each glass of his spirits, in order, to use his own words, "to take off their coldness." He soon after died a martyr to his intemperance.

Ministers of the gospel, of every denomination, in the United States! aid me with all the weight you possess in society, from the dignity and usefulness of your sacred office, to save our fellow men from being destroyed by the great destroyer of their lives and souls. In order more successfully to effect this purpose, permit me to suggest to you to employ the same wise modes of instruction, which you use in your attempts to prevent their destruction by other vices. You expose the evils of covetousness, in order to prevent theft; you point out the sinfulness of impure desires, in order to prevent adultery; and you dissuade from anger, and malice, in order to prevent murder. In like manner, denounce, by your preaching, conversation, and examples, the seducing influence of toddy and grog, when you aim to prevent all the crimes and miseries which are the offspring of strong drink.

We have hitherto considered the effects of ardent spirits upon individuals, and the means of preventing them. I shall close this head of our inquiry, by a few remarks upon their effects upon the population and welfare of our country, and the means of obviating them.

It is highly probable not less than 4000 people die annually, from the use of ardent spirits, in the United States. Should they continue to exert this deadly influence upon our population, where will their evils terminate? This question may be answered, by asking, where are all the Indian tribes, whose numbers and arms formerly spread terror among their civilized neighbours? I answer, in the words of the famous Mingo chief, "the blood of many of them flows not in the veins of any human creature." They have perished, not by pestilence, nor war, but by a greater foe to human life than either of them—ardent spirits. The loss of 4000 American citizens, by the yellow fever, in a single year, awakened general sympathy and terror, and called forth all the strength and ingenuity of laws, to prevent its recurrence. Why is not the same zeal manifested in protecting our citizens from the more general and consuming ravages of distilled spirits? Should the customs of civilized life preserve our nation from extinction, and even from an increase of mortality, by those liquors; they cannot prevent our country being governed by men, chosen by intemperate and corrupted voters. From such legislators, the republic would soon be in danger. To avert this evil, let good men of every class unite, and besiege the general and state governments with petitions to limit the number of taverns; to impose heavy duties upon ardent spirits; to inflict a mark of disgrace, or a temporary abridgment of some civil right, upon every man convicted of drunkenness; and finally to secure the property of habitual drunkards, for the benefit of their families, by placing it in the hands of trustees, appointed for that purpose by a court of justice.

To aid the operation of these laws, would it not be extremely useful for the rulers of the different denominations of christian churches to unite, and render the sale and consumption of ardent spirits a subject of ecclesiastical jurisdiction? The methodists, and society of friends, have, for some time past, viewed them as contraband articles to the pure laws of the gospel, and have borne many public and private testimonies against making them the objects of commerce. Their success, in this benevolent enterprise, affords ample encouragement for all other religious societies to follow their example.

We come now to the third part of this inquiry, that is, to mention the remedies for the evils which are brought on by the excessive use of distilled spirits.

These remedies divide themselves into two kinds.

I. Such as are proper to cure a fit of drunkenness, and

II. Such as are proper to prevent its recurrence and to destroy a desire for ardent spirits.

I. I am aware that the efforts of science and humanity, in applying their resources to the cure of a disease induced by an act of vice, will meet with a cold reception from many people. But let such people remember, the subjects of our remedies are their fellow creatures, and that the miseries brought upon human nature, by its crimes, are as much the objects of divine compassion (which we are bound to imitate) as the distresses which are brought upon men by the crimes of other people, or which they bring upon themselves by ignorance or accidents. Let us not then pass by the prostrate sufferer from strong drink, but administer to him the same relief we would afford to a fellow creature, in a similar state, from an accidental, and innocent cause.

1. The first thing to be done to cure a fit of drunkenness, is to open the collar, if in a man, and remove all tight ligatures from every other part of the body. The

head and shoulders should at the same time be elevated, so as to favour a more feeble determination of the blood to the brain.

2. The contents of the stomach should be discharged, by thrusting a feather down the throat. It often restores the patient immediately to his senses and feet. Should it fail of exciting a puking,

3. A napkin should be wrapped round the head, and wetted for an hour or two with cold water, or cold water should be poured in a stream upon the head. In the latter way I have sometimes seen it used, when a boy, in the city of Philadelphia. It was applied, by dragging the patient, when found drunk in the street, to a pump, and pumping water upon his head for ten or fifteen minutes. The patient generally rose, and walked off, sober and sullen, after the use of this remedy.

Other remedies, less common, but not less effectual for a fit of drunkenness, are,

4. Plunging the whole body into cold water. A number of gentlemen who had drunken to intoxication, on board a ship in the stream, near Fell's point, at Baltimore, in consequence of their reeling in a small boat, on their way to the shore, in the evening, overset it, and fell into the water. Several boats from the shore hurried to their relief. They were all picked up, and went home, perfectly sober to their families.

5. Terror. A number of young merchants, who had drunken together, in a compting-house, on James river, above thirty years ago, until they were intoxicated, were carried away by a sudden rise of the river, from an immense fall of rain. They floated several miles with the current, in their little cabin, half filled with water. An island in the river arrested it. When they reached the shore that saved their lives, they were all sober. It is probable terror assisted in the cure of the persons who fell into the water at Baltimore.

6. The excitement of a fit of anger. The late Dr. Witherspoon used to tell a story of a man in Scotland, who was always cured of a fit of drunkenness by being made angry. The means chosen for that purpose was a singular one. It was talking against religion.

7. A severe whipping. This remedy acts by exciting a revulsion of the blood from the brain to the external parts of the body.

8. Profuse sweats. By means of this evacuation, nature sometimes cures a fit of drunkenness. Their good effects are obvious in labourers, whom quarts of spirits taken in a day will seldom intoxicate while they sweat freely. If the patient be unable to swallow warm drinks, in order to produce sweats, they may be excited by putting him in a warm bath, or wrapping his body in blankets, under which should be placed half a dozen hot bricks, or bottles filled with hot water.

9. Bleeding. This remedy should always be used, when the former ones have been prescribed to no purpose, or where there is reason to fear, from the long duration of the disease, a material injury may be done to the brain.

It is hardly necessary to add, that each of the above remedies should be regulated by the grade of drunkenness, and the greater or less degree in which the intellects are affected in it.

II. The remedies which are proper to prevent the recurrence of fits of drunkenness, and to destroy the desire for ardent spirits, are religious, metaphysical, and medical. I shall briefly mention them.

1. Many hundred drunkards have been cured of their desire for ardent spirits, by a practical belief in the doctrines of the christian religion. Examples of the divine efficacy of christianity for this purpose have lately occurred in many parts of the United States.

2. A sudden sense of the guilt contracted by drunkenness, and of its punishment in a future world. It once cured a gentleman in Philadelphia, who, in a fit of drunkenness, attempted to murder a wife whom he loved. Upon being told of it when he was sober, he was so struck with the enormity of the crime he had nearly committed, that he never tasted spirituous liquors afterwards.

3. A sudden sense of shame. Of the efficacy of this deep seated principle in the human bosom, in curing drunkenness, I shall relate three remarkable instances.

A farmer in England, who had been many years in the practice of coming home intoxicated, from a market town, one day observed appearances of rain, while he was in market. His hay was cut, and ready to be housed. To save it, he returned in haste to his farm, before he had taken his customary dose of grog. Upon coming into his house, one of his children, a boy of six years old, ran to his mother, and cried out, "O, mother! father is come home, and he is not drunk." The father, who heard this exclamation, was so severely rebuked by it, that he suddenly became a sober man.

A noted drunkard was once followed by a favourite goat to a tavern, into which he was invited by his master, and drenched with some of his liquor. The poor animal staggered home with his master, a good deal intoxicated. The next day he followed him to his accustomed tavern. When the goat came to the door, he paused: his master made signs to him to follow him into the house. The goat stood still. An attempt was made to thrust him into the tavern. He resisted, as if struck with the recollection of what he suffered from being intoxicated the night before. His master was so much affected by a sense of shame, in observing the conduct of his goat to be so much more rational than his own, that he ceased from that time to drink spirituous liquors.

A gentleman, in one of the southern states, who had nearly destroyed himself by strong drink, was remarkable for exhibiting the grossest marks of folly in his fits of intoxication. One evening, sitting in his parlour, he heard an uncommon noise in his kitchen. He went to the door, and peeped through the key hole, from whence he saw one of his negroes diverting his fellow servants, by mimicking his master's gestures and conversation when he was drunk. The sight overwhelmed him with shame and distress, and instantly became the means of his reformation.

4. The association of the idea of ardent spirits with a painful or disagreeable impression upon some part of the body, has sometimes cured the love of strong drink. I once tempted a negro man, who was habitually fond of ardent spirits, to drink some rum (which I placed in his way) and in which I had put a few grains

of tartar emeric. The tartar sickened and puked him to such a degree, that he supposed himself to be poisoned. I was much gratified by observing he could not bear the sight, nor smell, of spirits for two years afterwards.

I have heard of a man who was cured of the love of spirits, by working off a puke by large draughts of brandy and water, and I know a gentleman, who in consequence of being affected with a rheumatism, immediately after drinking some toddy, when overcome with fatigue and exposure to the rain, has ever since loathed that liquor, only because it was accidentally associated in his memory with the recollection of the pain he suffered from his disease.

This appeal to that operation of the human mind, which obliges it to associate ideas, accidentally or otherwise combined, for the cure of vice, is very ancient. It was resorted to by Moses, when he compelled the children of Israel to drink the solution of the golden calf (which they had idolized) in water. This solution, if made, as it most probably was, by means of what is called hepar sulphuris, was extremely bitter, and nauseous, and could never be recollected afterwards, without bringing into equal detestation the sin which subjected them to the necessity of drinking it. Our knowledge of this principle of association upon the minds and conduct of men should lead us to destroy, by means of other impressions, the influence of all those circumstances, with which the recollection and desire of spirits are combined. Some men drink only in the *morning*, some at *noon*, and some only at *night*. Some men drink only on a *market day*, some at *one* tavern only, and some only in one *kind* of company. Now by finding a new and interesting employment or subject of conversation for drunkards, at the usual times in which they have been accustomed to drink, and by restraining them by the same means from those places and companions, which suggested to them the idea of ardent spirits, their habits of intemperance may be completely destroyed. In the same way the periodical returns of appetite, and a desire of sleep, have been destroyed in a hundred instances. The desire for strong drink differs from each of them, in being of an artificial nature, and therefore not disposed to return, after being chased for a few weeks from the system.

5. The love of ardent spirits has sometimes been subdued, by exciting a counter passion in the mind. A citizen of Philadelphia had made many unsuccessful attempts to cure his wife of drunkenness. At length, despairing of her reformation, he purchased a hogshead of rum, and, after tapping it, left the key in the door of the room in which it was placed, as if he had forgotten it. His design was to give his wife an opportunity of drinking herself to death. She suspected this to be his motive, in what he had done, and suddenly left off drinking. Resentment here became the antidote to intemperance.

6. A diet consisting wholly of vegetables cured a physician in Maryland of drunkenness, probably by lessening that thirst, which is always more or less excited by animal food.

7. Blisters to the ankles, which were followed by an unusual degree of inflammation, once suspended the love of ardent spirits, for one month, in a lady in this city. The degrees of her intemperance may be conceived of, when I add, that

her grocer's account for brandy alone amounted, annually, to one hundred pounds, Pennsylvania currency, for several years.

8. A violent attack of an acute disease has sometimes destroyed a habit of drinking distilled liquors. I attended a notorious drunkard, in the yellow fever in the year 1798, who recovered, with the loss of his relish for spirits, which has, I believe, continued ever since.

9. A salivation has lately performed a cure of drunkenness, in a person of Virginia. The new disease excited in the mouth and throat, while it rendered the action of the smallest quantity of spirits upon them painful, was happily calculated to destroy the disease in the stomach which prompts to drinking, as well as to render, the recollection of them disagreeable, by the laws of association formerly mentioned.

10. I have known an oath, taken before a magistrate, to drink no more spirits, produce a perfect cure of drunkenness. It is sometimes cured in this way in Ireland. Persons who take oaths for this purpose are called affidavit men.

11. An advantage would probably arise from frequent representations being made to drunkards, not only of the certainty, but of the *suddenness* of death, from habits of intemperance. I have heard of two persons being cured of the love of ardent spirits, by seeing death suddenly induced by fits of intoxication; in the one case, in a stranger, and in the other, in an intimate friend.

12. It has been said, that the disuse of spirits should be gradual, but my observations authorise me to say, that persons who have been addicted to them should abstain from them *suddenly*, and *entirely*. "Taste not, handle not, touch not," should be inscribed upon every vessel that contains spirits, in the house of a man who wishes to be cured of habits of intemperance. To obviate, for awhile, the debility which arises from the sudden abstraction of the stimulus of spirits, laudanum, or bitters infused in water, should be taken, and perhaps a larger quantity of beer or wine, than is consistent with the strict rules of temperate living. By the temporary use of these substitutes for spirits, I have never known the transition to sober habits to be attended with any bad effects, but often with permanent health of body, and peace of mind.

Chapter 5

A Powerful Statement against All Alcohol by a Distinguished Preacher

Lyman Beecher (1775–1863), the father of the preacher Henry Ward Beecher and the social reformers Catharine Beecher and Harriet Beecher Stowe, was one of the preeminent preachers of his time. His Six Sermons (1826) is the full statement of the first American temperance movement. Beecher extended Rush's condemnation of distilled spirits and, through an inexorable logic, found fault with any beverage containing alcohol, including whiskey, wine, and beer. This short book was distributed in the United States and abroad with powerful effect. By all accounts a moving speaker, Beecher wrote his sermons in the style and voice of a passionate advocate.

When I first asked students to read the Six Sermons in the 1970s, they saw Beecher as quaint and out of touch with real life. Now another opinion has surfaced: that not only did Beecher understand the dangers of alcohol but also his recommendations for changing popular attitudes were, in many respects, modern. While Beecher's statements have not changed, we have become more sensitive to the dangers of alcohol.

Beecher added to Hales's arguments another, moral, reason for opposing alcohol: drunkenness interfered with achieving salvation. Beecher believed that a sober individual could cooperate in his or her salvation, but a mind under the influence of alcohol could not. The end result would be eternity in Hell rather than Heaven. Through this argument Beecher and like-minded clergy dramatically increased the perception of the significance of alcohol abuse. Whereas Rush viewed hanging or suicide as the extreme end point of drunkenness, Beecher raised the stakes to Divine Judgment.

Six Sermons on the Nature, Occasions, Signs, Evils and Remedy of Intemperance

Lyman Beecher

Sermon I: The Nature and Occasions of Intemperance

Proverbs, xxiii. 29–35

Who hath wo? who hath sorrow? who hath contentions? who hath babbling? who hath wounds without canse? who hath redness of eyes?

They that tarry long at the wine; they that go to seek mixed wine.

Look not thou upon the wine when it is red, when it giveth his colour in the cup, when it moveth itself aright. At the last it biteth like a serpent, and stingeth like an adder. Thine eye shall behold strange women, and thine heart shall utter perverse things. Yea, thou shalt be as he that lieth down in the midst of the sea, or as he that lieth upon the top of a mast. They have stricken me, shalt thou say, and I was not sick; they have beaten me, and I felt it not: when shall I awake? I will seek it yet again.

This is a glowing description of the sin of intemperance. None but the pencil of inspiration, could have thrown upon the canvass so many and such vivid traits of this complicated evil, in so short a compass. It exhibits its woes and sorrows, contentions and babblings, and wounds and redness of eyes; its smiling deceptions in the beginning, and serpent-bite in the end; the helplessness of its victims, like one cast out upon the deep; the danger of destruction, like that of one who sleeps upon the top of a mast; the unavailing lamentations of the captive, and the giving up of hope and effort. "They have stricken me, and I was not sick; they have beaten me, and I felt it not: when shall I awake? I will seek it yet again;" again be stricken and beaten; again float upon the deep, and sleep upon the mast.

No sin has fewer apologies than intemperance. The suffrage of the world is against it; and yet there is no sin so naked in its character, and whose commencement and progress is indicated by so many signs, concerning which there is among mankind such profound ignorance. All reprobate drunkenness; and yet, not one of the thousands who fall into it, dreams of danger when he enters the way that leads to it.

The soldier, approaching the deadly breach, and seeing rank after rank of those who preceded him swept away, hesitates sometimes, and recoils from certain death. But men behold the effects upon others, of going in given courses, they see them begin, advance, and end, in confirmed intemperance, and unappalled rush heedlessly upon the same ruin.

A part of this heedlessness arises from the undefined nature of the crime in its early stages, and the ignorance of men, concerning what may be termed the experimental indications of its approach. Theft and falsehood are definite actions. But intemperance is a state of internal sensation, and the indications may exist long, and multiply, and the subject of them not be aware that they are the signs of intemperance. It is not unfrequent, that men become irreclaimable in their habits, without suspicion of danger. Nothing, therefore, seems to be more important, than a description of this broad way, thronged by so many travellers, that the temperate, when they come in sight of it, may know their danger and pass by it and turn away.

What I shall deliver on this subject, has been projected for several years, has been delayed by indisposition, and the pressure of other labors, and is advanced now without personal or local reference.

Intemperance is the sin of our land, and, with our boundless prosperity, is coming in upon us like a flood; and if anything shall defeat the hopes of the world, which hang upon our experiment of civil liberty, it is that river of fire, which is rolling through the land, destroying the vital air, and extending around an atmosphere of death.

It is proposed in this and the subsequent discourses, to consider the nature, the occasions, the signs, the evils, and the remedy of intemperance. In this discourse we shall consider THE NATURE AND OCCASIONS OF INTEMPERANCE.

The more common apprehension is, that nothing is intemperance, which does not supersede the regular operations of the mental faculties and the bodily organs. However much a man may consume of ardent spirits, if he can command his mind, his utterance, and his bodily members, he is not reputed intemperate. And yet, drinking within these limits, he may be intemperate in respect to inordinate desire, the quantity consumed, the expense incurred, the present effect on his health and temper, and moral sensibilities, and what is more, in respect to the ultimate and inevitable results of bodily and mental imbecility, or sottish drunkenness.

God has made the human body to be sustained by food and sleep, and the mind to be invigorated by effort and the regular healthfulness of the moral system, and the cheering influence of his moral government. And whoever, to sustain the body, or invigorate the mind, or cheer the heart, applies habitually the stimulus of ardent spirits, does violence to the laws of his nature, puts the whole system into disorder, and is intemperate long before the intellect falters, or a muscle is unstrung.

The effect of ardent spirits on the brain, and the members of the body, is among the last effects of intemperance, and the least destructive part of the sin. It is the moral ruin which it works in the soul, that gives it the denomination of giant-wickedness. If all who are intemperate, drank to insensibility, and on awaking, could arise from the debauch with intellect and heart uninjured, it would strip the crime of its most appalling evils. But among the woes which the scriptures denounce against crime, one is, "wo unto them that are mighty to drink wine, and men of strength to consume strong drink." These are captains in the bands of intemperance, and will drink two generations of youths into the grave, before they go to lie down by their side. The Lord deliver us from strong-headed men, who can move the tongue when all are mute around them, and keep the eye open when all around them sleep, and can walk from the scene of riot, while their companions must be aided or wait until the morning.

It is a matter of undoubted certainty, that habitual tippling is worse than periodical drunkenness. The poor Indian, who, once a month, drinks himself *dead* all but simple breathing, will out-live for years the man who drinks little and often, and is not, perhaps, suspected of intemperance. The use of ardent spirits daily, as ministering to cheerfulness, or bodily vigor, ought to be regarded as intemperance. No person, probably, ever did, or ever will, receive ardent spirits into his system once a day, and fortify his constitution against its deleterious effects, or exercise such discretion and self government, as that the quantity will not be increased, and bodily infirmities and mental imbecility be the result, and, in more than half the instances, inebriation. Nature may hold out long against this sapping and mining of the constitution, which daily tippling is carrying on; but, first or last, this foe of life will bring to the assault enemies of its own formation, before whose power the feeble and the mighty will be alike unable to stand.

All such occasional exhilaration of the spirits by intoxicating liquors, as produces levity and foolish jesting, and the loud laugh, is intemperance, whether we regard those precepts which require us to be sober-minded, or the effect which such exhilaration and lightness has upon the cause of Christ, when witnessed in professors of religion. The cheerfulness of health, and excitement of industry, and social intercourse, is all which nature demands, or health or purity permits.

A resort to ardent spirits as a means of invigorating the intellect, or of pleasurable sensation, is also intemperance. It is a distraint upon nature, to extort, in a short time, those results of mind and feeling, which in her own unimpelled course would flow with less impetuosity, but in a more equable and healthful current. The mind has its limits of intellectual application, and the heart its limits of feeling, and the nervous system of healthful exhilaration; and whatever you gain through stimulus, by way of anticipation, is only so much intellectual and vital power cut off at the latter end of life. It is this occult intemperance, of daily drinking, which generates a host of bodily infirmities and diseases: loss of appetite—nausea at the stomach—disordered bile—obstructions of the liver—jaundice—dropsy—hoarseness of voice—coughs—consumptions—rheumatic pains—epilepsy—gout—colic—palsy—apoplexy—insanity—are the body-guards which attend intemperance, in the form of tippling, and where the odious name of drunkenness may perhaps be never applied.

A multitude of persons, who are not accounted drunkards, create disease, and shorten their days, by what they denominate a "prudent use of ardent spirits." Let it therefore be engraven upon the heart of every man, THAT THE DAILY USE OF ARDENT SPIRITS, IN ANY FORM, OR IN ANY DEGREE, IS INTEMPERANCE. Its effects are certain, and deeply injurious, though its results may be slow, and never be ascribed to the real cause. It is a war upon the human constitution, carried on ostensibly by an auxiliary, but which never fails to subtract more vital power than it imparts. Like the letting out of waters by little and little, the breach widens, till life itself is poured out. If all diseases which terminate in death, could speak out at the grave, or tell their origin upon the coffin-lid, we should witness the most appalling and unexpected disclosures. Happy the man, who so avoids the appearance of evil, as not to shorten his days by what he may call the prudent use of ardent spirits.

But we approach now a state of experience, in which it is supposed generally that there is some criminal intemperance. I mean when the empire of reason is invaded, and weakness and folly bear rule; prompting to garrulity, or sullen silence; inspiring petulance, or anger, or insipid good humour, and silly conversation; pouring out oaths, and curses, or opening the storehouse of secrets, their own and others. And yet, by some, all these have been thought insufficient evidence to support the charge of drinking, and to justify a process of discipline before the church. The tongue must falter, and the feet must trip, before, in the estimation of some, professors of religion can be convicted of the crime of intemperance.

To a just and comprehensive knowledge, however, of the crime of intemperance, not only a definition is required, but a philosophical analysis of its mechanical effects upon the animal system.

To those who look only on the outward appearance, the triumphs of intemperance over conscience, and talents, and learning, and character, and interest, and family endearments, have appeared wonderful. But the wonder will cease, when we consider the raging desire which it enkindles, and the hand of torment which it lays, on every fibre of the body and faculty of the soul.

The stomach is the great organ of accelerated circulation to the blood, of elasticity to the animal spirits, of pleasurable or painful vibration to the nerves, of vigor to the mind, and of fulness to the cheerful affections of the soul. Here is the silver cord of life, and the golden bowl at the fountain, and the wheel at the cistern; and as these fulfil their duty, the muscular and mental and moral powers act in unison, and fill the system with vigor and delight. But as these central energies are enfeebled, the strength of mind and body declines, and lassitude; and depression, and melancholy, and sighing, succeed to the high beatings of health, and the light of life becomes as darkness.

Experience has decided, that any stimulus applied statedly to the stomach, which raises its muscular tone above the point at which it can be sustained by food and sleep, produces, when it has passed away, debility—a relaxation of the over-worked organ, proportioned to its preternatural excitement. The life-giving power of the stomach falls of course as much below the tone of cheerfulness and health, as it was injudiciously raised above it. If the experiment be repeated often, it produces an artificial tone of stomach, essential to cheerfulness and muscular vigor, entirely above the power of the regular sustenance of nature to sustain, and creates a vacuum, which nothing can fill, but the destructive power which made it—and when protracted use has made the difference great, between the natural and this artificial tone, and habit has made it a second nature, the man is a drunkard, and, in ninety-nine instances in a hundred, is irretrievably undone. Whether his tongue falter, or his feet fail him or not, he will die of intemperance. By whatever name his disease may be called, it will be one of the legion which lie in wait about the path of intemperance, and which abused Heaven employs to execute wrath upon the guilty.

But of all the ways to hell, which the feet of deluded mortals tread, that of the intemperate is the most dreary and terrific. The demand for artificial stimulus to supply the deficiencies of healthful aliment, is like the rage of thirst, and the ravenous demand of famine. It is famine: for the artificial excitement has become as essential now to strength and cheerfulness, as simple nutrition once was. But nature, taught by habit to require what once she did not need, demands gratification now with a decision inexorable as death, and to most men as irresistible. The denial is a living death. The stomach, the head, the heart, and arteries, and veins, and every muscle, and every nerve, feel the exhaustion, and the restless, unutterable wretchedness which puts out the light of life, and curtains the heavens, and carpets the earth with sackcloth. All these varieties of sinking nature, call upon the wretched man with trumpet tongue, to dispel this darkness, and raise the ebbing tide of life, by the application of the cause which produced these woes, and after a momentary alleviation will produce them again with deeper terrors, and more urgent importunity; for the repetition, at each time renders the darkness deeper, and the torments of self-denial more irresistible and intolerable.

At length, the excitability of nature flags, and stimulants of higher power, and in greater quantities, are required to rouse the impaired energies of life, until at length the whole process of dilatory murder, and worse than purgatorial suffering, having been passed over, the silver cord is loosed, the golden bowl is broken, the wheel at the cistern stops, and the dust returns to the earth as it was, and the spirit to God who gave it.

These sufferings, however, of animal nature, are not to be compared with the moral agonies which convulse the soul. It is an immortal being who sins, and suffers; and as his earthly house dissolves, he is approaching the judgment seat, in anticipation of a miserable eternity. He feels his captivity, and in anguish of spirit clanks his chains and cries for help. Conscience thunders, remorse goads, and as the gulf opens before him, he recoils, and trembles, and weeps, and prays, and resolves, and promises, and reforms, and "seeks it yet again,"—again resolves, and weeps, and prays, and "seeks it yet again!" Wretched man, he has placed himself in the hands of a giant, who never pities, and never relaxes his iron gripe. He may struggle, but he is in chains. He may cry for release, but it comes not; and lost! lost! may be inscribed upon the door posts of his dwelling.

In the mean time these paroxysms of his dying moral nature decline, and a fearful apathy, the harbinger of spiritual death, comes on. His resolution fails, and his mental energy, and his vigorous enterprise; and nervous irritation and depression ensue. The social affections lose their fulness and tenderness, and conscience loses its power, and the heart its sensibility, until all that was once lovely and of good report, retires and leaves the wretch abandoned to the appetites of a ruined animal. In this deplorable condition, reputation expires, business falters and becomes perplexed, and temptations to drink multiply as inclination to do so increases, and the power of resistance declines. And now the vortex roars, and the struggling victim buffets the fiery wave with feebler stroke, and warning supplication, until despair flashes upon his soul, and with an outcry that pierces the heavens, he ceases to strive, and disappears.

A sin so terrific should be detected in its origin and strangled in the cradle; but ordinarily, instead of this, the habit is fixed, and the hope of reformation is gone, before the subject has the least suspicion of danger. It is of vast importance therefore, that the various occasions of intemperance should be clearly described, that those whose condition is not irretrievable, may perceive their danger, and escape, and that all who are free, may be warned off from these places of temptation and ruin. For the benefit of the young, especially, I propose to lay down a map of the way to destruction, and to rear a monument of warning upon every spot where a wayfaring man has been ensnared and destroyed.

The first occasion of intemperance which I shall mention, is found in the free and frequent use of ardent spirits in the family, as an incentive to appetite, an alleviation of lassitude, or an excitement to cheerfulness. In these reiterated indulgences, children are allowed to partake, and the tender organs of their stomachs are early perverted, and predisposed to habits of intemperance. No family, it is believed, accustomed to the daily use of ardent spirits, ever failed to plant the seeds of that dreadful disease, which sooner or later produced a harvest of wo. The material of so much temptation and mischief, ought not to be allowed a place in the family, except only as a medicine, and even then it would be safer in the hands of the apothecary, to be sent for like other medicine, when prescribed.

Ardent spirits, given as a matter of hospitality, is not unfrequently the occasion of intemperance. In this case the temptation is a stated inmate of the family. The utensils are present, and the occasions for their use are not unfrequent. And when there is no guest, the sight of the liquor, the state of the health, or even lassitude of spirits, may indicate the propriety of the "prudent use," until the prudent use becomes, by repetition, habitual use—and habitual use becomes irreclaimable intemperance. In this manner, doubtless, has many a father, and mother, and son, and daughter, been ruined forever.

Of the guests, also, who partake in this family hospitality, the number is not small, who become ensnared; especially among those whose profession calls them to visit families often, and many on the same day. Instead of being regarded, therefore, as an act of hospitality, and a token of friendship, to invite our friends to drink, it ought to be regarded as an act of incivility, to place ourselves and them in circumstances of such high temptation.

Days of public convocation are extensively the occasions of excess which eventuate in intemperance. The means and temptations are ostentatiously multiplied, and multitudes go forth prepared and resolved to yield to temptation, while example and exhilarated feeling secure the ample fulfilment of their purpose.—But when the habit is once acquired of drinking even *"prudently,"* as it will be called, on all the days of public convocation which occur in a year, a desire will be soon formed of drinking at other times, until the healthful appetite of nature is superseded by the artificial thirst produced by ardent spirits.

Evening resorts for conversation, enlivened by the cheering bowl, have proved fatal to thousands. Though nothing should be boisterous, and all should seem only the "feast of reason, and the flow of soul," yet at the latter end it biteth like a serpent and stingeth like an adder: many a wretched man has shaken his chains and cried out in the anguish of his spirit, oh! that accursed resort of social drinking; there my hands were bound and my feet put in fetters; there I went a freeman and became a slave, a temperate man and became a drunkard.

In the same class of high temptation are to be ranked all convivial associations for the purpose of drinking, with or without gambling, and late hours. There is nothing which young men of spirit fear less, than the exhilaration of drinking on such occasions; nor any thing which they are less able to resist, than the charge of cowardice when challenged to drink. But there is no one form of temptation before which more young men of promise have fallen into irretrievable ruin. The connexion between such beginnings and a fatal end is so manifest, and the presumptuous daring of Heaven is so great, that God in his righteous displeasure is accustomed to withdraw his protection and abandon the sinner to his own way.

Feeble health and mental depression are to be numbered among the occasions of intemperance. The vital sinking, and muscular debility, and mental darkness, are for a short time alleviated by the application of stimulants. But the cause of this momentary alleviation is applied and repeated, until the habit of excessive drinking is formed and has become irresistible.

Medical prescriptions have no doubt contributed to increase the number of the intemperate. Ardent spirits, administered in the form of bitters, or as the medium of other medicine, have let in the destroyer; and while the patient was seeking health at the hand of the physician, HE was dealing out debility and death.

The distillation of ardent spirits fails not to raise up around the establishment a generation of drunkards. The cheapness of the article, and the ease with which families can provide themselves with large quantities, the product of their own labor, eventuate in frequent drinking, and wide spread intemperance.

The vending of ardent spirits, in places licensed or unlicensed, is a tremendous evil. Here, those who have no stated employment loiter away the day for a few potations of rum, and here, those who have finished the toils of the day meet to spend a vacant hour; none content to be lookers on: all drink, and none for any length of time drink temperately. Here too the children of a neighborhood, drawn in by enticements, associate for social drinking, and the exhibition of courage and premature manhood. And here the iron hand of the monster is fastened upon them, at a period when they ought not to have been beyond the reach of maternal observation.

The continued habit of dealing out ardent spirits, in various forms and mixtures, leads also to frequent tasting, and tasting to drinking, and drinking to tippling, and tippling to drunkenness.

A resort to ardent spirits as an alleviation of trouble, results often in habits of confirmed intemperance. The loss of friends, perplexities of business, or the wreck of property, bring upon the spirits the distractions of care and the pressure of sorrow; and, instead of casting their cares upon the Lord, they resort to the exhilarating draught, but, before the occasion for it has ceased, the remedy itself has become a calamity more intolerable than the disease. Before, the woes were temporary; now, they have multiplied and have become eternal.

Ardent spirits employed to invigorate the intellect, or restore exhausted nature under severe study, is often a fatal experiment. Mighty men have been cast down in this manner never to rise. The quickened circulation does for a time invigorate intellect and restore exhausted nature. But, for the adventitious energy imparted, it exhausts the native energy of the soul, and induces that faintness of heart, and flagging of the spirits, which cry incessantly, "give, give," and never, but with expiring breath, say it is enough.

The use of ardent spirits, employed as an auxiliary to labor, is among the most fatal, because the most common and least suspected, causes of intemperance. It is justified as innocent, it is insisted on as necessary: but no fact is more completely established by experience than that it is utterly useless, and ultimately injurious, beside all the fearful evils of habitual intemperance, to which it so often leads. THERE IS NO NUTRITION IN ARDENT SPIRIT. ALL THAT IT DOES IS, TO CONCENTRATE THE STRENGTH OF THE SYSTEM FOR THE TIME, BEYOND ITS CAPACITY FOR REGULAR EXERTION. It is borrowing strength for an occasion, which will be needed for futurity, without any provision for payment, and with the certainty of ultimate bankruptcy.

The early settlers of New-England endured more hardship, and performed more labor, and carried through life more health and vigor, than appertains to the existing generation of laboring men. And they did it without the use of ardent spirits.

Let two men, of equal age and firmness of constitution, labor together through the summer, the one with and the other without the excitement of ardent spirits, and the latter will come out at the end with unimpaired vigor, while the other will be comparatively exhausted. Ships navigated as some now are without the habitual use of ardent spirits—and manufacturing establishments carried on without—and extended agricultural operations—all move on with better industry, more peace, more health, and a better income to the employers and the employed. The workmen are cheerful and vigorous, friendly and industrious, and their families are thrifty, well fed, well clothed and instructed; and instead of distress and poverty, and disappointment and contention—they are cheered with the full flow of social affection, and often by the sustaining power of religion. But where ardent spirit is received as a daily auxiliary to labor, it is commonly taken at stated times—the habit soon creates a vacancy in the stomach, which indicates at length the hour of the day with as much accuracy as a clock. It will be taken besides, frequently, at other times, which will accelerate the destruction of nature's healthful tone, create artificial debility, and the necessity of artificial excitement to remove it; and when so much has been consumed as the economy of the employer can allow, the growing demand will be supplied by the evening and morning dram, from the wages of labor—until the appetite has become insatiable, and the habit of intemperance nearly universal—until the nervous excitability has obliterated the social sensibilities, and turned the family into a scene of babbling and wo—until voracious appetite has eaten up the children's bread, and abandoned them to ignorance and crime—until conscience has become callous, and fidelity and industry have disappeared, except as the result of eye service; and wanton wastefulness and contention, and reckless wretchedness characterize the establishment.

Sermon II: The Signs of Intemperance

PROVERBS, xxiii. 29–35

Who hath wo? who hath sorrow? who hath contentions? who hath babbling? who hath wounds without cause? who hath redness of eyes?

They that tarry long at the wine; they that go to seek mixed wine.

Look not thou upon the wine when it is red, when it giveth his colour in the cup, when it moveth itself aright. At the last it biteth like a serpent, and stingeth like an adder. Thine eye shall behold strange women, and thine heart shall utter perverse things. Yes, thou shalt be as he that lieth down in the midst of the sea, or as he that lieth upon the top of a mast. They have stricken me, shalt thou say, and I was not sick; they have beaten me, and I felt it not: when shall I awake? I will seek it yet again.

In the preceding discourse I considered the nature and occasions of intemperance. In this I shall disclose some of the symptoms of this fearful malady, as they affect both the body and the mind, that every one, who is in any degree addicted to the sin, may be apprised of his danger, and save himself before it be too late.

In the early stages of intemperance reformation is practicable. The calamity is, that intemperance is a sin so deceitful, that most men go on to irretrievable ruin, warned indeed by many indications, but unavailingly, because they understand not their voice.

It is of vast importance, therefore, that the symptoms of intemperance should be universally and familiarly known; the effects of the sin upon the body, and upon the mind, should be so described in all its stages, from the beginning to the end, that every one may see, and feel, and recognise these harbingers of death as soon as they begin to show themselves upon him.

1. One of the early indications of intemperance may be found in the associations of time and place.

In the commencement of this evil habit, there are many who drink to excess only on particular days, such as days for military exhibition, the anniversary of our independence, the birth-day of Washington, Christmas, new year's day, election, and others of the like nature. When any of these holidays arrive, and they come as often almost as saints' days in the calendar, they bring with them, to many, the insatiable desire of drinking, as well as a dispensation from the sin, as efficacious and quieting to the conscience, as papal indulgences.

There are some I am aware that have recommended the multiplication of holidays and public amusements, as a remedy for intemperance:—about as wise a prescription—as the multiplying gambling houses to supersede gambling, or the building of theatres to correct the evils of the stage.

There are others who feel the desire of drinking stirred up within them by the associations of place. They could go from end to end of a day's journey without ardent spirits, were there no taverns on the road. But the very sight of these receptacles of pilgrims awakens the desire "just to step in and take something." And so powerful does this association become, that many will no more pass the tavern than they would pass a fortified place with all the engines of death directed against them. There are in, every city, town, and village, places of resort, which in like manner, as soon as the eye falls upon them, create the thirst of drinking, and many, who, coming to market or on business, pass near them, pay toll there as regularly as they do at the gates; and sometimes both when they come in and when they go out. In cities and their suburbs, there are hundreds of shops at which a large proportion of those who bring in produce stop regularly to receive the customary beverage.

In every community you may observe particular persons also who can never meet without feeling the simultaneous desire of strong drink. What can be the reason of this? All men, when they meet, are not affected thus. It is not uncommon for men of similar employments to be drawn by association, when they meet, to the same topics of conversation:—physicians, upon the concerns of their profession:—politicians, upon the events of the day:—and Christians, when they meet, are drawn by a common interest to speak of the things of the kingdom of God. But this is upon the principle of a common interest in these subjects, which has no slight hold upon the thoughts and affections. Whoever then finds himself tempted on meeting his companion or friend to say, 'come and let us go and take something,' or, to make it his first business to set out his decanter and glasses, ought to understand that he discloses his own inordinate attachment to ardent spirits, and accuses his friend of intemperance.

2. A disposition to multiply the circumstances which furnish the occasions and opportunities for drinking, may justly create alarm that the habit is begun. When you find occasions for drinking in all the variations of the weather, because it is so hot or so cold—so wet or so dry—and in all the different states of the system—when you are vigorous, that you need not tire—and when tired, that your vigor may be restored, you have approached near to that state of intemperance in which you will drink in all states of the weather, and conditions of the body, and will drink with these pretexts, and drink without them whenever their frequency may not suffice. In like manner if, on your farm, or in your store, or workshop, or on board your vessel, you love to multiply the catches and occasions of drinking, in the forms of treats for new comers—for mistakes—for new articles of dress—or furniture—until in some places a man can scarcely wear an article of dress, or receive one of equipage or furniture, which has not been "wet," you may rely on it that all these usages, and rules, and laws, are devices to gratify an inordinate and dangerous love of strong drink; and though the master of the shop should not himself come down to such little measures, yet if he permits such things to be done, if he hears, and sees, and smiles, and sometimes sips a little of the forfeited beverage, his heart is in the thing, and he is under the influence of a dangerous love of that hilarity which is produced by strong drink.

3. Whoever finds the desire of drinking ardent spirits returning daily at stated times, is warned to deny himself instantly, if he intends to escape confirmed intemperance.

It is infallible evidence that you have already done violence to nature—that the undermining process is begun—that the over-worked organ begins to flag, and cry out for adventitious aid, with an importunity which, if indulged, will become more deep toned, and importunate, and irresistible, until the power of self-denial is gone, and you are a ruined man. It is the vortex begun, which, if not checked, will become more capacious, and deep, and powerful, and loud, until the interests of time and eternity are engulfed.

It is here then—beside this commencing vortex—that I would take my stand, to warn off the heedless navigator from destruction. To all who do but heave in sight, and with voice that should rise above the winds and waves, I would cry—"stand off!!!"—spread the sail, ply the oar, for death is here—and could I command the elements—the blackness of darkness should gather over this gateway to hell—and loud thunders should utter their voices—and lurid fires should blaze—and the groans of unearthly voices should be heard—inspiring consternation and flight in all who came near. For this is the parting point between those who forsake danger and hide themselves, and the foolish who pass on and are punished. He who escapes this periodical thirst of times and seasons, will not be a drunkard, as he who comes within the reach of this powerful attraction will be sure to perish. It may not be certain that every one will become a sot; but it is certain that every one will enfeeble his body, generate disease, and shorten his days. It may not be certain that every one will sacrifice his reputation, or squander his property, and die in the alms house; but it is certain that a large proportion will come to poverty and infamy, of those who yield daily to the periodical appetite for ardent spirits. Here is the stopping place, and though beyond it men may struggle, and retard, and modify their progress, none, comparatively, who go by it, will return again to purity of enjoyment, and the sweets of temperate liberty. The servant has become the master, and, with a rod of iron and a whip of scorpions, he will torment, even before their time, the candidates for misery in a future state.

4. Another sign of intemperance may be found in the desire of concealment. When a man finds himself disposed to drink oftener, and more than he is willing to do before his family and the world, and begins to drink slily and in secret places, he betrays a consciousness that he is disposed to drink more than to others will appear safe and proper, and what he *suspects* others may think, he ought to suppose they have *cause* to think, and reform instantly. For now he has arrived at a period in the history of intemperance, where, if he does not stop, he will hasten on to ruin with accelerated movement. So long as the eye of friendship and a regard to public observation kept him within limits, there was some hope of reformation; but when he cuts this last cord, and launches out alone with his boat and bottle, he has committed himself to mountain waves and furious winds, and probably will never return.

5. When a man allows himself to drink always in company so much as he may think he can bear without awakening in others the suspicion of inebriation, he will deceive himself, and no one beside. For abused nature herself will publish the excess in the bloated countenance, and flushed visage, and tainted breath, and inflamed eye; and were all these banners of intemperance struck, the man with his own tongue will reveal his shame. At first there will be something

strange in his appearance or conduct, to awaken observation, and induce scrutiny, until at length, with all his carefulness, in some unguarded moment he will take more than he can bear. And now the secret is out, and these unaccountable things are explained; these exposures will become more frequent, the unhappy man still dreaming that though he erred a little, he took such good care to conceal it, that no one knew it but himself. He will even talk when his tongue is palsied, to ward off suspicion, and thrust himself into company, to show that he is not drunk.

6. Those persons who find themselves for some cause always irritated when efforts are made to suppress intemperance, and moved by some instinctive impulse to make opposition, ought to examine instantly whether the love of ardent spirits is not the cause of it.

An aged country merchant, of an acute mind and sterling reputation, once said to me, "I never knew an attempt made to suppress intemperance, which was not opposed by some persons, from whom I should not have expected opposition; and I never failed to find, first or last, that these persons were themselves implicated in the sin." Temperate men seldom if ever oppose the reformation of intemperance.

7. We now approach some of those symptoms of intemperance which abused nature first or last never fails to give.

The eyes. Who hath redness of eyes? All are not of course intemperate whose visual organs become inflamed and weak. But there are few intemperate persons who escape this malady, and yet when it comes, they have no suspicion of the cause—speak of it without embarrassment—and wonder what the matter can be—apply to the physician for eye water, and drink on. But every man who is accustomed to drink ardent spirits freely, whose eye begins to redden and to weep, ought to know what the matter is, and to take warning; it is one of the signals which distressed nature holds out and waves in token of distress.

Another indication of intemperance is found in the fullness and redness of the countenance. It is not the fulness and freshness of health—but rather the plethora of a relaxed fibre and peccant humours, which come to occupy the vacancy of healthful nutrition, and to mar the countenance with pimples and inflammation. All are not intemperate of course who are affected with diseases of the skin. But no hard drinker carries such a face without a guilty and specific cause, and it is another signal of distress which abused nature holds out, while she cries for help.

Another indication of intemperance may be found in impaired muscular strength and tremour of the hand. Now the destroyer, in his mining process, approaches the citadel of life, and is advancing fast to make the keepers of the house tremble, and the strong men bow themselves. This relaxation of the joints, and trembling of the nerves, will be experienced especially in the morning—when the system, unsustained by sleep, has run down. Now all is relaxed, tremulous, and faint-hearted. The fire which sparkled in the eye, the evening before, is quenched—the courage which dilated the heart is passed away—and the tones of eloquence, which dwelt on the inspired tongue, are turned into pusillanimous complainings, until opium, or bitters, or both, are thrown into the stomach to wind up again the run-down machine.

And now the liver, steeped in fire, begins to contract, and refuses to perform its functions, in preparing the secretions which are necessary to aid digestion; and loss of appetite ensues; and indigestion, and fermentation, and acidity, begin to rob the system of nutrition, and to vex and irritate the vital organ, filling the stomach with air, and the head with fumes, and the soul with darkness and terror.

This reiterated-irritation extends by sympathy to the lungs, which become inflamed and lacerated, until hemorrhage ensues. And now the terrified victim hastens to the physician to stay the progress of a consumption, which intemperance has begun, and which medical treatment, while the cause continues, can not arrest.

About this time the fumes of the scalding furnace below begin to lacerate the throat, and blister the tongue and the lip. Here again the physician is called in to ease these torments; but until the fires beneath are extinct, what can the physician do? He can no more alleviate these woes than he can carry alleviation to the tormented, in the flames for which these are the sad preparations.

Another indication of intemperance is irritability, petulance, and violent anger. The great organ of nervous sensibility has been brought into a state of tremulous excitement. The slightest touch causes painful vibrations, and irritations, which defy self-government.—The temper becomes like the flash of powder, or ungovernable and violent as the helm driven hither and thither by raging winds, and mountain waves.

Another indication of intemperance is to be found in the extinction of all the finer feelings and amiable dispositions of the soul; and, if there have ever seemed to be religious affections, of these also. The fiery stimulus has raised the organ of sensibility above the power of excitement by motives addressed to the finer feelings of the soul, and of the moral nature, and left the man a prey to animal sensation. You might as well fling out music upon the whirlwind to stay its course, as to govern the storm within by the gentler feelings of humanity. The only stimulant which now has power to move, is ardent spirits—and he who has arrived at this condition is lost. He has left far behind the wreck of what he once was. He is not the same husband, or father, or brother, or friend. The sea has made a clear breach over him, and swept away forever whatsoever things are pure, and lovely, and of good report.

And as to religion, if he ever seemed to have any, all such affections declined as the emotions of artificial stimulants arose, until conscience has lost its power, or survives only with vulture scream to flap the wing, and terrify the soul. His religious affections are dead when he is sober, and rise only to emotion and loquacity and tears when he is drunk. Dead, twice dead, is he—whatever may have been the hopes he once indulged, or the evidence he once gave, or the hopes he once inspired. For drunkards, no more than murderers, shall inherit the kingdom of God.

As the disease makes progress, rheumatic pains diffuse themselves throughout the system. The man wonders what can be the reason that he should be visited by such a complication of disease, and again betakes himself to the physician, and tries every remedy but the simple one of temperance. For these pains are only the murmurings and complainings of nature, through all the system giving signs of wo, that all is lost. For to rheumatic pains ensues a debility of the system, which becoming unable to sustain the circulation, the fluids fall first upon the feet, and, as the deluge rises, the chest is invaded, and the breath is shortened, until by a sudden inundation it is stopped. Or, if in this form death is avoided, it is only to be met in another—more dilatory but no less terrific; for now comes on the last catastrophe—the sudden prostration of strength and appetite—an increased difficulty of raising the ebbing tide of life by stimulants—a few panic struck reformations, just on the sides of the pit, until the last sinking comes, from which there is no resurrection but by the trump of God, and at the judgment day.

And now the woes, and the sorrows, and the contentions, and the wounds, and babblings, are over—the red eye sleeps—the tortured body rests—the deformed visage is hid from human observation—and the soul, while the dust crumbles back to dust, returns to God who gave it, to receive according to the deeds done in the body.

Such is the evil which demands a remedy. And what can be done to stop its ravages and rescue its victims?

This is not the place to say all that belongs to this part of the subject, but we cannot close without saying by anticipation a few things here; and,

1. There should be extended through the community an all-pervading sense of the danger there is of falling into this sin. Intemperance is a disease as well as a crime, and were any other disease, as contagious, of as marked symptoms, and as mortal, to pervade the land, it would create universal consternation: for the plague is scarcely more contagious or deadly; and yet we mingle fearlessly with the diseased, and in spite of admonition we bring into our dwellings the contagion, apply it to the lip, and receive it into the system.

I know that much is said about the prudent use of ardent spirits; but we might as well speak of the prudent use of the plague—of fire handed prudently around among powder—of poison taken prudently every day—or of vipers and serpents introduced prudently into our dwellings, to glide about as a matter of courtesy to visitors, and of amusement to our children.

First or last, in spite of your prudence, the contagion will take—the fatal spark will fall upon the train—the deleterious poison will tell upon the system—and the fangs of the serpent will inflict death. There is no prudent use of ardent spirits, but when it is used as a medicine. All who receive it into the system are not destroyed by it. But if any vegetable were poisonous to as many, as the use of ardent spirits proves destructive, it would be banished from the table; it would not be prudent to use it at all. If in attempting to cross a river upon an elastic beam—as many should fall in and be drowned, as attempt to use ardent spirits *prudently* and fail, the attempt to cross in that way would be abandoned—there would be no prudent use of that mode of crossing. The effect of attempting to use ardent spirits prudently, is destructive to such multitudes, as precludes the possibility of prudence in the use of it. When we consider the deceitful nature of this sin, and its irresistible power when it has obtained an ascendency—no man can use it prudently—or without mocking God can pray while he uses it, "lead us not into temptation." There is no necessity for using it at all, and it is presumptuous to do so.

2. A wakeful recollection should be maintained of the distinction between intemperance and drunkenness. So long as men suppose that there is neither crime nor danger in drinking, short of what they denominate drunkenness, they will cast off fear and move onward to ruin by a silent, certain course, until destruction comes upon them, and they cannot escape. It should be known therefore and admitted, that to drink daily, at stated times, any quantity of ardent spirits, is intemperance, or to drink periodically as often as days, and times, and seasons, may furnish temptation and opportunity, is intemperance. It may not be for any one time the intemperance of animal or mental excitement, but it is an innovation upon the system, and the beginning of a habit, which cannot fail to generate disease, and will not be pursued by one hundred men without producing many drunkards.

It is not enough therefore to erect the flag ahead, to mark the spot where the drunkard dies. It must be planted at the entrance of his course, proclaiming in waving capitals—THIS IS THE WAY TO DEATH!! Over the whole territory of "prudent use," it must wave and warn. For if we cannot stop men in the beginning, we cannot separate between that and the end. He who lets ardent spirits alone before it is meddled with, is safe, and he only. It should be in every family a contraband article, or if it is admitted, it should be allowed for medical purposes only. It should be labelled as we label laudanum—and TOUCH NOT, TASTE NOT, HANDLE NOT, should meet the eye on every vessel which contains it.

Children should be taught early the nature, symptoms, and danger of this sin, that they may not unwittingly fall under its power. To save my own children from this sin has been no small part of my solicitude as a parent, and I can truly say, that should any of my children perish in this way, they will not do it ignorantly, nor unwarned. I do not remember that I ever gave permission to a child to go out on a holiday, or gave a pittance of money to be expended for his gratification, unattended by the earnest injunction, not to drink ardent spirits, or any inebriating liquor; and I cannot but believe, that if proper exertions are made in the family to apprise children of the nature and danger of this sin, and to put them on their guard against it—opinions and feelings and habits might be so formed, that the whole youthful generation might rise up as a rampart, against which the fiery waves of intemperance would dash in vain, saying, hitherto shalt thou come, but no farther, and here shall thy proud waves be stayed. To all our schools instruction on this subject should be communicated, and the Sabbath schools now spreading through the land, may in this manner lend a mighty influence to prevent the intemperance of the rising generation.

In respect to the reformation of those over whom the habit of intemperance has obtained an ascendency, there is but one alternative—they must resolve upon immediate and entire abstinence.

Some have recommended, and many have attempted, a gradual discontinuance. But no man's prudence and fortitude are equal to the task of reformation in this way. If the patient were in close confinement, where he could not help himself, he might be dealt with in this manner, but it would be cruelly protracting a course of suffering through months, which might be ended in a few days. But no man, at liberty, will reform by gradual retrenchment.—Substitutes have also been recommended as the means of reformation, such as opium, which is only another mode of producing inebriation, is often a temptation to intemperance, and not unfrequently unites its own forces with those of ardent spirits to impair health, and destroy life. It is a preternatural stimulant, raising excitement above the tone of health, and predisposing the system for intemperate drinking.

Strong beer has been recommended as a substitute for ardent spirits, and a means of leading back the captive to health and liberty. But though it may not create intemperate habits as soon, it has no power to allay them. It will finish even what ardent spirits have begun—and with this difference only, that it does not rasp the vital organs with quite so keen a file—and enables the victim to come down to his grave, by a course somewhat more dilatory, and with more of the good natured stupidity of the idiot, and less of the demoniac frenzy of the madman.

Wine has been prescribed as a means of decoying the intemperate from the ways of death. But habit cannot be thus cheated out of its dominion, nor ravening appetite be amused down to a sober and temperate demand. If it be true that men do not become intemperate on wine, it is not true that wine will restore the intemperate, or stay the progress of the disease. Enough must be taken to screw up nature to the tone of cheerfulness, or she will cry "give," with an importunity not to be resisted, and long before the work of death is done, wine will fail to minister a stimulus of sufficient activity to rouse the flagging spirits, or will become acid on the enfeebled stomach, and brandy and opium will be called in to hasten to its consummation the dilatory work of self-destruction. So that if no man becomes a sot upon wine, it is only because it hands him over to more fierce and terrible executioners of Heaven's delayed vengeance.

If in any instance wine suffices to complete the work of ruin, then the difference is only that the victim is stretched longer upon the rack, to die in torture with the gout, while ardent spirits finish life by a shorter and perhaps less painful course.

Retrenchments and substitutes then are idle, and if in any case they succeed, it is not in one of a thousand. It is the tampering of an infant with a giant, the effort of a kitten to escape from the paw of a lion.

There is no remedy for intemperance but the cessation of it. Nature must be released from the unnatural war which is made upon her, and be allowed to rest, and then nutrition, and sleep, and exercise, will perform the work of restoration. Gradually the spring of life will recover tone, appetite will return, digestion become efficient, sleep sweet, and the muscular system vigorous, until the elastic heart with every beat shall send health through the system, and joy through the soul.

But what shall be done for those to whom it might be fatal to stop short? Many are reputed to be in this condition, probably, who are not—and those who are may, while under the care of a physician, be dealt with, as he may think best for the time, provided they obey strictly as patients his prescriptions. But if, when they are committed to their own care again, they cannot live without ardent spirits—then they must die, and have only the alternative to die as reformed penitents, or as incorrigibly intemperate—to die in a manner which shall secure pardon and admission to heaven, or in a manner which shall exclude them forever from that holy world.

As the application of this discourse, I would recommend to every one of you who hear it, immediate and faithful self-examination, to ascertain whether any of the symptoms of intemperance are beginning to show themselves upon you. And let not the consideration that you have never been suspected, and have never suspected yourselves of intemperance, deprive you of the benefit of this scrutiny. For it is inattention and self-confidence which supersede discretion, and banish fear, and let in the destroyer, to fasten upon his victim, before he thinks of danger or attempts resistance.

Are there then set times, days, and places, when you calculate always to indulge yourselves in drinking ardent spirits? Do you stop often to take something at the tavern when you travel, and always when you come to the village, town, or city. This frequency of drinking will plant in your system, before you are aware of it, the seeds of the most terrific disease which afflicts humanity. Have you any friends or companions whose presence, when you meet them, awakens the thought and the desire of drinking? Both of you have entered on a course in which there is neither safety nor hope, but from instant retreat.

Do any of you love to avail yourselves of every little catch and circumstance among your companions, to bring out "a treat?" "Alas, my lord, there is death in the pot."

Do you find the desire of strong drink returning daily, and at stated hours? Unless you intend to travel all the length of the highway of intemperance, it is time to stop. Unless you intend soon to resign your liberty forever, and come under a despotism of the most cruel and inexorable character, you must abandon the morning bitters, the noontide stimulant, and the evening bowl.

Do any of you drink in secret, because you are unwilling your friends or the world should know how much you drink? You might as well cut loose in a frail boat before a hurricane, and expect safety: you are gone, gone irretrievably, if you do not stop.

Are you accustomed to drink, when opportunities present, as much as you can bear without any public tokens of inebriation? You are an intemperate man now, and unless you check the habit, you will become rapidly more and more intemperate, until concealment becomes impossible,

Do your eyes, in any instance, begin to trouble you by their weakness or inflammation? If you are in the habit of drinking ardent spirits daily, you need not ask the physician what is the matter—nor inquire for eye water. Your redness of eyes is produced by intemperance; and abstinence, and that only, will cure them. It may be well for every man who drinks daily, to look in the glass often, that he may see in his own face the signals of distress, which abused nature holds out one after another, and too often holds out in vain.

Do any of you find a tremour of the hand coming upon you, and sinking of spirits, and loss of appetite in the morning? Nature is failing, and giving to you timely admonition of her distress.

Do the pains of a disordered stomach, and blistered tongue and lip, begin to torment you? You are far advanced in the work of self-destruction—a few more years will probably finish it.

Sermon III: The Evils of Intemperance

HABAKKUK, ii. 9–11, 15, 16

Wo to him that coveteth an evil covetousness to his house, that he may set his nest on high, that he may be delivered from the power of evil! Thou hast consulted shame to thy house by cutting off many people, and hast sinned against thy soul. For the stone shall cry out of the wall, and the beam out of the timber shall answer it.

Wo unto him that giveth his neighbor drink, that puttest thy bottle to him, and makest him drunken also, that thou mayest look on their nakedness! Thou art filled with shame for glory: drink thou also, and let thy foreskin be uncovered: the cup of the LORD's right hand shall be turned unto thee, and shameful spewing shall be on thy glory.

In the preceding discourses we have illustrated THE NATURE, THE OCCASIONS, AND THE SYMPTOMS OF INTEMPERANCE.

In this discourse we propose to illustrate THE EVILS OF INTEMPERANCE.

The physical and moral influence of this sin upon its victims, has of necessity been disclosed in giving an account of the causes and symptoms of this criminal disease. We shall therefore take a more comprehensive view of the subject, and consider the effect of intemperance upon national prosperity. To this view of the subject the text leads us. It announces the general principle, that communities which rise by a violation of the laws of humanity and equity, shall not prosper, and especially that wealth amassed by promoting intemperance, will bring upon the community intemperance, and poverty, and shame, as a providential retribution.

1. The effects of intemperance upon the health and physical energies of a nation, are not to be overlooked, or lightly esteemed.

No fact is more certain than the transmission of temperament and of physical constitution, according to the predominant moral condition of society, from age to age. Luxury produces effeminacy, and transmits to other generations imbecility and disease. Bring up the generation of the Romans who carried victory over the world, and place them beside the effeminate Italians of the present day, and the effect of crime upon constitution will be sufficiently apparent. Excesses unmake the man. The stature dwindles, the joints are loosely compacted, and the muscular fibre has lost its elastic tone. No giant's bones will be found in the cemeteries of a nation, over whom, for centuries, the waves of intemperance have rolled; and no unwieldy iron armour, the annoyance and defence of other days, will be dug up as memorials of departed glory.

The duration of human life, and the relative amount of health or disease, will manifestly vary, according to the amount of ardent spirits consumed in the land. Even now, no small proportion of the deaths which annually make up our national bills of mortality, are cases of those who have been brought to an untimely end, and who have, directly or indirectly, fallen victims to the deleterious influence of ardent spirits; fulfilling, with fearful accuracy, the prediction, "the wicked shall not live out half their days." As the jackal follows the lion to prey upon the slain, so do disease and death wait on the footsteps of inebriation. The free and universal use of intoxicating liquors for a few centuries cannot fail to bring down our race from the majestic, athletic forms of our Fathers, to the similitude of a despicable and puny race of men. Already the commencement of the decline is manifest, and the consummation of it, should the causes continue, will not linger.

2. The injurious influence of general intemperance upon national intellect, is equally certain, and not less to be deprecated.

To the action of a powerful mind, a vigorous muscular frame is, as a general rule, indispensable. Like heavy ordnance, the mind, in its efforts, recoils on the body, and will soon shake down a puny frame. The mental action and physical reaction must be equal—or, finding her energies unsustained, the mind itself becomes discouraged, and falls into despondency and imbecility. The flow of animal spirits, the fire and vigor of the imagination, the fulness and power of feeling, the comprehension and grasp of thought, the fire of the eye, the tones of the voice, and the electrical energy of utterance, all depend upon the healthful and vigorous tone of the animal system, and by whatever means the body is unstrung, the spirit languishes. Caesar, when he had a fever once, and cried "give me some drink, Titinius," was not that god who afterwards overturned the republic, and reigned without a rival—and Bonaparte, it has been said, lost the Russian campaign by a fever. The greatest poets and orators who stand on the records of immortality, flourished in the iron age, before the habits of effeminacy had unharnessed the body and unstrung the mind. This is true of Homer, and Demosthenes, and Milton; and if Virgil and Cicero are to be classed with them, it is not without a manifest abatement of vigor for beauty, produced by the progress of voluptuousness in the age in which they lived.

The giant writers of Scotland are, some of them, men of threescore and ten, who still go forth to the athletic sports of their youthful days with undiminished elasticity. The taper fingers of modern effeminacy never wielded such a pen as these men wield, and never will.

The taste may be cultivated in alliance with effeminacy, and music may flourish, while all that is manly is upon the decline, and there may be some fitful flashes of imagination in poetry, which are the offspring of a capricious, nervous excitability—and perhaps there may be sometimes an unimpassioned stillness of soul in a feeble body, which shall capacitate for simple intellectual discrimination. But that fulness of soul, and diversified energy of mind, which is indispensable to national talent in all its diversified application, can be found only in alliance with an undebased and vigorous muscular system.

The history of the world confirms this conclusion. Egypt, once at the head of nations, has, under the weight of her own effeminacy, gone down to the dust. The victories of Greece let in upon her the luxuries of the east, and covered her glory with a night of ages. And Rome, whose iron foot trode down the nations, and shook the earth, witnessed in her latter days—faintness of heart—and the shield of the mighty vilely cast away.

3. The effect of intemperance upon the military prowess of a nation, cannot but be great and evil. The mortality in the seasoning of recruits, already half destroyed by intemperance, will be double to that experienced among hardy and temperate men.

If in the early wars of our country the mortality of the camp had been as great as it has been since intemperance has facilitated the raising of recruits, New England would have been depopulated, Philip had remained lord of his wilderness, or the French had driven our Fathers into the sea, extending from Canada to Cape Horn the empire of despotism and superstition. An army, whose energy in conflict depends on the excitement of ardent spirits, cannot possess the coolness nor sustain the shock of a powerful onset, like an army of determined, temperate men. It was the religious principle and temperance of Cromwell's army, that made it terrible to the licentious troops of Charles the First.

4. The effect of intemperance upon the patriotism of a nation is neither obscure nor doubtful. When excess has despoiled the man of the natural affections of husband, father, brother, and friend, and thrust him down to the condition of an animal; we are not to expect of him comprehensive views, and a disinterested regard for his country. His patriotism may serve as a theme of sinister profession, or inebriate boasting. But, what is the patriotism which loves only in words, and in general, and violates in detail all the relative duties on which the welfare of country depends!

The man might as well talk of justice and mercy, who robs and murders upon the highway, as he whose example is pestiferous, and whose presence withers the tender charities of life, and perpetuates weeping, lamentation, and wo. A nation of drunkards would constitute a hell.

5. Upon the national conscience or moral principle the effects of intemperance are deadly.

It obliterates the fear of the Lord, and a sense of accountability, paralyses the power of conscience, and hardens the heart, and turns out upon society a sordid, selfish, ferocious animal.

6. Upon national industry the effects of intemperance are manifest and mischievous.

The results of national industry depend on the amount of well-directed intellectual and physical power. But intemperance paralyses and prevents both these springs of human action.

In the inventory of national loss by intemperance, may be set down—the labor prevented by indolence, by debility, by sickness, by quarrels and litigation, by gambling and idleness, by mistakes and misdirected effort, by improvidence and wastefulness, and by the shortened date of human life and activity. Little wastes in great establishments constantly occurring may defeat the energies of a mighty capital. But where the intellectual and muscular energies are raised to the working point daily by ardent spirits, until the agriculture, and commerce, and arts of a nation move on by the power of artificial stimulus, that moral power cannot be maintained, which will guaranty fidelity, and that physical power cannot be preserved and well directed, which will ensure national prosperity. The nation whose immense enterprise is thrust forward by the stimulus of ardent spirits, cannot ultimately escape debility and bankruptcy.

When we behold an individual cut off in youth, or in middle age, or witness the waning energies, improvidence, and unfaithfulness of a neighbor, it is but a single instance, and we become accustomed to it; but such instances are multiplying in our land in every direction, and are to be found in every department of labor, and the amount of earnings prevented or squandered is incalculable: to all which must be added the accumulating and frightful expense incurred for the support of those and their families, whom intemperance has made paupers. In every city and town the poor-tax, created chiefly by intemperance, is augmenting. The receptacles for the poor are becoming too strait for their accommodation. We must pull them down and build greater to provide accommodations for the votaries of inebriation; for the frequency of going upon the town has taken away the reluctance of pride, and destroyed the motives to providence which the fear of poverty and suffering once supplied. The prospect of a destitute old age, or of a suffering family, no longer troubles the vicious portion of our community. They drink up their daily earnings, and bless God for the poor-house, and begin to look upon it as, of right, the drunkard's home, and contrive to arrive thither as early as idleness and excess will give them a passport to this sinecure of vice. Thus is the insatiable destroyer of industry marching through the land, rearing poor-houses, and augmenting taxation: night and day, with sleepless activity, squandering property, cutting the sinews of industry, undermining vigor, engendering disease, paralysing intellect, impairing moral principle, cutting short the date of life, and rolling up a national debt, invisible, but real and terrific as the debt of England: continually transferring larger and larger bodies of men, from the class of contributors to the national income, to the class of worthless consumers.

Add the loss sustained by the subtraction of labor, and the shortened date of life, to the expense of sustaining the poor, created by intemperance; and the nation is now taxed annually more than the expense which would be requisite for the maintenance of government, and for the support of all our schools and colleges, and all the religious instruction of the nation. Already a portion of the entire capital of the nation is mortgaged for the support of drunkards. There seems to be no other fast property in the land, but this inheritance of the intemperate: all other riches may make to themselves wings and fly away. But until the nation is bankrupt, according to the laws of the State, the drunkard and his family must have a home. Should the pauperism of crime augment in this country as it has done for a few years past, there is nothing to stop the frightful results which have come upon England, where property is abandoned in some parishes, because the poor-tax exceeds the annual income. You who are husband-men; are accustomed to feel as if your houses and lands were wholly your own; but if you will ascertain the percentage of annual taxation levied on your property for the support of the intemperate, you will perceive how much of your capital is held by drunkards, by a tenure as sure as if held under mortgages, or deeds of warranty. Your widows and children do not take by descent more certainly, than the most profligate and worthless part of the community. Every intemperate and idle man, whom you behold tottering about the streets and steeping himself at the stores, regards your houses and lands as pledged to take care of him,—puts his hands deep, annually, into your pockets, and eats his bread in the sweat of your brows, instead of his own: and with marvellous good nature you bear it. If a robber should break loose on the highway, to levy taxation, an armed force would be raised to hunt him from society. But the tippler may do it fearlessly, in open day, and not a voice is raised, not a finger is lifted.

The effects of intemperance upon civil liberty may not be lightly passed over.

It is admitted that intelligence and virtue are the pillars of republican institutions, and that the illumination of schools, and the moral power of religious institutions, are indispensable to produce this intelligence and virtue.

But who are found so uniformly in the ranks of irreligion as the intemperate? Who like these violate the Sabbath, and set their mouth against the heavens—neglecting the education of their families—and corrupting their morals? Almost the entire amount of national ignorance and crime is the offspring of intemperance. Throughout the land, the intemperate are hewing down the pillars, and undermining the foundations of our national edifice. Legions have besieged it, and upon every gate the battle-axe rings; and still the sentinels sleep.

Should the evil advance as it has done, the day is not far distant when the great body of the laboring classes of the community, the bones and sinews of the nation, will be contaminated; and when this is accomplished, the right of suffrage becomes the engine of self-destruction. For the laboring classes constitute an immense majority, and when these are perverted by intemperance, ambition needs no better implements with which to dig the grave of our liberties, and entomb our glory.

Such is the influence of interest, ambition, fear, and indolence, that one violent partisan, with a handful of disciplined troops, may overrule the influence of five hundred temperate men, who act without concert. Already is the disposition to temporize, to tolerate, and even to court the intemperate, too apparent, on account of the apprehended retribution of their perverted suffrage. The whole power of law, through the nation, sleeps in the statute book, and until public sentiment is roused and concentrated, it may be doubted whether its execution is possible.

Where is the city, town, or village, in which the laws are not openly violated, and where is the magistracy that dares to carry into effect the laws against the vending or drinking of ardent spirits? Here then an aristocracy of bad influence has already risen up, which bids defiance to law, and threatens the extirpation of civil liberty. As intemperance increases, the power of taxation will come more and more into the hands of men of intemperate habits and desperate fortunes; of course the laws gradually will become subservient to the debtor, and less efficacious in protecting the rights of property. This will be a vital stab to liberty—to the security of which property is indispensable. For money is the sinew of war—and when those who hold the property of a nation cannot be protected in their rights, they will change the form of government, peaceably if they may, by violence if they must.

In proportion to the numbers who have no right in the soil, and no capital at stake, and no moral principle, will the nation be exposed to violence and revolution. In Europe, the physical power is bereft of the right of suffrage, and by the bayonet is kept down. But in this nation, the power which may be wielded by the intemperate and ignorant is tremendous. These are the troops of the future Caesars, by whose perverted suffrages our future elections may be swayed, and ultimately our liberties destroyed. They are the corps of irreligious and desperate men, who have something to hope, and nothing to fear, from revolution and blood. Of such materials was the army of Catiline composed, who conspired against the liberties of Rome. And in the French revolution, such men as Lafayette were soon swept from the helm, by mobs composed of the dregs of creation, to give place to the revolutionary furies which followed.

We boast of our liberties, and rejoice in our prospective instrumentality in disenthralling the world. But our own foundations rest on the heaving sides of a burning mountain, through which, in thousands of places, the fire has burst out, and is blazing around us. If they cannot be extinguished, we are undone. Our sun is fast setting, and the darkness of an endless night is closing in upon us.

Sermon IV: The Remedy of Intemperance

HABAKKUK, ii. 9–11, 15, 16

Wo to him that coveteth an evil covetousness to his house, that he may set his nest on high, that he may be delivered from the power of evil! Thou hast consulted shame to thy house by cutting off many people, and hast sinned against thy soul. For the stone shall cry out of the wall, and the beam out of the timber shall answer it.

Wo unto him that giveth his neighbor drink, that puttest thy bottle to him, and makes him drunken also, that thou mayest look on their nakedness! Thou art filled with shame for glory: drink thou also, and let thy foreskin be uncovered: the cup of the LORD's right hand shall be turned unto thee, and shameful spewing shall be on thy glory.

We now come to the inquiry, BY WHAT MEANS CAN THE EVIL OF INTEMPERANCE BE STAYED? and the answer is, not by any *one thing*, but by every thing which can be put in requisition to hem in the army of the destroyer, and impede his march, and turn him back, and redeem the land.

Intemperance is a national sin, carrying destruction from the centre to every extremity of the empire, and calling upon the nation to array itself, *en masse*, against it.

It is in vain to rely alone upon self-government, and voluntary abstinence. This, by all means, should be encouraged and enforced, and may limit the evil, but can never expel it. Alike hopeless are all the efforts of the pulpit, and the press, without something more radical, efficient and permanent. If knowledge only, or argument, or motive, were needed, the task of reformation would be easy. But argument may as well be exerted upon the wind, and motive be applied to chain down the waves. Thirst, and the love of filthy lucre, are incorrigible. Many may be saved by these means; but with nothing more, many will be lost, and the evil will go down to other ages. Alike hopeless is the attempt to stop intemperance by mere civil coercion.

There is too much capital vested in the importation, distillation, and vending of ardent spirits, and too brisk a demand for their consumption in the market, to render mere legal enactments and prohibitions, of sufficient influence to keep the practice of trafficking in ardent spirits within safe limits. As well might the ocean be poured out upon the Andes, and its waters be stopped from rushing violently down their sides. It would require an omniscient eye, and an almighty arm, punishing with speedy and certain retribution all delinquents, to stay the progress of intemperance in the presence of the all-pervading temptation of ardent spirits.

Magistrates WILL NOT, and CANNOT, if they would, execute the laws against the unlawful vending and drinking of ardent spirits, amid a population who hold the right of suffrage, and are in favor of free indulgence. The effort, before the public sentiment was prepared for it, would hurl them quick from their elevation, and exalt others who would be no terror to evil doers. Our Fathers could enforce morality by law; but the times are changed, and unless we can regulate public sentiment, and secure morality in some other way, WE ARE UNDONE.

Voluntary associations to support the magistrate in the execution of the law are useful, but after all are ineffectual—for though, in a single town, or state, they may effect a temporary reformation, it requires an effort to make them universal, and to keep up their energy, which never has been, and never will be made.

Besides, the reformation of a town, or even of a state, is but emptying of its waters the bed of a river, to be instantly replaced by the waters from above; or like the creation of a vacuum in the atmosphere, which is instantly filled by the pressure of the circumjacent air.

The remedy, whatever it may be, must be universal, operating permanently, at all times, and in all places. Short of this, every thing which can be done, will be but the application of temporary expedients.

There is somewhere a mighty energy of evil at work in the production of intemperance, and until we can discover and destroy this vital power of mischief, we shall labor in vain.

Intemperance in our land is not accidental; it is rolling in upon us by the violation of some great laws of human nature. In our views, and in our practice as a nation, there is something fundamentally wrong; and the remedy, like the evil, must be found in the correct application of general principles. It must be a universal and national remedy.

What then is this universal, natural, and national remedy for intemperance?

IT IS THE BANISHMENT OF ARDENT SPIRITS FROM THE LIST OF LAWFUL ARTICLES OF COMMERCE, BY A CORRECT AND EFFICIENT PUBLIC SENTIMENT; SUCH AS HAS TURNED SLAVERY OUT OF HALF OUR LAND, AND WILL YET EXPEL IT FROM THE WORLD.

Nothing should now be said, by way of crimination for the past, for verily we have all been guilty in this thing; so that there are few in the land, whose brother's blood may not cry out against them from the ground, on account of the bad influence which has been lent in some way to the work of destruction.

We are not therefore to come down in wrath upon the distillers, and importers, and venders of ardent spirits. None of us are enough without sin to cast the first stone. For who would have imported, or distilled, or vended, if all the nominally temperate in the land had refused to drink? It is the buyers who have created the demand for ardent spirits, and made distillation and importation a gainful traffick. And it is the custom of the temperate too, which inundates the land with the occasion of so much and such unmanageable temptation. Let the temperate cease to buy—and the demand for ardent spirits will fall in the market three fourths, and ultimately will fail wholly, as the generation of drunkards shall hasten out of time.

To insist that men, whose capital is embarked in the production, or vending of ardent spirits, shall manifest the entire magnanimity and self-denial, which is needful to save the land, though the example would be glorious to them, is more than we have a right to expect or demand. Let the consumer do his duty, and the capitalist, finding his employment unproductive, will quickly discover other channels of useful enterprise. All language of impatient censure, against those who embarked in the traffick of ardent spirits while it was deemed a lawful calling, should therefore be forborne. It would only serve to irritate and arouse prejudice, and prevent investigation, and concentrate a deaf and deadly opposition against the work of reformation. No *ex post facto* laws.—Let us all rather confess the sins which are past, and leave the things which are behind, and press forward in one harmonious attempt to reform the land, and perpetuate our invaluable blessings.

This however cannot be done effectually so long as the traffick in ardent spirits is regarded as lawful, and is patronised by men of reputation and moral worth in every part of the land. Like slavery, it must be regarded as sinful, impolitic, and dishonorable. That no measures will avail short of rendering ardent spirits a contraband of trade, is nearly self-evident.

Could intemperance be stopped, did all the rivers in the land flow with inebriating and fascinating liquids? But the abundance and cheapness of ardent spirits is such, that, surrounded as it is by the seductions of company, and every artifice of entertainment, it is more tempting and fatal than if it flowed freely as water. Then, like the inferior creation, men might be expected to drink when athirst, and to drink alone. But intemperance now is a social sin, and on that account exerts a power terrific and destructive as the plague.

That the traffick in ardent spirits is wrong, and should be abandoned as a great national evil, is evident from the following considerations.

1. It employs a multitude of men, and a vast amount of capital, to no useful purpose. The medicinal use of ardent spirits is allowed; for this however the apothecary can furnish an adequate supply: but considered as an article of commerce, for ordinary use, it adds nothing to animal or social enjoyment, to muscular power, to intellectual vigor, or moral feeling. It does, indeed, produce paroxysms of muscular effort, of intellectual vigor, and of exhilarated feeling, but it is done only by an improvident draught upon nature by anticipation, to be punished by a languor and debility proportioned to the excess. No man leaves behind him a more valuable product of labor, as the result of artificial stimulus, than the even industry of unstimulated nature would have produced; or blesses the world with better specimens of intellectual power; or instructs it by a better example; or drinks enjoyment from a fuller, sweeter cup, than that which nature provides. But if the premises are just, who can resist the conclusion? To what purpose is all this waste? Is it not the duty of every man to serve his generation in some useful employment? Is not idleness a sin? But in what respect does that occupation differ from idleness which adds nothing to national prosperity, or to individual or social enjoyment? Agriculture, commerce, and the arts are indispensable to the perfection of human character, and the formation of the happiest state of society; and if some evils are inseparable from their prosecution, there is a vast overbalancing amount of good. But where is the good produced by the traffick in ardent spirits, to balance the enormous evils inseparable from the trade? What drop of good does it pour into the ocean of misery which it creates? And is all this expense of capital, and time, and effort, to be sustained for nothing? Look at the mighty system of useless operations—the fleet of vessels running to and fro—the sooty buildings throughout the land, darkening the heavens with their steam and smoke—the innumerable company of boats, and wagons, and horses, and men—a more numerous cavalry than ever shook the blood-stained plains of Europe—a larger convoy than ever bore on the waves

the baggage of an army—and more men than were ever devoted at once to the work of desolation and blood. All these begin, continue, and end their days in the production and distribution of a liquid, the entire consumption of which is useless. Should all the capital thus employed, and all the gains acquired, be melted into one mass, and thrown into the sea, nothing would be subtracted from national wealth or enjoyment. Had all the men and animals slept the whole time, no vacancy of good had been occasioned.

Is this then the manner in which rational beings should be willing to spend their days—in which immortal beings should fill up the short period of their probation, and make up the account to be rendered to God of the deeds done in the body—in which benevolent beings, desiring to emulate the goodness of the great God, should be satisfied to employ their powers?

It is admitted that the trade employs and sustains many families, and that in many instances the profits are appropriated to useful purposes. But this is no more than might have been said of the slave trade. The same families might be as well sustained in some other way, and the same profits might be earned and applied to useful purposes in some other calling. The earth is not so narrow, nor population so dense, nor the useful avocations so overstocked, as that large portions of time, and capital, and labor, may be devoted to the purpose of sustaining life merely, without reference to public utility.

The merchant who deals in ardent spirits is himself a loser; for a temperate population consume more, and pay better, and live longer, than the intemperate; and among such a population merchants would do more business, and secure better profits than when they depend for any part of their gains upon the sale of ardent spirits. What merchant, looking out for a place where to establish himself in trade, would neglect the invitation of temperate, thrifty farmers and mechanics, and settle down in a village of riot and drunkenness—made up of tipplers, widows, and beggared children—of old houses, broken windows, and dilapidated fences?

I push not this argument reproachfully, but for the purpose of awakening conscientious investigation. We are a free people. No imperial *ukase*, or forest of bayonets, can make us moral and industrious, or turn us back if we go astray. Our own intelligence and moral energy must reclaim us, or we shall perish in our sins.

2. The amount of suffering and mortality inseparable from the commerce in ardent spirits, renders it an unlawful article of trade.

The wickedness is proverbial of those who in ancient days caused their children to pass through the fire unto Moloch. But how many thousands of children are there in our land who endure daily privations and sufferings, which render life a burden, and would have made the momentary pang of infant sacrifice a blessing? Theirs is a lingering, living death. There never was a Moloch to whom were immolated yearly as many children as are immolated, or kept in a state of constant suffering in this land of nominal Christianity. We have no drums and gongs to drown their cries, neither do we make convocations, and bring them all out for one mighty burning. The fires which consume them are slow fires, and they blaze balefully in every part of our land; throughout which the cries of injured children and orphans go up to heaven. Could all these woes, the product of intemperance, be brought out into one place, and the monster who inflicts the sufferings be seen personified, the nation would be furious with indignation. Humanity, conscience, religion, all would conspire to stop a work of such malignity.

We are appalled, and shocked, at the accounts from the east, of widows burnt upon the funeral piles of their departed husbands. But what if those devotees of superstition, the Brahmins, had discovered a mode of prolonging the lives of the victims for years amid the flames, and by these protracted burnings were accustomed to torture life away? We might almost rouse up a crusade to cross the deep, to stop by force such inhumanity. But, alas! we should leave behind us, on our own shores, more wives in the fire, than we should find of widows thus sacrificed in all the east; a fire too, which, besides its action upon the body, tortures the soul by lost affections, and ruined hopes, and prospective wretchedness.

It is high time to enter upon the business of collecting facts on this subject. The statistics of intemperance should be published; for no man has comprehended as yet the height, and depth, and length, and breadth of this mighty evil.

We execrate the cruelties of the slave trade—the husband torn from the bosom of his wife—the son from his father—brothers and sisters separated forever—whole families in a moment ruined! But are there no similar enormities to be witnessed in the United States? None indeed perpetrated by the bayonet—but many, very many, perpetrated by intemperance.

Every year thousands of families are robbed of fathers, brothers, husbands, friends. Every year widows and orphans are multiplied, and grey hairs are brought with sorrow to the grave—no disease makes such inroads upon families, blasts so many hopes, destroys so many lives, and causes so many mourners to go about the streets, because man goeth to his long home.

We have heard of the horrors of the middle passage—the transportation of slaves—the chains—the darkness—the stench—the mortality and living madness of wo—and it is dreadful. But bring together the victims of intemperance, and crowd them into one vast lazar-house, and sights of wo quite as appalling would meet your eyes.

Yes, in this nation there is a middle passage of slavery, and darkness, and chains, and disease, and death. But it is a middle passage, not from Africa to America, but from time to eternity, and not of slaves whom death will release from suffering, but of those whose sufferings at death do but just begin. Could all the sighs of these captives be wafted on one breeze, it would be loud as thunder. Could all their tears be assembled, they would be like the sea.

The health of a nation is a matter of vast importance, and none may directly and avowedly sport with it. The importation and dissemination of fevers for filthy lucre's sake, would not be endured, and he who should import and plant the seed of trees, which, like the fabled Upas, poisoned the atmosphere, and paved the earth around with bones, would meet with universal execration. The construction of morasses and stagnant lakes, sending out poisonous exhalations, and depopulating the country around, would soon be stopped by the interposition of law. And should a foreign army land upon our shores, to levy such a tax upon us as intemperance levies, and to threaten our liberties as intemperance threatens them, and to inflict such enormous sufferings as intemperance inflicts, no mortal power could resist the swelling tide of indignation that would overwhelm it.

It is only in the form of ardent spirits in the way of a lawful trade extended over the entire land, that fevers may be imported and disseminated—that trees of death may be planted—that extensive morasses may be opened, and a moral *miasma* spread over the nation—and that an armed host may land, to levy upon us enormous taxations, to undermine our liberties, bind our hands, and put our feet in fetters. This dreadful work is going on, and yet the nation sleeps. Say not that all these evils result from the abuse of ardent spirits; for as human nature is constituted, the abuse is as certain as any of the laws of nature. The commerce therefore, in ardent spirits, which produces no good, and produces a certain and an immense amount of evil, must be regarded as an unlawful commerce, and ought, upon every principle of humanity, and patriotism, and conscience, and religion, to be abandoned and proscribed.

Sermon V: The Remedy of Intemperance

HABAKKUK, ii. 9–11, 15, 16

Wo to him that coveteth an evil covetousness to his house, that he may set his nest on high, that he may be delivered from the power of evil! Thou hast consulted shame to thy house by cutting off many people, and hast sinned against thy soul. For the stone shall cry out of the wall, and the beam out of the timber shall answer it.

Wo unto him that giveth his neighbor drink, that puttest thy bottle to him, and makest him drunken also, that thou mayest look on their nakedness! Thou art filled with shame for glory: drink thou also, and let thy foreskin be uncovered: the cup of the LORD's right hand shall be turned unto thee, and shameful spewing shall be on thy glory.

We have endeavored to show that commerce in ardent spirits is unlawful,

1. Inasmuch as it is useless; and

2. As it is eminently pernicious.

We now proceed to adduce further evidence of its unlawfulness—and observe,

3. That it seems to be a manifest violation of the command, "Thou shalt love thy neighbor as thyself;" and of various other evangelical precepts.

No man can act in the spirit of impartial love to his neighbor, who for his own personal emolument, inflicts on him great and irreparable evil; for love worketh no ill to his neighbor. Love will not burn a neighbor's house, or poison his food, or blast his reputation, or destroy his soul. But the commerce in ardent spirits does all this inevitably and often. Property, reputation, health, life and salvation fall before it.

The direct infliction of what is done indirectly, would subject a man to the ignominy of a public execution. Is it not forbidden then by the command which requires us to love our neighbor as ourselves? "Whatsoever ye would that men should do to you, do ye even so to them." Be willing to do for others whatever you may demand of them, and inflict nothing upon them which you would not be willing to receive. But who is willing to be made a drunkard, and to have his property squandered, and his family ruined, for his neighbor's emolument? Good were it for the members of a family if they had never been born, rather than to have all the evils visited upon them, which are occasioned by the sale of ardent spirits.

It is scarcely a palliation of this evil that no man is destroyed maliciously—or with any direct intent to kill—for the certainty of evil is as great as if waters were poisoned which some persons would surely drink, or as if a man should fire in the dark upon masses of human beings, where it must be certain that death would be the consequence to some.

Those who engage in this traffick, are exposed to temptations to intemperance which no man will needlessly encounter who has that regard to the preservation of his own life and virtue, which the law of God requires. All who are employed in vending ardent spirits in small quantities, do not of course become intemperate. But the company in whose presence they pass so much of their time, and the constant habit of mixing and tasting, has been the means of casting down many strong men wounded. It is also a part of the threatened retribution, that those who amass property by promoting intemperance in others, shall themselves be punished by falling under the dominion of the same sin. "Wo unto him that giveth his neighbor drink, that puttest thy bottle to him, and makest him drunken also—Thou art filled with shame for glory: drink thou also, and let thy foreskin be uncovered: the cup of the Lord's right hand shall be turned unto thee, and shameful spewing shall be on thy glory."

The injustice which is so inseparable from the traffick in ardent spirits; evinces its unlawfulness.

Those who vend ardent spirits will continue to supply their customers, in many instances, after they have ceased to be competent to take care of their property. They are witnesses to their dealing with a slack hand, their improvidence, and the accumulation of their debts; and, to save themselves, must secure their own claims by obtaining mortgages on the property of these wretched victims, which they finally foreclose, and thus wind up the scene. And are they not in this way accessary to the melting away of estates, and the ruin of families around them? And can all this be done without violating the laws of humanity and equity? Human laws may not be able to prevent the wrong, but the cries of widows and orphans will be heard in heaven, and a retribution which human tribunals cannot award, will be reserved for the day of judgment. Is it not an "evil covetousness" that rolls up an estate by such methods? It is like "building a town with blood, and establishing a city by iniquity." And can those who do thus escape the wo denounced against him, "that giveth his neighbor drink, that putteth his bottle to him, and maketh him drunken?"

Can it be denied that the commerce in ardent spirits makes a fearful havock of property, morals, and life? Does it not shed blood as really as the sword, and more blood than is shed by war? In this point none are better witnesses than physicians, and, according to their testimony, intemperance is one of the greatest destroyers of virtue, health and life.

It is admitted that commerce generally lays a heavy tax upon life and morals. But it is an evil inseparable from a course of things which is actually indispensable to civilization. The entire melioration of the human condition seems to depend upon it, so that were commerce to cease, agriculture would fall back to the simple product of a supply without surplus, destroying the arts, and cutting the sinews of industry. But the commerce in ardent spirits stands on a different ground: its evils are compensated by no greater good; it promotes no good purpose which would not prosper better without it; it does not afford property to those who engage in it, which they might not accumulate in some other way; nor does it give the least adventitious aid to agriculture, or the arts. Every thing needful to a perfect state of society can exist without it; and with it, such a state of society can never be attained. It retards the accomplishment of that prophecy of scripture which foretells the time, when the knowledge of the Lord shall cover the earth, and violence and fraud shall cease.

The consideration, that those, to whose injury we are accessary by the sale of ardent spirits, are destroyed also by the perversion of their own free agency— and that the evil is silent, and slow-paced in its march—doubtless subtracts in no small degree, from the keen sense of accountability and crime, which would attend the administration of arsenic, or the taking of life by the pistol, or the dagger—as does also the consideration, that although we may withhold the cup, yet, from some other source, the deleterious potion will be obtained.

But all this alters not the case. He who deliberately assists his neighbor to destroy his life, is not guiltless because his neighbor is a free agent and is also guilty—and he is accessary to the crime, though twenty other persons might have been ready to commit the same sin, if he had not done it. Who would sell arsenic to his neighbor to destroy himself, because he could obtain it elsewhere? Who would sell a dagger for the known purpose of assassination, because, if it were refused, it could be purchased in another place? We are accountable for our own wrong-doing, and liable to punishment at the hand of God, as really as if it had been certain that no one would have done the deed, if we did not.

The ungodliness in time, and the everlasting ruin in eternity, inseparable from the commerce in ardent spirits, proscribe it as an unlawful article of traffick.

Who can estimate the hatred of God, of his word and worship, and of his people, which it occasions; or number the oaths and blasphemies it causes to be uttered—or the violations of the sabbath—the impurities and indecencies— violence and wrong-doing—which it originates? How many thousand does it detain every sabbath-day from the house of God—cutting them off from the means of grace, and hardening them against their efficacy! How broad is the road which intemperance alone opens to hell, and how thronged with travellers!

Why is all this increase of ungodliness and crime? Is not the desperate wickedness of the heart sufficient without artificial excitement? If the commerce were inseparable from all the great and good ends of our social being, we might endure the evil, for the sake of the good, and they only be accountable who abuse themselves. But here is an article of commerce spread over the land, whose effect is evil only, and that continually, and which increases a hundred-fold the energies of human depravity, and the hopeless victims of future punishment.

Drunkenness is a sin which excludes from heaven. The commerce in ardent spirits, therefore, productive only of evil in time, fits for destruction, and turns into hell multitudes which no man can number.

I am aware that in the din of business, and the eager thirst for gain, the consequences of our conduct upon our views, and the future destiny of our fellow men, are not apt to be realized, or to modify our course.

But has not God connected with all lawful avocations the welfare of the life that now is, and of that which is to come? And can we lawfully amass property by a course of trade which fills the land with beggars, and widows, and orphans, and crimes; which peoples the grave-yard with premature mortality, and the world of wo with the victims of despair? Could all the forms of evil produced in the land by intemperance, come upon us in one horrid array—it would appal the nation, and put an end to the traffick in ardent spirits. If in every dwelling built by blood, the stone from the wall should utter all the cries which the bloody traffick extorts—and the beam out of the timber should echo them back—who would build such a house?—and who would dwell in it? What if in every part of the dwelling, from the cellar upward, through all the halls and chambers—babblings, and contentions, and voices, and groans, and shrieks, and wailings, were heard, day and night! What if the cold blood oozed out, and stood in drops upon the walls; and, by preternatural art, all the ghastly skulls and bones of the victims destroyed by intemperance, should stand upon the walls, in horrid sculpture within and without the building!—who would rear such a building? What if at eventide, and at midnight, the airy forms of men destroyed by intemperance, were dimly seen haunting the distilleries and stores, where they received their bane—following the track of the ship engaged in the commerce—walking upon the waves—flitting athwart the deck—sitting upon the rigging—and sending up, from the hold within, and from the waves without, groans, and loud laments, and wailings! Who would attend such stores? Who would labor in such distilleries? Who would navigate such ships?

Oh! were the sky over our heads one great whispering gallery, bringing down about us all the lamentation and wo which intemperance creates, and the firm earth one sonorous medium of sound, bringing up around us from beneath, the wailings of the damned, whom the commerce in ardent spirits had sent thither;—these tremendous realities, assailing our sense, would invigorate our conscience, and give decision to our purpose of reformation. But these evils are as real, as if the stone did cry out of the wall, and the beam answered it—as real, as if, day and night, wailings were heard in every part of the dwelling—and blood and skeletons were seen upon every wall—as real, as if the ghostly forms of departed victims flitted about the ship as she passed o'er the billows, and showed themselves nightly about stores and distilleries, and with unearthly voices screamed in our ears their loud lament. They are as real, as if the sky over our heads collected and brought down about us all the notes of sorrow in the land—and the firm earth should open a passage for the wailings of despair to come up from beneath.

But it will be said,—What can be done?—and ten thousand voices will reply, 'Nothing—oh nothing—men always have drunk to excess, and they always will; there is so much capital embarked in the business of importation and distillation—and so much supposed gain in vending ardent spirits—and such an insatiable demand for them—and such ability to pay for them by high-minded, wilful, independent freemen—that nothing can be done.'

Then farewell, a long farewell, to all our greatness! The present abuse of ardent spirits has grown out of what was the prudent use of it, less than one hundred years ago; then there was very little intemperance in the land—most men, who drank at all, drank temperately. But if the prudent use of ardent spirits one hundred years ago, has produced such results as now exist, what will the present intemperate use accomplish in a century to come? Let no man turn off his eye from this subject, or refuse to reason, and infer—there is a moral certainty of a wide extended ruin, without reformation. The seasons are not more sure to roll, the sun to shine, or the rivers to flow—than the present enormous consumption of ardent spirits is sure to produce the most deadly consequences to the nation. They will be consumed in a compound ratio—and there is a physical certainty of the dreadful consequences. Have you taken the dimensions of the evil, its manifold and magnifying miseries, its sure-paced and tremendous ruin? And shall it come unresisted by prayer, and without a finger lifted to stay the desolation?

What if all men had cried out, as some did, at the commencement of the revolutionary struggle—'Alas! we must submit—we must be taxed—nothing can be done—Oh the fleets and armies of England—we cannot stand before them!!' Had such counsels prevailed, we should have abandoned a righteous cause, and forfeited that aid of Heaven, for which men are always authorized to trust in God, who are disposed to do his will.

Nothing can be done! Why can nothing be done? Because the intemperate will not stop drinking, shall the temperate keep on and become drunkards? Because the intemperate cannot be reasoned with, shall the temperate become madmen? And because force will not avail with men of independence and property, does it follow that reason, and conscience, and the fear of the Lord, will have no influence?

And because the public mind is now unenlightened, and unawakened, and unconcentrated, does it follow that it cannot be enlightened, and aroused, and concentrated in one simultaneous and successful effort? Reformations as much resisted by popular feeling, and impeded by ignorance, interest, and depraved obstinacy, have been accomplished, through the medium of a rectified public opinion,—and no nation ever possessed the opportunities and the means that we possess, of correctly forming the public opinion—nor was a nation ever called upon to attempt it by motives of such imperious necessity. Our all is at stake—we shall perish if we do not effect it. There is nothing that ought to be done, which a free people cannot do.

The science of self-government is the science of perfect government, which we have yet to learn and teach, or this nation, and the world, must be governed by force. But we have all the means, and none of the impediments, which hinder the experiment amid the dynasties and feudal despotisms of Europe. And what has been done justifies the expectation that all which yet remains to be done will be accomplished. The abolition of the slave trade, an event now almost accomplished, was once regarded as a chimera of benevolent dreaming. But the band of Christian heroes, who consecrated their lives to the work, may some of them survive to behold it achieved. This greatest of evils upon earth, this stigma of human nature, wide-spread, deep-rooted, and intrenched by interest and state policy, is passing away before the unbending requisitions of enlightened public opinion.

No great melioration of the human condition was ever achieved without the concurrent effort of numbers, and no extended, well-directed application of moral influence, was ever made in vain. Let the temperate part of the nation awake, and reform, and concentrate their influence in a course of systematic action, and success is not merely probable, but absolutely certain. And cannot this be accomplished?—cannot the public attention be aroused, and set in array against the traffick in ardent spirits, and against their use? With just as much certainty can the public sentiment be formed and put in motion, as the waves can be moved by the breath of heaven—or the massy rock, balanced on the precipice, can be pushed from its centre of motion;—and when the public sentiment once begins to move, its march will be as resistless as the same rock thundering down the precipice. Let no man then look upon our condition as hopeless, or feel, or think, or say, that nothing can be done. The language of Heaven to our happy nation is, "be it unto thee even as thou wilt," and there is no despondency more fatal, or more wicked, than that which refuses to hope, and to act, from the apprehension that nothing can be done.

Sermon VI: The Remedy of Intemperance

Habakkuk, ii. 9–11, 15, 16

Wo to him that coveteth an evil covetousness to his house, that he may set his nest on high, that he may be delivered from the power of evil! Thou hast consulted shame to thy house by cutting off many people, and hast sinned against thy soul. For the stone shall cry out of the wall, and the beam out of the timber shall answer it.

Wo onto him that giveth his neighbor drink, that puttest thy bottle to him, and makest him drunken also, that thou mayest look on their nakedness! Thou art filled with shame for glory: drink thou also, and let thy foreskin be uncovered: the cup of the LORD's right hand shall be turned unto thee, and shameful spewing shall be on thy glory.

Let us now take an inventory of the things which can be done to resist the progress of intemperance. I shall set down nothing which is chimerical, nothing which will not commend itself to every man's judgment, as entirely practicable.

1. It is entirely practicable to extend universal information on the subject of intemperance. Its nature, causes, evils, and remedy—may be universally made known. Every pulpit and every newspaper in the land may be put in requisition to give line upon line, on this subject, until it is done. The National Tract Society may, with great propriety, volunteer in this glorious work, and send out its warning voice by winged messengers all over the land. And would all this accomplish nothing? It would prevent the formation of intemperate habits in millions of instances, and it would reclaim thousands in the early stages of this sin.

2. It is practicable to form an association for the special purpose of superintending this great subject, and whose untiring energies shall be exerted in sending out agents to pass through the land, and collect information, to confer with influential individuals, and bodies of men, to deliver addresses at popular meetings, and form societies auxiliary to the parent institution. This not only may be done, but I am persuaded will be done before another year shall have passed away.* Too long have we slept. From every part of the land we hear of the doings of the destroyer, and yet the one half is not told. But when the facts are collected and published, will not the nation be moved? It will be moved. All the laws of the human mind must cease, if such disclosures as may be made, do not produce a great effect.

3. Something has been done, and more may be done, by agricultural, commercial, and manufacturing establishments, in the exclusion of ardent spirits as an auxiliary to labor. Every experiment which has been made by capitalists to exclude ardent spirits and intemperance, has succeeded, and greatly to the profit and satisfaction, both of the laborer and his employer. And what is more natural and easy than the extension of such examples by capitalists, and by voluntary associations, in cities, towns, and parishes, of mechanics and farmers, whose resolutions and success may from time to time be published, to raise the flagging tone of hope, and assure the land of her own self-preserving powers? Most assuredly it is not too late to achieve a reformation; our hands are not bound, our feet are not put in fetters—and the nation is not so fully set upon destruction, as that warning and exertion will be in vain. It is not too much to be hoped, that the entire business of the nation, by land and by sea, shall yet move on without

*These Discourses were composed and delivered at Litchfield, in the year 1826: since that time the American Society for the Promotion of Temperance has been formed, and is now in successful operation.

the aid of ardent spirits, and by the impulse alone of temperate freemen. This would cut off one of the most fruitful occasions of intemperance, and give to our morals and to our liberties an earthly immortality.

The young men of our land may set glorious examples of voluntary abstinence from ardent spirits, and, by associations for that purpose, may array a phalanx of opposition against the encroachments of the destroyer; while men of high official standing and influence, may cheer us by sending down the good example of their firmness and independence, in the abolition of long-established, but corrupting habits.

All the professions too may volunteer in this holy cause, and each lift up its warning voice and each concentrate the power of its own blessed example. Already from all clerical meetings the use of ardent spirits is excluded; and the medical profession have also commenced a reform in this respect which, we doubt not, will prevail. Nor is it to be expected that the bar, or the agricultural interest as represented in agricultural societies, will be deficient in magnanimity and patriotic zeal, in purifying the morals, and perpetuating the liberties of the nation. A host may be enlisted against intemperance which no man can number, and a moral power be arrayed against it, which nothing can resist.

All denominations of Christians in the nation may with great ease be united in the effort to exclude the use and the commerce in ardent spirits. They alike feel and deplore the evil, and, united, have it in their power to put a stop to it. This union may be accomplished through the medium of a national society. There is no object for which a national society is more imperiously demanded, or for which it can be reared under happier auspices. God grant that three years may not pass away, before the entire land shall be marshalled, and the evils of intemperance be seen like a dark cloud passing off, and leaving behind a cloudless day.

The churches of our Lord Jesus Christ, of every name, can do much to aid in this reformation. They are organized to shine as lights in the world, and to avoid the very appearance of evil. A vigilant discipline is doubtless demanded in the cases of members who are of a lax and doubtful morality in respect to intemperance. It is not enough to cut off those who are past reformation, and to keep those who, by close watching, can be preserved in the use of their feet and tongue. Men who are mighty to consume strong drink, are unfit members of that kingdom which consisteth not in "meat and drink," but in "righteousness and peace." The time, we trust, is not distant, when the use of ardent spirits will be proscribed by a vote of all the churches in our land, and when the commerce in that article shall, equally with the slave trade, be regarded as inconsistent with a credible profession of Christianity. All this, I have no doubt, can be accomplished with far less trouble than is now constantly occasioned by the maintenance, or the neglect of discipline, in respect to cases of intemperance.

The Friends, in excluding ardent spirits from the list of lawful articles of commerce, have done themselves immortal honor, and in the temperance of their families, and their thrift in business, have set an example which is worthy the admiration and imitation of all the churches in our land.

When the preceding measures have been carried, something may be done by legislation, to discourage the distillation and importation of ardent spirits, and to discountenance improper modes of vending them. Then, the suffrage of the community may be expected to put in requisition men of talents and integrity, who, sustained by their constituents, will not hesitate to frame the requisite laws, and to give to them their salutary power. Even now there may be an amount of suffrage, could it be concentrated and expressed, to sustain laws which might go to limit the evil; but it is scattered, it is a dispersed, unorganized influence, and any effort to suppress intemperance by legislation, now, before the public is prepared for an efficient cooperation, could terminate only in defeat. Republics must be prepared by moral sentiment for efficient legislation.

Much may be accomplished to discountenance the commerce in ardent spirits, by a silent, judicious distribution of patronage in trade.

Let that portion of the community, who would exile from society the traffick in ardent spirits, bestow their custom upon those who will agree to abandon it; and a regard to interest will soon produce a competition in well doing. The temperate population of a city or town are the best customers, and have it in their power to render the commerce in ardent spirits disadvantageous to those who engage in it. This would throw an irresistible argument upon the side of reformation. There are many now who would gladly be released from the necessity of dealing in spirituous liquors, but they think that their customers would not bear it. Let their sober customers, then, take off their fears on this hand, and array them on the other, and a glorious reformation is achieved. When the temperate part of the community shall not only declaim against mercantile establishments which thrive by the dissemination of moral contagion, but shall begin to act with a silent but determined discrimination, the work is done;—and can any conscientious man fail to make the experiment? "To him who knoweth to do good and doeth it not, to him it is sin." If we countenance establishments in extending and perpetuating a national calamity, are we not partakers in other men's sins? How many thousands may be saved from entering into temptation, and how many thousands rescued who have entered, if temperate families will give their custom to those who have abandoned the traffick in ardent spirits! And to how much crime, and suffering, and blood, shall we be accessary, if we fail to do our duty in this respect! Let every man, then, bestow his custom in the fear of the Lord, and as he expects to give an account with joy or grief, of the improvement or neglect of that powerful means of effecting moral good.

When all these preliminary steps have been taken, petitions may be addressed to the Legislatures of the States and to Congress, by all denominations, each under their own proper name, praying for legislative interference to protect the health and morals of the nation. This will call to the subject the attention of the ablest men in the nation, and enable them to touch some of the springs of general action with compendious energy. They can reach the causes of disastrous action, when the public sentiment will bear them out in it, and can introduce principles which, like the great laws of nature, will, with silent simplicity, reform and purify the land.

And now, could my voice be extended through the land, to all orders and descriptions of men, I would "cry aloud and spare not." To the watchmen upon Zion's walls—appointed to announce the approach of danger, and to say unto the wicked man, "thou shalt surely die"—I would say—can we hold our peace, or withhold the influence of our example in such an emergency as this, and be guiltless of blood? Are we not called upon to set examples of entire abstinence? How otherwise shall we be able to preach against intemperance, and reprove, rebuke, and exhort? Talk not of "habit," and of "prudent use," and a little for the "stomach's sake." This is the way in which men become drunkards. Our security and our influence demand immediate and entire abstinence. If nature would receive a shock by such a reformation, it proves that it has already been too long delayed, and can safely be deferred no longer.

To the churches of our Lord Jesus Christ,—whom he hath purchased with his blood, that he might redeem them from all iniquity, and purify them to himself, a peculiar people—I would say—Beloved in the Lord, the world hath need of your purified example;—for who will make a stand against the encroachments of intemperance, if professors of religion will not? Will you not, then, abstain from the use of it entirely, and exile it from your families? Will you not watch over one another with keener vigilance—and lift an earlier note of admonition— and draw tighter the bands of brotherly discipline—and with a more determined fidelity, cut off those whom admonition cannot reclaim? Separate, brethren, between the precious and the vile, the living and the dead, and burn incense between them, that the plague may be stayed.

To the physicians of the land I would cry for help, in this attempt to stay the march of ruin. Beloved men—possessing our confidence by your skill, and our hearts by your assiduities in seasons of alarm and distress—combine, I beseech you, and exert, systematically and vigorously, the mighty power you possess on this subject, over the national understanding and will. Beware of planting the seeds of intemperance in the course of your professional labors, but become our guardian angels to conduct us in the paths of health and of virtue. Fear not the consequence of fidelity in admonishing your patients, when diseased by intemperance, of the cause, and the remedy of their malady: and whenever one of you shall be rejected for your faithfulness, and another be called in to prophesy smooth things, let all the intemperate, and all the land know, that in the whole nation there are no false prophets among physicians, who, for filthy lucre, will cry peace to their intemperate patients, when there is no peace to them, but in reformation. Will you not speak out on this subject in all your medical societies, and provide tracts sanctioned by your high professional authority, to be spread over the land?

Ye magistrates, to whom the law has confided the discretionary power of giving license for the vending of ardent spirits, and the sword for the punishment of the violations of law—though you alone could not resist the burning tide, yet, when the nation is moved with fear, and is putting in requisition her energies to strengthen your hands—will you not stand up to your duty, and do it fearlessly and firmly? No class of men in the community possess as much direct power as you possess, and, when sustained by public sentiment, your official influence and authority may be made irresistible. Remember, then, your designation by Heaven to office for this self-same thing;—and, as you would maintain a conscience void of offence, and give up to God a joyful account—be faithful. Through you, let the violated law speak out—and righteousness and peace become the stability of our times.

To the governments of the states and of the nation, appointed to see to it, "that the commonwealth receives no detriment," while they facilitate and guide the energies of a free people, and protect the boundless results of industry—I would say—Beloved men and highly honored, how ample and how enviable are your opportunities of doing good—and how trivial, and contemptible, and momentary, are the results of civil policy merely, while moral principle, that mainspring of the soul, is impaired and destroyed by crime. Under the auspices of the national and state governments, science, commerce, agriculture and the arts flourish, and our wealth flows in like the waves of the sea. But where is the wisdom of filling up by a thousand streams the reservoir of national wealth, to be poured out again by as many channels of profusion and crime? Colleges are reared and multiplied by public munificence, while academies and common schools enlighten the land. But to what purpose—when a single crime sends up exhalations enough to eclipse half the stars and suns destined to enlighten our moral hemisphere, before they have reached their meridian.

The medical profession is patronised, and ought to be; and the standard of medical attainment is rising. But a single crime, unresisted, throws into the distance all the achievements of art, and multiplies disease and death much faster than the improvements in medical science can multiply the means of preventing them.

The improvements by steam and by canals augment the facilities and the motives to national industry. But, while intemperance rages and increases, it is only to pour the tide of wealth into one mighty vortex which swallows it up, and, with a voice of thunder, and the insatiable desire of the grave, cries, Give, give; and saith not, It is enough.

Republican institutions are guarantied to the states, and the whole nation watches with sleepless vigilance the altar of liberty. But a mighty despot, whose army is legion, has invaded the land—carrying in his course taxation, and chains, and fire, and the rack—insomuch that the whole land bleeds and groans at every step of his iron foot—at every movement of his massy sceptre—at every pulsation of his relentless heart. And yet in daylight and at midnight he stalks unmolested—while his myrmidons with infernal joy are preparing an ocean of blood in which our sun may set never to rise.

The friends of the Lord and his Christ, with laudable enterprise, are rearing temples to Jehovah, and extending his word and ordinances through the land, while the irreligious influence of a single crime balances, or nearly balances, the entire account.

And now, ye venerable and honorable men, raised to seats of legislation in a nation which is the freest, and is destined to become the greatest and may become the happiest upon earth—can you, will you behold unmoved the march of this mighty evil? Shall it mine in darkness, and lift fearlessly its giant form in daylight—and deliberately dig the grave of our liberties—and entomb the last hope of enslaved nations—and nothing be done by the national government to stop the destroyer? With the concurrent aid of an enlightened public sentiment, you possess the power of a most efficacious legislation; and, by your example and influence, you of all men possess the best opportunities of forming a correct and irresistible public sentiment on the side of temperance. Much power to you is given to check and extirpate this evil, and to roll down to distant ages, broader, and deeper, and purer, the streams of national prosperity. Save us by your wisdom and firmness, save us by your own example, and, "as in duty bound, we will ever pray."

Could I call around me in one vast assembly the temperate young men of our land, I would say—Hopes of the nation, blessed be ye of the Lord now in the dew of your youth. But look well to your footsteps: for vipers, and scorpions, and adders, surround your way—look at the generation who have just preceded you,—the morning of their life was cloudless, and it dawned as brightly as your own—but behold them bitten, swollen, enfeebled, inflamed, debauched, idle, poor, irreligious, and vicious,—with halting step dragging onward to meet an early grave! Their bright prospects are clouded, and their sun is set never to rise. No house of their own receives them, while from poorer to poorer tenements they descend, and to harder and harder fare, as improvidence dries up their resources. And now, who are those that wait on their footsteps with muffled faces and sable garments? That is a father—and that is a mother—whose grey hairs are coming with sorrow to the grave. That is a sister, weeping over evils which she cannot arrest—and there is the broken-hearted wife—and there are the children—hapless innocents—for whom their father has provided the inheritance only of dishonor, and nakedness, and wo. And is this, beloved young men, the history of your course—in this scene of desolation, do you behold the image of your future selves—is this the poverty and disease, which as an armed man shall take hold on you—and are your fathers, and mothers, and sisters, and wives, and children, to succeed to those who now move on in this mournful procession—weeping as they go? Yes—bright as your morning now opens, and high as your hopes beat, this is your noon, and your night, unless you shun those habits of intemperance which have thus early made theirs a day of clouds, and of thick darkness. If you frequent places of evening resort for social drinking—if you set out with drinking, daily, a little, temperately, prudently, it is yourselves which, as in a glass, you behold.

Might I select specific objects of address—to the young husbandman or mechanic—I would say—Happy man—your employment is useful, and honorable, and with temperance and industry you rise to competence, and rear up around you a happy family, and transmit to them, as a precious legacy, your own fair fame. But look around you;—are there none who were once in your condition, whose health, and reputation, and substance, are gone? What would tempt you to exchange conditions? And yet, sure as seed-time and harvest, if you drink daily, at stated times, and visit from evening to evening the resorts of social drinking, or stop to take refreshment as you enter or retire from the city, town, or village, yours will become the condition of those ruined farmers and artisans around you.

To another I would say—You are a man of wealth, and may drink to the extinction of life, without the risk of impoverishment—but look at your neighbor, his bloated face, and inflamed eye, and blistered lip, and trembling hand—he too is a man of wealth, and may die of intemperance without the fear of poverty.

Do you demand, "what have I to do with such examples?" Nothing—if you take warning by them. But if you too should cleave to the morning bitter, and the noon-tide dram, and the evening beverage, you have in these signals of ruin the memorials of your own miserable end; for the same causes, in the same circumstances, will produce the same effects.

To the affectionate husband I would say—Behold the wife of thy bosom, young and beautiful as the morning—and yet her day may be overcast with clouds, and all thy early hopes be blasted. Upon her the fell destroyer may lay his hand, and plant in that healthful frame the seeds of disease, and transmit to successive generations the inheritance of crime and wo. Will you not watch over her with ever-wakeful affection—and keep far from your abode the occasions of temptation and ruin? Call around you the circle of your healthful and beautiful children. Will you bring contagion into such a circle as this? Shall those sparkling eyes become inflamed—those rosy cheeks purpled and bloated—that sweet breath be tainted—those ruby lips blistered—and that vital tone of unceasing cheerfulness be turned into tremour and melancholy? Shall those joints so compact be unstrung—that dawning intellect beclouded—those affectionate sensibilities benumbed, and those capacities for holiness and heaven be filled with sin, and "fitted for destruction?" Oh thou father, was it for this that the Son of God shed his blood for thy precious offspring—that, abandoned and even tempted by thee, they should destroy themselves, and pierce thy heart with many sorrows? Wouldst thou let the wolf into thy sheep-fold among the tender lambs—wouldst thou send thy flock to graze about a den of lions?—Close, then, thy doors against a more ferocious destroyer—and withhold the footsteps of thy immortal progeny from places of resort more dangerous than the lion's den. Should a serpent of vast dimensions surprise in the field one of your little group, and wreath about his body his cold, elastic folds—tightening with every yielding breath his deadly gripe, how would his cries pierce your soul—and his strained eye-balls, and convulsive agonies, and imploring hands, add wings to your feet, and supernatural strength to your arms!—But in this case you could approach with hope to his rescue. The keen edge of steel might sunder the elastic fold, and rescue the victim, who, the moment he is released, breathes freely, and is well again. But the serpent intemperance twines about the body of your child a deadlier gripe, and extorts a keener cry of distress, and mocks your effort to relieve him by a fibre which no steel can sunder. Like Laocoon, you can only look on while bone after bone of your child is crushed, till his agonies are over, and his cries are hushed in death.

And now, to every one whose eye has passed over these pages—I would say—Resolve upon reformation by entire abstinence, before you close the book.

While the argument is clear, and the impression of it is fresh, and your judgment is convinced, and your conscience is awake, be persuaded, not almost, but altogether. The present moment may be the one which decides your destiny forever. As you decide now upon abstinence, or continued indulgence, so may your character be, through time and through eternity. Resolve also instantly to exclude ardent spirits from your family, and put out of sight the memorials of past folly and danger. And if for medicinal purposes you retain ardent spirits in your house, let it be among other drugs, and labelled, "Touch not, taste not, handle not."

As you would regulate your conduct by the Gospel, and give up your last account with joy, weigh well the arguments for abandoning the traffick in ardent spirits as unlawful in the sight of God. And "if thy right hand offend thee, cut it off. If thy right eye offend thee, pluck it out." Talk not of loss and gain—for who can answer for the blood of souls? and "what shall it profit a man, if he gain the whole world and lose his own soul?" "Wo to him that coveteth an evil covetousness to his house, that he may set his nest on high, that he may be delivered from the power of evil! Thou hast consulted shame to thy house by cutting off many people, and hast sinned against thy soul. For the stone shall cry out of the wall, and the beam out of the timber shall answer it. Wo to him that buildeth a town with blood, and stablisheth a city by iniquity! Behold, is it not of the Lord of hosts that the people shall labor in the very fire, and the people shall weary themselves for very vanity?"

Let the discourses upon the causes and symptoms of intemperance be read aloud in your family, at least once a year—that the deceitful, dreadful evil may not fasten unperceived, his iron gripe on yourself, or any of your household—and that, if one shall not perceive his danger, another may, and give the timely warning. Thousands every year may be kept back from destruction, by the simple survey of the causes and symptoms of intemperance. And,

Finally, when you have secured your own household—let your benevolence extend to those around you. Become in your neighborhood, and throughout the whole extent of your intercourse and influence, a humble, affectionate, determined reformer. It is to little purpose that the causes, symptoms, evils, and remedy of intemperance have been disclosed, if this little volume be left to work its obscure and dilatory way through the land: but if every one who approves of it will aid its circulation, it may find a place yet in every family, and save millions from temporal and eternal ruin.

I pant not for fame or posthumous immortality, but my heart's desire and prayer to God for my countrymen is, that they may be saved from intemperance, and that our beloved nation may continue free, and become great and good.

Chapter 6

The Woman's Crusade of 1873–74

Surely one of the reasons for the enthusiasm behind the powerful Woman's Crusade of 1873–74 was the rare opportunity it provided for women to take a public stance against the damage done to families by alcohol. The Woman's Crusade utilized religious activity, an arena in which women were more experienced and well-represented than men, in an attempt to change the public's attitude toward alcohol. In an era in which women's proper sphere was thought to be the home, their fervent hymn-singing and praying in the street in front of saloons and their demands that barkeeps throw out their wares and shut the doors of their establishments could be justified as efforts to protect and preserve home and family. Although the flurry of demonstrations faded, much of the movement continued under the auspices of the Woman's Christian Temperance Union. Eliza Thompson's recollections of the crusade were published in 1896.

HILLSBORO CRUSADE SKETCHES

Eliza Jane Trimble Thompson, Her Two Daughters and Frances E. Willard

I

Volumes have been written, and speeches without number made, setting forth most graphically the "Crusade of Woman against Rum." Yet strange to say, the call comes with greater and still greater earnestness to the leader of the little "band of seventy:" "Tell us more about the beginning of the Crusade in Hillsboro, and give us all the incidents connected with it, for the story must not die with the veterans of 1873 and 1874." As the shadows lengthen, and the number of that band counts fewer, I am reminded that what I do, I must do quickly.

Many years ago a friend wrote to me for a brief but plain account of the facts in connection with the starting of the Crusade in our town, and of my relation to it. Supposing at the time that it was for her own personal interest merely, I wrote freely, withholding no part of the truth as it occurred.

That narrative was adopted by Miss Willard in her work, "Woman and Temperance," and has become the "old, old story." After all these years I could not change the "facts and figures," and might not change the diction to profit;

therefore, with slight additions, I furnish it as the first of the promised series of Crusade sketches from the "Old Fort."

On the evening of December 22, 1873, Dio Lewis, a Boston physician and lyceum lecturer, delivered in Music Hall, Hillsboro, Ohio, a lecture on "Our Girls." He had been engaged by the Lecture Association, some months before, to fill one place in the winter course of lectures, merely for the entertainment of the people; but finding that he could remain another evening, and still reach his next appointment (Washington Court-house), he consented to give another lecture on the evening of the 23d. At the suggestion of Judge Albert Matthews, an old-line temperance man and Democrat, a free lecture on temperance became the order of the evening.

Dr. Lewis was our guest until the morning of the 23d, when my brother, Colonel Wm. H. Trimble, took him to his beautiful "Woodland" home, intending to send him across the country to Washington Court-house in his own carriage on the morning of the 24th.

I did not hear Dio Lewis lecture because of home cares that required my presence; but my son, a youth of seventeen, and my daughter were there, and they came to me upon their return home, and in a most earnest manner related the thrilling incidents of the evening; how Dr. Lewis told of his own mother, and several of her good Christian friends, uniting in prayer with and for the liquor-sellers of his native town, until they gave up their soul-destroying business. Dr. Lewis said, "Ladies, you might do the same thing in Hillsboro, if you had the same faith," and then turning to the ministers and temperance men who were upon the platform, added: "Suppose I ask the women of this audience to signify their opinions upon the subject?" They all bowed their consent, and fifty or more women stood up in token of approval. He then asked the men how many of them would stand as "backers," should the women undertake the work. Sixty or seventy arose. "And," continued my son, "you are on some committees to do work at the Presbyterian church in the morning, and the ladies expect you to go out with them to the saloons!"

My husband, who had returned from Adams County Court that evening and was feeling very tired, seemed asleep as he rested upon the sofa, while my children in an undertone had given me all the above facts; but as the last sentence was uttered, he raised himself up upon his elbow and said: "What tomfoolery is all that?" My dear children slipped out of the room quietly, and I betook myself to the task of consoling their father, with the promise that I should not be led into any foolish act by Dio Lewis, or any association of human beings, but added: "If the Lord should show me that it was his will for the women to visit places where liquors were sold and drunk, I should not shrink from it."

After some time my husband relaxed into a milder mood, continuing to call the whole plan, as he understood it, "tomfoolery." I ventured to remind him that the men had been in the "tomfoolery" business a long time, and suggested that it might be God's will that the women should now take their part.

Nothing farther was said upon the subject until the next morning after breakfast. "Are you going to the church this morning?" asked the children. I hesitated, and doubtless showed in my countenance the burden upon my spirit. My husband walked the length of the room several times, and finally said: "Children, you know where your mother goes to settle all vexed questions. Instead of family prayers this morning, let her alone to make her decision." I went to my room, kneeling before God and his Holy Word, to see what would be sent me, when I heard a step at the door, and upon opening it, my daughter stood there. With tearful eyes she handed me her small, open Bible and said with with trembling voice: "See what my eyes fell upon. It must be for you." She immediately left the room, and I sat down to read the wonderful message of the great "I Am" contained in the 146th Psalm. And as I read, new meaning seemed to attach to those promises (so often read before), and the Spirit said: "This is the way, walk ye in it." No longer doubting, I quickly repaired to the Presbyterian Church, and took my seat near the door. Several of my friends came, and urged me to go up to the front. While hesitating, I was unanimously chosen as president or leader, Mrs. General McDowell vice-president, and Mrs. D. K. Fenner secretary of the strange work that was to follow.

Appeals were drawn up to druggists, saloon-keepers, and hotel proprietors. Then the pastor of the Presbyterian Church, Rev. Dr. McSurely, who had up to this time occupied the chair, called upon the chairman-elect to "come forward to the post of honor." But your humble servant could not; her limbs refused to bear her. The dear ladies offered me assistance, but it was not God's time. My brother, Colonel Trimble, observing my embarrassed situation, said to Dr. McSurely: "I believe the ladies will do nothing until the gentlemen of the audience leave the house!"

After some moments, Dr. McSurely said: "I believe Colonel Trimble is right. Brethren, let us adjourn, and leave this work with God and the women."

As the last man closed the door after him, strength before unknown came to me, and without any hesitation or consultation I walked forward to the minister's table, and opened the large Bible, explained the incidents of the morning; then read, and briefly (as my tears would allow) commented upon its new meaning to me.

I then called upon Mrs. McDowell to lead in prayer; and such a prayer! It seemed as though the angel had brought down "live coals" from off the altar and touched her lips—she who, by her own confession, had never before heard her own voice in prayer!

As we arose from our knees (for all were kneeling that morning), I asked Mrs. Cowden, the Methodist Episcopal minister's wife, a grand singer of the "olden style," to start my favorite hymn, "Give to the winds thy fears," to the familiar tune of St. Thomas, and turning to the dear women, I said: "As we all join in singing this hymn, let us form in line, two and two, and let us at once proceed to our sacred mission, trusting alone in the 'God of Jacob.'"

It was all done in less time than it takes to write it. Every heart was throbbing and every woman's countenance betrayed her solemn realization of the fact that she was going "about her Father's business."

As this "band of mysterious beings" first encountered the outside gaze, and as they passed from the door of the old church and reached the street beyond the large churchyard, they were singing these prophetic words:

> "Far, far above thy thought
>   His counsel shall appear,
> When fully He the work hath wrought
>   That caused thy needless fear."

On we marched in solemn silence, looking neither to the right nor left, until we arrived at the drugstore of Dr. Wm. Smith on East Main Street. Mrs. Milton Boyd had been appointed to read "the appeal" on that morning, and proceeded to do so. From the minutes so carefully kept by our secretary, Mrs. D. K. Fenner, we extract the following:

> "Dr. Wm. Smith, after much persuasion, signed the 'druggists pledge,' with the understanding that he, as a physician, had a right to prescribe liquor and sell on his own prescription.
> "Seybert and Isaman signed very willingly, and assured the ladies of their good wishes.
> "Mr. James Brown, Sr., signed also willingly.
> "Mr. Wm. H. H. Dunn postponed his decision."
> "HILLSBORO, OHIO, December 24, 1873.

Before entering upon the second chapter, I yield to the entreaty of many friends and insert my husband's first impressions of this memorable morning.

Judge Thompson's account of this movement, taken from his History of the County of Highland: "The town of Hillsboro has always been noted for its interest in the encouragement of all systems of education, and few populations have excelled that of Hillsboro in the promotion of female education; the result of which has been to establish a high standard of refinement of both sexes, and an unusually independent order of thought and action between them, as is evidenced by the fact that the Woman's Temperance Crusade had its birth in the village, and has already breathed its infant breath throughout Christendom. Books have been written, voluminous reports have been made, and eloquent speeches have been uttered as to the minute details of the origin of the Woman's Temperance Crusade in Hillsboro, and most of them are true in statement and in fact; but nowhere has pen ventured a description of the band—the cohort, the troupe. No! rather the apparition of seventy women in sable black arrayed, and in settled line of march, moving as when first seen on the streets of Hillsboro.

"It was a dark, cloudy, cold, and still December day, no sun shining from above, no wind playing around, a little snow leisurely dropping down, and under the magic command of their own leaders, chosen on the instant at the hurried previous organization at the Presbyterian church, the procession moved with solemn steps, as if each woman had been trained for that day's work from the cradle.

'Not a drum was heard, not a funeral note,'

but the poetic mind instantly hummed the 'Ode of Charles Wolfe at the Burial of Sir John Moore.' Husbands saw their wives, sons and daughters their mothers, and neighbors their friends, moving along with the strange apparition, and knew not what it meant, until before some liquor saloon or hotel or drugstore, you could hear the singing of some familiar hymn warble through the air in tones of the most touching note; and then, solemn silence prevailing up and down street, the utterance of a soul-stirring prayer made by some lady, with all others kneeling around on curbstone or pavement or door-sill, could be heard ascending to the throne of God to avert the curse of intemperance.

"No crowd of shouting boys followed; no cliques of consulting men on the street corners were gathered; every countryman halted his team in awe; no vociferous angry words were heard, and no officer commanded the peace—for it was death-like peace. Throughout the day, songs and prayers were heard at all places kept for the sale of liquors, and at night consultation was resumed at the church, from whence the "Phœnix-like body," springing from the ashes of the "funeral pyre" of woman's immolation, had emerged in the morning; and there, in making reports, prayer, and singing in spirit as never before, was sung on Christmas Eve:

> 'Ring out the grief that saps the mind,
>   For those that here we see no more;
>   Ring out the feud of rich and poor,
> Ring in redress to all mankind.'

"They remained until the moon in the last quarter lighted their pathway to homes, whose inmates as spectators of the troupe when the first curtain was raised, stood around the hearth-stones in as much wonder as if a company of celestial beings had on that day come down from the skies.

"Such is a dim outline of the first parade of the Woman's Temperance Crusade at Hillsboro; and well may it be said of the 'opening of the heavens' on that memorable day, that 'He who made a decree for the rain and a way for the lightning' will alone limit its effects on the nations of the earth." . . .

III. Story of Saloon Visitation

At the time of the "new departure" on the part of the ladies of Hillsboro, there were four hotels, four drugstores, and thirteen saloons where intoxicating liquors could be obtained, there being little hindrance, save the conscientious scruples of individual cases!

When the "Praying Band," as it was called in ridicule, first started out upon its divinely-appointed mission, as the procession of somber-looking beings passed up High Street from the church where their first meeting of consecration had just been held, Dr. Dio Lewis was driven slowly by on his way from Colonel Trimble's home to Washington Court-house.

On the following morning, the 25th, many of the earnest women and quite a goodly number of zealous brethren assembled promptly at nine o'clock in the Presbyterian church to renew their consecration vows. After a season of fervent prayer, song, and testimony, it was voted to respect a previous appointment for religious services in the Episcopal church—quite a number of our band being members of that Church, and their rector, Rev. John Ely, one of our loyal supporters. It was also thought wise to give to our families the attention due the established usage of Christmas-day. Therefore, after adjournment, an informal prayer-meeting was held, which strengthened the hearts of all greatly, and better prepared the women for the services of the following morning.

The cold, clear, crisp morning of the 26th dawned upon us with a sparkling snow upon the ground, but paths were shoveled and swept by new hands that morning, and, as we passed, heads were uncovered and earnest benedictions showered upon us by many a manly heart, which dared to be on the right side. The nine o'clock prayer-meeting was opened by Scripture reading, prayer, and song; earnest exhortations and words of hearty support and encouragement were offered by Dr. McSurely and others.

The Committee of Visitation, after singing a hymn, adjourned to meet at the same time and place the next morning; then, forming in procession, it visited hotels and saloons in the following order—quoting from minutes:

"Mrs. Thompson was appointed to present appeal at hotels and saloons." "The first call was made at the Uhrig saloon, on East High Street. There we were met by smooth words and fair promises, but no signatures." "Kramer House proprietor—*not at home.*" "Ellicott House—the polite landlord said he did hope we would succeed, but could not close his bar unless the others would." "The kind proprietor of the Woodrow House half agreed to give up the miserable business, and said he certainly would if the other hotels of the town would close up."

It was quite evident to the minds of the ladies that the question with these gentlemen turned upon the pivot of popularity and financial success, and not upon any innate love of the curse, for the fact was too apparent that the effects of liquor-drinking had proven the hardest part of a landlord's office.

Fortified with hope in the evident unrest of these men, who were building upon sandy foundations—their hope of gain—our next call was at the saloon of John Bales. He was cool and polite, treated the subject-matter of our visit in a purely business way, proposed selling out his entire stock, billiard tables and all, at two-thirds of invoiced value, and *sell no more liquor!* As this was quite out of the line of our warfare against spiritual wickedness in high places, we turned our faces towards the first-class saloon (as it was called) kept by Robert Ward, on High Street, a resort made famous by deeds, the memory of which nerved the heart and paled the cheek of some among us, as the seventy entered the open door of the "witty Englishman" (as his patrons were wont to call the popular Ward). Doubtless he had learned of our approach, as he not only propped the heavy door open, but with the most perfect suavity of manner held it until the ladies all passed in; then, closing it, walked to his accustomed stand behind the bar.

Seizing the strange opportunity, the leader addressed him as follows: "Well, Mr. Ward, this must seem to you a strange audience! I suppose, however, that you understand the object of our visit?" "Robert" by this time began to perspire freely, and remarked that he would like to have a talk with Dio Lewis. Mrs. Thompson said: "Dr. Lewis has nothing whatever to do with the subject of our mission. As you look upon some of the faces before you, and observe the marks of sorrow, caused by the unholy business that you ply, you will find that it is no wonder we are here. We have come, however, not to threaten, not even to upbraid, but in the name of our Divine Friend and Savior, and in his spirit, to forgive, and to commend you to his pardon, if you will but agree to abandon a business that is so damaging to our hearts and to the peace of our homes!"

The hesitation and embarrassment of the famous saloon-keeper seemed to afford (as the leader thought) an opportunity for prayer; so, casting her eye around upon that never-to-be-forgotten group of earnest faces, she said, *very softly:* "Let us pray." Instantly all, even the poor liquor-seller himself, were upon their knees, Mrs. McSurely, wife of the Presbyterian minister, was asked by Mrs. Thompson to lead in prayer, but she declined. The spirit of utterance then came upon the latter, and, as a seal of God's approval upon the self-sacrificing work there inaugurated, the Holy Spirit touched all hearts. As we arose from our knees, dear Mrs. Doggett (now in heaven) broke forth in her sweet, pathetic notes, and all joined with her in singing:

> "There is a fountain filled with blood,
>   Drawn from Immanuel's veins;
> And sinners plunged beneath that flood,
>   Lose all their guilty stains."

The scene that followed, in a most remarkable manner portrayed the spirit of our holy religion. Poor wives and mothers, who the day before would have crossed the street to avoid passing by a place so identified with their heartaches, their woes, and their deepest humiliation, in tearful pathos were now pleading with this deluded brother to accept the world's Redeemer as his own. Surely, "God is Love!"

Shortly after the ladies retired from this their first saloon prayer-meeting, a message from Dr. Lewis, at Washington Court-house, was received by Colonel William H. Trimble to this effect: "The women over here are terribly in earnest." As the report of union in this strange work first greeted our ears and strengthened our hearts, "Praise ye the Lord" seemed more and more a fitting prelude to our "Magna Charta"—the 146th Psalm—and we entered upon the Saturday morning prayer service with renewed faith and courage.

Dr. Mathews, president of the Hillsboro Female College, the renowned and venerated educator of woman in our community for so many years, presided over the meeting, and spoke to our hearts such words of earnest commendation and sympathy that the "doubting ones" could but have been convinced as was Thomas of old.

William H. H. Dunn, the druggist, who was not at his place of business on the morning of the visit by the "band of ladies," sent in his reply to their "appeal." It read as follows:

> "Ladies,—In compliance with my agreement I give you this promise, that I will carry on my business in the future as I have in the past; that is to say, that in the sale of intoxicating liquors I will comply with the law, nor will I sell to any person whose father, mother, wife, or daughter send me a written request not to make such sale."

There was some discussion as to whether Mr. Dunn's pledge should be received as satisfactory. Remarks were made by the gentlemen as well as the ladies, but it was soon apparent that there were mothers in that audience who could never vote to have "his business" carried on "in the future as in the past." Action was therefore deferred.

Next in order came a message from Mr. Bennet, the master of the Hillsboro Grange: "Say to the ladies for me, *God bless them;* and, poor man that I am, I will back them with fifty dollars if it is needed."

It was resolved at this Saturday morning meeting to hold a mass temperance-meeting in the Methodist Episcopal Church on Sunday evening, December 28th, and a committee of three ministers—Rev. Dr. McSurely, of the Presbyterian Church; Rev. Mr. Cowden, of the Methodist; and Rev. John Ely, of the Episcopal Church—were chosen to take charge of said meeting, inviting both ladies and gentlemen to speak, Rev. Mr. Ely was also requested to invite Father Donahue, of the Catholic Church, and his temperance society, to join us in our work.

After uniting in a fervent prayer and singing part of a favorite hymn, the committee adjourned to meet on Monday morning, at the same time and place. Procession then formed, and visits were made at two hotels and three saloons. One of the saloon-keepers expressed a great desire to *get out of the business.* With this encouraging prospect we ended the first week of the "Crusade" in Hillsboro.

Chapter 7

The Woman's Christian Temperance Union

The Woman's Christian Temperance Union (WCTU), especially as led by Frances E. Willard, took up a host of women's causes — including legal equality, the right to vote, and raising the age of consent — as well as agitation for the prohibition of alcohol. In the last quarter of the nineteenth century the WCTU launched a campaign to require instruction in the public schools about the dangers of alcohol and narcotics. The union was quite successful in this mission, and state after state enacted laws mandating such education. Extracts appear here from an 1885 primer, one of the many produced under WCTU auspices.

Today the WCTU typically is remembered as an extreme anti-alcohol group out of touch with majority opinion, but in fact its history was distinguished by the determined fight for rights that now are accepted without question.

No. 14. Don't Let the Women Vote.

JENNIE SAYRE. J. W. HOLTON. By per.

1. Those temp'rance men do all they can, To keep their cause a - float;
2. Just let the wom- en prate and pray, By that they will do no harm;
8 We'll scare those temp'rance men somewhat, And tell them they'll lose the day.
4. If we get the temp'rance men to throw That suf - frage plank a - way.

I have no fear of what they may do, So long as the women don't vote.
But when they talk of letting them vote, My soul takes on a - larm.
If tney don't get rid of those women folks, And throw that plank a - way.
And drop the W. C. T. U. 'Twill be a mer - ry day.

Male Voices, 2nd Bass sing Alto Octave Lower

CHORUS.

Don't let the wo - men vote! Don't 'let the women vote! We'll
Don't let the wo - men vote! Don't let the women vote! It's
Don't let the wo - men vote! Don't let the women vote! The
Don't let the wo - men vote! Don't let the women vote! We

oh, no!

lose the bat - tle as sure as you live, If they let the women vote.
good bye whis- key, beer and rum, If they let the women vote.
whis- key traf - fic is gone for sure, When they let the women vote.
fear not God, and we fear not man, But we fear a women vote.

Copyright, 1888, by J. G. DAILEY,

No. 19. The "Practical" Temperance Man.

Words by Rev. T. C. JOHNSON. Music by W. A. WILLIAMS.

1. Oh the "prac-ti-cal" tem-per-ance man   Is a ver-y queer sort of a
2. He will vote ev-'ry time with his clan,   Though the rummies are all in the
3. He's a won-der-ful, won-der-ful plan   For put-ing rum un-der the
4. Since ev-er our coun-try be-gan,   Dis-cov-er his like if you
5. The vote of us cranks he will scan,   And call it a "flash in the

man. To kill the sa-loon, He will li-cense en-dorse, And
van; He'll whoop up his par-ty from morn-ing till night, And
ban. He'll vote for a pro-hi-bi-to-ry stat-ute, Then
can! He'll pray for the king-dom of heav-en to come, And
pan". He'll cud-gel us fel-lows for wast-ing our votes, By

choose a rum-sel-ler the law to en-force, A whis-key platform al-ways
shout for the tar-iff with all of his might, And "sympathize" on-ly, with
vote for a Judge that's a whis-key galoot, And for an at-tor-ney that
God's ho-ly will on the earth to be done, And still he will vote to per-
leav-ing the flocks of the fat whis-key goats, And casts a rum bal-lot, e-

CHORUS.

shaping his course, This "prac-ti-cal" tem-per-ance man.
temp'rance and right, This "prac-ti-cal" tem-per-ance man.
wont pros-e-cute, This "prac-ti-cal" tem-per-ance man.
pet-u-ate rum, This "prac-ti-cal" tem-per-ance man.
lect-ing the bloats,—This "prac-ti-cal" tem-per-ance man.

Ha! ha! ha! ha! ha! Just

The "Practical" Temperance Man.

look at this prac - ti - cal, ha! ha! ha! ha! This prac — ti - cal man, He's

lift - ing him-self by the straps of his boots, ha! ha! ha! ha! ha! ha! ha! ha!ha! And

out of both ends of his can - non he shoots, ha! ha! ha! ha!

ha! ha! ha! ha! And back from the foe like a crawfish he scoots, this "practical" temperance man.

Primer of Physiology and Hygiene

William Thayer Smith

Alcoholic Drinks

16. *Wines* are made of the juice of grapes or berries. *Beer, ale, porter,* and *whisky* are made from grain. *Brandy* is made from wine and cider and some other liquors. *Rum* is made from sugar-cane or molasses. All these drinks contain alcohol, and it is for the alcohol in them that they are used.

17. *Alcohol* looks like water. It burns the mouth like fire if it is taken clear. Brandy is about half alcohol. Wine is from one-tenth to one-fifth alcohol.

18. Many men spend more money to get alcoholic drinks than they spend for food or clothes or any thing else. Why do they want them so much?

You have already learned, that, when you take any stimulant for a while, you are likely to get fond of it, and to want more and more of it. This is especially so with alcoholic drinks. The appetite for them often keeps growing, until it is stronger than any other desire. A moderate drinker is always in some danger of becoming a drunkard, and a drunkard will give up every thing for liquor.

19. All stimulants are sometimes an injury to those who use them. But no other one has such power as alcohol. It can change a man into something worse than a beast. It can take away his property and his home. It can destroy his character.

It makes more people poor and unhappy and wicked than any other cause. . . .

Effects of Alcohol and Tobacco

Sect. IV.—**1.** Alcohol is a fiery *stimulant*. You remember what a stimulant does in your mouth,—such an one as pepper, for instance. Alcohol you could not keep in your mouth a moment.

2. The mouth and stomach are made for simple food. If we are well, they do not need any strong stimulants. Too much mustard or tea is bad for them.

3. Alcohol is a much more dangerous stimulant than these. Nobody drinks clear alcohol. The strongest drinks are about one-half alcohol, and the weakest have only three or four spoonfuls to a tumblerful.

4. But you have learned, that; when we like any stimulant, we are apt to want more and more of it, until we get so that we need a great deal to satisfy us.

No stimulant is so *enticing* as alcohol. It is very easy to get into the habit of using a great deal of it.

5. Since the stomach was not made to need strong stimulants, it *hurts it* to use them.

Dr. Beaumont found, that when St. Martin took wine, beer, or any of the intoxicating liquors freely for some days, the lining of his stomach looked red and inflamed and sore, and the gastric juice became thick and ropy.

6. If a boy handles a bat a good deal, he may get his hands blistered at first. By and by the skin will grow thick and hard. In the same way, the ends of a girl's fingers may get hardened by sewing. So, if the stomach is irritated constantly by alcohol, it will grow thick and tough.

7. An old toper can drink a great deal of strong liquor without feeling it. That is because his stomach has changed. It is a better stomach to hold alcohol, but not so good a stomach to digest food.

8. Drinking often causes *dyspepsia*. It takes away the appetite, and spoils the gastric juice.

After long use of alcohol, the stomach sometimes gets into such a condition that it will not bear food at all, without being first roused by drink.

9. Drinking often causes *diseases of the liver*. . . .

Effects of Alcohol and Tobacco

Sect. IV—1. When men take a little liquor, it makes them feel comfortable or gay. The brain and nerves are stimulated. If they take enough to get slightly intoxicated, they become talkative and boastful, or cross or silly. If they drink more, they lose their judgment. Their passions become violent. They are ready to be excited by small things, and to quarrel. Many of the murders and other crimes, of which we read every day in the papers, are done under the influence of alcohol. Men who when sober are quiet and kind, are changed by it into wild beasts. After the drunken fury is past, they are filled with remorse for what they have done. The brain ought to be the master of the whole body. In such men it becomes a slave. When the appetite sends in through the nerves a demand for liquor, it can not refuse.

2. The man who indulges freely in drink is likely to pay for it the next day. His head aches. He is low-spirited and weak. His stomach is foul. His appetite is gone. He then thinks that he never will take it again. But, when the nerves are accustomed to the excitement of drinking, they will not give it up easily.

3. *Delirium tremens* is one of the results of the free use of alcohol. This is a disease of the nervous system. The victim of it is wild and raving. He is filled with distress and horror. Death sometimes ends his misery. If he recovers, he is likely to have it again if he continues drinking.

4. *Insanity* is another result of drinking-habits. Many of the patients in insane-asylums are brought there by drink.

5. Discord in families, quarrels, murders, sickness, pauperism, insanity, and misery are some of the results of the action of alcohol on the nervous system.

Do not understand that alcohol always produces such results. Men sometimes use it through a long life without seeming to be harmed by it. But its victims are in every community, and among all classes of the people. . . .

Questions

SECT. I—**1.** What is it to feel nervous? Why does a drunken man fall?

SECT. IV—**1.** What is the effect of a small amount of alcohol on the nervous system? What is the effect of a larger amount? How does alcohol enslave the brain?

2–4. What is often the effect of the free use of alcohol on the nervous system the day after taking it? What diseases of the nervous system result from the use of alcohol?

5. What other results of the action of alcohol on the nervous system? Do these results always follow?

Chapter 8

Frances E. Willard

Frances E. Willard (1839–1898) began her working life as an educator, serving as dean of women at Northwestern University. In 1874 she became one of the founders of the WCTU and five years later was elected president, a post she held until her death. Willard traveled widely throughout the United States, speaking and organizing for the broad range of reforms embraced by the WCTU. She also took an active role in the Prohibition Party and later in the Populist Party, as she attempted to forge alliances in the drives for alcohol control and woman's suffrage. A statue of Frances Willard was placed by the state of Illinois in the National Statuary Hall of the United States Capitol in 1905, the first contribution given to the hall to honor a woman. The article by Willard excerpted here was published posthumously in 1910.

FRANCES E. WILLARD

Statuary Hall, Washington, February 17th, 1903

Katherine Lent Stevenson

How still she stands!
The snow-peak kissed by morning's glad first beam,
The violet, bending to the woodland stream,
The hush of twilight grey, before dawn's gleam,
  Are not more still.

How calm she stands!
Like ocean's voiceless peace, the waves below,
Like winter's quiet, 'neath its depth of snow,
Like the still heart of earth, where all things grow,
  Is her great calm.

How white she stands!
The lily glows beside her marble brow,
All palest things of earth gleam ruddy now;

Like to the Bride of Christ through solemn vow,
  Is her pure white.

  How great she stands!
A mountain-peak her soul; an ocean wide;
A river, sweeping on with full, free tide;
A sacred shrine where holiest things abide;
  How great she stands!

  How loved she stands!
Unnumbered souls their costliest incense bring;
O'er all the world her name doth heart-bells ring;
Love-notes to her e'en little children sing;
  How loved she stands!

  A Queen she stands!
In her our women-heart has found its throne;
Through her our kinship will all good is shown;
Her white life makes our royal birth-right known;—
  Our Queen she stands!

  A Seer she stands!
To her clear eyes Truth's radiant sweep unfolds;
She reads what, down the years, the fu-ture holds;
She sees things heavenly 'neath their earth-ly mould;
  A Seer she stands!

  A Knight she stands!
A maiden-knight, whom fear could not assail,
Whose eye flinched not, whose great heart did not fail;
Who sought, and found, e'en here, the Holy Grail;—
  Our Knight she stands!

  Stand, radiant soul!
Here, in the centre of our Nation's heart;
Forever of its best life thou'rt a part;
Here thou shalt draw they land to what thou art;
  Stand, radiant soul!

  Stand, conquering one!
Swift down the years already leaps the morn
Of holiest triumph, for which thou wert born;
"Sought out" our land shall be "no more forlorn,"
  Since thou dost stand!

Scientific Temperance Instruction in Public Schools

A Message of Fifteen Years Ago

Frances E. Willard

Suppose you take a watch, full jeweled; of finest Geneva workmanship, and put it into a case made of gold, then into one made of silver, then into one made of porcelain. You will find that it keeps just as good time in a cheap case as in a costly one, because there is no interdependence between the watch and its environment. But God has wound up a watch in this snug round box on the top of your heads and mine; warranted, with good usage, to tick right on with thoughts for eighty or a hundred years. A watch with the main-spring of reason, the balance-wheel of judgment, the fine jewels of imagination and fancy, the dial-plate of a human face divine, and the pointers of a character thereon, and this wonderful watch, the human brain, can not keep as good time in a coarse case as in a fine one, for there is the closest interdependence between the brain and its environment; between the tissues of the body and the temper of the soul.

Just as Theodore Thomas controls an orchestra with his baton, or an engineer his engine with the throttle-valve, or an operator his telegraph line, so the wonderful prisoner in the brain controls the body's intricate machinery. Given so much clear thought, and you will get so much clear action. Given so much crazed thought and you will get so much crazed action. There is not an axiom of mathematics more fixed than this physical law. The man who can't think his own thoughts, though nobody hinders him; can't speak his own words though everybody wishes that he could; can't use his own five senses though they were given him for that specific purpose; and whose cruelty is greatest toward those he loves the best, presents nature's supreme illustration of the law that alcoholic drinks have no business in the economics of a well-ordered physical life: and the time to teach this law is just as soon as a child's brain can take it in.

But the same truth is illustrated from another point of view. The geography of character is a "branch," sure to be taught some day in public schools. But character is bounded on the north by sobriety, on the east by integrity, on the west by industry, and on the south by gentleness. But these cardinal points are all determined by the first, sobriety. Clearly note first that this virtue must precede that of integrity. As George Eliot has said, with her almost preternatural discrimination, "We can not command veracity at will; the power of seeing and reporting truth is a form of health that has to be delicately guarded." Dr. Benjamin Ward Richardson, the leading specialist of England, has spent twenty-two years studying the effects of alcoholics. During a series of experiments he associated three hundred chief physicians with him in his study, and they met in London semi-annually to give results. In one conclusion all agreed, and it was this: No form of degeneracy produced by alcoholic beverages is more invariable than the drinker's untruthfulness in word and deed. The person who drinks will use all his ingenuity to conceal, first the fact itself, next its consequences, and soon the fine edge of perception and conscience is worn away, so that he is untrustworthy in everything. Therefore, sobriety outranks integrity as an essential of genuine character. . . .

This body that we live in is in a sense the universe to us. We get no light save that which comes in through this strange sky-light of the brain. The man wonderful lives in a house beautiful, and it is all in all to him. It was meant to be his perfect instrument and not his prison. Perfect obedience to its laws would make him the true microcosm—the mirror of the universe—nay, of its Creator. In his ignorance he began to use strong drinks, and honestly called them "a good creature of God." But the attractive ingredient in all these beverages is alcohol, a poison that has this changeless law, that it acts in exact proportion to the quantity imbibed, upon the brain and nervous system, precisely as fire acts upon water, lapping it up with a fierce and insatiable thirst. This affinity of alcohol for moisture is like a feverish and consuming passion, and the blistered nose, burnt brain, and parboiled stomach of the drinking man are nature's perpetual object lesson to illustrate the fact that alcohol must be the redoubtable enemy of an organization made up as the human being is, of seven in every eight parts of water. Put with this fact one other, viz.: That alcoholic beverages are the only ones on earth that have no power of self-limitation. One glass says two, and two say three, until as a general rule, from the power of self-perpetuation in this appetite, the life of a drinker of alcoholics has but two periods, in the first of which he could leave off if he would, and in the last, he would leave off if he could. But how shall the young and thoughtless avoid this supreme peril of their youth unless they know about it, and how shall they learn without a teacher, and how shall they teach except they be sent? This, then, is the rationale of scientific temperance instruction in the public schools. . . .

In the light of many years' work as teacher of total abstinence from alcoholic poison, I solemnly aver that had I the power our system of education should be so changed that the course of study for every pupil, from the kindergarten toddler to the high school graduate, should be grounded where God grounds our very being—on natural law. They should know the laws of health, since their physical being is the firm base of the whole pyramid of character. "According to law" is the method as it is the philosophic explanation of the universe so far as we can spell it out. The blessed word "health" once literally meant "holiness," and that means simply "wholeness." This body of ours was meant to be the temple of the Holy Spirit, but enemies have taken possession of it and dimmed or well nigh extinguished the Shekinah. The alcohol and nicotine poisons, leagued with bad food, unnatural dress, bad ventilation, and ill-proportioned exercise, are the demons that hold the sacred citadel. Yet we call ourselves a science-loving people and think we care to know God's reason why. . . .

In the school of the future, carefully trained hygienists will be steadily at work studying the habits of the children and teaching them, on scientific grounds, how they may form those upon which physical sanity is conditioned. Clothing that imposes a ligature upon any organ or member of the body will not be tolerated; the eating of highly seasoned food will be condemned; the use of the hog as an article of diet shown to be a relic of barbarism, and the physical sin of using alcoholic drinks and other narcotics denounced with all the emphasis of a "Thus saith the Lord." For we shall never get beyond that dictum of the wondrous Hebrew nation. It will be quoted when Aristotle's is forgotten. For there is One.

> In every age, by every clime adored,
> By Saint, by savage, and by sage,
> Jehovah, Jove, or Lord.

. . . As a beginning of this vital education I would teach on scientific grounds the unreasonableness of using alcoholic drinks. By every practical method of illustration and experiment I would set before my pupils that the tendency of yesterday is likely to become the habit of today and the bondage of tomorrow. They should be drilled into the fact that the alcoholic habit is cumulative, subtly strengthening by what it feeds upon, so that the ignorant claim that drinks like cider, beer, and wine, are preventives of drunkenness, should be an insult to their intelligence. . . .

Much has already been accomplished in this direction. In every state in our country but ten, more or less stringent laws have been enacted, requiring the study of hygienic physiology, with special reference to the effects of alcoholic drinks and other narcotics, to be pursued by all pupils under state control. May 17, 1886, the National Congress enacted a law making this study mandatory in all schools under Federal control, including all territories, our Military and Naval academies at West Point and Annapolis, all public schools in the District of Columbia, including our National Capital, and in Indian and colored schools.

Talking with teachers on this subject of scientific temperance teaching, I have found their sympathy almost universal, but they have often said: "We are already so over-crowded with duties that the practical difficulty is, how can we add this to our cares or find time for the children to take up another branch?" It seems to me that the Superintendent of Schools in a leading city of Massachusetts made a conclusive reply to this objection when he said recently in reply to the President of the W. C. T. U.: "This subject ought to be taught. If the schedule is too much crowded already, we will take something out and make room for this, because it is entitled to the right of way."

I believe this systematic instruction, which both forewarns and forearms them, to be the road out of bondage for the children of America. No other institution of the Republic reaches them all. Powerful as are the forces of pulpit and press; the former does not attract all ears, and the latter is largely influenced by the saloon in finance and the saloon in politics. But to the school-house door come white and black, native and foreign-born; inside its walls are invested their formative years; and the laws of their being, as set forth by science, must appeal to their self-love, an attribute upon which we may always confidently base our calculations! The German, who learns that the laws of nature take sides with total abstinence, will gradually cease the cry of "fanaticism." His boy comes home from school and tells him that in time of pestilence and sunstroke the beer-drinkers pay forfeit and total abstainers get off scot free; that these last are at a premium with the life insurance companies; that they win in the athletic games; that they are the successful explorers and victorious soldiers, and that chemistry, physiology and hygiene prove that this must always be so. Mein Herr scoffed at the crusading women, but the dignity of science, will do much to silence him, and it will convince his children. I beseech you then, as the truest guardians of the state and the most intelligent and helpful friends of the child in our midst, who is also in the market place, and who is sure to be auctioned off to the forces that bid highest for him, stand by the mothers of the Nation in their brave, tender, loving labors to save

> "The little soldiers newly mustered in
> To the army of temptation and of sin."

The Anti-Saloon League

The Anti-Saloon League was a strikingly successful single-issue organization. Working through Protestant congregations, the league began its activities in Ohio with the intellectual and theological support of Oberlin College, the home of many reform campaigns. The selection reproduced here is a 1913 talk by Wayne B. Wheeler (1869–1927), once one of the most familiar names in the United States and now forgotten. In the first quarter of the twentieth century "Wheelerism" represented political savvy, hard-nosed confrontation, and an exclusive devotion to the prohibition of alcohol that culminated in 1919 with passage of the Eighteenth Amendment to the Constitution.

PROCEEDINGS OF THE 1913 NATIONAL CONVENTION

The Fifteenth National Convention of the Anti-Saloon League of America, met in Memorial Hall in the city of Columbus, Ohio, on Monday evening, November 10, 1913, and was called to order by General Superintendent, Rev. P. A. Baker.

A brief song service was conducted by Prof. E. O. Excell, of Chicago.

Dr. P. A. Baker made several announcements and introduced Bishop Luther B. Wilson, the president of the Anti-Saloon League.

Bishop Wilson then took the chair and called for the singing of the first and last stanzas of "America."

Prayer was offered by Rev. Thomas H. Campbell.

President Wilson then said:

"I have a message from across the seas which I am very sure this convention will be pleased to hear. It comes from the city of London, Huston Station, and is addressed to the Superintendent of the Anti-Saloon League, and the message is as follows:

> 350 Railway men gathered at Huston Station, London, in annual convention from all parts of England, Wales and Scotland, representing over 60,000 railway men, send happy greetings, wishing your great convention God's speed in its efforts to destroy the power of the saloon, and overthrow the greatest enemy of the home, the church and the state.
>
> (Signed)
>
> Faulker, Chairman,
> Bateson, Secretary."

"It is a great thing to know, as we gather here, that they are thinking of us across the seas, and I am sure that you and I will together, may pray God's blessing upon that gathering in London and will join them in praying for this result that is specifically named in the message that they sent."

Address of Welcome by Wayne B. Wheeler

Mr. Wayne B. Wheeler, superintendent of the Ohio Anti-Saloon League, was then introduced, and gave the address of welcome as follows:

We welcome you to the greatest home coming of temperance forces ever seen in America. It is fitting that you should come to Ohio this year to celebrate the Twentieth Anniversary of the League for it was here that the first statewide application of League principles and methods had their trial. If any one had prophesied twenty years ago that such a gathering of anti-saloon forces would be possible at this time, he would have been considered an idle dreamer. This cause has been moving forward since those few earnest souls met in Oberlin in 1893 to lay the foundation of this great movement. Since that time practically every state of the Union has been organized on an omnipartisan, interdenominational basis. More than a score of men have gone from Ohio to lead these fights as superintendents and workers. The two superintendents of the National League, Dr. Howard H. Russell and Dr. Purley A. Baker, are Ohio trained warriors. We welcome our boys back home tonight as well as those of you who visit us for the first time.

Since 1893 when this League work started six new states have been added to the roll of dry states; about twenty-eight million people have voted out the liquor traffic, this means on the average a million and four hundred thousand per year have adopted prohibition as their policy. They are now ready and anxious to move forward all along the line and finish up the job.

Is it not time for a Jubilee? Is it not fitting that we point with pride to the past and with confidence to the future? If there is a pessimist among us tonight let him get out new citizenship papers and forget his fears and doubts and join this invincible army that know no defeat and expects nothing short of unconditional surrender from the enemy. An army that has sounded forth the trumpet that shall never call retreat.

We would be ungrateful at a time like this if we failed to impress you that you are thrice welcome here in Ohio, the home of temperance reform movements. Here the Crusade preceded the Anti-Saloon League by twenty years, just as we now mark the twenty years of progress from the inception of the League. Godly women in those early days prayed for and pleaded with the saloonkeeper to quit his iniquitous business until they shamed the manhood of our state and nation into action. The Crusade, and W. C. T. U. which followed were forerunners, or we might say foster Mothers of this Anti-Saloon Crusade that is now on.

When the Roll of Honor is called up yonder, the White Ribbon brigade will have crowns full of stars. On behalf of the W. C. T. U. of this state, which co-operates with the League in every forward movement against the liquor traffic we bid you a hearty welcome.

We welcome you, also, in the names of more than 5,000 loyal churches in this state. They have opened their doors and their pocketbooks each year for two decades in larger proportion. Each year they have given more money and more consecration and more loyal support. Without the loyal churches of Ohio, it would be impossible to make one successful, forward movement against the liquor traffic in the state. We welcome you, therefore, in the name of our loyal churches.

We welcome you, also, on behalf of the Ohio League. For twenty years it has battered away at the liquor traffic, moving forward, each year holding that which you have won and paving the way for larger victories. It started its work with no dry counties, and no dry cities and but very little dry territory in the smaller units. Today 1,300 out of 1,373 townships are dry; 550 villages and cities out of approximately 800 in the state are dry and a majority of the counties are dry. Eighty-five per cent of the territory is free from the saloon and with God's help, the remaining 15 per cent will be rolling along on the water wagon in the next few years.

We welcome you in the name of the best citizenship of the state. You will find it in old Western Reserve, which has taken no backward step on the moral issue in twenty years; and you will find it in our churches, our young people's societies, in our Christian homes and our W. C. T. U.'s, in the Granges and every agent for human uplift and they are here to welcome you.

We welcome you to Ohio where we are just now trying out the last brand of the 57 varieties of the Model License law. It is a perfect law—just as they are all perfect laws. It guarantees the making of saloons respectable and harmless. It is drunkard proof and jag tight. Its advocates tell us this law will solve the liquor problem. The brewers proclaimed to the state in the campaign for license that they stood for the restriction, regulation and limitation of the traffic. Did you ever hear that kind of campaign material?

At every turn in the constitutional convention that submitted license, and in the legislature that passed the license law the liquor traffic is on record as opposing every regulation and restriction which they advocated in their campaign. Their hypocritical cry of saloon regulation reminds me of the story of an Irishman and a colored boy who stole a watch. The Irishman stole the watch, but just before he was arrested, he handed it to the colored boy and told him to return it to its owner. At the trial the Irishman made up a first-class defense. He testified that he was simply sending the watch back to its owner through the colored boy. The innocent colored boy then took the stand almost white with fear. He made a poor showing. The judge endeavored to help him in his defense and said, "Rastus, tell the court and the jury in plain English what was your relation to this defendant and this whole transaction." The colored boy half scared to death looked up at the judge and said: "Judge I isn't related to that defendant at all, I am just scared is the reason I looked this way." The colored boy represents the liquor interests in the situation which we face in this country today. They don't mean anything by it when they say they want restrictions and regulations, they are simply scared for fear that something worse is coming in the way of state and national Prohibition.

The license law of Ohio will never eliminate the evil from the liquor traffic. You cannot make a saloon decent, respectable or harmless by license any more than you can make a polecat smell sweet by sprinkling it with rose water. The last approved definition of "license" which we have heard reads as follows:

"It was invented by the devil, patented by the politicians, operated by certain communities to coin buzzard dollars to lay on the eyes of a dead conscience, to make the corpse look respectable."

Such a system never has nor never will solve the liquor problem or any other. The only way to clean up the liquor business is to clean it out root and branch.

We welcome you last and most important of all to the launching of the most beneficent and far reaching movement since the Civil War. As Moses said to the children of Israel, "That they should go forward," just so the time has come for the moral forces of this great nation to march on against the last bulwarks of the enemy. A great national evil has been localized and quarantined. Over two-thirds of the saloons of America are now in ten states. They are localized more today than slavery was when the last stage of the conflict was reached. Our enemy realizes it. They say that "Prohibition is no longer our local issue. It is a great national danger." The people are growing restless as they observe these remaining wet centers pouring forth their floods of crime and misery upon society for the sober citizenship to care for and support. Like the muttering of a great storm you can hear the determined demand from every quarter, to attack the enemy all along the line for National Constitutional Prohibition.

No one who has looked over the situation doubts that Congress will eventually submit to the states for ratification an amendment to the constitution to prohibit the manufacture and sale of intoxicating liquor as a beverage. Then the battle is on in the states for ratification. Ratification of the amendment by a state closes the conflict in that state. That action cannot be repealed, but rejection of the amendment only invites another contest until the Prohibition forces finally win. We must now enlist for the war, and never quit fighting until the enemy are worn out, whipped and voted out of the nation. I do not know how you may feel about this, but I would rather die than run from such a conflict, that means so much for the future welfare of humanity and perpetuity of this nation.

Chapter 10

Congressional Debate over the Prohibition Amendment

From the extended debate in the Congress over the prohibition amendment proposed in 1914, we have selected two representative speeches by prominent supporters of each side. Richmond Pearson Hobson (1870–1937), a Democrat from Alabama, had been a naval hero in the Spanish-American War. He devoted his career, first, to prohibition and, later, to the control of narcotics and marijuana. As a celebrated speaker for the Anti-Saloon League, he honed a rhetorical style and core message exemplified by this speech.

Among the vigorous opponents of national prohibition was James R. Mann (1856–1922), a Republican from Illinois. Mann had championed reform legislation, including the Pure Food and Drug Act and the Mann Act, but balked at prohibiting alcohol. In this debate Mann makes traditional arguments against prohibitory legislation. In many respects, the outcomes he warns against came to pass during the Prohibition period.

The 1914 resolution failed, but a similar proposal passed in 1917 and was ratified as the Eighteenth Amendment to the Constitution.

HOUSE JOINT RESOLUTION NO. 168

Debated 22 December 1914

Whereas exact scientific research has demonstrated that alcohol is a narcotic poison, destructive and degenerating to the human organism, and that its distribution as a beverage or contained in foods lays a staggering economic burden upon the shoulders of the people, lowers to an appalling degree the average standard of character of our citizenship, thereby undermining public morals and the foundation of free institutions, produces widespread crime, pauperism, and insanity, inflicts disease and untimely death upon hundreds of thousands of citizens and blights with degeneracy their children unborn, threatening the future integrity and the very life of the nation: Therefore be it

Resolved by the Senate and House of Representatives of the United States of America in Congress assembled (two-thirds of each House concurring therein), That the following amendment of the Constitution be, and hereby is, proposed to the States, to become valid as part of the Constitution when ratified by the legislatures of the several States as provided by the Constitution.

ARTICLE _____

SECTION 1. The sale, manufacture for sale, transportation for sale, importation for sale and exportation for sale of intoxicating liquors for beverage purposes in the United States and all territory subject to the jurisdiction thereof are forever prohibited.

SECTION 2. Congress shall have the power to provide for the manufacture, sale, importation, and transportation of intoxicating liquors for sacramental, medicinal, mechanical, pharmaceutical, or scientific purposes, or for use in the arts, and shall have power to enforce this article by all needful legislation.

TESTIMONY BY REPRESENTATIVES HOBSON AND MANN

Mr. HOBSON. Mr. Speaker [applause], I desire to allot to myself at this time 10 minutes, and request that I be notified at the expiration of that time. The proposition is to take away, through the exercise of the organic law, the power of both the Federal Government and of the States to propagate the liquor traffic. The limitation is precisely the same for both, so there can be no change in the balance of power as between the two. A State has the right to be dry if it so desires, because in being dry it does not harm or menace any neighboring State; but no State has a real inherent right to be wet, because being wet, under the claims of the Liquor Trust itself, no neighboring State can be protected in its right to be dry. The liquor traffic is an interstate nuisance against which the States have no recourse, and Congress itself can not delegate to the States the right to protect themselves in interstate commerce. Consequently we are dealing with a proposition of protecting the absolute inherent rights of the States without changing the balance of power between the States and the Federal Government.

The method of changing the organic law is through the States. There is a clause in the Constitution that provides that no State, without its consent, shall be deprived of its equal representation in the Senate, not even by a change in the Constitution. I was astonished when I heard even a ripple of applause and commendation when one Member was reckless enough to announce that he would have the Constitution of the United States changed by a referendum majority vote of the people. Why, he could have that done only after a war of revolution. The foundation of our Government is a Union of the States, and the States themselves can not change the Constitution in that respect. The revolutionary suggestion of a popular vote to amend the Constitution has never been made before in the history of this Government until invoked to-day to protect the liquor traffic.

This question in the last analysis is really a matter of fact and not of opinion.

When the fact is established that opium and cocaine and other drugs are poisonous, no question has ever been raised as to the power and the right of the

Federal Government and the States to cooperate in the suppression of the popular distribution of such drugs. There never has been any serious conflict of authority in the enforcement of a just law to protect the public health and the public morals. Is alcohol such a habit-forming drug? I call the attention of Members to these posters giving samples of the findings of the great scientists of the world. Alcohol is a hydrocarbon derivative, a chemical compound whose general properties can be and have been established correctly and finally as the properties of other similar compounds. These are its properties: Being the excretion, the loathsome excretions of living organisms, the ferment of germs, alcohol belongs to the family of the toxins. Ferment germs being the lowest forms of life, their toxin, alcohol, is and must always be a poison to all life, a protoplasmic poison. The second finding is that alcohol is a habit-forming drug. The third finding is the most startling. Alcohol is not satisfied with attacking equally all tissues that build up life. It has an affinity, a deadly attack, for the top part of the brain, the line of human evolution. It attacks the line of evolution in plants and animals as well. In this top part of the brain of humanity resides the will power.

Every time a man drinks he takes that much away from his manhood; will power declines. An anesthetic, like chloroform and ether, that hides the pain and poisoning effect, alcohol fools you and leaves the craving behind, increasing steadily with the drinking. Then, with the will power declining, the habit in time becomes fixed. The use of this habit-forming drug is so widespread and its grip so powerful that to-day there are 5,000,000 American citizens, heavy drinkers and drunkards, who have shackles on their wrists, a ball and chain upon their ankles. A few thousand brewers and distillers to-day own 5,000,000 slaves.

Nature is not going to tolerate this tearing down where she is trying to build. Any living thing that so violates the evolutionary law of nature must pay the penalty—nature will proceed to exterminate.

I will refer you to these placards: Starting at 20, a young man as a total abstainer will live to be 65; as a moderate drinker he will die at 51. Do not extol temperate drinking, when it will cut 14½ years out of the life of the average man, though he never gets drunk in his life. The heavy drinker at 20 dies at 35; 30 years are cut out of his short life.

Alcohol is not satisfied with shortening life and bringing to an untimely end and premature death hundreds of thousands of our citizens every year; it blights the offspring; it attacks the tender tissues associated with reproduction in both male and female; it affects the tender system of embryo in the prenatal period. For both parents to be simply moderate drinkers, to drink but once a day beer or wine, will quadruple the chance of miscarriage for the mother, increasing 400 per cent the suffering and danger of maternity, will increase nearly 100 per cent the number of children that will die in the first year of infancy. The children of drinking parents die off at the rate of from four to five times as many as those of abstaining parents. Do not talk about prohibition invading the rights of individuals—liquor blights the rights of our citizens before they are born; it denies the rights of the children to be born with parental love; it throws the boys on the streets and into the mines and factories, preventing them from getting the education they are entitled to. It attacks our young during the whole period of minority. It tramples upon the rights of communities, the rights of counties and States. All of this for what purpose? So that this monster may continue to fatten upon the weaknesses and woes of humanity. The liquor interests can not teach old men to drink, so they must teach the boys.

Sixty-eight per cent of our drunkards had contracted their habits before they were 21 years old, 30 per cent before 16, 7 per cent before 12. What is the inevitable result of this terrible shortening of life and blighting of the offspring? It means that no family, no State, no nation, no empire, no civilization can permanently flourish and prosper and survive unless it is sober.

Who is the agent that teaches the boys to drink? Drinking men do not teach boys to drink. I have never yet found a drinking man who made a habit of teaching boys to drink. Who teaches them? These thousands and tens of thousands of agents of the Liquor Trust who are all over the land. You need not think the bootlegger is simply sustained by his peddling; he is sustained by the great National Liquor Trust. They must get those boys, and they go after them systematically. Why do they do it? What is the motive? Not to harm the boys. I am not fanatical on this question. They do it to get the profits from the sale of their goods. We propose to remove the motive; we propose to cut out the sale and everything that pertains to sale. . . .

Mr. MANN. Mr. Speaker, I am for morality and against immorality. I am for decency and against indecency. I am for temperance and against drunkenness. I am for virtue and against vice. I am for law and order and against crime and disorder. I am for the right and against the wrong. So are we all. But, notwithstanding my sentiments and our sentiments universally. I am not able to vote for the resolution now pending or for what I suppose will be offered as a substitute for it. The gentleman from Alabama [Mr. HOBSON] has introduced in this Congress nine distinct, separate prohibition amendments to the Constitution. Just which one of them we will be called upon to vote for I do not know. They all differ, and I venture to say that in now considering this constitutional amendment there is not a Member of this House besides the gentleman from Alabama who knows what the differences are in these different prohibition resolutions offered by him; and I do not believe that he knows. [Laughter.]

The tendency of governments everywhere has always been toward centralization, and whenever that tendency has proceeded until local powers have been transferred from the local governments to the central government history shows that from its own weight the government has broken down and either revolution occurred or dissolution of the country.

What is the proposition now before us? To-day alcohol is one of the cheapest and most easily produced products. A man with a book before him can manufacture an alcohol still from which he can produce alcohol at a cost of probably not to exceed 15 to 30 cents a gallon, privately, without publicity, except that the Government of the United States, now levying a very high tax upon the production of alcohol, finds it necessary, in order to protect its revenue, to follow up the producers of alcohol unless they pay the Government tax. And the Government tax is very high, so that the main cost of alcohol to-day is the Government tax upon it.

As I understand this proposition, it is not intended that the Government shall hereafter levy tax upon the production of alcohol or alcoholic beverages. The Government's interest in protecting the revenue no longer exists. The National Government is no longer directly interested, so far as revenue is concerned, in preventing the cheap production of alcohol. And not only that, this resolution does not prohibit the manufacture of alcohol ad libitum. There is not a word in the resolution or the proposed amendment which looks to the prohibition of the manufacture of alcohol, or even of alcoholic beverages, unless they are for sale. We can not reach the manufacture of alcohol.

Now, how will this amendment be enforced? The Government of the United States will either do one of two things. It will either have a Government agent spying out the places in every locality in the United States—Government spies everywhere—or else the Government will not attempt to prohibit the manufacture for sale of alcoholic beverages. It is the tendency everywhere. I know, for the local authorities to endeavor to have the General Government enforce a law, make a law upon matters where the local authorities fall, upon the idea, which is not correct, that the Government in Washington can better enforce a law in California than the people of California can enforce it. And so long as the Government has the incentive through the raising of the revenue the Government attempts to enforce the law concerning the manufacture of alcohol. Do you propose by this amendment to have the Government or a Government officer or agent or spy, as you may please to call him, in every township in the United States to detect the production of an article which a farmer or a laborer in his cellar can produce without expense and without publicity, and which when produced is still legal under the amendment unless it be made for sale?

I know it is suggested that you can confer the power of enforcement both upon the General Government and upon the States. It is impossible as a governmental matter to make each of two sovereigns supreme. You can not confer upon the General Government the power to enforce a law or a constitutional amendment and at the same time confer the same power upon the States without inevitable conflict and disaster. The Government would not enforce such an amendment. But you have taken away the governmental control of license. The Government now keeps track—or attempts to do so—of every manufacturer of alcoholic liquor, of every blender of alcoholic liquor, of every rectifier of alcoholic liquor, of every wholesale and retail dealer in alcoholic liquors; but when you forbid by this amendment these things the Government can no longer keep track of them by license or otherwise. It then becomes a matter of detection or spying. The Government of the United States will not be permitted by the people in the different localities in the long run to foster and put upon them thousands of agents or spies to affect them in their immediate locality. And the result will be, if this amendment should be adopted, that liquor will become free, easily made, will sell for 25 or 30 or 40 or 50 cents a gallon, with no prohibition on its manufacture, no penalty for its sale, unless you catch the man at it with a Government spy, the Government itself no longer having any financial interest in detecting the crime. You have practically taken away from the State the power to make and enforce their own laws on the subject. You can not have Government control and State control at the same time.

You say the States can not control it. If the people of a locality can not enforce their local laws, it will never be possible for the National Government successfully to enforce them. It is proposed, is it, where a man has manufactured alcohol at a cost of 30 cents a gallon in his cellar, legitimately, permitted by the law, and has secretly sold it to somebody else, to have the Government agent seize him and carry him a hundred or two hundred miles to be tried in a Federal court instead of being tried in local State courts? Is it the proposition that the enforcement of these ordinary police regulations which must always depend in the main for their enforcement upon the sentiment of the local community shall be brought about by having the offenders dragged into the Federal courts for trial?

If that is attempted, it will break down of its own weight. The result will be as it was years ago, before the Federal Government imposed a high tax upon alcoholic spirits, that whenever a farmer, a laborer, a merchant, or otherwise, desires, he will produce alcohol and give it to his men, like they used to dole out liquor in the harvest fields. It cost nothing to produce it, there was no tax upon it, and no way of preventing it. You have taken away with this resolution the authority of the local governments to protect themselves. You attempt to confer that upon Washington. Well, you will not get Washington unduly excited, or the government in Washington unduly excited, because some man is illegally selling whisky in Portland, Me., or in Portland, Oreg. They do not get too much excited when they sell liquor illegally in the city of Washington.

Mr. SMALL. Will the gentleman pardon a very brief interruption right there, so that I may ask him just one question?

Mr. MANN. Yes.

Mr. SMALL. May I ask the gentleman if there is anything in this proposed amendment which prohibits the manufacture of intoxicating liquors for exportation?

Mr. MANN. It prohibits the manufacture of liquors for exportation for sale.

Mr. SMALL. Exportation, I mean.

Mr. MANN. Exportation for sale. There is nothing in the resolution which prohibits the manufacture of anything. It prohibits the manufacture of intoxicating beverages for sale, and you can make intoxicating beverages of any kind or description, with the proper recipes and a small addition of brown sugar and a few other ingredients, out of plain, pure alcohol, and nobody pretends that you prohibit alcohol or its production.

I understand very well how a wave of excitement goes through and over a country. The bitterest persecutions that have ever been had have been had under the name of religious fervor. People get the impression that they want to accomplish a certain good, as they used to when they proposed to make a man profess a certain religion in order to save his soul, and if he would not save his soul in that way they would destroy his body. Good purposes, laudable desires; but you must test a proposition by its natural results, by the evolution which comes from it; and I declare to you that in my opinion, as a student of government for years, the effort to confer upon the National Government the power to control the manufacture of alcoholic liquors for sale and to prohibit them will result in no tax, no license, no control over the production and sale, and will render them cheap and easy to obtain in every part of the United States, with no government properly equipped to prevent it, and that instead of prohibiting you will have made liquor almost free.

I live in a prohibition district in the city of Chicago, created by an ordinance which I drew years ago, largely enforced by the aid of the good people, its enforcement aided by the saloon keepers on the outskirts. To-day the whisky manufacturers aid the Government as far as they can in the enforcement of the law requiring the payment of a heavy tax upon whisky, because it is to their interest to prevent "moonshine" whisky being made, and most of the information which comes to the Government in regard to attempted illicit stills comes from liquor men, who feel the competition and put the Government on notice and on guard. But when the tax is all removed they will no longer have that incentive. Who will give the information? How will you discover the manufacture and sale of these beverages? The Government is far away. The local people may not be in favor of the enforcement of the law there, as many of them are not in favor of the enforcement of all law.

The prohibitionists, so called, are on the wrong track. I respect their sentiments. I have great regard for them personally. But the way to obtain the restriction of the sale of alcoholic beverages, like the way to enforce any other moral propaganda, is through local authorities, and not by depending upon a strong central government located far away. [Applause.]

Chapter 11

A Classic Tract by the Highest-Paid Speaker of the Anti-Saloon League

The basic attack on alcohol that Richmond Hobson reiterated in his many lectures and in the book from which this excerpt is taken, Alcohol and the Human Race *(1919), is summarized in the congressional testimony reproduced in the preceding selection. In the excerpt here, from the foreword to his book, Hobson gives an account of his interest in the alcohol question. Note that he emphasizes scientific research, a body of knowledge that transcends religious differences and provides an alternative to morality as justification for alcohol control.*

ALCOHOL AND THE HUMAN RACE

Richmond Pearson Hobson

In 1908 the Legislature of Alabama, after enacting a Prohibition statute, submitted a Prohibition Amendment to the State constitution as a referendum to be voted on by the people early the following year.

I was then a member of Congress from that State. My political advisers, in whose wisdom I had confidence, urged me to come out against the Amendment, as most of the men in public life in the State were doing, and I had about decided to follow their advice, for, though taught in childhood to be abstemious, eighteen years of life in the United States Navy and the superficial observation of an average man of the world, had led me to look upon the liquor question as a mere matter of police regulation which would be out of place in the organic law. The thought that my mother, if alive, would have been for the Amendment, led me to decide, before announcing myself, to make an investigation as to whether any issue of a deep abiding nature, fit for incorporation in the organic law of a state, were involved.

I recognized at once that the question was wholly one of fact rather than judgment, and that it hinged on the actual properties of alcohol, a chemical compound. I therefore proceeded, with the aid of the Librarian of Congress, to assemble all available scientific information on the subject. I was startled to find, almost at the outset, that alcohol is not a product built up of grain, grapes and other food materials, but is the toxin of yeast or ferment germs, which, after devouring the food materials, excrete alcohol as their waste product. Though abstemious myself, the thought that intoxicating liquors were really built up of the excretions of living organisms removed all glamour from the cup, and produced a reaction of loathing. Soon I was shocked to find that this toxin causes degeneracy in all living things, disrupts the germ plasm, blights offspring, and, in the end, entails sterility and extinction. I saw at once that instead of being a mere matter of local police regulation its handling was the most fundamental and organic question confronting society, involving not only the integrity of free institutions, but the lives of nations, and the perpetuity of the race. I could not understand how my ignorance had been so dense regarding so important a scientific matter since, at Annapolis and at the Ecole d' Application du Génie Maritime, I had been trained for a scientific profession—that of Naval Constructor and Marine Engineer. After beginning the study of alcohol, however, I never ceased. This book is the product of scientific investigations continued steadily from 1908 until now—investigations in which I have always sought only "the truth, the whole truth and nothing but the truth."

During the past ten years I have endeavoured to take my knowledge of this subject to my fellow countrymen, chiefly by the spoken word. Now that democracy has conquered in its age-long struggle, and must face the reconstruction of the world, I am hoping and praying that I may be helpful in some degree in carrying this vital truth to the ends of the earth through the written word. If the peoples of the earth do get this truth, a no-license world will follow as day follows night, democracy will endure, and a new era will dawn for the sobering world.

To those who wish to examine original experimental data, I would suggest the following:

First—Publications of the Carnegie institution at Washington on experimental investigations by Drs. Benedict and Dodge, on the effect of moderate doses of alcohol. These investigations establish that alcohol is always a depressant poison, no matter how small the quantity taken, and set at rest the controversy over the imagined food value of alcohol, "temperate drinking," "the use of light wine, of beer, etc."

Second—Reports of Dr. Stockard of experiments conducted at the Cornell Medical College, as to the effect of alcohol taken by mammals upon offspring and progeny, published in the "American Naturalist," and in the Proceedings of the Society of Experimental Biology on Medicines. These experiments upon lower animals show the disruptive effect of drinking upon the germ plasm, producing degeneracy in the offspring, and finally possible sterility and extinction in the progeny.

Third—Reports of Dr. Laitinen of the University of Helsingfors, investigations—covering thousands of families—into the effects of drinking of parents upon their children, published in the Proceedings of International Congresses on Alcoholism, especially the Congress of London, 1909. These investigations uncover the degenerating effect of even the most temperate drinking by parents upon children, showing that the general use of "light wine" or "light beer" must in time bring about the disintegration of any family, and the decline and downfall of any nation.

To those who wish to examine an assemblage of experimental data, and the searching analysis of poisonous effects of alcohol, I would suggest the "Psychology of Alcoholism" by George B. Cutten.

The basic facts about alcohol are now established so thoroughly by the scientific world that for brevity I have omitted all my copious bibliography, and have cut down the citations of authorities. The question has really passed the controversial stage—elucidation and interpretation are now in order.

R.P.H.

Chapter 12

Is Alcohol Dangerous to the Fetus? Part 1: Yes

The animal experiments Dr. Charles R. Stockard describes in this 1912 report were cited explicitly by Richmond Hobson as support for his anti-alcohol arguments (see preceding selection). Other temperance crusaders similarly seized on scientific work, even with animal subjects, to bolster their cause.

There is an interesting twist in the applications of Stockard's research: by the 1930s his studies were used to cast doubt on the proposition that maternal alcohol consumption presents a danger to the fetus. For instance, in his chapter "The Effects of Alcohol in Development and Heredity" (in Alcohol and Man: The Effects of Alcohol on Man in Health and Disease, *ed.* Haven Emerson, M.D. [New York: Macmillan, 1932], *reprinted in (*Alcohol and Man [New York: Arno, 1981]), *Stockard writes, "Results from these experiments on the embryos of lower animals justify only the conclusion — that if comparisons with human embryos are possible they indicate that the content of alcohol in human blood is fortunately never sufficiently high to present a danger to the developing embryo" (p. 111). Two other documents in this anthology (see Haggard and Jellinek and the health caution on Fetal Alcohol Syndrome) trace the later history of this question.*

THE INFLUENCE OF ALCOHOLISM ON THE OFFSPRING

Charles R. Stockard

Two years ago I showed that almost all known gross deformities of the brain could be produced by treating developing fish embryos with alcohol and a number of anæsthetics.

Since that time these experiments have been extended to birds and mammals. The work of Feré with hen's eggs has been repeated and his results confirmed. When these eggs are subjected to the fumes of alcohol the shell is penetrated and the developing embryo is affected. The rate of development is reduced and a large number of monstrosities occur.

Guinea pigs have been put into a state of chronic alcoholism by treating them for six days per week with alcohol fumes to almost the point of intoxication. Forty full-term matings of various combinations have been made with these alcoholic animals. Treated males have been paired with normal females (test of paternal influence on offspring), treated females paired with normal males (maternal influence plus the direct effect on the developing embryo) and finally treated males and females were paired. The outcome of these matings has been most striking.

Twenty-five matings gave no result or the embryos were aborted early and eaten by the mother. Fifteen matings produced in all 25 young, of these two have lived to reach maturity and are apparently normal, four are still young but seem normal. Of the other 19, eight were stillborn or aborted shortly before term, seven lived for a few days after birth and all died in convulsions, four were *in utero* when the mothers were killed and one of these was deformed.

All of the control matings were successful, all of the young lived and were vigorous.

Chapter 13

Constitutional Prohibition

The Senate approved the text of the Eighteenth Amendment on June 11, 1917, and the House of Representatives followed on December 16, 1917. The measure then went to the states for approval. On January 16, 1919, with the vote of Nebraska, the required thirty-six states had ratified the amendment. It passed into law one year later, on January 16, 1920.

THE EIGHTEENTH AMENDMENT

Section 1. After one year from the ratification of this article the manufacture, sale, or transportation of intoxicating liquors within, the importation thereof into, or the exportation thereof from the United States and all territory subject to the jurisdiction thereof for beverage purposes is hereby prohibited.

Section 2. The Congress and the several states shall have concurrent power to enforce this article by appropriate legislation.

Section 3. This article shall be inoperative unless it shall have been ratified as an amendment to the Constitution by the legislatures of the several states, as provided in the Constitution, within seven years from the date of the submission hereof to the states by the Congress.

Chapter 14

Enforcing the Eighteenth Amendment

The Volstead Act of October 1919, named for the Minnesota Democrat Andrew J. Volstead (1869–1947), detailed the workings of national Prohibition. In addition to promulgating the detailed procedures for enforcement of the Eighteenth Amendment, which was scheduled to come into effect on January 16, 1920, this measure affirmed the enactment of so-called wartime prohibition, which had begun on July 1, 1919. The six months of wartime prohibition are nowadays often forgotten, as is the result that the impact of alcohol prohibition began before the Eighteenth Amendment went into effect.

Only a few passages from the lengthy act are reprinted here. Note that alcohol purchased legally prior to Prohibition could be used in the home and served to guests. Furthermore, the Eighteenth Amendment did not make purchase of alcohol illegal.

THE VOLSTEAD ACT

An Act to prohibit intoxicating beverages, and to regulate the manufacture, production, use, and sale of high-proof spirits for other than beverage purposes, and to insure an ample supply of alcohol and promote its use in scientific research and in the development of fuel, dye, and other lawful industries.

Be it enacted by the Senate and House of Representatives of the United States of America in Congress assembled, That the short title of this Act shall be the "National Prohibition Act." . . .

Title II. Prohibition of Intoxicating Beverages.

SEC. 1. When used in Title II and Title III of this Act (1). The word "liquor" or the phrase "intoxicating liquor" shall be construed to include alcohol, brandy, whisky, rum, gin, beer, ale, porter, and wine, and in addition thereto any spirituous, vinous, malt, or fermented liquor, liquids, and compounds, whether medicated, proprietary, patented, or not, and by whatever name called, containing one-half of 1 per centum or more of alcohol by volume which are fit for use for beverage purposes: *Provided,* That the foregoing definition shall not extend not extend to dealcoholized wine nor to any beverage or liquid produced by the process by which beer, ale, porter or wine is produced, if it contains less than one-half of 1 per centum of alcohol by volume, and is made as prescribed in section 37 of this title, and is otherwise denominated than as beer, ale, or porter, and is contained and sold in, or from, such sealed and labeled bottles, casks, or containers as the commissioner may by regulation prescribe. . . .

Sec. 3. No person shall on or after the date when the eighteenth amendment to the Constitution of the United States goes into effect, manufacture, sell, barter, transport, import, export, deliver, furnish or possess any intoxicating liquor except as authorized in this Act, and all the provisions of this Act shall be liberally construed to the end that the use of intoxicating liquor as a beverage may be prevented.

Liquor for nonbeverage purposes and wine for sacramental purposes may be manufactured, purchased, sold, bartered, transported, imported, exported, delivered, furnished and possessed, but only as herein provided, and the commissioner may, upon application, issue permits therefor: *Provided*, That nothing in this Act shall prohibit the purchase and sale of warehouse receipts covering distilled spirits on deposit in Government bonded warehouses, and no special tax liability shall attach to the business of purchasing and selling such warehouse receipts.

Sec. 4. The articles enumerated in this section shall not, after, having been manufactured and prepared for the market, be subject to the provisions of this Act if they correspond with the following descriptions and limitations, namely:

(a) Denatured alcohol or denatured rum produced and used as provided by laws and regulations now or hereafter in force.

(b) Medicinal preparations manufactured in accordance with formulas prescribed by the United States Pharmacopœia, National Formulary of the American Institute of Homeopathy that are unfit for use for beverage purposes.

(c) Patented, patent, and proprietary medicines that are unfit for use for beverage purposes.

(d) Toilet, medicinal, and antiseptic preparations and solutions that are unfit for use for beverage purposes.

(e) Flavoring extracts and sirups that are unfit for use as a beverage, or for intoxicating beverage purposes.

(f) Vinegar and preserved sweet cider. . . .

Sec. 6. No one shall manufacture, sell, purchase, transport, or prescribe any liquor without first obtaining a permit from the commissioner so to do, except that a person may, without a permit, purchase and use liquor for medicinal purposes when prescribed by a physician as herein provided, and except that any person who in the opinion of the commissioner is conducting a bona fide hospital or sanatorium engaged in the treatment of persons suffering from alcoholism, may, under such rules, regulations, and conditions as the commissioner shall prescribe, purchase and use, in accordance with the methods in use in such institution, liquor, to be administered to the patients of such institution under the direction of a duly qualified physician employed by such institution. . . .

Nothing in this title shall be held to apply to the manufacture, sale, transportation, importation, possession, or distribution of wine for sacramental purposes, or like religious rites, except section 6 (save as the same requires a permit to purchase) and section 10 hereof, and the provisions of this Act prescribing penalties for the violation of either of said sections. No person to whom a permit may be issued to manufacture, transport, import, or sell wines for sacramental purposes or like religious rites shall sell, barter, exchange, or furnish any such to any person not a rabbi, minister of the gospel, priest, or an officer duly authorized for the purpose by any church or congregation, nor to any such except upon an application duly subscribed by him, which application, authenticated as regulations may prescribe, shall be filed and preserved by the seller. The head of any conference or diocese or other ecclesiastical jurisdiction may designate any rabbi, minister, or priest to supervise the manufacture of wine to be used for the purposes and rites in this section mentioned, and the person so designated may, in the discretion of the commissioner, be granted a permit to supervise such manufacture.

SEC. 7. No one but a physician holding a permit to prescribe liquor shall issue any prescription for liquor. And no physician shall prescribe liquor unless after careful physical examination of the person for whose use such prescription is sought, or if such examination is found impracticable, then upon the best information obtainable, he in good faith believes that the use of such liquor as a medicine by such person is necessary and will afford relief to him from some known ailment. Not more than a pint of spirituous liquor to be taken internally shall be prescribed for use by the same person within any period of ten days and no prescription shall be filled more than once. Any pharmacist filling a prescription shall at the time indorse upon it over his own signature the word "canceled," together with the date when the liquor was delivered, and then make the same a part of the record that he is required to keep as herein provided.

Every physician who issues a prescription for liquor shall keep a record, alphabetically arranged in a book prescribed by the commissioner, which shall show the date of issue, amount prescribed, to whom issued, the purpose or ailment for which it is to be used and directions for use, stating the amount and frequency of the dose.

SEC. 8. The commissioner shall cause to be printed blanks for the prescriptions herein required, and he shall furnish the same, free of cost, to physicians holding permits to prescribe. The prescription blanks shall be printed in book form and shall be numbered consecutively from one to one hundred, and each book shall be given a number; and the stubs in each book shall carry the same numbers as and be copies of the prescriptions. The books containing such stubs shall be returned to the commissioner when the prescription blanks have been used, or sooner, if directed by the commissioner. All unused, mutilated, or defaced blanks shall be returned with the book. No physician shall prescribe and no pharmacist shall fill any prescription for liquor except on blanks so provided, except in cases of emergency, in which event a record and report shall be made and kept as in other cases. . . .

SEC. 17. It shall be unlawful to advertise anywhere, or by any means or method, liquor, or the manufacture, sale, keeping for sale or furnishing of the same, or where, how, from whom, or at what price the same may be obtained. No one shall permit any sign or billboard containing such advertisement to remain upon one's premises. But nothing herein shall prohibit manufacturers and wholesale druggists holding permits to sell liquor from furnishing price lists; with description of liquor for sale, to persons permitted to purchase liquor, or from advertising alcohol in business publications or trade journals circulating generally among manufacturers of lawful alcoholic perfumes, toilet preparations, flavoring extracts, medicinal preparations, and like articles: *Provided, however,* That nothing in this Act or in the Act making appropriations for the Post Office Department, approved March 3, 1917 (Thirty-ninth Statutes at Large, Part 1, page 1058, et seq.), shall apply to newspapers published in foreign countries when mailed to this country.

SEC. 18. It shall be unlawful to advertise, manufacture, sell, or possess for sale any utensil, contrivance machine, preparation, compound, tablet, substance, formula direction, or recipe advertised, designed, or intended for use in the unlawful manufacture of intoxicating liquor.

SEC. 19. No person shall solicit or receive, nor knowingly permit his employee to solicit or receive from any person any order for liquor or give any information of how liquor may be obtained in violation of this Act.

SEC. 20. Any person who shall be injured in person, property means of support, or otherwise by any intoxicated person, or by reason of the intoxication of any person whether resulting in his death or not, shall have a right of action against any person who shall, by unlawfully selling to or unlawfully assisting in procuring liquor for such intoxicated person, have caused or contributed to such intoxication, and in any such action such person shall have a right to recover actual and exemplary damages. In case of the death of either party, the action or right of action given by this section shall survive to or against his or her executor or administrator, and the amount so recovered by either wife or child shall be his or her sole and separate property. Such action may be brought in any court of competent jurisdiction. In any case where parents shall be entitled to such damages, either the father or mother may sue alone therefor, but recovery by one of such parties shall be a bar to suit brought by the other.

SEC. 21. Any room, house, building, boat, vehicle, structure, or place where intoxicating liquor is manufactured sold, kept, or bartered in violation of this title, and all intoxicating liquor and property kept and used in maintaining the same, is hereby declared to be a common nuisance, and any person who maintains such a common nuisance shall be guilty of a misdemeanor and upon conviction thereof shall be fined not more than $1,000 or be imprisoned for not more than one year, or both. If a person has knowledge or reason to believe that his room, house, building, boat, vehicle, structure, or place is occupied or used for the manufacture or sale of liquor contrary to the provision of this title, and suffers the same to be so occupied or used, such room, house, building, boat, vehicle, structure, or place shall be subject to a lien for and may be sold to pay all fines and costs assessed against the person guilty of such nuisance for such violation, and any such lien may be enforced by action in any court having jurisdiction. . . .

Sec. 25. It shall be unlawful to have or possess any liquor or property designed for the manufacture of liquor intended for use in violating this title or which has been so used, and no property rights shall exist in any such liquor or property. A search warrant may issue as provided in Title XI of public law numbered 24 of the Sixty-fifth Congress, approved June 15, 1917, and such liquor, the containers thereof, and such property so seized shall be subject to such disposition as the court may make thereof. If it is found that such liquor or property was so unlawfully held or possessed, or had been so unlawfully used, the liquor, and all property designed for the unlawful manufacture of liquor, shall be destroyed, unless the court shall otherwise order. No search warrant shall issue to search any private dwelling occupied as such unless it is being used for the unlawful sale of intoxicating liquor, or unless it is in part used for some business purpose such as a store, shop, saloon, restaurant, hotel, or boarding house. The term "private dwelling" shall be construed to include the room or rooms used and occupied not transiently but solely as a residence in an apartment house, hotel, or boarding house. The property seized on any such warrant shall not be taken from the officer seizing the same on any writ of replevin or other like process. . . .

Sec. 29. Any person who manufactures or sells liquor in violation of this title shall for a first offense be fined not more than $1,000, or imprisoned not exceeding six months, and for a second or subsequent offense shall be fined not less than $200 nor more than $2,000 and be imprisoned not less than one month nor more than five years. . . .

Sec. 33. After February 1, 1920, the possession of liquors by any person not legally permitted under this title to possess liquor shall be prima facie evidence that such liquor is kept for the purpose of being sold, bartered, exchanged, given away, furnished, or otherwise disposed of in violation of the provisions of this title. Every person legally permitted under this title to have liquor shall report to the commissioner within ten days after the date when the eighteenth amendment of the Constitution of the United States goes into effect, the kind and amount of intoxicating liquors in his possession. But it shall not be unlawful to possess liquors in one's private dwelling while the same is occupied and used by him as his dwelling only and such liquor need not be reported, provided such liquors are for use only for the personal consumption of the owner thereof and his family residing in such dwelling and of his bona fide guests when entertained by him therein; and the burden of proof shall be upon the possessor in any action concerning the same to prove that such liquor was lawfully acquired, possessed, and used. . . .

Chapter 15

A Leading Economist Argues for Prohibition

Irving Fisher (1867–1947), an esteemed economist known as the "father of econometrics," devoted much of his prodigious energy to improving public health. He describes himself in the selection given here as a reluctant but convinced convert to the belief that Prohibition would be an effective strategy for improving the quality and length of life. Fisher regretted, however, that a broad measure intended to be permanent had been mandated before the nation fully had been won over to the reform, as might have happened with a true wartime prohibition trial. Fisher's book Prohibition at Its Worst *appeared in 1926, as the forces against Prohibition were starting to receive a better hearing. In this extract we see how the economist tries, through the use of reason, personal testimonies, and statistics, to demonstrate the achievements of Prohibition.*

The "Mr. Shirk" to whom Fisher refers here was Stanley Shirk, a lawyer and the research director of the Moderation League.

PROHIBITION AT ITS WORST

Irving Fisher

How I Became Interested

My Own Health

It is now twenty-five years since I was first attracted to the alcohol problem. When starting for Colorado in 1899 to repair my health I was warned by Dr. Trudeau not to let the Colorado doctors give me whisky; for at that time alcohol was still regarded by many physicians as a valuable medicine for numerous diseases.

While recovering my health I undertook a systematic study of how to get, and keep, well. In the course of this study I soon found that, according to the best evidence, alcohol is a physiological poison, and out of place in the human body. This conclusion is now commonly accepted by reputable physiologists. Some of the evidence for it is given in this book.

Having thus reached the conclusion that total abstinence, rather than "temperance," is the truer ideal, I soon became, for the sake of my own health, a teetotaler except for occasional sips of wine at my friends' tables. I also ceased to serve wine at my own table except when entertaining those who, I knew, especially desired and expected it.

I next applied the results of this study to my own professional subject, economics. I saw that the use of alcoholics was economically costly and wasteful to the nation, and in more ways than one.

Solution, Education of Youth

The problem of how best to reduce this waste puzzled me, just as it is now puzzling many other people. I was then far from thinking that Prohibition was the best solution. I knew that all laws affecting personal habits are resented by those whose personal habits are thereby reflected on, and that such laws are, therefore, difficult to enforce. I realized then, as I realize now, that laws without sufficient public sentiment behind them are apt to become a dead letter and to lead to disrespect for law in general. It was clear, therefore, that, even if Prohibition were eventually desirable—which I did not then believe—the first and most important step toward the great objective (reduction in the flow of alcohol down human throats) must be the *education of the public*. I even hoped, with youthful enthusiasm, that such moral suasion would be rapid and effective, and tried to do my part.

It soon became apparent, however, that there was a flaw in this program— the same flaw as in the program of moral suasion as a sufficient solution of the problem of narcotic drugs. In fact, the alcohol problem shaped itself in my mind as simply a special case of the narcotic problem.

The flaw in the moral suasion program as a complete solution of the problem of narcotics, alcohol included, is that *the will is weakened by the drug habit*.

Ordinarily, there is little or no use in preaching to a dope-fiend or a drunkard. His reason is convinced, but his will is not strong enough to follow his reason. His will has been destroyed by the drug habit and it is too late for the drug habit to be destroyed by the will.

I had noted that, occasionally, strong religious appeal does result in "conversion," as the Salvation Army is demonstrating every day. But no practical reformer expects any wholesale results from confirmed addicts. On the other hand, to the moderate users whose wills are only moderately impaired, the appeal to become total abstainers is itself only moderate. The moderate user generally sees no need of "reformation." He does not realize the subtle, steady damage being done to his body and mind, nor the seriousness of the risk he is running of becoming a confirmed addict.

Noting these things, I came to believe that the only class left to appeal to is the young, who have not yet reached even the half-way stages of the moderate users. The teaching of the effects of alcohol in the public schools, under the influence of the Women's Christian Temperance Union, seemed to me the basic educational fact underlying alcohol reform in the United States.

Also Necessary to Outlaw Saloon

But such education, if not supplemented by legislation, is painfully slow. Moreover, without help from legislation, any such education of children is sure to be largely offset by the examples of their elders and the allurements of the saloon. It became clear to me that it was the saloon which kept up and increased the liquor habit. The real problem is the problem of new recruits. We may well forget the confirmed addict of this generation if we can prevent others from taking his place in the next. The great objective is to break the chain by which the custom of drinking is passed on from generation to generation. The use of liquor is no more natural than the use of opium. When either is once discontinued it can stay discontinued.

As a practical student I reached the inevitable conclusion that, besides education, there must be some *legislation* to lessen, or abolish, the opportunity of the saloon-keeper, the brewer, etc., to ensnare new recruits.

Accordingly I studied the dispensary system and other devices to remove or reduce the profit-motive and diminish the advertising of liquors. These devices have undoubtedly some value in Scandinavia, but are disappointing as a complete solution of the problem.

Reluctantly Converted to Prohibition

At last I was reluctantly compelled to conclude that Prohibition is the ultimate solution, when public sentiment is adequate to enforce it. What finally converted me was the experience of the Western states which tried it. I was particularly impressed by the experience of the State of Washington. Certain cities there voted against State Constitutional Prohibition but were defeated by the country districts. Later, however, when the inevitable attempt came to "modify," and to permit so-called "light wines and beer," these same cities voted dry!

The reason was the surprising prosperity which followed State Prohibition. One city editor, who had predicted business depression and had pointed to definite saloon sites as destined to remain vacant and for rent, had the manhood to confess his error and advocate that Prohibition should remain unimpaired. This sort of experience beat down my conservatism. I found then, as I have found since, that we cautious Easterners have much to learn from the venturesome West.

War Conference on Alcohol

A new impulse was given to my study of the alcohol problem by the war. When the war broke out, I offered my services to the Council of National Defense. I expected to be assigned to some strictly economic task; but was asked to call a conference on Alcohol to meet with the conference being called by Colonel Snow on Venereal Disease, since Alcohol and Venereal Disease are always the twin obstacles to the soldiers' fitness to fight.

Accordingly, I called such a conference of leading economists and physicians at the New Willard Hotel in Washington in April, 1917. The conference recommended two war measures:

(1) The establishing of a Dry Zone around each Army Cantonment, and
(2) *War-time* Prohibition.

The first recommendation was transmitted, through various sub-committees, to the Council of National Defense; was approved by the Council, and was finally enacted into law. It was, I believe, a very important factor in keeping up the efficiency of our soldiers.

Brewers Block War-Time Prohibition

The second recommendation, that for War-time Prohibition, was likewise approved by the four successive committees through which it had to pass on its way to the Council of National Defense. Then something happened!

The recommendation was scheduled to be presented to the Council on April 17, 1917, together with that for a Dry Zone around the Cantonments. The spokesman to present the matter was selected. The small sub-committee that had it in charge met a half-hour before the Council convened in order to rehearse the program.

We were to have been met by Dr. Franklin Martin of the Council. He did not appear, however, until the half-hour had expired. He then said, cryptically, that only the Dry Zone recommendation could be presented. Thus War-time Prohibition went by the board—for the time.

Afterward, on inquiry, I learned what had happened. In the course of sounding out public opinion I had sent several hundred telegrams to business leaders and others, asking whether they favored War-time Prohibition. Most business men, and practically all economists, approved of Prohibition as a war measure. It so happened that one of the telegrams, reaching a business man who disapproved of the proposal, was handed to a brewer.

The brewers' forces had long been superbly organized for action and they proceeded at once to train their machine-guns on the members of the Council of National Defense. One member, Mr. Gompers, I was told, received fifty telegrams in a single day, protesting against any War-time Prohibition. Intimations or threats were made that, if any such action were taken, the Council of National Defense would be put out of business.

Daniel Willard, chairman of the Council, though personally favorable to Prohibition, felt it unwise, as did others, to permit the matter to be presented, and Dr. Martin was requested to call it off.

The special interest of the brewers won against the general interest of the nation.

Later, a permanent Sub-committee of the Council was appointed on Alcohol, and I was made chairman. This Committee also favored War-time Prohibition.

But its recommendations had no chance even to reach the Council. The brewers had effectually blocked any such action.

Blocked Again by Filibuster

The result was that those favoring War-time Prohibition—including the members of the Sub-committee just mentioned, namely, Dr. Haven Emerson, Dr. Eugene L. Fisk, Professor Alonzo Taylor, Rev. Charles Stelzle, and myself—took steps to press the matter directly with Congress. This had already been independently undertaken by the Anti-Saloon League.

The importance of War-time Prohibition for food conservation was conclusively proved, when Professor Alonzo Taylor showed that the barley used in beer production destroyed potentially eleven million loaves of bread a day.

In Congress the brewers' opposition again presented itself. But, at last, Congressman Randall succeeded in so amending the Lever Food bill as to provide for War-time Prohibition.

This food bill, with the War-time Prohibition amendment attached, passed the House of Representatives, but was blocked in the Senate by the brewing influences. The instant the House passed the bill, literally a trainload of brewers swarmed into Washington. As was subsequently brought out by a Senate investigation, the *Washington Times* was bought almost overnight by a well-known editor with money "loaned" to him, without interest, by C. W. Feigenspan, President of the United States Brewers Association.

Senator Penrose of Pennsylvania, a notorious Wet, and others threatened to prevent the passage of the food bill until, or unless, the War-time Prohibition clause was eliminated, and they sought to conceal their own guilt in delaying that measure by trying to cast the responsibility for delay on the other side. On one occasion Senator Penrose made a speech definitely accusing the Drys of delaying the passage of the bill, whereupon Senator Sheppard, for the Drys, stated that his side was ready for a vote then and there, and moved for unanimous consent to take the vote immediately. Senator Penrose looked sheepishly around to find some friend willing to object to such unanimous consent. But his friends merely smiled at his predicament and he was forced, amid laughter, to object himself and thereby to accept the responsibility for delay. He knew that to prevent a vote was, in fact, the only way to defeat War-time Prohibition, for there were plenty of votes in the Senate to pass it if it could be brought to a vote.

What was happening was what so often happens in our Senate, with its antiquated rules making it possible for a minority to block legislation by filibuster. When, as in war time, quick action is essential, an unpatriotic and selfish minority has the country by the throat.

It was imperative that the Lever Food bill should be passed at once. The War-time-Prohibition features of the bill were important, but not so important as other features.

It soon appeared that, in view of the attitude of the Wets in the Senate, the food bill would be delayed indefinitely unless the prohibition clauses were eliminated. Accordingly, President Wilson requested the Drys, through a letter addressed to the Anti-Saloon League, to withdraw these prohibition clauses.

I remember sitting up most of a June night in 1917 laboring with the Anti-Saloon League leaders to persuade them to accede to the President's request, in the interest of immediate food legislation, and in the expectation of bringing up War-time Prohibition again as a separate measure.

As is well known, the President's request was heeded. War-time Prohibition once more went down to defeat.

It was the brewers, primarily, who had won; for their influence had caused the filibuster that impelled the President to make his request.

Brewers Hoist with Their Own Petard

It was as an indirect result of this second defeat of War-time Prohibition that Constitutional Prohibition came about! The brewers found that, unwittingly, they had jumped out of the frying pan into the fire!

Personally I had been very reluctant to see Constitutional Prohibition tried until War-time Prohibition had been tried first. To me, Prohibition was, and is, merely an experiment in the long fight against alcohol; and I feared to see that the experiment tried permanently and irrevocably until after it had been tested temporarily.

My own program and that of the committees with which I had worked was to get War-time Prohibition enacted on its merits as a war measure for the duration of the war, and for one year thereafter.

Then, on the basis of the record of War-time Prohibition, and after all war hysteria was over, Permanent Prohibition might properly be submitted to the people for their deliberate and final decision.

But we all know what happens to the best laid plans of mice and men. Neither my plans to take one little step first, nor the brewers' plans to crush out all Prohibition, were to be realized.

National Prohibition Comes Too Soon

What actually happened was that Constitutional Prohibition came first. The resolution submitting to the States passed the Senate August 1, 1917, and the House December 18, 1917.

War-time Prohibition did come eventually. But when it came not only had Constitutional Prohibition been provided for, but the war itself was over! President Wilson signed the bill November 21, 1918, and the law became operative July 1, 1919. One could scarcely imagine a more illogical program.

The reason was that the Senators who had acceded to President Wilson's request to withdraw the War-time Prohibition clauses from the Food Act thereby so disappointed and angered their dry constituents that these Senators felt constrained to do *something* to set themselves right.

And the Anti-Saloon League very astutely took advantage of the situation to propose the Act submitting the Eighteenth Amendment. Other important agencies which helped to bring that Amendment about were the Women's Christian Temperance Union, the various church temperance organizations, especially the Methodist, the Methodist Church South, the Baptist, and the Presbyterian, the Order of Good Templars, and the Prohibition party.

It was easy even for wet Senators to let this act pass, on the theory that it did not really enact Prohibition, but merely submitted it to the States.

The Act was passed and Constitutional Prohibition was on its way.

When three-quarters of the States had ratified, the Amendment became a part of the Constitution. But under it Prohibition was not to be effective until one year later, namely, January 17, 1920.

War-Time Prohibition after War Time

Meantime, the measure for War-time Prohibition had been slowly making progress in Congress, in spite of all the opposition and delays; and after the Eighteenth Amendment was adopted and ratified by the States that opposition became helpless.

The result was that, though the war was over, the long pending War-time Prohibition bill was finally passed as a means of filling in the gap between the adoption of Constitutional Prohibition and its taking effect.

This was pretty hard on the brewers, who had counted on a year's breathing space; but the brewers received and deserved scant sympathy at that juncture.

At a meeting in Atlantic City soon after these events, Wayne B. Wheeler paid me the somewhat doubtful compliment of having "done more to bring about War-time Prohibition than any other man who wears shoe leather." "War-time" Prohibition, as such, never really existed. Nor did the act finally passed, and called War-time Prohibition, ever serve as a preliminary experiment by which we might judge of the value of Permanent Prohibition.

Evidently Constitutional Prohibition came on the country somewhat prematurely. That is to say, it came before certain sections, notably the East and the great cities, were prepared for it by education.

Why Turn Back Now?

But while, according to a logical program, Constitutional Prohibition was premature, can we and ought we, as a practical proposition, at this late date, go back and begin all over, only to end, in all probability, in Prohibition again at a later time, after the uselessness of other, halfway, measures shall have been demonstrated anew?

May it not be more practical to go forward instead of backward, and to do now the educating after Prohibition, which, by rights, should have been done before Prohibition?

Certainly, before taking any radical step, we ought to weigh carefully the facts presented to us during the last six years. We must "face the facts"—the facts good and bad, favorable and unfavorable, and be led by what they reveal.

That is the object of this book. If Prohibition at its worst, during these first trying years when New York, for instance, was far from ready for it, and when, consequently, it has proved so bewildering and offensive to many good people, is nevertheless actually accomplishing its main purpose of suppressing the saloon and lessening the use of alcohol, we may well think twice before giving it up until it is tried out further.

The most important question of fact is whether the new recruits among the youth are more or less numerous under Prohibition. . . . In Chapter II new evidence, never before presented, will be given on this question.

Drinking among the Youth

At the Nation's Capital

The exaggerations as to increased drinking among the youth of the country are next in order to be considered. And here Mr. Shirk is found not wanting in willingness to contribute to the testimony as to their corruption.

He declares that while there is little that is authoritative on the subject, records of arrests of young people for drunkenness are furnished by the police department of Washington, D.C. He reports:

> Arrests of persons under 22 years old average 44 a year for the four pre-prohibition years 1914–1917. A bone-dry law was enacted for Washington before National Prohibition became effective, and immediately youthful drunkenness increased. In 1918 it rose to 73 and by 1924 had reached 282, an increase of 540 per cent above the pre-prohibition level. . . . This condition in Washington merely confirms what is known to exist in the rest of the country (1, p. 346).

Now it would be interesting to learn the proportion of young people in Washington to total population in war time and during the years following the war, as compared with the years from 1914 to 1917. No sooner was war declared than the capital of the nation became a vast encampment, surrounded by army concentration camps and filled with young men in newly created civilian stations drawn from every part of the country. Washington was immediately a city charged with the excitements of mobilization, war preparations, organization of industries and all manner of activities on a national scale, and it became a Mecca for the youth of the country. The doubling and trebling of the government personnel remained to a large extent even after the war, because the bureaus and commissions had become permanently enlarged. The artificial atmosphere and stimulations of the nation's capital might easily produce among certain of the youth who flocked there a record of excesses that would hardly be typical of conditions among the youth in other parts of the country. It is unfortunate for Mr. Shirk's contentions that he fails to present such a record for any other city. Moreover, the Superintendent of the Police Department of Washington reports:

Prior to July 1, 1923, it was not an offense to be intoxicated in the District of Columbia.*

Here is another case of increased severity of arrests, as enjoined by law, to explain Mr. Shirk's charts based on raw statistical data.

Prohibition in the Colleges

There is ample testimony concerning the effect on youth of Prohibition—not only the testimony already given, including the diminishing totals of first offenders on the charge of drunkenness, but quite as typical a record of Prohibition enforcement in the colleges.

The case of Yale University, in fact, presents a unique test of a change of custom in the face of disapproving opinion.

There can be no doubt that the prevailing sentiment among Yale students is wet. The statistics of the Senior class of Yale College, published early in 1926, showed that 80 per cent of that class were wet in their sympathies. This is a larger proportion than the figures for Harvard reported during 1925, and far larger than the recent survey of eleven colleges, mostly Middle Western, which show that two-thirds of the men and four-fifths of the women students favor strict enforcement.

Not only is the Yale student sentiment prevailingly wet, but the city and state in which Yale is located are among the wettest in the Nation. Connecticut did not ratify the Eighteenth Amendment, and recently refused an opportunity to tighten up its inadequate enforcement legislation. The newspapers of New Haven are uniformly wet. Many judges are wet. Besides living in this damp atmosphere, the students largely come from the great wet cities, especially New York, and a large fraction of the students are from homes of the well-to-do who can support wine cellars. Thus tradition and environment conspire to moisten these young men's minds, if not their throats. Moreover, the students are just at the age at which, we are so often told, Prohibition is corrupting the youth.

If, therefore, anywhere in this great country, Prohibition ought to prove a rank failure, it should be among such a group of susceptible young men as we have at Yale. I have taken great pains to ascertain the actual facts in the case. Not relying on my own impressions, I went to those who had the recorded facts of students in disciplinary cases, the eight authorities who knew the facts at first hand, and far better than others. At least two of these eight men I know to be strongly opposed to Prohibition. One I know to be strongly in favor. The attitude of the other five I do not know positively, but I believe that it is mostly opposed to Prohibition. The facts at Yale, as these authorities have given them to me in writing, are summarized as follows:

Frederick S. Jones, outgoing Dean of Yale College, says:

*Report sent to Irving Fisher, August, 1926, by Major Edwin B. Hesse, Superintendent, Police Department, Washington, D.C.

I think, on the whole, there is decidedly less drinking than before Prohibition, and conditions have been improving with time. On the other hand, the cases with which I have to deal are often more acute than those encountered before Prohibition. The college fraternities have forbidden liquor in their houses, and are living up to this rule.

C. W. Mendell, incoming Dean of Yale College:

I should say on the whole that Fay Campbell's summary [see below] of the matter was reasonably good, and as near to the facts as one could hope to come. It seems to me, however, that he has overlooked one very important fact, that there is more drinking of hard liquor now than there was before Prohibition. This, I think, cannot be questioned. In the old days the staple drink was beer, and I am inclined to think that it led to very little harm. The present drinking of hard liquor almost always results in trouble of some sort, so that scenes of public disgrace are rather worse than they used to be. The drinking is more occasional, but more disastrous. Personally, I am not a believer in Prohibition.

E. Fay Campbell, Secretary of the Yale University Christian Association:

The police feel that this year there was less drinking at the junior prom, than at any time in many years. There was a great deal of drinking at the games. I am perfectly sure, however, that there was not nearly as much drinking as in 1915 when I was a sophomore.

Charles H. Warren, Dean of the Sheffield Scientific School:

Four years ago I was appalled at the drinking among the students. The alumni were even worse. Since that time there has been a very steady improvement. I think there is less drinking now than ever before in the University. The worst offenders are the returning alumni at the football games and at commencement.

Charles C. Clarke, Professor of Romance Languages:

I am not a prohibitionist and have never been. I will admit to you, however, that the effect of Prohibition at Yale University has been good. I know whereof I speak, for I have been a member of the committee on discipline from a time dating back many years before Prohibition. I know conditions intimately. I do not pretend that the students are prohibitionists or are not drinking. But the change has been simply revolutionary. In the old days our committee was constantly busy with cases involving intoxication and the disorders arising from it. Now we have practically no business of the kind at all to transact. Moreover, this is in spite of the fact that in the old days we rarely troubled ourselves about a case of mere intoxication if it had not resulted in some kind of public disorder, whereas now intoxication of itself is regarded as calling for the severest penalty.

Roswell P. Angier, former Dean of Freshmen:

Among freshmen the situation got distinctly better from year to year of my administration, September, 1920, to June, 1924.

Percy T. Walden, present Dean of Freshmen:

There was much more open traffic in liquor at the games this year. The freshmen found more drinking places this year than formerly, at least since Prohibition came in.

James R. Angell, President of Yale University:

The impression which I get from all well-informed alumni with whom I talk is that, despite the all too frequent violation of the law, the amount of drinking at present, and particularly the amount of excessive drinking, is very much less than it was in earlier years.

I would summarize my own conclusions, based on the authorities quoted, on my own observations, and on conversations with others informed on the situation, as follows:

(1) The number of discipline cases at Yale in which drinking is a factor is now very much smaller than before Prohibition.

(2) The improvement has been especially noticeable in the last few years.

(3) Such drinking as still remains at Yale is often more concentrated and uproarious than before the Prohibition period. When liquor that was largely beer was easily obtainable, many got it, got it often, and got it in small quantities. Now that it is harder to get, fewer get it, get it more seldom, but when they do get it, make up for lost time.

(4) Prohibition created a defiant attitude in many students. It is unpopular even among many who do not try to circumvent the law.*

The various canvasses of student opinion in the colleges of the United States are interesting chiefly as reflecting the opinion of the students' elders, wet or dry, according to the general prevalence of opinion in their localities.

The testimony of more than two hundred college and university heads who answered the questionnaire sent out by the *Literary Digest* to approximately all such institutions of the country, brought answers declaring the beneficial effect of Prohibition on the student bodies and on youth in general.

To the question whether drinking had increased or decreased during Prohibition as they had observed it, 213 college heads representing 44 states and nearly a third of the total of higher colleges and universities, almost unanimously reported that drinking in the colleges and drinking by the younger generation as a whole had decreased. The conclusion of the *Literary Digest*, drawn from such testimony, is that, "there are actually fewer drinkers in the colleges now than in the days when there were only one-third the present number of students," (53, p. 30.)

*A poll taken at Yale University at the time of Prohibition hearings at Washington in April, 1926, recorded the belief of a large majority of students that Prohibition has increased drinking. But, as they were on an average thirteen years old when Prohibition came into effect and were not at Yale University at the time but scattered all over the United States, their opinion cannot carry much weight.

Fewer Juvenile Delinquents

Another good measure of the moral improvement of the rising generation is to be derived from the statistics of juvenile delinquency, . . . [which show] a rapid decline of the curve of juvenile delinquency in New York City. Here is a typical major exhibit illustrating the benefits of National Prohibition in a wet city, undefended by a local law such as most cities benefit by in coöperation with the Federal Prohibition enforcement agents. Despite this handicap, juvenile delinquency has been cut in half in New York City.

Chapter 16

A Pamphlet from the Association against the Prohibition Amendment

The Association against the Prohibition Amendment (AAPA) was organized even before the adoption of the Eighteenth Amendment but did not assume leadership in the fight against Prohibition until it was taken over by public figures such as Pierre du Pont (a former president of General Motors), John J. Raskob (chairman of the Democratic National Committee), and James W. Wadsworth, Jr. (a former Republican senator from New York). Another product of the elite opposition to Prohibition was the Woman's Organization for National Prohibition Reform (WONPR), which countered the WCTU's claim to speak for women in this debate. Many of the prominent leaders of the AAPA later lost public stature due to their involvement in the ultraconservative Liberty League.

Like the Anti-Saloon League's testaments in favor of Prohibition, the arguments adduced by the AAPA for repeal were part of a political campaign and, as such, often were more dramatic than accurate. The 1926 pamphlet excerpted here offers a good example.

A Criticism of National Prohibition

Foreword

The most serious affliction of our Government and our people today is so-called National Prohibition.

Every normal American citizen must resent it and does resent it. No greater curse has ever befallen America. The evidence of it is seen daily through the press. It is found upon our court dockets, in our jails and penitentiaries, in our asylums for the blind and the insane, in our high schools and colleges, and in the very weave and woof of our whole social fabric.

The very existence of the 18th Amendment and the Volstead Law constitutes an offense against the rights and privileges of every American citizen greater than any crime they undertake to define and punish; and no amount of men or money will ever make them effective. Their continuance means the continuance of crime and corruption, of bitter strife and dangerous discord.

The influences, however well intentioned, that led us into the horrible mess of National Prohibition, should now lead us out of it; but this they refuse to do. Their fight is for prohibition—fanatical Prohibition, our fight is for Temperance—

temperance in all things. We can have sobriety, law, order and decency, but we cannot have National Prohibition too.

National Prohibition means the destruction of American liberty under the law. The first ten Amendments to the Federal Constitution, commonly known as the Bill of Rights, contain in concrete form the principles of the liberty of the individual established by centuries of struggle in England, suffered for by our ancestors at Valley Forge, and upheld by our fathers at Gettysburg and on many a hard-fought field in Virginia. These great principles of liberty for which our forefathers died have been impaired (indeed, it is hardly too much to say, destroyed) in the effort to enforce the Volstead Act.

We are face to face with the greatest issue since that of slavery.

I. Prohibition vs. Regulation

1. The use of fermented drinks has been general since prehistoric times, and the use of distilled liquors has been prevalent in Europe since about the time of the Norman Conquest of England. Efforts to reduce or prevent the use of all alcoholic beverages are almost an ancient as their use.

2. The use of alcoholic beverages in small quantities is not harmful and their prohibition is, therefore, unreasonable.

(a) Expectation of life is no less among moderate drinkers, who form the great majority of those who drink at all, than it is among total abstainers.

(b) Most virile and successful races have used and do use alcoholic drinks.

(c) Any temporary decrease in mental alertness or efficiency in the individual caused by their proper use is more than compensated for by the pleasure and relief from nervous strain they afford.

3. Christians should not condemn their use as sinful, for Christ made them and use them.

4. Their abuse or use to excess is a great and terrible evil. The problems of crime and poverty are closely bound up with the vice of drunkenness. Therefore the manufacture, sale and use of alcoholic liquors is a proper subject of regulation by government.

General Considerations

Prohibition awakens resentment. Reasonable regulation appeals to common sense.

Prohibition decreases the use of fermented liquors, for their bulk makes them easy of detection; but leads to increased use of the more dangerous and more easily hidden spirits. Regulation can be made to discourage the use of spirits and foster the use of beer and wine, the milder beverages. This has been accomplished under various systems; for instance, under the laws of various Canadian Provinces.

Prohibition enriches bootleggers and criminals. Regulation enriches the government.

Prohibition endangers public health, but regulation protects it; for the purity of prohibited liquors cannot be guaranteed, while liquors produced under governmental regulation can be tested at every stage of manufacture or sale.

No system of regulation yet devised is perfect, but several have been measurably successful in reducing drunkenness and commanding public respect and support. Prohibition has never succeeded except in small or sparsely settled communities, and not even in them if any considerable minority of the people have opposed it.

Prohibition turns over the liquor traffic to the criminal classes, and makes the community their partner. Regulation puts it in the hands of a better and more respectable class.

Prohibition means intemperance among the rich and the reckless, the young and the foolish. It restrains only the poor and the cautious. Regulation bears hard upon the abuse of liquor, but leaves a reasonable freedom for its use in moderation.

Prohibition can never really prevent the use of liquor, but regulation can control it.

Prohibition weakens self-control. Regulation encourages moderation.

Prohibition means bad liquor drunk in secret by sneaks and hypocrites. Regulation means good liquor used in the light of day by self-respecting men.

Prohibition drives the manufacture of liquor into the home and teaches the habit of drinking to children. Regulation discourages home-brewing and distilling, and forbids indulgence by children.

II. The Conflict between the Principles of the Federal Constitution and the 18th Amendment

1. What is the Federal Constitution?

It is a statement of the fundamental organization of this nation. To it our laws and statutes must conform, but it is not itself a statute or a law in the ordinary sense of that word.

2. What subjects does the Constitution properly deal with?
(a) The structure of the Federal Government.
(b) The relations between the Federal Government and the states.
(c) Protection of the liberty of the individual citizen.

3. What is the 18th Amendment?
(a) A statute, law, or police regulation.
(b) The only denial of liberty contained in the Constitution.

A chief reason for the existence of the Constitution is to limit the power of the majority to oppress the minority. Therefore no denial of liberty, and no law or police regulation, should appear in it, for the majority should always have power to gain more freedom and to legislate freely for the public good, provided such legislation does not interfere with the rights of citizens described as inalienable in the Declaration of Independence. The 18th Amendment is a strait-jacket violating the fundamental rule that a Constitutional provision should deal with principles only, and leave the Government free to deal with their application.

4. What are the consequences of such a violation of the principles of the Constitution, as the insertion in it of a statute, as in the case of the 18th Amendment?

Loss of respect for the Constitution.

(a) An American reveres the principles of the Constitution, but reserves the freedom to criticise their application in laws made thereunder. For example, the Constitution grants Congress power to lay duties upon importations, and Congress has always exercised this power, the tariff bills varying as to what imported articles are taxed, and how heavily, according to whether high protectionists or low tariff men have for the time a majority. If Congress should pass a Free Trade Act, criticism would be directed against the Act, but if the Constitution itself provided for Free Trade, criticism would be directed against the Constitution.

(b) If the 18th Amendment were a mere grant of power to Congress to enact a national prohibition law, the resentment of opponents of prohibition would be directed against the law that Congress might then pass. Such a constitutional grant of power might be criticised as unwise, and out of keeping with the three fundamental matters with which only the Constitution ought to deal, but it could not cause disloyalty to the Constitution, as legislative freedom and consequently the rightful power of the majority would remain unimpaired.

5. Was the 18th Amendment properly adopted and ratified?

(a) Legally, perhaps; as exactly the same process—adoption by two-thirds vote of a quorum of both Houses of Congress, and ratification by a majority vote of three-fourths of the state legislatures—was followed, as in the case of all the other Amendments.

(b) Morally, unquestionably no; for an amendment denying to the people rights formerly appertaining to them should have been submitted to Constitutional Conventions in the several states elected for the purpose. Two methods of ratification of an Amendment are provided in the Constitution.

1. By State Legislatures. This method may properly be used for Amendments altering the structure of the Federal Government, or its relation with the States, or further protecting the liberty and privileges of citizens.
2. By Constitutional Conventions in the various states. This method ought to be used for any Amendment granting to the Federal Government any powers restricting the rights and freedom of the people of the United States, who created the Constitution, as is shown by its preamble.

6. How can the 18th Amendment be repealed, or itself amended?

(a) Congress must call a Constitutional Convention for this purpose if petitioned to do so by a majority vote of two-thirds of the State Legislatures. An Amendment adopted by such a convention must be ratified by the legislatures of three-fourths of the states, or by state conventions in three-fourths of the states, as Congress may specify.

(b) Congress may itself adopt a new amendment repealing or altering the 18th Amendment by a vote of two-thirds of a quorum of each house, and an Amendment so adopted must be ratified by the legislatures of three-fourths of the states, or by Conventions in three-fourths thereof as Congress may specify.

(c) An Amendment adopted by either of the above methods might take the form of—

1. Outright Repeal of the 18th Amendment, which would leave the states in possession of the same powers they had before its adoption to regulate or prohibit the manufacture, sale and transportation of intoxicating beverages.
2. Changing it into a grant of power to Congress to regulate or prohibit the manufacture, sale or transportation of intoxicating beverages, instead of a mandate to Congress to do so, as it is now considered to be.
3. Any other proposed alteration which might obtain the necessary vote.

Chapter 17

Pierre S. du Pont Urges Repeal

Pierre S. du Pont, at the time president of the United Repeal Council, delivered this speech over the radio shortly before the Democratic and Republican National Conventions in 1932. Du Pont's discussion was businesslike and dealt much with statistics, although his deepest opposition to Prohibition arose from his objection to the invasion of personal liberty by the federal government that it represented. He argued that repeal of Prohibition should be combined with reinstitution of alcohol taxes. This measure, he claimed, would bring in as much revenue as the personal income tax, which then could be eliminated. Certainly that outcome would be a boon to the wealthy du Pont.

This radio program, preserved on an aluminum disk in the Eleutherian Mills Historical Library, is also noteworthy as the earliest known recording of the voice of Edward R. Murrow, later to become a legendary figure in radio and television news broadcasting. Murrow introduces du Pont.

RADIO SPEECH

Pierre S. du Pont

ANNOUNCER: This afternoon's broadcast is the last of a series of six presented over this network by the National Student Federation of America on the subject "Prohibition Plainly Put." The speaker today is Mr. Pierre S. du Pont who will be introduced by Mr. [Edward R.] Murrow.

MURROW: The National Student Federation is indeed fortunate to be able to close this series of broadcasts by presenting Mr. du Pont. We have been attempting to place before the American people the facts of Prohibition and particularly those dealing with the economic issues involved. The National Student Federation of America is a non-partisan, undergraduate organization representing over 260 colleges and universities. The comments received from our constituency concerning these broadcasts have been very encouraging and demonstrate that American students are giving consideration to some of the fundamental issues involved in the discussion of Prohibition.

Mr. du Pont is a graduate of the Massachusetts Institute of Technology. He is a director of General Motors Corporation and a member of the American Philosophical Society. As a result of his wide experience with American business and finance Mr. du Pont is particularly well qualified to discuss the situation that confronts the country today. It is a pleasure for us to present at this time Mr. Pierre S. du Pont.

DU PONT: The national supply of food and drink is a subject of paramount importance, but today we are not troubled because of abundance but by fear of famine. Our surplus food weighs upon our producers and our abundant supply of drink has prevailed in face of twelve years of fruitless endeavor to bring about its complete obstruction. How to rid ourselves of drink has been the outstanding question of recent years. No subject has more concerned the government, the churches or has more fully occupied the printed page of books, magazines and daily papers. It is probably true that resentment against the politically controlled saloon caused many states to contribute to prohibit the retail sale of liquor. But nowhere at anytime throughout the whole United States was this [presentment?] of petition to even suggest the prohibition of the use of intoxicants. When the 18th Amendment was proposed more than 90% of the American people lived — and had voted to live under conditions — where liquor was legally obtainable, legally possessed and legally consumed. We had gradually developed the mistaken belief, however, that condemnation of the saloon by a large part of our people carried with it a desire to discontinue the use of liquor. This led us to undertake the impossible task of changing — by force of law only — the drinking habits of nation of over one hundred million people. Had our efforts been directed against the excesses of those who drink, a condition of satisfactory temperance might have been obtained. Unfortunately, we chose to attempt the absolute prevention of the use of liquor by forbidding its manufacture, sale and transportation only. This was done in full knowledge that nature herself was pitted against us, prepared to make alcohol at any time or anyplace or from nearly any material of the vegetable kingdom. We had complained of the illegal acts of the sellers of liquor as a class but very many hotels and saloons were conducted in an exemplary manner under the law. Today every manufacturer and seller of liquor must be a lawbreaker and a criminal. He must use the device of the criminal world for his own protection. Wholesale bribery and corruption of political offices and servants . . . circumventing the law have replaced the fairly well conducted enforcement of former years. Under these conditions and the continued magnitude of the liquor business [we have] a situation that seriously affects the economic affairs of the nation. The cost of attempted enforcement amounting to millions of dollars annually is large, but insignificant when compared to the billion of dollars paid for liquor and not accounted for on the books of . . . industries. We know that 100 per cent proof alcohol can be produced and sold profitably at not more than one dollar per gallon. Modern whisky gin and other liquids are not much more than a mixture of alcohol and water. At five dollars per nominal quart the selling price of the 160 million gallons minimum consumption now estimated brings in today's market about four billion dollars. This shows a profit of three billion six hundred million dollars. One hundred sixty million has become four billion. Who benefits from this 25 fold increase in value? Not legitimate industry or effort. Cost of manufacture, sales and transportation of liquor under continual risk of discovery is enormously expensive. More important, the ever increasing demand for graft arises in all quarters in order to pacify hungry office-holders. Finally, a very large profit must be exacted to warrant the risk of a business operated entirely outside the law. Waste, graft, corruption and crime have been the benefactors. Never before in the history of the world has government so persistently been the enemy of law and order. Never has the outlaw been so bountifully endowed financially by law itself.

Prohibitionists confronted by this disaster to their efforts have taken refuge in a challenge to recommend a better plan of procedure. The plan offered is: return to the states the right to decide all questions of liquor control for themselves. Any uniform system of control would fail to meet the views of all of the states. Kansas and New York cannot both be reconciled to any one procedure. Hence, national control and administration is impossible as it must be of a uniform nature.

In order to make clear the financial losses arising out of prohibition, let us compare our present situation with one obtainable under the least acceptable of all plans, that is, under the return of the saloon. Surely, any other condition would be more acceptable and therefore more advantageous. Fortunately, we have before us a very perfect demonstration of the saloon method as applied in the year 1932 and contrasted to the year 1912. This period of twenty years has brought about many changes in many things. The saloon is no exception to the rule. England had a saloon known as the public house or pub in 1912. At that time the consumption of alcohol was nearly double that of the United States. Today without prohibition it has been reduced to six-tenths of that amount and liquor in the form of spirits has fallen to forty per cent of former consumption. This reduction has been accompanied by a corresponding decrease in drunkenness, in deaths from alcoholism and in crimes related to drunkenness. It is not surprising to find also [less drunkenness among] young persons as well as less committed drunkenness in the saloon. The number of places licensed for sale has been greatly reduced and the condition of these places improved. Thus under a saloon system England has made advances in the administration and control of the liquor traffic in all particulars greater than the advances made by the United States under Prohibition. The quantity of spirits drunk is less and the results obtained are shown in the decrease of alcoholism and cirrhosis, in less arrests for drunkenness and reduction in crime and imprisonment. Moreover, the cost of liquor per capita is not greater than in the United States; the quality is certainly much better. England with a foresight we have not shown has consistently maintained a tax on liquor thus furnishing one fifth of her total state revenue. Had we elected to continue taxation of the industry at British rate we should have enjoyed one billion seven hundred million dollars additional revenue each year during the past twelve years. This policy continued until the year 1932 would have enabled us to retire the entire national debt, and to have accumulated a cash surplus about equal to the debts of foreign nations to the United

States. Instead of a bankrupt treasury we should have today no debt and a surplus of five to ten billions of dollars. The income tax would not be necessary in the future and half of the revenue applied to the budget, reduced by the absence of interest and debt charges, would be furnished by the tax on liquor alone. As an alternative, the continued levy of a very modest income tax would permit the abolishment of all of the so-called nuisance taxes now in force.

Some of the most marked improvements in the administration of liquor control in England relate to the betterment and character of public houses or saloons. Those unsuited to sanitary operation and convenient inspection have been gradually abolished. Those remaining as well as the newly added establishments are greatly improved. The standards of the liquor traffic have been raised so much that at the opening of a new and modern public house in London, Queen Mary herself stood behind the bar and witnessed the drawing of beer. Would that the First Lady of our land [let] herself inspect the opening of a like [project], not only to admit the supply of well-made beer but to loose a flood of revenue for balancing our budget and at the same time relieving our heavy tax burden and shutting off the tremendous money resources of the underworld.

Chapter 18

FDR Stumps for Repeal

The Depression had an enormous impact on support for the repeal of Prohibition. As late as 1928 dry forces in Congress were increasing in number, but the national financial disaster put Prohibition in a different light, as Americans looked for any measure that might ease bad times and give succor to the unemployed.

By 1932 the forces of repeal were dominating the discussion. The Democrats advocated repeal in their party platform of that year, while the Republicans tried to straddle the issue. In the first speech excerpted here, Franklin Roosevelt, the presidential nominee of the Democrats, calls Prohibition a failure at promoting temperance and reducing crime. His approach in the second speech, given as the Depression deepened, is economic: beverage-alcohol taxation will help to supply the dire need for more revenue. Roosevelt notes that, while it urges modification of the Volstead Act, the Democratic Party opposes reestablishment of the "oldtime saloon."

CAMPAIGN ADDRESS ON PROHIBITION

Franklin Delano Roosevelt

(*Prohibition — Repeal of the Eighteenth Amendment.*)

My friends:

. . . . However we may differ as to method, we all agree that temperance is one of the cardinal virtues. In dealing with the great social problems in my own State, such as the care of the wards of the States, and in combating crime, I have had to consider most earnestly this question of temperance. It is bound up with crime, with insanity and, only too often, with poverty. It is increasingly apparent that the intemperate use of intoxicants has no place in this new mechanized civilization of ours. In our industry, in our recreation, on our highways, a drunken man is more than an objectionable companion, he is a peril to the rest of us. The hand that controls the machinery of our factories, that holds the steering wheel of our automobiles, and the brains that guide the course of finance and industry, should alike be free from the effects of over-indulgence in alcohol.

But the methods adopted since the World War with the purpose of achieving a greater temperance by the forcing of Prohibition have been accompanied in most parts of the country by complete and tragic failure. I need not point out to you that general encouragement of lawlessness has resulted; that corruption, hypocrisy, crime and disorder have emerged, and that instead of restricting, we have extended the spread of intemperance. This failure has come for this very good reason: we have depended too largely upon the power of governmental action instead of recognizing that the authority of the home and that of the churches in these matters is the fundamental force on which we must build. The recent recognition of this fact by the present Administration is an amazing piece of hindsight. There are others who have had foresight. A friend showed me recently an unpublished letter of Henry Clay, written a hundred years ago. In this letter Clay said that the movement for temperance "has done great good and will continue to do more" but "it will destroy itself whenever it resorts to coercion or mixes in the politics of the country." . . .

We threw on the table as spoils to be gambled for by the enemies of society the revenue that our Government had theretofore received, and the underworld acquired unparalleled resources thereby. The multiplication of enforcement agencies created resentment and a cynical and complacent attitude toward lax enforcement resulting from connivance between such agencies and the law breakers. The general disregard for and defiance of such law of nationwide application bred disrespect for other law. The attempt to impose the practice of virtue by mandate of the fundamental law produced an attitude of intolerance to other forms of restraint and a denial even of the basis of authority. The violation of fundamental principles set in motion a chain of consequences that no one not politically blind could fail to see; and all the time a steady flow of profits, resulting from the exactions of a newly created industry, was running into the pockets of racketeers. The only business of the country that was not helping to support the Government was in a real sense being supported by the Government. This was the business that was the direct product of the 18th Amendment and the Volstead Law—a business which is lucrative, vicious and corrupting in its influence on the enforcement agencies of Government.

Unquestionably our tax burden would not be so heavy nor the forms that it takes so objectionable if some reasonable proportion of the uncounted millions now paid to those whose business has been reared upon this stupendous blunder could be made available for the expenses of Government . . .

So that there can be no possible misunderstanding, let me read the provisions of the Democratic platform on this point. It begins:

"We advocate the repeal of the Eighteenth Amendment. To effect such repeal we demand that the Congress immediately propose a Constitutional Amendment to truly representative conventions in the States called to act solely on that proposal."

So much for repeal. Now what does it tell the States to do:

"We urge the enactment of such measures by the several States as will actually promote temperance, effectively prevent the return of the saloon and bring the liquor traffic into the open under complete supervision and control by the States."

It then clearly states what the President either accidentally overlooked or deliberately misrepresented:

"We demand that the Federal Government effectively exercise its power to enable the States to protect themselves against importation of intoxicating liquors in violation of their laws." It then goes on to speak of the Volstead Law:

"Pending repeal, we favor immediate modification of the Volstead Act to legalize the manufacture and sale of beer and other beverages of such alcoholic content as is permissible under the Constitution and to provide therefrom a proper and needed revenue."

Thus the Democratic platform expressly and unequivocally opposes the return of the saloon and with equal emphasis it demands that there be Federal control of the liquor traffic to protect dry States.

Campaign Address on the Federal Budget

Franklin Delano Roosevelt

I have sought to make two things clear: First, that we can make savings by reorganization of existing departments, by eliminating functions, by abolishing many of those innumerable boards and those commissions which, over a long period of years, have grown up as a fungus growth on American Government. These savings can properly be made to total many hundreds and thousands of dollars a year.

Second, I hope that it will not be necessary to increase the present scale of taxes, and I call definite attention to the fact that just as soon as the Democratic platform pledge is enacted into legislation modifying the Volstead Act, a source of new revenue amounting to several hundred millions of dollars a year will be made available toward the balancing of the budget. I refer specifically to a Federal tax on beer, which would be raised through the sale of beer in those States and those States only which by State law allow the sale of beer. At the same time I reiterate the simple language of the Democratic platform which in good faith opposes the return of the old-time saloon.

"We urge the enactment of such measure by the several States as will actually promote temperance, effectively prevent the return of the saloon and bring the liquor traffic into the open under complete supervision and control by the State."

The above two categorical statements are aimed at a definite balancing of the budget. At the same time, let me repeat from now to election day so that every man, woman and child in the United States will know what I mean: If starvation and dire need on the part of any of our citizens make necessary the appropriation of additional funds which would keep the budget out of balance, I shall not hesitate to tell the American people the full truth and ask them to authorize the expenditure of that additional amount.

These have been unhealthy years for prophets, and I hasten to disclaim such a role. But one thing I know: A powerful cause contributing to economic disaster has been this inexcusable fiscal policy and the obscurity and uncertainty that have attended and grown out of it. There it remains for all to see—a veritable cancer in the body politic and economic. Is it prophecy to assure you that if we remove that destructive growth we shall move on to better health and better life?

To my mind, that is so plain and persuasive as scarcely to be open to argument. As I said in the beginning, this is the one field in which business is wholly in the grip of Government. It is a field where Government can make a great contribution to recovery.

To that contribution I here pledge the utmost of my faith and my ability. I am as certain as mortal man can be certain of anything in the future, that from the moment that you and I set our hands openly and frankly and courageously to that problem, we shall have reached the end of our long, hard, downward road. We shall have started on the upward trail. We shall have built for economic recovery a firm footing, on a path that is broad, true and straight. Join me, and "let's go!"

Chapter 19

Prohibition Is Repealed

Several of the values that haunted the alcohol debates and that sometimes were placed in competition with one another are evoked by the president in this public statement on repeal, published in the New York Times *in 1933. With the end of Prohibition, he avows, individual freedom has been restored. State and federal power will protect against the reemergence of corruption and criminality. "Reasonable" taxation of liquor will ease the tax burden elsewhere. The government will aid in educating citizens about the dangers of overindulgence and trusts in their "good sense" to insure temperance.*

ROOSEVELT PROCLAIMS REPEAL; URGES TEMPERANCE IN NATION

President Roosevelt's proclamation of the repeal of the Eighteenth Amendment was as follows:

By the President of the United States of America

A Proclamation

Whereas the Congress of the United States in the second session of the Seventy-second Congress, begun at Washington on the fifth day of December in the year one thousand nine hundred and thirty-two adopted a resolution in the words and figures following: to wit —

JOINT RESOLUTION

Proposing an amendment to the Constitution of the United States.

Resolved by the Senate and House of Representatives of the United States of America in Congress assembled (two-thirds of each House concurring therein), That the following article is hereby proposed as an amendment to the Constitution of the United States; which shall be valid to all intents and purposes as part of the Constitution when ratified by conventions in three-fourths of the several States:

ARTICLE

Section 1. The Eighteenth Article of amendment to the Constitution of the United States is hereby repealed.

Section 2. The transportation or importation into any State, Territory or possession of the United States for delivery or use therein of intoxicating liquors, in violation of the laws thereof, is hereby prohibited.

Section 3. This article shall be inoperative unless it shall have been ratified as an amendment to the Constitution by conventions in the several States, as provided in the Constitution, within seven years from the date of the submission hereof to the States by the Congress.

Declares Amendment Repealed

Whereas, Section 217 (a) of the Act of Congress entitled "An act to encourage national industrial recovery, to foster competition and to provide for the construction of certain useful public works, and for other purposes," approved June 16, 1933, provides as follows:

> Section 217 (a) The President shall proclaim the date of:
> (1) the close of the first fiscal year ending June 30 of any year after the year 1933, during which the total receipts of the United States (excluding public-debt receipts) exceed its total expenditures (excluding public-debt expenditures other than those chargeable against such receipts), or
> (2) the repeal of the Eighteenth Amendment to the Constitution, whichever is the earlier.

Whereas it appears from a certificate issued Dec. 5, 1933, by the Acting Secretary of State that official notices have been received in the Department of State that on the fifth day of December, 1933, conventions in thirty-six States of the United States, constituting three fourths of the whole number of the States had ratified the said repeal amendment;

Now, therefore, I Franklin D. Roosevelt, President of the United States of America, pursuant to the provisions of Section 217 (a) of the said Act of June, 16, 1933, do hereby proclaim that the Eighteenth Amendment of the Constitution of the United States was repealed on the fifth day of December 1933.

Legal Purchases Asked

Furthermore, I enjoin upon all citizens of the United States and upon others residents within the jurisdiction thereof, to cooperate with the government in its endeavor to restore greater respect for law and order, by confining such purchases of alcoholic beverages as they may make solely to those dealers or agencies which have been duly licensed by State or Federal license.

Observance of this request, which I make personally to every individual and every family in our nation, will result in the consumption of alcoholic beverages which have passed Federal inspection, in the break-up and eventual destruction of the notoriously evil illicit liquor traffic and in the payment of reasonable taxes for the support of government and thereby in the superseding of other forms of taxation.

I call specific attention to the authority given by the Twenty-first Amendment to the government to prohibit transportation or importation of intoxicating liquors into any State in violation of the laws of such State.

I ask the whole-hearted cooperation of all our citizens to the end that this return of individual freedom shall not be accompanied by the repugnant conditions that obtained prior to the adoption of the Eighteenth Amendment and those that have existed since its adoption. Failure to do this honestly and courageously will be a living reproach to us all.

Urges People to Sobriety

I ask especially that no State shall be law or otherwise authorize the return of the saloon in its old form or in some modern guise.

The policy of the government will be to see to it that the social and political evils that have existed in the pre-prohibition era shall not be revived nor permitted again to exist. We must remove forever from our midst the menace of the bootlegger and such others as would profit at the expense of good government, law and order.

I trust in the good sense of the American people that they will not bring upon themselves the curse of excessive use of intoxicating liquors, to the detriment of health, morals and social integrity.

The objective we seek through a national policy is the education of every citizen towards a greater temperance throughout the nation.

In witness whereof, I have hereunto set my hand and caused the seal of the United States to be affixed.

Done at the City of Washington, this fifth day of December in the year of our Lord nineteen hundred and thirty-three, and of the Independence of the United States of America the one hundred and fifty-eighth.

By THE PRESIDENT.

WILLIAM PHILLIPS
Acting Secretary of State

Chapter 20

Recovery from Alcoholism

Alcoholics Anonymous (AA) is a self-help, volunteer organization begun in the mid-1930s that views alcoholism as a disease, not a defect of will. Its founders, themselves alcoholics, maintained that persons with the disease should completely stop drinking, but they did not condemn those who could handle alcohol. This position contrasted with the premises of most temperance advocates, who saw drinking as a moral choice and opposed any alcohol use by anyone.

The Twelve Steps embody the wisdom of the founders of AA about pursuing ongoing recovery from alcoholism. The procedure they describe has evolved into one of the most successful programs for helping alcoholics. Many antidrug treatment programs also have based themselves on the Twelve Steps.

THE TWELVE STEPS OF ALCOHOLICS ANONYMOUS

The relative success of the A.A. program seems to be due to the fact that an alcoholic who no longer drinks has an exceptional faculty for "reaching" and helping an uncontrolled drinker.

In simplest form, the A.A. program operates when a recovered alcoholic passes along the story of his or her own problem drinking, describes the sobriety he or she has found in A.A., and invites the newcomer to join the informal Fellowship.

The heart of the suggested program of personal recovery is contained in Twelve Steps describing the experience of the earliest members of the Society:

1. We admitted we were powerless over alcohol—that our lives had become unmanageable.
2. Came to believe that a Power greater than ourselves could restore us to sanity.
3. Made a decision to turn our will and our lives over to the care of God as we understood Him.
4. Made a searching and fearless moral inventory of ourselves.
5. Admitted to God, to ourselves and to another human being the exact nature of our wrongs.
6. Were entirely ready to have God remove all these defects of character.
7. Humbly asked Him to remove our shortcomings.

8. Made a list of all persons we had harmed, and became willing to make amends to them all.

9. Made direct amends to such people wherever possible, except when to do so would injure them or others.

10. Continued to take personal inventory and when we were wrong promptly admitted it.

11. Sought through prayer and meditation to improve our conscious contact with God as we understood Him, praying only for knowledge of His will for us and the power to carry that out.

12. Having had a spiritual awakening as the result of these steps, we tried to carry this message to alcoholics and to practice these principles in all our affairs.

Newcomers are not asked to accept or follow these Twelve Steps in their entirety if they feel unwilling or unable to do so.

They will usually be asked to keep an open mind, to attend meetings at which recovered alcoholics describe their personal experiences in achieving sobriety, and to read A.A. literature describing and interpreting the A.A. program.

Chapter 21

Is Alcohol Dangerous to the Fetus? Part 2: No

In the middle decades of the twentieth century, physicians and researchers continued to explore the question of possible physiological connections between parental drinking and negative consequences — spontaneous abortion or mental or physical defects — for the child.

Howard W. Haggard and E. M. Jellinek were key figures in the Yale Center of Alcohol Studies, a post-repeal research group based at Yale University. The goal of the Yale Center was to analyze the alcohol problem scientifically, rather than as a moral or religious issue. In this selection from their book Alcohol Explored *(1942), Haggard and Jellinek take up the question of whether drinking by a parent can produce hereditary problems, as often had been claimed. This association would be valid, they claim, only if alcohol could cause damage to the "germ cell," the egg or sperm. Their understanding of the "physiology of alcohol" and of the "properties of the germ," which they delineate, rules out the possibility that alcohol "is the cause of any abnormality in the child."*

In an answer in their regular Queries section, the editors of the Journal of the American Medical Association *confirm that in 1942 physicians still felt that pregnant women could consume "large amounts" of alcohol without risk to their developing offspring.*

Alcohol Explored

Howard W. Haggard and E. M. Jellinek

The dramatic effects of acute intoxication and the bodily deterioration of chronic alcoholism have often led to the question as to whether or not the germ, that is, the egg of the mother or the sperm of the father, becomes affected by the action of alcohol to alter heredity. . . .

The belief that intoxication at the time of procreation might cause damage to the child is so ancient that we find it expressed in the myths of the Romans. Vulcan, the blacksmith of the gods, was supposed to have been born lame because his father, Jupiter, begot him while he was intoxicated. Many old rites and customs reflect this same view. Thus in Carthage the bridal couple was ritualistically forbidden to drink wine on their wedding night in order that defective children might not be conceived.

This belief, reflected in myth and custom, has maintained itself up to present times. As long as the physiology of alcohol and properties of the germ were not known, the question of hereditary damage through acute intoxication was a cogent one. On the basis of present knowledge, however, it may be dismissed.

It is true that the alcohol that is drunk passes into the tissues of the reproductive organs and into the spermal fluids. The concentration of alcohol there is approximately the same as that in the blood; that is, in severe intoxication the concentration of alcohol is between 0.2 and 0.5 per cent and, in rare instances, between 0.5 and 1.0 per cent. Within this range, alcohol concentration becomes dangerous to human life. But even in these concentrations, alcohol could be put in the eye, or even on raw flesh, without irritation or injury, or any painful sensation.

In intoxication so severe as to cause death in man, no injury to the tissues of the body has been found. Intoxication results from the disturbances in the functions of the nervous system caused by alcohol and not from injury to it; death is due to failure of respiration. Germ cells do not have nerves; they do not become intoxicated, and they are injured by alcohol only when it is present in concentrations far higher than those causing death from failure of respiration—concentrations which are strong enough to be "germicidal." Thus, in a sense, the body protects the germ cells; it is sacrificed before they can be injured. There may be exceptions to any general rule in this regard when the action of the injuring agent can be directed specifically on the germ cells and immediate flesh, and not, as with alcohol, on the whole body. Thus radium emanations allowed to act on the sex glands may injure the germ cells.

There are reports of old experiments carried out on dogs and other higher animals which were presumed, at one time, to show effects of acute intoxication on the offspring. But the experiments were poorly designed and they were "uncontrolled"; that is, there was no assurance given that the abnormalities in the offspring might not have occurred even when no alcohol was given.

And in this same category fall the efforts of those investigators who have tried to gather evidence of the birth of idiots and other types of defective children conceived while the parents were said to have been in a state of acute intoxication. Such spectacular studies do not yield valid evidence; they belong more in the realm of rumormongering than in that of scientific study.

The fact is that no acceptable evidence has ever been offered to show that acute alcoholic intoxication has any effect whatsoever on the human germ, or has any influence in altering heredity, or is the cause of any abnormality in the child. All facts point to the contrary. This is a question to which much study has been given; it is also a question which must be dealt with within the proper limitations. We are dealing only with heredity—the germ cell—and not with the influence of the poor nutrition of an alcoholic mother on her unborn child, or the influence of the alcoholic parents on the home life of the child. In many of the studies intended to show damage to the germ cell by chronic alcoholism, these limitations have not been maintained.

Damage to the reproductive organs has occurred in animals given very large amounts of alcohol daily for long periods of time. These amounts of alcohol were much greater, proportionately, than even the heaviest drinker could consume; the animals were kept deeply intoxicated, even unconscious, most of the time. Damage to the reproductive organs has also been observed in human beings who are chronic alcoholics. It does not follow, however, that damage to the organs of reproduction means damage to the germ cells. Similar changes, even without the use of alcohol, may occur from diseases of the liver and from certain infections. It has never been suggested that these disturbances alter the germ cells. Consequently the finding of changes in the reproductive organs cannot be taken as an indication that if an individual thus affected were able to have a child, the child would be injured.

Moreover, as far as human beings are concerned, there is an additional feature to be considered. The changes in the reproductive organs due to chronic alcoholism usually occur after the age of 45. Statistics show that in the United States only 6.0 per cent of all births occur after the father is 45.

The child of the inebriate may suffer great handicaps, but these handicaps are inherent not in the germ but in the unfavorable environment which the inebriety of the parent creates. If the child of the inebriate is exposed to bodily and mental damage it may seem petty to lay stress on the fact that the effect is not that of alcohol itself but of environment and to imply an exculpation of alcohol. However, when the belief is held that the ill effects are due to germ damage, the prevention seems hopeless. Hereditary weakness cannot be remedied after the child is born. When, however, it is realized that the effect is not due to fundamental weakness of the child, but instead to home and social conditions, its remedy is no longer impossible.

Statistical studies made on the question of heredity and chronic alcoholism in human beings show results as conflicting as those made on animals. Often, however, in the light of modern knowledge, an explanation for the results can now be given. These studies have been directed toward comparing the families in which one or both parents was a chronic alcoholic with those in which neither was an alcoholic, in respect to:

1. The number of children.
2. The number of miscarriages.
3. The infant mortality.
4. The occurrence of feeble-mindedness, epilepsy, and mental disorders.

The conclusions reached in many of the older studies on these points cannot be accepted; it is agreed by modern investigators that the statistical procedures used were at fault. Many of the observations can, however, be used and reinterpreted in the light of modern knowledge. In studies made today it is pointed out that comparisons should not be made as between alcoholic and temperate families but between children of the same parents before and after the parents became alcoholics. Scientifically this principle is correct, but unfortunately it has not given much practical help since, in most instances, it is impossible to determine when drinking by parents became excessive. We are therefore forced to use information obtained from the comparison of alcoholic and temperate families, a fact which demands great caution in interpretation of the information. Unfortunately this caution is not always exercised, and many erroneous and harmful conclusions have been made and widely publicized.

EFFECT OF SINGLE LARGE ALCOHOL INTAKE ON FETUS

To the Editor:—A patient is worried about the effects of alcohol when taken early during pregnancy on the future child. Specially, this woman drank about 36 ounces of beer shortly after conception and before she knew she was pregnant. What is the present opinion in this respect as to imbibing that amount of alcohol on only one occasion early in pregnancy? M.D., New Jersey.

ANSWER.—The patient need have no worries about the effect of her beer debauch on her unborn baby. The amount of alcohol even in 36 ounces of beer is scarcely large enough to injure a fertilized ovum. In fact, in human beings it is difficult to prove that alcohol has a deleterious effect on babies in utero, even when large amounts are taken. Vignes (*Revue anthropologique* 51:33 [April–June] 1941) maintains that acute alcoholism is a frequent cause of congenital defects, but whereas this is true among animals it has not been definitely proved for human beings. Likewise Vignes believes that acute alcoholism favors premature interruption of pregnancy.

Chapter 22

Definitions of Alcoholism

E. M. Jellinek was the leading American expert on alcoholism in the 1940s and 1950s. Although the concept of alcoholism as a disease can be traced back to Benjamin Rush, in modern times its most thorough advocate has been Jellinek. He distinguished among several varieties of alcoholism, and the book from which this selection is taken, The Disease Concept of Alcoholism *(1960), served as the bible for a national campaign to convince physicians and the public that alcoholism did not stem from a flaw of character or will but instead was a well-defined physical disorder. In the late twentieth century the debate over whether alcoholism is a disease resurfaced as part of a protest against the medicalization of response to undesirable behavior.*

THE DISEASE CONCEPT OF ALCOHOLISM

E. M. Jellinek

III.1 Notes on Terminology

Before entering on the discussion of the various conceptions of "alcoholism" as a disease, it may be in order to give some enumeration of terms and to comment upon them. First, explanations of the term alcoholism and of other terms denoting its various species will be presented without any intention of suggesting their acceptance. They are stated for the purpose of making it clear what is meant by certain terms in the present study. It is not intended here to go into a critique of current definitions. . . .

III.1.2. Alcoholism and Its Species

Many nations the world over . . . have various highly vexatious problems which they term "alcoholism," problems whose seriousness cannot be denied but which would not be designated in America by that term. It would not be doing justice to the nations concerned if one were to belittle those problems by shrugging them off as not representing "alcoholism."

Every country that has alcohol problems has "alcoholism" in the sense in which we are accustomed to think of it in America; but in many of those countries there are other problems arising from the use of alcoholic beverages, and these problems may be so extensive or so grievous that they may overshadow those species of alcoholism for which the term is reserved in America. Furthermore those other problems exist in America, too.

By adhering strictly to our American ideas about "alcoholism" and "alcoholics" (created by Alcoholics Anonymous in their own image) and restricting the term to those ideas, we have been continuing to overlook many other problems of alcohol which need urgent attention.

In this connection it may be mentioned that while in the American alcoholism literature, by and large, alcoholism means true addiction—let us say, for the time being, the type prevalent in Alcoholics Anonymous—there are a number of American students of alcoholism who would include, under that term, heavy weekend drinkers as well as "relief drinkers" who never become addicted. In order to do justice to these international, as well as our own national differences, we have termed as *alcoholism any use of alcoholic beverages that causes any damage to the individual or society or both*. Vague as this statement is, it approaches an operational definition.

It may be said that such a loose definition has little operational value. With such a vague definition we cannot even ask whether alcoholism is an illness. Obviously there are species of alcoholism—so defined—which cannot be regarded as illnesses. One may well say that such a vague definition is useless. But in this uselessness lies its utility, for it forces us to single out species of alcoholism (in the above sense) and to speak of them in stringent terms. We must be particularly definite about those forms which we wish to examine as possibly constituting illnesses. Furthermore, in view of our broad and vague statement of alcoholism we cannot say that alcoholics are those who suffer from alcoholism as defined above. We shall have to make a distinction between alcoholism and alcoholics.

In speaking about the species of alcoholism and alcoholics I shall give brief descriptions and attach labels to them without any pretension to formal definitions. Only those species of alcoholism will be described and labeled here that may come at all into consideration as disease processes or symptoms of disease processes. In addition, some statements will be made concerning certain terms that are frequently used in the formulations of the conception of alcoholism as an illness. Some of those statements may be true definitions, some may be merely "delimitations" and operational definitions, and some may comply neither with the formal requirements of definition nor with the desiderata of "delimitation."

For the labeling of the species of alcoholism considered here, I am taking recourse to letters of the Greek alphabet. Letter symbols arouse perhaps less misgivings than names which may have different connotations for many students of alcoholism. Of course the letters can be replaced by word labels according to the preferences of readers. Nevertheless, adherence to the letter symbols will cause the least degree of controversy.

Alpha alcoholism represents a *purely* psychological *continual* dependence or reliance upon the effect of alcohol to relieve bodily or emotional pain. The drinking is "undisciplined" in the sense that it contravenes such rules as society tacitly agrees upon—such as time, occasion, locale, amount and effect of drinking—*but does not lead to "loss of control" or "inability to abstain."* The damage caused by this species of alcoholism may be restricted to the disturbance of interpersonal relations. There may also be interference with the family budget, occasional absenteeism from work and decreased productivity, and some of the nutritional deficiencies of alcoholism, but not the disturbances due to withdrawal of alcohol. *Nor are there any signs of a progressive process.*

The relief of bodily pain or emotional disturbance implies an underlying illness and thus the "undisciplined" use of alcoholic beverages may be regarded as a symptom of the pathological conditions which it relieves. *This species of alcoholism cannot be regarded as an illness per se.*

Of course, it is quite possible that in many instances alpha alcoholism may develop into gamma alcoholism, i.e., that it may often be a developmental stage. On the other hand, it is well known that this species of alcoholism may be seen in a drinking career of 30 or 40 years without any signs of progression. When we speak here of alpha alcoholism we mean this latter "pure culture" but not the development stage of gamma alcoholism.

Alpha alcoholism as described here is sometimes called problem drinking, but that expression just as frequently includes physical dependence upon alcohol. The terms problem drinking and problem drinker will not be used in the present study.

Beta alcoholism is that species of alcoholism in which such alcoholic complications as polyneuropathy, gastritis and cirrhosis of the liver may occur without either physical or psychological dependence upon alcohol. The incentive to the heavy drinking that leads to such complications may be the custom of a certain social group in conjunction with poor nutritional habits. The damage in this instance is of course the nutritional deficiency diseases, but impaired family budget and lowered productivity as well as a curtailed life span may also occur. Withdrawal symptoms, on the other hand, do not emerge.

Beta alcoholism too may develop into gamma or delta alcoholism, but such a transition is less likely than in the instance of alpha alcoholism.

Gamma alcoholism means that species of alcoholism in which (1) acquired increased tissue *tolerance to alcohol,* (2) adaptive cell metabolism, (see below), (3) withdrawal symptoms and "craving," i.e., *physical dependence,* and (4) *loss of control* are involved. In gamma alcoholism there is a definite progression from psychological to physical dependence and marked behavior changes . . . . Alpha and beta alcoholism, as already noted, may develop under given conditions into gamma alcoholism.

This species produces the greatest and most serious kinds of damage. The loss of control, of course, impairs interpersonal relations to the highest degree. The damage to health in general and to financial and social standing are also more prominent than in other species of alcoholism.

Gamma alcoholism is apparently (but not with certainty) the *predominating* species of alcoholism in the United States and Canada, as well as in other Anglo-

Saxon countries. It is what members of Alcoholics Anonymous recognize as alcoholism to the exclusion of all other species. Of course they use loss of control and "craving" as the criteria par excellence but these necessarily involve the other characteristics of gamma alcoholism mentioned above. As I have said before, Alcoholics Anonymous have naturally created the picture of alcoholism in their own image, although at least 10 to 15 per cent of their membership are probably specimens of alpha alcoholism who conform in their language to the A.A. standards. I base this statement on the fact that in a sample of slightly over 2,000 A.A. members I have found 13 per cent who never experienced loss of control. More likely than not only a small percentage of those with alpha alcoholism would seek the help of Alcoholics Anonymous, and almost none of those with beta alcoholism. The latter may be seen most frequently in general hospitals.

In spite of the respect and admiration to which Alcoholics Anonymous have a claim on account of their great achievements, there is every reason why the student of alcoholism should emancipate himself from accepting the exclusiveness of the picture of alcoholism as propounded by Alcoholics Anonymous.

Delta alcoholism shows the first three characteristics of gamma alcoholism as well as a less marked form of the fourth characteristic—that is, instead of loss of control there is *inability to abstain*. In contrast to gamma alcoholism, there is no ability to "go on the water wagon" for even a day or two without the manifestation of withdrawal symptoms; the ability to control the amount of intake on any given occasion, however, remains intact. The incentive to high intake may be found in the general acceptance of the society to which the drinker belongs, while pre-alcoholic psychological vulnerability, more often than not, may be of a low degree. This species of alcoholism and its underlying drinking pattern have been [seen] in connection with the *pre-dominant species of alcoholism ("inveterate drinking") in France* and some other countries with a large wine consumption. . . . Delta alcoholism would rarely be seen in Alcoholics Anonymous, since the alcoholic afflicted with this species of alcoholism does not go through the distressing social and psychological experiences of the gamma alcoholic and manifests only a few of the behavior changes of the latter.

There are, of course, many other species of alcoholism—if it is defined as any drinking that causes any damage—and all the remaining 19 letters of the Greek and if necessary other alphabets are available for labeling them.

Among these other species is *periodic alcoholism,* which in Europe and Latin America is still designated as dipsomania, a term in disuse in North America. We may denote it as *Epsilon alcoholism* but it will be neither described nor defined here, as it seems to be the least known species of alcoholism. In the course of their periodic bouts, epsilon alcoholics may cause serious damage. I should like to point out that in the last 20 or 25 years a phenomenon which may be called pseudoperiodic alcoholism has turned up. It would appear that some gamma alcoholics who have not benefited to the full extent from the A.A. program or from therapy in clinics or by private psychiatrists are able to resist drinking for 3, 6 or 12 months, but then find no other solution than intoxication, after which they remorsefully return to "sobriety."

Other species of alcoholism (accepting the criterion of damage through drinking) are, of course, "explosive drinking" as well as what the French call "alcoolisation," i.e., the undermining of health and curtailing of the life span (to the exclusion of other "alcoholic complications" and physical or psychological dependence). Then there is the excessive weekend drinking which follows a cultural pattern and causes damage through rowdiness, absenteeism and impairment of the family budget. Still other species cause damage, for instance, "fiesta drinking" and occasional drinking that causes accidents. I do not propose to list, describe or discuss all these species of alcoholism, but should like to point out that the student of the problems of alcohol cannot afford to overlook these behaviors, whether or not he is inclined to designate them as species of alcoholism.

Returning to the question whether alcoholism is a disease, only alpha, beta, gamma, delta and epsilon alcoholism can come into consideration at all. Alpha alcoholism may be ruled out as it is the symptom of an underlying disturbance; this, of course, does not deny that the person suffering from this species of alcoholism is a sick person. As to beta alcoholism, it too must be ruled out, being neither a disease per se nor even a symptom, unless we regard the drinking that produces the damage (certain alcoholic diseases) as social pathology, a rather diffuse concept. No doubt polyneuropathy, cirrhosis of the liver and gastritis are serious diseases, but in this instance they are purely effects of the excessive drinking, and in this species the excess in drinking itself does not indicate any physical or psychological pathology and no dependence develops.

This leaves us with the gamma, delta and epsilon species of alcoholism. The first two of these may come into consideration as diseases, since it is the adaptation of cell metabolism, and acquired increased tissue tolerance and the withdrawal symptoms, which bring about "craving" and loss of control or inability to abstain. These species involve that use of alcoholic beverages which has induced Bacon to say that "alcoholics do not drink," although Bacon is not thinking merely of the loss of control but, quite rightly, of certain drinking behaviors which precede the loss of control. In gamma alcoholism, the adaptation of cell metabolism and the other characteristics mentioned above indeed represent physiopathological changes analogous to those in drug addiction as well as psychopathological conditions which differ from those of any possible pre-alcoholic psychopathology. With the exception of the psychological changes and the loss of control, which is replaced by the inability to abstain, the same changes are involved in delta alcoholism.

If it should be conceded that morphine, heroin and barbiturate addiction involve grave physiopathologic processes which result in "craving," then they may be designated as diseases (and they are included in the American Medical Association's nomenclature of diseases). The gamma and delta species of alcoholism may be regarded so by the same tokens (and alcoholism is included, too, in the list of the American Medical Association). Of course it is a matter of opinion whether or not such processes are designated as diseases. On the other hand, the presence of the physiopathological changes leading to craving cannot be denied in the addictions, whether to narcotic drugs or to alcohol. The current majority opinion to which the present writer subscribes, and subscribed before it was a majority opinion, is that anomalous forms of the ingestion of narcotics and alcohol, such as drinking with loss of control and physical dependence, are caused by physiopathological processes and constitute diseases.

Whether epsilon alcoholism, i.e., periodic alcoholism, is a disease per se or the symptom of an underlying disease cannot be asserted at our present state of knowledge concerning that species of alcoholism. Pseudoperiodic alcoholism or pseudoepsilon alcoholism is a relapse into a disease, but I must add that the occasion for the relapse is a voluntary one and does not form a part of the disease process, except perhaps in a psychopathological sense.

As I have said before, the definition of alcoholism which I have adopted here, namely that alcoholism is any drinking that leads to any damage, does not permit of designating as alcoholics all those who occasion some kind of damage through their use of alcoholic beverages. I would call alcoholics only those who manifest the alpha, beta, gamma, delta and epsilon varieties of alcoholism. This is admittedly an arbitrary distinction. Some may wish to exclude the alpha or beta alcoholics or both, and others may be inclined to include the "explosive drinkers," the "alcoholized drinkers," or perhaps all who cause any damage through any use of alcoholic beverages. I shall have no quarrel with them as I made these statements only in order to assure what the terms used mean in the present study.

Chapter 23

Is Alcohol Dangerous to the Fetus? Part 3: Yes

For nearly four decades after the 1930s the view that alcohol could not harm the fetus was generally accepted. Then in 1970 a pediatrics resident, at the University of Washington, Dr. Uleland, noted what she thought was a curious similarity in the facial appearance of several babies born to welfare mothers who were regular and heavy users of alcohol. From this small observation, research into the danger of alcohol to the fetus grew. Once the danger was established to the satisfaction of numerous authorities as fact, the existence of the condition named Fetal Alcohol Syndrome, or FAS, become a well-known and influential factor in the changing attitude toward alcohol. In the early 1970s the Surgeon General warned pregnant women against consuming more than three average-size alcoholic drinks a day, but by the 1980s this recommendation had fallen to no drinks whatsoever. In 1977 the Department of Health, Education and Welfare issued the following statement on drinking and Fetal Alcohol Syndrome.

HEALTH CAUTION ON FETAL ALCOHOL SYNDROME

Recent research reports indicate that heavy use of alcohol by women during pregnancy may result in a pattern of abnormalities in the offspring, termed The Fetal Alcohol Syndrome, which consists of specific congenital and behavioral abnormalities. Studies undertaken in animals corroborate the initial observations in humans and indicate as well as increased incidence of stillbirths, resorptions and spontaneous abortions. Both the risk and the extent of abnormalities appear to be dose-related, increasing with higher alcohol intake during the pregnancy period. In human studies, alcohol is an unequivocal factor when the full pattern of the Fetal Alcohol Syndrome is present. In cases where all of the characteristics are not present, the correlation between alcohol and the adverse effects is complicated by such factors as nutrition, smoking, caffeine and other drug consumption.

Given the total evidence available at this time, pregnant women should be particularly conscious of the extent of their drinking. While safe levels of drinking are unknown, it appears that a risk is established with ingestion above 3 ounces of absolute alcohol or 6 drinks per day. Between 1 ounce and 3 ounces, there is still uncertainty but caution is advised. Therefore, pregnant women and those likely to become pregnant should discuss their drinking habits and the potential dangers with their physicians.

Chapter 24

Warning Labels Are Mandated on Containers of Alcoholic Beverages

The identification of Fetal Alcohol Syndrome, which included the correlate that this kind of damage to a fetus was preventable, served as a direct impetus for the passage of a new law. Under Title II of the Anti–Drug Abuse Act of 1988, beginning on November 18, 1989, all alcoholic beverage containers had to carry a warning label — evidence that increasingly Americans viewed alcohol as another dangerous drug, rather than a beverage harmless if taken in "moderation."

THE ANTI–DRUG ABUSE ACT OF 1988

An Act to prevent the manufacturing, distribution, and use of illegal drugs, and for other purposes.

Be it enacted by the Senate and House of Representatives of the United States of America in Congress assembled,
SECTION 1. Short Title.
This Act may be cited as the "Anti–Drug Abuse Act of 1988".....

Title II — Alcoholic Beverage Labeling

Short Title

[smSec. 201. This title may be cited as the "Alcoholic Beverage Labeling Act of 1988".

Declaration of Policy and Purpose

SEC. 202. The Congress finds that the American public should be informed about the health hazards that may result from the consumption or abuse of alcoholic beverages, and has determined that it would be beneficial to provide a clear, nonconfusing reminder of such hazards, and that there is a need for national uniformity in such reminders in order to avoid the promulgation of incorrect or misleading information and to minimize burdens on interstate commerce. The Congress finds that requiring such reminders on all containers of alcoholic beverages is appropriate and necessary in view of the substantial role of the Federal Government in promoting the health and safety of the Nation's population. It is therefore the policy of the Congress, and the purpose of this title, to exercise the full reach of the Federal Government's constitutional powers in order to establish a comprehensive Federal program, in connection with the manufacture and sale of alcoholic beverages in or affecting interstate commerce, to deal with the provision of warning or other information with respect to any relationship between the consumption or abuse of alcoholic beverages and health, so that—

(1) the public may be adequately reminded about any health hazards that may be associated with the consumption or abuse of alcoholic beverages through a nationally uniform, nonconfusing warning notice on each container of such beverages; and

(2) commerce and the national economy may be—

(A) protected to the maximum extent consistent with this declared policy,

(B) not impeded by diverse, nonuniform, and confusing requirements for warnings or other information on alcoholic beverage containers with respect to any relationship between the consumption or abuse of alcoholic beverages and health, and

(C) protected from the adverse effects that would result from a noncomprehensive program covering alcoholic beverage containers sold in interstate commerce, but not alcoholic beverage containers manufactured and sold within a single State.

Labeling Requirement; Conspicuous Statement

Sec. 204. (a) On and after the expiration of the 12-month period following the date of enactment of this title, it shall be unlawful for any person to manufacture, import, or bottle for sale or distribution in the United States any alcoholic beverage unless the container of such beverage bears the following statement:

"GOVERNMENT WARNING: (1) According to the Surgeon General, women should not drink alcoholic beverages during pregnancy because of the risk of birth defects. (2) Consumption of alcoholic beverages impairs your ability to drive a car or operate machinery, and may cause health problems."

Chapter 25

How to Speak about Alcohol and Drugs: Government Recommendations

As part of the renewed attack on drugs in the late 1980s, the Office (now Center) for Substance Abuse Prevention (OSAP) was created in the Department of Health and Human Services. A major goal of OSAP was to promote prevention materials intended to discourage drug and alcohol use. In 1989 the office issued guidelines for evaluating such materials. They included scientific criteria by which materials submitted were to be judged and also an editorial sheet containing a list of words and phrases commonly used in reference to drugs or alcohol yet judged by OSAP to be false or misleading. Opposite each proscribed term was a recommended substitute. Significantly, alcohol is amalgamated with drugs.

Note that the guidelines describe consumption of any amount of alcohol as a risk and proscribe the term "responsible use." Compare this with the arguments of Lyman Beecher against "prudent" drinking. OSAP opposes the concept of a "designated driver," which, it argues encourages others to drink excessively. Similarly, the passage on the Fetal Alcohol Syndrome is interesting for its formulation of a strict no-alcohol position for pregnant women. Questioning of this view is prohibited. OSAP distributed the editorial guidelines not only to health professionals but also to others who might allude to drugs and alcohol, including television and film writers.

MESSAGE AND GUIDELINES

Office for Substance Abuse Prevention

The Office for Substance Abuse Prevention (OSAP), in the Alcohol, Drug Abuse, and Mental Health Administration (ADAMHA), has implemented a review program to help prevention workers screen for appropriateness, accuracy, credibility, appeal, and so forth. The cornerstone of the OSAP program is the Communications Message and Material Review Process, a detailed manual designed to assess a product's conformance to public health policies and principles, scientific accuracy, and appropriateness of communication strategies. . . .

Scientific Review Guidelines

1. The material is scientifically significant, based on valid assumptions, supported by accurate citations, and appropriately used. If the developers are working from hypotheses, theories, or models but not from statistically significant and conclusive research which has been replicated, this should be noted under comments: for example, this appears to be based on a promising prevention hypothesis, which is in the testing phase. This would not be rated unacceptable unless the National Institute on Drug Abuse (NIDA) or the National Institute on Alcohol Abuse and Alcoholism (NIAAA) believe that harm could result from further testing; for example, an applied theory has resulted in increased drug use or application may result in misperception or other harm.

2. The scientific methods and approaches used are adequate, appropriate, and clearly described. These include the methods of basic biomedical research, behavioral research, and applied research. Clinical studies use and describe sound modalities.

3. Findings reported are accurate, current, applicable to the subject matter, and appropriately interpreted. The findings follow from the methods and approach used. For instance, facts should not be exaggerated nor purposely understated.

4. Recommendation: rate as acceptable or unacceptable. If rated unacceptable, an overall rating of unacceptable should be recorded on the Product Description Form.

5. Comments: complete per instructions above. Highlight positive aspects and problems.

OSAP Policy Review Guidelines

1. Material makes clear that illegal and unwise drug use (including alcohol for those under 21) is unhealthy and harmful for all persons.

   There are five kinds of illegal or unwise drug use:

   - Use of any legally prohibited drug. For example, heroin, cocaine, PCP, and "designer drugs" are all legally prohibited drugs—it is unlawful to produce, distribute or purchase these drugs under any circumstances.

- Use of a drug for a purpose other than its prescribed use (e.g., tranquilizer or diet pill for purposes other than prescribed).
- Use of any product or substance that can produce a drug-like effect (e.g., using glues, gasoline, or aerosols as inhalants).
- Use of any legal drug, including alcohol or tobacco, by individuals legally underage for its use.
- Illegal or unwise use of a legal drug; for example, public intoxication or operation of a car after drinking or other drug-taking.

Materials should communicate clearly that all the above are either illegal and/or potentially harmful. Look for "red flag" phrases incorrectly implying that there is a "safe" use of illegal drugs. For example, materials that

- Use the term "mood-altering" as a euphemism for "mind-altering" drugs or
- Imply that there are no "good" or "bad" drugs, just "improper use, misuse, or abuse."

2. Material gives a clear message that risk is associated with using any form or amount of alcohol or other drugs.

It is misleading to state or imply that there are any risk-free or fully safe levels of use of alcohol or other drugs. Even small amounts of alcohol and other drugs can increase risk of injury or to health.

If the message is that some people use alcohol to relax or to celebrate, it also should say that alcohol is a drug and, as with any drug, there are risks associated with use. No materials should give or imply mixed messages: for example, it's safe to drink as much as you want as long as you don't drive; using drugs "recreationally" or "experimentally" is safe but don't get hooked; beer drinkers can't become alcoholic; or marijuana is a "soft" drug and heroin is a "hard" drug, implying that one is safe and the other is dangerous.

Materials recommending a designated driver should be rated unacceptable. They encourage heavy alcohol use by implying that it is okay to drink to intoxication as long as you don't drive.

Materials that carry messages, either implicitly or explicitly, that drinking alcoholic beverages is universal or the norm for virtually all occasions are unacceptable. For instance, a publication that states you should not drink to the point of intoxication and drive, but encourages "moderate" use on other occasions as a norm, should be considered primarily promotional and rated as unacceptable.

3. Material gives a clear message of no alcohol use for persons under 21 years of age, pregnant women, recovering alcoholics and drug addicts, and persons taking prescription or nonprescription drugs.

Persons Under 21 Years of Age

Clearly young people must go through a decision-making process regarding alcohol use. Learning how to make wise decisions is an important skill. However, the material should make it clear that a nonuse decision is best and give support for this decision.

Be sure that materials targeting underage college students convey the alcohol "no use" message. If materials addressing this audience are not age specific, assume that most undergraduate college students are under the legal drinking age of 21.

All youth materials should adhere to a strict abstinence message. Any material that talks about drinking and driving should be aimed at adults, not at underage youth. Materials recommending designated drivers should be rated unacceptable as they are giving a mixed "no use" message to youth—they imply that it's okay to drink as long as you don't drive.

Pregnant Women

Material for pregnant women should give a clear abstinence message. The U.S. Surgeon General says that "the safest choice is not to drink at all during pregnancy or if you are planning pregnancy." Abstinence during pregnancy removes the risk of producing a child with alcohol-related birth defects. Material that merely warns about the dangers of drinking during pregnancy without stating an abstinence message should be rated as unacceptable. For example, this is unacceptable: "you owe it to yourself and your unborn child to be informed about drinking during pregnancy and to avoid excessive or abusive drinking."

Materials stating that "research is inconclusive" or "not enough is known to make a judgment" or "some believe this ... while others believe that" are waffling. In fact, since not enough is known about how much alcohol is acceptable, for whom, and during which stages of pregnancy, the safest choice is not to drink during pregnancy. This message should be clearly stated.

Recovering Alcoholics

Abstinence from alcohol is regarded as a major goal of treatment for alcoholics in the United States. Those in treatment are urged to abstain from drinking and also are counseled to avoid psychoactive drugs. Clinical and scientific evidence seems to support the view that once physical dependence has occurred, the alcoholic no longer has the option of returning to social drinking. Materials indicating that controlled drinking or an occasional social drink is alright for recovering alcoholics, should be rated as unacceptable. Many treatment professionals also support the hypothesis that recovering addicts also should not use alcohol—but additional testing is required before assessing materials based on this concept.

Individuals Using Prescription or Nonprescription Medications

Materials should state that persons taking medications should not drink alcohol. An alcohol and drug combination may alter a drug's effectiveness. The physical reactions are unpredictable and sometimes fatal. Also, many medications contain alcohol.

4. Material states clearly that pregnant women must not use any drugs (prescription or nonprescription) without first consulting their physicians.

Although scientists do not know, and may never know, about the exact effects of all drugs on unborn babies, animal research and the unfortunate thalidomide tragedy have provided important clues about the possibility of prenatal damage. Materials should clearly state that pregnant women should consult their physician before buying any new drug, refilling a prescription, or taking medication on hand for common ailments, such as headaches and colds.

Common over-the-counter drugs that should be avoided by pregnant women without first consulting their physicians are antacids, aspirin, laxatives, nose drops, nasal sprays, and vitamins. Likewise, commonly prescribed drugs that can be dangerous to a fetus are antibiotics, antihistamines, antimigraines, antinauseants, diuretics, hormones, such as in oral contraceptives, vaccinations, tranquilizers, and sedatives. Materials must state clearly that these and other drugs should only be used by pregnant women on the advice of their physicians or other medical practitioners.

5. Material does not glamorize or glorify the use of alcohol and other drugs.

Materials should not portray alcohol and other drug use as a positive experience. For youth, the first temptation to use alcohol and other drugs often comes as pressure to be "one of the gang." Depicting alcohol and other drug use as a way to have a good time, a way to "fit in," be sexy, or attain social and financial status may lure potential users. Rate as unacceptable materials that depict alcohol and other drug use in a positive or attractive light.

6. Prevention material does not contain illustrations or dramatizations that could teach people ways to prepare, obtain, or ingest illegal drugs, and whenever feasible materials for youth contain no illustrations of drugs. Intervention material does not contain illustrations or dramatizations that may stimulate recovering addicts or alcoholics to use drugs.

Prevention materials that illustrate drug paraphernalia and methods of illegal drug use in such a way that they may inadvertently instruct an individual about how to use or obtain illegal other drugs are unacceptable. Prevention materials targeting youth should contain no illustrations of illegal drugs unless when making a non-use point that cannot be made in any other way. Illegal drugs should not be used as graphic "filler."

Intervention materials depicting action scenes of consumption or ingestion of alcohol and other drugs may negatively influence the audience they are intended to help. For example, scenes of people injecting drugs, sniffing cocaine, or drinking alcohol may stimulate the behavior. A powerful craving for cocaine has been found to be very common for all cocaine addicts and can be easily stimulated by the sight of this drug and by objects, people, paraphernalia, places, and emotions associated in the addict's mind with cocaine. Therefore, explicit illustrations or dramatizations of drugs or drug use should not be used in materials targeted to recovering persons. All materials containing such illustrations or dramatizations should be rated unacceptable. Caution is actually wise in depicting any illegal drug use for any population, since it is unclear as to who may be most likely to use alcohol or other drugs after seeing such depictions.

7. Material does not "blame the victim."

Addiction is an illness. Therefore, material should focus on preventing and treating the disease and not on berating the individual. Materials that focus on an individual's shortcomings as a reason for usage or addiction are "blaming the victim" and should be rated as unacceptable. This is not to imply that a person should not take responsibility for his or her alcohol and other drug problems, which may be related to addiction, dependence, and even just very unwise use. The material, however, should also include encouraging the person to take responsibility for seeking help, if alcohol and other drug problems continue and/or dependence is suspected. The material should include resources for seeking help.

Materials using insulting terms about the victims of drug or alcohol abuse do not conform to OSAP policy and should be rated unacceptable. For example, information that refers to those who consume alcohol and illegal drugs as "drunks," "skid row burns," "pot heads," or "dope fiends" should be rejected.

8. Material targeting youth does not use recovering addicts or alcoholics as role models.

Prevention education materials targeting youth that use recovering addicts or alcoholics as role models do not conform to OSAP policy. While the power of the confession may be useful in an intervention program counseling high-risk students or adults who are recovering users, it often has the opposite effect on children.

Focus group testing has shown children and adolescents enrolled in prevention education programs (most of whom are not recovering users) may get a different message than what is intended from the testimony of recovering addicts and alcoholics. Rather than the intended "don't do as I did" message, children may hear the message that the speaker used alcohol and other drugs and survived very well or even became wealthy and famous. An exception may be made for role models who clearly show they have been negatively affected by the use of alcohol and other drugs, such as someone now visibly handicapped or injured as a result of alcohol and other drug use.

Materials targeting adults that use these individuals as role models may be acceptable, provided they meet all of the other criteria.

9.   Material supports abstinence as a viable choice.

Materials need to give a clear message that abstinence is a feasible choice for everyone. For example, they should not imply that the only solution for a headache is an over-the-counter analgesic or that the only way to celebrate a special event is with an alcoholic toast. Materials focusing on reducing or limiting the amount of alcohol or other drugs taken are unacceptable if they don't also present the message that abstinence is another viable choice. This in no way implies that valid medical attention, including appropriate drugs, should be withheld from anyone for any reason.

10.   Cultural and ethnic sensitivity.

Examples must be culturally and ethnically sensitive. Materials must not be biased and must not perpetuate myth or stereotype. They should reflect the social, economic, and familial norms of the intended audience and reflect the physical appearance of the audience. Extreme care should be taken in detecting subtle racist or sexist biases. For example, everything "good" is portrayed with white symbols and everything "bad" or "wrong" is portrayed with brown, black, or dark colors; or only males being arrested for alcohol-impaired driving. Norms and symbols important to the culture of the audience also must be reflected; e.g., groups are more important than individuals among some audiences; spiritual symbols are very important among some populations. Materials also need to both reflect and respect such cultural factors as the importance of the extended family, key role of grandparents, and religion.

11.   Recommendation: rate as acceptable or unacceptable. If rated unacceptable, an overall rating of unacceptable should be recorded on the Product Description Form.

12.   Comments: highlight positive aspects and problems.

Editorial Guidelines

Because uniformity in terminology is desirable when communicating prevention messages, we encourage our readers to use the following guidelines adopted by OSAP and ADAMHA for their publications. Because prevention is a relatively new science, we expect that this style sheet occasionally will be expanded.

DO NOT USE	USE
Drunk Driving	Alcohol-Impaired Driving (Because a person does not have to be drunk to be impaired)
Liquor (for any alcoholic beverages)	Beer, Wine, Distilled Spirits, or Alcoholic Beverages
Substance Abuse	Alcohol and Other Drug Abuse
Abuse when sentence refers to anyone under 21	Use (DHHS aims to prevent the use, not just abuse, of alcohol and other drugs by youth)
Drug Abuse Prevention or Alcohol Abuse Prevention	Except when referring to adults, use "to prevent alcohol and other drug problems"
Hard or Soft Drugs	Drugs (since all illicit drugs are harmful)
Recreational Use of Drugs	Use (since no drug use is recreational)
Responsible Use	Use (since there is a risk associated with all use
Accidents, when referring to alcohol and other drug use	Crashes (since the term "accident" suggests the event could not have been avoided)

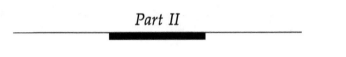

Part II

Drugs

Introduction
Opiates, Cocaine, Cannabis, and Other Drugs

America's recurrent enthusiasm for drugs and subsequent campaigns for abstinence present a problem to policy makers and the public. The peaks of these dramatic episodes are so far apart, about a lifetime, that citizens rarely have an accurate or even a vivid recollection of the last wave of cocaine or opiates. A second problem is that the phase of growing intolerance has in the past been fueled with such fear and anger that the record of times favorable toward drug taking has been either erased from public memory or so distorted as to be useless for policy formation. In the attack on drug taking, total denigration of the preceding but contrary mood has seemed necessary for public welfare. Such a vigorous rejection may have value in further reducing demand, but the long-term effect is to destroy a realistic perception of the past, of the conflicting attitudes toward mood-altering substances that have characterized our national history.

Having no grasp of earlier and formative encounters with drugs unnecessarily impedes our already difficult effort to establish a workable and sustainable drug policy, perhaps a policy that can survive the great attitudinal changes characterizing the nineteenth and twentieth centuries or, even more optimistically, a policy that can moderate future swings. The wave of drug use that peaked around 1900 illuminates our present encounter.

For millennia cocaine and morphine had been available only in the natural product that was chewed, drunk, or taken in some way that similarly diluted the impact of the active ingredient. Then the nineteenth century brought a remarkable rise in organic chemistry: morphine was isolated from opium in the first decade, cocaine from coca by 1860, and in 1874 heroin was synthesized from morphine. By midcentury the hypodermic syringe was perfected and by 1870 it had become a familiar instrument to American physicians and patients. Meanwhile, the astounding growth of the pharmaceutical industry intensified the impact of these accomplishments. Throughout the century, manufacturers grew more adept at identifying a marketable innovation, moving into mass production, and distributing and advertising throughout the world.

During the nineteenth century these powerful drugs were much more available in the United States than in most nations due to the peculiarity of the United States Constitution. Each individual state assumed responsibility for health issues, such as control of medical practice and pharmacy. The federal government responded to communicable diseases and health care for the merchant marine and government dependents, such as Native Americans. In nations with a less restricted central government, such as Britain and Prussia, a single, preeminent pharmacy law controlled availability of dangerous drugs; physicians would have their right to practice similarly granted by a central authority. America, in contrast, had as many laws regarding health professions as it had states. Indeed, for much of the nineteenth century many states chose to have no controls at all; their legislatures reacted to the conflicting claims of contradictory health theories by allowing free enterprise for all practitioners.

Therefore, when we consider consumption of opium, opiates, coca, and cocaine in nineteenth-century America, we are looking at an era of wide availability, unrestrained advertising claims, and an initial enthusiasm for the purified substances that was unsullied by any substantial doubts or fear. It was an "experiment in nature" that has been largely forgotten, even repressed, as a result of the extremely negative reaction to that wave of drug use peaking around 1900.

Opium

Crude opium, alone or dissolved in some liquid such as alcohol or acetic acid, was brought by European explorers and settlers to North America. Colonists regarded opium as a familiar resource for pain relief. Benjamin Franklin regularly took laudanum, opium in an alcohol extract, for the pain of kidney stones during the last few years of his life. At about the same time, William Coleridge, then a student at Oxford, began using laudanum for pain and developed a lifelong addiction to the drug.

Americans recognized the potential danger of continually using opium long before the availability of morphine and the hypodermic's popularity. The *American Dispensatory* of 1806 warned that habitual use of opium would lead to "tremors, paralysis, stupidity and general emaciation." Balancing this danger, the text noted the value of opium in a multitude of ailments ranging from cholera to asthma. Considering the other treatments then in vogue—blistering, vomiting, and bleeding—we can understand why opium was as cherished by patients as by their physicians.

The per capita consumption of opium rose gradually during the nineteenth century, reaching a peak in the 1890s. It then declined until at least 1915, when new federal laws severely restricted legal imports. We are able to track its rise and fall through the U.S. import/consumption statistics while opium and morphine importation was legal and carried moderate tariffs. Smoking opium exhibits an interesting divergence from this pattern: per capita consumption rose until the 1909 act outlawing its importation.

Americans had quickly associated smoking opium with Chinese immigrants who arrived after the Civil War to work on railroad construction. Here was one of the earliest examples of a powerful theme in American perception of drugs, that is, linkage between a drug and a feared or rejected group within our society.

Cocaine and marijuana would be similarly linked in the first third of the twentieth century.

Because of opium's growing use in the nineteenth century, many people fell under the power of a substance that demanded regular consumption or the penalty of withdrawal, a painful although rarely life-threatening experience. Whatever the cause—overprescribing by physicians, patent medicines, self-indulgence, or "weak will"—opium addiction brought shame. As consumption increased, so did the apparent frequency of addiction.

Ironically, neither physicians nor others at first considered the introduction of the hypodermic syringe and the availability of pure morphine to be adding to the danger of addiction. Because pain could be controlled with less morphine when injected, the assumption followed that this procedure was less likely to addict. Regrettably, sufferers from chronic pain, such as arthritis, could obtain syringes and morphine with ease whether they had a physician or not.

Late in the century local and state laws were enacted to limit morphine to a physician's prescription and some laws forbade refilling these prescriptions. The lack, however, of any control over interstate commerce (the responsibility of the federal government) combined with the lack of uniformity among the state laws and the further lack of effective enforcement meant that the rising tide of laws directed at opiates—and later cocaine—was more a reflection of changing public attitude toward these drugs than an effective shutoff of supplies to users. The decline noted after the mid-1890s probably was due mostly to the public's growing fear of addiction and casual use of habit-forming substances. Of course, the health professions developed more specific treatments for painful disease as well as an appreciation for the danger of the hypodermic, which had caused many examples of addiction. Likewise, the public now feared the careless—and possibly addicted—physician. In a *Long Day's Journey into Night*, Eugene O'Neill dramatized the painful and shameful impact of his mother's physician-induced addiction.

Campaign for a National Anti-Narcotic Law

In a spirit not unlike our own times, Americans in the last decade of the nineteenth century grew increasingly concerned about the environment, adulterated foods, destruction of the forests, and the widespread use of dangerous drugs. The Anti-Saloon League (founded in 1895) led a temperance movement toward prohibition, which was achieved in 1920.

After overcoming years of resistance by patent medicine manufacturers, the federal government enacted the Pure Food and Drug Act in 1906. This act did not prevent sales of dangerous drugs like opiates and cocaine, but it did require accurate labeling of contents for all over-the-counter remedies sold in interstate commerce. Still, there was no nationally uniform restriction on the availability of opiates or cocaine, a problem whose solution would require growing concern, legal ingenuity, and an unexpected involvement of the federal government with the international trade in narcotics through acquisition of the Philippines Islands.

Responsibility for the Philippines after 1898 added an international dimension to the growing domestic alarm at drug abuse. It also revealed that Congress, if given the opportunity, would prohibit nonmedical use of opium among its new dependents. Governor-General William Howard Taft proposed reinstituting a Spanish opium monopoly and using the profits to help pay for a massive public education campaign. President Theodore Roosevelt vetoed this plan, and Congress in 1905 mandated an absolute prohibition of opium for any purpose other than medicinal. In order to deal efficiently with the antidrug policy established for the Philippines, a committee from the Islands visited various territories in the area to see how others dealt with the opium problem. The desirability of dealing with narcotics at the international level became apparent.

In early 1906 China had instituted a campaign against opium, especially smoking opium, in an attempt to modernize and make the empire more able to cope with Western encroachments on its sovereignty. In the same year Chinese anger at maltreatment of their nationals in the United States seethed into a voluntary boycott of American goods. Partly to appease the Chinese by aiding their anti-opium campaign, and partly to deal with uncontrollable smuggling within the Philippine archipelago, the United States, at the urging of the Protestant Episcopal bishop of the Philippines, Charles Henry Brent, convened a meeting of powers linked to the area and the opium trade. In this way, the United States launched a campaign for worldwide narcotics traffic control extending in an unbroken diplomatic sequence through the League of Nations to the present efforts of the United Nations.

The International Opium Commission, a gathering of thirteen nations, met in Shanghai in February 1909. Bishop Brent was chosen to preside and resolutions were adopted noting problems with opium and opiates. These resolutions did not constitute a treaty, however, and no actions bound the nations attending the commission. In diplomatic parlance, what was needed was a conference, not a commission. The United States pursued this goal with determination.

The American anti-narcotic campaign had several motivations. Appeasement of China was certainly one factor for officials of the State Department. The department's opium commissioner, Dr. Hamilton Wright (whose report is excerpted here), thought the whole matter could be "used as oil to smooth the troubled water of our aggressive commercial policy there." Another reason was the belief, still strongly held by the United States government, that controlling crops and traffic in the producing countries could most efficiently stop nonmedical consumption of drugs in the United States.

To restrict opium and coca production required worldwide agreement and, therefore, an international conference. After threats and intense diplomatic activity, such a conference was convened in the Hague in December 1911. Again, Bishop Brent was chosen to preside and on January 23, 1912, the convention was signed by the dozen nations represented. Provision was made for the other international powers to adhere prior to bringing the treaty into force, for no producing or manufacturing nation wanted to leave the market to the benefit of nonratifying nations.

The convention required each nation to enact domestic legislation controlling the traffic in narcotics. The goal was a world in which every nation restricted narcotics to medicinal purposes and respected the desire of other nations to do the same. Both the producing and consuming nations would have control over their boundaries.

After his return from Shanghai, Wright labored to craft a comprehensive federal antinarcotic law in accord with the Hague Convention. In his path loomed the problem of states' rights. The health professions were considered a major cause of addiction, and yet how could federal law interfere with the prescribing practices of physicians or require that pharmacists keep records? Wright settled upon the federal government's power to tax; the result, after prolonged bargaining with pharmaceutical, import/export, and medical interests, was the Harrison Act, passed in December 1914 and excerpted here.

Representative Francis Burton Harrison's association with the act was just an accident of his introduction of the administration's bill. If the chief proponent and negotiator was to be given eponymic credit, it should have been called the Wright Act. It could even have been called a second Mann Act, after Representative James Mann, who actually saw the bill through to passage in the House of Representatives, for by that time Harrison had become Governor-General of the Philippines.

The act required a strict accounting of opium and coca and their derivatives from entry into the United States to the point of dispensing to a patient. A small tax had to be paid at each transfer and permits had to be obtained upon application to the Treasury Department. Only the patient paid no tax and needed no permit and, in fact, was not allowed to obtain one.

Initially, Wright and the Justice Department argued that the Harrison Act forbade indefinite maintenance of addiction unless there was a specific medical reason such as cancer or tuberculosis. This was rejected in 1916 by the Supreme Court, although the Justice Department argued that the Harrison Act was the domestic implementation of the Hague Opium Convention and therefore took precedence over states' rights. Then in 1919 the Supreme Court, led by Oliver Wendell Holmes and Louis Brandeis, changed its mind by a five-to-four vote. In the *Webb* and *Doremus* decisions (excerpted here), the Court declared that indefinite maintenance for "mere addiction" was outside legitimate medical practice and consequently prohibiting it did not constitute interference with a state's right to regulate physicians. Second, because the person receiving the drugs for maintenance was therefore not a bona fide patient but just a receiver of drugs, the transfer of narcotics defrauded the government of taxes required under the Harrison Act.

During the 1920s and 1930s the opiate problem, chiefly morphine and heroin, declined in the United States until much of the problem was confined to the periphery of society and the outcasts of urban areas. This was not invariably the case with opiates: health professionals and a few others of middle-class or higher status continued to take up opiates, but nevertheless a downward trend from the numbers reasonably estimated earlier in the century was apparent when viewed from the 1940s.

A curious sidelight on the Hague Convention and the effort to obtain broad ratification was the proposal by the British and American governments to add the convention to the Versailles Treaty that ended World War I. As a result, to ratify the Peace Treaty was to simultaneously ratify the Hague Convention that required a domestic law controlling narcotics. This is the origin of the British Dangerous Drugs Act of 1920, not a raging heroin epidemic in Britain. Beginning in the 1940s, some in the United States have promoted the argument that the "British system" provided heroin to addicts and, by not relying on law enforcement, reduced to almost a vanishing point the opiate problem. In fact, Britain had no problem to begin with. This is an interesting example of simplifying or distorting a foreign drug situation in the desperate attempt to locate a solution to the much larger one in the United States.

Cocaine

Purified cocaine became commercially available in the United States in 1884. At first the wholesale cost was very high—five to ten dollars a gram—but after a few years fell to about twenty-five cents a gram and remained there until the price inflation of World War I. Problems with cocaine were evident almost from the beginning, but the preponderance of popular opinion and the voices of leading medical experts depicted cocaine as a remarkable and harmless stimulant. Dr. William A. Hammond, one of America's most prominent neurologists, extolled cocaine in print and lectures. By 1887, Hammond was assuring his audiences that cocaine was no more habit-forming than coffee or tea and told them of the cocaine-wine he had perfected with the help of a New York druggist: two grains of cocaine to a pint of wine. This, he claimed, was a much more effective tonic than the popular foreign wine of coca, probably a reference to Vin Mariani, which he complained had only half a grain of cocaine to the pint.

Coca-Cola was also introduced in 1886 as a drink with the advantages of coca but without the danger of alcohol, a temperance coca beverage. Cocaine was removed in 1900, before an Atlanta City Ordinance of 1901 (and a state statute the following year) prohibited provision of any cocaine to a consumer without a prescription.

Cocaine is the most powerful central nervous system euphoriant. This fact underlay cocaine's quickly growing consumption and the ineffectiveness of the early warnings. How could anything that made users so confident and happy be bad?

Within a year of cocaine's introduction, the Parke-Davis Company provided coca and cocaine in fifteen forms, including coca cigarettes, cocaine for injection, and cocaine for sniffing. The company also outfitted a handy cocaine kit with various forms of the drug and a hypodermic syringe. Parke-Davis proudly supplied a drug that, it announced, "can supply the place of food, make the coward brave, the silent eloquent . . . and render the sufferer insensitive to pain." Reflecting how rapidly cocaine spread throughout the nation, a physician in Puyallup, Washington Territory, reported in September 1886 an adverse reaction to cocaine during an operation. As the years progressed, reports of overdoses and idiosyncratic reactions shifted to the social and behavioral effects of long-term cocaine use. The ease with which experimenters evolved to regular users and the increasing instances of cocaine being linked with violence and paranoia gradually took hold in popular and medical thought.

In New York state an attempt was made in 1905 to shift the responsibility for cocaine's availability from the open market to medical control. Assemblyman Al Smith, later governor and 1928 Democratic presidential candidate, sponsored a law to that effect. The cost of cocaine on New York City streets, as revealed by newspaper and police accounts after the law's enactment, was typically twenty-five cents a packet of "deck." Although this may seem cheap, actually it was slightly higher than the average hourly industrial wage at that time, which was about twenty cents. In these packets, usually a glassine envelope, there were one to two grains (65 to 130 milligrams), or about a tenth of a gram. The going rate was roughly ten times that of the wholesale price, a ratio not unlike recent cocaine street prices, although in the last few years the street price has actually been lower in real value than that in 1910.

Several similar reports from the years before the Harrison Act of 1914 suggest that both the profit margin and the street price of cocaine were unaffected by the legal availability of cocaine from a physician. Perhaps the formality of medical consultation and the growing antagonism among physicians as well as the public to providing cocaine helped sustain the illicit market.

In 1910 President Taft sent to Congress a report that cocaine was the most serious drug problem America had ever faced. Four years later President Wilson signed into law the Harrison Act permitting cocaine only through prescriptions. It also forbade any trace of cocaine in over-the-counter remedies, the most severe restriction on any habit-forming drug to that date. Although the press continued to reveal Hollywood scandals and underworld cocaine practices during the 1920s, cocaine gradually declined as a problem. The laws probably hastened its decline, and certainly the overwhelming public fear reduced demand. By 1930, New York City's Mayor's Committee on Drug Addiction reported, "During the last 20 years cocaine as an addiction has ceased to be a problem."

Marijuana

The practice of smoking cannabis leaves arrived in the United States with Mexican immigrants, who had come north during the 1920s to work in agriculture, and extended to white and black jazz musicians. As the Great Depression of the 1930s settled over America, the immigrants became an unwelcome minority linked with violence and with growing and smoking marijuana. Western states pressured the federal government to control marijuana use. The first federal response was to urge adoption of a uniform state antinarcotic law. Then a new approach became feasible in 1937 when the Supreme Court upheld the National Firearms Act. This act prohibited the transfer of machine-guns between private citizens without purchase of a transfer tax stamp and the government would not issue the necessary stamp. It was prohibition through the taxing power of the federal government.

Within a month of the Supreme Court's decision, the Treasury Department was testifying before Congress for a bill to establish a marijuana transfer tax. The Marihuana Tax act was passed in 1937 (see excerpt included here) and until the Comprehensive Drug Abuse Act of 1970, marijuana was legally controlled through a transfer tax for which no stamps or licenses were available to private citizens.

Certainly some were smoking marijuana in the 1930s, but not until the 1960s did its use spread widely among youthful Americans. Around the time of the Marijuana Tax Act the federal government released dramatic and exaggerated portrayals of marijuana's effects. Scientific publications during the 1930s also described marijuana's dangers. Even Dr. Walter Bromberg, who thought that marijuana made only a small contribution to major crimes, nevertheless reported that his research indicated the drug to be "a primary stimulus to the impulsive life with direct expression in the motor field" (Bromberg's report is excerpted here). This was not marijuana's image in the 1960s, when it was said that marijuana use at the gigantic Woodstock gathering kept peace in contrast to what might have happened if alcohol had been the drug of choice. In the shift to drug toleration in the late 1960s and early 1970s investigators found it difficult to locate any problems with marijuana. The 1930s and 1940s had marked the nadir of drug toleration in the United States, and possibly the mood of both times affected professional perception of this controversial plant.

After the Harrison Act the severity of federal laws against dealing in and possession of opiates, cocaine, and marijuana gradually rose. As drug use declined, penalties increased until 1957, when the death penalty was introduced as an option by the federal government for anyone over eighteen providing heroin to anyone under eighteen (no one was ever actually executed under this possibility), and mandatory minimum prison sentences were extended to twenty years.

A youthful counterculture discovered marijuana in the 1960s and the substance grew in popularity until about 1978, when the favorable attitude toward it reached a peak. In 1972 the National Commission on Marihuana and Drug Abuse had recommended "decriminalization" of marijuana, that is, legal possession of a small amount for personal use (the commission's report is excerpted here), In 1977 the Carter administration formally advocated the decriminalization of marijuana for amounts up to an ounce. A Gallup poll on relaxation of laws against marijuana is instructive, paralleling the changes in attitude among high school students revealed by a survey conducted by the Institute of Social Research at the University of Michigan. The decline in favorable attitudes toward marijuana that began in the late 1970s continues and in the last few years we have seen penalties rise again against users and dealers and such impressive reversals as the recriminalization of marijuana by popular vote in Alaska.

Antidrug Strategies

In addition to the increase in penalties, two other strategies, silence and exaggeration, were implemented in the 1930s to keep drug use low and prevent a recurrence of the decades-long, frustrating, and fearful antidrug battle of the late nineteenth and early twentieth centuries. As the problem declined but while drug use was still noticeable, grade and high schools instituted educational programs against drugs. Then policies shifted amidst fears that talking about cocaine or heroin to young people, who now had less exposure to drugs, would arouse their curiosity. This concern led to a decline in information on drugs. For example, the Motion Picture Association of America in 1934 refused a seal of approval for any of its motion pictures that even showed narcotics, a prohibition that was enforced with one exception until *Man with the Golden Arm* was successfully exhibited in 1959 without a seal.

Associated with a decline in drug information was a second and apparently paradoxical strategy, exaggeration of the effects of drugs. In 1924 Richmond P. Hobson, a nationally prominent campaigner against drugs, declared that one ounce of heroin could addict two thousand persons, and in 1936 an article in the *American Journal of Nursing* warned that a marijuana user "will suddenly turn with murderous violence upon whomever is nearest to him. He will run amuck with knife, axe, gun, or anything else that is close at hand, and will kill or maim without any reason."[1] A goal of this well-meaning exaggeration was to describe drugs so repulsively that anyone reading or hearing of them would not be in the least tempted to experiment with the substances. One contributing factor to such a publicity campaign, especially regarding marijuana, was that the Depression permitted little money for any other course of action.

Severe penalties, silence, and, if silence was not possible, exaggeration became the basic strategies against drugs after the decline of their first wave of use. As much as we can sympathize with the goals of this policy, the effect was to create ignorance and false images that would present no real obstacle to a renewed enthusiasm for drugs in the 1960s. Then, enforcing draconian and mandatory penalties would have filled to overflowing all jails and prisons with just the users of marijuana. Exaggeration fell to the realities of drug use and led to a loss of credibility regarding any government pronouncement on drugs. Lack of information wiped away any awareness of the first epidemic, including the gradually obtained and hard-won public insight into the shortcomings of cocaine and the opiates. Public memory was a casualty of the antidrug strategies.

Conclusion

The first wave of drug use primarily involved opiates and cocaine. The nation's full experience with marijuana is now in process, since marijuana's prohibition in 1937 was not the result of any lengthy or broad experience with the plant. The popularity and growth in demand for opiates and cocaine derived from a simple factor: the effect on most people's physiology and emotions was enjoyable. Americans have recurrently hoped that the technology of drugs would maximize their potential. That opiates could relax and cocaine energize seemed wonderful opportunities for finetuning their efforts.

Two other factors allowed a long and substantial rise in consumption in America of the last century. The first is that casualties accumulate gradually. Not everyone taking cocaine or opiates becomes hooked on it; in the case of opiates, a few users have become addicted for a lifetime and have still been productive. Yet casualties have mounted as those who could not handle occasional use have succumbed to domination by drugs and drug seeking. These addicts become not only miserable themselves but also objects of fear and pity to their families and friends. Of course, such pathetic cases are legion today in our larger cities, but the percentage of those who try a substance and get into serious trouble is not 100 percent. For cocaine, the estimate varies from 3 percent to 20 percent and so it is a matter of time before cocaine is recognized as a likely danger to ourselves. Early in the cycle the explanation for casualties is that those who succumb have a physiological idiosyncrasy or foolish trait and so a personal disaster should be viewed as an exception to the rule. Another factor minimizing the sense of risk is our narcissistic belief in our own invulnerability—that general warnings do not include us. Such faith reigns in the years of greatest initiation to drug use, ages fifteen to twenty-five. Resistance to a drug that makes a user feel confident and exuberant, that we are assured causes few problems—and even those we feel we can avoid—takes many years to permeate a society as large and complex as the United States. The question is not why people take drugs, the interesting question is, why do we stop taking drugs?

We perceive risk differently as we begin to reject drugs. One can see a 3 percent risk from taking cocaine either as an assurance of 97 percent safety, or as one would react if told that 3 percent of New York–Washington shuttle flights crash. Noting the accumulation of personal disasters as we are exposed to drug problems at work, in our neighborhood, and within our families shifts our perception and gradually shakes our sense of invulnerability.

Cocaine causes the most dramatic change in estimating risk. From a grand image as the ideal tonic, cocaine's reputation degenerates into that of the most dangerous of drugs, linked in our minds with stereotypes of mad, violent behavior. Opiates have never fallen so far in esteem, nor have they ever been repressed to the extent of cocaine between 1930 and 1970.

We are experiencing the obverse of an earlier era when the technology of drug use promised an extension of our natural potential. Increasingly we see drug consumption as reducing what we could achieve on our own with healthy food and exercise. Our change of attitude about drugs is connected to our concern over air pollution, food adulteration, and fears for the health of the environment. Ours is an era not unlike that early in the twentieth century, when Americans made similar positive efforts and initiated an assault on habit-forming drugs.

Perhaps as we become more aware of the policies adopted in the decline phase of the earlier epidemic we will settle on more successful strategies to put drug use in perspective and to retain our public memory of the recent decades. Americans are the least likely to accept the inevitability of historical cycles. If, however, we do not appreciate the history of the past century, we may again become captive to the powerful emotions that led to draconian penalties, exaggeration, or silence.

NOTE

1. Victor Lewitus, "Marihuana," *American Journal of Nursing* 36 (July 1936): 678.

I. Opiates

Chapter 26

The Pleasures of Laudanum

Laudanum is a liquid preparation of opium. It was easily available in the eighteenth and nineteenth centuries, by prescription or otherwise. At times, it could be a kind of opium cocktail. One recipe called for dissolving crude opium in sherry and adding saffron and cloves to disguise the bitter taste of the drug. Included here is a selection from Thomas De Quincey's book in praise of opium, Confessions of an English Opium-Eater, *first published in 1822. This excerpt is from the last edition published during his lifetime. In spite of his own struggles with addiction, De Quincey makes opium taking sound exciting and glamorous. He was accused of enticing readers into opium use.*

CONFESSIONS OF AN ENGLISH OPIUM-EATER

Thomas De Quincey

It is very long since I first took opium; *so* long that, if it had been a trifling incident in my life, I might have forgotten its date: but cardinal events are not to be forgotten; and, from circumstances connected with it, I remember that this inauguration into the use of opium must be referred to the spring or is the autumn of 1804; during which seasons I was in London, having come thither for the first time since my entrance at Oxford. And this event arose in the following way:—From an early age I had been accustomed to wash my head in cold water at least once a-day. Being suddenly seized with toothache, I attributed it to some relaxation caused by a casual intermission of that practice, jumped out of bed, plunged my head into a basin of cold water, and with hair thus wetted went to sleep. The next morning, as I need hardly say, I awoke with excruciating rheumatic pains of the head and face, from which I had hardly any respite for about twenty days. On the twenty-first day I think it was, and on a Sunday, that I went out into the streets; rather to run away, if possible, from my torments, than with any distinct purpose of relief. By accident, I met a college acquaintance, who recommended opium. Opium! dread agent of unimaginable pleasure and pain! I had heard of it as I had heard of manna or of ambrosia, but no further. How unmeaning a sound was opium at that time! what solemn chords does it now strike upon my heart! what heart-quaking vibrations of sad and happy remembrances! Reverting for a moment to these, I feel a mystic importance attached to the minutest circumstances connected with the place, and the time, and the man (if man he was), that first laid open to me the paradise of opium-eaters. It was a Sunday afternoon, wet and cheerless; and a duller spectacle this earth of ours has not to show than a rainy Sunday in London. My road homewards lay through Oxford Street; and near "the *stately* Pantheon" (as Mr. Wordsworth has obligingly called it) I saw a druggist's shop. The druggist (unconscious minister of celestial pleasures), as if in sympathy with the rainy Sunday, looked dull and stupid, just as any mortal druggist might be expected to look on a rainy London Sunday; and, when I asked for the tincture of opium, he gave it to me as any other man might do; and, furthermore, out of my shilling returned to me what seemed to be real copper halfpence, taken out of a real wooden drawer. Nevertheless, and nothwithstanding all such indications of humanity, he has ever since figured in my mind as a beatific vision of an immortal druggist, sent down to earth on a special mission to myself. And it confirms me in this way of considering him that, when I next came up to London, I sought him near the stately Pantheon, and found him not; and thus to me, who knew not his name (if, indeed, he had one), he seemed rather to have vanished from Oxford Street than to have fitted into any other locality, or (which some abominable man suggested) to have absconded from the rent. The reader may choose to think of him as, possibly, no more than a sublunary druggist; it may be so, but my faith is better. I believe him to have evanesced. So unwillingly would I connect any mortal remembrances with that hour, and place, and creature that first brought me acquainted with the celestial drug. . . .

First, then, it is not so much affirmed as taken for granted by all who ever mention opium, formally or incidentally, that it does or can produce intoxication. Now, reader, assure yourself, *meo periculo*, that no quantity of opium ever did, or could, intoxicate. As to the tincture of opium (commonly called laudanum), *that* might certainly intoxicate, if a man could bear to take enough of it; but why? Because it contains so much proof spirits of wine, and not because it contains so much opium. But crude opium, I affirm peremptorily, is incapable of producing any state of body at all resembling that which is produced by alcohol; and not in *degree* only incapable, but even in *kind*; it is not in the quantity of its effects merely, but in the quality, that it differs altogether. The pleasure given by wine is always rapidly mounting, and tending to a crisis, after which as rapidly it declines; that from opium, when once generated, is stationary for eight or ten hours: the first, to borrow a technical distinction from medicine, is a case of acute, the second of chronic, pleasure; the one is a flickering flame, the other a steady and equable glow. But the main distinction lies in this—that, whereas wine disorders the mental faculties, opium, on the contrary (if taken in a proper manner), introduces amongst them the most exquisite order, legislation, and harmony. Wine robs a man of his self-possession; opium sustains and reinforces it. Wine unsettles the judgment, and gives a preternatural brightness and a vivid exaltation to the contempts and the admirations, to the loves and the hatreds, of the drinker; opium, on the contrary, communicates serenity and equipoise to all the faculties, active or passive; and, with respect to the temper and moral feelings in general, it gives simply that sort of vital warmth which is approved by the judgment, and which would probably always accompany a bodily constitution of primeval or antediluvian health. Thus, for instance, opium, like wine, gives an expansion to the heart and the benevolent affections; but, then, with this remarkable difference, that, in the sudden development of kindheartedness which accompanies inebriation, there is always more or less of a maudlin and a transitory character, which exposes it to the contempt of the bystander. Men shake hands, swear eternal friendship, and shed tears—no mortal knows why; and the animal nature is clearly uppermost. But the expansion of the benigner feelings incident to opium is no febrile access, no fugitive paroxysm; it is a healthy restoration to that state which the mind would naturally recover upon the removal of any deep-seated irritation from pain that had disturbed and quarrelled with the impulses of a heart originally just and good. True it is that even wine up to a certain point, and with certain men, rather tends to exalt and to steady the intellect; I myself, who have never been a great wine-drinker, used to find that half-a-dozen glasses of wine advantageously affected the faculties, brightened and intensified the consciousness, and gave to the mind a feeling of being "ponderibus librata suis"; and certainly it is most absurdly said, in popular language, of any man, that he is *disguised* in liquor; for, on the contrary, most men are disguised by sobriety, and exceedingly disguised; and it is when they are drinking that men display themselves in their true complexion of character; which surely is not disguising themselves. But still, wine constantly leads a man to the brink of absurdity and extravagance; and, beyond a certain point, it is sure to volatilise and to disperse the intellectual energies; whereas opium always seems to compose what had been agitated, and to concentrate what had been distracted. In short, to sum up all in one word, a man who is inebriated, or tending to inebriation, is, and feels that he is, in a condition which calls up into supremacy the merely human, too often the brutal, part of his nature; but the opium-eater (I speak of him simply *as* such, and assume that he is in a normal state of health) feels that the diviner part of his nature is paramount—that is, the moral affections are in a state of cloudless serenity, and high over all the great light of the majestic intellect.

Chapter 27

Morphine Is Isolated

The credit for isolating morphine from crude opium is generally given to Friedrich Wilhelm Sertürner (1783–1841), a German pharmacist. He found that crude opium contained an alkaloid that caused the actions of opium with which the medical profession was familiar. Although the discovery seems to have taken place in 1804, it was not until 1817 that he was given credit by the scientific community. His work encouraged further analyses of plant alkaloids that led to useful and powerful drugs. By 1826 the Merck Company of Darmstadt was producing morphine in substantial qualities. In the 1830s pharmaceutical manufacturers in Philadelphia became a major source for Americans. Some writers state that Sertürner himself became addicted to morphine. Although this allegation has not been substantiated, it is known that he led an erratic life characterized by boasting and ostentatious behavior.

FRIEDRICH WILHELM SERTÜRNER
AND THE DISCOVERY OF MORPHINE

Rudolf Schmitz

The rather contrived dispute as to whether Sertürner was successful in discovering morphine in 1803, 1804 or 1805 is, historically speaking, meaningless. If one considers the chronological possibilities, the probable date of discovery is 1804. Sertürner delivered the first short note about his discovery, "Säure im Opium," to the publisher of the *Journal der Pharmacie*, the Erfurt professor and pharmacist, J. B. Trommsdorff (1770–1837), who published it in 1805. This publication as well as the following one on the "Darstellung der reinen Mohnsäure (Opiumsäure)," which appeared in the same journal in the same year, remained unnoticed. Six years later he tried again to draw attention to his work, this time under the title, "Ueber das Opium und dessen krystallisirbare Substanz," but again without success. The breakthrough finally came with the publication. "Ueber das Morphium, eine neue salzfähige Grundlage, und die Mekonsäure als Hauptbestandtheil des Opiums," which appeared in Ludwig Wilhelm Gilbert's (1769–1824) *Annalen der Physik* in Leipzig in 1817. This publication attracted the attention of the French physician, Joseph Louis Gay-Lussac (1778–1850), who, realizing its fundamental importance, had his student Pierre Jean Robiquet (1780–

1840) rework it. The dispute about the priority of the discovery of morphine between Sertürner and the French pharmacist Charles Louis Derosne (1780–1846), who, in 1803, had isolated a narcotic morphine mixture that was being distributed as "Sel de Derosne," was settled when Sertürner received the Montyon Prize of the Institut de France for recognizing the alkaline nature of morphine.

Chapter 28

The Invention of the Hypodermic Syringe

The introduction of the hypodermic syringe is credited to Dr. Alexander Wood, who, first, in 1855 used a syringe constructed by a Mr. Ferguson and later improved on that original design. Invention of the hypodermic syringe depended on a combination of earlier advances. Hollow tubes, such as goose quills, long had been available. The trick was to create a reliable, reusable syringe, making it practical to inject into the tissues or to place the needle into a vein or artery.

Securing a smooth fit between the plunger and the barrel of the syringe proved difficult for early experimenters. Another key step was successful graduation of the syringe, which enabled physicians to introduce measured amounts of drugs into the body, advancing progress toward scientific therapy. Experimenters also debated whether syringes should be manufactured from metal, which was strong but opaque, or from transparent but fragile glass.

Throughout the latter part of the nineteenth century, the syringe continued to evolve, until gradually it settled into a widely agreed-upon shape and construction. The major innovation in more recent times is reliance in the developed countries on plastic syringes intended for onetime use. Acceptance of this practice eliminated the need to sharpen needles as they became dull with use.

A CRITICAL STUDY OF THE ORIGINS AND EARLY DEVELOPMENT OF HYPODERMIC MEDICATION

Norman Howard-Jones

1. Introduction

The effects of the bites of venomous snakes and insects pointed clearly to the possibility of the introduction of drugs through punctures in the skin. In primitive societies, the application for therapeutic purposes of plant and animal products through cutaneous incisions is practiced, and the use of poisoned arrows may be regarded as a crude precursor of hypodermic and intramuscular medication. Nevertheless, it was not until the nineteenth century that hypodermic medication was initiated, although percutaneous medication had been empirically employed since ancient times in the form of baths, ointments, and cataplasms. The hypodermic was in fact the last of the commonly employed routes to be adopted: the inhalation of medicated vapors; rectal, intraurethral, intrauterine, and intravenous injections; and the injection treatment of hydrocele all preceded hypodermic medication. Intravenous medication had been practiced intermittently, both in animals and in man, since the seventeenth century.

It was not until just before the beginning of the nineteenth century that methodical attempts were made to employ the skin as a medium for the absorption of medicaments. Before 1800, Brera systematically employed percutaneous administration of drugs by inunction, to which he gave the name "anatripsology." Chrestien developed the technique under the name *méthode iatroleptique*, to which the term *cipnoische Medizin* was also applied.

In 1828 Lembert published a monograph of 124 pages on the *méthode endermique*, which had previously been described by Lesieur. This technique consisted of the application of a vesicant to remove the epidermis, after which the drug, usually one of the recently isolated alkaloids, was applied to the denuded cutis as a powder, solution, or ointment. The method won considerable popularity and was adopted by Trousseau among others. Eulenburg suggested that it should properly be described as the emplastro-endermic (*emplastro-endermatische*) method.

In 1809, Magendie reported the lethal effects in dogs of a Javanese arrow-poison, of which the active principle was later found to be strychnine. Magendie administered the poison by applying it to the extremity of a wooden barb, which was thrust into the dog's buttock. In spite of the interest aroused by these and subsequent experiments demonstrating the absorption of poisons via the subcutaneous and muscular tissues, it was not until nearly thirty years later that drugs were administered therapeutically by mechanical penetration of the skin.

It may be noted in passing that Sir Robert Christison in 1831 suggested that whales might be killed by fastening a phial of prussic acid to a harpoon "in such a way that the phial should break when a strain was put upon the harpoon after entering the body of the animal." This method would appear to have been used, although precise information on the results is lacking . . .

3. Subcutaneous Administration of Fluids

a. Rynd's Retractible Trocar. In 1845 a new treatment was described by Rynd, of the Meath Hospital and County Infirmary, Dublin. A woman of 59, who from Rynd's description appears to have been suffering from trigeminal neuralgia, was admitted to the hospital on May 1844.

> On the 3rd of June a solution of fifteen grains of acetate of morphia, dissolved in one drachm of creosote, was introduced to the supra-orbital nerve, and along the course of the temporal, malar, and buccal nerves, by four punctures of an instrument made for the purpose.

Rynd here gives no description of the instrument used. He claims the relief was practically instantaneous, and that the patient slept better that night than she had done for months. The operation was repeated one week later, and after a few weeks more in hospital the patient was discharged well and did not return.

In a second case, that of a man of 28 with symptoms typical of sciatica, "fluid was introduced" (10 grains of morphine acetate in 1 drachm of creosote) in two sites along the course of the sciatic nerve. This was repeated after 3 days, and the patient was discharged "well" 13 days after the second injection.

It was not until 1861, by which time the use of the hypodermic syringe was well known, that Rynd published a description of his instrument. It was not a syringe, but an elaborate trocar and cannula. Pressure on a catch caused retraction of the trocar, and this permitted descent of the fluid which had been poured into the lumen of the cannula, whence it reached the tissues by gravity. Rynd's own description of his instrument follows:

> The canula (A) screws on the instrument at (B); and when the button (C), which is connected to the needle (F), and acted on by a spring, is pushed up, the small catch (D) retains it in its place. The point of the needle then projects a little beyond the canula. The fluid to be applied is now to be introduced through the hole (E), either from a common writing-pen or the spoon-shaped extremity of a silver director; a small puncture through the skin is to be made with a lancet, or the point of the instrument itself is to be pressed through the skin, and on to the depth required; light pressure now made on the handle raises the catch (D), the needle is released, and springs backwards, leaving the canula empty, and allowing the fluid to descend.

Rynd claims:

> The subcutaneous introduction of fluids, for the relief of neuralgia, was first practised in this country by me, in the Meath Hospital, in the month of May, 1844.

b. Alexander Wood's "New Method of Treating Neuralgia." In 1855 Dr. Alexander Wood of Edinburgh published the first account of the subcutaneous injection of solutions of drugs for therapeutic purposes. He was apparently unaware of Rynd's earlier publication, which in any case gave no details of the procedure adopted. Wood opens his paper by reference to improvements in the treatment of neuralgic affections consequent on Valleix's observation that sensitive points could be identified along the course of affected nerves, and on Valleix's advocacy of blistering over such points and, in some cases, the endermic applications of morphine (emplastro-endermic method). Wood says that he has "almost invariably" used a morphine-containing paste to dress the blistered surface, but that it has often occurred to him that the direct application of a narcotic to the nerve or its immediate neighborhood might be more efficacious. Describing how he came to use a syringe subcutaneously, he tells us that he had made several attempts

> to introduce morphia directly by means of puncture needles and otherwise, but without success. Having occasion, however, about the end of 1853, to endeavor to remove a naevus by injection with the acid solution of perchloride of iron, I pro-

cured one of the elegant little syringes constructed for the purpose by Mr. Ferguson of Giltspur Street, London. While using this instrument for the naevus, it occurred to me that it might supply the means of bringing some narcotic to bear more directly than I had hitherto been able to accomplish on the affected nerve in neuralgia. I resolved to make the attempt, and did not long lack the opportunity.

Wood then describes how an elderly spinster, suffering from "cervico-brachial neuralgia," had been unable to sleep, the usual remedies, with the exception of opium, for which she had an idiosyncrasy, having failed.

> Under these circumstances, I resolved to put into practice the plan which I had so long revolved in my mind. Accordingly, on November 28th, I visited her at 10 p.m. to give the opiate the benefit of the night. Having ascertained that the most tender spot was the post clavicular point of Valleix, I inserted the syringe within the angle formed by the clavicle and acromion, and injected twenty drops of a solution of muriate of morphia, of a strength about double that of the official preparation.

Pereira gives the Morphiae Muriatis Solutio of the Edinburgh Pharmacopoeia as containing I grain of morphine hydrochloride in about 106 minims of solution. Taking a drop as equivalent to a minim, twenty drops of the solution used by Wood would therefore contain about $\frac{2}{5}$ grain of morphine. Ten minutes after receiving this dose, the old lady complained of giddiness and confusion of ideas, and in ½ hour her pain had subsided. Wood visited her again on the following morning at about 11.00 a.m., and he was

> a little annoyed to find that she had never wakened; the breathing was also somewhat deep, and she was roused with difficulty. Under the use of somewhat energetic stimuli, however, these symptoms disappeared, and from that time to this the neuralgia has not returned.

Wood then describes eight further successful cases, and adds particulars of two others treated by a Dr. Thomas Wright, F.R.C.P. In all except Wood's first case, "Battley's sedative solution" was injected.

Towards the end of his paper, Wood refers to Lafargue's first technique:

> Inoculation . . . has been proposed by M. Lafargue St Emilion [sic], to be extended so as to secure the application of remedies. This method was brought before the Westminster Medical Society in February 1837, by Dr. Bureaud, but from the account given in the "Lancet" he does not seem to have been very successful, as only a slight local effect was produced.

Wood then refers to the report made in 1836 by Martin-Solon who, he asserts,

> comes to the somewhat damaging conclusion that the effect produced was very much the same, whatever agent was inoculated, even when the experiments were made with agents as dissimilar as belladonna, strychnine, the gastric juice, chyme.

This is a most unfair comment, as Martin-Solon was in this context referring to the non-specificity of the cutaneous reaction which was suggested by Lafargue as a test for the presence of opiates. Wood reveals that he has engaged in experiments on "an improved apparatus" designed to cause less injury to the tissues.

The writer has been unable to trace an illustration of the Ferguson syringe, but in the museum of the Royal College of Surgeons of Edinburgh there is a broken glass syringe which is said to have been used by Wood. This syringe is not graduated, as was the improved model that Wood describes in 1858, and, assuming its authenticity, it seems reasonable to regard it as an example of the original Ferguson syringe. A description and photograph of the syringe are given by Comrie.

The barrel, piston-rod, and piston are of glass. Cotton-wool has been wrapped round the piston. The metal parts are tarnished, but are almost certainly of silver. The conical metallic extremity terminates in a male screw, upon which the hollow needle was fixed. Wood's reference to the improvements upon which he is experimenting indicates that the Ferguson syringe was not without defects and, particularly, that it traumatized the tissues.

Gaujot says that the Fergusson [*sic*] syringe is not sufficiently accurate, owing to the large size of the *canule*. Nevertheless, he pays tribute to Ferguson for having introduced "le principe ingénieux de la canule-trocart," the hollow needle with a sharpened extremity which could penetrate the skin while screwed on to the syringe.

Jousset describes the Fergusson [*sic*] syringe as having a hollow steel needle with a very sharp fluted extremity which, however, penetrated the skin with difficulty and caused pain. He also criticizes it on the grounds that it is badly made and that the barrel is not graduated. Currie says of the Fergusson [*sic*] syringe that the needle "being of too large calibre, in penetrating the tissues tears them, and occasions thereby severe pain."

In a second paper published on 28 August 1858, Wood gives the following description of the syringe which subsequently became known by his name:

> The instrument is of the simplest construction, and is a modification of Mr. Ferguson's already alluded to. It consists of a small glass syringe graduated like a drop measure, and to this is attached a small needle, hollow, and having an aperture near to the point like the sting of a wasp.

From this description, it is clear that Wood's modifications of the Ferguson syringe consisted of improvements to the cutting extremity of the needle and the addition of graduation to the barrel. His reference to a "small needle" may perhaps indicate that he reduced the bore of the needle, although this is not specifically mentioned. In the following week (4 September), Wood published a letter in which he states, in answer to a number of inquiries, that "the instrument" may be purchased from Mr. Young of Edinburgh, and refers his inquirers to an advertisement in the same journal.

In his paper of 1858, Wood is able to say "In Edinburgh, I may mention, the use of this instrument has become nearly universal. . . ."

It is remarkable that no attention appears to have been paid to Wood's first paper, either in England or on the Continent. As will be seen later, it was his second paper, published 3 years later in the *British Medical Journal*, that resulted in the extension of the method beyond the borders of Scotland.

Comparison of the 1855 and 1858 papers shows the development of a desire to emphasize the originality of his technique. Whereas, in the earlier paper, Wood pays tribute to the influence of Valleix in directing his mind towards the invention, he is at some pains to disown his debt in the later paper. Valleix's method of blistering sensitive points along the course of the affected nerve was

> not nearly so successful as he led me to expect. I then varied the application very much. I raised the blister, removed the cuticle, and applied morphia (both in a liquid form and as a powder in ointments) on the surface, and found contrary to the experience of Valleix, that the patient derived decided benefit from it.

Three years before, he had referred to the "immense improvement . . . effected in our treatment of neuralgic affections" by Valleix's observations, and by his "plan of treatment, which, as an external remedy I have largely employed ever since my attention was first directed to his work in 1842." . . .

8. The Belated Recognition of Addiction to Hypodermically-Administered Morphine

It is improbable that the cruder methods of endermic and hypodermic administration of morphine were ever practiced with sufficient regularity or frequency to produce addiction. With the coming of hypodermic injection, however, morphine was injected with reckless frequency, and apparently without a thought of the possibility of addiction. Three years after he had introduced hypodermic injection, Wood casually speaks of having given over 100 injections to a female patient with neuralgia. When hypodermic injection was universally adopted, physicians and patients alike unwittingly became slaves to morphine. Leiter describes patients as well as doctors as having their own hypodermic syringes. In an editorial comment on a publication by Prof. Nussbaum of Munich, in which he described the accidental injection of morphine into a vein, with disagreeable consequences, the *Medical Times & Gazette* writes in 1865:

> Suffering from neuralgia, he had injected morphia under his own skin more than 2000 times—sometimes to the extent of five grains of morphia in twenty-four hours.

The large number of injections, and the high dosage employed, are not considered worthy of comment, and there is no reference to addiction.

Hunter recommended morphine injection as a "nerve tonic in cases of great nervous exhaustion, or of irritability or great mental depression."

The committee on hypodermic injection of the Royal Medical and Chirurgical Society reported in 1867 that:

> To confirmed opium-eaters this method has been found of much service, smaller doses than those previously taken by mouth being requisite.

The typical attitude of a patient to "the puncture" may be well imagined by reference to the words which Lafitte in 1875, illustrating only the popularity of morphine injections, says are heard on all sides:

> Docteur, docteur, vite une injection, je souffre comme une possédée, j'ai ma névralgie, etc.

It was from Thomas Clifford Allbutt that the first considered warning of the dangers of morphinism came in 1870:

> Among the numerous essays and records concerning the hypodermic use of morphia which have been published of late, both at home and abroad, I cannot call to mind one in which its possible dangers have been considered; . . . while my fears were indefinite, I felt the time had not come for me to speak. Now my experience has been greater, I have a large number of cases before me, and yet the uncomfortable fear of mischief is growing rather than diminishing.

Is it not true, he asks,

> that we are now often consulted by patients who have been injecting themselves daily or more than daily during long periods of time, for neuralgias which seem, nevertheless, as far from cure as they were at the outset?

Allbutt then refers to nine patients suffering from "various forms of neuralgia" in whom

> the hypodermic use of morphia has been constantly practised for periods varying from nine months to three years. . . .
>   They seem as far from cure as they ever were, they all find relief in the incessant use of the syringe, and they all declare that without the syringe life would be insupportable.

In a postscript to his paper, Allbutt quotes a relevant passage from a German writer, Niemeyer, to which his attention had been drawn by Dr. Fothergill of Leeds, and which refers to the development of an irresistible need for injections, which is often described as a sort of "hangover" (*Katzenjammer*).

Allbutt's point of view was, however, by no means popular, although there must have been an abundance of evidence to support the fears that he expressed. Doubtless many physicians did not care to admit their own addiction. Moreover, the very urgency of their patients' demands for morphine, added to the fact that oft-repeated injections must have been a substantial source of income, may have contributed to the tendency to rationalize or ignore the disagreeable truth. Oliver followed Allbutt with an admission that addiction occurred, but claimed rather unconvincingly that it was justifiable to "set up a morphia-habit, and then get safely over this habit by firmly withholding the morphia. . . ." A more question-begging solution can scarcely be imagined! Anstie followed Oliver by an even more unrealistic approach. He admits that

> the subcutaneous injection of morphia has become a comparatively common household remedy among certain classes of society for some years past. More especially among the very numerous persons, chiefly women, who suffer either from neuralgia

of greater or less severity, or even from attacks of nervous depression and sleeplessness without positive pain, it has become a too common practice to inject themselves, or to get injected by their servants, whenever they feel symptoms of their
besetting trouble.

While disagreeing with self-injection, Anstie claims that small and "purely stimulant doses of morphia" are "perfectly legitimate" in elderly patients with
chronic diseases, such as sciatica. He defines such doses as of $\frac{1}{12}$th to $\frac{1}{4}$ grain,
with which there is "no vestige of *narcotic* action"!

As late as 1880, Eulenburg speaks blandly of having given over 1200 injections
of morphine to a patient with neuralgic pains. In another context he refers to the
increasing incidence of "Morphiumsucht," or morphiophilia, which, he says, has
to a certain extent discredited morphine injection in the eyes both of the medical
profession and the public. However, his admission of the existence of morphine
addiction is a grudging one, and he is inclined to regard it as a consequence of
the abuse of hypodermic injection by patients. He points out, in defence of the
administration of morphine by injection, that there are extensive abuses of drugs
when they are taken by the more usual method of oral ingestion. Apart from the
obvious example of opiophagy, he says, it is necessary to recall only the considerable consumption of chloral in England and America, and the arsenic-eaters of
Steiermark.

Enough has been said to show that the dangers inherent in morphine injection
were not anticipated, and were for several years quite unrecognized. Even when
morphine addiction had developed on a wide scale, the medical profession was
extraordinarily slow to admit its significance, and sought refuge from unwelcome
truths in sophistry and rationalizations. . . .

13. Conclusions

The following conclusions may be drawn from this study. They refer only to
events which were steps in the continuous evolution of hypodermic medication,
and do not take into account collateral developments, such as the therapeutic
injection of solutions into abscess-cavities.

1. *Lafargue* systematically employed hypodermic medication, first by the "in-
oculation" of solid drugs as a paste, then by the subcutaneous implantation of
pellets—a technique which was revived in 1937. Lafargue's intention was to
exert a local action upon the peripheral nerves, although he recognized that
absorption and systemic action occurred.

2. *Rynd* practiced the hypodermic administration of a solution of morphine,
with the intention of exerting a local action upon the peripheral nerves. He
published no observations on systemic effects. Rynd did not employ a syringe,
and his procedure was a hypodermic infusion.

3. *Wood* devised the technique of hypodermic injection in 1853 and introduced
it as a therapeutic procedure. His intention was to secure a local analgesic action

on peripheral nerves, and although he clearly recognized the occurrence of systemic effects, he failed to appreciate their significance.

4. *Hunter* adopted Wood's technique of local injection. The occurrence of infection at the site of injection in his first two patients led him to make remote injections. He recognized that the remote injections were as effective as the local injections, and correctly argued that the subcutaneous route was effective by reason of systemic absorption. Hunter introduced the word "hypodermic" to distinguish his use of subcutaneous injection as a mode of systemic administration from Wood's use of the same technique for its supposed local action.

5. It was at first assumed that the hypodermic injection of morphine would be free from the habit-forming property of orally-ingested opiates. Recognition of addiction to hypodermically-administered morphine was reluctant and belated, and there was for some years a widespread abuse of morphine injection.

6. The danger of sepsis as a result of hypodermic injection was generally discounted, and when sepsis occurred it was commonly attributed to multiple injections at the same site or to the use of irritating solvents.

7. Several retrospective claims to priority of hypodermic injection have been considered, but none had a direct bearing on the evolution of hypodermic medication. . . .

Chapter 29

Narcotic Use in the Civil War

*The Civil War is commonly cited as the starting point of the American drug problem.
The accepted argument is that physicians, employing the new technology of the hypodermic syringe, gave so many injections of morphine to injured and ill soldiers that returning troops brought addiction home with them. The definitive study of the war's impact
on drug use is yet to be written, but the following passage from the official Civil War
medical history suggests that hypodermic syringes came into use very late in the conflict,
if at all.*

The Medical and Surgical History of the Civil War

Opium, which was used so frequently in the form of Dover's powder in the early
stages to control fever and allay cerebral excitement, and at a later date with
astringents to restrain diarrhœa, was also largely used when an aggravation of
the abdominal pain suggested a possibility of peritoneal inflammation. The frequent occurrence, in the course of the fever, of therapeutic indications which
could be best fulfilled by means of this drug rendered it an important agent. In
fact, it may be said of some hospitals that opium and brandy constituted the
essentials of treatment. In cases 13 and 14 of the *post-mortem* series, from the
Ladies' Home hospital, New York, the treatment is said to have been effected in
the one case by laudanum, brandy, beef-extract and milk, and in the other by
anodynes, alcoholic stimulants and sustaining diet. Cases 19, 20, 82 and 226 of
the same series may be noted as illustrations of the use of opium to alleviate the
intense pain of peritoneal inflammation; in 50, the drug was given by enema on
account of gastric irritability. The hypodermic syringe had not yet found its way
into the hands of our officers.[1]

NOTE

1. It was not until after the close of the war that hypodermatic medication began to be
discussed in our medical journals. Ruppaner's treaties on *Hypodermic Injections* was not
published until 1865, although in 1860, in the *Boston Medical and Surgical Journal*, its author

called the attention of the profession to the value of the syringe in the treatment of neuralgia. BARTHOLOW, in his *Manual of Hypodermic Medication*, Philadelphia, 1869, ascribes the new art to the discovery of the practicability and utility of introducing medicines under the skin for the relief of local pain, by ALEXANDER WOOD of Edinburgh in 1843, and the demonstration by Mr. CHARLES HUNTER of London in 1859 of the important fact that the application of the injection to the painful points, as contended for by Wood, was really unnecessary, as equally good effects followed the introduction of the injection into a distant part. During the war Mr. HUNTER was engaged in extending the use of the hypodermic method from Edinburgh and Dublin, where it was first employed. It was tried and reported upon favorably by COUNTY of Montpeiller, BÉHEIR of Paris, SCANZONI of Wurtzburg, OPPOLZEE of Vienna, GRAETE of Berlin and many others who established its use in Europe; and very shortly afterwards the hypodermic syringe became naturalized in this country.

Chapter 30

Upsurge in Opium Use

In addition to the official medical accounts, which raise doubt about the widespread use of hypodermic syringes during the Civil War, a second source of questions about the role of that war in starting a drug epidemic is this study of opium use in Massachusetts published in 1877 by the state board of health. Although the study reports significantly increased use of opium and opiates, neither the invention of the syringe nor the addiction of returning veterans is considered a significant factor in the rise of drug use. The two main factors cited are the medical route to opiates, whether by prescription or in the increasing numbers of patent remedies, and the alcohol temperance movement, which, the board speculates, leads former drinkers to search for alternative "stimulants."

The Use and Abuse of Opium

F. E. Oliver

The well-attested fact of the increased and increasing consumption of opium in the United States, during the past few years, has suggested the inquiry whether, and to what extent, the so-called opium habit can be traced among our own inhabitants, and to what causes it may fairly be attributed. If it be true that this practice, so long an endemic in Eastern and Southern Asia, has appeared among us, and, according to a recent and careful observer, is rapidly gaining ground "in a ratio very considerably increasing as every successive year arrives," it is not too soon to look about us and see how far it has intruded upon our soil, that we may be the better prepared to meet, if need be, so insidious a foe. It is obvious, in an investigation of this nature, with the limited opportunity at command, that to reach more than an approximate result would be difficult, if not impossible. Many important sources of information are carefully guarded, and the habit is so unobtrusive as often to pass unnoticed by the casual observer, the professional eye alone detecting the secret in the haggard countenance, or in some maniacal propensity characteristic of the opium eater. It will not be surprising, therefore, if the statistics thus far obtained, although suggestive, seem meagre, and in many respects unsatisfactory. The following are the questions addressed to the physicians throughout the State:—1st. Are preparations of opium used by the people except for the relief of pain? 2d. We would like to know whether the injurious use of opium has increased of late years, and, if so, the causes of such increase? Of the one hundred and twenty-five physicians from whom replies have been received, forty report, in answer to the first question, that they know of no case of opium eating. The remaining eight-five state that opium is used to a greater or less extent in their respective circuits. In many of the smaller towns where the habit exists, the number of those addicted to it is reported as nearly as could be ascertained. In the returns from others, the terms "few," "many" and "several" are alone given, and in still others the number is altogether omitted. From such uncertain data, it would, of course, be impossible to arrive at anything like an accurate computation. The number in the towns where it is given varies from one to twelve, the latter being the largest reported in any one. In the larger towns,—as Boston, Charlestown, Worcester and New Bedford,—the number is necessarily much larger. On inquiry among the druggists of Boston, we learn that their experience is various, there being those who have little call for the drug, and who make it a rule never to sell it without a written prescription; while others have many regular customers. One druggist states that, although he never sells it without a physician's order, he has, on an average, five or six applications for it daily, in some one of its forms. Two other prominent druggists have each six habitual purchasers. Several report one or two. Much seems to depend on locality. In the more public streets, and in parts of the city where those addicted to the habit mostly reside, the sales are much larger. In Worcester, one druggist reports that "opium is used to an alarming extent in that community." In Charlestown, inquiry was made at all the eighteen druggists' shops. Of these, "eleven have at present no regular customers; one never sells, except on prescription; the remaining six report sales to regular purchasers of opium, as follows:—each shop has an average of two, the largest number to any one being four."

In Chicopee, the druggists report that they have a great many regular customers. Many others in various parts of the State speak of the habit as quite prevalent. A prominent druggist of Boston states that "the sales of opium preparations to the country trade is out of all proportion to those of other drugs." From these statements the inference is unavoidable that the opium habit is more or less prevalent in many parts of the State; and, although it may be impossible to estimate it, the number addicted to the drug must be very considerable. The number of opium eaters in the United States, says a late anonymous writer, has been computed, from the testimony of druggists in all parts of the country, as well as from other sources, to be not less than from eighty to one hundred thousand. How far Massachusetts contributes toward her numerical quota, must, for the present, be a matter of conjecture. The daily amounts of opium reported as taken vary with the habit and idiosyncrasy of the taker. Few even approach De Quincey, whose daily laudanum potations amounted to more than half a pint, equivalent to about three hundred and twenty grains of the gum. In the town of Athol, of twelve opium eaters reported, "one person takes an ounce of laudanum daily; another, nine ounces weekly; another, two ounces monthly; two take one drachm of sulphate of morphia each, weekly; two take half that quantity in the same time; and two take a drachm of this salt each, monthly; one takes one ounce of opium, and one twice this quantity every month." In Charlestown, the largest monthly sale of the sulphate of morphia is ten drachms; the average to each of five is eight drachms monthly; of laudanum, two persons are reported who each buy thirty ounces per month; one buys eight ounces of crude opium in the same time; one uses about one ounce of opium monthly; and two others two ounces each. In Leyden, one person is reported who takes one drachm of the sulphate of morphia weekly. In Shrewsbury, "of seven habitual opium eaters, one drachm of the sulphate of morphia, weekly, is the largest amount used."

In Shirley, one drachm of the sulphate of morphia is taken, by the one opium eater reported, in three weeks. In Swampscott, one person is reported who takes two ounces of laudanum daily. In Boston, one druggist sells to a customer one ounce of laudanum daily,—two ounces being ordered on Saturday. It will be noted that the largest quantity of crude opium taken was eight ounces per month, or about one hundred and twenty-eight grains daily. The largest reported daily amount of laudanum was one ounce. The largest monthly sale of the sulphate of morphia was ten drachms, at the rate of one-third of a drachm daily, and equivalent to not far from one hundred grains of the gum. A Boston druggist informs us that not long since, an habitual customer bought a drachm of the sulphate of morphia, one-half of which he took on the spot, and, on the following day, having disposed of the remainder, called for a draught containing an ounce and a half each of laudanum and brandy. No apparent effect followed the dose referred to. The question as to the increase "in the injurious use of opium," and the causes of such increase, where this exists, seems to have received but partial attention. Of the eighty-five correspondents above mentioned, thirty-nine make no allusion to this inquiry. Twelve are of the opinion that the habit is decidedly on the increase, twenty-eight, that it is not increasing, and six, that it is diminishing, in their respective districts. These opinions, not always based upon very accurate observation, must be taken for what they are worth. The more general opinion among the best informed druggists throughout the State is that the habit is increasing. The following extract from a communication received from one of the State Assayers, Mr. S. Dana Hayes, will be found of especial interest in this connection:—"In reply to your inquiries, it is my opinion that the consumption of opium in Massachusetts and New England is increasing more rapidly in proportion than the population. There are so many channels through which the drug may be brought into the State, that I suppose it would be almost impossible to determine how much foreign opium is used here; but it may easily be shown that the home production increases every year. Opium has been recently made from white poppies, cultivated for the purpose, in Vermont, New Hampshire and Connecticut, the annual production being estimated by hundreds of pounds, and this has generally been absorbed in the communities where it is made. It has also been brought here from Florida and Louisiana, while comparatively large quantities are regularly sent east from California and Arizona, where its cultivation is becoming an important branch of industry, ten acres of poppies being said to yield, in Arizona, twelve hundred pounds of opium. This domestic opium is often improperly manufactured in the form of expressed juice from the whole poppy plant, including the stems, leaves and flowers, instead of the exuded sap obtained by scarifying the capsules of the plant. It is generally deficient in morphia, and is sold in balls of sticky paste, covered with green leaves, or as a semi-fluid, like thick-boiled molasses, in boxes. That which is not used where it is produced, including the shipments from California and the West, together with inferior and damaged parcels of foreign opium received and condemned at this port, is sent to Philadelphia, where it is converted into morphia and its salts, and is thus distributed through the country. "Opium and morphia are not only freely used in patent and commercial medicines, but they have now become common ingredients in many family remedies, which were formerly made at home from simple herbs and roots,—such as cough mixtures, tooth washes, lotions, liniments, enemas, poultices, healing tinctures and decoctions. Opium is consumed in the form of pills often made by very unskilful hands, and it has been found in alcoholic liquors, especially in the brandy which was sold publicly in one of the western towns of this State. "Among the most dangerous preparations of morphia are those now prescribed and sold by uneducated or villainous individuals as so-called 'cures' for persons afflicted with the uncontrollable appetite for opium—'Relief for the Opium Eater'—, and the very existence of such nostrums certainly indicates the extent of the disease. One of these preparations consisted of a clear solution of sulphate of morphia, colored pinkish by aniline fuschine, and sweetened; the directions accompanying it were not very definite, but a dose containing about two grains of sulphate of morphia was to be taken three times a day, "if necessary," by the patient, when suffering badly from depression and other symptoms.

"I need only refer to the frequency of wilful and accidental poisoning and narcotization by morphia or opium, as you are familiar with such cases; but they are certainly increasing every year in this State."

In . . . letters of our correspondents, . . . frequent mention is made of this habit, as caused by the injudicious and often unnecessary prescription of opium by the physician. So grave a statement, and one so generally endorsed, should not be allowed to pass unnoticed by those who, as guardians of the public health, are in no small measure responsible for the moral, as well as physical, welfare of their patients. It is unnecessary here to do more than allude to the other physical causes that occasionally lead to excess in the use of opium, dependent upon a depressed condition of the nervous system, induced either by occupation, overwork with deficient nutrition; or by a vicious mode of life, as prostitution, and sometimes, intemperance. Those more generally exempt from this vice are out-of-door laborers, and others whose occupations allow an abundance of fresh air and nourishing food, with regular hours of sleep. A deficiency in these natural stimuli, so essential to sound health, promotes a desire for artificial substitutes, and opium, where others are unavailable, is often resorted to. In England, and we suspect the same would be found true, although to a less extent, in our own country, the opium habit is especially common among the manufacturing classes, who are too apt to live regardless of all hygienic laws. The taste for opium eating among soldiers retired from the army is alluded to by a few of our correspondents. It seems also to have been noticed in England, and is probably due to the habit acquired in the service, or to shattered health, the result of campaign exposure. The fact generally remarked that women constitute so large a proportion of opium takers, is due, perhaps, more to moral than to physical causes. Doomed, often, to a life of disappointment, and, it may be, of physical and mental inaction, and in the smaller and more remote towns, not unfrequently, to utter seclusion, deprived of all wholesome social diversion, it is not strange that nervous depression, with all its concomitant evils, should sometimes follow,— opium being discreetly selected as the safest and most agreeable remedy. We must not omit, however, one other most important cause of this habit referred to by our correspondents, and the most general one of all that predispose to it. We allude to the simple desire for stimulation,—in the words of another, "that innate propensity of mankind to supply some grateful means of promoting the flow of agreeable thoughts, of emboldening the spirit to perform deeds of daring, or of steeping in forgetfulness the sense of daily sorrows." No climate and no soil is without some product of its own which furnishes, at man's bidding, a stimulating ingredient to meet this universal want. In an age, too, like our own, of unprecedented mental and physical activity, the constant over-exercise of all the faculties, together with the cares and perplexities incident to a condition of incessant unrest, create a keener appetite for some sort of stimulus. No clearer confirmation of the truth of this statement is needed than the present enormous consumption of alcohol and tobacco, as well as of those milder stimulants, tea and coffee, for which there is an ever-increasing demand.

The selection of opium in preference to other stimulants, due more often to a taste, natural or acquired, is sometimes prompted, as appears in our reports, by motives of expediency—the facility, perhaps, with which it can be procured and taken without endangering the reputation for sobriety. In one town mentioned, it was thought "more genteel" than alcohol.

The question how far the prohibition of alcoholic liquors has led to the substitution of opium, we do not propose to consider. It is a significant fact, however, that both in England and in this country, the total abstinence movement was almost immediately followed by an increased consumption of opium. In the five years after this movement began in England, the annual importations of this drug had more than doubled; and it was between 1840 and 1850, soon after teetotalism had become a fixed fact, that our own importations of opium swelled, says Dr. Calkins, in the ratio of 3.5 to 1, and when prices had become enhanced by fifty per cent. "The habit of opium chewing," says Dr. S, "has become very prevalent in the British Islands, especially since the use of alcoholic drinks has been to so great an extent abandoned, under the influence of the fashion introduced by total abstinence societies, founded upon mere social expediency, and not upon that religious authority which enjoins temperance in all things, whether eating or drinking, whether in alcohol or in opium." And, in other countries, we find that where the heat of the climate or religious enactments restrict the use of alcohol, the inhabitants are led to seek stimulation in the use of opium. Morewood, also, in his comprehensive *History of Inebriating Liquors*, states that the general use of opium and other exhilarating substances, among the Mahometans, may date its origin from the mandate of the Prophet forbidding wine. These statements accord with the observations of several of our correspondents, who attribute the increasing use of opium to the difficulty of obtaining alcoholic drinks. It is a curious and interesting fact, on the other hand, that in Turkey, while the use of wine of late years has increased, that of opium has as certainly declined. We had almost omitted to mention one source of the opium appetite, more than once referred to by our correspondents: we allude to the taste implanted in infancy and childhood by nursery medication. When it is remembered that nearly all the various soothing sirups contain this drug, or some one of its preparations, in greater or less proportion, it will not be surprising that such a result should sometimes follow.

Chapter 31

The Benefits of Nonmedical Opium Use

George Wood was a leader of the medical community in Philadelphia and served as president of the American Philosophical Society. Although he warns in the extract below from his popular Treatise on Therapeutics and Pharmacology (1868) *that immoderate use of opium could cause discomfort, including addiction, he comments extensively on the favorable effects of judicious use. Opium produces "an elevation and expansion of the whole moral and intellectual nature." As opposed to alcohol, furthermore, it does not cause "erotic excitement" and does not affect movement and coordination.*

While casual use later was condemned as dangerous toying with a drug that could easily lead to addiction, Wood's views were typical of the years during which society, including the medical profession, was unsure what restrictions, if any, to put on the opioids.

A Treatise on Therapeutics and Pharmacology

George Wood

It may be said of opium, in general terms, that, being at first moderately stimulant to the parts to which it may be applied, and to the circulation, and energetically so to the nervous system generally, and especially to the brain, it subsequently operates with even greater energy and universality as an apparent sedative. But little idea of the real powers of the medicine would be obtained from such a definition of its effects. In order to form an exact and profitable conception of its influence, so far as known, it is necessary to follow it through the different functions, and trace its operation carefully in each, step by step. Its vast importance, and diversified applicability, call for more minute details than are necessary or advisable in relation to most other medicines. I shall consider it in relation *first* to the nervous system, *secondly* to the circulatory and respiratory system, *thirdly* to the other functions or organs, *fourthly* to the part with which it may be directly brought into contact.

1. *Action upon the Nervous System.* From a full dose of opium taken internally, no other immediate effect is experienced than a slight feeling of warmth, or perhaps of weight in the stomach. But in a short time, varying somewhat according to the form in which the medicine is used, and the state of the stomach, but

seldom exceeding ten or fifteen minutes, and often much less, a sensation of fullness is felt in the head, soon followed by a universal feeling of delicious ease and comfort, with an elevation and expansion of the whole moral and intellectual nature, which is, I think, among the most characteristic of its effects. There is not the same uncontrollable excitement as from alcohol, but an exaltation of our better mental qualities, a warmer glow of benevolence, a disposition to do great things, but nobly and beneficently, a higher devotional spirit, and withal a stronger self-reliance, and consciousness of power. Nor is this consciousness altogether mistaken. For the intellectual and imaginative faculties are raised to the highest point compatible with the individual capacity. The poet never has brighter fancies, or deeper feelings, or greater felicity of expression, nor the philosopher a more penetrating or profounder insight, than when under the influence of opium in this stage of its action. It seems to make of the individual, for the time, a better and a greater man. Sometimes there may be delusion; but it is not so much in relation to the due succession or dependence of thought, as in the elevation of the imagination and the soul above the level of reality. The hallucinations, the wildness, the delirious imaginations of alcoholic intoxication, are, in general, quite wanting. Along with this emotional and intellectual elevation, there is also increased muscular energy; and the capacity to act, and to bear fatigue, is greatly augmented.

If the quantity of opium taken has been just insufficient to induce sleep, this delightful exaltation may continue for hours, supporting the mind and body under an amount of exertion, to which they would be wholly inadequate in their ordinary condition.

In two remarkable points, besides those mentioned, the operation of opium differs from that of alcohol; in the absence, namely, of that erotic excitement, and that incapacity of combined muscular movement for a given purpose, which are so strongly characteristic of alcoholic stimulation.

With the psychological phenomena above mentioned, there is very frequently a roaring, singing, or buzzing in the head, of which there is scarcely a consciousness, unless the attention is specially directed towards it. Sometimes these noises, combined with throbbings or thumpings in the brain, are somewhat disagreeable; but they are seldom sufficiently so, to call back the mind from its higher flights, or the spirit from its keen enjoyments.

After a length of time varying, according to the dose of the drug and the susceptibility of the individual, from half an hour, to two, three, or four hours, or even longer, this exaltation sinks into a corporeal and mental calmness, which is scarcely less delicious than the previous excitement, and in a short time ends in sleep. Perhaps, in most instances, where a full dose has been taken, this result occurs within an hour. But, when the quantity of opium is insufficient for this effect, the individual will remain awake for hours, sometimes for many hours, even for the whole night, supposing the drug to have been given at bedtime, lying calmly and placidly, without mental effort or uneasiness, and submitting himself to a current of vague, but generally pleasing fancies.

Should the dose be sufficient only to induce a light sleep, there will be a constant succession of dreams, having the vividness almost of reality, usually pleasant in their character, but sometimes very much the reverse. I have repeatedly known patients to complain of excessively disagreeable effects from opium, and chiefly of horrible dreams with which they have been tormented during the night, and to declare that nothing would ever induce them to take the medicine again; but I have almost invariably found, under such circumstances, that by increasing the dose on a subsequent occasion, or by giving an additional quantity when such symptoms may have presented themselves, that sound sleep is induced, and all discomfort vanishes. So real do these dreams appear, and so much like waking thoughts, that patients will often assert that they have not closed their eyes all night, when the fact is that they have scarcely been awake during that time.

The illusions of opium are so strong that one who uses the drug habitually can sometimes scarcely distinguish them from realities; and I have known intelligent, well educated men, having the ordinary regard for opinion, and perfectly free from any suspicion of insanity, to make statements, in the presence of numbers, as to occurrences which were known to every one present to be impossible, but were as fully believed by themselves as any other event of ordinary life; and I have been able to explain such aberrations, only upon the supposition that the dreams produced by opium had been mistaken for realities. I have no doubt that perfectly truthful persons have thus got the credit of habitual mendacity, when in fact their only immorality was the habitual use of opium, perhaps to relieve sufferings otherwise intolerable.

When opium exercises its full soporific influence, the sleep is usually profound and dreamless, and continues for about eight or ten hours. Should the patient be awakened before the direct effect of the medicine has been exhausted, the feelings of comfort or *bienaise* before experienced will often continue for hours in the following day; and I have known the same thing to happen repeatedly even after a good night's rest. But generally, upon awaking from the full uninterrupted effects of opium, the patient experiences a state of greater or less depression, indicated by languor and listlessness, a relaxed surface, a rather feeble pulse, and not unfrequently loss of appetite, nausea, and even vomiting. This, however, gradually passes away, and the system returns to its ordinary condition, without having experienced any appreciable disadvantage.

A remarkable *diminulion of sensibility* attends the narcotic operation of opium, beginning even before the soporific effect, and continuing in a greater or less degree throughout the direct action of the medicine, and even into the secondary stage of depression. It is the general sensibility, or that to painful impressions, which is first and most prominently affected; but the special senses are in some degree involved, especially under the influence of very large doses; though I have met with no instance, even of opium poisoning, in which, until the advanced stage when profound coma had set in, the patient could not hear and see when roused. In this respect opium differs strikingly from some other narcotic medicines, and especially belladonna.

2. *Action upon the Circulation.* It was long an undecided point, whether opium

was to be regarded as stimulant or sedative. The experiments of Dr. Crumpe, published in 1793, decided, what any one might have determined for himself by counting his own pulse under a dose of opium, that, in its first operation, it is stimulant at least to the circulation. Within ten or fifteen minutes after its administration, the pulse is, in general, moderately increased in frequency, fullness, and force, and at the same time the surface of the body becomes warmer, and the face somewhat flushed. When the period of general excitement is past, and that of calmness or drowsiness supervenes, the pulse either resumes its original condition as to frequency, or, under a large dose of the opium, becomes somewhat slower, retaining, however, its fullness and for a time its force. In this condition it continues for some time during the period of sleep; but then gradually relaxes, and becomes soft with the relaxing surface, and in the end, participates in the general depression which attends the cessation of the direct influence of the medicine.

With the increased frequency of the pulse, the respiration is also somewhat quickened; and, as the former becomes slower, the latter undergoes a similar change, and generally even in a greater degree. Under the full influence of opium, one of the most striking phenomena is the relative slowness of the breathing, which is sometimes even stertorous, when the sleep is profound.

Corresponding with the condition of the circulatory and respiratory movements is that of the blood itself. Retaining its florid color for a time, it may give a bright tint to the complexion during the stage of excitement; but, with the diminished influence from the respiratory centres, the change from venous to arterial is less thoroughly effected, and the blood becomes darker-hued. This is not very obvious from ordinary doses of opium; but, when it has been very largely taken, the venous hue upon the surface, and particularly in the face, is often conspicuous. . . .

Coffee is another remedy which may be employed to qualify the effects of opium. It acts, probably, more nearly in the capacity of an antidote than any other agent. Its use was suggested by its well-known tendency to produce wakefulness. It should be taken freely, and as strong as possible; never, however, to the exclusion of other means. Caffeine has been substituted for coffee in several cases, with encouraging results.

Belladonna has recently acquired no little reputation from its supposed antagonistic powers to those of opium. That there is, in some respects, an antagonism between these two narcotics, I have no doubt; but I do not believe that it extends to those points in their action which entitle them both to the name of cerebral stimulants; and it would be extremely hazardous to trust the poisonous action of opium to the antidotal powers of belladonna. But in the advanced stage of the poisoning, when the immediate effects of the opium are passed, and the chief danger consists in the prostration of the nervous power, belladonna may be used with great propriety; and I can readily conceive that, under these circumstances, it may sometimes save the life of the patient. . . . This subject will be more fully discussed under the head of belladonna.

Chronic Poisoning. The extremely grateful effects of opium on most persons, in its first stimulant action, and in the calming influence which follows, has led to an enormous abuse of the drug, which, though less injurious either to the individual or to society than a similar abuse of alcohol, is often very pernicious in its effects on the health of those who give way to it. Like the alcoholic beverages, though employed habitually, provided its use be restrained within certain limits, it does little apparent injury, even through a long course of years, and does not seem, obviously, at least, to shorten life. We are told, on the most reliable authority, that in India and China, in the mode in which it is commonly employed by those of respectable position, who have a character to maintain, its effects are in general not such as to produce any seeming unfitness for the ordinary duties of life, or materially to shorten its duration. In our own country, the apothecaries inform us of sales of opium or its preparations to a vast amount, beyond any possible calls for it as a medicine; yet the number of instance are comparatively few, in which its ill effects are brought under the notice of the physician. The vice is indulged secretly, and does not betray itself by any disorder in the acts, or, so far as known, in the health of the individual; and the best British writers make the same statements relative to the abuse of the drug in their country. But the danger is that, as its pleasing effects cease to be felt, at least with the same zest, from the original dose, the temptation is always present to increase the quantity used, and to go on increasing it until it becomes a source of great and undeniable evil.

If the ordinary operation of opium be compared with that of alcohol the cause will be obvious why life is so much less endangered by the former than the latter. The stimulant influence of opium, either on the part to which it is applied, or generally on the circulation, is very much less than that of alcohol; nor does it equally excite the functions of the lungs, liver, and kidneys. Hence it is much less liable to induce either chronic inflammation of the different organs, or that organic degeneration, which almost necessarily attends the debility consequent upon excessive vascular excitement. Operating mainly on the functions, the disordering influence of opium is witnessed chiefly in the functions.

Occasionally the medical man is consulted in this country by the slaves of opium, and has the opportunity of witnessing the consequences of its excessive abuse. In his own therapeutic observation, he also witnesses frequent disturbance of the functions from its medicinal employment, and necessarily infers that the same disturbances must exist in those who use it as a luxury within the same limits. The greatest sufferings experienced by the opium-eater are those which attend the state of nervous depression, always existing when its direct influence is no longer felt. There are excessive restlessness, a universal and indescribable uneasiness, feelings of intolerable distress, especially in the epigastrium and lower extremities, an irksome sense, moreover, of incapacity both for intellectual exertion, and for mental or emotional enjoyment, constituting together a state of exquisite misery, from which the only relief is by renewed recourse to the stimulus, which, if taken in an increasing dose, renders him happy again, and again capable of exertion; and thus he goes on, in an alternation of lessening comfort and increasing misery, to the end. At the same time, there is a gradual depravation of the functions, which impairs the degree of health, though it may not very materially shorten life, unless the indulgence be carried to great excess. The ordinary derangements of the organic functions are impaired appetite and digestion, habitual constipation, and defective action of the liver those of the animal functions, tremors, wakefulness, weakened memory and intellect, and loss of interest in the usual concerns of life and social relations. The lowest stage of degradation has been attained, when the indulgence ends in a total loss of self-respect, and indifference to the opinions of the community; and everything is sacrificed to the insatiable demands of the vice. Not unfrequently, this habit of excess has been engendered by the supposed necessity of obtaining relief from painful affections, such as cancer, and certain incurable cases of neuralgia; but, though some palliation, this is no satisfactory excuse; for, by proper management, considerable relief of pain can generally be obtained, without an excess sufficient to degrade the mind, or even materially the general health; and it is rather a weak yielding to the seductive pleasure opium, than any necessity for its anodyne influence, that leads to the lowest depths of the evil.

The effects of the vice of opium-eating, and opium-smoking, among the lower class of the Orientals, have been frequently described, and with such warm colouring that a suspicion is apt to arise of some interference of the imagination in the pictures given; especially as we do not meet their exact counterparts among those, who perhaps equally abandon themselves to the vice among ourselves. It is possible that the fumes of opium inhaled may exercise a more deleterious influence on the health than the drug taken into the stomach; and this may explain the incompatibility of the descriptions of travelers with our own observation. Dr. Oppenheim, one of the most recent and reliable observers, gives the following account of what he has himself witnessed in European and Asiatic Turkey. The opium-eater usually begins with from half a grain to two grains, and gradually increases to two drachms and sometimes more in a day. He is readily recognized by his appearance. "A total attenuation of body, a withered yellow countenance, a lame gait, a bending of the spine frequently to such a degree as to assume a circular form, and glossy deep-sunken eyes, betray him at the first glance. The digestive organs are in the highest degree disturbed, the sufferer eats scarcely anything, and has hardly one evacuation in a week; his mental and bodily powers are destroyed; he is impotent." Finding the stimulant effect of the poison at length almost lost, he conjoins with it the use of corrosive sublimate, gradually increasing the latter till it amounts to ten grains daily. He becomes subject finally to neuralgic pains, to which the opium yields no relief; and if he has begun the use of the drug early in life, seldom attains the age of forty. (*Brit. and For. Med. Rev.*, iv. 394.) It is unnecessary to state, that the corrosive sublimate has probably quite as much to do with the fatal result as the opium.

It is satisfactory to know that this evil habit may be corrected, without great difficulty, if the patient is in earnest; and, as the disorders induced by it are mainly functional, that a good degree of health may be restored. It will not answer to break off suddenly. No fortitude is sufficient to support the consequent misery, and life might be scarified in the effort. Of the particular phenomena which might result I have no experience; for I have met with no case in which the attempt has been made, or at any rate more than momentarily preserved in. Dr. B. H. Coates, however, states that he has seen well characterized cases, in which delirium tremens occurred (*N. Am. Med. and Surg. Journ.*, iv. 34.); and this result might be reasonably anticipated. The proper method of correcting the evil is by gradually withdrawing the cause; a diminution of the dose being made every day, so small as to be quite imperceptible in its effects. Supposing, for example, that a fluidounce of laudanum is taken daily, the abstraction of a minim every day would lead to a cure in somewhat more than a year; and the progress might be much more rapid than this. Time, however, must be allowed for the system gradually to regain the healthy mode of action, which it had gradually lost.

Chapter 32

The Importance of Prevention

The following letter by a young middle-class woman, describing the ill effects of her addiction to laudanum, was published in Britain in 1889. The belief — widely held in the United States as well as Britain in the nineteenth century — that intense studying can damage the female mind is at least suggested, though it is not explicitly stated. As signs of the "moral idiocy" caused by addiction, the writer cites her laziness, inefficiency, memory loss, attempts to hide overdosing, and indifference to the admonitions and concern of siblings and parents. She does a reasonably good job of describing withdrawal and closes with a plea for prevention: young people should be warned that occasional laudanum taking can slip into dangerous habitual use.

PLEA FROM A YOUNG LAUDANUM ADDICT

Dear Sir,—

Perhaps you may remember a lady calling on you with her daughter about the middle of August, to ask you if there was any way of curing the habit of taking opium, which the girl had contracted. I, who write, am that same girl, and think you may perhaps be interested to hear how I got on. It is hateful to me to think of that horrible time, and one of my chief reasons for writing to you is to beg you to try and make known, by every means in your power, what a terrible thing opium-eating is. . . .

When I came home from school I insisted on practising [music] seven hours a day, and the family put up with it, though it was a great infliction to them. It would have been better for me had they not done so, for I was naturally so tired-out at night that I could not sleep, and, knowing that sleep would come easily with a little laudanum, it was difficult to resist taking it. Of course, it didn't become habitual all at once; the first time I got it was at school, after a concert, when its effects were so soothing, that it became quite usual for me to get it. . . .

None but those who have as completely succumbed to it as I did, could guess the mischief it would do. Even you, with an experience which must be extremely varied, being as you are, in such a good place for studying people's brains, (or rather their want of them) cannot know the amount of harm it did to me morally, though I must say you did seem to have a pretty fair idea of it. It got me into such a state of indifference, that I no longer took the least interest in anything, and did nothing all day but loll on the sofa reading novels, falling asleep every now and then, and drinking tea. Occasionally I would take a walk or drive, but not often. Even my music I no longer took much interest in, and would play only when the mood seized me, but felt it too much of a bother to practise. I would get up about ten in the morning, and make a pretence of sewing; a pretty pretence, it took me four months to knit a stocking. Worse than all, I got so deceitful, that no one could tell when I was speaking the truth. It was only this last year it was discovered; those living in the house with you are not so apt to notice things, and it was my married sisters who first began to wonder what had come over me. They said I always seemed to be in a half dazed state, and not to know what I was doing. However they all put it down to music. Mother had let me go to all the Orchestral Concerts in the winter, and they thought it had been too much for me. By that time it was a matter of supreme indifference to me what they thought, and even when it was found out, I had become so callous that I didn't feel the least shame. Even mother's grief did not affect me, I only felt irritated at her; this is an awful confession to have to make, but it is better to tell the whole truth when you once begin, and it might be some guide to you in dealing with others. If you know of anyone indulging in such a habit, especially girls, just tell them what they will come to. . . .

No one need think they will escape without punishment in some form or other. Unfortunately those who are strong can go on for a long time with impunity. But sooner or later retribution is sure to follow, and as I don't believe anyone's friends would put up with them as mine did with me, there would be nothing for it but to either voluntarily go where you suggested I should, or, if their reason was gone (which you also politely suggested with regard to me) they would be sent. I must say you have a pretty plain way of putting things. It is rather startling to a young lady to be told that she'll have to pay a six months' visit to a lunatic asylum, even when such varied attractions as "needlework, drawing and walking," are held out. However, perhaps the thought of living in such a palatial residence might reconcile some people to it. All the same, it would be a pity to make the place too comfortable, people might miss it when they got out. . . .

There's just one thing I would like to know, and that is—whether you could tell that I had not left off laudanum that day we called. Surely you must know the state one gets into when suddenly deprived of it; they could no more sit up and speak as I did than fly. By that time I had brought myself down to a quarter of an ounce a day, and as you had put mother on her guard, I had no means of getting any more, (I hate having to own that I tried to do so) so the day after we saw you was the last I had any. Then began a time I shudder to look back upon, I don't like owning to bodily suffering, but will not deny that I suffered then. I wonder if leaving off opium has the same effect on everyone! My principal feeling was one of awful weariness and numbness at the end of my back; it kept me tossing about all day and night long. It was impossible to lie in one position for more than a minute, and of course sleep was out of the question. I was so irritable that no one cared to come near me; mother slept on the sofa in my room, and I nearly kicked her once for suggesting that I should say hymns over to myself, to try and make me go to sleep. Hymns of a very different sort were in my mind, I was once or twice very nearly strangling myself, and I am ashamed to say that the only thing that kept me from doing so was the thought that I would be able to get laudanum somehow. Oh, I did feel miserable! Poor mother had a hard time of it, she said she never had such a heart-rending time in all her life; any time any of us were ill before there was always some remedy, but this time there was none, there was nothing for it but to bear it. . . .

Oh, dear, surely I shall never touch opium again! Besides the remembrance of what I endured in giving it up, there is my gratitude to all the family, especially my dear mother, for their extreme kindness to me when little better than a brute. Here I must state that I think you are right about a lunatic asylum being the only place for one to be cured of opium-eating. In my own case I can truly state that I could easily have procured it loads of times if I had wished, for though mother watched me very strictly at first, she soon relaxed, and if I had not by that time possessed the wish to be cured, I should probably be as bad as ever now. However, my parents very firmly told me that this was my last chance, that they would not stand any more of it. . . .

Oh, why do you doctors not try prevention as well as cure? You have it in your power to warn those who take laudanum now and then for toothache or a headache, what an insidious thing it is, and how easily they may become the victims of it. I began that way, and see what it came to. Even now I often wonder if I've quite got over its effects. Does anyone who has gone up to three or four ounces a day, and is suddenly deprived of it, live to tell the tale? I can hardly believe it. My own sufferings were bad enough, and I had got down to a quarter of an ounce. I'll end this by alluding again to the object of my writing, namely, the prevention of people getting into such a state as I was: if they were to know the state of moral idiocy to which they would in the end be brought, would they ever allow themselves to once begin the habit? They need not say to themselves "Oh, we can stop it when we like;" opium takes away their power to do that. There can't be a more determined person that I am naturally, and what good did that do me! I determined a hundred times to stop it, but never succeeded, and at last I got that I didn't care a rap what became of me, all the reasoning and affection expended on me, being a mere waste of time and love. You doctors know all the harm those drugs do, as well as the "victims" of them, and yet you do precious little to prevent it.

Chapter 33

Treatment of Chronic Diseases with Opiates

As the hypodermic syringe grew in popularity, users could obtain a set — as it was called — without any restriction and could also easily obtain morphine. Physicians thought that needle delivery was safer than oral administration because less of the drug was required to reach the same level of pain relief. Soon, however, the practice of recommending morphine by syringe over an indefinite period for chronic ailments such as arthritis came to be suspected of causing addiction even more rapidly than had the simpler opiate-consumption methods that antedated syringe use. The following are late-nineteenth-century accounts of addiction that followed unrestricted hypodermic use of morphine.

ON THE ABUSE OF HYPODERMIC INJECTIONS OF MORPHIA

Clifford Allbutt

Now that the hypodermic use of morphia is brought into sensation novels as a melodramatic device, it may indeed be said to have reached the height of fashion. We may thank our stars if one of us be not seen ere long, syringe in hand, between Aspasia and Clodius in the windows of the Burlington Arcade.

It is not for me to say that I do not run this risk as nearly as anyone, for what I have written upon the subject hitherto has been to record the virtues of this admirable remedy, and to extend its applications. At the same time it seems the duty of those who use so potent a medicine, to consider the full bearings of their practice, and to make themselves as well aware of its dangers as of its virtues. For my part, although I have found the hypodermic use of morphia of great value in the relief of the painful spasmodic or inflammatory elements of many and very various diseases; and although I may, therefore, seem to have used morphia very extensively, yet I cannot compare myself with those practitioners of whom the syringe and phial are as constant companions as was the lancet to their fathers. There is another side of the question, however, of which we must admit that we are still very ignorant: that while on the one hand we know the eminent virtues of morphia when administered under the skin, and feel how sadly crippled we should now be without it; on the other hand, little or nothing has been said of any harm which may result from it, or of the evils which may come of its careless use. Among the numerous essays and records concerning the hypodermic use of morphia which have been published of late, both at home and abroad, I cannot call to mind one in which its possible dangers have been considered; but I feel that the time has come when the attention of the profession will be called to this less pleasant side of the account. Thoughts of this kind have gradually gained a firmer footing in my own mind during the last three years; but while my fears were indefinite, I felt the time had not come for me to speak. Now my experience has been greater, and I have a larger number of cases before me, and yet the uncomfortable fear of mischief is growing rather than diminishing. Setting aside the mere obstructive reasoning of those prejudiced against any new thing, especially if it claims much of their attention, I would raise the further question whether the hypodermic injection of morphia which avoids many of those discomforts and evils which belong to morphia taken by mouth, has any special dangers of its own, which may be none the less for being deferred? I ask this question not as one having an answer at hand, nor, indeed, as being able myself to contribute very much to the answer which is to come, but as one having some grounds to be uneasy, and seeking information from those who have it.

It is not true that we are now often consulted by patients who have been injecting themselves daily or more than daily during long periods of time for neuralgias which seem, nevertheless, as far from cure as they were at the outset? Such at least is my own experience. I have now nine patients in my mind who are or who have been under my own care, and in whom the hypodermic use of morphia has been constantly practised for periods varying from nine months to three years. These patients suffer from various forms of neuralgia—from abdominal, uterine, facial, cervico-brachial, sciatic and other pains—they seem as far from cure as ever they were, they all find relief in the incessant use of the syringe, and they all declare that without the syringe life would be insupportable. I have been much struck by what seems to me the formation of a new class of patients, patients suffering not monthly, nor weekly, but even daily, from neuralgias which are only kept at bay by repeated injections, which return when the influence of the injection has passed off, and which resist all curative treatment with wearisome obstinacy, but which do not seem in themselves to be necessarily intractable. Not only so, but there are certain further symptoms which are common to these patients. The ease and recreation which naturally follows the arrest of intense pain, has passed by insidious gradations into a substantive sensation of well-being, of conscious activity, and of cheerfulness which is more than negative; which is more, I mean, than the mere recovery of natural elasticity on relief from pain. It has a certain tonic and stimulant effect which in the course of time is prized for its own sake, and is innocently enough welcomed as the evidence of a renewal of life. Here lies, to me, the anxious responsibility of the medical adviser. Is he to withhold that means which relieves pain, which restores appetite, which encourages activity and promotes ease and cheerfulness? I honestly confess that, during a long period, I could not see my way to forbidding the repetitions of the morphia. Injected morphia seemed so different to swallowed morphia, no one had experience of any ill effects from it, and we all had the daily experience of it as a means of peace and comfort, while pain on the other hand was as certainly the forerunner of wretchedness and exhaustion. Gradually, however, the conviction began to force itself upon my notice, that injections of morphia, though free from the ordinary evils of opium-eating, might, nevertheless, create the same artificial want and gain credit for assuaging a restlessness and depression of which it was itself the cause. Certainly, all the patients I have named fall off in the same way when the morphia fades from the system, and in all there is an indescribable depression and irritability which alone the morphia can relieve, and for which it is accordingly again and again administered. They are all satisfied that without the morphia the pain must return and will keep them in agony, and, when efforts are made to omit the dose, the pains do return until the fortitude of the patient is broken down, and the morphia is called for. At such times I have certainly felt it a great responsibility to say that pain, which I know is an evil, is less injurious than morphia, which may be an evil. Here experience is needed. Does morphia tend to encourage the very pains it pretends to relieve; or if not, does it at any rate induce in those who use it constantly, an artificial state which makes its further use a necessity? Are the subjects of morphia injection, that is, liable to become depressed, relaxed, irritable, and dependent upon a new habit of constant intoxication? If this be so, we are incurring a grave risk in bidding people to inject whenever they need it, and in telling them that the morphia can have no ill effects upon them so long as it brings with it tranquillity and well-being. With regard to the question of the perpetuation of the morbid condition under the mask of a seeming relief, I have been struck, for example, with the apparently bad results of the hypodermic injection in acute rheumatism and in gout. In consulting practice it must of course be remembered that the cases which do well are not the subjects of consultations, but those which do badly. Still I cannot rid myself of the notion that in three cases of acute rheumatism and one of acute gout, which have come under my notice, the very bad result was due to the treatment by injection of morphia alone. In these three cases, which were followed by visceral complications, and in which an abiding crippling pain seemed to outlive all other changes, the treatment throughout had been by morphia injection alone. The use of this remedy as a solace from pain during the careful use of other therapeutical means can do nothing but good; but I repeat that, in the cases in question, I have much reason to suspect that a reliance upon hypodermic morphia only ended in that curious state of perpetuated pain, of irritability and depression, and of artificial need of a certain stimulant, which I have observed in the nine cases of neuralgia. I now leave the matter open, but I sincerely hope that some one more competent to deal with it than myself will continue the discussion.

There must by this time be a vast amount of experience of this remedy in the profession, and I would inquire whether any of my brethren have met with such cases as I have described, and if so, whether we are to see in them the victims of a treacherous remedy; or whether they are but instances of those cases of inveterate neuralgia which we can now relieve by hypodermic morphia, but which formerly raged unrestrained.

OPIUM AND THE OPIUM-APPETITE

Alonzo Calkins

In Constantinople the bazaars are adorned in a style more accordant with the Asian pomp of the Ottoman. The visitor, having placed himself reclining upon a dais, the servitor in waiting, with a *tactus eruditus* such as ever designates the trained expert, deftly lays a single lozenge upon the tongue of the recipient, like as is the manner in a Christian country with the knight of the mortar and pestle, who

> "(Most mild of men!)
> Bids you put *out* your tongue,
> Then put it *in* again."

As between pipe and bolus, in view of their pathologic consequences, says Surgeon Smith, there is little to choose. The chandoo being partially denarcotized, has the advantage in respect of purity, an advantage evenly counterbalanced if not more than that in this, that the area of cellular surface in the expanded lungs directly exposed to the narcotizing action is in excess so many times over of that of the stomach-membrane.

A third mode of bringing the system under the desired influence, is the *Hypodermic* method—subcutaneous injection by means of a syringe. In this way one-third the quantity that would ordinarily be taken by the mouth suffices, i.e. the same amount exerts a triple force. The practice, as favoring the habit, appears to be less hazardous in instances, but not certainly. Eulenberg in a case of disease made 1200 injections in all, and without manifest injury appertaining. For withdrawal he advises graduated reductions, with atropia incorporated in proportionately increased quantities. Any reliance placed upon this form of use, however, for its supposed comparative security, is likely to prove delusive. Dr. Sewall of N.Y. has just reported two cases. In the first, the practice, after a two months continuance, was arrested, but not without much embarrassment; the second patient still continues on, writhing as helplessly as if, Laocoon-like, he were wound around in the coils of some monster-serpent. This gentleman, now of middle life, having suffered much from a diseased ankle, was advised (professionally) to use morphine hypodermically. The immediate effect being found most soothing and satisfactory, an indefinite continuance was suggested; and now, after a habituation for two years, the invalid is hopelessly delivered over, an abject slave to the habit, enervated in body and enfeebled in mind. The thigh of the affected limb is literally studded with punctures, to be counted by the score.

Morbid Craving for Morphia

Edward Levinstein

Morbid craving for morphia means the uncontrollable desire of a person to use morphia as a stimulant and tonic, and the diseased state of the system caused by the injudicious use of the said remedy.

Under this head we do not include those cases which necessitate the use of morphia for special medical purposes. Its proper use in these cases prevents the patient getting accustomed to the drug, because the injections are discontinued as soon as the disease passes away. But this can only be decided by the medical man, who has himself administered the injections, and never by the patient, if perchance they have been left in his hands. All painful diseases accompanied with sleeplessness make the convalescents nervous and melancholy; they continually worry themselves about their bodily health, greatly magnifying the importance of every trifling bodily change, of which a healthy person would not have taken the slightest notice. If, then, they should have by them a remedy, such as injection of morphia, which has previously proved of great benefit to them, they will at once resort to its use, either to prevent pain coming on, or to avoid the recurrence of a restless night. Such are the causes of the habitual use of morphia, of the seeming impossibility of doing without it, and, finally, the morbid craving for it.

The originators and propagators of this disease are the medical men who, in cases more or less painful and protracted, have advised the patients to themselves use the injection of morphia. They must not be blamed for acting as they did, as it was done in the hope of affording relief to their patients, none of them thinking of the attendant danger. The evil was still further spread by those suffering from craving for morphia, who highly praised it as a remedy of which they knew the beneficial effects.

The injections of morphia not only relieve sleeplessness and pain, but their action at the same time induces a change in the entire system. It produces a state of mental excitement that can only be compared to that produced by the use of alcohol. The temper is altered; depressed persons will become lively; to the fainting person it imparts strength; to the weakly it restores energy; the taciturn become eloquent; shy persons lose their bashfulness; and the consciousness of power and ability is greatly increased. But as soon as the morphia has left the system, a reaction sets in, and the period of great mental and bodily excitement is followed by a state of deep despondency.

This narcotic remedy will soon be indispensable to those who have it often injected, as, by doing so, they know that they are able to banish all physical and moral trouble; hence they resort to morphia as the drunkard to the dram bottle. They drown their anger, their domestic sorrows, and their business cares; and, like the drunkard with his morning draught, they steady their shaking limbs by the use of morphia. And when the effect of the latter passes off, and the mental and bodily depression that follows makes them feel their sad and helpless condition (similar to the misery that follows the abuse of spirits), and their morally and physically miserable life, they again and again make use of another injection of this poison, in the hope of forgetting the misery partly brought on by themselves.

But the lucid intervals which allow them to lead an existence worthy of human beings become shorter and shorter; the craving for morphia increases daily; the vicious circle draws closer and closer around them, until, at last, all power of resistance having failed, they succumb under its action.

Inebriety, or Narcomania

Norman Kerr

The most frequent apology with which I have been favoured by opium and morphine inebriates has been, that they first had recourse to the drug to procure sleep. Many persons are terribly afflicted with insomnia, an increasing trouble in these days of mental over-pressure and over-strain. These have chiefly been literary workers and members of the learned professions. A sedative for the relief of pain has been the origin of the habit with nearly as many. In one case, that of male of 55 years of age, who had morphine injected under the skin some 2,000 times, the first injections were for the alleviation of the acute pain caused by a gastric ulcer. In another case, that of an educated and talented medical practitioner, the laudanum indulgence to the extent of one ounce every morning, with the morbid craving for the matutinal narcotic had been the effect of a few medicinal doses for the assuaging of pain arising from inflammatory stricture of the urethra. Obscure and intense neuralgic pains being generally relieved as by a charm by morphine introduced subcutaneously, this also is a frequent inauguration of the habit. Opium is also taken by some persons of education and refinement to promote increased intellectual activity, brilliancy of thought, imagination, and speech. Though much less in vogue with women than with men, those of the former sex who have been enslaved by it have taken to an opiate narcotic to calm the perturbation of a delicate organization, or for the relief of natural pain. The enormous amount of opium given to children in the form of soothing syrups has much to answer for in the increase among us of opium indulgence.

In a small proportion of cases I have found the alcoholic precede the opiate inebriety, the latter drug with a very few so taking the place of the former that alcoholic intoxicants became less grateful to the palate.

Speaking broadly, I have generally found the hypodermic method to have taken its origin from a resort to morphine thus applied to assuage severe local distress; while for the wooing of sleep the solid and sometimes the liquid preparations of opium have been sought. In my experience the smoking of opium has rarely been attributed to any therapeutic necessity; but has almost always taken its birth from the pursuit of pleasure, the few exceptions having been for the relief of the asthmatic paroxysm, in which this drug is very unreliable. Moderate indulgence has been ventured upon, but in many cases the power of the narcotic has insensibly increased until it took possession of the whole man, holding him in an iron grip from which there has seemed little chance of his escape.

In the United States the intense nerve activity and exhaustion of the people, and, within extensive tracts of country, the prevalence of malarial fevers of a low type, with their depressant sequelæ, are the principal introductions to opium inebriety. In China and Burmah a desire for the illusory pleasures of narcotic imagining is probably the general inducement. Crombie ascribes 90 per cent. of the opium taken by the Bengal peasantry to a longing for relief from the pain of chronic rheumatism, chronic diarrhœa, chronic dysentery, and malarial fever.

AGE:—With opium as with alcohol, the greatest liability is between 30 and 50 years of age, the number of cases below and above that age being comparatively few. With alcohol there is this difference, that a considerable proportion of cases enter on their career of excess below 20 and above 50.

Though the effects of the drug may be somewhat modified by the idiosyncrasy of the individual opium *habitué*, there is a certain train of symptoms which usually follows the consumption of a dose sufficient to procure the characteristic action. A few minutes after the does, with a shorter interval when given hypodermically, the face is suffused with a blush, with probably a well-defined hectic spot. The eyes sparkle with unwonted brilliance. The countenance is ruddy and the expression animated. This is the stage of excitement or exhilaration. The pulse beats faster, and muscular activity is increased.

In the second stage there is a pleased feeling of satisfaction, partaking of delight and ineffable composure. This is a stage of complete repose. The pulse beats more slowly, the muscles are less active.

A vacant look, with an occasional gleam of momentary consciousness, ushers in the third stage. The opiized gradually sinks into a state of torpor, from which he is with difficulty aroused. The only effectual means of arousing him is to administer a fresh dose of the narcotizing agent. The face looks pale or dusky, the skin is withered, the pupils are contracted to the size of a pin's head.

The vascular system is relaxed in the first stage, and slightly tightened up in the second, this contraction being intensified in the third.

The awakening from the third stage of torpor-prostration, and apparently impending death, is most wretched. Tremors are succeeded by growing restlessness, and with returning consciousness there is an overwhelming sense of intolerable uneasiness, distress, and depression, which imperiously craves for a renewal of the witching soporific. In this state of reaction the agony, or desperation, is sometimes so acute that suicide or homicide has been the issue.

Opium and morphine inebriates are often very chilly.

Opium exerts a soothing influence. Under its powerful sway, the cantankerous and quarrelsome are transformed for the moment into the most amiable and peaceful of beings. Rarely does violence proclaim this inebriate's downward march to a premature grave.

Evanescent albuminuria at times occurs, during the exhibition of the drug and also after its discontinuance. It is apt to last for a few days at a time and to recur at intervals. Symptoms resembling ague are occasionally seen, in both the presence and absence of the narcotic. There are high temperature and shivering, like the cold and hot stages of intermittent fever. There is also an opiate and morphine trembling delirium, exclusive of the acute wakeful and trembling delirious state supervening on sudden withdrawal. No one can describe the torture experienced by opium inebriates on the failure of the supply of a fresh dose at the accustomed time. While in this fatuous, listless, irritable condition, the patient will at once become lively, clear-headed, and brilliant, on the exhibition of a sufficient dose. This depraved physical state is a pathological condition, a physical depression which clamours for a renewal of the potion as soon as the pleasurable effects of the preceding dose have disappeared. Chronic dysentery, not very often seen in alcohol inebriety, is a frequent complication in confirmed opiomania. Many of the complicatory diseases which excite to inebriety in alcohol or opium are either alike or akin. Dyspeptic and neuralgic painful troubles are among the most common ailments, thus provocative of, or intercurrent with alcoholomania and opiomania. But cirrhotic and nephritic disorders are less frequently seen with opium. It is almost a tradition of the medical world that disease of the kidneys is apt to occur in the person of morphinomaniacs and opiomaniacs; but, though I have always been expecting to discover albuminuria in this group of narcomaniacs I have never yet detected albumen in their urine, except when the kidneys were affected with organic kidney disease prior to the development of the narcotic symptoms.

A true impulse or crave for both alcohol and opium is often the direct effect of previous moderate use. In cases with no narcotic heredity the continued taking in limited quantity of either substance has set up, *de novo*, a persistent and overmastering craze. In these cases the narcomaniac greedily drinks his alcoholic intoxicant or smokes his opiate, not for pleasure, but to gratify a crave begotten of prior indulgence.

In some localities, especially in China, the opium degradation is so terrible that gross immorality abounds. Sometimes men think nothing of gratifying their mania for this narcotic from the proceeds of their wife's prostitution. Even little children are torn from their maternal embrace and sold into slavery to procure supplies of the demoralizing drug for the abject slave of this most dreadful and brutalizing of all forms of narcomania.

So intense is the crave that a man has been known to mortgage his mother and sell his wife to gratify it. One man sold his wife for £12 and smoked the proceeds. This crave robs a man of his resources, unfits him for work, and hurries him to an untimely end.

The quantity taken is sometimes enormous. In one case of female addiction I have known as much as one pint of laudanum drunk daily; in a male case 150 grains of solid opium eaten in the same period, and 30 grains taken at one dose. One male patient injected 20 grains of morphine per diem in divided doses under the skin. Another took 60 grains on an average each day. But the ordinary amount of the narcotic usually taken by opium inebriates is very much less than any of these extraordinarily excessive quantities. In my observation the average daily allowance of laudanum has been rather over one ounce, of opium about thirty grains, and of the hypodermic self-administration of morphine salts about eight grains. These quantities, as well as the more excessive, have sometimes been taken daily for periods of months and years.

One young woman, unmarried, age 30, regularly consumed 1½ ounces of laudanum daily, and often double that quantity, for many years. She used to take the 1½ ounces in a quart of beer. The wife, aged 45, of a medical practitioner, drank an average of 1¾ ounces daily for seven months. Another married lady, aged 46, took a daily allowance of seven ounces of equal parts of tincture of opium, spirits of lavender, and chloric ether. A man, aged 50, for many years drank regularly every day 2½ ounces of laudanum and 1½ ounces of paregoric.

Though the opium habit does not seem to me to be spreading so rapidly amongst us in England as is often asserted, the result of my observation is that the practice of opium smoking, eating, and drinking, and of morphine injection, is undoubtedly on the increase. The number of helpless children who are dosed to death, though not intentionally killed, with opium or other narcotics to keep them quiet, is, especially in certain localities, simply appalling. My experience is, that among male adults the increase is chiefly in opium smoking and morphine injection, and, among females, mainly in laudanum. I have found about one per cent of alcoholic inebriates take some form of opiate. The unsuspected, yet large increase of laudanum drinking, among persons of restricted means, in London, was illustrated by the report of an inquest on a milliner in North Kensington two years ago, who had died from poisoning by tk. opii. A chemist deposed that one of his customers spent ten shillings a week on laudanum, and another drank two ounces at a sitting. He added that the habit was very common.

There has also been an enormous increase of opium inebriety in China. The consumption by the Chinese has been stimulated largely, if not mainly, by the removal of the local tax on the drug, which has thereby been substantially reduced in price. It is humiliating to Englishmen to reflect that the local tax abolition has been at the instance of England, a dishonourable and infamous action which cries aloud for speedy and effectual redress.

Like alcohol, opium is a poison, though the poisonous process is marked by somewhat different symptoms. That many human beings can without *apparent* harm consume "moderate" or even somewhat liberal quantities of such substances cannot be gainsayed; but the use of neither is absolutely free from peril. There is some risk inseparable from the social use of all intoxicants. Opium is a poison which excites, intoxicates, and enervates the whole man; by repeated indulgence inducing bodily and mental prostration and moral perversion.

Chapter 34

Morphinism

Writing in 1908 in the Journal of Inebriety, *Dr. Charles W. Carter carefully analyzes conceptions of morphinism, that is, addiction to morphine. After dismissing the ideas that this addiction arises from habit, moral laxity, or organic disease, Carter defines it as a disorder brought about and maintained by self-poisoning, in an attempt to relieve physical and mental distress. The particular characteristics and circumstances of the individual create "variations or types" of the morphine disease.*

What Is the Morphine Disease?

Charles W. Carter

In using the term "morphine habit" we do not mean what we say. A drug habit is not a habit. A habit is the result of education or of accumulated experiences, by which repeated conscious efforts have at last become automatic and are performed sub-consciously, or even unconsciously. By habit we come to have characteristic ways of speaking, walking, eating, adjusting our clothing, doing our accustomed tasks, and performing most of the various and multitudinous duties that make up the sum of each day's life. Habit makes no impress upon our being, other than to give us easier ways of doing things, or peculiarities, tricks, and mannerisms that comprise those outward appearances we recognize as personality. Habit makes no change in the organism. The man who acquires a habit is the same man he was before. Compel him to give up this habit, or acquire a new one, and we find no change in the man.

But in a drug habit we have a very different picture. The man who acquires a drug habit is a different man from what he was before. Compel him to forego indulgence in his habit, and he is still another individual. A drug habit grips the being with a tighter clutch than does a true habit, and in a different way. It stamps an impression upon the organism impossible to be imprinted by the elements responsible for the formation of a true habit, and conscious effort and mere repetition of themselves can have little to do with the formation of that condition we call drug habituation. If that were all, then we might equally expect to have the bread and butter habit, the beefsteak habit or the milk habit, because we practice the frequent taking of these agreeable substances.

It ought to be equally evident that morphinism is not a moral perversion, and yet it would appear that most laymen, including a majority of moralists and reformers, and very many physicians also, regard it not only as a habit, but also as a variety of dissipation, a vice, a sin, a folly, or other evidence of moral obliquity. It is true that weak, vicious, and degenerate characters more readily and more often lapse into drug abuse, but it is also true that persons of the highest moral type not infrequently become equally subject to narcotic addiction. They are often in no sense morally perverted. Their ideals may remain as high, and their lives in private as before the public, as faultless as before their addiction began, or after it has been abandoned. If weak-willed, depraved, and vicious natures more readily acquire drug habits, and are restored with greater difficulty, and with less certainty of permanent restoration, it is probably due to their natural tendency to slip and drift, to follow in the path of least resistance, rather than to a distinctively moral degeneracy.

The moral nature, of itself, probably plays only a minor rôle in the formation of a drug habit, and until this is more generally recognized to be a fact, a large part of well meant temperance and reform work will continue to be misdirected and must prove ineffective; and a great deal of injustice must be perpetrated upon unfortunate persons who are entitled to sympathy and encouragement instead of meriting criticism and condemnation.

Morphinism is not an immorality, but according to the most advanced medical thought a physical or psychophysical disorder, or a condition of disease. Just what it is that constitutes the disease in this condition can not be said to be determined beyond question. It appears that no explanation thus far given is wholly convincing and satisfactory. There are indications of an approaching unanimity of opinion among the most diligent observers, but probably the mass of the profession nominally subscribing to this opinion still feel much uncertainty as to the exact nature of the morphine disease.

The truth is, the condition which we know as morphinism presents the greatest imaginable variety and complexity of symptoms—as great, apparently, as are the variations in human temperament. Unlike the majority of well defined diseases, it has no characteristic or pathognomonic symptoms, no marks or signs by which its presence may be recognized with certainty in either the living or the dead subject, no organic lesions or tissue changes discoverable either on the post-mortem table or under the microscope, directly or essentially referable to the drug. In other words, morphinism is not in any sense an organic disease, but a derangement of function, a change in the mode of action of the organism, not a change in its structure.

In watching the effects of the administration of a medicinal dose of morphine, we observe two sets of symptoms: one, the specific effect of the drug itself, and the other, secondary to conditions brought about by the morphine. As a result of the morphine action itself we observe paralysis of the higher centers of the brain and cord, with consequent dulling of the perceptive faculties, and retardation of both sensory and motor nerve impulses. The intellectual centers are inhibited; their perception of the annoyances and distractions of the outer world has been dulled, and distresses originating within the body likewise fail to rouse the usual recognition of their existence. Hence the calmness, the dreaminess, the sense of well-being, the relief from pain and weariness enjoyed by the narcotized subject.

At the same time, and due to the same inhibiting or paralyzing effect of the drug upon the nervous apparatus, we have a retardation of the whole metabolic function of the organism, a diminution of glandular secretion and of excretion, a crippling of digestion and a paralysis of peristalsis. The whole machinery of nutrition and elimination is retarded in its action. It moves dully, haltingly, and imperfectly as under a spell. As a consequence the toxines constantly elaborated through normal cell action and through putrefactive and other changes in the contents of the intestinal tract are hindered in their escape from the body, and the organism is thus subjected not alone to the poisonous action of the morphine, but also to the deleterious effect of its own waste matters.

This is the effect of a single dose of the drug. If this were all, then if the dose were not sufficiently great to be overwhelmingly poisonous, in a little time the somnolent kidneys, skin, bowels and other avenues of elimination would manage to carry off the poisons, both of the drug and of the organism itself, and as soon as this were accomplished the system would be returned to its former state of equilibrium. But this is not all. From what we know of the results of faulty elimination of toxines, we should expect the characteristic symptoms of these poisons to be manifested, and so we find, after the morphine action has ceased, the usual picture of auto-intoxication, namely: languor, headache, constipation, scanty, high colored urine, nausea, deranged digestion, coated tongue, foul breath, neuralgic pains, uneasiness, mental depression, and a host of indefinite distresses commonly following auto-intoxication, whether brought on by the paralyzing effects of morphine or from gluttony or from constipation or from any other cause whatever, and to avoid which we are accustomed to follow the medicinal use of morphine with salines, enemas, and other eliminative agents.

But instead of eliminating these toxines from the system, and thus removing the discomforts which they occasion, we might cover up their effects and relieve the patient by administering another dose of morphine. We would then again lull the intellectual faculties to quietude, render each nerve cell again indifferent to its duty, and the pain centers deaf to the calls for relief. The secretions and excretions would be still further diminished, and thus the quantity of toxines retained in the system would be still further increased. The poisoning would be intensified, but the usual discomforts arising from toxemia would be put to rest under the comforting touch of the narcotic. And thus this condition might be indefinitely continued, or for as long a time as the organism would be able to endure the continued toxemia, the morphine aggravating the poisoning, the toxemia demanding more morphine.

This is what the drug victim does for himself. He is self-poisoned to an extreme degree, and suffers all the myriad distresses ordinarily arising from the auto-toxemic state. He is also affected by a hypersensitiveness to pain, or a morbid intolerance of any kind of distress, and a degree of mental incompetency probably always more or less present in pronounced auto-toxemias, which render his self-control and his judgment inadequate to a rational course of action. He suffers. His suffering is actually great. To his astigmatic inner eye it seems even greater than it is. He does not recognize the real source of his distress, but interprets it as a cry of deprivation from the inner self. He wants relief, and needs relief, but he is sure of only one means of obtaining it. He knows that in morphine, is a certain quick and pleasant cure for his discomfort, and though he may know that the relief is but temporary, he does just what most of us would probably do in the same circumstances, he takes the morphine.

This, I take it, is the morphine disease, a condition of auto-intoxication for the relief of whose discomforts morphine is taken. It is a condition of double poisoning, first and least by the drug, and secondly and mostly by the toxines of the body itself, the morphine exercising its peculiarly deleterious effect upon the psychical centers and upon the physical functions, the auto-toxemia likewise, damaging both the bodily functions and the mental health. If the toxines were not present there would not be the pains and discomforts that call so beseechingly for the forgetfulness of opium; if the opium were not given the toxic condition would cease to be aggravated. Eliminate either factor, and the morphine disease would not exist.

I do not mean to suggest that this is all there is to morphinism. We cannot ignore the part played by unfortunate heredity, vicious environment, and instabilities arising from other sources, not one of which is negligible in a full consideration of this condition; but the chief feature that looms up before us in the practical management of morphinism, and the one at which our remedial attack is best directed, is as above suggested, the state of toxemia—mainly auto-toxemia—and effects directly traceable to auto-engendered poisoning.

If this view is correct, it does a great deal to clear away the haziness, surrounding the subject of morphinism, simplifying our conception of the condition, and rationalizing our treatment. We can understand why, instead of a pathological entity with clear cut, essential symptoms, such as we meet in malaria or diphtheria, or a host of easily recognizable ailments, we find in the morphine disease as many variations or types as there are varieties of mentality, of temperament, of character, of physical resistance and physical susceptibility; for all of these things respond in various ways both to the narcotism of morphine and to constitutional poisoning from auto-toxemia.

And if this is true, then not only will our treatment vary in accordance with conditions in each individual case, and thus be more intelligently and more certainly directed to a successful issue, but we will also be enabled to deal with the distressed and unhappy morphinist with a larger sympathy and a more enduring patience, for we know of no tortures of mind or body that surpass those arising from a poison saturated system, and none that more irresistibly appeals to us for relief.

Chapter 35

Treating the Morphia Habit

Sir William Osler was the most distinguished physician in the English-speaking world in the decades around 1900. His textbook The Principles and Practices of Medicine *went through numerous editions after its initial appearance in 1894. Because for many physicians Osler was the last word on any medical topic, his views on addiction were extremely important. Here Osler details the symptoms and treatment of morphine addiction in cool, scientific terminology but ends with a strong caution against medical practices that can lead to addiction.*

Interestingly, while Osler was writing this book, he served as the physician of Dr. William Stewart Halsted (1852–1922), later known as the "father of American surgery," who was addicted to morphine from about 1890 until the end of his life. One wonders what Halsted thought when he read this passage.

THE PRINCIPLES AND PRACTICES OF MEDICINE

William Osler

Morphia Habit

This habit arises from the constant use of morphia—taken at first, as a rule, for the purpose of allaying pain. The craving is gradually engendered, and the habit in this way acquired. The injurious effects vary very much, and in the East, where opium-smoking is as common as tobacco-smoking with us, the ill effects are, according to good observers, not so striking.

The habit is particularly prevalent among women and physicians who use the hypodermic syringe for the alleviation of pain, as in neuralgia or sciatica. The acquisition of the habit as a pure luxury is rare in this country.

The symptoms at first are slight, and moderate doses may be taken for months without serious injury and without disturbance of health. There are exceptional instances in which for a period of years excessive doses have been taken without deterioration of the mental or bodily functions. As a rule, the dose necessary to obtain the desired sensations has gradually to be increased. As the effects wear off the victim experiences sensations of lassitude and mental depression, accompanied often with slight nausea and epigastric distress, symptoms which are relieved by another dose of the drug. The confirmed opium-eater presents a very characteristic appearance. There is a sallowness of the complexion which is almost pathognomonic, and he becomes emaciated, gray, and prematurely aged. He is restless, irritable, and unable to remain quiet for any time. Itching is a common symptom. The sleep is disturbed, the appetite and digestion are deranged, and except when directly under the influence of the drug the mental condition is one of depression. Occasionally there are profuse sweats, which may be preceded by chills. The pupils, except when under the direct influence of the drug, are dilated, sometimes unequal. Persons addicted to morphia are inveterate liars, and no reliance whatever can be placed upon their statements. In many instances this is not confined to matters relating to the vice. In women the symptoms may be associated with those of pronounced hysteria or neurasthenia. The practice may be continued for an indefinite time, usually requiring increase in the dose until ultimately enormous quantities may be needed to obtain the desired effect. Finally a condition of asthenia is induced, in which the victim takes little or no food and dies from the extreme bodily debility.

The *treatment* of the morphia habit is extremely difficult, and can rarely be successfully carried out by the general practitioner. Isolation, systematic feeding, and gradual withdrawal of the drug are the essential elements. As a rule, the patients must be under control in an institution and should be in bed for the first ten days. It is best in a majority of cases to reduce the morphia gradually. The diet should consist of beef, juices, milk, and egg-white, which should be given at short intervals. The sufferings of the patients are usually very great, more particularly the abdominal pains, sometimes nausea and vomiting, and the distressing restlessness. Usually within a week or ten days the opium may be entirely withdrawn. In all cases the pulse should be carefully watched and, if feeble, stimulants should be given, with the aromatic spirits of ammonia and digitalis. For the extreme restlessness a hot bath is serviceable. The sleeplessness is the most distressing symptom, and various drugs may have to be resorted to, particularly hyoscine and sulphonal and sometimes, if the insomnia persists, morphia itself.

It is essential in the treatment of a case to be certain that the patient has no means of obtaining morphia. Even under the favorable circumstances of seclusion in an institution, and constant watching by a night and a day nurse, I have known a patient to practice deception for a period of three months. After an apparent cure the patients are only too apt to lapse into the habit.

The condition is one which has become so common, and is so much on the increase, that physicians should exercise the utmost caution in prescribing morphia, particularly to female patients. Under no circumstances whatever should a patient with neuralgia or sciatica be allowed to use the hypodermic syringe, and it is even safer not to intrust this dangerous instrument to the hands of the nurse.

Chapter 36

The Towns Cure

No one else in the addiction field enjoyed so astounding a rise in public and professional esteem, and later such a fall from grace, as that experienced by Charles B. Towns. In the early years of the twentieth century, as new laws restricted the availability of drugs, pressures to find a cure for addiction grew. One consideration was that taking drugs away from addicts without treatment caused them cruel suffering and even the risk of death. Another, from a different perspective, was that if a cure were available, the addict could be held responsible for continuing his behavior. A former successful insurance salesman and stockbroker with no medical training, Towns bought a "cure" from a stranger and started an addiction treatment program that became the leading method of its time. The regimen Towns established was quite brutal but followed the medical theories of the day in prescribing strong laxatives and drugs that countered the effects of withdrawal.

One of the keys to Towns's success lay in his persuading a nationally prominent physician, Dr. Alexander Lambert (later president of the American Medical Association), to endorse his cure. The following article from 1909 marks Lambert's first description of the treatment. Later Lambert came to understand that detoxification from an opiate, the effective result of programs like Towns's, does not signify cure of the craving for the drug. By about 1920 Lambert and much of the rest of the medical community had withdrawn their approval from Towns's cure. Towns, undeterred, continued for the rest of his life to promote his method. In time he added to his crusade against opiates warnings about the dangers of other substances, including coffee, tea, and tobacco.

THE OBLITERATION OF THE CRAVING FOR NARCOTICS

Alexander Lambert

If some years ago any one had told me that it was possible to take away the desire for morphin, cocain, or alcohol in less than five days with a minimum of discomfort and suffering to the patient, I should have felt justified in treating the statement with a polite skepticism. Such, however, is the fact, if the treatment which is about to be described in this article is carefully carried out. I do not doubt that in my turn I shall be met with skepticism, and perhaps ridicule, and more especially from those members of the profession who have struggled and toiled to break up the morphin and cocain habits. Heretofore there has been nothing so discouraging, so trying to both physician and patient, as the endeavor to eradicate the craving for these drugs.

In my service in the alcoholic wards of Bellevue Hospital most of the patients were simply in the various stages and degrees of alcoholism, but there was always about 1 per cent among the men and 2 per cent among the women who were addicted to morphin and cocain. Many of these patients did not wish to be cured; many did earnestly desire to be rid of their enslaving habit. Many were the forms of treatment and drugs with which I tried to break off the habit and take away the craving. In a very few cases I sometimes believed that I had succeeded, but even in these cases there was always a doubt in my mind. In the vast majority of patients I knew that I had failed.

Five years ago Mr. Charles B. Towns, of New York City, informed me that he had a treatment by the use of which it was possible in about three days to remove the craving for morphin and cocain and also for alcohol. After this desire for the narcotics was gone the patients would be able to remain free from the use of morphin, and if it was worth while to the patients it was possible for them to abstain from the use of cocain and alcohol. Mr. Towns, not being a physician, was not bound to tell me the ingredients of this treatment. I begged him to publish it and to put it on an ethical basis, as otherwise I could not use it, but at the time it did not seem expedient for him to do so. Recently he has made the treatment known in all its details to the Opium Congress at Shanghai, and on his return from China he has given me the full details of the treatment and I have been using it in Bellevue Hospital during the last two months.

While the treatment was still unknown to me, and before I used it, I watched Mr. Towns treat various patients addicted to morphin, cocain and alcohol, and found that the claims he made for the treatment were true. I have, therefore, watched patients who ceased the use of their drug five years ago and have not returned to it, and recently I have myself carried out the treatment indicated below.

There are so many factors to be considered in treating those addicted to narcotic drugs that there is no intention here to claim an infallible cure. We are dealing very often with the morally perverted, with those who have been suffering mental or physical pain, with those who have endeavored to stimulate their flagging abilities to ward off failure in life and to spur themselves on by means of these drugs in the hope of succeeding where failure seemed inevitable. Every morphin habitué knows the ease and sureness with which morphin will relieve pain and distress, and if once off the drug and the temptation returns there is a full knowledge of how it may all be relieved. There is no stimulant like cocain, which so fully gives the feeling of being able to do all that one hopes and dreams possible; and there is no drug which so gives the feeling of physical and mental well-being. Added to this, after a few months' use of cocain, there arises a form of persecutory insanity which convinces those addicted to the drug that every one and all the world is against them, and they refuse to listen to any advice. Most alcoholics do not desire to cease from their drinking. When once the habit becomes thoroughly formed, they do not become drunk from haphazard drinking, but they deliberately drink to excess that they may blunt the knowledge of their unhappiness and the realization of their misery and their environment. Alcohol also in many cases brings with it actual physical lesions in the nervous tissues, so that with a deteriorated mentality the higher functions of the mind are destroyed.

The specific in this treatment is the old 15 per cent tincture of belladonna and the fluid extract of xanthoxylum (prickly ash) and the fluidextract of hyoscyamus mixed in the following proportions:

℞	gm.	
Tincture belladonnæ	02	℥ii
Fluidextracti xanthoxyli		
Fluidextracti hyoscyami . . . āā	31	℥i

While this specific is being given, the patients do not suffer from the intense diarrhea which usually accompanies the withdrawal of morphin. On the contrary, the most energetic, drastic, cathartic medication is necessary to obtain the desired elimination and to make their bowels move satisfactorily. This cathartic medication forms one of the crucial points in the treatment. Unless it is properly carried out the treatment will fail and the patients suffer intensely and to no avail. If properly carried out, according to the directions given below, the sufferings of the patient are actually but little, and the treatment goes on to a successful issue.

The most useful combinations in my hands have been the compound cathartic pills of the Pharmacopoeia, which contains:

℞	gm.	
Extracti colorynthidis compositi	08	gr.i⅓
Hydrargyri chloridi mitis.	06	gr.i
Cambogiæ	016	gr.¼
Resinæ jalapæ.	02	gr.⅓

And also the pilule catharticæ vegetabilis:

℞	gm. or c.c	
Extracti colocynthidis compositi	06	gr.i.
Extracti hyoseyami		
Extracti jalapæ . . . . āā	03	gr.ss
Extracti leptandræ		
Extracti resina podophylli . . . . āā	015	gr.¼
Olei menthæ piperitæ	008	M.⅛

To these last I have added in each pill 1/10 (6 mg.) of a grain of the oleoresin of capsicum, ½ gr. (30 mg.) of ginger, and ¹⁄₂₅ minim (.0025 c.c.) of croton oil. I also found that the ordinary stock preparations of compound cathartic pills were too dry to be effective. I, therefore, had made up fresh masses of these preparations, and the mass equivalent to each pill put into a capsule. The preparations kept their freshness, and their effectiveness was very noticeably increased. I also had put in capsules blue mass in five-grain doses. I have thus gone into details because of their importance.

For brevity, I shall hereafter refer to the compound cathartic pills as C. C. pills, and the vegetable cathartic pills, as modified above, as B. B. pills.

The treatment of a case of morphin or cocain is as follows: Before beginning the treatment, give four C. C. pills and five grains of blue mass. It is also wise at this time to give an enema of soapsuds to clean out the rectum and sigmoid thoroughly. When these pills have begun to act, begin with the specific, 6 to 8 minims, and give it every hour throughout the treatment, or until some signs of belladonna intoxication are observed. Every six hours, increase the specific 2 minims until 14 or 16 minims are being taken every hour. Do not increase above 16 minims. If the signs of belladonna intoxication are noticed, such as dilated pupils, dryness of the throat, red rash, or a rapidity and incisiveness of speech, or sometimes a beginning delirium, stop the specific. When these belladonna symptoms have subsided begin the specific again in 8-minim doses. Some patients are very susceptible to belladonna, and one may have to begin again with 4, 5 or 6 minims. Give with the first dose of the specific from one-half to two-thirds of the usual total daily dose of opium, morphin, or cocain which the patient is taking at the time of his treatment. Divide this amount of narcotic in three doses and give them at half-hour intervals, by mouth or by hypodermic as the patient is accustomed to take it. After the first dose of the specific, wait fourteen hours and then give four C. C. pills and five grains of blue mass; again, six hours later, repeat the four C. C. pills or give four to six B. B. pills. It is essential that the cathartic should act at this time, and, if the above amounts do not produce the desired action within three or four hours, they must be repeated with five to ten grains of blue mass. It is astonishing how difficult it sometimes is to obtain a cathartic action at this period, but cathartics must be persisted in until a movement is obtained. If this is not done, the patients are liable to begin to vomit, and the distressing symptoms of the narcotic withdrawal will come out in full force. An ox-gall enema is sometimes of assistance.

After the bowels have acted, but not before, one-third or one-half the original dose of the narcotic may be given. This will make the patient comfortable and contented and ready for the final stage.

Twelve hours after the second dose of the narcotic again give 4 C. C. pills or 4 to 6 B. B. pills with five grains of blue mass, and six hours later give an ounce or more of castor-oil disguised in coffee or orange juice, but not in whiskey. Just before the castor-oil acts, one may have to give from two to five grains of codein phosphate hypodermically or by mouth to quiet the nervousness and discomfort. This is not always necessary, but it adds to the comfort of the patient and does not tie up the secretions as does opium or morphin. The castor-oil at this time will produce a characteristic stool, which shows that the entire treatment may cease. This is a liquid green stool, composed of mucus and bile. When this stool occurs, or shortly afterward, the patients often will feel suddenly relaxed and comfortable, and their previous discomfort ceases. The transition from discomfort to relaxation and contentment is often strikingly marked.

After the patient has been under treatment for thirty hours, one should begin to give some cardiac stimulant, such as strychnin, $\frac{1}{30}$ to $\frac{1}{60}$ grain, every three hours, or digitalis or strophanthus, either one of these separately or in combination. These tend to overcome the relaxation of the vascular system, which in these patients often produces a feeling of exhaustion.

During the treatment the patients should be given a regular diet of easily digested food, such as eggs, cereals, bread and butter, and vegetables; coffee or tea if they desire it. Many of these patients have a good appetite throughout and eat abundantly; some, of course, do not, and, beginning in a poor physical condition, do not begin to eat abundantly until after the treatment is ended. After they are through the treatment, their appetite becomes voracious, and during the first week care must be taken that they do not overeat, which they are very prone to do. If their stomachs should become overloaded the discomfort will often make them feel as if they were suffering from the symptoms of withdrawal of their accustomed narcotic. If this occurs, the best thing to do is to give them an emetic, and their distressing symptoms will soon cease . . .

The treatment of alcoholics with this specific differs slightly from the treatment of the morphin or cocain habitué. The same specific is used and in the same dosage, but it does not have to be continued for so long a time, although there may be some exceptions. Much closer observation is necessary in treating the alcoholic in regard to the symptoms of the intoxication of belladonna. The alcoholic is more sensitive to the belladonna effects. This is only a general rule, because, no matter what narcotic drug an individual may take, or how accustomed he may be to enormous doses of any given narcotic, he may have a marked idiosyncrasy toward any other drug. If, however, there is an idiosyncrasy against belladonna this sensitiveness will show within six or eight hours, no matter which one of the three narcotics under discussion the patient has been taking. The alcoholic is more prone to show a slight delirium from belladonna than are the patients who take morphin or cocain, and often a good deal of shrewd observation is necessary to differentiate the beginning delirium of belladonna from the ordinary delirium of alcohol. The belladonna delirium is, I think, a less furious and less pugnacious delirium than that of alcohol. The patients are more persistent and more insistent in their ideas, and more incisive in their speech concerning their hallucinations than is the alcoholic. The hallucinations of alcohol are usually those of an occupation delirium; those of belladonna are not. The various hallucinations of alcohol follow each other so quickly that a man is busily occupied in observing them one after another. The belladonna delirium is apt to be confined to one or two ideas in which the patient is very insistent.

In the above description of the treatment for morphin, cocain or alcohol, I have spoken as if the patient was taking a single drug. Very frequently we encounter patients who are taking morphin and cocain or morphin and alcohol. When this treatment is given to the cocain habitué who is taking only cocain, or when morphin and cocain are combined, the patients sleep almost continuously throughout the treatment. Cocain is usually taken as a stimulant, an antidote against the depressing effects of the morphin, and this should never be forgotten; therefore, the initial dose of the morphin, in the very beginning of the treatment, when the two drugs are combined, should be smaller than when morphin alone is taken. Cocain is so strong a stimulant that when it is withdrawn it is often necessary, from the very beginning of the treatment, to give a stimulant, such as strychnin, instead of waiting thirty hours, as stated above.

The familiar symptoms in morphin withdrawal, such as intense diarrhea, intense joint and abdominal pains, and muscular contraction, do not occur when this treatment is properly carried out. They are most likely to appear just before the second cathartic acts, and for that reason, as emphasized above, the cathartic action must be obtained at this time. If this is not done, the patients are certain to have trouble . . .

As is well known, morphin is often taken to smother the pain of some under-lying disease, or the distress of some disturbance of function. If these causes still exist after the morphin has been eliminated, the evidence of this former disease or this disturbed function will come to the surface again. At times the narcotic addiction is but a symptom of some abnormal mental state which is only diag-nosticated after the narcotic craving in the patient has been removed. This treat-ment is not a cure-all for disease, a rehabilitator of all the disturbed functions of the body, but if properly carried out it will obliterate the craving for the narcotic and the patient starts anew where he was before taking the narcotic.

The details of this treatment have been given so minutely because it is neces-sary that they should be carried out, for the success of this treatment depends on the conscientious adherence to its many details. Unless this adherence is given, this treatment will probably not succeed. A successful issue is endangered when an attempt is made to carry out the treatment in the patients' homes and in their accustomed environment. They must be placed where they are alone and where they can be carefully watched. Morphin habitués never begin a treatment with any confidence of its success, but invariably with a dread of the distressing withdrawal symptoms. They will secrete the drug in the most unexpected places, and they are the most sly and resourceful creatures on earth, especially those who have ever tried to break it off. No physician is capable of taking this treatment himself and carrying it through successfully. If it is attempted, the old medical adage that the doctor who treats himself has a fool for a patient will be strikingly exemplified.

This treatment does not offer a cure of the perverted habits of the human race, or a regeneration of the mentally defective. It will obliterate the craving for narcotic drugs, and that is all that is claimed for it.

Chapter 37

The Burden of Morphine

Written in 1941 but set in 1912, Long Day's Journey into Night *by Eugene O'Neill re-creates the burden on his family, here called the Tyrones, caused by the mother's addiction to morphine. Like thousands of others — particularly women — in the late nineteenth century, Mary Tyrone was given morphine by her physician and was unaware of the dangers of addiction until too late. The shame often felt by such addicts and their families helped spur the rising demand in the 1910s and 1920s for severe laws to curtail both medical and nonmedical use of opiates.*

The family story represented in this play, which included other sources of conflict besides drug taking, was so painful to O'Neill that in his will he prohibited its performance for twenty-five years after his death. However, his wife, mindful that the persons portrayed all had died and that the work was a masterpiece, allowed it to be shown beginning in 1956, three years after O'Neill's death.

In this passage it is evening in the Tyrones' summer cottage. The father, James Tyrone, a touring actor, is playing cards with his younger son, Edmund. Earlier in the day, Edmund (who represents Eugene O'Neill) has been told that he has tuberculosis. As their card game continues, they hear noises from upstairs.

Long Day's Journey into Night

Eugene O'Neill

Edmund: For God's sake, Papa! Why don't you pick up your hand?

Tyrone: Picks it up — dully. Yes, let's see what I have here. *They both stare at their cards unseeingly. Then they both start. Tyrone whispers.* Listen!

Edmund: She's coming downstairs.

Tyrone: Hurriedly. We'll play our game. Pretend not to notice and she'll soon go up again.

Edmund: Staring through the front parlor — with relief. I don't see her. She must have started down and then turned back.

Tyrone: Thank God.

Edmund: Yes. It's pretty horrible to see her the way she must be now. *With bitter misery.* The hardest thing to take is the blank wall she builds around her. Or it's more like a bank of fog in which she hides and loses herself. Deliberately, that's the hell of it! You know something in her does it deliberately—to get beyond our reach, to be rid of us, to forget we're alive! It's as if, in spite of loving us, she hated us!

Tyrone: Remonstrates gently. Now, now, lad. It's not her. It's the damned poison.

Edmund: Bitterly. She takes it to get that effect. At least, I know she did this time! *Abruptly.* My play, isn't it? Here. *He plays a card.*

Tyrone: Plays mechanically — gently reproachful. She's been terribly frightened about your illness, for all her pretending. Don't be too hard on her, lad. Remember she's not responsible. Once that cursed poison gets a hold on anyone—

Edmund: His face grows hard and he stares at his father with bitter accusation. It never should have gotten a hold on her! I know damned well she's not to blame! And I know who is! You are! Your damned stinginess! If you'd spent money for a decent doctor when she was so sick after I was born, she'd never have known morphine existed! Instead you put her in the hands of a hotel quack who wouldn't admit his ignorance and took the easiest way out, not giving a damn what happened to her afterwards! All because his fee was cheap! Another one of your bargains!

Tyrone: Stung — angrily. Be quiet! How dare you talk of something you know nothing about! *Trying to control his temper.* You must try to see my side of it, too, lad. How was I to know he was that kind of a doctor? He had a good reputation—

Edmund: Among the souses in the hotel bar, I suppose!

Tyrone: That's a lie! I asked the hotel proprietor to recommend the best—

Edmund: Yes! At the same time crying poorhouse and making it plain you wanted a cheap one! I know your system! By God, I ought to after this afternoon!

Tyrone: Guiltily defensive: What about this afternoon?

Edmund: Never mind now. We're talking about Mama! I'm saying no matter how you excuse yourself you know damned well your stinginess is to blame—

Tyrone: And I say you're a liar! Shut your mouth right now, or—

Edmund: Ignoring this. After you found out she'd been made a morphine addict, why didn't you send her to a cure then, at the start, while she still had a chance? No, that would have meant spending some money! I'll bet you told her all she had to do was use a little will power! That's what you still believe in your heart, in spite of what doctors, who really know something about it, have told you!

Tyrone: You lie again! I know better than that now! But how was I to know then? What did I know of morphine? It was years before I discovered what was wrong. I thought she'd never got over her sickness, that's all. Why didn't I send her to a cure, you say? *Bitterly.* Haven't I? I've spent thousands upon thousands in cures! A waste. What good have they done her? She always started again.

A Federal Antinarcotic Law

The Harrison Act of 1914 is a milestone in the history of drug control in the United States. Passage of the act completed a campaign to move control of opiates and cocaine to the national level, replacing the patchwork quilt of antinarcotic laws in the various states. The law was designed to operate under the taxing power of the federal government. All transfers and sales of opiates, except those between doctor or pharmacist and patient, required payment of a tax. The regulations promulgated by the Treasury Department forbade any addiction maintenance — that is, the supply of drugs to those with long-standing addictions — in cases where addiction was unrelated to medical illnesses.

The problem faced by the framers of the law was that any attempt to control the practices of health professionals was likely to violate the police powers retained by the states. The first stratagem employed to bypass this obstacle was to argue that the statute was in fulfillment of the Hague Opium Convention of 1912 and, therefore, could invade the states' police powers per Article VI of the Constitution. This argument as it regarded the prohibition of addiction maintenance was rejected by the Supreme Court in 1916. The Court held that the prohibition of maintenance was not mandated by the treaty.

THE HARRISON ACT

An Act to provide for the registration of, with collectors of internal revenue, and to impose a special tax upon all persons who produce, import, manufacture, compound, deal in, dispense, sell, distribute, or give away opium or coca leaves, their salts, derivatives, or preparations, and for other purposes.

Be it enacted by the Senate and House of Representatives of the United States of America in Congress assembled, That on and after the first day of March, nineteen hundred and fifteen, every person who produces, imports, manufactures, compounds, deals in, dispenses, sells, distributes, or gives away opium or coca leaves or any compound, manufacture, salt, derivative, or preparation thereof, shall register with the collector of internal revenue of the district his name or style, place of business, and place or places where such business is to be carried on: . . .

It shall be unlawful for any person required to register under the terms of this Act to produce, import, manufacture, compound, deal in, dispense, sell, distribute, or give away any of the aforesaid drugs without having registered and paid the special tax provided for in this section. . . .

That the Commissioner of Internal Revenue, with the approval of the Secretary of the Treasury, shall make all needful rules and regulations for carrying the provisions of this Act into effect.

SEC. 2. That it shall be unlawful for any person to sell, barter, exchange, or give away any of the aforesaid drugs except in pursuance of a written order of the person to whom such article is sold, bartered, exchanged, or given, on a form to be issued in blank for that purpose by the Commissioner of Internal Revenue. Every person who shall accept any such order, and in pursuance thereof shall sell, barter, exchange, or give away any of the aforesaid drugs, shall preserve such order for a period of two years in such a way as to be readily accessible to inspection by any officer, agent, or employee of the Treasury Department duly authorized for that purpose, and the State, Territorial, District, municipal, and insular officials named in section five of this Act . . . Nothing contained in this section shall apply—

(a) To the dispensing or distribution of any of the aforesaid drugs to a patient by a physician, dentist, or veterinary surgeon registered under this Act in the course of his professional practice only: *Provided,* That such physician, dentist, or veterinary surgeon shall keep a record of all such drugs dispensed or distributed, showing the amount dispensed or distributed, the date, and the name and address of the patient to whom such drugs are dispensed or distributed, except such as may be dispensed or distributed to a patient upon whom such physician, dentist or veterinary surgeon shall personally attend; and such record shall be kept for a period of two years from the date of dispensing or distributing such drugs, subject to inspection, as provided in this Act. . . .

SEC. 4. That it shall be unlawful for any person who shall not have registered and paid the special tax as required by section one of this Act to send, ship, carry, or deliver any of the aforesaid drugs from any State or Territory or the District of Columbia, or any insular possession of the United States, to any person in any other State or Territory or the District of Columbia or any insular possession of the United States: . . .

SEC. 5. That the duplicate-order forms and the prescriptions required to be preserved under the provisions of section two of this Act, and the statements or returns filed in the office of the collector of the district, under the provisions of section three of this Act, shall be open to inspection by officers, agents, and employees of the Treasury Department duly authorized for that purpose; and such officials of any State or Territory, or of any organized municipality therein, or of the District of Columbia, or any insular possession of the United States, as shall be charged with the enforcement of any law or municipal ordinance regulating the sale, prescribing, dispensing, dealing in, or distribution of the aforesaid drugs. . . .

SEC. 6. That the provisions of this Act shall not be construed to apply to the sale, distribution, giving away, dispensing, or possession of preparations and remedies which do not contain more than two grains of opium, or more than one-fourth of a grain of morphine, or more than one-eighth of a grain of heroin, or more than one grain of codeine, or any salt or derivative of any of them in one fluid ounce, or, if a solid or semisolid preparation, in one avoirdupois ounce; or to liniments, ointments, or other preparations which are prepared for external use only, except liniments, ointments, and other preparations which contain cocaine or any of its salts or alpha or beta eucaine or any of their salts or any synthetic substitute for them: *Provided*, That such remedies and preparations are sold, distributed, given away, dispensed, or possessed as medicines and not for the purpose of evading the intentions and provisions of this Act. The provisions of this Act shall not apply to decocainized coca leaves or preparations made therefrom, or to other preparations of coca leaves which do not contain cocaine. . . .

Sec. 8. That it shall be unlawful for any person not registered under the provisions of this Act, and who has not paid the special tax provided for by this Act, to have in his possession or under his control any of the aforesaid drugs; and such possession or control shall be presumptive evidence of a violation of this section, and also of a violation of the provisions of section one of this Act: *Provided*, That this section shall not apply to any employee of a registered person, or to a nurse under the supervision of a physician, dentist, or veterinary surgeon registered under this Act, having such possession or control by virtue of his employment or occupation and not on his own account; or to the possession of any of the aforesaid drugs which has or have been prescribed in good faith by a physician, dentist, or veterinary surgeon registered under this Act; or to any United States, State, county, municipal, District, Territorial, or insular officer or official who has possession of any said drugs, by reason of his official duties, or to a warehouseman holding possession for a person registered and who has paid the taxes under this Act. . . .

Sec. 9. That any person who violates or fails to comply with any of the requirements of this Act shall, on conviction, be fined not more than $2,000 or be imprisoned not more than five years, or both, in the discretion of the court.

Chapter 39

The *Doremus* and *Webb* Decisions

Between 1916 and 1919 concern over drugs escalated for several reasons. It seemed likely that there would be new addicts among the soldiers returning from the war in Europe. National prohibition of alcohol clearly was on the horizon, and many experts believed that eradicating one drug would only turn inebriates, those vulnerable to addiction, to another. Therefore, they thought it necessary to repress all drugs simultaneously. An additional factor was the report of a special committee established by the Treasury Department to look into the drug problem. That committee concluded that there were a million or more addicts in the United States. This was cause for alarm, as it was widely believed that drugs drove the user to commit crimes simply for the thrill of it. Adding all these forces together, the Supreme Court was under considerable pressure to reconsider its views on addiction maintenance. Two cases, heard together in 1919, supplied the opportunity.

*In the **Doremus** case the Supreme Court ruled on the question of whether the federal government exceeded its powers in taxing drug transactions and, concurrently, regulating the dispensation of drugs by physicians. The Court found that the government was acting within its powers, thereby upholding the constitutionality of the Harrison Act, which provided that physicians could dispense drugs only "in the course of . . . professional practice," through "prescriptions."*

*The **Webb** case was an appeal brought by a physician and a pharmacist who had been convicted for supplying drugs to an addict for no other reason than to support his addiction. The issue was whether such an action fell within the legitimate practice of medicine. It did not, the Court ruled, asserting that to call "such an order for the use of morphine a physician's prescription would be so plain a perversion of meaning that no discussion of the subject is required." Ominously, the decision was five to four, with the conservatives voting in the minority against an invasion of states' rights and the more liberal justices (including Holmes and Brandeis) voting to uphold the Harrison Act. In spite of the close decision, the U.S. government opposed maintenance until the 1960s, when methadone began to be approved as a maintenance opioid for heroin addicts.*

UNITED STATES V. DOREMUS

Mr. Assistant Attorney General Porter and *Mr. W.C. Herron* for the United States:

A reading of the indictment shows that the first two counts and each succeed-

ing two counts must be read together in order to make out the offense intended
to be charged.

Looking at § 2 of the [Harrison] act, in connection with the title and all the
other provisions thereof, it is clear that the key to its meaning is in the distinction
made between producers of, and dealers in, these drugs, on the one hand, and
consumers of them on the other. The former must register and pay the special
tax; the latter not. The incidence of the tax is placed upon the former by the title
of the act, and by its first section, while the latter are not directly dealt with by
the act at all. This distinction is believed to be fundamental. Assuming it to be
the practical object in the mind of Congress, the natural end to be accomplished
by the act in this connection would be to see that the drugs in question, in so far
as the incidence of the tax upon them was concerned, came really and honestly
into the hands of consumers, and did not, through the passport of a druggist or
doctor, come into the hands of a dealer who would not register, would not pay
the special tax, and whose dealings would not be supervised by the Bureau of
Internal Revenue. The facility with which they may be transferred, and the ease
therefore with which the tax upon dealers may be evaded are evident, and
therefore methods and means, which seem at first drastic, may nevertheless be
properly deemed by Congress necessary to secure the assessment of all producers
and dealers, while relieving genuine consumers.

Congress, consequently, provided for the producers and dealers in the provisions of §§ 1 and 2. It required the transferrer and the transferee both to register in
the normal case, and to pay the tax, and to use official order forms in their dealings
with each other, so as to secure that both should so register and pay the tax.

It recognized, however, consumers in paragraphs (*a*) and (*b*) of § 2. It permitted the sale of the drugs to them either from a physician directly or from him
indirectly through a prescription to a druggist. In order, however, to prevent
frauds on the revenue by the obtaining of the drugs under the guise of *bona fide*
consumers by persons who in truth intended to deal in them without registering
and paying the special tax, it required that physicians dispensing the drugs
directly should do so only to "patients" treated in the course of professional
practice, and that druggists should dispense the drugs only on "prescriptions"
issued by physicians, and that neither of them should procure the drugs on order
forms for any purpose other than the distribution of them to *bona fide* consumers
—that is, genuine patients of a physician. The act thus looked at hangs together.
It is true, of course, that it also had the moral purpose of discouraging the use of
the drugs except as a medicine, but its main purpose as a revenue measure was
to see that dealers in the drugs do not escape the tax. . . .

The same presumption prevails in favor of the constitutionality of the means
adopted by Congress to effectuate its exercise of the taxing power as prevails
regarding the exercise of the power itself. Where Congress has acted clearly in
the exercise of its taxing power, the means employed to effectuate this legitimate
functioning are in their nature practical, belonging to the field of experiment and
experience, and outside of the field of judicial knowledge. Hence, if it once be
determined that the main provision of the act levying the tax and defining its

incidence is constitutional, the means devised by Congress for the collection of the tax and the prevention of frauds in connection with it will, except in the most extraordinary case, be held to be within the proper scope of the legislative power. . . .

MR. JUSTICE DAY delivered the opinion of the court. . . .

There are ten counts in the indictment. The first two were treated by the court below as sufficient to raise the constitutional question decided. The first count in substance charges that: Doremus, a physician, duly registered, and who had paid the tax required by the first section of the act, did unlawfully, fraudulently, and knowingly sell and give away and distribute to one Ameris a certain quantity of heroin, to wit, five hundred one-sixth grain tablets of heroin, a derivative of opium, the sale not being in pursuance of a written order on a form issued on the blank furnished for that purpose by the Commissioner of Internal Revenue.

The second count charges in substance that: Doremus did unlawfully and knowingly sell, dispense and distribute to one Ameris five hundred one-sixth grain tablets of heroin not in the course of the regular professional practice of Doremus, and not for the treatment of any disease from which Ameris was suffering, but as was well known by Doremus, Ameris was addicted to the use of the drug as a habit, being a person popularly known as a "dope fiend," and that Doremus did sell, dispense, and distribute the drug, heroin, to Ameris for the purpose of gratifying his appetite for the drug as an habitual user thereof.

Section 1 of the act requires persons who produce, import, manufacture, compound, deal in, dispense, sell, distribute, or give away opium or coca leaves or any compound, manufacture, salt, derivative or preparation thereof, to register with the collector of internal revenue of the district his name or style, place of business, and place or places where such business is to be carried on. At the time of such registry every person who produces, imports, manufactures, compounds, deals in, dispenses, sells, distributes, or gives away any of the said drugs, is required to pay to the collector a special tax of $1.00 per annum. It is made unlawful for any person required to register under the terms of the act to produce, import, manufacture, compound, deal in, dispense, sell, distribute, or give away any of the said drugs without having registered and paid the special tax provided in the act. . . .

It is made unlawful for any person to obtain the drugs by means of the order forms for any purpose other than the use, sale or distribution thereof by him in the conduct of a lawful business in said drugs, or the legitimate practice of his profession.

It is apparent that the section makes sales of these drugs unlawful except to persons who have the order forms issued by the Commissioner of Internal Revenue, and the order is required to be preserved for two years in such way as to be readily accessible to official inspection. But it is not to apply (a) to physicians, etc., dispensing and distributing the drug to patients in the course of professional practice, the physician to keep a record thereof, except in the case of personal attendance upon a patient; and (b) to the sale, dispensing, or distributing of the drugs by a dealer upon a prescription issued by a physician, etc., registered under the act. Other exceptions follow which are unnecessary to the consideration of this case.

Section 9 inflicts a fine or imprisonment, or both, for violations of the act.

This statute purports to be passed under the authority of the Constitution, Article I, § 8, which gives the Congress power "To lay and collect taxes, duties, imposts and excises, to pay the debts and provide for the common defence and general welfare of the United States; but all duties, imposts and excises shall be uniform throughout the United States."

The only limitation upon the power of Congress to levy excise taxes of the character now under consideration is geographical uniformity throughout the United States. This court has often declared it cannot add others. Subject to such limitation Congress may select the subjects of taxation, and may exercise the power conferred at its discretion. Of course Congress may not in the exercise of federal power exert authority wholly reserved to the States. Many decisions of this court have so declared. And from an early day the court has held that the fact that other motives may impel the exercise of federal taxing power does not authorize the courts to inquire into that subject. If the legislation enacted has some reasonable relation to the exercise of the taxing authority conferred by the Constitution, it cannot be invalidated because of the supposed motives which induced it. . . .

Nor is it sufficient to invalidate the taxing authority given to the Congress by the Constitution that the same business may be regulated by the police power of the State.

The act may not be declared unconstitutional because its effect may be to accomplish another purpose as well as the raising of revenue. If the legislation is within the taxing authority of Congress—that is sufficient to sustain it.

The legislation under consideration was before us in a case concerning § 8 of the act, and in the course of the decision we said: "It may be assumed that the statute has a moral end as well as revenue in view, but we are of opinion that the District Court, in treating those ends as to be reached only through a revenue measure and within the limits of a revenue measure, was right." Considering the full power of Congress over excise taxation the decisive question here is: Have the provisions in question any relation to the raising of revenue? That Congress might levy an excise tax upon such dealers, and others who are named in § 1 of the act, cannot be successfully disputed. The provisions of § 2, to which we have referred, aim to confine sales to registered dealers and to those dispensing the drugs as physicians, and to those who come to dealers with legitimate prescriptions of physicians. Congress, with full power over the subject, short of arbitrary and unreasonable action which is not to be assumed, inserted these provisions in an act specifically providing for the raising of revenue. Considered of themselves, we think they tend to keep the traffic aboveboard and subject to inspection by those authorized to collect the revenue. They tend to diminish the opportunity of unauthorized persons to obtain the drugs and sell them clandestinely without paying the tax imposed by the federal law. This case well illustrates the possibility which may have induced Congress to insert the provisions limiting sales to registered dealers and requiring patients to obtain these drugs as a medicine from physicians or upon regular prescriptions. Ameris, being as the indictment charges an addict, may not have used this great number of doses for himself. He might sell some to others without paying the tax, at least Congress may have deemed it wise to prevent such possible dealings because of their effect upon the collection of the revenue.

We cannot agree with the contention that the provisions of § 2, controlling the disposition of these drugs in the ways described, can have nothing to do with facilitating the collection of the revenue, as we should be obliged to do if we were to declare this act beyond the power of Congress acting under its constitutional authority to impose excise taxes. It follows that the judgment of the District Court must be reversed.

Reversed.

THE CHIEF JUSTICE dissents because he is of opinion that the court below correctly held the act of Congress, in so far as it embraced the matters complained of, to be beyond the constitutional power of Congress to enact because to such extent the statute was a mere attempt by Congress to exert a power not delegated, that is, the reserved police power of the States.

MR. JUSTICE MCKENNA, MR. JUSTICE VAN DEVANTER and MR. JUSTICE MCREYNOLDS concur in this dissent.

WEBB ET AL. *v.* UNITED STATES

MR. JUSTICE DAY delivered the opinion of the court . . .

"Webb was a practicing physician and Goldbaum a retail druggist, in Memphis. It was Webb's regular custom and practice to prescribe morphine for habitual users upon their application to him therefor. He furnished these 'prescriptions,' not after consideration of the applicant's individual case, and in such quantities and with such direction as, in his judgment, would tend to cure the habit or as might be necessary or helpful in an attempt to break the habit, but without such consideration and rather in such quantities as the applicant desired for the sake of continuing his accustomed use. Goldbaum was familiar with such practice and habitually filled such prescriptions. Webb had duly registered and paid the special tax as required by § 1 of the act. Goldbaum had also registered and paid such tax and kept all records required by the law. Goldbaum had been provided with the blank forms contemplated by § 2 of the act for use in ordering morphine, and, by the use of such blank order forms, had obtained from the wholesalers, in Memphis, a stock of morphine. It had been agreed and understood between Webb and Goldbaum that Goldbaum should, by using such order forms, procure a stock of morphine, which morphine he should and would sell to those who desired to purchase and who came provided with Webb's so-called prescriptions. It was the intent of Webb and Goldbaum that morphine should thus be furnished to the habitual users thereof by Goldbaum and without any physician's prescription issued in the course of a good faith attempt to cure the morphine habit. In order that these facts may have their true color, it should also be stated that within a period of eleven months Goldbaum purchased from wholesalers in Memphis, thirty times as much morphine as was bought by the average retail druggist doing a larger general business, and he sold narcotic drugs in 6,500 instances; that Webb regularly charged fifty cents for each so-called prescription, and within this period had furnished, and Goldbaum had filled, over 4,000 such prescriptions; and that one Rabens, a user of the drug, came from another state and applied to Webb for morphine and was given at one time ten so-called prescriptions for one drachm each, which prescriptions were filled at one time by Goldbaum upon Rabens' presentation, although each was made out in a separate and fictitious name."

Upon these facts the Circuit Court of Appeals propounds to this court three questions:

"1. Does the first sentence of § 2 of the Harrison Act prohibit retail sales of morphine by druggists to persons who have no physician's prescription, who have no order blank therefor and who cannot obtain an order blank because not of the class to which such blanks are allowed to be issued?

"2. If the answer to question one is in the affirmative, does this construction make unconstitutional the prohibition of such sale?

"3. If a practicing and registered physician issues an order for morphine to an habitual user thereof, the order not being issued by him in the course of professional treatment in the attempted cure of the habit, but being issued for the purpose of providing the user with morphine sufficient to keep him comfortable by maintaining his customary use, is such order a physician's prescription under exception (b) of § 2?

"If question one is answered in the negative, or question two in the affirmative, no answer to question three will be necessary; and if question three is answered in the affirmative, questions one and two become immaterial."

What we have said of the construction and purpose of the act in No. 367, plainly [*U.S. v. Doremus*] requires that question one should be answered in the affirmative. Question two should be answered in the negative for the reasons stated in the opinion in No. 367. As to question three—to call such an order for the use of morphine a physician's prescription would be so plain a perversion of meaning that no discussion of the subject is required. That question should be answered in the negative.

Answers directed accordingly.

For the reasons which prevented him from assenting in No. 367, THE CHIEF JUSTICE also dissents in this case.

MR. JUSTICE McKENNA, MR. JUSTICE VAN DEVANTER and MR. JUSTICE McREYNOLDS concur in the dissent.

Chapter 40

The Demonization of Opium

Sara Graham-Mulhall held the office of the first deputy commissioner in the Department of Narcotic Drug Control in New York state from 1919 until the repeal of legislation for that department two years later. She took a hard line on drugs, and her description of a battle over pain control between a nurse and a physician in this selection from Opium: The Demon Flower *(1926) is particularly interesting. One can see the attitude being inculcated into physicians during the 1920s, a great fear of addicting patients, regardless of their pain. In recent years a very different approach toward pain control has arisen, and its advocates would look at the anecdote below with disgust.*

OPIUM: THE DEMON FLOWER

Sara Graham-Mulhall

In 1855 Dr. Alexander Wood, of Edinburgh, after much experimentation, invented the hypodermic syringe, which medical authorities consider chiefly responsible for the scourge of modern addiction. After the syringe had been in use for about ten years, the effect of it was shown to be so disastrous in many instances that the London *Lancet* published in 1864 a series of forceful papers on the dangers of morphine addiction through subcutaneous administration of the drug. This seed of warning fell on stony ground.

The prestige of the hypodermic syringe was greatly enhanced in 1866, when it was introduced for use in the French army for service both in the field and in the hospital. Attention thus focused on it resulted in the use of the hypodermic syringe in medical ranks everywhere. However, even then there were physicians in France and in Germany who vainly protested against the indiscriminate use of this dangerous implement.

To our country, in 1856, Dr. Fordyce Barker brought for the first time a hypodermic syringe from Edinburgh, the home city of its inventor. Dr. Barker employed what was a small syringe for the subcutaneous administration of morphine and other medication. By our time physicians licensed to deal in narcotics under the federal and state laws had come to give children 15 grains of heroin and a hypodermic needle for self-administration! Who can wonder that nations and world conferences have found regulation necessary even of prescriptions?

There is another danger which even the conscientious physician could not escape. One who was deeply concerned gave me this warning, which I tell as nearly verbatim as possible.

"One night," he said, "the nurse called me up and reported alarming symptoms in the patient. 'Can't we do something to ease the pain?' she asked me. Of course I knew what she meant. She wanted instructions to give him more morphine. I did not give it, because I dread the danger of drug addiction which often begins by giving the patient oft-repeated doses.

" 'I'll come in myself, but I'm very busy,' I said, 'I can't get there for an hour or two. Keep up the medicine you have and wait till I get there.' Of course, I knew and the nurse knew it also, that another quarter of a grain would do the work—put the patient to sleep. But I hesitated to take the chance of increasing the dose. It is about as dangerous to increase the tolerance of the body to morphine as it is to fight the patient's bodily weakness without it. I believe in avoiding morphine entirely except after surgical operations when it should be given with the utmost caution and under no circumstances leaving the dosage to the judgment of the nurse. On making my rounds in the evening I found the patient quiet and went away more hopefully. At midnight, however, the nurse telephoned me again.

" 'Doctor, the patient is in agony again. What shall I do?' " she asked.

" 'Now, you know my rule is never to use the stuff,' I said to her.

" 'But what shall I do?' asked the distracted nurse, tired out with the strain of a raving sick patient.

" 'Well, wait and see, I cannot allow morphine if there is any way under heaven to avoid using it,' I said.

" 'Very well, you're the doctor, but the symptoms of collapse are alarming,' said the nurse, giving me the technical report from the sick chart.

" 'Um, well, we'll see. If things get worse, well, we'll see,' I said.

"At four o'clock in the morning I was roused again. The nurse told be that morphine was imperative. By this time I was so tired and exhausted that I did not want to be disturbed again. The nurse's voice was a trifle impatient. Perhaps I was over-scrupulous, I thought, other physicians use the drug.

" 'Very well, an eighth of a grain, but no more. Be careful about that now, no more till I get around myself in the morning,' I said.

The foregoing is not hypothetical or exceptional, it is what happens in many other cases. No one can find fault with the physician who stands guard over his patient against the drug. No one can criticise the nurse at the bedside, standing between life and death, as she does, in the long night watches. And yet this is one of the side doors in our present civilization through which morphine, opium's chief alkaloid, invades the spirit of resistance.

"The patient recovered," concluded the physician, "but there were other doses of morphine injected before that time arrived. Later, there were recurrences of pain and the patient applied to me for a drug prescription. Then the spiritual battle began, with me explaining the danger of the drug and firmly refusing it, on the one side; on the other side, the patient, under the whispering spell of the drug itself, obstinately pressing me to the wall, with arguments that it was my duty to relieve suffering, that it was I myself who first gave it, that if I would not do as I was asked, there were other physicians who would prescribe it. I knew of course that this was true, but I stood my ground and lost a patient.

"It is a small loss, however, to the self-respecting physician, to the man who does not betray his calling. I made my protest, and the patient went to another physician of equally high standing and reputation in his profession, and got the drug. Not only once, but as the patient was rich, he could have his bottle of morphine constantly in his pocket, properly prescribed by a physician whose reputation as an authority on how a drug addict should be treated is respectfully accepted."

Chapter 41

Drug Addiction as Chronic Disease

Dr. Ernest Bishop was a martyr to his theory of opiate addiction. Like some experts from the first decade of the twentieth century, Bishop had become convinced that drug addiction was a physical disease. He went on to argue, as in these passages from his 1920 book, that the addict seeks out the drug not because of weak character or moral depravity, but because "his body require[s] it." At this time, in the wake of the Doremus *and* Webb *decisions, the belief that addiction was a disease, especially a disease that required indefinite maintenance, conflicted with the announced determination of the federal government to outlaw drug dispensation to addicts. Bishop, who had issued prescriptions in accord with his theory, was indicted by the federal government for violation of the narcotic laws. The Justice Department, believing that this action would reduce Bishop's stature as a prominent therapist, kept him under indictment for five years without trial. Ultimately the charges were dropped because of his ill health. Bishop died shortly afterwards.*

THE NARCOTIC DRUG PROBLEM

Ernest Bishop

It is a fact becoming more and more obvious that too little study and effort to interpret their physical condition have been given to those unfortunates suffering from narcotic drug addiction.

We have neglected their disease in its origin and subsequent progress and formed our conception of its character from fully developed conditions and spectacular end-results. We have seen some of them during or after our fruitless efforts at treatment, their tortures and poor physical condition overcoming their resolutions, until they plead for and attempted to obtain more of their drug. We have seen others exhausted, starved, with locked-up elimination, toxic from self-made poisons of faulty metabolism, worn with the struggle of concealment and hopeless resistance, and for the time being more or less irresponsible beings, made so, not because of their addiction-disease itself, but because they were hopeless and discouraged and did not know which way to turn for relief.

What literature has appeared on the subject has usually pictured them as weak-minded, deteriorated wretches, mental and moral derelicts, pandering to morbid sensuality; taking a drug to soothe them into supposed dream states and give them languorous delight; held by most of us in dislike and disgust, and regarded as so depraved that their rescue was impossible and they unworthy of its attempt.

We have overlooked, ignored or misinterpreted intense physical agony and symptomatology, and regarded failure to abstain from narcotics as evidence of weak will-power or lack of desire to forego supposed morbid pleasure. We have prayed over our addicts, cajoled them, exhorted them, imprisoned them, treated them as insane and made them social outcasts; either refused them admission to our hospitals or turned them out after ineffective treatment with their addiction still fastened to them. To a great extent the above has been their experience and history.

In great numbers they have realized our failure to appreciate their condition and to remedy it, and have after desperate trials of quacks, charlatans and exploited "cures," finally accepted their slavery and by regulation of their drug and life, their addiction unsuspected, maintained a socially and economically normal existence. Some failing in this, perhaps broken and impoverished, their addiction recognized, have become social and economic derelicts and often public charges.

From these last, together with the addicted individuals from the class of the fundamentally unfit, we have painted our addiction picture. Confined and observed by the custodial official and the doctor of the institution of correction and restraint, or concealed as family skeletons in many homes, descriptions of them have given to the narcotic addicts as a whole their popular status—cases of mental and moral disorder due to supposed drug action or habit deterioration, and based upon inherent lack of mental and moral stamina.

It was with the above conception of these addiction conditions that I began my work in the Alcoholic, Narcotic and Prison Service of Bellevue Hospital, attracted to the service not by hope of helping nor by interest in "jags" and "dope fiends" as I then considered them, but by the mass of clinical material available for surgical and medical diagnosis and study which was daily admitted to those wards. When I left the service after sixteen months of day and night observation, with personal oversight and attempt to care for in the neighborhood of a thousand admissions a month, my early and faulty conception of narcotic addicts was replaced by a settled conviction that these cases were primarily medical problems. I realized that these patients were people sick of a definite disease condition, and that until we recognized, understood and treated this condition, and removed the stigma of mental and moral taint from those cases in which it did not exist, we should make little headway towards solution of the problem of addiction.

It is a fact that the narcotic drugs may afford pleasurable sensations to some of those not yet fully addicted to them, and that this effect has been sought by the mentally and morally inferior purely for its enjoyment for the same reasons and in the same spirit that individuals of this type tend to yield themselves to morbid impulses, curiosities, excesses and indulgences. Experience does not teach them intelligence in the management of opiate addiction and they tend to complicate it with cocaine and other indulgence, increasing their irresponsibility and conducing to their earlier self-elimination.

Wide and varied experience, however, hospital and private, with careful analysis of history of development, and consideration of the individual case, demonstrates the fact that a majority of narcotic addicts do not belong to this last described type of individuals. It will be found upon careful examination that they are average individuals in their mental and moral fundamentals. Among them are many men and women of high ideals and worthy accomplishments, whose knowledge of narcotic administration was first gained by "withdrawal" agonies following cessation of medication, who have never experienced pleasure from narcotic drug, are normal mentally and morally, and unquestionably victims of a purely physical affliction.

The neurologist, the alienist, the psychologist, the lawmaker, the moralist, the sociologist and the penologist have worked in the field of narcotic addiction in the lines of their special interests, and interpreted in the lights of their special experiences. Each has reported conditions and results as he saw them, and advised remedies in accordance with his understanding. With very few exceptions little has been heard from the domain of clinical medicine and from the internist. It is only here and there that the practitioner of internal medicine has been sufficiently inspired by scientific interest to seriously consider narcotic drug addiction and to make a clinical study of its actual physical manifestations and phenomena.

The idea that narcotic drug addiction should be accorded a basis of weakness of will—neurotic or otherwise, inherent or acquired—and should be classed as a morbid appetite, a vice, a depraved indulgence, a habit, has been generally unquestioned and the prevailing dogma for many years. It is very unfortunate that we have paid so little attention to material facts and have made so little effort to explain constant physical symptomatology on a basis of physical cause, and that there has not been a wider recognition and more general acceptation of scientific work that has been done.

Despite the years of effort that have been devoted to handling the narcotic addict on the basis of inferiority and neurotic tendencies, and of weakness of will and perverted appetite—in spite of exhortation, investigation, law-making and criminal prosecution—in spite of the various specific and special cures and treatments—narcotic addiction has increased and spread in our country until it has become a recognized menace calling forth stringent legislation and desperate attempts at administrative and police control. And though a large amount of money has been spent in custodial care and sociological investigation on the prevailing theories, and in various legislation, much of it necessary and much of it wisely planned, we have made but little progress in the real remedy of conditions.

It is becoming apparent that in spite of all the work which has been done—in spite of all the efforts which have been made—there has been practically no change in the general situation, and there has been no solution of the drug problem.

In analyzing results of efforts and arriving at causes for failure, it seems to me that it is always wise to begin at the beginning, and to ask ourselves whether we have not started out with an entirely erroneous conception of our basic problem. Is it not possible that instead of punishing a supposedly vicious man, instead of restraining and mentally training a supposedly inherent neuropath and psychopath, we should have been treating an actually sick man? Is it not possible that the addict did not want his drug because he enjoyed it but that he wanted it because his body required it? This is not only possible—it is fact—and the whole secret of our failure has been the misconception of our problem based on our lack of understanding of the average narcotic drug addict and his physical conditions.

In my own experience as a medical practitioner I know that non-appreciation of this fact was the cause of my early failures; and I further know that from the beginning of appreciation of this fact dates whatever progress I have made and whatever success I have attained. In my early efforts as Resident Physician to the Alcoholic and Prison Wards of Bellevue Hospital, devoid of previous experience in the treatment of narcotic addiction, directed by my available literature and by the teachings of those in my immediate reach, I followed the accepted methods. I tried the methods of the alienist; I tried the exhortations of the moralist; I tried sudden deprivation of the drug; I tried rapid withdrawal of the drug; I tried slow reduction of the drug; I tried well-known special "treatment." In other words I exhausted the methods of handling narcotic drug addiction of which I knew. My results were, in these early efforts, one or two possible "cures," but as a whole suffering and distress without relief; in a word failure.

The blame I placed not where it belonged—on the shoulders of my medical inefficiency and lack of appreciation and knowledge of the disease I was treating—but upon what I supposed was my patient's lack of co-operation and unwillingness to forego what I supposed to be the joys of his indulgence. In discouragement and despair I held the addict to be a degenerate, a deteriorated wretch, unworthy of help, incurable and hopeless. Strange as it seems to me now, possessing as I did good training in clinical observation and being especially interested in clinical medicine, in calm reliance upon the correctness of the theories I followed, I ignored the presence of obvious disease.

As to the existing opinion that the addict does not want to be cured, and that while under treatment he cannot be trusted and will not co-operate, but will secretly secure and use his drug—I can only quote from my personal experience with these cases. During my early attempts with the commonly known and too frequently routinely followed procedures of sudden deprivation, gradual reduction and special or specific treatment, etc., my patients beginning with the best intentions in the world, often tried to beg, steal or get in any possible way the drug of their addiction. Like others, I placed the blame on their supposed weakness of will and lack of determination to get rid of their malady. Later I realized the fact that the blame rested almost entirely upon the shoulders of my medical inefficiency and my lack of understanding and ability to observe and interpret. The narcotic addict as a rule will co-operate and will suffer if necessary to the limit of his endurance. Demanding co-operation of a completely developed case of opiate addiction during and following incompetent withdrawal of the drug is asking a man to co-operate for an indefinite period in his own torture. There is a well-defined limit to every one's power of endurance of suffering.

Abundant evidence of what I have written is easily found among the many sufferers from the disease of opiate addiction who have maintained for years a personal, social and economic efficiency—their affliction unknown and unsuspected. These cases are not widely known but there are a surprising number of them. When one of them becomes known his success in handling his condition and its problems is generally attributed to his being on a rather higher moral and mental plane than his fellow sufferers and possessed of will-power sufficient to resist temptation to over-indulge his so-called appetite. We have not as a rule considered any other explanation nor sought more at length for the cause of his apparent immunity to the hypothetical opiate stigmata. It would have been wiser and more profitable for us to have respectfully listened to his experiences and learned something about his disease.

The facts in such cases are that instead of being men of unusual stamina and determination, they are simply men who have used their reasoning ability. They have tried various methods of cure without success. They have realized the shortcomings and inadequacy of the usual understanding and treatment of their condition. Being average practical men, and making the best of the inevitable, they have made careful and competent study of their own cases and have achieved sufficient familiarity with the actions of their opiate upon them and their reactions to the opiate to keep themselves in functional balance and competency and control. The success of these people is not due to determined moderation in the indulgence of a morbid appetite. It is due to their ability to discover facts; to their wisdom in the application of common-sense to what they discover; and to rational procedure in the carrying out of conclusions reached through their experiences. They have simply learned to manage their disease so as to avoid complications. When I tried to account for some of the things I saw by questioning these men who had studied and learned upon themselves, I soon obtained a clearer conception of what opiate addiction was.

When we eliminate the distracting and misleading complications, mental and physical, and study the residue of physical symptomatology left, we make some very surprising and striking observations.

We find that we are dealing fundamentally with a definite condition whose disease manifestations are not in any way dependent in their origin upon mental processes, but are absolutely and entirely physical in their production, and character. These symptoms and physical signs are clearly defined, constant, capable of surprisingly accurate estimation, yielding with a sureness almost mathematical in their response to intelligent medication and the recognition and appreciation of causative factors; forming a clean-cut symptom-complex peculiar to opiate addiction. Any one—whether of lowered nervous, mental and moral stamina, or a giant of mental and physical resistance—will, if opiates are administered in continuing doses over a sufficient length of time, develop some form of this symptom-complex. It represents causative factors, and definite conditions which are absolutely and entirely due to changed physical processes which fundamentally underlie all cases of opiate addiction, and which proceed to full development through well-marked stages.

During the past years I have had under my care a number of excellent and competent physicians of unusual mental and nervous balance and control in whom there could be no hint of lack of courage, nor of deficient willpower, nor of lack of desire to be free from their affliction. Possessing, some of them, unusual medical training and scientific ability, having added to this the actual experiences of opiate addiction, they with others have co-operated and aided in experiment, study and analysis, and the result has been in their minds as in mine, complete confirmation of the facts above stated.

Primarily, there are two phrases I should like to see eliminated from the literature of opiate drug addiction. I believe they have worked great injustice to the opiate addict and have played no small part in the making of present conditions. It seems to me that to speak and write as we still often do of "drug habit" and "drug fiends" is placing upon the opiate addict a burden of responsibility which he does not deserve. If long ago we had discarded the word "habit" and substituted the word "disease" I believe we would have saved many people from the hell of narcotic drug addiction. I believe if it had not been for the use of the word "habit" that the medical profession would long ago have recognized and investigated this condition as a disease. A man, physician or layman, believes that he can control a habit when he would fear the development of a disease. Until now, however, the description has been "drug habit." And the man who acquires one of the most terrible diseases to be encountered in the practice of medicine is unconscious of his being threatened with a physical disease process until this process has become so developed and so rooted that it is beyond average human power to resist its physical demands.

In the near future, I earnestly hope the true story and the real facts concerning the opiate drug addict will become universally known. Without familiarity with them and understanding of them, and comprehension and appreciation of their disease, we shall never make real progress in the solution of the narcotic drug problem. From the present day trend of articles and stories in the newspapers and lay and medical magazines it cannot be doubted that the time is not far distant when in the lay press will appear, in plain, sober, unvarnished truth, the true story of the experiences and struggles of the opiate drug addict. I have marked a rapidly growing appreciation of facts and a steadily increasing activity in the investigation of conditions. This is sooner or later bound to be followed by intelligent public and scientific demand for competent and common-sense explanation and solution.

Chapter 42

Richmond P. Hobson Takes on Drugs

Cheered by the success of the antialcohol movement in achieving Prohibition, Richmond Pearson Hobson went on to the drug problem. In this campaign, too, he talked and wrote in extravagant terms, here comparing heroin addicts to lepers who would spread their traits among the healthy population. He also exaggerated the number of addicts: Hobson sometimes claimed that there were four million users in the United States, while the federal government's estimate was 100,000 to 200,000. Danger lurked everywhere. At one point, Hobson urged women to have their face powder checked for traces of heroin. The following from his 1928 pamphlet is a good example of the propaganda that influenced American attitudes toward drug users in the 1920s and 1930s.

MANKIND'S GREATEST AFFLICTION AND GRAVEST MENACE

Richmond P. Hobson

Exploitation of Narcotic Drug Addiction

The human race is consuming every year many thousands of tons of poisonous narcotic drugs, not one percent of which is necessary for strictly medicinal purposes. Nearly all of this great quantity is consumed by addicts who number in the world scores of millions who are abject slaves, who consider getting their drug supply as the supreme consideration, in many cases as a matter of life and death. The production and distribution of these drugs constitute a profitable traffic of vast proportions extending to all corners of the earth.

The motive and urge that constantly drive the traffic on are the enormous profits, the jobber and retailer between them often realizing thousands of per cent profit. Add to this the lure for the armies of impoverished addicts of getting the drug for themselves through recruiting and supplying the new addicts. It is not surprising that the amount of narcotic drugs produced is probably thirty times the amount required for medicinal purposes. The profits are so great because the poor addict, under the awful depression and torture of withdrawal symptoms, feels that he must have the drug, no matter what the cost or the consequences, whether he has to steal to get the money, whether he has to rob or even to commit murder.

Like the invasions and plagues of history, the scourge of Narcotic Drug Addiction came out of Asia. However, it was the European in Asia who discovered the vast profit in opium smoking and eating and proceeded with the commercial culture of the poppy and the widening circle of exploitation.

In the progress of modern science, a French chemist, something over a century ago, discovered how to extract morphine from opium, making it suitable for medical practice. While the opium traffic radiating from Asia started centers of infection in seaports of Europe and America, the spread of addiction was still comparatively slow. With morphine, however, the train of addiction quickly spread around the world and a new problem of morphine addiction was superimposed upon the old problem of opium addiction. About a half a century later, an Austrian chemist discovered how to extract cocaine from coca leaves, and cocaine addiction was further superimposed upon the morphine and opium addiction, making the problem more difficult and more dangerous, adding a serious factor of criminology especially inherent in cocaine addicts.

In 1898, a German chemist discovered how to produce heroin by treating morphine with acetic acid. Heroin addiction has placed the cap on the whole structure of cocaine-morphine-opium addiction. The crime symptoms of cocaine suddenly sprang into a veritable crime wave and a new "Banditry" with the spread of heroin. The white man is in graver peril than the yellow man.

Narcotics are soluble in fat, so they penetrate the fatty sheathing that protects the brain from most harmful substances in the blood current, and in this way the poison comes quickly in contact with the delicate highly organized gray matter. Similarly these poisons attack the delicate, carefully protected organs of reproduction, impairing the sexual powers of the male, causing the female addict to become sterile, and undermining the germ plasm, by virtue of which the species renews its life from generation to generation.

In the case of cocaine and heroin the degeneration of the upper brain is so swift that the elements of character crumble in a few months. Complete demoralization follows, and often the life of crime joins with physical ills and the spur of torture of the drug, to hasten the end.

Incalculable Suffering

When the drug begins to subside, a condition of torture sets in. Pains often succeed each other as though a sword were being thrust through the body. In advanced cases this suffering (called "withdrawal symptoms") is considered the most acute torture ever endured by man. The drug of addiction will quickly relieve this torture. Naturally, the addict comes to consider getting his supply of the drug as a matter of life and death.

The mental suffering and anguish endured are commensurate with the physical sufferings. The fear of not being able to get the drug supply is perpetual, and the thought of the torture of "withdrawal symptoms" brings abject submission to a pitiless master. The sympathies of mankind have always been aroused for the sufferings of slaves in the days of the slave trade. Their bondage was easy and light compared to the "LIVING DEATH" of drug addicts. It would be hard for any normal person to appreciate the anguish of mind and of soul that comes to an addict as he gradually realizes his helplessness and sees his own elements of character, his own morals, his own principles disintegrate, and beholds the sufferings of his family and friends and the scorn and hate of Society as it pursues him. Drug addicts endure more suffering and anguish, physical and mental, than any other group of sufferers.

We have only to bear in mind that the drug addicts of the Orient are numbered in tens of millions and the drug addicts of the Occident in hundreds of thousands. The suffering of the average addict, multiplied by the number of addicts, makes a product incredibly huge.

The sufferings of the families of addicts are second only to the sufferings of the addicts themselves. First comes the shock of discovering that a dear one is an addict. Then the long period of efforts at rescue, with hopes rising, only to be wrecked, witnessing the physical, intellectual, moral and spiritual disintegration of a dear one in the grip of progressive addiction, tear asunder the heartstrings of loved ones as nothing else can do. The dissipation of family substance, the humiliation from the conduct of the addict member as he sinks deeper in moral turpitude, the silent, perpetual shame of it all, the mockery, the despair, constitute a cup of suffering second only to that of the "LIVING DEATH." Multiply the total number of addicts by five to get the number of close of kin, and multiply this product by the suffering of the average kin, and think what the grand product must be. Of course, more distant relatives and friends also suffer keenly and their number is very large.

The Sufferings of Society Are Difficult to Over-Estimate

A citizen asset, becoming an addict, is turned into the worst form of liability. The economic wastage is heavy, the producer becoming not only a dependent, but a destructive parasite. It is estimated that CRIME NOW PLACES A BURDEN EXCEEDING TEN BILLIONS OF DOLLARS YEARLY UPON THE AMERICAN PEOPLE. Drug addicts constitute overwhelmingly the biggest group of convicts in Federal penitentiaries. It would be conservative to estimate at one-third of the total burden of crime the part that comes from DRUG ADDICTION. THE PUBLIC HEALTH is equally menaced, the drug addict being the principal incubator and carrier of vice diseases as well as the other diseases that menace the public health. PUBLIC MORALS suffer from the prevalence of drug addicts even more heavily than the health and the public safety. Before drug addiction, all the moral and spiritual attributes of men upon which the institutions of civilized society are built, utterly disintegrate. A sufficient spread of drug addiction must insure the disintegration and obstruction of any civilization.

Adding up the suffering of the armies of the addicts themselves, "THE LIVING DEAD," the sufferings of the families, the kin and friends of these addicts, making up vastly larger armies, and the sufferings of society with all the institutions of our complex civilization, it is manifest that NARCOTIC DRUG ADDICTION NOW INFLICTS UPON MANKIND ITS GREATEST MEASURE OF SUFFERING.

While many methods have been found for getting the victim off the drug, the scientific world and the medical profession recognize no sure and permanent cure. Only a small percentage of morphine and opium addicts remain permanently off the drug, while the number of heroin addicts is practically negligible. So helpless is the victim, and so pitiless the master, that the heroin addicts are termed "THE LIVING DEAD."

The Crime Wave, A Symptom

The transformation in character is swift, especially in the young and swifter with cocaine and heroin than with the other narcotics. In an incredibly short time a youth of either sex "hooked" with the "snow gang," loses the result of good heredity and of careful home training. Self-respect, honor, obedience, ambition, truthfulness, melt away. Virtue and morality disintegrate. The question of securing the drug supply becomes absolutely dominant. To get this supply the addict will not only advocate public policies against the public welfare, but will lie, steal, rob and if necessary, commit murder. Thus we can understand how intimately addiction is connected causatively with crime.

In addition to the general anti-social traits of all addicts, the heroin addict has two special characteristics: First, for a period after taking the drug he experiences an "exaltation of the ego," looks upon himself as a hero. Bent upon getting money to buy his drug, he will dare anything, thinks he can accomplish anything. The daylight holdups, robberies, murders committed by these young criminal heroin addicts eclipse in daring all the exploits of Jesse James and his gang. This can be said also of cocaine addicts.

Spreading Like Infection

The heroin addict has a mania to bring everybody else into addiction. It may be said in general that all addicts have a desire for company and wish others to share with them the problem of securing the drug supply, but in the case of the heroin addict it is an absolute mania for recruiting. He thinks, he dreams, he plots to bring all whom he contacts into addiction. All addiction tends to spread. Heroin addiction can be likened to a contagion. Suppose it were announced that there were more than a million lepers among our people. Think what a shock the announcement would produce! Yet drug addiction is far more incurable than leprosy, far more tragic to its victims, and is spreading like a moral and physical scourge.

Capture of the books of a "dope ring" in Chicago revealed 18,000 addicts among the customers, involving yearly payments of $39,000,000. This was but one ring in one city. More than half of all prisoners in moral turpitude cases in the prisons of New York City are now addicts, over 90 percent of these being young heroin addicts, although heroin addiction has been in exploitation only a few years. The number of prisoners in Federal penitentiaries convicted for offenses against Narcotic laws is three times that of those convicted on any other law. Offenses against Federal Narcotic Laws were about 1,000 a year until the exploitation of heroin set in in America. From this level in 1917 the number doubled in two years, in 1919 exceeding 2,000. This second number doubled in two years, in 1921 exceeding 4,000. This number has now doubled, exceeding 8,000.

Progress in synthetic chemistry is very rapid, stimulated by military experimentation in the development of poison gases and other materials of war. This progress is not only sure to discover new habit-forming narcotic drugs more powerful and more menacing even than heroin, but is also certain to find additional sources of material from which to manufacture, especially utilizing coal tar bases. The human race is thus in the midst of a new environment of peril for which it is not adapted. Adaptation to this environment is a biological necessity if the race is to live and flourish upon the earth. Certainly a problem such as this, having reached such vast proportions, with the attendant ravages so vitally affecting every department of human life, should arouse the solicitude of our Government and the governments of other lands and all thoughtful citizens who are devoted to the uplifting of mankind.

The Defense

Manifestly, no normal youth, or for that matter, normal adult, would deliberately embrace this "LIVING DEATH" of drug addiction if he knew what it meant. The whole reruiting system is based on the ignorance of the victim, and thorough education would literally sweep away the very foundation of this hideous traffic.

This exploitation partakes of the nature of a parasite and the nature of a beast of prey or inherent enemy. Therefore governmental and legal processes are logical weapons of society to invoke and organize for its defense. Since its victims are the chief instruments through which the enemy preys upon society, the isolation and rehabilitation of those victims constitute an integral part of the treatment. The defense of society against Narcotic Drug Addiction must therefore embrace processes of education, processes of law, and processes of reclamation. The International Narcotic Education Association is undertaking to bring into operation organizations for all these processes.

Chapter 43

No Mercy for Drug Violations

During the middle decades of the twentieth century, the center of the federal response to illicit drug use was the Federal Bureau of Narcotics (FBN), founded in 1930 and headed from that date until 1962 by the legendary Harry J. Anslinger. Within the bureau opinion held that stringent laws accounted for the decline in drug use observed in the first third of the century. When heroin use rose somewhat around 1950, the FBN's reaction was to call for increased penalties.

Mandatory minimum sentences, long desired by Commissioner Anslinger, were enacted by Congress in 1951, in the measure known as the Boggs Act, after Representative Hale Boggs of Louisiana. Five years later the Narcotic Control Act of 1956 lengthened minimum sentences and allowed imposition of the death penalty on anyone over eighteen who provided heroin to one under that age. A separate section of the act required that all those still legally in possession of heroin (pharmacists, for instance) turn the drug over to the government, after which time heroin would be considered contraband. In spite of these severe measures, illicit drug use would skyrocket in the mid-1960s.

The Boggs Act

An Act to amend the penalty provisions applicable to persons convicted of violating certain narcotic laws, and for other purposes.

Be it enacted by the Senate and House of Representatives of the United States of America in Congress assembled, That section 2 (c) of the Narcotic Drugs Import and Export Act, as amended (U.S.C., title 21, sec. 174), is amended to read as follows:

"(c) Whoever fraudulently or knowingly imports or brings any narcotic drug into the United States or any territory under its control or jurisdiction, contrary to law, or receives, conceals, buys, sells, or in any manner facilitates the transportation, concealment, or sale of any such narcotic drug after being imported or brought in, knowing the same to have been imported contrary to law, or conspires to commit any of such acts in violation of the laws of the United States, shall be fined not more than $2,000 and imprisoned not less than two or more than five years. For a second offense, the offender shall be fined not more than $2,000 and imprisoned not less than five or more than ten years. For a third or subsequent offense, the offender shall be fined not more than $2,000 and impris-

oned not less than ten or more than twenty years. Upon conviction for a second
or subsequent offense, the imposition or execution of sentence shall not be suspended and probation shall not be granted. . . .

"Whenever on trial for a violation of this subdivision the defendant is shown
to have or to have had possession of the narcotic drug, such possession shall be
deemed sufficient evidence to authorize conviction unless the defendant explains
the possession to the satisfaction of the jury."

THE NARCOTIC CONTROL ACT OF 1956

An Act to amend the Internal Revenue Code of 1954 and the Narcotic Drugs
Import and Export Act to provide for a more effective control of narcotic drugs
and marihuana, and for other related purposes.

*Be it enacted by the Senate and House of Representatives of the United States of America
in Congress assembled.* That this Act may be cited as the "Narcotic Control Act of
1956."

Title I — Amendments to the 1954 Code, The Narcotic Drugs Import and Export Act, Etc.

SEC. 101. Unlawful Acquisition, etc., of Marihuana.

Subsection (a) of section 4744 of the Internal Revenue Code of 1954 (unlawful
acquisition of marihuana) is amended to read as follows:

"(a) PERSONS IN GENERAL.—It shall be unlawful for any person who is a
transferee required to pay the transfer tax imposed by section 4741 (a)—

"(1) to acquire or otherwise obtain any marihuana without having paid such
tax, or
"(2) to transport or conceal, or in any manner facilitate the transportation or
concealment of, any marihuana so acquired or obtained.

Proof that any person shall have had in his possession any marihuana and shall
have failed, after reasonable notice and demand by the Secretary or his delegate,
to produce the order form required by section 4742 to be retained by him shall
be presumptive evidence of guilt under this subsection and of liability for the tax
imposed by section 4741 (a)."

SEC. 102. Unlawful Transportation of Marihuana.

Subsection (b) of section 4755 of the Internal Revenue Code of 1954 (unlawful
transportation of marihuana) is amended to read as follows:

"(b) Transportation—Except as otherwise provided in this subsection, it shall
be unlawful for any person to send, ship, carry, transport, or deliver any mari-

huana within any Territory, the District of Columbia, or any insular possession of the United States, or from any State, Territory, the District of Columbia, or insular possession of the United States. Nothing contained in this subsection shall apply—

"(1) to any person who shall have registered and paid the special tax as required by sections 4751 to 4753, inclusive;

"(2) to any common carrier engaged in transporting marihuana;

"(3) to any employee acting within the scope of his employment for any person who shall have registered and paid the special tax as required by sections 4751 to 4753, inclusive, or to any contract carrier or other agent acting within the scope of his agency for such registered person;

"(4) to any person who shall deliver marihuana which has been prescribed or dispensed by a physician, dentist, veterinary surgeon, or other practitioner registered under section 4753 and employed to prescribe for the particular patient receiving such marihuana;

"(5) to any person carrying marihuana which has been obtained by the person from a registered dealer in pursuance of a written prescription referred to in section 4742 (b) (2), issued for legitimate medical uses by a physician, dentist, veterinary surgeon, or other practitioner registered under section 4753, if the bottle or other container in which such marijuana is carried bears the name and registry number of the druggist, serial number of prescription, name and address of the patient, and name, address, and registry number of the person issuing such prescription;

"(6) to any person carrying marihuana which has been obtained by the person as a patient from a registered physician, dentist, or other practitioner in the course of his professional practice if such marihuana is dispensed to the patient for legitimate medical purposes; or

"(7) to any United States, State, county, municipal, District, Territorial, or insular officer or official acting within the scope of his official duties."

SEC. 103. Violations of Narcotic Drug and Marihuana Laws.

Section 7237 of the Internal Revenue Code of 1954 (violations of laws relating to narcotic drugs and marihuana) is amended to read as follows:

"SEC. 7237. Violation of Laws Relating to Narcotic Drugs and to Marihuana.

"(a) WHERE NO SPECIFIC PENALTY IS OTHERWISE PROVIDED.—Whoever commits an offense, or conspires to commit an offense, described in part I or part II of subchapter A of chapter 30 for which no specific penalty is otherwise provided, shall be imprisoned not less than 2 or more than 10 years and, in addition, may be fined not more than $20,000. For a second offense, the offender shall be imprisoned not less than 5 or more than 20 years and, in addition, may be fined not more than $20,000. For a third or subsequent offense, the offender shall be imprisoned not less than 10 or more than 40 years and, in addition, may be fined not more than $20,000.

"(b) SALE OR OTHER TRANSFER WITHOUT WRITTEN ORDER.—Whoever commits an offense, or conspires to commit an offense, described in section 4705 (a) or section 4742 (a) shall be imprisoned not less than 5 or more than 20 years and, in addition, may be fined not more than $20,000. For a second or subsequent offense, the offender shall be imprisoned not less than 10 or more than 40 years and, in addition, may be fined not more than $20,000. If the offender attained the age of 18 before the offense and—

"(1) the offense consisted of the sale, barter, exchange, giving away, or transfer of any narcotic drug or marihuana to a person who had not attained the age of 18 at the time of such offense, or

"(2) the offense consisted of a conspiracy to commit an offense described in paragraph (1),

the offender shall be imprisoned not less than 10 or more than 40 years and; in addition, may be fined not more than $20,000. . . .

"(d) No SUSPENSION OF SENTENCE; NO PROBATION; ETC.—Upon conviction—

"(1) of any offense the penalty for which is provided in subsection (b) of this section, subsection (c), (h), or (i) of section 2 of the Narcotic Drugs Import and Export Act, as amended, or such Act of July 11, 1941, as amended, or

"(2) of any offense the penalty for which is provided in subsection (a) of this section, if it is the offender's second or subsequent offense,

the imposition or execution of sentence shall not be suspended, probation shall not be granted, section 4202 of title 18 of the United States Code shall not apply, and the Act of July 15, 1932 (47 Stat. 696; D. C. Code 24–201 and following), as amended, shall not apply. . . .

SEC. 105. Importations, etc., of Narcotic Drugs.

Section 2 (c) of the Narcotic Drugs Import and Export Act, as amended (U.S.C., title 21, sec. 174), is amended to read as follows:

"(c) Whoever fraudulently or knowingly imports or brings any narcotic drug into the United States or any territory under its control or jurisdiction, contrary to law, or receives, conceals, buys, sells, or in any manner facilitates the transportation, concealment, or sale of any such narcotic drug after being imported or brought in, knowing the same to have been imported or brought into the United States contrary to law, or conspires to commit any of such acts in violation of the laws of the United States, shall be imprisoned not less than five or more than twenty years and, in addition, may be fined not more than $20,000. For a second or subsequent offense (as determined under section 7237 (c) of the Internal Revenue Code of 1954), the offender shall be imprisoned not less than ten or more than forty years and, in addition, may be fined not more than $20,000.

"Whenever on trial for a violation of this subsection the defendant is shown to have or to have had possession of the narcotic drug, such possession shall be deemed sufficient evidence to authorize conviction unless the defendant explains the possession to the satisfaction of the jury. . . .

SEC. 106. Smuggling of Marihuana.

Section 2 of the Narcotic Drugs Import and Export Act, as amended, is amended by adding at the end thereof the following:

"(h) Notwithstanding any other provision of law, whoever, knowingly, with intent to defraud the United States, imports or brings into the United States marihuana contrary to law, or smuggles or clandestinely introduces into the United States marihuana which should have been invoiced, or receives, conceals, buys, sells, or in any manner facilitates the transportation, concealment, or sale of such marihuana after being imported or brought in, knowing the same to have been imported or brought into the United States contrary to law, or whoever conspires to do any of the foregoing acts, shall be imprisoned not less than five or more than twenty years and, in addition, may be fined not more than $20,000. For a second or subsequent offense (as determined under section 7237 (c) of the Internal Revenue Code of 1954), the offender shall be imprisoned for not less than ten or more than forty years and, in addition, may be fined not more than $20,000.

"Whenever on trial for a violation of this subsection, the defendant is shown to have or to have had the marihuana in his possession, such possession shall be deemed sufficient evidence to authorize conviction unless the defendant explains his possession to the satisfaction of the jury. . . .

SEC. 107. Sale of Heroin to Juveniles—Penalties.

Section 2 of the Narcotic Drugs Import and Export Act, as amended, is further amended by adding at the end thereof the following:

"(i) Notwithstanding any other provision of law, whoever, having attained the age of eighteen years, knowingly sells, gives away, furnishes, or dispenses, facilitates the sale, giving, furnishing, or dispensing, or conspires to sell, give away, furnish, or dispense, any heroin unlawfully imported or otherwise brought into the United States, to any person who has not attained the age of eighteen years, may be fined not more than $20,000, and shall be imprisoned for life, or for not less than ten years, except that the offender shall suffer death if the jury in its discretion shall so direct.

"Whenever on trial for a violation of this subsection the defendant is shown to have had heroin in his possession, such possession shall be sufficient proof that the heroin was unlawfully imported or otherwise brought into the United States unless the defendant explains his possession to the satisfaction of the jury. . . .

Title II — Amendments to Title 18 of the United States Code

SEC. 201. Addition of New Chapter—Narcotics.

Part I of title 18 of the United States Code is amended by inserting after chapter 67 the following new chapter:

"*Chapter 68 — Narcotics*

"§ 1401. Definitions
    "As used in this chapter—
    "The term 'heroin' shall mean any substance identified chemically as diacetyl-morphine or any salt thereof. . . .
"§ 1402. Surrender of heroin—procedure
    Any heroin lawfully possessed prior to the effective date of this Act shall be surrendered to the Secretary of the Treasury, or his designated representative, within one hundred and twenty days after the effective date of the Act, and each person making such surrender shall be fairly and justly compensated therefor. The Secretary of the Treasury, or his designated representative, shall formulate regulations for such procedure. All quantities of heroin not surrendered in accordance in with this section and the regulations promulgated thereunder by the Secretary of the Treasury, or his designated representative, shall by him be declared contraband, seized, and forfeited to the United States without compensation. All quantities of heroin received pursuant to the provisions of this section, or otherwise, shall be disposed of in the manner provided in section 4733 of the Internal Revenue Code of 1954, except that no heroin shall be distributed or used for other than scientific research purposes approved by the Secretary of the Treasury, or his designated representative.

Chapter 44

The AMA and the ABA on the Limits of Law Enforcement

While the FBN held the line against viewing addiction as a disease that might require maintenance, agitation grew among physicians and lawyers who believed that a new approach was needed, one that relied more on public health measures and rather less on the criminal justice system. Debate raged over maintenance, but the lack of almost any treatment programs other than the Lexington and Fort Worth hospitals, to which addicted convicts were remanded and which accommodated small numbers of voluntary patients, concerned reformers on both sides of that question. Under the joint aegis of the American Bar Association (ABA) and the American Medical Association (AMA), a study of the drug problem was conducted. The results, published in 1961, greatly irritated Commissioner Anslinger, who took a "no tolerance" position on the drugs he oversaw — the opioids, cocaine, and marijuana. In his view no changes were necessary, only the strict enforcement of the law.

DRUG ADDICTION: CRIME OR DISEASE?

Joint Committee of the American Bar Association and the American Medical Association on Narcotic Drugs

Recommendation

The joint committee recommends to the House of Delegates of the American Bar Association and the House of Delegates of the American Medical Association that its activities as a special committee be terminated; and that the study of the narcotic drug traffic and related problems, initiated by it, be carried forward cooperatively through appropriate instrumentalities and research facilities within the permanent structures of the two associations.

Report

In this report the Joint American Bar Association–American Medical Association Committee on Narcotic Drugs is completing its original assignment as set forth in the A.B.A. House of Delegates resolution of February 22, 1955, "To explore with the American Medical Association the possibilities of a jointly conducted study of the narcotic drug traffic and related problems...." Its principal conclusions are two: that present methods of dealing with narcotic addiction and narcotic addicts raise questions which are urgently in need of study; and that the legal and medical professions, equally concerned, can most fruitfully pursue the subject in close cooperation through their respective associations. In passing, it is noted with great satisfaction that the joint committee's two years' work has been, in view of all concerned, a rewarding and eminently successful experiment in inter-professional cooperation.

The joint committee offers its observations and tentative conclusions here, and recommends its own dissolution, because it has reached a point where it believes the full resources of its parent associations must be called into play. The research it deems necessary seems too extensive to be undertaken by a temporary committee—when both associations support permanently organized research foundations precisely designed for such projects; and the policy determinations which must ultimately be made lie within the jurisdiction of permanently constituted divisions within both parent bodies.

With the aid of a grant from the Russell Sage Foundation, the joint committee has completed a factual analysis of present policies and present knowledge concerning narcotic addiction and the control of narcotic drugs, which was submitted with its interim report to the A.M.A. and A.B.A. House of Delegates last year. This interim report, with its appendices, contains information concerning the medical, social and legal problems confronted in dealing with drugs and drug addiction in the light of existing policies and available knowledge. It does not attempt to provide solutions, but does reflect a degree of dissatisfaction within the legal and medical professions concerning current policies which tend to emphasize repression and prohibition to the exclusion of other possible methods of dealing with addicts and the drug traffic.

The interim report recommends additional research in five major areas:

1. An experimental facility for the outpatient treatment of drug addicts, to explore the possibilities of dealing with at least some types of addicted persons in the community rather than in institutions.
2. An extensive study of relapse and causative factors in drug addiction.
3. The development of sound and authoritative techniques and programs for the prevention of drug addiction.
4. A critical evaluation of present legislation on narcotic drugs and drug addiction.
5. A study and analysis of the administration of present narcotic laws.

The joint committee urges that the above projects and studies be carried on under the auspices of its parent associations, in order to provide additional experience and data needed to appraise alternative methods of controlling narcotic addiction and dealing with the drug addict.

In making these recommendations, the joint committee is aware that they may encounter opposition from those who tend to view the drug problem as essentially a problem of criminal law enforcement, and specifically that the United States Narcotics Bureau has indicated that it will oppose them. The joint committee regrets this attitude demonstrated by the Narcotics Bureau. In the committee's opinion, the Narcotics Bureau, together with all other persons and agencies interested in the problem, should welcome research in the areas which have been indicated. The narcotics problem is too important to be insulated from intensive study and investigation.

While zealous law-enforcement efforts have unquestionably played a part in reducing drug addiction—and will indisputedly continue to be required in curbing the illicit drug traffic—experience has not demonstrated that the laws and enforcement policies urged by the United States Narcotics Bureau provide the full answer to the problem. On the contrary, experience suggests that further investigation of the problem is essential. The joint committee trusts that nothing will be permitted to hamper inquiries which may lead to fruitful results, and which should, at the very least, provide a factual basis for appraising alternative approaches to the problem.

On the basis of its studies and deliberations, the joint committee has reached the following conclusions concerning narcotic addiction and methods of dealing with narcotic addicts, which it submits for the purpose of indicating the need for further studies along the lines recommended above, and with the hope that these conclusions, although subject to reappraisal in the light of additional data, will be serviceable guides:

1. There appears to have been a considerable increase in drug addiction in the United States immediately following World War II; the increase was most apparent in the slum areas of large metropolitan centers and especially among minority groups in the population.

2. As a result, the federal government and many states passed legislation imposing increasingly severe penalties upon violators of the drug laws, as a means of dealing with the apparent increase in addiction.

3. This penal legislation subjects both the drug peddler and his victim, the addict, to long prison sentences, often imposed by mandatory statutory requirements without benefit of the probation and parole opportunities afforded other prisoners.

4. Though drug peddling is acknowledged to be a vicious and predatory crime, a grave question remains whether severe jail and prison sentences are the most rational way of dealing with narcotic addicts. And the unusual statutory basis of present drug-law enforcement, substantial federal domination in a local police-power field established by means of an excise measure enforced by a federal fiscal agency, invites critical scrutiny.

5. The narcotic drug addict because of his physical and psychological dependence on drugs and because of his frequently abnormal personality patterns should be as much a subject of concern to medicine and public health as to those having to do with law enforcement. But the ordinary doctor is not presently well

equipped to deal with the problems of the narcotic addict, and even his authority to do so is in doubt.

6. The role of medicine and public health in dealing with drug addiction and the drug addict should be clarified. There must be a new determination of the limits of good medical practice in the treatment of drug addiction, and an objective inquiry into the question whether existing enforcement policies, practices and attitudes, as well as existing laws, have unduly or improperly interfered with good medical practice in this area. As part of this evaluation, consideration should also be given to the possibility of helping both the addict and persons formerly addicted through open clinic facilities as well as in closed institutions such as Lexington and Fort Worth.

7. It can be stated emphatically that no acceptable evidence whatsoever points to the indiscriminate distribution of narcotic drugs as a method of handling the problem of addiction. On the contrary, the use of such drugs, except for legitimate medical needs, should be discouraged by the best available means. Individuals who have become addicted should be given the benefit of all known medical and paramedical procedures to encourage them to withdraw from dependence on narcotic drugs voluntarily; those who have withdrawn should be given psychiatric and social-agency help as long as necessary to assure against relapse. We need much more information than is presently available about the best means of handling addicts who, despite the best professional efforts, continue to be dependent on drugs. An experiment conducted by experts (as proposed above in this report) should be charged with getting information on this point.

8. There is a high rate of relapse on the part of addicts who have been in the care of narcotics hospitals and installations for the treatment of addiction. The real reasons for this must be determined. Factors to be considered include the physical and personality make-up of the individual, the social pressures applied to him, both adverse and constructive, and the attitude and sophistication of medicine and the law regarding addicts and addiction.

9. Some responsible authorities state that the physical and psychological dependence of addicts on narcotic drugs, the compulsion to obtain them, and the high price of the drugs in the illicit market are predominantly responsible for the crimes committed by addicts. Others claim that the drug itself is responsible for criminal behavior. The weight of evidence is so heavily in favor of the former point of view that the question can hardly be called a controversial one. But this point is so fundamental to the development of a sound philosophy of management of the problem that any residue of reasonable doubt must be resolved. In this connection the joint committee deplores the hysteria which sometimes dominates the approach to drug addiction problems by persons in positions of public trust. In terms of numbers afflicted, and in ill effects on others in the community, drug addiction is a problem of far less magnitude than alcoholism. Crimes of violence are rarely, and sexual crimes are almost never, committed by addicts. In most instances the addicts' sins are those of omission rather than commission; they are ineffective people, individuals whose great desire is to withdraw from the world and its troubles into a land of dreams.

10. It appears that neither compulsory hospitalization of all addicts nor permanent isolation is practicable at the present time. Hospital facilities to deal with narcotic addicts are not adequate in numbers, staff or program, and the permanent isolation of addicts, even if feasible, would not be a solution but only a temporizing maneuver—the very antithesis of the medical and scientific approach to the physical and behavioral problems of man.

The foregoing recommendation and report will be submitted to the House of Delegates of the American Medical Association with resolutions similar to those appended hereto, merely conformed to adapt the language of the resolutions to A.M.A. purposes. The object of the resolutions is to continue cooperation between the two associations in further mutual efforts along the lines suggested in this report and the joint committee's interim report.

It is firmly believed by the joint committee that the work it has already done clearly indicates a need for further joint efforts, carried on by both associations through permanent instrumentalities which have greater continuity, more facilities, and a broader mandate than the joint committee. Accordingly, favorable action on this report and its appended resolutions is respectfully urged.

Chapter 45

A Presidential Commission Suggests a Medical Approach

Gradually and gingerly the federal government began to incorporate some of the positions taken by critics of the Federal Bureau of Narcotics. Anslinger retired in 1962, and the Kennedy and Johnson administrations oversaw a great revival of the faith in medical research and treatment of drug users that last had existed in the 1910s. The medical attitude displaced criminal justice approaches now viewed as crude and indiscriminate weapons against those with drug problems. Still, the public held extremely negative opinions on drug users, and the government moved cautiously, as will be seen in the following excerpts from a 1967 presidential task force report.

NARCOTICS AND DRUG ABUSE

Task Force on Narcotics and Drug Abuse, President's Commission on Law Enforcement and Administration of Justice

In 1962 a White House Conference on Narcotic and Drug Abuse was convened in recognition of the fact that drug traffic and abuse were growing and critical national concerns. Large quantities of drugs were moving in illicit traffic despite the best efforts of law enforcement agencies. Addiction to the familiar opiates, especially in big-city ghettos, was widespread. New stimulant, depressant, and hallucinogenic drugs, many of them under loose legal controls, were coming into wide misuse, often by students. The informed public was becoming increasingly aware of the social and economic damage of illicit drug taking. . . .

The President's Advisory Commission on Narcotic and Drug Abuse was created in 1963 to translate this commitment into a program of action. The Commission's final report, issued in November of that year, set forth a strategy designed to improve the control of drug traffic and the treatment of drug users. The 25 recommendations of that report have been the basis for most of the subsequent Federal activity in this field. Many of them, notably those pertaining to civil commitment for narcotic addicts and the need for Federal controls on the distribution of nonnarcotic drugs, have been or are in the process of being implemented.

This Commission has not and could not have undertaken to duplicate the comprehensive study and report on drug abuse so recently completed by another Presidential Commission. Yet any study of law enforcement and the administration of criminal justice must of necessity include some reference to drug abuse and its associated problems. In the course of the discussion in this chapter, recommendations are made where they seem clearly advisable. In many instances these recommendations parallel ones made by the 1963 Commission.

There have been major innovation in legal procedures and medical techniques during the last few years. There are new Federal and State laws and programs designed to provide treatment both for narcotic addicts charged with or convicted of crime, and for those who come to the attention of public authorities without criminal charge. These laws and programs signify that the Nation's approach to narcotic addiction has changed fundamentally. They are a creative effort to treat the person who is dependent on drugs. . . .

Careful implementation, evaluation, and coordination of the new programs, some of which are not yet in operation will be absolutely essential. These are among today's first needs. New ideas are only a first step. Unless the programs they lead to are provided with sufficient money and manpower and are completely administered, no improvement in drug abuse problems can be expected.

The Commission recommends:

Research should be undertaken devoted to early action on the further development of a sound and effective framework of regulatory and criminal laws with respect to dangerous drugs. In addition, research and educational programs concerning the effects of such drugs should be undertaken. . . .

The Results

Judgments about enforcement results are hard to make. Experience with the opiate laws has been the longest. There are persuasive reasons to believe that enforcement of these laws has caused a significant reduction in the flow of these drugs. The best evidence is the high price, low quality, and limited availability of heroin today as contrasted with the former easy availability of cheap and potent heroin. Arguments based on comparisons of the number of addicts in the general population at different points in time are difficult to assess because of the uncertainties in the estimates being compared. However, there is a widespread conviction that the incidence of addiction in the general population has declined since the enactment and enforcement of the narcotic control laws.

The brunt of enforcement has fallen heavily on the user and the addict. In cases handled by the Bureau of Narcotics, whose activities are directed against international and interstate traffickers, more than 40 percent of the defendants prosecuted are addicts. However, these addicts almost invariably are also peddlers, who are charged with sale rather than mere possession. It is fair to assume that the percentage of addicts among the defendants prosecuted by State and local drug enforcement agencies is even higher. The enforcement emphasis on the addict is due to his constant exposure to surveillance and arrest and his potential value as an informant.

The Need to Strengthen Law Enforcement

More customs enforcement is not a simple formula for progress. To begin with, it must be understood that illegal importations of drugs can never be completely blocked. The measures necessary to achieve or even approach this goal, routine body searches being one obvious example, would be so strict and would involve such a burden on the movement of innocent persons and goods that they would never be tolerated. Moreover, the demand and the profits being what they are in the drug traffic, there will always be people willing to take whatever risks are necessary to pass the customs barrier. These conditions make the impact of any enforcement buildup hard to determine in advance. Nevertheless the ports and borders are the neck of the illicit traffic, and it is at these points that the Commission believes a commitment of more men would achieve the most. Illicit drugs regularly arrive at these points in significant quantities and in the hands of people who, while not at the highest, are at least not at the lowest level of the traffic. More frequent interceptions of both the drugs and the people could reasonably be expected if the capacity to enforce customs laws was increased. Other important benefits, in the form of larger revenue collections and the suppression of smuggling generally, would also follow.

Three separate studies of the manpower needs of customs enforcement operations have been made within the last 5 years. Each has arrived independently at the same recommendation: That the enforcement staff be increased by a total of about 600 positions. But only a small fraction of this total has, in fact, been authorized. In the meantime, the overall customs workload, from which the enforcement workload is naturally derived, has increased by 5 or 10 percent a year, a rate exceeding every advance estimate. The need for more enforcement staff is thus more urgent now than ever. . . .

The Commission recommends:

The enforcement and related staff of the Bureau of Customs should be materially increased.

There are no convenient devices, such as the rate of incoming persons or merchandise, to measure the workload of the Bureau of Narcotics. The need for more funds and more staff is thus hard to document. Yet the simple fact is that the Bureau has numerous complex tasks to perform. It bears the major Federal responsibility for suppression of traffic in illicit narcotics and marijuana. It assists foreign enforcement authorities within their own countries. It assists in training local enforcement personnel in this country. It not only enforces the penal statutes relating to narcotics and marihuana but also administers the laws relating to the legitimate importation, manufacture, and distribution of these drugs. The

Commission believes that the Bureau's force of some 300 agents, spread across 10 foreign countries and throughout the United States, is not sufficient. It certainly does not enable the Bureau to divert personnel from the business of making arrests, seizing drugs, and obtaining convictions, to the work of intelligence. Yet given the pyramidal structure of the illicit drug traffic and the limited exposure of those at the top, intelligence activity has a vital place in the enforcement effort.

The Commission recommends:

The enforcement staff of the Bureau of Narcotics should be materially increased. Some part of the added personnel should be used to design and execute a long-range intelligence effort aimed at the *upper echelons* of the illicit drug traffic.

The Commission also notes that the Federal Government undertook responsibility in respect to dangerous drugs with the enactment of the Drug Abuse Control Amendments of 1965. It is essential that adequate resources be provided to the Bureau of Drug Abuse Control to enable it to carry out these responsibilities.

In enacting the 1965 Drug Abuse Control Amendments, Congress sought to control the traffic in dangerous drugs predominantly by a system of registration, inspection, and recordkeeping. The amendments apply to drugs in intrastate as well as interstate commerce. Thus, once a drug has been placed under control of the amendments, State law cannot exempt from regulation even intrastate commerce in that drug. . . .

The Commission recommends:

Those States which do not already have adequate legislation should adopt a model State drug abuse control act similar to the Federal Drug Abuse Control Amendments of 1965.

The recordkeeping and inspection provisions of the 1965 amendments are at the heart of the Federal dangerous drugs regulatory scheme. They are designed to serve several purposes: To furnish information regarding the extent of the dangerous drug problem and the points in the chain of distribution where diversions of drugs occur; to facilitate the detection of violations; and to deter violations. Yet at present the 1965 amendments specifically state:

> No separate records, nor set form or forms for any of the foregoing records (of manufacture, receipt, and disposition), shall be required as long as records containing the required information are available.

There are about 6,000 establishments, including 1,000 manufacturers and 2,400 wholesalers, which are required to register and keep records under the amendments. In addition, there are about 73,000 other establishments that are required to maintain records but not required to register. This group includes some 54,000 pharmacies or other retail drug outlets, some 9,000 hospitals and clinics, some 8,000 dispensing practitioners, and some 2,000 research facilities. The Commission simply does not believe that a proper and productive audit of such a mass of records is possible without, at the very least, a provision requiring the records to be segregated or kept in some other manner permitting rapid identification and inspection.

The Commission recommends:

The recordkeeping provisions of the 1965 amendments should be amended to require that records must be segregated or kept in some other manner that enables them to be promptly identified and inspected.

Drug Abuse and Crime

Drug addicts are crime-prone persons. This fact is not open to serious dispute, but to determine its meaning is another matter. Analysis is best restricted to heroin because of the applicable laws, because of the information available, and because drugs with addiction liability present the clearest issues. In order to obtain an accurate idea of the drug-crime relationship, it is necessary to make a clear distinction between the drug offenses and the non-drug offenses committed by addicts.

Drug Offenses

Addiction itself is not a crime. It never has been under Federal law, and a State law making it one was struck down as unconstitutional by the 1962 decision of the Supreme Court in *Robinson* v. *California*. It does not follow, however, that a state of addiction can be maintained without running afoul of the criminal law. On the contrary, the involvement of an addict with the police is almost inevitable. By definition, an addict has a constant need for drugs, which obviously must be purchased and possessed before they can be consumed. Purchase and possession, with certain exceptions not relevant in the case of an addict, are criminal offenses under both Federal and State law. So is sale, to which many addicts turn to provide financial support for their habits. In many States, the nonmedical use of opiates is punishable, as is the possession of paraphernalia such as needles and syringes designed for such use. In other States, vagrancy statutes make it punishable for a known or convicted addict to consort with other known addicts or to be present in a place where illicit drugs are found.

Thus, the addict lives in almost perpetual violation of one or several criminal laws, and this gives him a special status not shared by other criminal offenders. Together with the fact that he must have continuous contact with other people in order to obtain drugs, it also gives him a special exposure to police action and arrest, and, in areas where the addiction rate is high, a special place in police statistics and crime rate computations.

Nondrug Offenses

The nondrug offenses in which the heroin addict typically becomes involved are of the fund-raising variety. Assaultive or violent acts, contrary to popular belief, are the exception rather than the rule for the heroin addict, whose drug has a calming and depressant effect. . . .

The projected totals [of addicts committing crimes] are so impressive that they lead one into the easy assumption that addicts must be responsible for most crimes against property where addiction is widespread. But this assumption cannot so easily be verified.

Records complied by the New York City Police Department indicate that 11.1 percent of those arrested in 1965 for those felonies against property most often committed by addicts were admitted drug (mostly heroin) users. The comparable figure for 1964 was 12.5 percent; for 1963 it was 11.7 percent. The involvement of admitted drug users in arrests for selected felonies against the person was much lower—on the order of 2 percent. . . .

The 4,385 people who were identified [by the FBI in 1966] as heroin users had an average criminal career (the span of years between the first and last arrest) of 12 years during which they averaged 10 arrests. Six of these arrests on an average were for offenses other than narcotics. Of the total arrests accumulated by heroin users in the property crime and violent crime categories, 26 percent were arrests for violent crimes and 74 percent were arrest for property crimes. On the other hand, all criminal offenders in the program (over 150,000) averaged 23 percent arrests for violent crimes and 77 percent for property crimes. Seventy-two percent of all heroin users had an arrest for some other criminal act prior to their first narcotic arrest.

The simple truth is that the extent of the addict's or drug user's responsibility for all nondrug offenses is unknown. Obviously it is great, particularly in New York City, with its heavy concentration of users; but there is no reliable data to assess properly the common assertion that drug users or addicts are responsible for 50 percent of all crime.

More broadly, the Commission's examination of the evidence on the causal connection between drug use and crime has not enabled it to make definitive estimates on this important issue. Since there is much crime in cities where drug use is not thought to be a major problem, to commit resources against abuse solely in the expectation of producing a dramatic reduction in crime may be to invite disappointment. While crime reduction is one result to be hoped for in eliminating drug abuse, its elimination and the treatment of its victims are humane and worthy social objectives in themselves.

Penalties

Since early in the century we have built our drug control policies around the twin judgments that drug abuse was an evil to be suppressed and that this could most effectively be done by the application of criminal enforcement and penal sanctions. Since then, one traditional response to an increase in drug abuse has been to increase the penalties for drug offenses. The premise has been that the more certain and severe the punishment, the more it would serve as a deterrent. Typically this response has taken the form of mandatory minimum terms of imprisonment, increasing in severity with repeated offenses, and provisions making the drug offender ineligible for suspension of sentence, probation, and parole. . . .

In its recommendations on mandatory minimums, the President's 1963 Advisory Commission sought to avoid the evils of treating all narcotics and marihuana offenders alike by dividing offenses into four groups:

- The smuggling or sale of large quantities of narcotics or the possession of large quantities for sale. This would subject the offender to mandatory minimum sentences. Probation, suspension of sentence, and parole would be denied.
- The smuggling or sale of small quantities of narcotics, or the possession of small quantities for sale. This would subject the offender to some measure of imprisonment but not to any mandatory minimum terms. Suspension of sentence would not be available but parole would.
- The possession of narcotics without intent to sell. The sentencing judge would have full discretion as to these offenses.
- All marihuana offenses. The sentencing judge would have full discretion.

This Commission believes that these gradations as to the seriousness of offense are sound in principle. But it does not believe they should rigidified into legislation. Rather, judges and correctional officials should be relied on to take account of the nature of the offense and the record and status of the offender in making their decisions.

The Commission recommends:

State and Federal drug laws should give a large enough measure of discretion to the courts and correctional authorities to enable them to deal flexibly with violator taking account of the nature and seriousness of the offense, the prior record of the offender and other relevant circumstances.

It should be noted that parole rights have already been reinstated for Federal marihuana violators by a provision of Public Law 89–793.

In submitting the foregoing recommendations, the Commission also wishes to record its concurrence in the view of the Bureau of Narcotics that long terms of imprisonment for major drug violators are essential. The Commission is opposed only to features of existing law that deny to judges and correctional officials the flexibility to deal with the infinitely varied types of violations and offenders in accordance with facts of each case rather than pursuant to prescribed rigid rules.

Marihuana

In addition to suggesting that the penalties provided for narcotics and marihuana offenses be made more flexible, the Commission would like to comment specially on marihuana, because of questions that have been raised concerning the appropriateness of the substantive law applicable to this drug.

The basic Federal control statute, the Marihuana Tax Act, was enacted in 1937 with the stated objectives of making marihuana dealings visible to public scrutiny, raising revenue, and rendering difficult the acquisition of marihuana for nonmedical purposes (the drug has no recognized medical value) and noncommercial use (the plant from which the drug comes has some commercial value in the production of seed and hemp). . . .

The act raises an insignificant amount of revenue and exposes an insignificant number of marihuana transactions to public view, since only a handful of people are registered under the act. It has become, in effect, solely a criminal law imposing sanctions upon persons who sell, acquire, or possess marihuana.

Marihuana was placed under a prohibition scheme of control because of its harmful effects and its claimed association with violent behavior and crime. Another reason now advanced in support of the marihuana regulations is that the drug is a steppingstone or forerunner to the use of addicting drugs, particularly heroin.

The law has come under attack on all counts, and the points made against it deserve a hearing.

The Effects

Marihuana is equated in law with the opiates, but the abuse characteristics of the two have almost nothing in common. The opiates produce physical dependence. Marihuana does not. A withdrawal sickness appears when use of the opiates is discontinued. No such symptoms are associated with marihuana. The desired dose of opiates tends to increase over time, but this is not true of marihuana. Both can lead to psychic dependence, but so can almost any substance that alters the state of consciousness.

The Medical Society of the County of New York has classified marihuana as a mild hallucinogen, and this is probably as good a description as any, although hallucinations are only one of many effects the drug can produce. It can impair judgment and memory; it can cause anxiety, confusion, or disorientation; and it can induce temporary psychotic episodes in predisposed people. Any hallucinogenic drug, and many of the other dangerous drugs, can do the same. Marihuana is probably less likely to produce these effects than such moderately potent hallucinogens as peyote, mescaline, and hashish (another derivative of the plant from which marihuana comes), and much less likely to do so than the potent hallucinogen LSD.

Marihuana, Crime, and Violence

Here differences of opinion are absolute and the claims are beyond reconciliation. One view is that marihuana is a major cause of crime and violence. Another is that marihuana has no association with crime and only a marginal relation to violence. . . .

One likely hypothesis is that, given the accepted tendency of marihuana to release inhibitions, the effect of the drug will depend on the individual and the circumstances. It might, but certainly will not necessarily or inevitably, lead to aggressive behavior or crime. The response will depend more on the individual than the drug. This hypothesis is consistent with the evidence that marihuana does not alter the basic personality structure.

Marihuana as a Prelude to Addicting Drugs

The charge that marihuana "leads" to the use of addicting drugs needs to be critically examined. There is evidence that a majority of the heroin users who come to the attention of public authorities have, in fact, had some prior experience with marihuana. But this does not mean that one leads to the other in the sense that marihuana has an intrinsic quality that creates a heroin liability. There are too many marihuana users who do not graduate to heroin, and too many heroin addicts with no known prior marihuana use, to support such a theory. Moreover there is no scientific basis for such a theory. The basic text on pharmacology, Goodman and Gilman, *The Pharmacological Basis of Therapeutics* (Macmillan 1960) states quite explicitly that marihuana habituation does not lead to the use of heroin.

The most reasonable hypothesis here is that some people who are predisposed to marihuana are also predisposed to heroin use. It may also be the case that through the use of marihuana a person forms the personal associations that later expose him to heroin.

The amount of literature on marihuana is massive. It runs to several thousand articles in medical journals and other publications. Many of these are in foreign languages and reflect the experience of other countries with the use of the drug and with other substances derived from the hemp plant. The relevance of this material to our own problem has never been determined. Indeed, with the possible exception of the 1944 LaGuardia report, no careful and detailed analysis of the American experience seems to have been attempted. Basic research has been almost nonexistent, probably because the principal active ingredient in marihuana has only recently been isolated and synthesized. Yet the Commission believes that enough information exists to warrant careful study of our present marihuana laws and the propositions on which they are based.

The Commission recommends:

The National Institute of Mental Health should devise and execute a plan of research, to be carried on both on an intramural and extramural basis, covering all aspects of marihuana use. . . .

Treatment

Until quite recently treatment opportunities for opia addicts were largely restricted to the two Federal narcotic hospitals at Lexington, Ky., and Fort Worth, Texas. Within the past decade, numerous new programs for the treatment of addiction have been developed. However there are virtually no programs for the treatment of use of the other dangerous drugs.

Lexington and Fort Worth

The Public Health Service hospitals were established in 1935 and 1938 respectively, for the primary purpose of providing treatment to Federal prisoners who were addicted to narcotic drugs. Voluntary patients, who make up almost one-half the hospital population at any given time, are admitted on a space-available basis after Federal prisoners have been accommodated. Since 1935 there have been more than 80,000 admissions of addict patients to the two hospitals. The constructed capacity of Lexington is 1,042 beds and of Fort Worth 777 beds.

There is no effective aftercare or supervision in the community, except in the case of a prisoner-patient who is granted parole. The relapse rate is high, but there is growing evidence that it is not as high as the 94-percent rate found in one short-term followup study. Much depends on whether relapse is taken to mean return to drugs once during a period of time or to refer to the drug status of the patient at the end of a period of time. One recent long-term (12-year) followup, using the second method of classification, found that, although 90 of the 100 heroin addicts studied had returned to drug use at some time, 46 of them were drug-free in the community at the time of death or last contact. Among the 30 who were considered to have made the best adjustment, the average length of abstinence was 7 years. Significantly, the best outcomes were found among those who had undergone some form of compulsory supervision after discharge.

The California Rehabilitation Center

This facility, operated by the California Youth and Adult Corrections Agency, was established in 1961. Most admissions are of addicted misdemeanants and felons convicted in California courts and committed by order of the court.

The program involves a combination of inpatient and outpatient treatment. The addicts are required to remain on inpatient status for at least 6 months, although the average is close to 15 months. During this period they are divided into 60-patient units for purpose of treatment. Work therapy, vocational courses, and a full academic course through high school also are offered.

Upon release to outpatient status, the patients are supervised by caseworkers with special training and small caseloads. Patients are chemically tested for the presence of drugs five times a month, both on a regular and a surprise basis, for at least the first 6 months. Failure of the test or other indications of relapse to drugs results in return to the institution. A halfway house, the Parkway Center, provides guidance for those making a marginal adjustment in the community. The patient becomes eligible for final discharge after 3 drug-free years as an outpatient.

The capacity of the Rehabilitation Center is 2,300 patients. Between September 15, 1961, and December 31, 1965, there were 5,300 admissions. During this period 3,243 persons were transferred to outpatient status. Although many were returned to the center, 1,700 persons remained on such status as of December 31, 1965; 27 persons had been finally discharged.

New York State Program

Between the effective date of the Metcalf-Volker Act, January 1, 1963, and June 30, 1966, there were 6,799 admissions of addicts to treatment units maintained by the State Department of Mental Hygiene. The majority of these were persons who chose treatment in lieu of prosecution for a crime. The treatment units were located in six State hospitals having a total of 555 beds for addict-patients; they could handle over 2,200 addicts a year. Both impatient and outpatient phases of treatment were provided.

A new and more comprehensive program for the treatment and prevention of addiction is now planned in New York under legislation passed in 1966 and administered by a new agency, the State Narcotic Control Commission. Facilities will be greatly expanded, as indicated by a $75 million appropriation for capital construction. The Commission is authorized, among other things, to conduct basic, clinical, and statistical research; to operate rehabilitation and aftercare centers; and to establish a unified program of education, prevention, care, and community referral.

Synanon

This is a private antiaddiction society founded in 1958. The central location is in Santa Monica, but there are other installations inside and outside California. The organization is made up and managed entirely by ex-addicts, aided by a volunteer medical staff. Membership is voluntary and not always available. The addict who seeks admission must first be screened by a committee. Once admitted, his compulsion to take drugs is countered by "attack" therapy and group pressure. If he does not respond, he can be expelled. If he does, he can move upward to levels of responsibility within the society, perhaps to an executive position. Some members return to the community; others become permanent

Synanon residents. As of March 1964, according to its officers, there were 400 drug-free persons affiliated with Synanon.

Daytop Lodge

This is a voluntary program serving addicts placed on probation by the local courts in Brooklyn, N.Y. It resembles Synanon in approach, but is supported by a Federal grant and is under court sponsorship. Its capacity, presently 25 addicts, is being expanded.

Methadone Maintenance

This is an experimental method of treatment for heroin addiction. Its principal sponsors are Drs. Vincent P. Dole and Marie Nyswander. They began their program of research in January 1964, at the Rockefeller University Hospital in New York City. Subsequently treatment units were established at Manhattan General and other New York hospitals. Patients are admitted on a voluntary but selective basis. Motivation and a past record of treatment failures are among the important selection criteria. The patients are free to leave the program at any time. Of the 108 heroin addicts admitted prior to February 1, 1966, 101 were still in the program on that date. The other seven had been dismissed from the program.

The first phase of the treatment involves hospitalization and withdrawal from heroin. The patient is then started on daily doses of methadone, a synthetic opiate that is itself addicting. The daily doses are gradually increased and finally become stable. The median stable dose is 100 milligrams per day. This phase of the program lasts about 5 weeks. It is followed by release to the outpatient phases of the treatment. These involve supportive contacts with the hospital staff and hopefully lead the patient to a secure and responsible position in society. Many of the outpatients are, in fact, employed or in school. No attempt has yet been made to withdraw any outpatient from methadone.

As used in the maintenance program, the methadone is dissolved in fruit juice and taken orally under supervision. It is always dispensed from a hospital pharmacy, and the outpatients are required to return each day for their doses. No prescriptions have been given to patients for the purchase of methadone at drug stores. The patients must also give daily urine samples for analysis.

According to the sponsors of the maintenance program, methadone given in adequate doses blocks the euphoric effects of heroin and does not itself produce euphoria, sedation, or distortion of behavior. The patients allegedly remain alert and functionally normal.

The question being tested here is whether an opiate drug, regularly administered as part of a medical program, can contribute to the rehabilitation of a heroin addict. The emphasis is on drawing the patient out of the addict community and away from a career of crime and into new social attitudes and relationships. The social rehabilitation of the addict is seen as a more important treatment goal than the medical cure of addiction itself.

The results of the methadone maintenance research are fragmentary. No final judgments about its suitability as treatment or as a public health approach are yet possible.

Cyclazocine Treatment

This method involves daily administration of a new drug, cyclazocine, which is a long-acting opiate antagonist and blocks the effects of heroin. The drug is not itself a narcotic. This treatment has been tried, with urinalysis to detect heroin use, on a pilot basis in New York.

Parole

Parole is of course not a medical technique, but it may fairly be classified as a form of treatment insofar as it is used to overcome a person's dependence on drugs. Several parole projects, with specially trained staffs carrying small caseloads, are in operation. The theory is that a parole agency, with its authority over the addict, is ideally situated to arrange and coordinate his adjustments in the community. Frequent contact and intensive supervision are necessary. The outpatient phase of the California rehabilitation program mentioned above is a special parole project in method, if not in name. The prototype of such a project, however, was developed in New York.

The 1960 final report of the Special Narcotic Project of the New York State Division of Parole described the results of a study of 344 addict-parolees supervised between 1956 and 1959. Of the total number supervised, 119 offenders had never been declared delinquent, and another 36 had been declared delinquent for reasons not related to drug use. Thus 155, or 45 percent, were found to be abstinent. A followup study of the same project parolees reported that, by the end of 1962, the abstinence rate had fallen to 32 percent. The median length of supervision of the 344 addict-parolees was 15 months in 1962, as against 8 months in 1959. The New York project now operates as the Narcotic Treatment Bureau. As of December 1966, there were 22 parole officers in the Bureau with an average caseload of 30 parolees.

Treatment of narcotic addiction is by no means a certain or perfected medical art. The most remarkable feature of the treatment programs mentioned above, and these represent only a sample, is their diversity of method. Careful and continuing evaluation of these programs, which has often been absent in the past, is imperative. There is great need for better standards for measuring the outcome of treatment. To think only in terms of "cure" is not very meaningful in the case of a chronic illness such as addiction. There is little knowledge about why a good outcome is achieved for one addict but not another, by one method but not another. More trained personnel are desperately needed. Methods of treatment for abusers of nonopiate drugs must be developed and there is a general need for research effort in the whole area of personality disorder, of which drug abuse is usually a symptom. New facilities will certainly be needed. The $15 million authorized by the Narcotic Addict Rehabilitation Act of 1966 for fiscal 1967 and for fiscal 1968 for grants to State and local governments is a bare minimum. States with drug abuse problems but without specialized treatment program must initiate such programs. Hospitals and medical schools must devote more attention to drug abuse. This is the beginning of what needs to be done.

Two subjects associated with treatment deserved particular mention. One is civil commitment; the other is the use of drugs in medical practice.

Civil Commitment

The enactment of laws authorizing or compelling commitment of drug addicts for purposes of treatment has been the most important development in recent years in the drug abuse field. This trend has broad public acceptance; perhaps it has even assumed the proportions of movement. In candor it must be said that commitment of addicts began as an experiment, born less out of an established body of medical and scientific knowledge than out of a sense of frustration with orthodox procedure and a demand for new approaches. There was growing awareness that drug addiction was a medical illness and that a clearer distinction, which would make some allowance for the quality of compulsion in addiction, should be made between addicts and other offenders.

California was the first State to initiate new procedures enacting a Civil Addict Commitment Law in 1961. New York followed with the Metcalf-Volker Act in 1962, but this legislation was revised and broadened in 1966. Also in 1966 a Federal commitment law, the Narcotic Addict Rehabilitation Act, was enacted. These statutes represent the most significant legislation in the field.

The results are still too fragmentary, and experience still too limited, to permit anything more than tentative judgments. A process of trial and error still lies ahead. The Commission therefore considers it imperative that the treatment programs be flexible enough to follow each promising idea and technique as it emerges. Most of all it is essential that the commitment laws be construed and executed to serve the purpose for which they were intended and by which alone they can be justified. This purpose is treatment in fact and not merely confinement with the pretense of treatment.

The expression "civil commitment" is misleading. The fact is that these commitments usually take place at some point during a criminal proceeding. They are denominated "civil" because they suspend that criminal proceeding and because they do not result in penal confinement. . . .

The Arguments Pro and Con

The involuntary commitment of noncriminal addicts and the voluntary commitment of criminal addicts are controversial and raise difficult issues.

The most heated debate centers on the involuntary commitment of the addict who is not accused of crime. Its proponents compare it to the practices of involuntarily committing the mentally ill, or isolating persons with serious contagious diseases; they argue that the addict is both a health risk to himself and a crime risk to others; they point to the evidence that addiction is spread by social contact with addicts rather than by the recruiting efforts of peddlers. These premises, buttressed by the right of a State to protect the general health and welfare of its citizens, lead them to the conclusion that commitment for treatment offers the maximum benefit to the individual and the minimum risk to society. Its opponents dispute both the premises and the conclusions. They contend that at the very least there should be a specific finding that the person to be committed is reasonably likely to commit dangerous acts; that mere proof of addiction is not a sufficient showing that a person is dangerous to himself or others; and that, in any event, the commitment is a subterfuge—it holds out the promise of a known method of treatment, or a reasonable prospect of cure, which does not exist.

These questions are not easily resolved. However, the Commission believes that involuntary civil commitment offers sufficient promise to warrant a fair test. But it must not become the civil equivalent of imprisonment. The programs must offer the best possible treatment, including new techniques as they become available, and the duration of the commitment, either within or outside an institution, must be no longer than is reasonably necessary.

Another group of issues is raised by voluntary commitment to treatment, before conviction, of addicts charged with crimes. The claimed advantages of such a commitment are that the addict can receive immediate treatment and avoid the stigma of criminal conviction. The eligible addict is given the choice of proceeding to trial or being committed. If he elects commitment, the criminal case is suspended pending the completion of treatment.

The objection in principle to this form of commitment is that a defendant, even though mentally competent in a legal sense, can avoid trial simply by asserting the fact of his addiction in a preliminary proceeding. Thus, so contend the critics, the ultimate issue of guilt or innocence is never reached at all. . . .

Medical Practice and Addiction

What limits does the law set on the right of a physician to prescribe or administer narcotic drugs to a narcotic addict? This short question raises issues that have been warmly debated for a long time—issues that are not resolved by reference to the general proposition that the statutory and regulatory measures for the control of narcotic drugs are not intended to interfere with the administration of such drugs in legitimate medical practice. The important issues are: How and by whom is the concept of legitimate medical practice defined and given content? Does legitimate medical practice mean the same thing as that practice accepted and followed by a majority of doctors in the community or as that approved by official spokesmen of the medical profession? If so, and if adverse legal consequences attend any departure from legitimate medical practice, how can new medical ideas and techniques safely be developed? What allowance is made for the good faith of a doctor who departs from standard treatment procedures while acting in what he considers to be the best interests of his patient?

Some background is necessary to put these issues into perspective. The Harrison Narcotic Act of 1914 regulates the distribution of narcotics. It requires those whose usual business involves transactions in narcotic drugs (including physicians) to register and pay an occupational tax, and it imposes a commodity tax evidenced by stamps on all narcotics manufactured. It further requires that all narcotics be distributed and transferred in original stamped packages, pursuant to order forms provided by the Treasury Department. Failure to comply with these provisions is a criminal offense. Specifically exempted from the operations of the act, however, are prescriptions issued by a physician "for legitimate medical uses" and distribution of drugs to a patient "in the course of his professional practice only." The very obvious but very important point to note here is that the medical practice exemption is part of a criminal statute. A prescription of drugs that falls outside this exemption is much more than a professional mistake on the part of a doctor. It is a prosecutable offense.

The American Medical Association has adopted and issued several statements on the use of narcotics in medical practice. The most recent, which appeared in 1963, and is currently in the process of revision, was prepared in collaboration with the National Research Council of the National Academy of Sciences. It may be summarized as follows:

- Continued administration of drugs for the maintenance of addiction is not a bona fide attempt at cure. In other words withdrawal of the drug must be accomplished before the rehabilitation phase of the treatment can begin.
- Withdrawal is most easily carried out in a drug-free environment, in specialized wards or installations for narcotic addicts. Under certain circumstances withdrawal may be carried out in other institutional settings, such as psychiatric wards of general hospitals.
- Withdrawal on an ambulatory basis (outside an institution) is, as a general matter, medically unsound and not recommended on the basis of present knowledge.
- Ambulatory clinic plans (dispensing drugs to outpatient addicts through clinics established for that purpose) or any other form of ambulatory maintenance (giving stable doses to outpatient addicts) are also medically unsound on the basis of present knowledge.
- It is proper ethical practice, after consultation and subject to keeping adequate records, to administer narcotics over a prolonged period to patients with chronic incurable and painful conditions, when reasonable al-

ternate procedures have failed, or to maintain an aged or infirm addict, when withdrawal would be dangerous to life. Finally it is ethical to administer maintenance does generally of methadone, a synthetic narcotic, to an addict who is awaiting admission to a narcotic facility, and to administer limited and diminishing doses to an addict during a process of withdrawal.

- Research on the problems of narcotics addiction is absolutely necessary and present concepts are open to revision based on the results of such research.

The AMA-NRC statement touches on areas of active controversy—maintenance, clinic plans, and ambulatory treatment. The Bureau of Narcotics accepts it as the authoritative definition of legitimate medical practice against which all medical practice is to be measured. However, there is a small but vocal minority, composed of reputable men within the medical profession, who do not consider it either authoritative or complete. At least some of these men do not regard withdrawal of the addict from drugs as the first, perhaps not even as the ultimate, treatment objective. Some would permit addicts to continue on stable doses of narcotics, either by means of a clinic arrangement or in some other medical setting. . . .

The inescapable fact is that medical science has not come very far or very fast in this extremely puzzling field. The need for expanded research is fundamental. It is in the interest of both the medical profession and good law enforcement that no obstacles be put in the way of such research.

Education

In 1963 the President's Advisory Commission on Narcotic and Drug Abuse found that public and professional education in the field was inadequate. It found the problem clouded by misconceptions and distorted by persistent fallacies. Unfortunately these conclusions are as valid today as they were 3 years ago. Misinformation about drugs and their effects is still prevalent, and the measures taken by the Federal Government to correct them are still limited, fragmented, and sporadic. The National Clearinghouse for Mental Health Information within the National Institute of Mental Health (NIMH) collects and disseminates information, but drug abuse is only one of its many concerns, and its audience is largely made up of researchers and other specialists. Similarly, the educational efforts of the Bureau of Narcotics and the Bureau of Drug Abuse Control, while well intended and well executed, are not on the necessary scale. There is a clear present need for a single agency, having a specific mandate for education, to prepare and distribute a broad range of materials, from pamphlets to films, suitable for presentation to target segments of the public, such as college students. The materials must above all be factual.

The Commission recommends:

A core of educational and informational materials should be developed by the National Institute of Mental Health.

This same recommendation was made by the 1963 Commission. Since that time a Center for Studies on Narcotics and Drug Abuse has been established within NIMH. This unit might be the appropriate one to charge with the major Federal responsibility for education. Wherever the responsibility is placed, it should be discharged with the cooperation of other Federal agencies, State and local agencies, universities, and private organizations. Adequate staff and funding should be provided on a priority basis.

The urgent need for a Federal response in education produced at least one hopeful start in 1966. A program to increase understanding of drug problems on college campuses has been undertaken by the National Association of Student Personnel Administrators under a contract with the Bureau of Drug Abuse Control. Regional seminars will be held for the benefit of campus officials. Written materials will be prepared and disseminated, and methods of communicating effectively with students will be explored. This is a useful, but only a very preliminary step. It is aimed at college students only. Moreover the work will end when the contract expires in 1967. The Federal responsibility for education will not expire at the same time.

The Commission believes that the education function must be given continuing and central direction by a single agency.

Chapter 46

Explosion of Drug Use

The sudden rise in drug use after the mid-1960s created a situation unfamiliar to all but the most elderly Americans. When the severe antidrug laws of the 1950s failed to halt the onslaught of illicit drug use, Congress pulled back from mandatory sentences and softened penalties for marijuana possession. At the same time, a national commission was established to review the whole range of drug use and to make recommendations for future legislation. In these excerpts from the commission's second report (1973), note the radical change from the hard-driving FBN approach to a program that favors "de-emotionaliz[ing]" the drug issue, reducing the size of the "drug abuse industrial complex," and combining "law enforcement, education and rehabilitation" in a "realistic" program of "short and long term goals."

DRUG USE IN AMERICA: PROBLEM IN PERSPECTIVE

National Commission on Marihuana and Drug Abuse

Like Alice on the other side of the looking glass, our two year examination of drug use, misuse and "abuse" has given us a constantly reinforced perception that all is not as it seems and that beliefs and realities are not always equal. All too often, familiar guideposts and landmarks, which we assumed could give us direction and purpose faded, changed shape or simply disappeared when carefully scrutinized. All too often, plans and policies conceived in good will and high hopes had unanticipated negative aspects which created as many problems as they did solutions. Because of the scope of the drug issue, we realized that the old definitions, the old ways of looking at these signs and symptoms of social dysfunction, required a new set of working terms and a new perspective. This is what we have attempted to do in this Report.

By direction of the Congress, we were named the "Commission on Marihuana and Drug Abuse". Whereas it was relatively easy to define the term "marihuana", such is not the case with the term "drug abuse". While a technical meaning can be ascribed to "marihuana", with "drug Abuse" it is more difficult. Drug abuse has become an emotional term that cannotes societal disapproval and elicits a sense of uneasiness and disquiet. It is a term that changes meaning depending on time and place. According to one's society, his place on the continuum of human history and his reason for using a particular drug, such use is regarded as either socially desirable or undesirable. Therefore, as a definition, drug abuse is of doubtful utility. For these reasons, this term will be abandoned in favor of other more descriptive terms which focus principally on the personal *risks* involved with drug use and the *social costs* which result from drug-induced and drug-using behavior and must be borne by the larger society.

As pointed out above, unless a term has an accepted meaning that bears a precise relationship to what is being described, it must be redefined or replaced. The vocabulary which defines drug use is imprecise; for example, "addiction," "narcotic," "treatment," "prevention" and "dependence" are all terms of variable meanings. Some, such as "addiction" and "narcotic," must be discarded; the others require careful redefinition. Unless agreement can be reached on terminology, attempts to direct groups or ideas into more productive channels to deal with the issues will fail.

Our mandate is broad Congress stated:

> The Commission is further directed to conduct a comprehensive study of the causes of drug abuse (not limited to marihuana use) and their relative significance, to make such interim reports as it deems advisable, and within two years after the date funds first become available to carry out the study to submit to the President and Congress a final report, including such legislative and administrative recommendations as it deems appropriate. It is the intent of the committee that the Commission should include in its study an examination of such subjects as the relationship, if any, to drug abuse by the young of individual personality with reference to personality traits which may make an individual prone to drug abuse; peer group relationships; patterns of family relations which appear to provide greater susceptibility than others to drug abuse; the degree to which societal tensions within the immediate community and Nation relate to drug abuse, including consideration of poverty, urban decay, war, and social permissiveness; availability and exposure to hard drugs; leisure activity; personal and family use of alcoholic beverages and drugs; movies, lyrics of rock music; advertising; underground newspaper; and other influences in the general social environment.

After carefully reviewing our mandate, the Commission recognizes the Congress was well aware of the symptomatic aspects of drug use in our society. The mandate requires us to deal, not only with the symptom, drug use, but also to determine whether the underlying assumptions that have been made regarding drugs are valid and whether official responses have produced workable programs. In many instances they have not.

Most of the discussion at the policy level tends to focus on the drugs themselves, ascribing to them an inordinate capacity for overpowering the human mind. Very often, policy makers characterize drugs as earlier generations did witchcraft and black magic. The social goal is exorcism. Each new treatment, educational or prevention technique is launched as the latest stratagem for quashing the forces of evil.

While the chemical properties of the various drugs are important, there is nothing mystical or supernatural about their effects. It is the behavior that may be associated with drugs use, such as crime, loss of productivity, disruption of the family unit and economic drain on the larger society, that should form the basis for policy planning. These are practical and tangible effects that we all can understand. Yet, these are problems that are associated with many factors, only one of which is drug use. It is with reference to all these factors that the plan of action must be formulated. Poverty, urban decay, lack of identity, the need to escape, boredom, apathy and other factors, as well as drug use, influence anti-social and asocial conduct.

Another aspect of the drug problem that this Report examines and which is the cause for much concern on the part of the Commission is the rapid institu-tionalization of the "drug abuse problem." The high degree of public concern has generated a shifting of large quantities of money, manpower and other resources at the federal, state and local levels to meet the problem and lessen the public concern. This response has created, in the short span of four years, a "drug abuse industrial complex."

With spending at the federal level alone of upwards of one billion dollars annually, with a rapid growth in bureaucracy, with an almost compulsive spend-ing on drug projects without benefit of evaluation or goal setting, the drug abuse industrial complex has firmly established itself as a fixture of government and society.

The Commission is concerned that the underlying assumptions about the problem and the organizational response of the "complex" may, rather than resolve or de-emotionalize the issue, tend to perpetuate it as an ongoing part of the American way of life. There is a real need to evaluate the present system to ensure that the government directs its efforts toward the achievement of success rather than the perpetuation of government activity.

There is an apparent unspoken assumption in this country that our drug problem is unique. Our travels to over 36 nations around the world showed us pointedly that such is not the case. Many other countries throughout the world have a drug problem. Some, such as Sweden and Japan, have recognized it publicly and have engaged in formal public efforts like our own. Others have not, either because they do not characterize the drug taking as a major govern-mental concern or because such behavior is well down the list of their national priorities.

Regardless of the nation involved, drug use, drug-induced behavior and drug dependence are common threads in the social fabric of humanity, from which almost no peoples or parts of the world are immune. How drug-using behavior is viewed depends in large measure on the unique conditions of each country. How the issue is resolved depends on how much effort a particular nation is willing to undertake and how much affluence there is to support large scale drug use. It is fair to say that a number of nations simply dismiss drugs as a problem by denying that it exists as a major problem in their country. We as a nation have not been willing to do this.

In this country, we have always had problems with drugs to some extent. The use of alcohol and tobacco is not a new phenomenon. The use of cocaine and opiate derivatives date from the Civil War and the use of marihuana dates from the early part of this century. To be sure, the use of drugs has increased, but what makes drugs such an issue now is their spread to all segments of society and the high visibility of their adverse impact on the public, especially through the mass media.

The perception that certain nations are more prone to drug use than others has a corollary between generations. Many Americans equate drug misuse with youth. While youth constitute a high risk group in our society and drug misuse is one of the high risk activities in which they engage, we must recognize that drug misuse is prevalent among the over-30 generation as well. Different drugs and different activities appeal more strongly to one age group than to another, if only because of conditioning and the maturation process. The use of alcohol, marihuana, barbiturates, heroin and other drugs appeals to different age groups because of their effects. The reasons people use drugs vary depending on their purported need for the drug. The drinking of alcohol may increase with age while the use of marihuana may decrease. The use of barbiturates may remain constant with age, but the pattern of use, moving from intermittent to continuous, may change as one grows older. The problem of drugs can and does affect all ages, although the reasons for and patterns of use may change markedly from person to person and from one community to another.

The vastness of our mandate, rather than causing us to despair, has caused us to reevaluate the problem. By examining the underlying causes of drug use and misuse, and by examining how we, as a nation, are responding both publicly and privately, we have concluded that we can come to grips with the drug issue by redefining our objectives realistically and by utilizing existing institutions more effectively. Unattainable goal setting and nearsighted responses to untested assumptions rather than realities will defeat us. We as a nation must make a commitment to a course of action, but only after we have carefully evaluated and tested our underlying assumptions. We must be willing to rethink the problem so that both short and long term goals are achieved. We must be willing to recognize that any institutional response to the problem will merely deal with the symptoms and that unless our citizens are genuinely committed to the values and goals, we can do no more than conduct a holding action. Law enforcement, education and rehabilitation can make inroads on the problem, but, together or separately, they cannot resolve it. Such resolution can only be achieved when we, as a nation, decide to abide by a fundamental decision to minimize drugs usage and to deal with the underlying needs and causes.

The Appendices which form the technical reservoir from which the Report was drawn contain more specific information and supporting data which both the public and the research community can utilize in exploring various aspects of the drug issue in greater detail. The Commission published these materials to create a baseline of current knowledge in this field from which further studies can be undertaken.

This Report has been written on two levels; first, to determine what can be done now to move us towards a more socially satisfactory situation *vis a vis* drug use and second, to project into the not too distant future further refinements or changes if the present recommendations do not achieve any more success than we have had in the past. These two levels of recommendations are necessary since drug use patterns and institutional responses change over a period of time. Since drugs and their use vary according to changes in other aspects of the society, there should be no hesitancy to adjust public policy to meet or intercept the circumstances of the times. We must be willing to experiment; we must be willing to explore alternatives to what we are now doing. We must be willing to change when change is indicated.

Chapter 47

New Laws from the 1960s to the 1980s

In 1965 Congress enacted legislation dealing not with the traditional illicit drugs — the opiates, cocaine, and marijuana — but with barbiturates, LSD, and amphetamine stimulants. This was followed in 1970 by passage of the Comprehensive Drug Abuse Prevention and Control Act, which reformed all existing drug laws, from the Harrison Act on. They no longer were to be based on the tax power of the federal government but instead were derived from the interstate commerce clause of the Constitution. In addition, this act introduced a system by which drugs were divided into categories depending on their abuse potential. Provision was made for moving drugs from one category to another. No longer would it be necessary to enact legislation drug by drug.

The 1980s brought a new fear, with the appearance and rapid rise in use of crack cocaine. Two major anti–drug abuse acts, those of 1986 and 1988, reinstituted mandatory minimum sentences and the death penalty. These two acts mark a return to the "zero-tolerance" position of an earlier era as faith in treatment declined and the fear of drugs and drug users rose.

THE DRUG ABUSE CONTROL AMENDMENTS OF 1965

An Act to protect the public health and safety by amending the Federal Food, Drug, and Cosmetic Act to establish special controls for depressant and stimulant drugs and counterfeit drugs, and for other purposes.

Be it enacted by the Senate and House of Representatives of the United States of America in Congress assembled, That this Act may be cited as the "Drug Abuse Control Amendments of 1965".

Findings and Declaration

SEC. 2. The Congress hereby finds and declares that there is a widespread illicit traffic in depressant and stimulant drugs moving in or otherwise affecting interstate commerce; that the use of such drugs, when not under the supervision of a licensed practitioner, often endangers safety on the highways (without distinction of interstate and intrastate traffic thereon) and otherwise has become a threat to the public health and safety, making additional regulation of such drugs necessary regardless of the intrastate or interstate origin of such drugs; that in order to make regulation and protection of intrastate commerce is also necessary because, among other things, such drugs, when held for illicit sale, often do not bear labeling showing their place of origin and because in the form in which they are so held or in which they are consumed a determination of their place of origin is often extremely difficult or impossible; and that regulation of interstate commerce without the regulation of intrastate commerce in such drugs, as pro-vided in this Act, would discriminate against and adversely affect interstate commerce in such drugs.

Control of Depressant and Stimulant Drugs

SEC. 3. (a) Section 201 of the Federal Food, Drug, and Cosmetic Act (21 U.S.C. 321) is amended by adding at the end thereof the following:

"(v) The term 'depressant or stimulant drug' means—

"(1) any drug which contains any quantity of (A) barbituric acid or any of the salts of barbituric acid; or (B) any derivative of barbituric acid which has been designated by the Secretary under section 502 (d) as habit forming;

"(2) any drug which contains any quantity of (A) amphetamine or any of its optical isomers; (B) any salt of amphetamine or any salt of an optical isomer of amphetamine; or (C) any substance which the Secretary, after investigation, has found to be, and by regulation designated as, habit forming because of its stimulant effect on the central nervous system; or

"(3) any drug which contains any quantity of a substance which the Secretary, after investigation, has found to have, and by regulation designates as having, a potential for abuse because of its depressant or stimulant effect on the central nervous system or its hallucinogenic effect. . . ."

(b) Chapter V of such Act (21 U.S.C., chap. 9, such. V) is amended by adding at the end thereof the following new section.

Depressant and Stimulant Drugs

SEC. 511. (a) No person shall manufacture, compound, or process any depressant or stimulant drug, except that this prohibition shall not apply to the following persons whose activities in connection with any such drug are solely as specified in this subsection:

"(1) (A) Manufacturers, compounders, and processors. . . .
"(B) Suppliers (otherwise qualified in conformance with local laws) of manu-facturers, compounders, and processors referred to in subparagraph (A).
"(2) Wholesale druggists. . . .
"(3) Pharmacies, hospitals, clinics, and public health agencies,

"(4) Practitioners licensed by law to prescribe or administer depressant or stimulant drugs, while acting in the course of their professional practice.

"(5) Persons who use depressant or stimulant drugs in research, teaching, or chemical analysis and not for sale.

"(6) Officers and employees of the United States, a State government, or a political subdivision of a State, while acting in the course of their official duties. . . .

"(c) No person, other than a person described in subsection (a) or subsection (b) (2), shall possess any depressant or stimulant drug otherwise than (1) for the personal use of himself or a member of his household, or (2) for administration to an animal owned by him or a member of his household. . . ."

Penalties

SEC. 7. (a) Section 303 (a) of the Federal Food, Drug, and Cosmetic Act (21 U.S.C. 333 (a)) is amended by inserting after the final word "fine" and before the period the following: ":*Provided, however*, That any person who, having attained his eighteenth birthday, violates section 301 (q) (2) by selling, delivering, or otherwise disposing of any depressant or stimulant drug to a person who has not attained his twenty-first birthday shall, if there be no previous conviction of such person under this section which has become final, be subject to imprisonment for not more than two years, or a fine of not more than $5,000, or both such imprisonment and fine, and for the second or any subsequent conviction for such a violation shall be subject to imprisonment for not more than six years, or a fine of not more than $15,000, or both such imprisonment and fine".

THE COMPREHENSIVE DRUG ABUSE PREVENTION AND CONTROL ACT OF 1970

An Act to amend the Public Health Service Act and other laws to provide increased research into, and prevention of, drug abuse and drug dependence; to provide for treatment and rehabilitation of drug abusers and drug dependent persons; and to strengthen existing law enforcement authority in the field of drug abuse.

Be it enacted by the Senate and House of Representatives of the United States of America in Congress assembled, That this Act may be cited as the "Comprehensive Drug Abuse Prevention and Control Act of 1970". . . .

Title I. — Rehabilitation Programs Relating to Drug Abuse

Programs Under Community Mental Health Centers Act. Relating to Drug Abuse

SECTION 1.

... (c) Part D of such Act [Community Mental Health Centers Act] is further amended by redesignating sections 253 and 254 as sections 254 and 255, respectively, and by adding after section 252 the following new section:

Drug Abuse Education

"SEC. 253. (a) The Secretary is authorized to make grants to States and political subdivisions thereof and to public or nonprofit private agencies and organizations, and to enter into contracts with other private agencies and organizations, for—

"(1) the collection, preparation, and dissemination of educational materials dealing with the use and abuse of drugs and the prevention of drug abuse, and

"(2) the development and evaluation of programs of drug abuse education directed at the general public, school-age children, and special high-risk groups. . . ."

Research Under the Public Health Service Act in Drug Use, Abuse, and Addiction

SEC. 3 (a) Section 303(a) of the Public Health Service Act (42 U.S.C. 242a(a)) is amended by adding after and below paragraph (2) the following:

"The Secretary may authorize persons engaged in research on the use and effect of drugs to protect the privacy of individuals who are the subject of such research by withholding from all persons not connected with the conduct of such research the names or other identifying characteristics of such individuals. Persons so authorized to protect the privacy of such individuals may not be compelled in any Federal, State, or local civil, criminal, administrative, legislative, or other proceedings to identify such individuals."

Medical Treatment of Narcotic Addiction

SEC. 4. The Secretary of Health, Education, and Welfare, after consultation with the Attorney General and with national organizations representative of persons with knowledge and experience in the treatment of narcotic addicts, shall determine the appropriate methods of professional practice in the medical treatment of the narcotic addiction of various classes of narcotic addicts, and shall report thereon from time to time to the Congress.

Title II — Control and Enforcement

Part A — Short Title; Findings and Declaration; Definitions

Short Title

SEC. 100. This title may be cited as the "Controlled Substances Act".

Findings and Declarations

SEC. 101. The Congress makes the following findings and declarations:

(1) Many of the drugs included within this title have a useful and legitimate medical purpose and are necessary to maintain the health and general welfare of the American people.

(2) The illegal importation, manufacture, distribution, and possession and improper use of controlled substances have a substantial and detrimental effect on the health and general welfare of the American people.

(3) A major portion of the traffic in controlled substances flows through interstate and foreign commerce. Incidents of the traffic which are not an integral part of the interstate or foreign flow, such as manufacture, local distribution, and possession, nonetheless have a substantial and direct effect upon interstate commerce because—

(A) after manufacture, many controlled substances are transported in ion interstate commerce,

(B) controlled substances distributed locally usually have been transported in interstate commerce immediately before their distribution, and

(C) controlled substances possessed commonly flow through interstate commerce immediately prior to such possession.

(4) Local distribution and possession of controlled substances contribute to swelling the interstate traffic in such substances.

(5) Controlled substances manufactured and distributed intrastate cannot be differentiated from controlled substances manufactured and distributed interstate. Thus, it is not feasible to distinguish, in terms of controls, between controlled substances manufactured and distributed interstate and controlled substances manufactured and distributed intrastate.

(6) Federal control of the intrastate incidents of the traffic in controlled sub-

stances is essential to the effective control of the interstate incidents of such traffic.

(7) The United States is a party to the Single Convention on Narcotic Drugs, 1961, and other international conventions designed to establish effective control over international and domestic traffic in controlled substances. . . .

Part B — Authority to Control; Standards and Schedules

Authority and Criteria for Classification of Substances

SEC. 201. (a) The Attorney General shall apply the provisions of this title to the controlled substances listed in the schedules established by section 202 of this title and to any other drug or other substance added to such schedules under this title. Except as provided in subsections (d) and (e), the Attorney General may by rule—

(1) add to such a schedule or transfer between such schedules any drug or other substance if he—
   (A) finds that such drug or other substance has a potential for abuse, and
   (B) makes with respect to such drug or other substance the findings prescribed by subsection (b) of section 202 for the schedule in which such drug is to be placed; or
(2) remove any drug or other substance from the schedules if he finds that the drug or other substance does not meet the requirements for inclusion in any schedule.

Rules of the Attorney General under this subsection shall be made on the record after opportunity for a hearing pursuant to the rulemaking procedures prescribed by subchapter II of chapter 5 of title 5 of the United States Code. Proceedings for the issuance, amendment, or repeal of such rules may be initiated by the Attorney General (1) on his own motion, (2) at the request of the Secretary, or (3) on the petition of any interested party.

(b) The Attorney General shall, before initiating proceedings under subsection (a) to control a drug or other substance or to remove a drug or other substance entirely from the schedules, and after gathering the necessary data, request from the Secretary a scientific and medical evaluation, and his recommendations, as to whether such drug or other substance should be so controlled or removed as a controlled substance. In making such evaluation and recommendations, the Secretary shall consider the factors listed in paragraphs (2), (3), (6), (7), and (8) of subsection (c) and any scientific or medical considerations involved in paragraphs (1), (4), and (5) of such subsection. The recommendations of the Secretary shall include recommendations with respect to the appropriate schedule, if any, under which such drug or other substance should be listed. The evaluation and the recommendations of the Secretary shall be made in writing and submitted to the Attorney General within a reasonable time. The recommendations of the Secretary to the Attorney General shall be binding on the Attorney General as to such scientific and medical matters, and if the Secretary recommends that a drug or other substance not be controlled, the Attorney General shall not control the drug or other substance. If the Attorney General determines that these facts and all other relevant data constitute substantial evidence of potential for abuse such as to warrant control or substantial evidence that the drug or other substance should be removed entirely from the schedules, he shall initiate proceedings for control or removal, as the case may be, under subsection (a).

(c) In making any finding under subsection (a) of this section or under subsection (b) of section 202, the Attorney General shall consider the following factors with respect to each drug or other substance proposed to be controlled or removed from the schedules:

(1) Its actual or relative potential for abuse.
(2) Scientific evidence of its pharmacological effect, if known.
(3) The state of current scientific knowledge regarding the drug or other substance.
(4) Its history and current pattern of abuse.
(5) The scope, duration, and significance of abuse.
(6) What, if any, risk there is to the public health.
(7) Its psychic or physiological dependence liability.
(8) Whether the substance is an immediate precursor of a substance already controlled under this title.

(d) If control is required by United States obligations under international treaties, conventions, or protocols in effect on the effective date of this part, the Attorney General shall issue an order controlling such drug under the schedule he deems most appropriate to carry out such obligations, without regard to the findings required by subsection (a) of this section or section 202(b) and without regard to the procedures prescribed by subsections (a) and (b) of this section. . . .

Schedules of Controlled Substances

SEC. 202. (a) There are established five schedules of controlled substances, to be known as schedules I, II, III, IV, and V. Such schedules shall initially consist of the substances listed in this section. The schedules established by this section shall be undated and republished on a semiannual basis during the two-year period beginning one year after the date of enactment of this title and shall be updated and republished on an annual basis thereafter.

(b) Except where control is required by United States obligations under an international treaty, convention, or protocol, in effect on the effective date of this part, and except in the case of an immediate precursor, a drug or other substance may not be placed in any schedule unless the findings required for such schedule are made with respect to such drug or other substance. The findings required for each of the schedules are as follows:

(1) SCHEDULE I.—

    (A) The drug or other substance has a high potential for abuse.

    (B) The drug or other substance has no currently accepted medical use in treatment in the United States.

    (C) There is a lack of accepted safety for use of the drug or other substance under medical supervision.

(2) SCHEDULE II.—

    (A) The drug or other substance has a high potential for abuse.

    (B) The drug or other substance has a currently accepted medical use in treatment in the United States or a currently accepted medical use with severe restrictions.

    (C) Abuse of the drug or other substances may lead to severe psychological or physical dependence.

(3) SCHEDULE III.—

    (A) The drug or other substance has a potential for abuse less than the drugs or other substances in schedules I and II.

    (B) The drug or other substance has a currently accepted medical use in treatment in the United States.

    (C) Abuse of the drug or other substance may lead to moderate or low physical dependence or high psychological dependence.

(4) SCHEDULE IV.—

    (A) The drug or other substance has a low potential for abuse relative to the drugs or other substances in schedule III.

    (B) The drug or other substance has a currently accepted medical use in treatment in the United States.

    (C) Abuse of the drug or other substance may lead to limited physical dependence or psychological dependence relative to the drugs or other substances in schedule III.

(5) SCHEDULE V.—

    (A) The drug or other substance has a low potential for abuse relative to the drugs or other substances in schedule IV.

    (B) The drug or other substance has a currently accepted medical use in treatment in the United States.

    (C) Abuse of the drug or other substance may lead to limited physical dependence or psychological dependence relative to the drugs or other substances in schedule IV.

The Anti–Drug Abuse Act of 1986

An Act to strengthen Federal efforts to encourage foreign cooperation in eradiocating illicit drug crops and in halting international drug traffic, to improve enforcement of Federal drug laws and enhance interdiction of illicit drug shipments, to provide strong Federal leadership in establishing effective drug abuse prevention and education programs, to expand Federal support for drug abuse treatment and rehabilitation efforts, and for other purposes.

Be it enacted by the Senate and House of Representatives of the United States of America in Congress assembled,

SECTION 1. SHORT TITLE.

This Act may be cited as the "Anti–Drug Abuse Act of 1986". . . .

Title I — Anti-Drug Enforcement

Subtitle A — Narcotics Penalties and Enforcement Act of 1986

SEC. 1001. Short Title.

This subtitle may be cited as the "Narcotics Penalties and Enforcement Act of 1986".

SEC. 1002. Controlled Substances Act Penalties.

Section 401(b)(1) of the Controlled Substances Act (21 U.S.C. 841(b)(1)) is amended—

(1) by redesignating subparagraph (C) as subparagraph (D); and

(2) by striking out subparagraphs (A) and (B) and inserting the following in lieu thereof:

"(1)(A) In the case of a violation of subsection (a) of this section involving—

"(i)   1 kilogram or more of a mixture or substance containing a detectable amount of heroin;

"(ii) 5 kilograms or more of a mixture or substance containing a detectable amount of—

"(I)   coca leaves, except coca leaves and extracts of coca leaves from which cocaine, ecgonine, and derivatives of ecgonine or their salts have been removed;

"(II) cocaine, its salts, optical and geometric isomers, and salts of isomers;

"(III) ecgonine, its derivatives, their salts, isomers, and salts of isomers; or

"(IV) any compound, mixture, or preparation which contains any quantity of any of the substance referred to in subclauses (I) through (III)";

"(iii) 50 grams or more of a mixture or substance described in clause (ii) which contains cocaine base;

"(iv) 100 grams or more of phencyclidine (PCP) or 1 kilogram or more of a mixture or substance containing a detectable amount of phencyclidine (PCP);

"(v) 10 grams or more of a mixture or substance containing a detectable amount of lysergic acid diethylamide (LSD);

"(vi) 400 grams or more of a mixture or substance containing a detectable amount of N-phenyl-N-[1-(2-phenylethyl)-4-piperidinyl] propanamide or 100 grams or more of a mixture or substance containing a detectable amount of any analogue of N-phenyl-N-[1-(2-phenylethyl)-4-piper-idinyl] propanamide; or

"(vii) 1000 kilograms or more of a mixture or substance containing a detectable amount of marihuana;

such person shall be sentenced to a term of imprisonment which may not be less than 10 years or more than life and if death or serious bodily injury results from the use of such substance shall be not less than 20 years or more than life, a fine not to exceed the greater of that authorized in accordance with the provisions of title 18, United States Code, or $4,000,000 if the defendant is an individual or $10,000,000 if the defendant is other than an individual, or both. . . .

"(B) In the case of a violation of subsection (a) of this section involving—

"(i) 100 grams or more of a mixture or substance containing a detectable amount of heroin;

"(ii) 500 grams or more of a mixture or substance containing a detectable amount of—

"(I) coca leaves, except coca leaves and extracts of coca leaves from which cocaine, ecgonine, and derivatives of ecgonine or their salts have been removed;

"(II) cocaine, its salts, optical and geometric isomers, and salts of isomers;

"(III) ecgonine, its derivatives, their salts isomers, and salts of isomers; or

"(IV) any compound, mixture, or preparation which contains any quantity of any of the substance referred to in subclauses (I) through (III);

"(iii) 5 grams or more of a mixture or substance described in clause (ii) which contains cocaine base;

"(iv) 10 grams or more of phencyclidine (PCP) or 100 grams or more of a mixture or substance containing a detectable amount of phencyclidine (PCP);

"(v) 1 gram or more of a mixture or substance containing a detectable amount of lysergic acid diethylamide (LSD);

"(vi) 40 grams or more of a mixture or substance containing a detectable amount of N-phenyl-N-[1-(2-phenylethyl)-4-piperidinyl] propanamide

or 10 grams or more of a mixture or substance containing a detectable amount of any analogue of N-phenyl-N-[1-(2-phenylethyl)-4-piper-idinyl] propanamide; or
"(vii) 100 kilograms or more of a mixture or substance containing a detectable amount of marihuana;

such person shall be sentenced to a term of imprisonment which may not be less than 5 years and not more than 40 years and if death or serious bodily injury results from the use of such substance shall be not less than 20 years or more than life, a fine not to exceed the greater of that authorized in accordance with the provisions of title 18, United States Code, or $2,000,000 if the defendant is an individual or $5,000,000 if the defendant is other than an individual, or both. If any person commits such a violation after one or more prior convictions for an offense punishable under this paragraph, or for a felony under any other provision of this title or title III or other law of a State, the United States, or a foreign country relating to narcotic drugs, marihuana, or depressant or stimulant substances, have become final, such person shall be sentenced to a term of imprisonment which may not be less than 10 years and not more than life imprisonment and if death or serious bodily injury results from the use of such substance shall be sentenced to life imprisonment, a fine not to exceed the greater of twice that authorized in accordance with the provisions of title 18, United States Code, or $4,000,000 if the defendant is an individual or $10,000,000 if the defendant is other than an individual, or both. Any sentence imposed under this subparagraph shall, in the absence of such a prior conviction, include a term of supervised release of at least 4 years in addition to such term of imprisonment and shall, if there was such a prior conviction, include a term of supervised release of at least 8 years in addition to such term of imprisonment. Notwithstanding any other provision of law, the court shall not place on probation or suspend the sentence of any person sentenced under this subparagraph. No person sentenced under this subparagraph shall be eligible for parole during the term of imprisonment imposed therein. . . .

Subtitle B — Drug Possession Penalty Act of 1986

Sec. 1051. Short Title.
    This subtitle may be cited as the "Drug Possession Penalty Act of 1986"
Sec. 1052. Penalty for Simple Possession.
    Section 404 of the Controlled Substance Act (21 U.S.C. 844) is amended to read as follows:

"Penalty for Simple Possession

"Sec. 404. (a) It shall be unlawful for any person knowingly or intentionally to possess a controlled substance unless such substance was obtained directly, or pursuant to a valid prescription or order, from a practitioner, while acting in the course of his professional practice, or except as otherwise authorized by this title or title III. Any person who violates this subsection may be sentenced to a term of imprisonment of not more than 1 year, and shall be fined a minimum of $1,000 but not more than $5,000, or both, except that if he commits such offense after a prior conviction under this title or title III, or a prior conviction for any drug or narcotic offense chargeable under the law of any State, has become final, he shall be sentenced to a term of imprisonment for not less than 15 days but not more than 2 years, and shall be fined a minimum of $2,500 but not more than $10,000, except, further, that if he commits such offense after two or more prior convictions under this title or title III, or two or more prior convictions for any drug or narcotic offense chargeable under the law of any State, or a combination of two or more such offenses have become final, he shall be sentenced to a term of imprisonment for not less than 90 days but not more than 3 years, and shall be fined a minimum of $5,000 but not more than $25,000. The imposition or execution of a minimum sentence required to be imposed under this subsection shall not be suspended or deferred. . . .

"(b)(1) If any person who has not previously been convicted of violating subsection (a) of this section, any other provision of this subchapter or subchapter II of this chapter, or any other law of the United States relating to narcotic drugs, marihuana, or depressant or stimulant substances, is found guilty of a violation of subsection (a) of this section after trial or upon a plea of guilty, the court may, without entering a judgment of guilty and with the consent of such person, defer further proceedings and place him on probation upon such reasonable conditions as it may require and for such period, not to exceed one year, as the court may prescribe. Upon violation of a condition of the probation, the court may enter an adjudication of guilt and proceed as otherwise provided. The court may, in its discretion, dismiss the proceedings against such person and discharge him from probation before the expiration of the maximum period prescribed for such person's probation. If during the period of his probation such person does not violate any of the conditions of the probation, then upon expiration of such period the court shall discharge such person and dismiss the proceedings against him. Discharge and dismissal under this subsection shall be without court adjudication of guilt, but a nonpublic record thereof shall be retained by the Department of Justice solely for the purpose of use by the courts in determining whether or not, in subsequent proceedings, such person qualifies under this subsection. Such discharge or dismissal shall not be deemed a conviction for purposes of disqualifications or disabilities imposed by law upon conviction of a crime (including the penalties prescribed under this part for second or subsequent convictions) or for any other purpose. Discharge and dismissal under this section may occur only once with respect to any person.

"(2) Upon the discharge of such person and dismissal of the proceedings against him under paragraph (1) of this subsection, such person, if he was not over twenty-one years of age at the time of the offense, may apply to the court for an order to expunge from all official records (other than the nonpublic records to be retained by the Department of Justice under paragraph (1)) all recordation relating to his arrest, indictment or information, trial, finding of guilty, and dismissal and discharge pursuant to this section. If the court determines, after hearing, that such person was dismissed and the proceedings against him discharged and that he was not over twenty-one years of age at the time of the offense, it shall enter such order. The effect of such order shall be to restore such person, in the contemplation of the law, to the status he occupied before such arrest or indictment or information. No person as to whom such order has been entered shall be held thereafter under any provision of any law to be guilty of perjury or otherwise giving a false statement by reason of his failures to recite or acknowledge such arrest, or indictment or information, or trial in response to any inquiry made of him for any purpose.

"(c) As used in this section, the term 'drug or narcotic offense' means any offense which proscribes the possession, distribution, manufacture, cultivation, sale, transfer, or the attempt or conspiracy to possess, distribute, manufacture, cultivate, sell or transfer any substance the possession of which is prohibited under this title."

Subtitle C — Juvenile Drug Trafficking Act of 1986

SEC. 1101. Short Title.

This subtitle may be cited as the "Juvenile Drug Trafficking Act of 1986".

SEC. 1102. Offense.

Part D of the Controlled Substances Act is amended by adding after section 405A a new section as follows:

"Employment or use of Person under 18 Years of Age in Drug Operations

"SEC. 405B. (a) It shall be unlawful for any person at least eighteen years of age to knowingly and intentionally—

  "(1) employ, hire, use, persuade, induce, entice, or coerce, a person under eighteen years of age to violate any provision of this title or title III; or
  "(2) employ, hire, use, persuade, induce, entice, or coerce, a person under eighteen years of age to assist in avoiding detection or apprehension for any offense of this title or title III by any Federal, State, or local law enforcement official.

"(b) Any person who violates subsection (a) is punishable by a term of imprisonment up to twice that otherwise authorized, or up to twice the fine otherwise authorized, or both, and at least twice any term of supervised release otherwise authorized for a first offense. Except to the extent a greater minimum sentence is otherwise provided, a term of imprisonment under this subsection shall not be less than one year."

THE ANTI–DRUG ABUSE ACT OF 1988

An Act to prevent the manufacturing, distribution, and use of illegal drugs, and for other purposes.

Be it enacted by the Senate and House of Representatives of the United States of America in Congress assembled,
SECTION 1. Short Title.
This Act may be cited as the "Anti-Drug Abuse Act of 1988". . . .

Title I — Coordination of National Drug Policy

Subtitle A — National Drug Control Program

SEC. 1001. Short Title.
This subtitle may be cited as the "National Narcotics Leadership Act of 1988".
SEC. 1002. Establishment of Office.
(a) Establishment of Office.—There is established in the Executive Office of the President the "Office of National Drug Control Policy".
(b) Director and Deputy Directors.—(1) There shall be at the head of the Office of National Drug Control Policy a Director of National Drug Control Policy.
(2) There shall be in the Office of National Drug Control Policy a Deputy Director for Demand Reduction and a Deputy Director for Supply Reduction.
(3) The Deputy Director for Demand Reduction and the Deputy Director for Supply Reduction shall assist the Director in carrying out the responsibilities of the Director under this Act.
(c) Bureau of State and Local Affairs.—(1) There is established in the Office of National Drug Control Policy a Bureau of State and Local Affairs.
(2) There shall be at the head of such bureau an Associate Director for National Drug Control Policy.
(d) Access by Congress.—The location of the Office of National Drug Control Policy in the Executive Office of the President shall not be construed as affecting access by the Congress or committees of either House to—

(1) information, documents, and studies in the possession of, or conducted by or at the direction of the Director; or
(2) personnel of the Office of National Drug Control Policy. . . .

SEC 1003. Appointment and Duties of Director, Deputy Directors, and Associate Director.

... (3) The Director shall—

(A) review each drug control budget request transmitted to the Director under paragraph (2);

(B) certify in writing as to the adequacy of such request to implement the objectives of the National Drug Control Strategy for the year for which the request is submitted; and

(C) notify the program manager, agency head, or department head, as applicable, regarding the Director's certification under subparagraph (B).

(4) The Director shall maintain records regarding certifications under paragraph (3)(B). . . .

SEC. 1004. Coordination with Executive Branch Departments and Agencies.

(a) ACCESS TO INFORMATION.—(1) Upon request of the Director, and subject to laws governing disclosure of information, the head of each National Drug Control Program agency shall provide to the Director such information as may be required for drug control. . . .

SEC. 1005. Development and Submission of National Drug Control Strategy.

(a) DEVELOPMENT AND SUBMISSION OF THE NATIONAL DRUG CONTROL STRATEGY.—(1) Not later than 180 days after the first Director is confirmed by the Senate, and not later than February 1 of each year thereafter, the President shall submit to the Congress a National Drug Control Strategy. Any part of such strategy that involves information properly classified under criteria established by an Executive order shall be presented to the Congress separately.

(2) The National Drug Control Strategy submitted under paragraph (1) shall—

(A) include comprehensive, research-based, long-range goals for reducing drug abuse in the United States;

(B) include short-term measurable objectives which the Director determines may be realistically achieved in the 2-year period beginning on the date of the submission of the strategy;

(C) describe the balance between resources devoted to supply reduction and demand reduction; and

(D) review State and local drug control activities to ensure that the United States pursues well-coordinated and effective drug control at all levels of government.

(3)(A) In developing the National Drug Control Strategy, the Director shall consult with—

(i)   the heads of the National Drug Control Program agencies;

(ii) the Congress;

(iii) State and local officials;

(iv) private citizens with experience and expertise in demand reduction; and

(v)   private citizens with experience and expertise in supply reduction.

(B) At the time the President submits the National Drug Control Strategy to the Congress, the Director shall transmit a report to the Congress indicating the persons consulted under this paragraph.

(4) Beginning with the second submission of a National Drug Control Strategy, the Director shall include with each such strategy a complete evaluation of the effectiveness of drug control during the preceding year.

(b) GOALS, OBJECTIVES, AND PRIORITIES.—Each National Drug Control Strategy shall include—

(1) a complete list of goals, objectives, and priorities for supply reduction and for demand reduction;

(2) private sector initiatives and cooperative efforts between the Federal Government and State and local governments for drug control;

(3) 3-year projections for program and budget priorities and achievable projections for reductions of drug availability and usage;

(4) a complete assessment of how the budget proposal transmitted under section 1003(c) is intended to implement the strategy and whether the funding levels contained in such proposal are sufficient to implement such strategy;

(5) designation of areas of the United States as high intensity drug trafficking areas in accordance with subsection (c); and

(6) a plan for improving the compatibility of automated information and communication systems to provide Federal agencies with timely and accurate information for purposes of this subtitle.

II. Cocaine

Chapter 48

Cocaine Is Isolated

Albert Niemann, a graduate student in the laboratory of the great German chemist Friedrich Wöhler, was given the task of isolating the active ingredient of coca leaves. Sacks of these leaves had been sent to Wöhler as a gift from an Austrian exploratory expedition to Peru in the 1850s. Niemann was successful, and, in his dissertation in 1860, he named the compound cocaïne, in parallel with morphine, nicotine, and other plant alkaloids. Niemann died the following year, leaving development of uses for the drug to others. This 1860 article from the American Journal of Pharmacy *reports on Niemann and his findings.*

A New Alkaloid in Coca

American Journal of Pharmacy

Coca is the name under which the leaves of several species of Erythroxylon are and have been known in Peru from time immemorial, and which, especially among the Indians, are used for chewing, mixed with a little unslacked lime or wood ashes. Numerous and somewhat fabulous accounts are given of their physiological action, as for instance in "Tschudi's Travels in Peru." A moderate use is said to produce excitement of the functions, to enable the chewer to remain some time without food, and to bear the greatest bodily exertions; while an immoderate chewing of coca, like that of opium, frequently becomes an habitual vice, producing all the deleterious symptoms and consequences of narcotics, such as a state of half intoxication, half of drowsiness, with visionary dreams, premature decay, complete apathy, and idiocy. These peculiar symptoms rendered the presence of a narcotic principle very probable, and have induced Prof. Wœhler and Dr. Niemann, of Goettingen, to undertake the investigation of the substance. The material was furnished by Dr. Scherzer, the naturalist of the exploring expedition in the Austrian frigate Novara. The examination has so far succeeded, by the usual method for the separation of alkaloids, in eliminating a crystallizable base, *cocaïne,* crystallizing in small prisms, devoid of color or odor, slightly soluble in water, more readily in alcohol, and very easily in ether. It possesses a strongly marked alkaline reaction, and a bitter taste, and acts in so far peculiarly, as it transiently benumbs, or almost paralyzes the part of the tongue which it touches. It bears some resemblance to atropine in its chemical relations, and forms perfect salts with the acids. It is, however, without action on the eye, and its compound with the chloride of gold is remarkable for forming benzoic acid in large proportion upon being heated. Further experiments will throw light on its physiological properties.

Chapter 49

Praise for Coca Extract

Although the Merck Company manufactured a small amount of the drug annually after its isolation in 1860, the real impact of pure cocaine would not be unleashed until the 1880s. In the intervening years, extracts of coca leaves were used to obtain a stimulating effect. Dr. G. Archie Stockwell's description of coca extract in this 1877 article presents good evidence of the positive attitude some physicians held toward this milder form of cocaine.

Erythroxylon Coca

G. Archie Stockwell

Coca is the dried leaf of the shrub *Erythroxylon coca* or *Erythroxylum Peruvianum; order*, trigynia; *class*, decandria; *habitation*, mountainous districts of Peru and Bolivia, two thousand feet and upwards above the level of the sea.

To the native Peruvian and Bolivian coca holds the same relation as the betel-nut to the Malay, the tea-plant to the Celestial, poppy and Indian hemp to the Oriental, and tobacco to the Caucasian. To it he is as much the slave as were Dr. Johnson and Gilbert Stuart to rappee. Beyond the confines of the country to which it is native but little seems to be known of coca; nevertheless it is, without doubt, one of the most remarkable products of the torrid zone. When we consider its peculiar properties, it is astonishing that it has so long remained unnoticed. Were it a product of the jungles of interior Africa, or extremely difficult to obtain, this neglect could be accounted for; on the contrary, hundreds of European and North American vessels annually frequent the harbors of Peru and Bolivia, or the metropolis of the Amazon, where it may be obtained in large quantities, and where it has been as long known as the cinchona; yet the tonic, stimulating, and narcotic properties of this shrub are just beginning to attract the attention of the medical world.

Like the cinchona, the peculiar powers of coca have been introduced to the notice of the Caucasian by the aboriginal inhabitants of the country to which it is indigenous. No historical record informs us when it was introduced to their notice, or who first discovered the hidden properties of its leaves. When the empire of Atahualpa was overthrown by the rapacious Pizarro, coca was as well known to the Peruvians as at the present day, and played an important part in their religion, being used in all public ceremonies as an offering to the sun god. . . .

It is a remarkable fact that those who regularly use the coca require but little food, and with increased indulgence are enabled to undergo the greatest fatigues without tasting anything else. Pöppig ascribes this astonishing increase of endurance to a temporary excitement, which must necessarily be succeeded by a corresponding collapse, and therefore asserts that the use of coca is highly injurious. This is in accordance with the exploded attempt to apply the dynamic law that "action and reaction are equal and opposite" to the phenomena of stimulation. Those who are ignorant of the physiological action of stimulant narcotics repeatedly affirm that tobacco, opium, hemp, alcohol, coca, and kindred drugs which are used as stimulants produces a corresponding recoil, whereas the so-called recoil is simply the advent of narcosis, owing to a large impregnation of the blood with the agent after stimulation from a small dose. Coca never produces a depressing action, except as the result of an overdose or of small quantities so frequently repeated as to cause the narcotic effect by accumulation. Careful observations lead me to believe that, so far from being injurious, the moderate consumption of coca is not only wholesome but frequently beneficial. Tschudi cites as examples several Indians who, never allowing a day to pass without at least three coceadas, attained the truly patriarchal age of one hundred and thirty years. As the ordinary food of the native Peruvian consists almost exclusively of roasted maize, barley, or seeds of the quinoa, which are eaten without any addition, they suffer with frequent and obstinate obstructions and derangements of the digestive system, which are entirely obviated by the use of coca. From the time the native becomes a coquero these troubles cease, never to recur, except with the abandonment of the habit.

Travelers in the Andes have found in coca a preventive of those asthmatic symptoms that are produced by the rarefied air of high altitudes. Tschudi invariably drank a strong infusion before undertaking his hunting excursions in the Puna, fourteen thousand feet above the sea level, and not only found it to afford great relief, but asserts that he suffered no greater difficulty in breathing while in the rapid pursuit of game than would have been the case upon the coast.

Although the moderate use of coca is thus beneficial, its abuse is attended with serious results, and if persisted in the digestive functions are deranged, and there is brought about a structural degeneration of nerve material, the consequences of which are to be seen in delirium, brain softening, and general paralysis. The permanent pathological effect induced does not allow of as ready an impression by the drug as before; hence the coquero continually demands more and more of his accustomed narcotic to produce the desired effect. Such a man may be readily distinguished by his trembling limbs and hollow cheeks, his sunken, lustreless, black-rimmed eyes, sallow complexion, incoherent speech, and stolid apathy; seemingly oblivious to all surroundings, he neither notices a friend nor fears a foe. His character is irresolute, suspicious, and false; in the prime of life he has all the appearance of senility, and in later years he sinks into complete idiocy. With the confirmed coquero no increase of temperature or acceleration of the circulation is induced by the use of the drug; on the contrary, the heart's action is slow and intermittent, and the pulse thin and thread-like. The forehead is frequently clammy and cold, while the extremities may be at a fever heat. The symptoms point strongly to the medulla oblongata as the part affected, which undoubtedly becomes partially paralyzed. In moderate doses, coca causes increased arterial action, stimulates the alimentary secretions and peristaltic action, diminishes weariness, strengthens the pulse, calms nervous excitement, retards waste, facilitates repair, alleviates spasms, and increases mental activity; in fact, it is an economizer of vital energy and an effective aid to nutrition. It invariably contributes to mental cheerfulness, and withal not unfrequently causes unequivocal aphrodisia. Although one cannot look upon coca as a food, it will be found second only to alcohol in its food-replacing power; for this reason it will undoubtedly prove of value in low forms of fever. In larger doses it has a decided action upon the kidneys, producing also watery stools, and, when long continued, gives to both urine and faeces a highly offensive odor, and renders the latter so acrid as almost instantaneously to destroy all vegetation with which they may come in contact; it also renders other excretions, as those of the lungs and skin, offensive. In these large doses it does not seem to affect the visual organs, as the pupils will be found freely contractible on the approach of light, and unless the doses are very heavy the eye presents an expression of combined merriment and cunning. Hunger seems never to be induced, but rather the contrary; yet if the patient be coaxed to partake of food set before him he eats voraciously.

According to one writer, loosened teeth with foul, ulcerous gums are among the effects of prolonged coquerism, and he cites as instances the Indians employed in certain of the mines of Peru, who, he discovered, not only consumed enormous quantities of coca, but "were afflicted with ulcerous gums, foul breath, and loosened teeth, the sufferings from which could only be allayed by death." The writer in question must have been wofully ignorant, or he has wantonly endeavored to mislead his renders, as the mines in question were the famous quicksilver workings of Peru. He speaks of them as silver, but ignores the fact that it was not argentiferous metal that was obtained, but mercury.

Of the physiological and therapeutical action of coca there is much to be discovered. It has been lauded as a hypnotic, yet its uncertainty of action will prevent its ever superseding the many other drugs of far greater value that we possess. It is, however, both anodyne and antispasmodic, exerting special influence upon the brain and spinal cord, and from its action upon the pneumogastric it will undoubtedly prove of benefit in certain forms of asthma. Its antispasmodic action has been vouched for by numerous South Americans. It is used by the natives to promote uterine contraction. Where inertia has supervened, I am told by Spanish American physicians that its effect is both speedy and certain. In melancholia, or where nervous depression exists, its action in promoting cheerfulness is marked, and its influence upon the digestive function, before noticed, will doubtless cause coca to be prescribed for many of the diseases of so-called dyspeptic character and those irregularities arising from non-assimilation of food.

It is said that certain of the Bolivian Indians inherit from their ancestors a mode of preparing and administering this drug so as to produce a cataleptic state so profound as to stimulate death beyond detection, from which the patient may be aroused after the lapse of a few hours without serious results. I believe a mixture of cannabis indica, opium, and certain other narcotics is used for the same purpose by the initiated among Orientals.

Coca will produce sleep oftentimes when opium has failed if given in repeated small doses for a little time before retiring to rest, in order to allow the preliminary stage of excitement to pass off; but, as a rule, it is inferior to the opiates, its action being extremely variable.

For the last few years it has been fashionable to claim for every new drug a decided antiperiodic action, vaunting for it all the powers of quinia, and coca has not escaped. A careful and thorough experimentation with the drug will, however, convince the most incredulous that it possesses no antiperiodic properties. Administered in conjunction with quinia it will, I doubt not, like opium, oftentimes prove a valuable adjunct. Give quinine to a confirmed coquero, at the same time depriving him of his solace, and you will frequently be disappointed in its results. Restore him his coca, and the action of the salt will be both speedy and certain. I have observed like results when prescribing for consumers of tobacco.

From the action of coca as observed, the writer would give it to a patient suffering from cholera with the expectation of happy results; its action is rapid, and vomiting and cramps would, I think, speedily yield to its influence. Larabie, Williams, and other travelers have experienced almost instantaneous relief from coca when suffering from cholera morbus. Dr. Carvallo informs me that he has observed similar results from an infusion, and has known even the chewing of the leaf to act favorably. I have witnessed the same effects myself. It would not be at all surprising if it were proven that the coca caused a marked increase of the biliary secretions. I should also expect marked results from it in congestive chills, particularly with flannels wet with ammonia spirits in which quinine had been dissolved to saturation, applied to the abdomen, as practiced in Central America. But it is in hypochondriacal diseases that we may look for the greatest benefit from coca.

I trust that the profession will thoroughly examine into the merits and demerits of the article, and give the full negative results of their investigations. I say *negative*, for that is the evidence demanded at the present day. We are overrun with positive evidence, all virtues being ascribed to all remedies to such an extent that we become lost in seeking information. What we now need to know is what medicines will *not* do.

It will probably be found that the dose required for our climate will be much larger than that demanded in Peru. The best mode of administering is in the form of an infusion, the dose being about two drachms. The greatest drawback to its use is the liability to gather moisture, which renders it worthless. The fluid extract I would have but little faith in, for obvious reasons. If an extract to be made of erythroxylon coca one pound, rectified spirit four pints, prepared by maceration for seven days, pressing out the tincture and evaporating to a proper consistence, I think it would be satisfactory. The dose of such an extract should be one fourth of a grain to two grains or more.

Chapter 50

The Therapeutic Value of Cocaine

William A. Hammond (1828–1900), a pioneering neurologist, was also a novelist and playwright. As an authority on mental illness and brain disease, Hammond was the kind of expert one would logically consult on the safety of a new drug. Hammond became interested in cocaine, used it himself, and recommended it for many common ailments. He did not believe that there was such a phenomenon as a cocaine habit: in this 1887 article he assured readers that cocaine users could stop whenever they so wished.

COCA: ITS PREPARATIONS AND THERAPEUTICAL QUALITIES

William A. Hammond

It is not my intention to consume the time of the Society by entering into the clinical history of the erythroxylon coca, or of the voluminous literature of which it and its active principle have been the subject; neither shall I devote much attention to the observations, interesting though they be, of other physicians and surgeons. I shall confine my remarks, therefore, almost entirely to an account of my own experience with these very important remedies. That experience, based as it is upon the results obtained by the administrations of coca and its preparations to others, as well as those drawn from a large personal experience of coca and the hydrochlorate of cocaine, will I trust be of interest to the members of the Medical Society of Virginia.

I have employed three preparations of the coca leaves—the fluid extract, the wine, and the hydrochlorate of cocaine. . . .

Disappointed in the result of my administration of these wines of coca, and recognizing the fact that wine is the best menstruum through which the active principle can be given, I represented to Messrs. Thurber, Whyland & Co., prominent grocers and druggists in New York, and who I knew had an exceedingly competent chemist in their employ, the expediency of preparing a wine of coca that should contain a fixed proportion of cocaine, and at the same time be free from the tannin, resin, and other inert or deleterious substances present in the leaves. I also insisted upon the point that the wine used in its manufacture should be full-bodied and absolutely pure. In a short time they submitted to me a wine of coca containing two grains of the hydrochlorate of cocaine to the pint, and absolutely free from tannin and resinous matter. This preparation leaves nothing to be desired; the wine used in its manufacture is the juice of the grape uncontaminated by foreign substances. The taste would be pronounced pleasant by everybody, and the proportion of cocaine is large enough to give a medium dose, about the sixth of a grain, to each wineglassful. . . .

I made some use of this wine of coca as a special *tonic to the vocal apparatus*, and I am quite sure that it possessed great value in which fatigue follows the excessive use of the voice, or in which the voice breaks down in the midst of some supreme effort. Where such fatigue or failure is to be feared a full claret glass of the wine taken just before beginning to speak or sing will almost invariably accomplish the object in view. Several of my patients—lawyers, clergymen, actors and other public speakers—have, after taking it according to my directions, avoided the unpleasant consequences which had previously followed their efforts. A lady, an opera singer, not however a patient of mine, but under the care of a brother physician, was apprehensive that she would have to give up her profession in consequence of a notable failure of her voice after an hour's work. There did not appear to be in her case any disease of the larynx other than a functional paralysis of the vocal chords, probably of hysterical origin. However that may be, a wineglassful of the wine of coca, taken after she had been singing a few minutes, effectually prevented the catastrophe, and in a few weeks entirely cured her so that she was able to do without the agent.

But I have made more use of this wine of coca in cases of *cerebral hyperæmia* than in any other affection. This disorder is generally the result of excessive mental exertion or of intense emotional disturbance. Nothing can be more beneficial in its action than is this remedy; dispensing with all other stimulants, I advise the patient to take a claret glassful of wine with each meal. The influence is felt almost immediately, the vital powers seem to be at once restored, and the mind soon regains its former vigor. If the sleep has been disturbed or absent it becomes regular and insufficient quantity after the remedy has been taken for a few days. These cases, passing as they do under the names of nervous prostration and neurasthenia, general debility, etc., are those in which the influence of the wine of coca is most distinctly shown.

In another form of mental depression which is not infrequently an accompaniment of hysteria in the female, or of a like condition in the male, and in which there is usually some disorder of the generative system, this wine of coca is invaluable, and may be often relied upon to effect a cure without the administration of any other medicinal agent. Under its use the emotions become more expansive, the disposition to brood over imaginary, or at least very slight troubles, disappear. Tears are no longer shed over mere nothings; the countenance loses its expression of utter hopelessness and thus an important step toward a successful therapeutical result is at once obtained. In such cases I give the wine continuously for several months. I have never had any difficulty in causing the patient to stop its use.

What is true of the wine of coca is true, though in a more marked degree, of its active principle, the *hydrochlorate of cocaine*, and which even for internal administration should often be preferred. In regard to this substance my experience has also led me to very definite conclusions. The hydrochlorate of cocaine is best known as a local anæsthetic in operations about the eye, nasal cavities, etc. But it is likewise an inestimable remedy in certain affections of the nervous system in which a speedy and decided result is desired.

About two years ago I undertook a series of experiments with this agent on myself, with the object of obtaining more satisfactory information relative to its action than it seemed possible for me to get otherwise. I began by injecting a grain of the substance under the skin of the forearm, the operation being performed at 8 o'clock, P.M.

The first effect ensued in about five minutes, and consisted of a pleasant thrill which seemed to pass through the whole body. This lasted about ten minutes and shortly after its appearance was accompanied by a sensation of fullness in the head and heat of the face. There was also noticed a decided acceleration of the pulse with increase of force. This latter symptom was probably, judging from subsequent experiments, the very first to ensue, but my attention being otherwise engaged it was overlooked. On feeling the pulse five minutes after making the injection, it was found to be 91, while immediately before the operation it was only 82.

With these physical phenomena there was a sense of exhilaration and an increase of mental activity that were well marked and not unlike in character those that ordinarily follow a glass or two of champagne. I was writing at the time, and I found that my thoughts flowed with increased freedom, and were unusually well expressed. The influence was well felt for two hours, when it gradually began to fade. At 12 o'clock, four hours after the injection, I went to bed, feeling, however, no disposition to sleep. I lay awake till daylight, my mind actively going over all the events of the previous day. When I at last fell asleep it was only for two or three hours, and then I awoke with a severe frontal headache. This passed off after breakfast.

On the second night following, at 7 o'clock, I injected two grains of the hydrochlorate of cocaine into the skin of the forearm. At that time the pulse was 84, full and soft. In four minutes and a half it had increased to 92, was decidedly stronger than before and somewhat irregular in rhythm. The peculiar thrill previously mentioned was again experienced. All the phenomena attendant on the first experiment were present in this, and to an increased degree. In addition there were twitching of the muscles of the face, and a slight tremor of the hands noticed especially in writing. In regard to the mental manifestations there was a similar exhilaration as in the last experiment, but much more intense in character. I felt a great desire to write, and did so with a freedom and apparent clearness that astonished me. I was quite sure, however, at the time, that on the following morning, when I came to read it over, I would find my lucubrations to be of no value; I was therefore agreeably disappointed when I came to pursue it, after the effects of the drug had passed off, that it was entirely coherent, logical, and as good, if not better in general character, as anything I had previously written.

The effects of this dose did not disappear till the middle of the next day, nor until I had drunk two or three cups of strong coffee. I slept little or none at all, the night being passed in tossing from side to side of the bed, and in thinking of the most preposterous subjects. I was, however, at no time unconscious, but it seemed as though my mind was to some extent perverted from its usual course of action. The heat of the head was greatest at about 12 o'clock, and at that time my pulse was 112, the highest point reached. I had no headache until after arising, and the pain disappeared in the course of the morning.

Four nights subsequently I injected four grains of the hydrochlorate of cocaine into the skin of the left forearm. The effects were similar in almost every respect with those of the other experiments except that they were much more intense. The mental activity was exceedingly great, and in writing, my thoughts as before appeared to be lucidly and logically expressed. I wrote page after page, throwing the sheets on the floor without stopping to gather them together. When, however, I came to look them over on the following morning, I found that I had written a series of high flown sentences altogether different from my usual style, and bearing upon matters in which I was not in the least interested. The result was very striking as showing the difference between a large and excessive dose of the drug, and yet it appeared to me at the time that what I was writing consisted of ideas of very superior character and expressed with a beauty of diction of which I was in my normal condition altogether incapable.

The disturbance of the action of the heart was also exceedingly well marked, and may be described best by the word "tumultuous." At times, beginning within three minutes after the injection, and continuing with more or less intensity all through the night, the heart beat so rapidly that its pulsations could not be counted, and then its action would suddenly fall to a rate not exceeding 60 in a minute, every now and then dropping a heat. This irregularity was accompanied by a disturbance of respiration of a similar character, and by a sense of oppression in the chest that added greatly to my discomfort.

On subsequent nights I took 6, 8, 10 and 12 grains of the cocaine at a dose, but I will not detain the Society with a detailed account of the effects produced. It will be sufficient to say that they were similar in general characteristics though of gradually increasing intensity in accordance with the dose taken to that in which 4 grains were injected. In all there was great mental excitement, increased fluency of thought, and exaggerated disposition to write, the matter written being disconnected and at times almost incoherent, though, it appeared to me at the moment to be wonderfully logical and profound. In one, that in which 12 grains were taken, I was conscious of a tendency to talk, and as far as my recollection extends, I believe I did make a long speech on some subject of which I had no remembrance the next day. In all, the action of the heart was increased, was irregular in rhythm and force to such an extent that I was apprehensive of serious results. Insomnia was a marked characteristic, and there was invariably a headache the following morning. In all cases, however, the effects passed off about midday, and by evening I was as well as ever.

Up to this time I certainly had not taken a poisonous dose of cocaine, or one that had produced any serious inconvenience. My experience had satisfied me that a much larger dose than any I had up to that time injected might, in my case at least, be taken with impunity. A consideration of the phenomena observed appeared to show that the effects produced by 12 grains were not very much more pronounced than those following 6 grains. I determined, therefore, to make one more experiment, and to inject 18 grains. I knew that in a case of attempted suicide 23 grains had been taken into the stomach without seemingly injurious effect, and that in another case 32 grains were taken within the space of three hours without symptoms following of greater intensity than those I had experienced.

I had taken the doses of 8, 10 and 12 grains in divided quantities, and this dose of 18 grains I took in four portions within five minutes of each other. At once an effect was produced upon the heart, and before I had taken the last injection the pulsations were 140 to the minute and characteristically irregular. In all the former experiments, although there was great mental exaltation, amounting at times almost to delirium, it was nevertheless distinctly under my control, and I am sure that at any time under the influence of a sufficiently powerful incentive I could have obtained entire mastery over myself, and have acted after my normal manner. But in this instance, within five minutes after taking the last injection, I felt that my mind was passing beyond my control, and that I was becoming an irresponsible agent. I did not feel exactly in a reckless mood, but I was in such a frame of mind as to be utterly regardless of any calamity or danger that might be impending over me. I do not think I was in a particularly combative condition, but I was elated and possessed of a feeling as though exempt from the operation of deleterious influences. I do not know how long this state of mind continued, for I lost consciousness of all my acts within, I think, half an hour after finishing the administration of the dose. Probably, however, other moods supervened, for the next day when I came downstairs, three hours after my usual time, I found the floor of my library strewn with encyclopaedias, dictionaries, and other books of reference, and one or two chairs overturned. I certainly was possessed of the power of mental and physical action in accordance with the ideas by which I was governed, for I had turned out the gas in the room and gone upstairs to my bed-chamber and lighted the gas, and put the match used in a safe place, and undressed, laying my clothes in their usual place, had cleaned my teeth and gone to bed. Doubtless these acts were all automatic, for I had done them all in pretty much the same way for a number of years. During the night the condition which existed was, judging from the previous experiments, certainly not sleep, and yet I remained entirely unconscious until 9 o'clock the following morning, when I found myself in bed, with a splitting headache and a good deal of cardiac and respiratory disturbance. For several days afterward I felt the effects of this extreme dose in a certain degree of languor and indisposition to mental or physical exertion; there was also a difficulty in concentrating the attention, but I slept soundly every night without any notable disturbance from dreams.

Certainly in this instance I came very near taking a fatal dose, and I would not advise anybody to repeat the experiment. I suppose that if I had taken the whole quantity in one single injection instead of in four, over a period of twenty minutes, the result might have been disastrous. Eighteen grains of cocaine are equivalent to about 3600 grains of coca leaves, and of course, owing to its concentration, capable of acting with very much greater intensity.

I am not aware that a fatal dose of cocaine has yet been indicated by actual fact. Probably 18 grains would kill some people, and perhaps even smaller quantities might, with certain individuals, be fatal. But these are inferences and not facts; but so far as I know there is not an instance on record of a person dying from the administration of cocaine. So far as my experiments extend (and I think it will be admitted that they have gone as far as is safe) I am inclined to think that a dose sufficient to produce death would do so by its action on the heart. Certainly it was there that in my case the most dangerous symptoms were perceived. The rapidity, force, and marked irregularity of the pulse all showed that the innervation of the heart was seriously affected.

It is surprising that no marked influence appeared to be exercised upon the spinal cord or upon the ganglia at the base of the brain. Thus there were no disturbances of sensibility (no anesthesia, no hyperæsthesia) and no interference with motility, except that some of the muscles, especially those of the face, were subjected to slight twitchings. In regard to sight and hearing, I noticed that both were affected, but that while the sharpness of vision was decidedly lessened, the hearing was increased in acuteness. At no time were there any hallucinations.

Acting from the data thus obtained, I have used the hydrochlorate of cocaine to a considerable extent in my practice, but always by hypodermic injections when employing it in its pure state. For internal administration, I have, as already mentioned, used the wine in preference; but recognizing the power of the substance when locally applied to mucous membranes to diminish the calibre of the blood-vessels of the part and to produce anesthesia I should use it in certain affections of the stomach upon the same principle as it is at present applied to the nasal mucous membrane, the larynx, and the larynx, should cases requiring its employment come under my observation.

I have derived great benefit from its administration hypodermically in cases of *melancholia*, and in others of *hysteria* characterized by great depression of spirits. In such case a half grain may be injected under the skin, and if necessary the quantity gradually increased to two grains. I have never given more than this quantity to a patient at one time, but I have frequently reached this point without having yet witnessed any deleterious effects. One injection given daily for three or four days will often make the most dismal melancholic cheerful, and what is remarkable is the fact that the improvement is permanent. In the case of a woman strongly hysterical, and who had not spoken a word for several months, a single injection of a grain (a rather large dose to begin with, but one which I thought proper under the circumstances) broke the spell in less than five minutes, and there has up to this date—and nearly a year has elapsed—been no return of any hysterical symptom. . . .

We have heard a good deal of the *cocaine habit*, a habit which I am very sure has *no existence* as such. I do not deny that there are morphi-eaters who, having heard that cocaine is an antidote to the morphia habit, have endeavored to cure themselves with it, and being deprived of full powers of judgment and of will, have ingrafted the cocaine on the morphia habit, producing thereby an exceedingly bad combination. But that there is any such thing as a cocaine habit pure and simple which the individual cannot of his own effort altogether arrest, I emphatically deny. The injection of half a grain to a grain produces a certain degree of mental exhilaration which is pleasurable, and which attends upon a repetition of the dose; but there is no weakening of the will power, such as is produced by morphia, and no craving for the drug such as opium and its preparations cause. I have given it to many patients, male and female, for several weeks continuously, and have never had a single one object to its administration being stopped. There is not so much trouble in ceasing its use as there is in giving up tea or coffee, and nothing like so much as is experienced by those who cease using alcohol or tobacco. Within a space of a few months, Dr. Bosworth, of New York, took, I think, between 500 and 600 grains, and stopped without suffering the least inconvenience.

Chapter 51

Freud as Cocaine User and Advocate

Sigmund Freud was attracted to cocaine by reading American accounts of its use as a cure for morphine and alcohol habits. Like Hammond and other physicians, he took the drug himself and approving of its effects, recommended it broadly for several years, until it was established that cocaine was not a cure for morphine and alcohol addiction and that use of this drug could become compulsive and damaging.

Freud's praise of coca and cocaine appears in three articles: "Über Coca" [On coca] (July 1884), from which the selection here is taken, "Beitrag zur Kenntniss der Cocawirkung" [Contribution to the knowledge of the effect of cocaine] (January 1885), and Über die Allgemeinwirkung des Cocaïns [On the general effect of cocaine] (August 1885). His fourth and last essay on the drug, "Bemerkungen über die Anwendung des Cocaïn" [Remark on craving for and fear of cocaine] (July 1887), took the form of a defense of his work against the condemnation of another physician, Dr. Albrecht Erlenmeyer. In his counterattack Freud quoted Hammond on the harmlessness of cocaine.

Über Coca

Sigmund Freud

In England A. Bennett carried out the first experiments on animals in 1874; in 1876 the reports of the president of the British Medical Association, Sir Robert Christison, created a considerable stir; and when a correspondent of the *British Medical Journal* claimed that a Mr. Weston (who had astonished scientific circles in London by his remarkable walking feats) chewed coca leaves, coca became, for a time, a subject of general interest. In the same year (1876) Dowdeswell published the results of a completely ineffective experiment carried out in the laboratory of University College, after which coca seems to have found no one in England willing to undertake further research.[1] . . .

The earlier . . . investigations . . . led, on the whole, to great disillusionment and to the conviction that effects from the use of coca such as had been reported so enthusiastically from South America could not be expected in Europe. Investigations such as those carried out by Schroff, Fronmüller, and Dowdeswell produced either negative or, at the most, insignificant results. There is more than one explanation for these failures. Certainly the quality of the preparations used was largely to blame. In a number of cases the authors themselves express doubt as to the quality of their preparations; and to the extent that they believe the reports of travelers on the effects of coca, they assume that these effects must be attributed to a volatile component of the leaf. They base this assumption on the report of Poeppig, among others, that even in South America leaves which have been stored for a long time are considered worthless. The experiments carried out recently with the cocaine prepared by Merk [sic] in Darmstadt alone justify the claim that cocaine is the true agent of the coca effect, which can be produced just as well in Europe as in South America and turned to good account in dietetic and therapeutic treatment. . . .

The Effect of Coca on the Healthy Human Body

I have carried out experiments and studied, in myself and others, the effect of coca on the healthy human body; my findings agree fundamentally with Mantegazza's description of the effect of coca leaves.

The first time I took 0.05g. of *cocaïnum muriaticum* in a 1% water solution was when I was feeling slightly out of sorts from fatigue. This solution is rather viscous, somewhat opalescent, and has a strange aromatic smell. At first it has a bitter taste, which yields afterwards to a series of very pleasant aromatic flavors. Dry cocaine salt has the same smell and taste, but to a more concentrated degree.

A few minutes after taking cocaine, one experiences a sudden exhilaration and feeling of lightness. One feels a certain furriness on the lips and palate, followed by a feeling of warmth in the same areas; if one now drinks cold water, it feels warm on the lips and cold in the throat. On other occasions the predominant feeling is a rather pleasant coolness in the mouth and throat.

During this first trial I experienced a short period of toxic effects, which did not recur in subsequent experiments. Breathing became slower and deeper and I felt tired and sleepy; I yawned frequently and felt somewhat dull. After a few minutes the actual cocaine euphoria began, introduced by repeated cooling eructation. Immediately after taking the cocaine I noticed a slight slackening of the pulse and later a moderate increase.

I have observed the same physical signs of the effect of cocaine in others, mostly people of my own age. The most constant symptom proved to be the repeated cooling eructation. This is often accompanied by a rumbling which must originate from high up in the intestine; two of the people I observed, who said they were able to recognize movements of their stomachs, declared emphatically that they had repeatedly detected such movements. Often, at the outset of the cocaine effect, the subjects alleged that they experienced an intense feeling of heat in the head. I noticed this in myself as well in the course of some later experiments, but on other occasions it was absent. In only two cases did coca give rise to dizziness. On the whole the toxic effects of coca are of short duration, and much less intense than those produced by effective doses of quinine or salicylate of soda; they seem to become even weaker after repeated use of cocaine. . . .

By way of an experiment, Sir Robert Christison—who is seventy-eight years old—tired himself to the point of exhaustion by walking fifteen miles without partaking of food. After several days he repeated the procedure with the same result: during the third experiment he chewed 2 drams of coca leaves and was able to complete the walk without the exhaustion experienced on the earlier occasions; when he arrived home, despite the fact that he had been for nine hours without food or drink, he experienced no hunger or thirst, and woke the next morning without feeling at all tired. On yet another occasion he climbed a 3000-foot mountain and arrived completely exhausted at the summit; he made the descent upon the influence of coca, with youthful vigor and no feeling of fatigue. . . .

The Therapeutic Uses of Coca

It was inevitable that a plant which had achieved such a reputation for marvelous effects in its country of origin should have been used to treat the most varied disorders and illnesses of the human body. . . .

a) *Coca as a stimulant.* The main use of coca will undoubtedly remain that which the Indians have made of it for centuries: it is of value in all cases where the primary aim is to increase the physical capacity of the body for a given short period of time and to hold strength in reserve to meet further demands—especially when outward circumstances exclude the possibility of obtaining the rest and nourishment normally necessary for great exertion. Such situations arise in wartime, on journeys, during mountain climbing and other expeditions, etc.—indeed, they are situations in which the alcoholic stimulants are also generally recognized as being of value. Coca is a far more potent and far less harmful stimulant than alcohol, and its widespread utilization is hindered at present only by its high cost. Bearing in mind the effect of coca on the natives of South America, a medical authority as early as Pedro Crespo recommended its use by European navies; Neudörfer, Clemens and Surgeon-Major E. Charles recommended that it should be adopted by the armies of Europe as well; and Aschenbrandt's experiences should not fail to draw the attention of army administrators to coca. If cocaine is given as a stimulant, it is better that it should be given in small effective doses (0.05–0.10g) and repeated so often that the effects of the doses overlap. Apparently cocaine is not stored in the body; I have already stressed the fact that there is no state of depression when the effects of coca have worn off.

At present it is impossible to assess with any certainty to what extent coca can be expected to increase human mental powers. I have the impression that protracted use of coca can lead to a lasting improvement if the inhibitions manifested before it is taken are due only to physical causes or to exhaustion. To be sure, the instantaneous effect of a dose of coca cannot be compared with that of a morphine injection; but, on the good side of the ledger, there is no danger of general damage to the body as is the case with the chronic use of morphine.

Many doctors felt that coca would play an important role by filling a gap in the medicine chest of the psychiatrists. It is a well-known fact that psychiatrists have an ample supply of drugs at their disposal for reducing the excitation of nerve centers, but none which could serve to increase the reduced functioning of the nerve centers. Coca has consequently been prescribed for the most diverse kinds of psychic debility—hysteria, hypochondria, melancholic inhibition, stupor, and similar maladies. Some successes have been reported: for instance, the Jesuit, Antonio Julian tells of a learned missionary who was freed from severe hypochondria; Mantegazza praises coca as being almost universally effective in improving those functional disorders which we now group together under the name of neurasthenia; Fliessburg reports excellent results from the use of coca in cases of "nervous prostration"; and according to Caldwell, it is the best tonic for hysteria. . . .

d) *Coca in the treatment of morphine and alcohol addiction.* In America the important discovery has recently been made that coca preparations possess the power to suppress the craving for morphine in habitual addicts, and also to reduce to negligible proportions the serious symptoms of collapse which appear while the patient is being weaned away from the morphine habit. According to my information (which is largely from the *Detroit Therapeutic Gazette*), it was W. H. Bentley who announced, in May 1878, that he had substituted coca for the customary alkaloid in the case of a female morphine addict. Two years later, Palmer, in an article in the *Louisville Medical News*, seems to have aroused the greatest general interest in this treatment of morphine addiction; for the next two years "*Erythroxylon coca* in the opium habit" was a regular heading in the reports of the *Therapeutic Gazette*. From then on information regarding successful cures became rarer: whether because the treatment became established as a recognized cure, or because it was abandoned, I do not know. Judging by the advertisements of drug dealers in the most recent issues of American papers, I should rather conclude that the former was the case.

There are some sixteen reports of cases in which the patient has been successfully cured of addiction; in only one instance is there a report of failure of coca to alleviate morphine addiction, and in this case the doctor wondered why there had been so many warm recommendations for the use of coca in cases of morphine addiction. The successful cases vary in their conclusiveness. Some of them involve large doses of opium or morphine and addictions of long standing. There is not much information on the subject of relapses, as most cases were reported within a very short time of the cure having been effected. Symptoms which appear during abstention are not always reported in detail. There is especial value in those reports which contain the observation that the patients were able to dispense with coca after a few weeks without experiencing any further desire for morphine. Special attention is repeatedly called to the fact that morphine cachexia gave way to excellent health, so that the patients were scarcely recognizable after their cure. Concerning the method of withdrawal, it should be made clear that in the majority of cases a gradual reduction of the habitual dose of the drug, accompanied by a gradual increase of the coca dose, was the method chosen; however, sudden discontinuation of the drug was also tried. In the latter case Palmer prescribes that a certain dose of coca should be repeated as often during the day as the desire for morphine recurs. The daily dose of coca is lessened gradually until it is possible to dispense with the antidote altogether. From the very beginning the attacks experienced during abstinence were either slight or else became milder after a few days. In almost every case the cure was effected by the patient himself, whereas the cure of morphine addiction without the help of coca, as practiced in Europe, requires surveillance of the patient in a hospital.

I once had occasion to observe the case of a man who was subjected to the type of cure involving the sudden withdrawal of morphine, assisted by the use of coca; the same patient had suffered severe symptoms as a result of abstinence in the course of a previous cure. This time his condition was tolerable; in particular, there was no sign of depression or nausea as long as the effects of coca lasted; chills and diarrhea were now the only permanent symptoms of his abstinence. The patient was not bedridden, and could function normally. During the first days of the cure he consumed 3dg of *cocaïnum muriaticum* daily, and after ten days he was able to dispense with the coca treatment altogether.

The treatment of morphine addiction with coca does not, therefore, result merely in the exchange of one kind of addiction for another—it does not turn the morphine addict into a *coquero*; the use of coca is only temporary. Moreover, I do not think that it is the general toughening effect of coca which enables the system weakened by morphine to withstand, at the cost of only insignificant symptoms, the withdrawal of morphine. I am rather inclined to assume that coca has a directly antagonistic effect on morphine, and in support of my view I quote the following observations of Dr. Josef Pollak on a case in point:

"A thirty-three-year-old woman has been suffering for years from severe menstrual migraine which can be alleviated only by morphia injections. Although the lady in question never takes morphia or experiences any desire to do so when she is free of migraine, during the attacks she behaves like a morphine addict. A few hours after the injection she suffers intense depression, biliousness, attacks of vomiting, which are stopped by a second morphine injection; thereupon, the symptoms of intolerance recur, with the result that an attack of migraine, along with all its consequences, keeps the patient in bed for three days in a most wretched condition. Cocaine was then tried to combat the migraine, but the treatment proved unsuccessful. It was necessary to resort to morphine injections. But as soon as the symptoms of morphine intolerance appeared, they were quickly relieved by 1dg of cocaine, with the result that the patient recovered from her attack in a far shorter time and consumed much less morphine in the process."

Coca was tried in America for the treatment of chronic alcoholism at about the same time as it was introduced in connection with morphine addiction, and most reports dealt with the two uses conjointly. In the treatment of alcoholism, too, there were cases of undoubted success, in which the irresistible compulsion to drink was either banished or alleviated, and the dyspeptic complaints of the drinkers were relieved. In general, however, the suppression of the alcohol craving through the use of coca proved to be more difficult than the suppression of morphomania; in one case reported by Bentley the drinker became a *coquero*. One need only suggest the immense economic significance which coca would acquire as a "source of savings" in another sense, if its effectiveness in combating alcoholism were confirmed. . . .

f) *Coca as an aphrodisiac.* The natives of South America, who represented their goddess of love with coca leaves in her hand, did not doubt the stimulative effect of coca on the genitalia. Mantegazza confirms that the *coqueros* sustain a high degree of potency right into old age; he even reports cases of the restoration of potency and the disappearance of functional weaknesses following the use of coca, although he does not believe that coca would produce such an effect in all individuals. Marvaud emphatically supports the view that coca has a stimulative effect; other writers strongly recommend coca as a remedy for occasional functional weaknesses and temporary exhaustion; and Bentley reports on a case of this type in which coca was responsible for the cure.

Among the persons to whom I have given coca, three reported violent sexual excitement which they unhesitatingly attributed to the coca. A young writer, who was enabled by treatment with coca to resume his work after a longish illness, gave up using the drug because of the undesirable secondary effects which it had on him.

g) *Local application of coca.* Cocaine and its salts have a marked anesthetizing effect when brought in contact with the skin and mucous membrane in concentrated solution; this property suggests its occasional use as a local anesthetic, especially in connection with affections of the mucous membrane. According to Collin, Ch. Fauvel strongly recommends cocaine for treating diseases of the pharynx, describing it as *"le tenseur par excellence des chordes vocales."* Indeed, the anesthetizing properties of cocaine should make it suitable for a good many further applications.

NOTE

1. For the collation of literature, I relied on the article, "Erythroxylon coca" in the Index Catalogue of the Library of the Surgeon-General's office, vol. IV, 1883, which can almost be considered as a complete index of the literature. Because of the inadequacy of our own public libraries, I was able to acquaint myself with a part of the literature which I have referred to on coca only by way of references and second-hand reports; I hope, however, that I have read enough to achieve my aim in this essay: to gather together all the existing information on coca.

Chapter 52

Recognizing Addiction

Dr. J. B. Mattison found Hammond's advocacy of cocaine to the public a gross dereliction of professional responsibility, Mattison collected many examples of death or other catastrophes that befell cocaine users. As this 1887 article attests, information on the negative side of cocaine was available from an early date, but that did not stop a striking rise in consumption. General opposition to cocaine was not manifested until ten or fifteen years after the introduction of the drug in the mid-1880s.

COCAINE DOSAGE AND COCAINE ADDICTION

J. B. Mattison

The recent sad story of the Russian surgeon's suicide from sorrow or remorse due to his belief that a patient had died from an overdose of cocaine points a moral, the import of which demands more than a passing notice. No advent in the therapeutic arena during the last decade has been attended with such varied and extensive claims for favour as cocaine. Its marvellous effect in ophthalmic surgery roused a spirit of experimental research in other directions which has added largely to its well-proved power for good; but, as has been well observed, a potency for good implies a potency for harm, and the risk impends of its ardent advocates being carried by over-enthusiasm beyond the limit of a safe regard for the welfare of their patients or themselves, that may imperil an otherwise well-founded success. Surely it is high time to draw the line, to revoice a warning as to the use and abuse of this valued but at the same time toxic drug, lest the roll of alarming, dangerous, and fatal effects from its ignorant or incautious use be sadly extended, and a reaction ensue that, by creating distrust within and without the profession, will damage its good repute, and hinder its use in cases where it would be almost certain of serving us well. And the need of this seems all the more called for in view of opinions expressed during the past year, in certain quarters, affirming the harmless character of cocaine—opinion which, I am convinced, are at variance with well-accredited facts, and should not be allowed to pass uncontradicted.

Cocaine seems to have secured for itself a more than usual share of attention apart from the professional press. One metropolitan daily, in particular, has again and again given its columns to a discussion of the topic, and in a somewhat lengthy article not long ago an "eminent but unnamed specialist"—Dr. Francke H. Bosworth—was reported as saying, "There is not a well-authenticated case on record as yet where cocaine has effected injury." In view of cases cited in this paper, and others elsewhere recorded, such a statement is no longer tenable, and any conclusion based thereon as to the harmless nature of cocaine is misleading and incorrect. And the evidence herewith presented weighs even more heavily against an assertion by Dr. Wm. A. Hammond, at a recent meeting of the New York Neurological Society, in the course of his "Remarks on Cocaine and the so-called Cocaine Habit," when, after narrating his taking of eighteen grains as a subcutaneous dose, he asserted "he did not believe any dose that could be taken was dangerous." What might be the outcome of such an opinion put in practice? The Russian surgeon's error of judgment, fatal to his patient and himself, was largely due to his reliance on the asserted use by other surgeons of large doses without ill effect. Might not a like result follow an incautious dependence on Dr. Hammond's disbelief in the toxic power of cocaine? The *Medical Record* (New York) well said of Professor Kolomnin's case, "The experience, though so sad, may not be without its lesson," and put a very pertinent query as to whether "there are not other surgeons who could report very serious if not fatal results from injudiciously or ignorantly using too large a dose of cocaine." Fifty cases herewith noted attest a power in this drug on some patients that warrants caution with all.

Germane to the subject of acute cocaine toxæmia is that of cocaine addiction—these notes are preliminary to a more extensive paper on cocaine inebriety,—the existence of which Dr. Hammond denies. He took half a dozen doses, at intervals of from one to four days, and says "be acquired no habit." But to argue from that that there is no danger of addiction is absurd. Such evidence is worthless. Dr. Hammond might do the same thing with morphia; more, he might take morphia subcutaneously daily for a month or two without creating a "habit"—albeit its ensnaring power is well admitted,—and yet that would not prove its freedom from danger. Not at all; it would merely show his exceptional strength to resist. Many, under a like pressure, would surely succumb. Supporting this opinion, I quote from the last report of Dr. Orpheus Everts (Cincinnati Sanitarium), a gentleman well known in alienistic circles, which report was kindly sent me after my paper was written, who says: "A distinguished physician of New York has recently reported personal experiences tending to discredit the claim that a cocaine habit corresponding to the morphine habit is acquirable. The judgment of this distinguished physician is based upon the evidence of personal experience reported by himself, he having failed to acquire the habit, or any especial fondness for the specific effects of the drug experienced by the hypodermic injection of one, two, three, and finally eighteen grains of the salt, on five or six different occasions in the evening before going to bed. But for the great reputation of this physician as an author and observer of facts, this denial would have but little weight. The testimony is both bad and insufficient. Bad, because reported by himself: the testimony of an intoxicated person respecting his experiences while intoxicated being proverbially untrustworthy; and insufficient, because the experiment was not continued long enough. Many instances might be cited of total failure to establish the morphine habit or habitual drunkenness by the use of six or seven doses of morphine, or six or seven drinks of whisky, one a day, for six or seven days in succession. It is often the case that such experiences end with disgust for the drugs used, instead of a desire to continue their use. There is also much and accumulating testimony by competent observers to the fact of such a habit as is alleged respecting cocaine, which a single opinion will not invalidate, however worthy of consideration."

Cocainism is not the outcome of using the drug at long intervals. Its transient effect and the demand of an impaired nerve status compel frequent taking—more than alcohol or opium,—so that *habitués* have been known to take it ten, twenty, or more times daily; and it is this—growing by what it feeds on—that tends to create and continue the disease. In the early days of chloral one point claimed in its favour was a freedom from risk of "habit," a claim long ago exploded, as cases of chloralism well prove; and yet I venture to assert that there are more cases of cocaine taking in this country to-day—less than three years since its arrival—than of chloral after a period more than six times as long. Dr. Hammond says there may be instances of cocainism as rare as chronic tea taking, and of cases with or after habitual alcohol or opium using; but, as for giving up the use of the drug, he believes every cocaine taker could if he chose. The same opinion regarding opium obtains among some medical men, and the only effective argument against such a fallacy is to place those who hold it under power of that drug, and then have them prove their precept by their practice. While admitting that most instances of cocaine taking are, for obvious reasons, in those who have been or are alcohol or opium *habitués*, especially the latter, I maintain there are cases of pure, primary addiction, and that the number is increasing at home and abroad. Foreign writers have noted them, and they will figure in our records. Notes of one such are here given; others are at command. My experience with a number of cocaine cases makes to me two things certain—there is a pernicious power *per se* in this drug, and it finds in the opium *habitué* a peculiar condition that specially favours its ill effects, making it, for such patients, as has well been said, the "devil's own device" to still further enslave. And this opinion is that of others, for it is the testimony, without exception, so far as I know, of those who have had to do with this disease, that as an intoxicant cocaine is more dangerous than alcohol or opium, and that inebriety resulting from its use is more marked and unyielding than any other form. Dr. Shrady, in the *Medical Record* of Nov. 28th, 1885, says: "To some persons nothing is more fascinating than indulgence in cocaine. It relieves the sense of exhaustion, dispels mental depression, and produces a delicious sense of exhilaration and well-being. The after-effects are at first slight, almost imperceptible, but continual indulgence finally creates a craving which must be satisfied; the individual then becomes nervous, tremulous, sleepless, without appetite, and he is at last reduced to a condition of pitiable neurasthenia." Dr. A. B. Shaw, Physician to St. Vincent Asylum for the Insane, St. Louis, asserts: "Once a man flies to cocaine for relief from 'cares that annoy,' he generally continues with such rapid strides towards such complete subjugation to its bewitching thraldom as but few will ever be rescued from by any power of will which they may be able to bring to their aid." Dr. Everts writes: "It is not only not an antidote to opium poisoning—or, more properly speaking, the organic demand for such drug effects as have been acquired by use,—but is itself a fascinating and dangerous intoxicant, the effects of which may be more difficult to counteract and renounce than are those of opium or its derivatives." Dr. Hughes declares it "a remedy to be used with extreme caution and prudence internally, and the large doses reported as having been given are not ordinarily safe. It will bear watching. It crazes and kills quicker than opium. The possibilities for immediate harm are only not great, but the likelihood of remote damage when tolerance is established is not small. The cocaine habit, more pernicious than the morphine neurosis, is the certain entailment of its frequent administration, and its thraldom is far more tyrannical than the slavery of opium." Erlenmeyer calls cocaine the third scourge of humanity, alcohol and opium being the first and second; and Erlenmeyer is right as to toxic neuroses. He says: "Its characteristic effects are vaso-motor paralysis, accelerated pulse, profuse sweats, dyspnœa and syncope, failure of general nutrition, eyes sunken, skin cadaveric, with mental trouble that sometimes needs restraint"; and I am positive, from cases under my care, that he is correct. I think it for many, notably the large and enlarging number of opium and alcohol *habitués*, the most fascinating, seductive, dangerous, and destructive drug extant; and while admitting its great value in various disordered conditions, earnestly warn all against its careless administration in these cases, and especially insist on the great danger of self-injecting, a course almost certain to entail added ill. To the man who has gone down under opium, and who thinks of taking to cocaine in the hope of being lifted out of the mire, I would say, "Don't," lest he sink the deeper. I have yet to learn of a single instance in which such an effort reached success, but know of many cases where failure followed, or worse—cocaine or coca morphia addiction. And the need of caution against free and frequent use obtains in other cases, for there may come a demand for continued taking that will not be denied.

To summarise. Cocaine may be toxic, sometimes deadly, in large doses. It may give rise to dangerous, or even fatal, symptoms in doses usually deemed safe. The danger, near and remote, is greatest when given under the skin. It may produce a diseased condition, in which the will is prostrate and the patient powerless—a true toxic neurosis, more marked and less hopeful than that from alcohol or opium. Such being my belief, I regard Dr. Hammond's statements mistaken and his conclusions rash and dangerous.

Chapter 53

The Difficulties of Treating Cocaine Addicts

As cocaine use became widespread, cost fell, and users could take as much of the drug as they wanted for as long as they desired, casualties mounted. At this time there was no specific cure for "cocaino-mania," as it is called in this 1898 article from the Journal of Inebriety. *Those suffering from addiction to this new kind of drug were integrated into treatment designed for a fundamental "inebriety" that was thought also to explain overuse of alcohol or opium.*

The Treatment of Chronic Cocaine Poisoning, or Cocaino-Mania

The following complete review of this subject is to be found in *Sajons' Annual and Cyclopedia of Practical Medicine:* The F. A. Davis Co., Philadelphia and Chicago.

The treatment of the cocaine habit, or chronic cocaine intoxication, is very much more difficult. It is more essential to have complete control of the cocaino-maniac and his actions than even in chronic alcohol or morphine mania. There is less to work upon in the brain and nerve centers of the chronic cocainist than in those of the chronic alcoholist or chronic morphinist. There is less mental and moral elasticity, less desire to be freed from the narcotic bondage, less conscious-ness of the bondage itself, a more helpless and hopeless wreck being difficult to find. Cocainomaniacs, however, are, in a few cases cured without seclusion. In these hopeful cases there generally has been a greater stock of inhibition from the first. Again, the indulgence having been periodical and ordinarily provoked only by some recurrent pain or distress and leaving intervals of shorter or longer non-narcotic consumption between, inhibition has not been so paralyzed, and thus there has been more resisting power left. In the latter group of cases it is imperative to direct the treatment to the abolition or counteraction of the exciting influences.

In the mass of cases the main hope of cure rests in therapeutic seclusion. The patient must be treated as a diseased person. Diet, at first simple and readily assimilable, should be carefully attended to. Milk, with soda or lime-water and effervescents if nausea and emesis are present; arrowroot or other farinacious or malted food, and other peptonized preparations are excellent. Gradually, broths and plain soups, oysters, fish, poultry, and, lastly, mutton and red meat, with an ample supply of fruit and vegetables, may be given. But there are cases in which a non-fish-and-flesh dietary agrees better with the patient. Each case must be carefully observed to determine the most suitable dietic instructions.

In the first week, exercise and fresh air may usually be insisted on, with massage to improve the wasted condition of the muscles. Meals should be regular, and exercise graduated.

Alcoholic beverages are best avoided; and, though in a few cases, tobacco in limited quantities may be allowed to aid in staying the morbid impulse or crave, yet most cocainomaniacs would be better without it in any form. Tobacco is apt, in many patients, to impair digestion and depress the heart's action, the healthy state of both vital processes being points of the highest importance in the treatment of this mania.

To combat the wearing insomnia of most cases I know of nothing better than the hot, wet pack. Of all the medicinal hypnotics, I have found phenacetin the most useful, in doses of five grains, repeated, if necessary, every hour: no more than three doses (fifteen grains) to be taken in one night. Other physicians have found chloral and sulphonal serviceable.

An important practical point is the method of complete withdrawal of the cocaine, which complete withdrawal is essential to cure. In most cases I have not felt justified in immediate withdrawal, though I have done this where practicable. I spread the reduction period over from seven to nine days, beginning, whatever the quantity which had been taken daily or how long, with a reduction of one-half. Dr. Welch Brauthwaite informs me that in five cases he at once, after only one dose, stopped the cocaine, without trouble. These were cases in which morphine had also been freely used. In the cases in which I gradually reduced the dose of cocaine, morphine had not been habitually taken in large doses. Where morphine is also freely and regularly taken, it is easier to withhold the cocaine without delay.

The best treatment of cocainism has been, in my hands, the administration of chloral in large doses. Opium was found to be feeble in its action, while some relief was obtained under the action of bromide of potassium by itself, or, better, in combination with the chloral. This latter alone is to be preferred, especially when there is weakness of the pulse.—Andrew Fullerton (*Lancet*, September 19, '91).

All complications must be attacked, but, in the main, besides hygienic measures, nervine tonics are indicated in the endeavor to restore the lost energy and will power which really constitute the disease. Of these tonics, nux vomica and strychnine are the most effectual. Arsenic also is useful. I have found this, as in other forms of narcomania, that an occasional replacement of the stronger nerve tonics by milder ones is advantageous; I mean such as quinine, calumba, and gentian. Galvanism has, in appropriate cases, its value.

Though it is often asserted that three to six months suffice to effect a cure, my observation has been that twelve months constitute the shortest time in which such a result can be hoped for. There are, at the same time, a few exceptional cases in which a good result has been secured in a shorter period.

Medico-Legal Relations.—As many cocainists will not apply for curative detention of their own accord, it ought to be the duty of the constitutional authorities to lay hold on these miserable and utterly helpless diseased persons, and insist on their reception and therapeutic seclusion for a given time, in a retreat, home, or hospital provided for the special treatment of such cases, with provision for persons with limited resources and for the very poorest. Such a provision would, in the long run, prove as economical as it would be invaluable to the welfare, physical and moral, of the whole community.

I am unaware of any trial for murder or for administering cocaine with intent to injure another person; but cocaine has been employed to commit suicide. It has been stated recently that forty cocainomaniacs appeared in the police courts of Chicago within the period of a few months in 1897. The habit was said to have been induced, in some cases, by the use of popular preparations as cures for colds, etc. In the charters of various special institutions in the United States power is given to the managers to receive and compulsorily detain habitual inebriates who are addicted to excess in any narcotic or inebriant, including cocaine; but in England only excess in alcoholic liquors renders applicants eligible for admission into retreats under the voluntary provisions of the Inebriates' Acts.

Chapter 54

Investigating Drug Abuse

By the mid-1890s there were enough problems associated with cocaine that restrictions were publicly discussed. After a decade of easy availability, would cocaine be banned entirely? In 1894 the Connecticut State Medical Society investigated the problems the drug had caused. There were not a great many deaths recorded, but habituation did occur, with attendant difficulties for the users, their families, and their employers. On the other hand, Connecticut physicians found that cocaine was a valuable surface and nerve anesthetic. They concluded that the state should restrict the use of cocaine by requiring a physician's prescription and supervision. Physicians should discontinue the practice of giving patients appliances that, like the atomizers used for controlling hay fever, allowed self-administration of this drug.

REPORT ON COCAINE

Connecticut State Medical Society

To the suggested danger of cocaine poisoning or of cocaine addiction were opposed the widely published views and experience of Dieulafoy in France, of Hammond and Bosworth in our country, and of many others. Doses of thirty, forty and even more grains were employed by Dieulafoy for operative purposes. Hammond, experimenting upon himself, injected as much as eighteen grains, pronouncing it safe in any supposable dose, and affirming that no cocaine habit could be acquired. A year after Koller's announcement, Dr. Robert Abbe wrote: "The value of cocaine as an extraordinary aid in the surgical field is daily demonstrated to the wonderment of all. Since the adoption of cocaine, ether has been used in less than half the operative cases at St. Luke's Hospital and bids fair to be further curtailed." Abbe so wrote in 1886. Before the year closed there occurred in Russia the tragic case of Prof. Kolomin, who injected twenty-four grains at different points into the perirectal tissues in order to curette and cauterize an ulcer in a young woman of twenty-three. The operation was not rendered painless: the patient died of collapse; Kolomin killed himself. A year later at the University College Hospital in England some twenty grains caused the death of a man to whom it was administered by mistake, and afterwards in our own country, Simes of Philadelphia reported a fatality due to the injection into the urethra of a dram of twenty per cent solution. Dr. J. B. Mattison of Brooklyn has collected about twenty cases of fatal cocaine poisoning and of a much greater number of cocaine addiction, in which the habit has indirectly caused or hastened death. The library of the Surgeon General at Washington contains more than one hundred references to cocaine poisoning. Many of these are of course repetitions, cases being copied into various journals. As to fatal cases, Mattison's list perhaps includes all reported, but those who constantly employ the local anesthetic no longer think of publishing an occasional instance of mild cocaine intoxication.

Such was the introduction of cocaine into our practice and such the doses advocated. Since 1884 as stated above, twenty deaths have been reported, some of these from the enormous doses at first employed, some from the accidental administration of the drug: few from the small quantities now commonly used. Considering the world-wide popularity of the new anesthetic, the showing is not such as to make the safety of its administration other than a legitimate subject for our investigation. . . .

REPORT OF TOXIC CASES.—Of two hundred and thirty-eight who have answered our questions, fifty-one have seen alarming results from the use of cocaine. Of these who have observed such toxic effects, thirty appear to make no less frequent use of the local anesthetic in consequence. Some of the observations reported were made in hospitals without the State and at a time when large doses were freely used: in others the symptoms were mild and only the patient alarmed—cases chiefly, perhaps, of nervous shock. Some were persons addicted to the use of the drug; others followed accidental administration. . . .

No deaths have been reported in this State, and when we consider that the observations cover the introduction of the drug with the large doses first advocated as safe, and the subsequent period of perhaps undue apprehension, surely cases in which severe toxic symptoms not due to mental impression or nervous shock but directly chargeable to the anesthetic, have been but rarely observed by our members.

Statistics often mislead and it is natural to turn to the experience of those who are most familiar with the use and effects of cocaine. We quote from Dr. H. L. Swain: "I have used cocaine many times daily nearly every working day for the past nine years and have never had any results which were at all alarming. I have frequently had people look a little pallid and feel faint, but could not separate these feelings from ordinary faintness due to operation, except perhaps two or three times."

Dr. W. T. Bacon. "Have never seen any alarming effects follow the use of cocaine. Subcutaneously use two or three drops of a two per cent solution."

Dr. F. S. Crossfield. "Have seen no such effects. Find it indispensable in my work (throat and nose). Never give it to a patient to use ad libitum."

Dr. T. D. Crothers. "Not a safe remedy in any case."

Perhaps your Committee can reconcile something of this seemingly wide difference of experience and expression. While we have no knowledge of death occurring in this State at any time from the induction of local anesthesia by cocaine, many cases of addiction are reported to us. Of such cases Dr. Crothers has seen some fifty, "four-fifths of which had been given the drug for catarrhal and other inflammations for local effect, and the effects had been so pleasant that they have not abandoned its use." Dr. Crothers claims no experience with the use of cocaine in minor surgery, and it may be noted that quite a number of the instances of cocaine intoxication reported to us (in persons not addicted) have resulted from the employment of a spray in the nose or throat, or the introduction of a solution by means of the medicine-dropper (as reported by Dr. Meek.) Perhaps the difference of views according to standpoint of observer may appear still more natural when we consider the doses and the mode of application in which cocaine is at this time chiefly used by those making most frequent employment of the local anesthetic. . . .

We have shown that cocaine was enthusiastically introduced into practice as safe in any dose and for every purpose: That despite a world-wide popularity and the employment of enormous doses but few deaths, hardly more than twenty, have resulted, in some of which it was taken by mistake, but that an enormously greater number of cases of addiction have occurred. Reaction and distrust were inevitable. Perhaps had cocaine always been employed in the moderate doses and weak solutions now advocated, no such distrust would have arisen and cases of intoxication would have excited less apprehension. True, instances occur in which fainting and even convulsive action follow operations in which only small quantities are employed. But the frequency of syncope and of hysterical symptoms whenever surgical procedures are undertaken without an anesthetic is to be remembered. Mental impressions due to the sight of instruments, the stroke of the knife and the flow of blood are prevented by ether, not by local anesthesia. Often it is a chief advantage of ether or chloroform that consciousness is abolished and with it the nervous shock of seeing and knowing.

The safety of cocaine as now used is so far established that recent investigations have been directed to the facilitating with its aid anesthesia from ether and chloroform. Dr. Gerster in the Annals of Surgery for January, 1896, published a series of one hundred consecutive cases from his service in the German Hospital in which cocainization of the nares was practiced after the method of Paul Rosenberg. The advantages claimed by Rosenberg are:

1. Prevention of the feeling of suffocation.
2. Cutting short the stage of excitement.
3. Infrequent vomiting.

Gerster concludes the report of his own series of cases: "On the whole, it is safe to conclude that in view of the ease and simplicity of the procedure, of the absence of apparent risk, and on account of the undeniable diminution of the trying subjective effects upon the patient caused by the use of cocaine upon the nasal mucous membrane, its extended and systematic trial deserves encouragement."

From consideration of the material placed at our disposal by the members of the Society, we conclude:

That the internal administration of cocaine is not increasing.

That the danger of addiction outweighs the little efficacy attributed to the remedy.

That the local use of cocaine self-administered as in form of spray or solution is open to the same danger and in greater degree than attends the internal use.

That in neurotic persons and those in whom there is great dread of the operation, small doses may intensify nervous or hysterical phenomena; what we call idiosyncrasy is potential.

That subcutaneously in minor surgery and by application to the mucous membrane for the purpose of local anesthesia the use of cocaine is increasing, but in smaller doses and weaker solutions.

That so used with the precautions available to restrict the application and to minimize the quantity to the requirement of the case, the employment of cocaine is practically free from danger.

Chapter 55

Cocaine Defined as Social Menace

The medical literature of the early twentieth century contained some of the most fearful, and racist, descriptions of cocaine use to be found. Two brief editorials from the Journal of the American Medical Association *(1900 and 1901) describe "a new form of vice"— addiction to cocaine among "negroes in some parts of the South." Lynching reached a peak at about this time, and Jim Crow laws were in force. The identification of cocaine use with African Americans, soon elaborated to a link between cocaine and supposed African American criminality, illustrates the tendency to find in drug use a simple explanation for complex social problems.*

The essay below by Dr. Edward Huntington Williams, published in 1914, is especially significant because he was a recognized drug expert. He spread alarm widely, including in an extensive interview in the New York Times, *also published in 1914, which bore the headline "Negro Cocaine Fiends a New Southern Menace." The central message embedded in William's scaremongering seems to be that alcohol prohibition (already far advanced at the state level in the South) has the effect of leading dangerous groups — that is, African Americans and poor whites — to the use of drugs, especially cocaine. Although Williams's article certainly betrays racist preconceptions, his prescription for action was more anti-Prohibition than anti–African American.*

A study of over two thousand consecutive admissions from 1909 to 1914 of African Americans to the Milledgeville State Asylum in Georgia had found only two individuals with a cocaine problem, and in both cases the drug use was only incidental to the reason for admission, an astounding contrast to assertions about race and cocaine then found in newspapers and magazines. This study irritated Williams, and he tries to minimize its value by claiming that "the negro drug-taker" would be confined in jail, not in a mental hospital. Nevertheless, the Milledgeville Asylum drew from the whole state, and the lack in its records of documented African American cocaine abusers is a powerful argument against Williams's claims.

THE COCAIN HABIT (1900)

The negroes in some parts of the South are reported as being addicted to a new form of vice—that of "cocain sniffing" or the "coke habit," as it appears to have this name also, A negro, it is said, will buy 5 cents' worth of cocain, which is sold in a little paper box for such purposes, and, taking it in the old-fashioned way of snuff-takers, proceed to indulge in a "coke drunk." The effects are described as much like those of an ordinary whisky drunk; some cocain "sniffers" are quarrelsome, some hilarious, some morose, and many are happy and indifferent like the opium smokers, while the intoxication lasts. It appears even that the habit is hoping to succeed to the recognized legal rights of whisky, for we read that one community licenses the sale, allowing, however, druggists to sell the alkaloid on physicians's prescriptions, but imposing heavy penalties on the doctor who prescribes it for other than patients requiring it medicinally. In this there is progress in a line not altogether encouraging. It is a pity that anything further in the way of intoxications should receive legal recognition. The world has heretofore got along without cocain exhilaration, and the necessity of it for the negroes of Kentucky, even could it be confined to them, can not be reasonably urged. The precedent is bad, and it is to be hoped the custom will not be followed elsewhere.

THE COCAIN HABIT (1901)

The cocain habit in the South, which has been already noticed by THE JOURNAL, seems to be extending. Measures have been taken to stop the indiscriminate sale of the drug in some cities where the evil is most pronounced, and similar ones are advocated in others. The cocain habit is said to have already invaded some northern cities, though in none of them is it as general a vice as among the negroes of the South. In New York some of the physicians interviewed in regard to the habit and its prevalence claimed that medical students were particularly liable to become its victims, others gave quack remedies as the chief cause of its spread, and the mistaken popular notion that it is a cure for drunkenness was also credited as an agency. Men in thus attempting to conquer one tendency become slaves to another, or both, and their last state is worse than their first. It may be that the danger is overestimated, but it is well to be informed as to the possibilities. In any case the sale of cocain should nowhere be unrestricted; this drug as well as morphin should be only obtainable on physicians' prescriptions and careful registry be kept of all sales. Its present freedom of sale in most sections, to any and every one who asks for it, is a special danger that is the more inexcusable as cocain is a comparatively new drug and the vice has not acquired, like that of alcohol, a time-honored common law sanction.

THE DRUG-HABIT MENACE IN THE SOUTH

Edward Huntington Williams

From the evidence offered by the State Hospital records it appears that there is a far higher percentage of drug habitués per capita in the South than in most of the Northern States. Moreover, in the Southern States drug habituation seems to be increasing rapidly in certain localities, whereas in many of the Northern States there appears to be an actual decline.

In 1912 the proportion of cases of drug psychoses admitted to the hospitals for the insane in New York State was only 1 to 386 of all other forms of aberration. During this same period the proportion in Georgia was 1 to 42; in North Carolina (Raleigh), 1 to 84; in the Eastern Hospital, Tenn., 1 to 74; in the Mississippi State Hospital (1911), 1 to 46; and in the Eastern Mississippi State Hospital, 1 to 23, during the same period. In other words the proportion of drug-takers admitted to the insane hospitals in the South was from five to fifteen times greater than in New York State.

One naturally assumes that the large negro population of the South is responsible for this striking difference in conditions. But this assumption is not sustained by the hospital records, at least as regards actual insanity. Thus in the Georgia State Hospital, where the proportion of negro patients to white is about three to four, there were only four cases of drug intoxication among the negroes in 1911, while the number of white patients was twenty-six. In 1912 the number of cases of this form of psychosis had risen to twenty-seven among the whites, while there were no cases among the negroes admitted. And a similar, although less striking, discrepancy is found in other hospitals where white and colored patients are admitted.

Apparently, then, the difference in race does not explain the relative difference in numbers of this form of psychosis. And yet there seems to be no question that drug-taking is practiced among the negroes to a far greater extent than among the white population, or that it has increased with alarming rapidity during the last four or five years.

The insane hospital records show that morphine is responsible for most of the committed cases of drug psychosis, while cocaine plays an insignificant and entirely subordinate part. Yet cocaine is the drug usually taken by the negro drug-taker—is, indeed, becoming a veritable curse to the colored race in certain regions. And when we turn from the hospital records to the records of the jails, work-houses, and prisons, we find ample explanation for the negro drug-taker's absence from the hospitals. He isn't in the hospital because he has stopped in the penal half-way house. In some places his numbers tax the capacity of these institutions.

Moreover, the authorities admit their inability to prevent the negro from getting his supply of cocaine, or even to determine where he gets it in most instances. They admit freely that there is an enormous underground traffic in the drug, and that any negro who can scrape together a few cents can get a supply whenever he wishes it. And of course this traffic is not confined to the negroes, but extends to the "poor whites" who occupy about the same social and intellectual plane.

In many of the towns and cities the bootblacks and newsboys act as common vendors—retailers, so to speak, who loyally refuse to reveal the sources of their supply even under most extreme pressure. They sell the commodity in the form of "snuff," a vile concoction composed of a small proportion of cocaine mixed with some white powder (such as Epson salts) to give it bulk. "Ten cents a sniff" is the usual price for an individual "dose." But the more affluent purchaser who can raise the sum of twenty-five cents may get a good day's supply for that price, which is dispensed in small paper pill-boxes.

Once the negro has reached the stage of being a "dope taker"—and a very few experimental sniffs of the drug make him an habitué—he is a constant menace to his community until he is eliminated. For his whole nature is changed for the worse by the habit. Sexual desires are increased and perverted, peaceful negroes become quarrelsome, and timid negroes develop a degree of "Dutch courage" that is sometimes almost incredible. A large proportion of the wholesale killings in the South during recent years have been the direct result of cocaine and frequently the perpetrators of these crimes have been hitherto inoffensive, law-abiding negroes. Moreover, the negro who has once formed the habit seems absolutely beyond redemption. Imprisonment "cures" him temporarily: but when released he returns to the drug almost inevitably.

But perhaps the most interesting feature of the effects of cocainism, at least from a medical standpoint, is the fact that the drug renders the user immune to *shock* to an astonishing degree—a condition adumbrated by Crile in his classic experiments of 1897. In the language of the police officer, "the cocaine nigger is sure hard to kill"—a fact that has been demonstrated so often that many of these officers in the South have increased the caliber of their guns for the express purpose of "stopping" the cocaine fiend when he runs amuck.

An experience of the Chief of Police, D. K. Lyerly, of Asheville, N.C., is illustrative. In attempting to arrest a hitherto peaceful negro who had become crazed by cocaine, Lyerly was forced to grapple with the man, who slashed him viciously with a long knife. In self-defense the officer drew his revolver, placed the muzzle over the negro's heart, and fired—"for I knew I had to kill him quick," the chief explained.

The revolver he used, be it understood, was not the short-cartridge, pocket weapon carried by most Northern policemen, but a heavy army model of .32-20 caliber—a cartridge which Lieut. Townsend Whelen, U.S.A., declares will kill any game in America. And yet this bullet did not even stagger the crazed negro, and neither did a second bullet which pierced the biceps muscle and entered the thorax. So that the officer had finally to "finish the man with his club." The following day Mr. Lyerly exchanged his .32-20 for a .38 caliber army model, the weapon carried by the men of our army and navy. And a similar exchange has been made by many of the officers in the South who have had experience with the homicidal negro, both before and since the days of cocaine-taking.

Needless to say this immunity to shock, together with the fearlessness, hallucinations, and homicidal tendencies that cocaine engenders, makes the "fiend" an object of special dread. But the drug has still another effect that makes him peculiarly dangerous. Unlike the effects of whisky, cocaine seems to put the muscular and nervous system of the user temporarily in a state of tense stability, so as to improve, rather than interfere with, his marksmanship.

It seems to be an established fact that the abuse of ardent spirits interferes with good shooting. But such an example as that of the cocaine-crazed negro in Asheville who killed five men dead in their tracks with one shot for each, shooting at long range in some instances, demonstrates that cocaine does not impair eyesight or muscular coordination. I doubt if this feat in marksmanship—actually killing, not merely wounding, five men with five shots—has been equalled in modern times. And undoubtedly the negro could not have accomplished it under the stimulus of any other known drug.

We should not, of course, draw too definite general conclusions from a single example. But there have been so many other instances in which the cocainized negro has exhibited deadly accuracy in shooting, such as the recent slaughter of nine persons at Harriston, Miss., and the shootings in Memphis, that there is no escaping the conclusion that cocaine, besides making the habitué homicidal, adds to his ability to carry out the homicidal intent.

The habit of cocaine-taking, while not entirely a novelty in the South, has developed into a veritable epidemic of alarming proportions only within the last few years. I was told by physicians and officers in many places that five years ago the "cocaine fiend" was practically unknown in their communities. A year or two later he had become a menace; and since that time the number of cocaine-takers has trebled and quadrupled in many places.

What is the cause of this sudden increase? And why does the negro and the poor white now take this hitherto little used, although long-known, stimulant?

For the purpose of trying to find a satisfactory answer to these questions, as well as to determine whether the drug-habits in the Southern States are really as common as the printed records indicate, I have recently taken an extended journey through certain regions of the South where these conditions seem to flourish. In this quest I visited State hospitals, county hospitals, jails, workhouses, and prisons, and interrogated patients, prisoners, physicians, and officers.

Everywhere I found evidence that the cocaine habit is increasing: there was not a single dissenting opinion. And since this universal belief is confirmed by police and hospital records, it may be accepted as a definitely established fact. I found also a unanimity of opinion, among those competent and in a position to judge, as to the cause of this appalling condition. A prisoner put the thing in a nutshell in answering my question as to why he began taking cocaine, when he said: " 'Cause I couldn't git nothin' else, Boss."

Ever since the emancipation of the slaves the South has been confronted by a problem that does not exist in the North. This problem is the control of the negro—particularly the low-class negro. Since numerically the colored people represent from 30 to 60 per cent of the population in these States (no Northern State has even 5 per cent) it is evident that any race-problem that concerns the negro in the South is one of first magnitude.

Of course the colored man, like his white neighbors everywhere, is likely to commit lawless acts when under the influence of strong liquors; and because of his inferior mental organization, sometimes perpetrates the most revolting crimes when intoxicated. And since the control of the sober negro offers a sufficiently difficult problem in communities where every other man is colored, it is naturally the earnest desire of the authorities to eliminate the added menace of the drunken negro. Moreover, since most of the Southern negroes are poor, illiterate, and shiftless, the controlling white men thought it would be a blessing to the colored man himself, as well as to the community at large, to put whisky out of his reach.

The simplest way to do this, it seemed, would be through the agency of prohibitive legislation. And so Georgia, Mississippi, North Carolina, Tennessee, South Carolina, and West Virginia, passed State-wide laws intended to abolish the saloon. These laws, of course, do not prevent the white man, or the well-to-do negro, from getting what liquor they wish, and, when they wish it, through legitimate channels, it is considerable trouble, to be sure, to write, send money, and receive packages by express; but the white men were ready to sacrifice this inconvenience if by doing so they could keep strong drink away from the shiftless and dangerous negro.

The task did not seem impossible, since active police work would close the saloons and dives. And by doing this they would (theoretically, at least) make it practically impossible for at least 25 per cent of the total population to obtain whisky. For the number of negroes, and poor whites, who have sufficient intelligence, education, and money to send away for their liquor is extremely limited. And so these States entered upon a hoped-for Utopian period by abolishing the saloons—"the blessing of prohibitive legislation," as some enthusiasts called it. But the "blessing" was not to prove an unmixed one by any means, as subsequent events have proved.

For the negro, and the white man, quickly discovered that there were other substances besides alcohol that produced pleasant intoxicant effects—substances that are measured in fractions of grains instead of fractions of gallons. Morphine and cocaine offered the most alluring attractions, although there were certain soda-fountain beverages, and drug-store nostrums, that could be requisitioned in a pinch. But eventually cocaine completely outstripped its rivals in popularity, because the substance could be readily obtained, and because its effects were produced quickly and certainly by the simple process of sniffling into the nose.

To supply the demand for this drug a steadily increasing cinudestine traffic was established, and flourishes despite the concerted efforts of Federal, State, and local authorities. In short, the South in trying to correct a bad condition, has created one intinitely worse, and one absolutely beyond the power of the authorities to suppress or even control.

Laws aimed to suppress illicit liquor traffic frequently fail because public sentiment, and public officials, are not in sympathy with the attempt. But such is not the case with the cocaine traffic. Public officials to a man are eager to suppress it, not merely for sentimental reasons, or from a sense of duty, but from the most potent and compelling motive, *fear*—a matter of self-preservation. Yet in the face of this all-powerful incentive for its suppression, the traffic is steadily increasing.

It is usually difficult to put a finger upon the exact cause of any important economic condition—or disease. Nevertheless a mass of evidence all pointing in one direction warrants our drawing certain conclusions about economic conditions and diseases. And in the case of the increasing drug-habits among the negroes and poor whites in the South the mass of evidence indicates that there is a direct relationship between this condition and the present method of controlling the liquor traffic.

It is significant that hospital and police records both show that during the last five years, the period of active prohibitive legislation, drug-habits have increased enormously. And these records are supplemented by concurrent opinions of physicians and officials.

The drug-users themselves are practically a unit in declaring that they began taking the drug because it was more easily obtained than their accustomed beverages. In considering the value of such statements we must, of course, make allowance for the characteristic untruthfulness of the drug habitué. But it is inconceivable that they should all hit upon the same statement without the existence of a groundwork of truth for their assertions. It is improbable, also, that physicians and officials should have reached the same conclusion without adequate reason for their belief.

Moreover, it is most significant that in cities such as Raleigh, Asheville, and Knoxville, where open drinking places have been abolished, cocaine-taking is increasing at an alarming rate. In Knoxville as many as seven cocaine-using women have been haled to police headquarters in a single day. On the other hand in such a place as Memphis, with its 70,000 negroes, where no attempt is made to stop the sale of liquor, there has been only a moderate increase in the number of drug-takers.

The fact that addiction to cocaine is rare among the better classes of whites and negroes is also significant. The offenders are found mostly among the shiftless class of both races; but unfortunately most of the negroes belong to this class, and in some localities represent fully half the total population. The upper classes can, and do, supply themselves with liquor through the agency of the express companies, whose records are open to inspection, and show a traffic in "gallon packages" that beggars belief. But none of these thousands of packages reach the poorer classes, whose financial status cannot ride above the ten-cent "sniff," or the twenty-five-cent pill-box mixture.

It is significant, also, that many persons who formerly found their way into hospitals and jails as alcoholics, now return as drug habitués.

In short, there is no escaping the conclusion from the mass of available evidence, that the enforcement of prohibition has created a demand for, and produced a traffic in habit-forming drugs among a dangerously large proportion of the lower classes in the South.

No one familiar with the horrors of the cocaine habit will question whether this substitution of the drug for alcohol is a change for the better. In the case of the habitual drunkard, of course, the substitution of the drug for alcohol is a change for the better. In the case of the habitual drunkard, of course, the substitution may be a good one; cocaine will kill him a little quicker. But it is a very different matter in the case of the ordinary temperate negro—the man who would take an occasional drink without ever becoming in any sense alcoholic. It is among this class that cocaine is working real havoc.

The negro does not appreciate that the penalty of taking a few sniffs of cocaine with convivial companions is very different from that of taking a few glasses of beer under the same circumstances. Like most normal white men, he can take liquor, or leave it alone, as he chooses; and unless he is tainted mentally he does not become an alcoholic. But it requires no mental taint to produce a cocaine fiend; and once the negro begins to dabble with the drug he is doomed. For there is no such thing as an "occasional" or "moderate" cocaine user. The line is very sharply drawn between the total abstainer and the "fiend," without any intermediate condition.

Rightfully, of course, the control of the cocaine habit, and conditions producing drug-habituation, belong to the domain of medicine just as surely as does the control and treatment of other forms of mental abnormalities or epidemics. But unfortunately some of the causes of cocainism are so hopelessly entangled with political issues that mere questions of what is right, or best, are completely subordinated. So that the physician must view with such complacency as he can the sight of a race being decimated by the abuse of a useful drug, until the tide of political contention has spent itself, or shifts to some other field of activity. The wisdom of this political policy is about on a par with that of calling in the surgeons to patch up the wounded after a battle, instead of averting the battle itself.

Chapter 56

The Shanghai Commission's Recommendations on Cocaine

Dr. Hamilton Wright served as a member of the U.S. delegation to the International Opium Commission held in Shanghai in 1909. The "new cocaine evil" was a concern at the commission. Although the international body took no action on the drug at the 1909 meeting, Wright included a section on cocaine in his report on the Shanghai meeting and on corresponding problems in the United States. His report was sent by President Taft to Congress in 1910.

Wright, like many other commentators of the time, asserts a cause-and-effect connection between cocaine use and crime. He repeats the charge that African Americans are particularly drawn to this drug and adds the warning that criminals use it to lure young girls into the world of "white-slave traffic." Wright used these fears in an attempt to neutralize southern legislators' opposition to federal intervention in the drug problem. These legislators viewed federal control of cocaine use as a violation of states' rights and a dangerous precedent for federal intervention in other areas, such as the recovery of voting rights extended during Reconstruction to African Americans.

REPORT ON THE INTERNATIONAL OPIUM COMMISSION AND ON THE OPIUM PROBLEM AS SEEN WITHIN THE UNITED STATES

Hamilton Wright

The necessity for an American Opium Commission was clearly set forth in House Document No. 926, Sixtieth Congress, first session. That document contains a letter from Secretary Root to President Roosevelt, in which the foreign aspect of the opium question is shortly reviewed, and particular mention made of the recent determination of China to finally rid herself of the evils of opium smoking. But, though particular attention was called to the Chinese aspect of the opium question, it was not lost sight of that there was within the United States itself an opium problem which had to be exposed and solved. As to the latter phase of the question, Secretary Root noted the extraordinary fact that in the year 1907 there was imported into the United States 728,530 pounds of opium, and that—

While the international investigation now proposed relates to opium in the Far East, an incidental advantage of the investigation may be to point out the necessity, and the best method of restricting the use of opium in the United States.

Secretary Root's letter was transmitted by President Roosevelt to the Senate and House of Representatives. It will be seen by the following document that there was an immediate appropriation of $20,000 to meet the expenses of the American delegates to the International Opium Commission which was to meet at Shanghai, January 1, 1909.

[H. R. 21260—Public, No. 141.]
AN ACT Making appropriations for sundry civil expenses of the Government
for the fiscal year ending June thirtieth, nineteen hundred and nine, and
for other purposes.

Be it enacted by the Senate and House of Representatives of the United States of America in Congress assembled, That the following sums be, and the same are hereby, appropriated, for the objects herein under expressed, for the fiscal year ending June thirtieth, nineteen hundred and nine, namely:

International investigation of opium evil: To enable the President to appoint not more than three commissioners to collate and complete on behalf of the United States information bearing on the opium question, and a secretary, who shall act as disbursing officer, and for traveling expenses, stationery, printing, and other incidental expenses connected with the investigation and the meeting of the commissioners for the purpose of finding common ground for joint and several recommendations and reports to their respective governments with a view to the suppression of the opium evil, twenty thousand dollars, or so much thereof as may be necessary.

Under the appropriation thus made three commissioners were appointed, the original commissioners being Judge Thomas Burke, of Seattle, Wash., Dr. Hamilton Wright, of Washington, D.C., and Dr. Charles D. Tenney, Chinese secretary to the American legation at Peking. Judge Burke found it impossible to serve on the commission and declined his appointment, his place being taken by Bishop Charles H. Brent, of the Philippine Islands. . . .

Tariff and Other Laws Governing the Importation, Manufacture, and Distribution of Cocaine

Mention has been made that in the study of the opium problem as it affected the United States the American opium commission found it necessary to take account of the new cocaine evil which threatens this country. A vast amount of reliable evidence has been furnished by the importers and manufacturers, pharmacy and police officials in this country on the evils that result from the misuse of this drug.

In the recent hearings before the Ways and Means Committee of the House and the Finance Committee of the Senate importers and manufacturers of this drug testified their desire that the importation and distribution of it should be

Imports of coca leaves and cocaine since the first years of their separate enumeration in the customs returns.

Fiscal year.	Coca leaves.	Rate of duty.	Value.	Cocaine.	Rate of duty.	Value.	Duty.
	Pounds			*Ounces*	*Per cent.*		
1898		Free	$53,752.00		24	$59,660	$14,915.00
1899		Free	26,388.00		25	40,141	10,035.25
1900		Free	591.00		25	112,375	23,093.75
1901		Free	483.00		25	170,949	44,237.00
1902		Free			25	254,704	63,576.00
1903		Free	249,798.00		25	224,453	56,113.25
1904		Free	323,405.00		25	74,446	18,611.30
1905		Free	342,518.00		25	10,391	2,597.75
1906	2,650,141	Free	488,545.00		25	10,782	2,695.20
1907	1,515,616	Free	212,424.00		25	37,585	9,396.25
1908	633,121	Free	76,109.00	3,792	25	4,108	1,025.00
1909	1,100,649	Free	126,891.00	32,272	25	49,343	12,086.00

strictly controlled by federal legislation. There follows a table showing our estimated importations of coca leaves to 1905 in dollars, and from that year onward the number of pounds of coca leaves imported per annum, with the rate of duty and the value. It will be noticed that there was a large importation of both coca leaves and cocaine in 1909 in anticipation of the duty changes made in the last tariff act.

There was no enumeration of the number of ounces of cocaine imported into this country until the fiscal year 1908, in which year, as the table shows, 3,792 ounces were imported. For the years previous to 1908 the value in dollars of imported cocaine is shown, and the rate of duty. Coca leaves, until the recent tariff was enacted, were admitted free, and cocaine paid 25 per cent ad valorem. The admission of coca leaves to this country was governed by paragraph 528 of the tariff act of July 24, 1897. Under this paragraph coca leaves were confounded with cacao leaves and were in the free list. The admission of cocaine was governed by paragraph 3 of section A of the same act, which placed a 25 per cent ad valorem duty on alkaloids amongst other things.

In the discussions and hearings on the food and drugs act the attention of Congress was called to the growth of the interstate traffic in cocaine, and in the act of May 27, 1908, making appropriations for the service of the Post-Office Department for the fiscal year ending June 30, 1909, there appeared a provision to the effect that—

No part of the appropriation herein made shall be used for the carrying in the mails of any malt, vinous or intoxicating liquors, or intoxicating liquors of any kind, or any cocaine or derivative thereof.

This provision was not repeated in the appropriation act of the following year. The provision in the act of June 30, 1909, does not seem to have been of much service in preventing the passage of cocaine through the mails.

Just how the cocaine evil has sprung into existence in the United States, how it has spread, and the best means for combating it by federal legislation will be dilated upon in later pages. . . .

Disposition of Cocaine within the United States

It is a generally known fact that during the last twenty years cocaine has been diverted from its original use by the surgeon to pander to the supposed needs of large numbers of our population. It is estimated, after wide consultation, that 15,000 or 20,000 ounces of this drug are sufficient to satisfy the demands of surgery in the United States. To-day there are manufactured at least 150,000 ounces of this drug, the larger part of which is put to improper uses.

Twenty years ago there was some use of this drug internally, but it was found that the anæsthetic effect of the drug on the mucous membrane of the stomach led to loss of appetite, and finally great emaciation and death, if the habit was not conquered. The ingenuity of certain pharmacists overcame the objection to the internal use of cocaine, and it was not long before various proprietary and patent preparations, catarrh remedies, etc., were put on the market which contained a large percentage of the drug. Those who had fallen to the habitual use of cocaine found that they could get the stimulating effect of the drug by snuffing it, and so absorbing it through the nasal mucous membrane. There is no doubt that the widespread abuse of cocaine is largely due to the fact that it was made accessible to those who wished to use it, in the form of catarrh powders and liquids. It was not long after the essential quality of the patent nostrums became known that disreputable physicians, druggists, and other dealers defied state and municipal laws by selling the drug pure or adulterated, more or less openly.

It is the unanimous opinion of every state and municipal body having to do with the enforcement of state and municipal antipoison acts that the misuse of cocaine is a direct incentive to crime, that it is perhaps of all factors a singular one in augmenting the criminal ranks. Quite apart from the criminal classes it converts the useful, orderly citizen who has become a habitué into a dangerous character. It wrecks him individually and jeopardizes the position of all who depend on him, and in the end drives him to crime. The illicit sale of the drug is the most difficult to cope with, and the habitual use of it temporarily raises the power of a criminal to a point where in resisting arrest there is no hesitation to murder. It is more appalling in its effects than any other habit-forming drug used in the United States.

In the report of the President's Homes Commission, 1909, Senate document No. 644, this question of the misuse of cocaine has been partially discussed and brought to the attention of the Government. But there is a phase of it that has not received due attention; that is the encouragement of the use of the drug among the humbler ranks of the negro population of the South. It has been stated on very high authority that the use of cocaine by the negroes of the South is one of the most elusive and troublesome questions which confront the enforcement of the law in most of the Southern States; and that it seems almost impossible to get at the facts when prosecutions are undertaken. Even after the police feel certain that they have facts on which to proceed they find it next to impossible to prove them by reliable witnesses. The cocaine seller and buyer are equally anxious to conceal their transaction; and, as the vendors of the drug usually put it up in small amounts, it is an easy matter to distribute it without detection. It would seem on first sight that much of what is known about the abuse of cocaine by the negroes of the South is based on gossip or irresponsible statements. But this is largely because of the difficulty experienced in tracing the sources of the drug.

It is certain, however, that the use of cocaine among the lower order of working negroes is quite common. This class of negro is not willing, as a rule, to go to much trouble or send to any distance for anything, and, for this reason, where he is known to have become debauched by cocaine, it is certain that the drug has been brought directly to him from New York and other Northern States where it is manufactured. It is current knowledge throughout the South that on many public works, levee and railroad construction, and in other working camps where large numbers of negroes congregate, cocaine is handled among them by some method largely obscure. Undoubtedly many irresponsible local druggists are to blame, but the main supply of the drug for a particular construction camp is procured from wholesale dealers and jobbers in another State and distributed to the working gangs by peddlers, commissary clerks, and even contractors. There is an enormous profit by this method of handling the drug. It can be bought for from $2.25 to $2.75 an ounce, and it is the custom of the panderers to this vice to dispense it in 1 or 2 grain packages, for which they charge 25 cents. When divided into small packages, it can be carried without detection and sold from the pocket of a vagrant negro man or woman who passes among the construction camps and other places where negroes are employed.

Attempts have been made to send special officers among the construction camps for the express purpose of buying the drug; but it has been found that juries are reluctant to convict on evidence submitted by a known spy or informer. In the South the drug is commonly sold in whisky dives, and it seems certain that a large quantity of the liquor sold in these illicit places is laced with cocaine. The combination of low-grade spirits and cocaine makes a maddening compound. Inquiries have been made as to whether or not cocaine is forced by contractors on the humble negro worker. There is some evidence that they do so under the impression that they can get more and better work from their employees.

Looking at the wider aspect of the use of cocaine throughout the United States, there is absolutely trustworthy information that the use of this drug has spread widely among the criminal classes of our large cities, that it is used by those concerned in the white-slave traffic to corrupt young girls, and that when the habit of using the drug has been established it is but a short time before the latter fall to the ranks of prostitution.

As an example of the free manner in which cocaine was distributed, it may be stated on reliable authority that it is only a short time since the drug was freely sold in the neighborhood of Mott street, in New York City, a conservative estimate being that at least a thousand ounces of the pure or adulterated drug were disposed of monthly, not only to habitués of that neighborhood, but to others from all over the city, who learned of the easy manner in which it could be procured. Here, again, as is the common practice, the drug was put up in small packages of from 1 to 5 grains and sold by the vendors from their pockets. These receptacles were at one time as common as cigarette stubs in the streets of certain sections of New York. Stringent laws have been passed by the State of New York and other States to meet the abnormal use of cocaine and prevent the sale of the drug except on a physician's prescription. These state laws have been partially successful, but they can not be made really effective until there is interstate control of the traffic. It has been authoritatively stated that cocaine is often the direct incentive to the crime of rape by the negroes of the South and other sections of the country.

Apart from the outlaw population, the use of cocaine threatens to creep into the higher social ranks of the country. It was stated in discussing the habit of smoking opium that no sign of this habit had appeared in the rank and file of the navy or army, in spite of the close contact of the services with the Far East. But there seems to be no doubt that an ever-increasing number of our soldiers and sailors are falling to the use of cocaine. This has grown out of the evil practice of lacing the alcoholic beverages sold to them in the lower class of saloons resorted to by the men.

The misuse of cocaine is undoubtedly an American habit, the most threatening of the drug habits that has ever appeared in this country, and there is no uncertain feeling in every State and municipality of the country that the habit will continue to spread unless there is some coordination of state laws and federal control of the manufacture and interstate commerce in the drug by the Federal Government.

Conclusions in Regard to the Foregoing

Such, then, was the state of the opium question and the use of other habit-forming drugs in the United States at the time of the appointment of the American Opium Commission.

The entire matter may be summed up in a few words: The opium traffic in the Far East has been steadily discountenanced by the United States through treaties made with far eastern countries resisting or prohibiting American citizens engaging in the traffic. Chinese subjects resident in the United States were excluded by the American-Chinese treaty of 1880 from the privilege of importing smoking opium into this country, and a statute had been passed to prevent American citizens from forcing opium on unprotected peoples of certain of the Pacific islands.

On the other hand, our Government had for half a century legalized the importation of opium prepared for smoking, which not only debauched the young, robust Chinese immigrant coolies who arrived on our Pacific slope before 1880, but the use of which had steadily spread to a large part of our outlaw population, and even into the higher ranks of society. A statute had been passed permitting the manufacture of this form of opium by American citizens; but, fortunately, the tax imposed had been sufficiently high to prevent American citizens attempting such manufacture. From the first scheduling of crude or medicinal opium there had been a continuous unrestricted import of it. The manufacture of morphia from this form of opium to supply our own population had come to be a monopoly of American manufacturers, and the production of it had grown enormously; large numbers in all social ranks had become debauched by the misuse of it. Nearly every State in the Union and nearly every large municipality had, from time to time, passed stringent pharmacy or police acts to control the misuse of the different forms of opium and its products; but these laws were largely ineffective because the Federal Government made no attempt to control the importation or manufacture and distribution of the drugs in interstate commerce. The police departments of our large cities had found it next to impossible to suppress the sale and use of smoking opium by Chinese to Chinese and to depraved Americans who frequented the resorts of the Chinese sections of our large cities.

A now drug problem appeared about twenty years ago, and had grown with a rapidity that marked the avidity of our criminal classes in acquiring a new vice; latterly it had exhibited a strong tendency to spread, corrupt, and ruin many who belonged to the higher ranks of society. This new vice, the cocaine vice, the most serious that has to be dealt with, has proved to be a creator of criminals and unusual forms of violence, and it has been a potent incentive in driving the humbler negroes all over the country to abnormal crimes. Thoughtful persons in every walk of life, not the least important of whom are the importers and manufacturers of these habit-forming drugs, had come to the conclusion that the time had arrived for a strict federal control of the importation, manufacture, and distribution of such drugs in interstate commerce. . . .

Recent Federal Laws in Regard to Cocaine

The activity of the Department of State in the international opium business and the passage of the act of February 9 last has caused considerable stir throughout the country in scientific, humanitarian, medical, and other societies. Boards of trade of our large cities have, by resolution, called the attention of the Federal Government not only to the widespread use of opium and its products, but also cocaine. On February 26, 1909, the Committee of One Hundred of the American Association for the Advancement of Science on National Health passed the following resolution:

> We favor a prohibitory tariff, internal-revenue tax, and other means which will restrict the use of cocaine, its substitutes and derivatives to medical purposes.

This resolution sums up views of nearly every authority consulted.

Attempts made by the Federal Government to control cocaine traffic are as follows: In the act of May 27, 1908, making appropriation for the service in the Post-Office Department for the fiscal year ending June 30, 1909, and for other purposes, a rider was added to the effect that no part of the appropriation should be used for the transmission of cocaine through the mails. But this provision does not seem to have been effective, and it did not reappear in the act of 1909 making appropriation for the service of the Post-Office Department. It would seem, however, that the Postmaster-General now has power to prevent the passage of cocaine and other drugs through the mails under the act approved March 4, 1909, entitled "An act to codify, revise, and amend the penal laws of the United States," which was effective January 1, 1910. . . .

During the Senate and House hearings on the recently enacted tariff law, pressure was brought to bear by the American manufacturers of cocaine to have a prohibitory duty placed upon it. It is the view of such manufacturers that the interstate traffic in cocaine can to some extent be controlled if the entry of the drug into this country is prohibited, for they contend it would be impossible for the illicit dealer under a prohibitory tariff to import his supplies from abroad, and they have expressed their willingness under law to account for the sale of their product. There can be no doubt of the earnestness of the American manufacturers of cocaine to control the illicit traffic. The leading manufacturer of the drug in this country is at the head of a serious movement to prohibit the use of the drug except for strictly surgical purposes.

Consonant with these views and as the result of the hearings on the last tariff act, what may prove to be a prohibitory impost was placed on cocaine. . . . Section 41 of the last tariff act provides, amongst other things, that there shall be paid on "Cocaine, cocaine, and all salts and derivatives of the same $1.50 per ounce (and on) coca leaves 5 cents per pound."

What Remains to Be Done to Control the Interstate Traffic in Habit-Forming Drugs

Before examining this phase of the subject, it should be pointed out that many state pharmacy laws now in force are defective, in that habit-forming drugs may be bought without the prescription of a physician. All that is required by such laws is that the dealer shall keep a record of sale, and the name of the person to whom, and the amount sold. The result is that it is possible in many grocery stores, as well as in pharmacies, for even children to buy small quantities of laudanum and other drugs. Under such laws oven scrupulous dealers are apt to look with complaisance on the sale of laudanum and paregoric—that is, the milder preparations of opium—forgetting that the unwise use of these forms inevitably lends to a confirmed opium habit, generally ending in the habitual use of morphine secured from unscrupulous dealers. Again, many state laws are defective in that they do not make illegal possession of habit-forming drugs evidence for conviction. They require that there shall be no sale except on a physician's prescription. Such laws are easily evaded, for many pharmacists are themselves registered physicians and prescribe their own stocks freely, while every community has its dishonorable physicians, dentists, or veterinarians, who regard their license to practice as a license to prescribe large quantities of these drugs for illicit use. It is no uncommon practice for a disreputable druggist to continue with a physician of that ilk, the latter being in attendance at the drug store during those hours when habitués swarm. Further, many unscrupulous physicians have fallen into the habit of dispensing habit-forming drugs in large quantities from their offices. It is almost impossible for state and municipal authorities to obtain reliable evidence-in-regard-to-illegal sales. If, as provided in the federal act of February 9 last, the States would make possession except for medical purposes evidence for conviction, there would be destroyed to a large extent the present enormous intrastate traffic in habit-forming drugs.

Judging by what followed on the passage of the national food and drugs act, there is no doubt that on the passage of a federal act to control the interstate traffic in habit-forming drugs defective state laws will be gradually amended to meet abnormal intrastate conditions. Several States have within the last few years so amended their laws—notably, as has been pointed out, the State of California—and an effort to make municipal laws more stringent is under way, with the result that the sale of narcotics in some of our large cities has been reduced to a minimum.

With an unfettered interstate commerce in these drugs such as now exists, it is possible and is a common practice for illicit dealers, disreputable physicians, and pharmacists in one State to send to neighboring or distant States for large supplies—many ruses being resorted to to accomplish their purpose. One of the commonest is for an illicit dealer to have a false letter head printed, having on it the name of a person and a legend stating that the person is a registered pharmacist. On such letter heads are written orders for large amounts of opium, morphine, or cocaine, and sent, say, from Boston to a reputable or disreputable dealer in New York, or vice versa, with a request that the order be filled. Reputable wholesalers and jobbers are frequently deceived by such orders and fill them. But the suspicion of a reputable house is soon aroused, and on investigation it is generally found that the address to which the drugs have been sent is that of a saloon, or a dressmaking or millinery establishment, and that from such centers the drugs are sold at enormous profit to regular patrons.

The practice just mentioned is no uncommon one. It obtains in several sections of the country, and it reduces the state and municipal authorities oftentimes to despair, for although they can, under state laws, detect and prosecute for the illicit sale of these drugs procured within the State, it is almost impossible for them to detect buyers who send outside of the state limits for their supplies.

After wide consultation with those interested in the control of the production and distribution of habit-forming drugs, the conclusion has been reached that there should be a federal act placing the interstate traffic in such drugs under the control of the Bureau of Internal Revenue of the Treasury Department, and that such an act should be based on the following general principles:

First. That such an act should demand the registration of every person who imports, produces, manufactures, compounds, distributes, or otherwise handles habit-forming drugs in interstate or foreign commerce.

Second. That importers, wholesale compounding pharmacists, and wholesale dealers should pay a small per-annum tax of $10, and that retail pharmacists and other retail dealers, including physicians who buy in interstate commerce and who carry large supplies of the drugs, should pay a tax of from $1 to $3 per annum; that every one engaged in handling drugs should register and pay a tax.

Third. That, without attempting to derive a revenue beyond the amount necessary to administer the act, all of the habit-forming drugs should have imposed upon them an internal-revenue tax of, say, 1 cent an ounce, and that such tax should be paid by affixing to packages or other receptacles containing the drugs, an engraved stamp, to be affixed and canceled according to law.

Fourth. That all compounds or preparations manufactured from the original tax-paid drugs should be marked or branded in such a manner as to show the payment of the tax on the original drug.

Fifth. That every person concerned in the importation, manufacture, remanufacture, or compounding, selling, or dispensing of habit-forming drugs and their preparations, should keep such books, render such returns, and give such bonds as may be determined by the Commissioner of Internal Revenue, with the approval of the Secretary of the Treasury.

Sixth. That it should be unlawful for any person to sell, give away, or otherwise dispose of in interstate commerce, any of the habit-forming drugs, their salts, derivatives, or preparations to any person other than a person who has registered and paid the special tax, public hospitals and scientific and public institutions excepted.

Seventh. That all of such drugs, their derivatives and preparations imported should pay an internal-revenue tax equal to that imposed on the home-produced drugs.

Eighth. That on trial for violation of such an act, illegal possession of such drugs should be deemed as sufficient evidence of such violation, unless the defendant shall explain the possession to the satisfaction of the jury.

Ninth. That all returns required by such an act should be filed and recorded in the office of the Commissioner of Internal Revenue, under such regulations as may be approved by the Secretary of the Treasury, and that these returns should be open to the inspection, and certified copies should be made to the proper officials of any State, Territory, or district under the jurisdiction of the United States who are charged with the enforcement of local laws regulating the prescribing, dispensing, sale, or use of such drugs.

Tenth. That heavy penalties, either by fine or imprisonment, or both, should be imposed on the violator of such an act.

A proposed bill embodying these principles has been drafted in consultation with those officials of the Treasury Department who would be charged with its enforcement should the bill pass and be approved. . . .

In drafting the suggested bill to control the interstate traffic in habit-forming drugs, it has been kept steadily in mind that state and municipal laws are now or can be made effective to control the intrastate relationship that should subsist between the physician who prescribes these drugs, the person he prescribes for, and the filling of such prescriptions by licensed pharmacists, if the importation, manufacture, and distribution of the drugs in interstate commerce is brought under effective federal control. This bill, as the others submitted, are offered as suggestions only.

It has been stated in the third principle laid down that no attempt should be made to derive a revenue from any opium act beyond the amount necessary to administer such an act. The reason for this should be apparent; the greatest obstacle to the solution of the opium problem as seen in the Far East is the practice that has obtained there of producing and distributing opium for revenue purposes. Could the present opium revenue of far eastern countries be immediately replaced, either by economy or by developing other sources of revenue, there is not the slightest doubt that the opium problem would be short lived. All the countries concerned have now pledged themselves to curtail the production and misuse of opium, and as a consequence the revenue derived therefrom. As the United States has taken the lead in this international movement, it would be both unseemly and impolitic for this Government to attempt to derive a revenue from any opium measure beyond the exact needs of administration.

In the suggested opium measure . . . a special tax of $10 is imposed on the wholesaler, importer, and jobber, and $1 on the retail druggist, or anyone dealing at retail, which would include large numbers of physicians, dentists, and veterinarians, who at present make it a practice to send outside their own States, where there are no large drug manufacturers, to other States where such manufacturers are located. There are in the United States about 500 houses importing, manufacturing, or dealing in drugs at wholesale, from which, under the special tax of $10 per annum, a revenue of $5,000 would be derived, and about 40,000 retail druggists who, under the special tax of $1 as provided for in the act, would yield a revenue of from $30,000 to $40,000. The number of ounces of the drugs named in the measure imported or manufactured in this country amounts at the present time to about 15,000,000. Under an efficient federal act to control the manufacture and interstate traffic in these drugs, and under the improved state laws being enacted, the number of ounces of such drugs imported or manufactured would be reduced at least one-third, leaving about 10,000,000 ounces to bear the special stamp tax of 1 cent an ounce, as provided for in the proposed bill, thus producing a revenue of about $100,000, or a total revenue form the projected measure of about $140,000. It may appear at first sight that a tax of 1 cent an ounce on the named drugs imported or manufactured in this country is merely nominal; but together with the special tax imposed by section 1 of the proposed act sufficient revenue would be derived to efficiently administer the act. The Commissioner of Internal Revenue is of the opinion that $125,000 is sufficient for this purpose.

Finally it should be pointed out that section 9 of the proposed act . . . , calling for an appropriation of $150,000 for the purpose of carrying into effect the provisions of the act is a necessary one, should the act be favorably considered during the coming fiscal year. The Commissioner of Internal Revenue has pointed out that the estimates of the Treasury Department for the next fiscal year have been made up, and that therefore it would be necessary to make a provision for carrying out the act.

Chapter 57

Cocaine Use Diminishes in the 1930s

By 1930 cocaine use appears to have been much reduced. Tellingly, in 1929, when the National Research Council of the National Academy of Sciences established its Committee on Drug Addiction, its focus was limited to the opiates. In the following report by a distinguished panel, cocaine is likewise seen as a problem of the past for New York City.

Report of the Mayor's Committee on Drug Addiction

At the time of admission heroine was the drug most commonly used, 263 cases. Morphine was taken by 31. It is interesting to note that cocaine, taken with either heroine or morphine, was recorded in but four instances. . . .

Drugs First Used

Heroin, 153 cases: 134 by sniffling and 19 by hypodermic. Opium (by smoking), 69 cases. Morphine, 58 cases: 47 by hypodermic and 11 by mouth. Cocaine (by sniffling), 33 cases. Maruahuana (hashish) (by smoking), 2 cases. Laudanum (by mouth), 2 cases. Morphine and atropine (by mouth), 1 case.

Drugs Used at Different Times

Heroin, 295 cases; morphine, 195 cases; cocaine, 130 cases; opium, 99 cases alcohol (to excess), 40 cases; maruahuana (hashish), 19 cases; paregoric 8 cases; laudanum, 6 cases; atropine, 5 cases; codeine, 4 cases; luminol, 3 cases; bromides, 3 cases; veronal, 2 cases; chloral, 2 cases; trional, 2 cases; dionine, 1 case; pantopon, 1 case; allonal, 1 case; amyl nitrite pearls, 1 case; hyoscine, 1 case. . . .

For 20 years, since the United States in 1909 drew attention to the international situation in regard to opium, there has been an aroused public opinion against the spread of narcotic addiction through opiates in this country. At that time Germany first exported heroin to the United States, with the assurance that it was a non-habit forming drug and produced its stimulation and narcotic effects without danger of habit formation, such as was connected with other opiates.

Cocaine, though often so classified, is not a narcotic, but produces only an intense overstimulation, which when continued brings about the happy mental condition of firm conviction that its addict possesses the power to obtain the fulfillment of all his hopes and dreams. Cocaine 20 years ago was a very prevalent addiction.

In 1913 a law was passed controlling the manufacture, sale and distribution of cocaine, and its possession made a crime. The arrests made at this time disclosed the fact that heroin was the drug chiefly used among the narcotic addicts, and the courts were powerless to control the situation. A year later the Boylan Bill included in affirmative statutes both narcotics and cocaine in the endeavor to control and prohibit the spread and use of these drugs. These restrictive and punitive measures did not control the situation. They caused the courts to take cognizance of the crime of possession of these narcotics, and to place the responsibility for rehabilitation of these addicts on the penal institutions during the period of custodial care.

During the last 20 years cocaine as an addiction has ceased to be a problem, not that those addicted to it ceased to use it, but because of the punishment involved. Cocaine addiction when persisted in over a certain period brings with it its own swift punishment by the development of acute mental disorders, and the fear and horror of this condition prevents its use as an addiction, even among the pathologic personalities of the criminal classes.

At the present time it does not enter as a disturbing problem into the situation.

Chapter 58

Cocaine Returns in the 1970s

Growing amounts of cocaine reappeared around 1970. Interestingly, the initial reaction of users, and some drug experts, paralleled the original responses to the drug in the 1880s. The White Paper of 1975 disseminated by the Ford administration, for instance, reveals a new toleration of recreational drug use that contrasted strongly with the Nixon administration's policy goal of eradicating the drug problem. This document is characteristic of the prevailing trend in the 1970s to accept some drug use as inevitable. The description of cocaine, although it acknowledges that problems could increase if "chronic" use spreads, seems especially low-keyed when compared to the official attitudes that came to predominate in the mid- and late 1980s. Note also that those who wrote and reviewed the White Paper appear to have been unaware of the earlier occurrence of a cocaine epidemic.

WHITE PAPER ON DRUG ABUSE

Domestic Council on Drug Abuse Task Force

Cocaine

Cocaine, though available for many years, is the new "in" drug, and the various implements and rituals associated with the use of cocaine have recently become subject to extensive commercial exploitation.

Historical Trends

Except for use in several highly publicized "in-groups" (e.g., musicians), cocaine use in this country was apparently insignificant as late as the early 1960's. Since then, however, use has increased rapidly, a trend which has received a great deal of attention in the press.

The increasing popularity of cocaine is reflected in law enforcement data. Since 1970, there has been a steady upward trend in the amount of cocaine seized en route to the United States from South America. DEA seizures and undercover purchases of cocaine have increased steadily in the last five years, both in the

United States and internationally. Cocaine arrests by State and Federal agents have also risen sharply.

Virtually all of the cocaine entering the United States come from South America and principally from Colombia, where the refining process is completed.[1]

Current Situation

. . . Rates of cocaine use vary greatly among specific groups within the general population. In a national survey conducted in 1972, 1.2 percent of junior high school students, 2.6 percent of senior high school students, and 10.4 percent of college students reported experience with cocaine. Almost half of those youths reported that their first use occurred recently—that is, during the previous twelve months. Additional studies indicate that as many as 16 percent of male high school graduates followed in a national sample had used cocaine at some time during the five years following graduation. There are other subpopulations in which use of cocaine is also high.

The data indicate that cocaine is used for the most part on an occasional basis (several times a month or less); usually in the company of others; and is likely to be taken in combination with alcohol, marihuana, or some other drug. Cocaine is not physically addictive.

About one percent of patients admitted to Federally funded treatment facilities reported cocaine as their primary drug of abuse; an additional 12 to 13 percent reported that they used cocaine in association with other drugs, mainly heroin. Thus, the data obtained from treatment programs and surveys generally reflect the fact that cocaine, as currently used, usually does not result in serious social consequences such as crime, hospital emergency room admissions, or death.[2] . . .

In summary, although the rate of increase of first use of cocaine is alarming, significantly less is known about cocaine use in the United States than about the other drugs described in this assessment.

NOTE

1. The finished cocaine is smuggled from Colombia into the United States by a variety of routes; direct, through Mexico, through the Caribbean, and even through Europe or Canada.

2. The phrase "as currently used" is important. The effects of cocaine if used intensively—particularly if injected—are not well known, but recent laboratory studies with primates, as well as reports of the effects of chronic cocaine injection during the early 1900's suggest that violent and erratic behavior may result. For this reason, the apparently low current social cost must be viewed with caution; the social cost could be considerably higher if chronic use began to develop.

Chapter 59

The Social Drug

Cocaine started to become available in the very late 1960s and spread throughout the 1970s into all quarters of society. Initially it was extremely expensive. In some circles conspicuous use and or gifts of the drug to friends or business associates were signs of financial success. As the cost of buying cocaine fell, it became a popular party drug. Cocaine jargon, references, and accessories proliferated. Users — who reported feeling strong, confident, competent, and sociable while high on cocaine — could see no harm in regular consumption. Some experts agreed that moderate regular use presented no health risk. The media recorded and magnified the widespread fascination with cocaine, as in this Newsweek *article from 1977.*

THE COCAINE SCENE

Richard Steele with Susan Agrest, Sylvester Monroe, Paul Brinkley-Rogers, and Stephan Lesher

Pinstriped Wall Street lawyers take it from 14-karat gold spoons at elegant parties. Ghetto kids huddle in tenements and sniff it off matchbook covers. Graduates of a North Miami high school hold a reunion every December to take it at a "White Christmas" bash, and a California corporate president dishes it out as a holiday bonus to his favorite secretaries. Some aficionados use nothing but $10 silver straws from Tiffany & Co. while others sniff it through rolled-up $100 bills. Cocaine—"the Cadillac of drugs"—was once known as the plaything of jazz musicians, kinky movie stars and the dissolute rich. No longer. To the delight of some and the alarm of others, cocaine is regularly bought, used and lavishly praised by hundreds of thousands of Americans. "Cocaine usage today is about where marijuana was four or five years ago," says one dealer. And its popularity has yet to peak. . . .

Penalties for the sale of cocaine or even the possession of more than a minimal amount are harsh. In New York, for instance, a person convicted of possessing 2 ounces of cocaine—57 grams—can be sentenced to life imprisonment. Cocaine ranks third on the DEA's list of law-enforcement priorities for dangerous drugs, behind heroin and amphetamines, barbiturates and hallucinogens, and just above marijuana. But cocaine is not a narcotic, is not addictive and causes no with-drawal symptoms. Taken in moderation, cocaine probably causes no significant mental or physical damage and a number of researchers have concluded that it can be safer than liquor and cigarettes when used discriminately. In a recent court case, a judge in Massachusetts ruled that since cocaine is not a dangerous narcotic drug, a state law barring its possession was unconstitutional. And there is today growing pressure to lessen the penalties for its use—and some argu-ments to de-criminalize cocaine altogether.

Cocaine's popularity has spread so vastly within the last few years that it has become the recreational drug of choice for countless Americans. Businessmen use it to get going in the morning and entertainers use it to keep going at night. College students and housewives use it, stockbrokers and fashion designers use it, rock singers and used-car salesmen use it. A Miami teen-ager estimates that 5 to 10 per cent of her classmates used cocaine "fairly frequently," and one Holly-wood producer reportedly budgeted $250,000 to keep his cast and crew happily high on cocaine during the filming of his new movie last summer.

Like Dom Perignon and Caviar

At certain restaurants in Aspen, Colo.—which one DEA official called "the cocaine capital of the U.S."—devotees can ask for "Booth D" to be assured of a table where they can safely take the drug. A University of California law student who pays her tuition with the money she makes from dealing cocaine concedes that she does have one problem. "Most of my profits go right up my nose," she says.

Among hostesses in the smart sets of Los Angeles and New York, a little cocaine, like Dom Perignon and beluga caviar, is now de rigueur at dinners. Some party-givers pass it around along with the canapés on silver trays; some fill ashtrays with cocaine and set them on the table. Other dispense it more grudgingly. "Hostesses say it ruins appetites," says one Hollywood partygoer, "and they get upset to see their guests playing with the beef Wellington." Even in circles where cocaine has long been popular, it is now taken far more openly. "Before, you would go to parties and the bathroom door was always locked," says one film star's manager. "I could never get into a bathroom when I needed to because people were in there sniffing cocaine . . . now it's become socially acceptable to see people doing it."

The drug itself has a fairly quick effect. When inhaled through the nose, it goes to the back of the nasal cavity, combines with mucus and drips down the back of the throat. The nose and upper gum go numb—and then the "high" begins. Cocaine is a stimulant—an "up"—and produces none of the blurred perception or memory lapse that often accompanies the use of marijuana. The user experiences a feeling of potency, of confidence, of energy. A Miami nurse reports: "I have such a beautiful feeling—like I could touch the moon." Even doctors who have studied the effects of cocaine agree that users generally experience an uplifting sensation. "It is one of the closest things to a pure feel-good drug," says Dr. Robert Byck of Yale University's School of Medicine.

Critics contend that the drug turns people unduly aggressive and hostile. "They become snappy," says one New Yorker who has sworn off. "And besides, coke talk is even more stupid than drunk talk." Cocaine also takes some getting used to. One New York City woman describes her first sniff: "My initial sensation was the same stinging, pungent feeling you get when you use nose drops. Within seconds, I developed a postnasal drip, and within minutes a numb nose. When the coke finally took hold of me, it was an exceedingly mild high—and it seemed to me that the whole thing was an expensive hype."

"Frosties" and "Lines"

There are many ways of taking cocaine. It can be dissolved in water, sprinkled into cocktails or dabbed onto a cigarette and smoked. It can be burned and the fumes inhaled or, like heroin, it can be taken intravenously. Some cocaine fanciers like what they call "frosties"—having a friend put cocaine on a piece of paper and blowing it into the back of their mouths. Most often it is sniffed—"snorted," in the argot of the cocaine culture—and the ritual at times seems as important as the drug itself. The cocaine powder is gently poured onto a clean flat surface, often a mirror to make it easier to spot each granule. Taking a razor blade, the user divides the powder into "lines," with a precision and concern for detail that a surgeon would envy. Then, using anything ranging from a plastic straw (the cocaine granules would stick to a paper straw) to rolled-up currency, the drug is inhaled into the nose.

The accouterments of the cocaine culture seem to be part of the kick. Some coke buffs wear neck chains with a razor blade and a tiny spoon dangling like amulets. Maxferd's, a San Francisco jewelry store, provides diamond-encrusted razor blades for $500 and custom-designed spoons that sell for as much as $5,000. The store, which sold $40,000 worth of cocaine spoons last year, also offers a double spoon. "We have to use calipers to measure the distance from one nostril to the other," says Maxferd's owner, Howard Cohn. "It can get quite funny."

Bookstores around the country have sold 50,000 copies of a slim, "how-to" volume called "Cocaine," and a Los Angeles store called Propinquity stocks vials of glass and 14-karat gold at $4,000 as well as bargain-basement coke kits (mirror, razor blade, spoon and cocaine container) at $10. At an L.A. boutique, a $150 sterling-silver fountain pen has a chamber to hold cocaine—and, just in case the buyer actually wants a pen, a cartridge that holds ink . . .

Most cocaine smugglers, however, are amateurs and independents. College students pool their funds and send a courier to South America to buy relatively large amounts. Tourists bring the drug back, planting it on their young children in hopes of escaping detection. One Hollywood movie mogul and a group of friends recently purchased 200 pounds—and turned more than $2 million profit in a space of five weeks. The ruses that the smugglers employ are many and varied, though not always successful. Customs agents and DEA officials have found cocaine sewn into an antique rug being imported by a 74-year-old woman, in a cage full of boa constrictors and pythons, in aerosol cans, in scuba divers' oxygen tanks, in diplomatic pouches and in bottles of Scotch (when the liquor is poured into a pan and evaporates, the cocaine remains) . . .

The adulterated dosages can then be resold at astounding profits. One 24-year-old Boston dealer, who has been selling narcotics since he was 13, has been able to pay for and renovate a triplex apartment and purchase a downtown bar with his profits. His income over the past five years: $700,000.

In some areas, cocaine dealers compose a genteel underworld. "When we bust someone, we always ask them what they know about heroin trafficking," says an agent in Detroit. "Most of them are quite outraged. They say things like, How would I know about that? That stuff ruins people's lives'." Other narcotics agents, however, contend that the subterranean world of cocaine dealers has grown increasingly violent. "A few years ago, none of the coke dealers armed themselves," notes a DEA official. "Now they're all packing pieces." Last year, an American agent was murdered in the course of a cocaine investigation in Bogota, Colombia.

As cocaine use rises, more people have come to regard the penalties for moderate, social indulgence as far too severe. Cocaine busts often net celebrities—and sometimes they are given only moderate sentences. Last May, for instance, television star Louise Lasser of "Mary Hartman, Mary Hartman" pleaded guilty to possession of cocaine, but the judge let her off on condition that she see a psychiatrist. A number of recent developments have encouraged cocaine cultists who look toward the day when the drug can be taken openly. The Massachusetts court's ruling last December was considered one important step in this direction. Spurred by the decision, the Judiciary Committee of the Massachusetts House of Representatives began hearings last month to put cocaine in a new—and lower—drug classification, and was considering lowering the penalty for possession from one year in jail to a mandatory six-month probation for first offenders.

President Carter's special assistant for health issues, Dr. Peter Bourne, says, "There's not a great deal of evidence of major health consequences from the use of cocaine." But Bourne, whom Carter has named to run the Office of Drug Abuse Policy, believes that if cocaine were less expensive and more easily obtained, users would indulge more heavily, perhaps creating greater health problems. There is little likelihood that Federal statutes will be revised in the immediate future. Despite the medical evidence that cocaine is a relatively harmless substance, the popular view is still that sniffing it can be dangerous to one's health—and few politicians seem inclined to risk the consequences of trying to lessen the penalties for doing so. But it is equally true that U.S. officials believe that "recreational" users of the drug are no more deterred by laws than marijuana smokers are. In short, the cocaine culture is sure to grow in coming months—and seems all but certain to hit a new high.

Chapter 60

The Danger of Cocaine

Gradually, reports of bad outcomes of cocaine use accumulated: damage to careers and families, paranoia, health problems, and movement toward complete absorption with getting and taking the drug. Then in 1986 Len Bias, a twenty-two-year-old college basketball star named as the first-round draft pick of the Boston Celtics, died after taking cocaine while celebrating his achievement. Shortly thereafter, Don Rogers, a professional football player, also died. Cocaine took on a very different image. At the same time well-publicized reports of accidents said to have been caused by drug use on the job—including bus crashes and train wrecks, for instance—and of drug-fueled outbursts of rage or violence created some public sympathy for drug "screening" of job applicants and for "random testing" of some categories of workers. As these 1986 Newsweek articles show, the federal and state governments began to move back to severe penalties for drug possession and sales.

COKE KILLS

They were the best days of his life: the legendary Boston Celtics had drafted him and he made a $1.6 million deal to endorse sneakers. He was celebrating with friends in his dorm at the University of Maryland, snorting so much cocaine that they told him to be careful. He is said to have laughed: "I can handle anything!" Then he collapsed.

The death of 22-year-old Len Bias riveted the nation's attention. It was suddenly clear cocaine, the glamour drug, could kill even the light user, striking at random. When crack, a cheap, highly addictive new form of the drug, appeared, a burn of anger spread across the country. Congress passed a sweeping, damn-the-expense drug bill. America finally believed that drugs weren't fun and games.

TRYING TO SAY "NO"

*Larry Martz with Mark Miller, Bob Cohn, George Raine,
and Ginny Carroll*

It is a formidable task, requiring no less than a basic shift of the national attitude toward drugs. But that is already happening in a piecemeal way, from vigilante committees in a dozen urban ghettos to drug-education programs in suburban high schools to crackdowns on local users from Michigan to North Carolina. And this week Ronald Reagan planned to scurry to the head of the growing parade by announcing his own demand-side drug program, a combination of moral suasion, education and drug testing for key government workers. In all, the plan looks to be far more jawbone than bite. But in an exclusive interview with NEWSWEEK (page 18), Reagan said it would "not be rhetoric . . . The main thrust has got to be to get the people themselves to turn off on [drugs]." . . .

The president decided it was time to move when his pollster Richard Wirthlin showed him a sharp rise on the fever chart of drug concern. A similar message has been received in Congress, where members are scrambling to write tough new drug laws and grab the credit in time for this year's elections. More than 300 members have signed a letter to the television networks for delivery this week, asking for a concerted campaign to educate young people to the dangers of drug abuse. But the congressional emphasis is still on the supply side of drugs: Democrats are working to put together an omnibus bill stiffening penalties for pushers, strengthening customs and border patrols, outlawing synthetic drugs, hitting at money laundering and beefing up treatment and prevention programs. Republicans plan amendments to make the bill even tougher, possibly including the death penalty for some drug dealers and tough new sanctions against countries that don't cooperate with drug-eradication programs. Price is no object, the lawmakers say. "We intend to bust the budget on this," vowed Democratic congressional campaign chairman Tony Coelho.

They had better be prepared for a sizable tab. Drug enforcement is already a $1.8 billion item, versus just $230 million spent on drug and alcohol treatment and education programs. At the cutting edge, the Drug Enforcement Administration is averaging 41 arrests a day, an increase of 18 percent in two years. Seizures of contraband cocaine soared to an annual rate of 43 tons in the first three months this year, up from 19 tons in all of last year and just 12 tons in 1984. Still, there is no shortage; indeed, if street prices are any guide, there may be a glut. According to necessarily iffy surveys, the number of regular cocaine users, which apparently peaked in the late '70s, has remained at about 5 million ever since. But individual consumption has been rising so fast that total cocaine use went up by 11 percent at last count, and the spread of riskier, high-purity cocaine and the potent new crack has heightened the sense of crisis. Heroin and marijuana consumption was down a bit, but total use of illegal drugs rose by 15 percent. And whether or not more enforcement will do any good, it will surely be costly. Democratic Rep.

Yes to Drug Tests

Some people think that periodic screening tests are a good idea to see whether individuals may be using drugs. Other people think such tests are a bad idea because they may not always be accurate or because they invade people's privacy. For each of the following groups, please tell me if you think it would be a good idea or a bad idea if they were required to take periodic drug-screening tests:

	Good Idea	Bad Idea
High-school teachers	64%	33%
Airline pilots	84%	14%
Police officers	85%	13%
TV, film and recording stars	52%	42%
High-school students	60%	37%
Professional athletes	72%	25%
Government workers	72%	25%
All other workers	50%	44%

Which *one* of the following actions do you think an employer should take against someone who is identified as a drug user through a screening test? Should the employer:

Report him to the police	5%
Fire him immediately	5%
Fire him after a set period of time if a test shows that he is still using drugs	15%
Don't fire him, but require his participation in a drug treatment program	60%
Do nothing unless his work is clearly affected by his drug use	13%

Do you think the possession of small amounts of marijuana should or should not be treated as a criminal offense?

	Current	1985	1980
Should	67%	50%	43%
Should not	27%	46%	52%

Priorities and Resources

Do you think the government spends too much money and effort fighting drug use—or is the government's expenditure of money and effort just about right?

Too much	9%
Too little	56%
About right	21%
Don't know	14%

There are many things that our government is doing to fight drug use. Which one of the following activities in the government's fight against drugs do you think deserves the most money and effort? Which is the next most important?

	Most Important	Second Most
Arresting the people in this country who sell drugs	23%	31%
Arresting the people who use drugs	3%	5%
Teaching young people about the dangers of drugs	42%	24%
Helping drug users to overcome their addiction	4%	12%
Working with foreign governments to stop the export of drugs to this country	25%	23%

Which of the following do you think is the most serious problem for society today: marijuana, alcohol abuse, heroin, crack, other forms of cocaine or other drugs?

Yes to Drug Tests (Continued)

Crack	22%
Other forms of cocaine	21%
Heroin	5%
Marijuana	4%
Alcohol abuse	34%
Other drugs	5%
Don't know	9%

For this Newsweek Poll, The Gallup Organization interviewed a representative national sample of 758 adults by telephone July 31 and Aug. 1. The margin of error is plus or minus 4 percentage points. Some "Don't know" responses omitted. The Newsweek Poll, © 1986 by Newsweek, Inc.

Glenn English of Oklahoma has introduced bills meant to stem the flood of drugs with more agents, planes, boats and radar. The added cost: nearly $1 billion. . . .

According to White House sources, Reagan saw Wirthlin's polling figures late in May and decided to make drugs a high priority; the schedule was speeded up after the cocaine death of basketball star Len Bias. The project touched off considerable debate in the administration, since it hit an ideological sore point that already divides conservatives: while authoritarians are happy to enforce traditional social values, the newer libertarian wing of the GOP wants to minimize the government's role. One school, led by Attorney General Edwin Meese, argued strongly for such measures as widespread drug testing of federal workers. But others, including communications director Pat Buchanan, argued that drug use should be a personal matter unless it endangered lives or national security.

In the end, Reagan chose the softer line, on the ground that any program touching off a firestorm of protest would be counter-productive. The death penalty for drug dealers was out, though some of his advisers urged it. So was stepped-up prosecution of casual users: not only did the budget makers worry about building enough prisons to hold them, but Reagan himself argued that the goal should be rehabilitation, not punishment. Details of the program are still evolving. Its outline:

- **Testing:** Department heads will be asked to designate federal workers who have security clearance or hold such sensitive jobs as air-traffic controllers or armed guards. If they refuse drug tests, they will be shifted to less sensitive jobs; if the tests turn up positive or they admit a drug problem, they will be offered treatment. Researching the proposal, aides found that federal insurance benefits for drug-abuse treatment were wiped out in a budget cut in 1982. Ways are being studied to restore them. But the government unions indignantly threaten to fight the whole plan in court.

- **Education:** The administration will encourage schools to suspend drug users and pushers. Some aides wanted to tie federal funding for schools to a showing that a school has a strong drug program, but Reagan was against it. The main goal is to create an atmosphere in which peer pressure can work against drug use.

- **Private Industry:** More than half of regular drug users are over 18, and the administration wants to reach them at work. It will encourage business to screen for drugs before hiring; federal contractors could be offered incentives to set up effective industrial drug programs.

- **Enforcement:** The Justice Department is working on proposals for stiffer drug penalties, including mandatory minimum terms for some dealers and possibly mandatory life sentences for convicted drug racketeers, but these will come later. For now, the president would only flick at the supply side with a reference to increased activities in the "southwest border initiative," newly named "Operation Alliance." . . .

One major hitch remains: nobody can show conclusively that drug-education programs do any good. Early in the century, programs based on moral arguments clearly failed to dent alcohol and drug abuse. Exaggerated scare tactics, like the pamphlet and film on "reefer madness," led only to ridicule. In the 1960s straightforward presentations of the pleasures and dangers of drugs proved equally futile and may even have made drugs more attractive to curious youths. The fashionable focus of educators now is on peer and family influences, trying to teach children simply to reject drugs as uncool. Practitioners are enthusiastic, but a NIDA review noted last year that the worth of this approach remains to be proved.

Reagan: Drugs Are the "No. 1" Problem

Newsweek: You've described America as "upbeat, optimistic" — why are drugs such a problem now?

Reagan: For one thing . . . the music world . . . has . . . made it sound as if it's right there and the thing to do, and rock-and-roll concerts and so forth. Musicians that young people like . . . make no secret of the fact that they are users. [And] I must say this, that the theater—well, motion-picture industry—has started down a road they'd been on before once, with alcohol abuse. I can remember when it was rather commonplace in films . . . to portray drunk scenes and so forth as being very humorous. And the motion-picture industry decided some time ago that that wasn't right for them to do . . . and they stopped. And yet, recently, there have been some pictures in which there was a gratuitous scene in there just for a laugh [about] drug use, that it made it look kind of attractive and funny, not dangerous and sad.

To what extent is the problem with Hollywood that a lot of people out there are using [drugs] themselves?

That again—that is at a level of society where . . . they have a dinner party and feel they have to put the drug out on the coffee table, as at a cocktail party. And yes, that has to be dealt with, that particular problem.

Chapter 61

The Crack Epidemic

Cocaine generally was ingested in powder form through sniffing or injection until about 1980, when the development of a dangerous procedure called "free-basing" meant that it could be inhaled into the lungs and rapidly transported to the brain, producing an intense euphoria. Free-basing, however, frequently caused fires. A safer procedure employed a new solid form of the drug called "crack cocaine," soon abbreviated to "crack." By applying heat to create vaporization, the user could inhale the drug and achieve the same powerful "high" the free-baser experienced.

Dr. Robert Byck, a professor of psychiatry and pharmacology at Yale, had studied the use of coca and cocaine in Peru in the late 1970s. Some youths, he found, had learned that an intermediate stage of cocaine production, coca paste, could be smoked. But, unlike coca leaves and cocaine powder, coca paste created enormous problems among users, who could not stop smoking and who experienced severe health effects and interference with thinking processes. There never had been such a problem with coca or cocaine in Peru's history. In 1979 Byck appeared before a congressional committee and warned that a health crisis was on its way, that the appearance of an inhalable form of the drug would create an explosion of dangerous cocaine use. When this explosion did in fact occur, it came to be called the "crack epidemic." It is not clear whether any action was taken as a result of Byck's warning.

Testimony before the Select Committee on Narcotics Abuse and Control

Robert Byck

Mr. Chairman, distinguished members of the Committee on Narcotics Abuse and Control: Thank you for the opportunity to testify before this committee. My name is Robert Byck and I reside at 1405 Yale Station, New Haven, Connecticut. I am a physician and a psychiatrist and am Professor of Psychiatry and Pharmacology at Yale University School of Medicine. I practice as a clinical psychiatrist, teach in the Yale University School of Medicine, and do research and consultation as a clinical pharmacologist. A clinical pharmacologist is a scientist who studies the effects, action, and disposition of drugs in man. I was a Burroughs Wellcome

Scholar in Clinical Pharmacology from 1972 to 1977 and have been involved since 1974 in clinical studies on the actions of cocaine in man . . .

I hope to give you a modern perspective on cocaine, an overview of dangerous drugs, a statement of a new problem, and suggestions as to what can be done to deal with problems of cocaine use and abuse. The new problem, smoking of coca paste or free base, calls for immediate action on the part of the government . . .

"Coca Paste" and "Free Base"

Reports from South America and in this country have indicated that there is an increasing use of crude coca paste or free base cocaine taken by smoking. When the leaves of coca are converted into cocaine, in order to decrease their volume a crude material known as coca paste is prepared in South America. This coca paste, which contains from 40–85 percent cocaine, is now utilized by smoking in cigarettes, in which it is combined with tobacco or marijuana. This I believe is a serious new problem and cocaine suddenly could become a dangerous drug used in this way.

Drs. Jatlow and Bailey of our group at Yale developed a method for measuring the amount of cocaine in the blood. We recently reported to the American Psychiatric Association in Chicago the effects of smoking coca paste in young men. Those experiments were done in Peru in collaboration with Dr. Raul Jeri of the University of San Marcos. Dr. Jeri had previously reported 148 cases of psychiatric hospitalizations of individuals who had been smoking coca paste. This was striking; Peru has had cocaine available for thousands of years and has never had a serious drug abuse problem prior to the advent of smoking.

We were particularly interested in what happened when individuals smoked coca paste under their usual circumstances. We found that the amounts of cocaine in the blood after two minutes of coca paste smoking were greater than those found an hour after similar doses by the intranasal route. There was an extremely rapid rise in the amount of cocaine in the blood when coca paste was smoked. It was obvious that this route of administration appeared much closer in its effects to an injection than it did to the usual intranasal route.

The person who smokes coca paste has a very intense euphoria almost immediately after he starts smoking the cigarette. Within 15 minutes after smoking one cocaine containing cigarette, his elevated mood decreases and, although he is still feeling the drug effect, he has painful anguish, depression, and drug yen. At the time of that anguish he still has significant levels of cocaine in his blood. In order to cure the anguish and intense drug craving, he will light up again and continue to smoke.

The difference between coca paste smoking behavior and the usual use of cocaine in this country depends on that intense bad feeling and desire for additional use of the drug. The patterns of use are compulsive and continuous. Users become totally dependent on the drug, will do anything to get it, and may use it to the extent where they become paranoid, are totally involved with drug taking, and become social cripples. Continuous coca paste smoking may lead to psychiatric hospitalization. At the conference in Lima, Andrew Weil, a student of coca and cocaine, told me that a woman he had met who smoked coca paste had said, "It's nice but it has a hook in it."

I think that this is a point to which the Committee should direct its attention. There is a hook in smoked cocaine. People become compulsive users. For that reason it is important that we bring attention to this use pattern and, by research and comparative sociological and ethnographic study, examine the dangers of this new pattern of cocaine use. In the U.S. manufacturers have been advertising smoking pipes and chemical kits for conversion of street cocaine to a material known as free base, which is similar to coca paste. I believe this is a dangerous habit and can represent the same threat that the speed epidemics of the 1960's represented in their time. Let me emphasize that, although cocaine itself can be a relatively safe material, this new route of administration can change that picture. We do not yet have an epidemic of free base or coca paste smoking in the United States. The possibility is strong that this might occur. It is occurring in the countries of South America. We must learn about this route of administration and its effects. Cocaine smoking represents a serious health hazard.

Of course the other routes of administration are not entirely innocuous and recurrent and repeated use of any drug can never be deemed medically safe. However cocaine has a far worse reputation than its pharmacology indicates and so, as with marijuana, it would be unwise to represent falsely the health dangers of its use. Our society has chosen to select what intoxicants will be legal and illegal. We have made an unfortunate choice in taking two of the most dangerous, alcohol and tobacco, and making them the drugs of choice for legality in our society. We should not confuse the use of cocaine with either criminality or aggressiveness. There is no evidence that cocaine causes an increase in aggression but there is ample evidence that alcohol does. There is no evidence that cocaine causes an impairment in performance in acute use but alcohol does. There is no evidence that, in the commonly used routes in the U.S., cocaine represents an acute or chronic health hazard of any significance, but there is no question that tobacco does.

In summary, cocaine should be regarded as a medically useful drug but making it freely available would be medically and socially unwise. Even though it is a relatively benign drug, pharmacologically cocaine is often abused. It can be used repeatedly by either the intranasal or oral route, as well as by the intravenous and smoked route. Although it does cause a euphoria, excessive use of this or any other drug may interfere with an individual's productivity and his contribution to society. Because cocaine is so intensely pleasing to the user it will always be smuggled into the U.S. We should pay serious consideration to decreasing the profits of this trade. These, however, are political and sociological issues and are in the domain of government, not science.

On the other hand, we know that cocaine, like amphetamine, can be used safely. We should attempt to maintain our reason and increase our knowledge and not to choose pharmacological villains. We should recognize that there is a danger of a drug abuse epidemic of cocaine because of a new route of administration rather than because of new properties of the drug. For that reason I would suggest that an intensive cross-cultural investigation be made of coca paste smoking, and that a commission be formed to examine ways of prevention and education. The advertising of cocaine smoking by the paraphernalia manufacturers should be restricted by agreement.

Cocaine has been glamorized in the media and by its association with well known, wealthy, and popular figures. Television, newspapers, and magazines must recognize that when they report on cocaine in a fashionable context they are providing the most effective advertising for the use of the drug. The media should use caution in reporting about it. The results of the reporting should not have the effect of advertisement for cocaine but rather should present a reasoned and informed truth about the subject. Caution is therefore indicated.

I don't think we can wait a long time for this research and planned educational campaign to get under way. We are on the brink of a dangerous drug use phenomenon. We should do something about it as rapidly as possible. This might involve collaborative research with South American countries and application of our best thinking in order to avert the problem. It is particularly important that research continue to be supported so that actions of the drug, as well as reasons why people use drugs in particular patterns, can be investigated. It is finally, equally important that legislators, scientists, educators, and the press get together to open a discourse on how to deal with problems of drug abuse in more effective ways.

III. Cannabis

Chapter 62

Hashish

Fitz Hugh Ludlow (1836–1870) became a hashish user while in college and, at the age of twenty-one, was one of the first Americans to write a description of the drug, a resin derived from the marijuana plant. Ludlow was the son of a minister, an excellent writer, and a student of literature who attended Princeton and was graduated from Union College. He was described by friends as charming and good-hearted. Unfortunately, he was unable to break from the use of hashish and, according to the Dictionary of American Biography, *his health steadily declined until he died at the age of thirty-four. Hashish was at this time also used by the French literati.*

The Hasheesh Eater

Fitz Hugh Ludlow

To pull out a broad and shallow cork was the work of an instant, and it revealed to me an olive-brown extract, of the consistency of pitch, and a decided aromatic odor. Drawing out a small portion upon the point of my penknife, I was just going to put it to my tongue when "Hold on!" cried the doctor; "do you want to kill yourself? That stuff is deadly poison." "Indeed!" I replied; "no, I can not say that I have any settled determination of that kind;" and with that I replaced the cork, and restored the extract, with all its appurtenances, to the shelf.

The remainder of my morning's visit in the sanctum was spent in consulting the Dispensatory under the title "Cannabis Indica." The sum of my discoveries there may be found, with much additional information, in that invaluable popular work, Johnston's Chemistry of Common Life. This being universally accessible, I will allude no further to the result of that morning's researches than to mention the three following conclusions to which I came.

First, the doctor was both right and wrong; right, inasmuch as a sufficiently large dose of the drug, if it could be retained in the stomach, would produce death, like any other narcotic, and the ultimate effect of its habitual use had always proved highly injurious to mind and body; wrong, since moderate doses of it were never immediately deadly, and many millions of people daily employed it as an indulgence similarly to opium. Second, it was the hasheesh referred to by Eastern travelers, and the subject of a most graphic chapter from the pen of Bayard Taylor, which months before had moved me powerfully to curiosity and admiration. Third, I would add it to the list of my former experiments.

In pursuance of this last determination, I waited till my friend was out of sight, that I might not terrify him by that which he considered a suicidal venture, and then quietly uncapping my little archer a second time, removed from his store of offensive armor a pill sufficient to balance the ten grain weight of the sanctorial scales. This, upon the authority of Pereira and the Dispensatory, I swallowed without a tremor as to the danger of the result.

Making all due allowance for the fact that I had not taken my hasheesh bolus fasting, I ought to experience its effects within the next four hours. That time elapsed without bringing the shadow of a phenomenon. It was plain that my dose had been insufficient.

For the sake of observing the most conservative prudence, I suffered several days to go by without a repetition of the experiment, and then, keeping the matter equally secret, I administered to myself a pill of fifteen grains. This second was equally ineffectual with the first.

Gradually, by five grains at a time, I increased the dose to thirty grains, which I took one evening half an hour after tea. I had now almost come to the conclusion that I was absolutely unsusceptible of the hasheesh influence. Without any expectation that this last experiment would be more successful than the former ones, and indeed with no realization of the manner in which the drug affected those who did make the experiment successfully. I went to pass the evening at the house of an intimate friend. In music and conversation the time passed pleasantly. The clock struck ten, reminding me that three hours had elapsed since the dose was taken, and as yet not an unusual symptom had appeared. I was provoked to think that this trial was as fruitless as its predecessors.

Ha! what means this sudden thrill? A shock, as of some unimagined vital force, shoots without warning through my entire frame, leaping to my fingers' ends, piercing my brain, startling me till I almost spring from my chair.

I could not doubt it. I was in the power of the hasheesh influence. My first emotion was one of uncontrollable terror—a sense of getting something which I had not bargained for. That moment I would have given all I had or hoped to have to be as I was three hours before.

No pain any where—not a twinge in any fibre—yet a cloud of unutterable strangeness was settling upon me, and wrapping me impenetrably in from all that was natural or familiar. Endeared faces, well known to me of old, surrounded me, yet they were not with me in my loneliness. I had entered upon a tremendous life which they could not share. If the disembodied ever return to hover over the hearth-stone which once had a seat for them, they look upon their friends as I then looked upon mine. A nearness of place, with an infinite distance of state, a connection which had no possible sympathies for the wants of that hour of revelation, an isolation none the less perfect for seeming companionship.

Still I spoke; a question was put to me, and I answered it: I even laughed at a bon mot. Yet it was not my voice which spoke; perhaps one which I once had far away in another time and another place. For a while I knew nothing that was going on externally, and then the remembrance of the last remark which had been made returned slowly and indistinctly, as some trait of a dream will return after many days, puzzling us to say where we have been conscious of it before.

A fitful wind all the evening had been sighing down the chimney; it now grew into the steady hum of a vast wheel in accelerating motion. For a while this hum seemed to resound through all space. I was stunned by it—I was absorbed in it. Slowly the revolution of the wheel came to a stop, and its monotonous din was changed for the reverberating peal of a grand cathedral organ. The ebb and flow of its inconceivably solemn tone filled me with a grief that was more than human. I sympathized with the dirge-like cadence as spirit sympathizes with spirit. And then, in the full conviction that all I heard and felt was real, I looked out of my isolation to see the effect of the music on my friends. Ah! we were in separate worlds indeed. Not a trace of appreciation on any face.

Perhaps I was acting strangely. Suddenly a pair of busy hands, which had been running neck and neck all the evening with a nimble little crochet-needle over a race-ground of pink and blue silk, stopped at their goal, and their owner looked at me steadfastly. Ah! I was found out—I had betrayed myself. In terror I waited, expecting every instant to hear the word "hasheesh." No, the lady only asked me some question connected with the previous conversation. As mechanically as an automaton I began to reply. As I heard once more the alien and unreal tones of my own voice, I became convinced that it was some one else who spoke, and in another world. I sat and listened; still the voice kept speaking. Now for the first time I experienced that vast change which hasheesh makes in all measurements of time. The first word of the reply occupied a period sufficient for the action of a drama; the last left me in complete ignorance of any point far enough back in the past to date the commencement of the sentence. Its enunciation might have occupied years. I was not in the same life which had held me when I heard it begun.

And now, with time, space expanded also. At my friend's house one particular arm-chair was always reserved for me. I was sitting in it at a distance of hardly three feet from the centre-table around which the members of the family were grouped. Rapidly that distance widened. The whole atmosphere seemed ductile, and spun endlessly out into great spaces surrounding me on every side. We were in a vast hall, of which my friends and I occupied opposite extremities. The ceiling and the walls ran upward with a gliding motion, as if vivified by a sudden force of resistless growth.

Oh! I could not bear it. I should soon be left alone in the midst of an infinity of space. And now more and more every moment increased the conviction that I was watched. I did not know then, as I learned afterward, that suspicion of all earthly things and persons was the characteristic of the hasheesh delirium.

In the midst of my complicated hallucination, I could perceive that I had a dual existence. One portion of me was whirled unresistingly along the track of this tremendous experience, the other sat looking down from a height upon its double, observing, reasoning, and serenely weighing all the phenomena. This calmer being suffered with the other by sympathy, but did not lose its self-possession. Presently it warned me that I must go home, lest the growing effect of the hasheesh should incite me to some act which might frighten my friends. I acknowledged the force of this remark very much as if it had been made by another person, and rose to take my leave. I advanced toward the centre-table. With every step its distance increased. I nerved myself as for a long pedestrian journey. Still the lights, the faces, the furniture receded. At last, almost unconsciously, I reached them. It would be tedious to attempt to convey the idea of the time which my leave-taking consumed, and the attempt, at least with all minds that have not passed through the same experience, would be as impossible as tedious. At last I was in the street.

Beyond me the view stretched endlessly away. It was an unconverging vista, whose nearest lamps seemed separated from me by leagues. I was doomed to pass through a merciless stretch of space. A soul just disenthralled, setting out for his flight beyond the farthest visible star, could not be more overwhelmed with his newly-acquired conception of the sublimity of distance than I was at that moment. Solemnly I began my infinite journey.

Before long I walked in entire unconsciousness of all around me. I dwelt in a marvelous inner world. I existed by turns in different places and various states of being. Now I swept my gondola through the moonlit lagoons of Venice. Now Alp on Alp towered above my view, and the glory of the coming sun flashed purple light upon the topmost icy pinnacle. Now in the primeval silence of some unexplored tropical forest I spread my feathery leaves, a giant fern, and swayed and nodded in the spice-gales over a river whose waves at once sent up clouds of music and perfume. My soul changed to a vegetable essence, thrilled with a strange and unimagined ecstasy. The palace of Al Haroun could not have bought me back to humanity.

I will not detail all the transmutations of that walk. Ever and anon I returned from my dreams into consciousness, as some well-known house seemed to leap out into my path, awaking me with a shock. The whole way homeward was a series of such awakings and relapses into abstraction and delirium until I reached the corner of the street in which I lived.

Here a new phenomenon manifested itself. I had just awaked for perhaps the twentieth time, and my eyes were wide open. I recognized all surrounding objects, and began calculating the distance home. Suddenly, out of a blank wall at my side a muffled figure stepped into the path before me. His hair, white as snow, hung in tangled elf-locks on his shoulders, where he carried also a heavy burden, like unto the well-filled sack of sins which Bunyan places on the back of his pilgrim. Not liking his manner, I stepped aside, intending to pass around him and go on my way. This change of our relative position allowed the blaze of a neighboring street-lamp to fall full on his face, which had hitherto been totally obscured. Horror unspeakable! I shall never, till the day I die, forget that face. Every lineament was stamped with the records of a life black with damning crime; it glared upon me with a ferocious wickedness and a stony despair which only he may feel who is entering on the retribution of the unpardonable sin. He might have sat to a demon painter as the ideal of Shelley's Cenci. I seemed to grow blasphemous in looking at him, and, in an agony of fear, began to run away. He detained me with a bony hand, which pierced my wrist like talons, and, slowly taking down the burden from his own shoulders, laid it upon mine. I threw it off and pushed him away. Silently he returned and restored the weight. Again I repulsed him, this time crying out, "Man, what do you mean?" In a voice which impressed me with the sense of wickedness as his face had done, he replied, "You *shall* bear my burden with me," and a third time laid it on my shoulders. For the last time I hurled it aside, and, with all my force, dashed him from me. He reeled backward and fell, and before he could recover his disadvantage I had put a long distance between us.

Through the excitement of my struggle with this phantasm the effects of the hasheesh had increased mightily. I was bursting with an uncontrollable life; I strode with the thews of a giant. Hotter and faster came my breath; I seemed to pant like some tremendous engine. An electric energy whirled me resistlessly onward; I feared for myself lest it should burst its fleshly walls, and glance on, leaving a wrecked frame-work behind it.

At last I entered my own house. During my absence a family connection had arrived from abroad and stood ready to receive my greeting. Partly restored to consciousness by the naturalness of homefaces and the powerful light of a chandelier which shed its blaze through the room, I saw the necessity of vigilance against betraying my condition, and with an intense effort suppressing all I felt, I approached my friend, and said all that is usual on such occasions. Yet recent as I was from my conflict with the super natural, I cast a stealthy look about me, that I might learn from the faces of the others if, after all, I was shaking hands with a phantom, and making inquiries about the health of a family of hallucinations. Growing assured as I perceived no symptoms of astonishment, I finished the salutation and sat down.

It soon required all my resolution to keep the secret which I had determined to hold inviolable. My sensations began to be terrific—not from any pain that I felt, but from the tremendous mystery of all around me and within me. By an appalling introversion, all the operations of vitality which, in our ordinary state go on unconsciously, came vividly into my experience. Through every thinnest corporeal tissue and minutes vein I could trace the circulation of the blood each inch of its progress. I knew when every valve opened and when it shut; every sense was preter-naturally awakened; the room was full of a great glory. The beating of my heart was so clearly audible that I wondered to find it unnoticed by those who were sitting by my side. Lo, now, that heart became a great fountain, whose jet played upward with loud vibrations, and, striking upon the roof of my skull as on a gigantic dome, fell back with a splash and echo into its reservoir. Faster and faster came the pulsations, until at last I heard them no more, and the stream became one continuously pouring flood, whose roar resounded through all my frame. I gave myself up for lost, since judgment, which still sat unimpaired above my perverted senses, argued that congestion must take place in a few moments, and close the drama with my death. But my clutch would not yet relax from hope. The thought struck me, Might not this rapidity of circulation be, after all, imaginary? I determined to find out.

Going to my own room, I took out my watch, and placed my hand upon my heart. The very effort which I made to ascertain the reality gradually brought perception back to its natural state. In the intensity of my observations, I began to perceive that the circulation was not as rapid as I had thought. From a pulseless flow it gradually came to be apprehended as a hurrying succession of intense throbs, then less swift and less intense, till finally, on comparing it with the second-hand, I found that about 90 a minute was its average rapidity. Greatly comforted, I desisted from the experiment. Almost instantly the hallucination returned. Again I dreaded apoplexy, congestion, hemorrhage, a multiplicity of nameless deaths, and drew my picture as I might be found on the morrow, stark and cold, by those whose agony would be redoubled by the mystery of my end. I reasoned with myself; I bathed my forehead—it did no good. There was one resource left: I would go to a physician.

With this resolve, I left my room and went to the head of the staircase. The family had all retired for the night, and the gas was turned off from the burner in the hall below. I looked down the stairs: the depth was fathomless; it was a journey of years to reach the bottom! The dim light of the sky shone through the narrow panes at the sides of the front door, and seemed a demon-lamp in the middle darkness of the abyss. I never could get down! I sat me down despairingly upon the topmost step.

Suddenly a sublime thought possessed me. If the distance be infinite, I am immortal. It shall be tried. I commenced the descent, wearily, wearily down through my league-long, year-long journey. To record my impressions in that journey would be to repeat what I have said of the time of hasheesh. Now stopping to rest as a traveler would turn aside at a wayside inn, now toiling down through the lonely darkness, I came by-and-by to the end, and passed out into the street.

Chapter 63

Physiological Effects and Dangers of Cannabis Use

Victor Robinson, a medical historian, was the son of a prominent physician. In this selection from his book Essay on Hashish *(1912) he comments on the consequences of the use of cannabis products, largely as described in the* Therapeutics and Materia Medica *(4th rev. ed; New York: Harper, 1874) of Alfred Stillé, a distinguished physician at the Philadelphia School of Medicine in the previous generation.*

Encouraged by stories of hashish's peculiar effects, Robinson experimented on his friends and recorded the results. The extreme behavior believed in 1912 to be unleashed by hashish ranged from making socialistic speeches to arguing for women's right to vote.

Robinson did not provide valid criteria for his list of recommended uses for cannabis. His anecdotal accounts include the description of an impossible relief of rabies symptoms, along with more likely therapeutic successes. Until Mexican immigrants brought the smoking of cannabis leaves to the United States in about 1920, smoking the more powerful resin was the usual form of ingestion.

AN ESSAY ON HASHEESH

Victor Robinson

The results of the prolonged use of large doses of Cannabis are thus epitomized by Alfred Stillé: "The habitual use of this drug entails consequences no less mischievous than are produced by alcohol and opium; the face becomes bloated, the eyes injected, the limbs weak and tremulous, the mind sinks into a state of imbecility, and death by marasmus is the ultimate penalty paid for the over-strained pleasure it imparts."

Poisoning by hasheesh is treated by the administration of emetics (what poison isn't), lemon-juice, tannin, coffee, ammonia, strychnine, atropine, spirit of nitrous ether. Electricity and artificial respiration are often useful.

A strange thing about hasheesh is that an overdose has never produced death in man or the lower animals. Not one authentic case is on record in which Cannabis or any of its preparations destroyed life. We thus have a poison which lacks a maximum and a fatal dose. Indeed, if we desire to be finical, we can claim that according to what is now considered the best definition of a poison, Cannabis is no poison at all, for the aforesaid best definition defines a poison as "any substance which is capable of causing death, otherwise than mechanically, when ingested. . . .

No drug in the entire Materia Medica is capable of producing such a diversity of effects as cannabis indica. "Of the action of hasheesh," writes Professor Stillé, "many and various descriptions have been given which differ so widely among themselves that they would scarcely be supposed to apply to the same agent, had we not every day a no less remarkable instance of the same kind before us in the case of alcohol. As the latter enlivens or saddens, excites or depresses, fills with tenderness, or urges to brutality, imparts vigor and activity, or nauseates and weakens, so does the former give rise to even a still greater variety of phenomena, according to the natural disposition of the person, and his existing state of mind, the quantity of the drug, and the combinations in which it is taken." . . .

This brings us to the physiological action of Cannabis. It primarily stimulates the brain, has a mydriatic effect upon the pupil, slightly accelerates the pulse, sometimes quickens and sometimes retards breathing, produces a ravenous appetite, increases the amount of urine, and augments the contractions of the uterus. In other words, it has an effect on the nervous, respiratory, circulatory, digestive, excretory and genito-urinary systems.

As a therapeutic agent hasheesh has its eulogizers, tho like many other drugs it has been replaced by later remedies in various disorders for which it was formerly used. Old drugs, like old folks, must give way to the new, and even the therapeutic master-builders must beware when the young generation of healing-agents knocks on the door of health.

In medicinal doses Cannabis is used as an aphrodisiac, for neuralgia, to quiet maniacs, for the cure of chronic alcoholism and morphine and chloral habits, for mental depression, hysteria, softening of the brain, nervous vomiting, for distressing cough, for St. Vitus' dance, and for the falling sickness so successfully simulated by Kipling's Sleary—epileptic fits of a most appalling kind. It is used in spasm of the bladder, in migraine, and when the dreaded *Bacillus tetanus* makes the muscles rigid. It is a uterine tonic, and a remedy in the headaches and hemorrhages occurring at the final cessation of the menses. It has been pressed into the service of the diseases that mankind has named in honor of Venus. According to Osler, cannabis is sometimes useful in locomotor ataxia. Christison reports a case in which Cannabis entirely cured the intense itching of eczema, while the patient was enjoying the delightful slumber which the hemp induced. It is much employed as an hypnotic in those cases where opium because of long-continued use has lost its efficiency. As a specific in hydrophobia it is sometimes marvelous, for Dr. J. W. Palmer writes that he himself has seen a sepoy, an hour before furiously hydrophobic, under the influence of cannabis drinking water freely and pleasantly washing his face and hands! Its function in this unspeakable affliction should be investigated carefully, for it will be a gala day for mankind when it can cease to fear Montaigne's terrible line: "The saliva of a wretched dog touching the hand of Socrates, might disturb and destroy his intellect."

Chapter 64

Hemp Growing for Farmers

The Pharmacopoeia of the United States of America *(1936) offers a straightforward description of the cannabis plant and its powdered form, as does the subsequent document, a 1920 publication for farmers, in which the Agriculture Department includes hemp (Cannabis sativa) among recommended drug-yielding plant crops. At that time, an acre of harvested hemp was worth about $100. The average agricultural worker received about $500 per year, and the average manufacturing worker about three times as much.*

Definition of Cannabis

The Pharmacopoeia of the United States of America

Cannabis

Cannab.—Cannabis indicæ herba P.I.

Cannabis consists of the dried flowering tops of the pistillate plants of *Cannabis saliva* Linné (Fam. *Moraceæ*).

It contains not more than 10 per cent of its fruits, large foliage leaves, and stems over 3 mm. in diameter, and not more than 2 per cent of other foreign organic matter. It yields not more than 5 per cent of acid-insoluble ash.

Description and physical properties—

Unground Cannabis—In separate tops or more or less agglutinated masses or fragments, consisting of the short stems with their leaf-like bracts and pistilate flowers or more or less developed fruits; color green to dark green or greenish-brown; odor agreeable, somewhat heavy and narcotic; taste somewhat acrid and pungent.

Leaves digitately compound, usually broken. Leaflets when entire, linear-lanceolate, nearly sessile, margin deeply serrate. Bracts ovate, pubescent, each enclosing 1 or 2 pistillate flowers or more or less developed fruits. Calyx dark green, pubescent and somewhat folded around the ovary. Styles 2, filiform and pubescent. Ovary with a single campylotropous ovule. Stems cylindrical, longitudinally furrowed, light green to light brown or purplish-brown, strigose-pubescent.

Structure of Stem—Cortex composed of collenchyma and several layers of parenchyma, in the larger stems, the phloem with numerous strands of more or less lignified bast-fibers; the xylem with strongly lignified wood having medullary rays 1-cell wide; pith, often hollow; rosette aggregates of calcium oxalate numerous.

Powdered Cannabis—Dark green; epidermis from lower surface of leaves with sinuate vertical walls and numerous oval stomata, from upper surface with straight walls and no stomata; non-glandular hairs numerous, unicellular, rigid, curved, with a very slender pointed apex and an enlarged base usually containing a cystolith; glandular hairs of two kinds, one with a short 1-celled stalk, the other with a long multicellular, tongue-shaped stalk, the head being globular and consisting of 8 to 16 cells; fragments of bracts and leaves showing yellowish-brown laticiferous vessels, numerous rosette aggregates of calcium oxalate, 0.005 to 0.030 mm. in diameter, and strands of spiral tracheæ and phloem; fragments of fruits with palisade-like, non-lignified cells with yellowish-brown finely porous walls; tissues of embryo and endosperm with numerous oil globules and aleurone grains, the latter from 0.005 to 0.010 mm. in diameter and displaying crystalloids and globoids.

Diluted hydrochloric acid added to powdered Cannabis causes effervescence visible under the microscope.

Preparations—Extractum Cannabis, Fluidextractum Cannabis.

DRUG PLANTS UNDER CULTIVATION

U.S. Department of Agriculture

Cannabis

The drug cannabis or Indian hemp (*Cannabis sativa*), consists of the dried flowering tops of the female plants. It grows well over a considerable portion of the United States, but the production of the active principle of this plant is believed to be favored by a warm climate. For drug purposes, therefore, this crop appears to be adapted to the Southern rather than to the Northern States.

Cannabis is propagated from seeds, which should be planted in the spring as soon as conditions are suitable, in well-prepared sandy of clayey loam at a depth of about an inch in rows 5 or 6 feet apart. The seeds may be dropped every two or three inches in the row or planted in hills about a foot apart in the row, 6 to 10 seeds being dropped into each hill. Two or three pounds of seed per acre should give a good stand. About half the seeds will produce male plants, which must be removed before their flowers mature; otherwise, the female plants will set seed, thereby diminishing their value as a drug. The male plants can be recognized with certainty only by the presence of stamens in their flowers.

Ordinary stable or barnyard manure plowed in deeply is better for use as a fertilizer than commercial preparations and may be safely applied at the rate of 20 tons per acre. However, good results may be obtained with commercial fertilizers, such as are used for truck crops and potatoes, when cultivated in between the rows at the rate of 500 or 600 pounds per acre.

When the female plants reach maturity, a sticky resin forms on the heavy, compact flower clusters, and harvesting may then be begun. The tops of the plants comprising the flower clusters are cut and carefully dried in the shade to preserve the green color as far as possible. Drying can best be done, especially in damp weather, by the use of artificial heat, not to exceed 140° F.

For several years cannabis of standard (U.S.P.) quality has been grown on a commercial scale in this country, chiefly in South Carolina and Virginia. After the flowering tops are harvested they are thoroughly dried under cover, then worked over by hand, and all the stems and large foliage leaves removed. This process gives a drug of high quality but greatly reduces the net or marketable yield per acre, which usually ranges from 350 to 400 pounds. Some growers do not remove the stems and leaves, thus increasing the acreage yield but reducing the market value of their product. The quality of cannabis can be determined only by special laboratory tests, which most dealers are not equipped to make; consequently, they are usually unwilling to pay growers as high prices as they would if the low-grade cannabis were kept off the market.

The market price in June, 1920, for tested (U.S.P.) domestic cannabis was 30 to 35 cents; for nontested, 20 to 25 cents a pound.

Chapter 65

Vipers in the Jazz Age and After

Milton "Mezz" Mezzrow parted with his white middle-class family background for life "on the corner": gang fighting, shooting pool, joyriding in stolen cars. In the reformatory he learned to play the blues on an alto saxophone and determined to become "a Negro musician." Mezzrow immersed himself in African American music and culture while playing saxophone, flute, and clarinet in bands in Chicago, New Orleans, and New York in the 1920s and 1930s. As he describes in this excerpt from his 1946 memoir, he liked the feeling that marijuana gave him, and he liked its effect on his playing, in contrast to the influence of alcohol or opium. He became a steady user, a viper. Before long, Mezzrow was known as a reliable source of marijuana; indeed, one of the common nicknames for a marijuana cigarette was a "mezz." In later years, Mezzrow claimed that he introduced marijuana to Harlem.

The 1938 New Yorker *article "Tea for a Viper" gives the perspective of the curious white intellectual sophisticate on the contemporary Harlem "tea" (marijuana) party.*

REALLY THE BLUES

Milton "Mezz" Mezzrow and Bernard Wolfe

It was that flashy, sawed-off runt of a jockey named Patrick who made a viper out of me after Leon Rappolo failed. Back in the Arrowhead Inn, where I first met Patrick, he told me he was going to New Orleans and would be back one day with some marihuana, real golden-leaf. He asked me did I want some of the stuff, and coming up tough I said sure, bring me some, I'd like to try it. When Patrick marched into the Martinique one night I began to look for the nearest exit, but it was too late. "Hi ya, boy," he said with a grin bigger than he was hisself, "let's you and me go to the can, I got something for you." That men's room might have been a deathhouse, the way I kept curving away from it, but this muta-mad Tom Thumb latched on to me like a ball-and-chain and steered me straight inside.

From Milton "Mezz" Mezzrow and Bernard Wolfe, *Really the Blues* (New York: Citadel, 1946), 71–77, 213–16. © 1946 by Citadel Press, all rights reserved. Reprinted by permission of Citadel Press/Kensington Publishing Corp., www.kensingtonbooks.com.

As soon as we were alone he pulled out a gang of cigarettes and handed them to me. They were as fat as ordinary cigarettes but were rolled in brown wheat-straw paper. We both lit up and I got halfway through mine, hoping they would break the news to mother gently, before he stopped me. "Hey," he said, "take it easy, kid. You want to knock yourself out?"

I didn't feel a thing and I told him so. "Do you know one thing?" he said. "You ain't even smokin' it right. You got to hold that muggle so that it barely touches your lips, see, then draw in air around it. Say *tfff, tfff*, only breathe in when you say it. Then don't blow it out right away, you got to give the stuff a chance." He had a tricky look in his eye that I didn't go for at all. The last time I saw that kind of look it was on a district attorney's mug, and it caused me a lot of inconvenience.

After I finished the weed I went back to the bandstand. Everything seemed normal and I began to play as usual. I passed a stick of gauge around for the other boys to smoke, and we started a set.

The first thing I noticed was that I began to hear my saxophone as though it was inside my head, but I couldn't hear much of the band in back of me, although I knew they were there. All the other instruments sounded like they were way off in the distance; I got the same sensation you'd get if you stuffed your ears with cotton and talked out loud. Then I began to feel the vibrations of the reed much more pronounced against my lip, and my head buzzed like a loudspeaker. I found I was slurring much better and putting just the right feeling into my phrases—I was really coming on. All the notes came easing out of my horn like they'd already been made up, greased and stuffed into the bell, so all I had to do was blow a little and send them on their way, one right after the other, never missing, never behind time, all without an ounce of effort. The phrases seemed to have more continuity to them and I was sticking to the theme without ever going tangent. I felt I could go on playing for years without running out of ideas and energy. There wasn't any struggle; it was all made-to-order and suddenly there wasn't a sour note or a discord in the world that could bother me. I began to feel very happy and sure of myself. With my loaded horn I could take all the fist-swinging, evil things in the world and bring them together in perfect harmony, spreading peace and joy and relaxation to all the keyed-up and punchy people everywhere. I began to preach my millenniums on my horn, leading all the sinners on to glory.

The other guys in the band were giggling and making cracks, but I couldn't talk with my mouthpiece between my lips, so I closed my eyes and drifted out to the audience with my music. The people were going crazy over the subtle changes in our playing; they couldn't dig what was happening but some kind of electricity was crackling in the air and it made them all glow and jump. Every so often I opened my eyes and found myself looking straight into a girl's face right in front of the bandstand, swinging there like a pendulum. She was an attractive, rose-complexioned chick, with wind-blown honey-colored hair, and her flushed face was all twisted up with glee. That convulsed face of hers stirred up big waves of laughter in my stomach, waves that kept breaking loose and spreading up to my head, shaking my whole frame. I had to close my eyes fast to keep from exploding with the joy.

It's a funny thing about marihuana—when you first begin smoking it you see things in a wonderful soothing, easygoing new light. All of a sudden the world is stripped of its dirty gray shrouds and becomes one big bellyful of giggles, a spherical laugh, bathed in brilliant, sparkling colors that hit you like a heatwave. Nothing leaves you cold any more; there's a humorous tickle and great meaning in the least little thing, the twitch of somebody's little finger or the click of a beer glass. All your pores open like funnels, your nerve-ends stretch their mouths wide, hungry and thirsty for new sights and sounds and sensations; and every sensation, when it comes, is the most exciting one you've ever had. You can't get enough of anything—you want to gobble up the whole goddamned universe just for an appetizer. Them first kicks are a killer, Jim.

Suppose you're the critical and analytical type, always ripping things to pieces, tearing the covers off and being disgusted by what you find under the sheet. Well, under the influence of muta you don't lose your surgical touch exactly, but you don't come up evil and grimy about it. You still see what you saw before but in a different, more tolerant way, through rose-colored glasses, and things that would have irritated you before just tickle you. Everything is good for a laugh; the wrinkles get ironed out of your face and you forget what a frown is, you just want to hold on to your belly and roar till the tears come. Some women especially, instead of being nasty and mean just go off bellowing until hysteria comes on. All the larceny kind of dissolves out of them—they relax and grin from ear to ear, and get right on the ground floor with you. Maybe no power on earth can work out a lasting armistice in that eternal battle of the sexes, but muggles are the one thing I know that can even bring about an overnight order to "Cease firing."

Tea puts a musician in a real masterly sphere, and that's why so many jazzmen have used it. You look down on the other members of the band like an old mother hen surveying her brood of chicks; if one of them hits a sour note or comes up with a bad modulation, you just smile tolerantly and figure, oh well, he'll learn, it'll be better next time, give the guy a chance. Pretty soon you find yourself helping him out, trying to put him on the right track. The most terrific thing is this, that all the while you're playing, really getting off, your own accompaniment keeps flashing through your head, just like you were a one-man band. You hear the basic tones of the theme and keep up your pattern of improvisation without ever getting tangled up, giving out with a uniform sequence all the way. Nothing can mess you up. You hear everything at once and you hear it right. When you get that feeling of power and sureness, you're in a solid groove.

You know how jittery, got-to-be-moving people in the city always get up in the subway train two minutes before they arrive at the station? Their nerves are on edge; they're watching the clock, thinking about schedules, full of that high-powered mile-a-minute jive. Well, when you've picked up on some gauge that clock just stretches its arms, yawns, and dozes off. The whole world slows down and gets drowsy. You wait until the train stops dead and the doors slide open, then you get up and stroll out in slow motion, like a sleepwalker with a long night ahead of him and no appointments to keep. You've got all the time in the world. What's the rush, buddy? Take-it-easy, that's the play, it's bound to sweeten it all the way.

I kept on blowing, with my eyes glued shut, and then a strange thing happened. All of a sudden somebody was screaming in a choked, high-pitched voice, like she was being strangled, "Stop it, you're killing me! Stop! I can't stand it!" When I opened my eyes it seemed like all the people on the dance floor were melted down into one solid, mesmerized mass; it was an overstuffed sardine-can of an audience, packed in an olive-oil trance. The people were all pasted together, looking up at the band with hypnotic eyes and swaying—at first I saw just a lot of shining eyes bobbing lazily on top of a rolling sea of flesh. But off to one side there was discord, breaking the spell. An entertainer, one of the girls who did a couple of vocals and specialized in a suggestive dance routine, was having a ball all to herself. She had cut loose from her partner and was throwing herself around like a snake with the hives. The rhythm really had this queen; her eyes almost jumped out of their sockets and the cords in her neck stood out stiff and hard like ropes. What she was doing with the rest of her anatomy isn't discussed in mixed company.

"Don't do that!" she yelled. "Don't do that to me!" When she wasn't shouting her head off she just moaned way down in her soundbox, like an owl gargling.

Then with one flying leap she sailed up on the bandstand, pulled her dress up to her neck, and began to dance. I don't know if dance is the right word for what she did—she didn't move her feet hardly at all, although she moved practically everything else. She went through her whole routine, bumps and grinds and shakes and breaks, making up new twists as she went along, and I mean twists. A bandstand was sure the wrong place to do what she was trying to do that night. All the time she kept screaming, "Cut it out! It's murder!" but her body wasn't saying no.

It was a frantic scene, like a nightmare walking, and it got wilder because all the excitement made us come on like gangbusters to accompany this palsy-bug routine. Patrick and his gang of vipers were getting their kicks—the gauge they picked up on was really in there, and it had them treetop tall, mellow as a cello. Monkey Pollack stood in the back, moving a little less than a petrified tree, only his big lips shaking like meatballs with the chills, and the Ragtime Cowboy Jew was staring through the clouds of smoke as though he was watching a coyote do a toe-dance. That girl must have been powered with Diesel engines, the way she kept on going. The sweat was rolling down her screwed-up face like her pores were faucets, leaving streaks of mascara in the thick rouge. She would have made a scarecrow do a nip-up and a flip.

The tension kept puffing up like an overstuffed balloon, and finally it broke.

There was the sharp crack of pistol shots ringing through the sweat and strain. Fear clamped down over the sea of faces like a mask, and the swaying suddenly stopped.

It was only Mac, our gunplayful cowboy bartender. Whenever he got worked up he would whip out his pistols and fire at the ceiling, catching the breaks in our music. The excitement that night was too much for him and to ease his nerves he was taking potshots at the electric bulbs, with a slap-happy grin on his kisser. Every time he pulled the trigger another Mazda crossed the Great Divide— he may have been punchy but his trigger finger didn't know about it.

The girl collapsed then, as though somebody had yanked the backbone right out of her body. She fell to the floor like a hunk of putty and lay in a heap, quivering and making those funny noises way down in her throat. They carried her upstairs and put her to bed, and I guess she woke up about six weeks later. Music sure hath charms, all right, but what it does to the savage breast isn't always according to the books.

The bandstand was only a foot high but when I went to step down it took me a year to find the floor, it seemed so far away. I was sailing through the clouds, flapping my free-wheeling wings, and leaving the stand was like stepping off into space. Twelve months later my foot struck solid ground with a jolt, but the other one stayed up there on those lovely soft clouds, and I almost fell flat on my face. There was a roar of laughter from Patrick's table and I began to feel self-conscious and nauseous at the same time. I flew to the men's room and got there just in time. Patrick came in and started to laugh at me.

"What's the matter, kid?" he said. "You not feeling so good?" At that moment I was up in a plane, soaring around the sky, with a buzz-saw in my head. Up and around we went, saying nuts to Newton and all his fancy laws of gravitation, but suddenly we went into a nosedive and I came down to earth, sock. Ouch. My head went spattering off in more directions than a hand grenade. Patrick put a cold towel to my temples and I snapped out of it. After sitting down for a while I was all right.

When I went back to the stand I still heard all my music amplified, as though my ear was built right into the horn. The evening rolled away before I knew it. When the entertainers sang I accompanied them on the piano, and from the way they kept glancing up at me I could tell they felt the harmonies I was inventing behind them without any effort at all. The notes kept sliding out of my horn like bubbles in seltzer water. My control over the vibrations of my tones was perfect, and I got a terrific lift from the richness of the music, the bigness of it. The notes eased out like lava running down a mountain, slow and sure and steaming. It was good. . . .

One of my friends, a fine musician, cornered me one day and we began to discuss our outcome with the tea. I wasn't selling it yet, and we tried to analyze the difference there was between gauge and whisky.

"Man, they can say what they want about us vipers," he said, "but you just dig them lushhounds with their old antique jive, always comin' up loud and wrong, whippin' their old ladies and wastin' up all their pay, and then the next day your head feels like all the hammers in the piano is beatin' out a tune on your brain. Just look at the difference between you and them other cats, that come uptown juiced to the gills, crackin' out of line and passin' out in anybody's hallway. Don't nobody come up thataway when he picks up on some good grass."

I sure knew what he was talking about. The very same thing, that contrast between the lushies and the vipers, had hit me hard way back in Chicago and Detroit, and I told him so.

"Yeah," he said, "and then for instance you take a lot of ofay liquor-heads, when they come up here and pass the jug around. Half of them will say they had enough 'cause some spade just took a drink out of it, and those that do take it will hem and haw, tryin' to rub the top off the bottle so's you can't see them, 'fore they put it to their chops. Now with vipers it's different. You don't have to pass a roach to a viper, he'll take it right out of your hand and go to puffin' on it not even thinkin' about who had it in his chops before. Them Indians must of had some gauge in that pipe of peace that they passed around, at least they had the right idea, ha ha! Now, far as hurtin' anybody is concerned, you know and I know that we can wake up the next day and go on about our business, marihuana or mary-don't-wanna, and that's that. It ain't against the law and you told me they couldn't put it under the Harrison Act because it wasn't habit-forming, so let's carry on from here. We'll both smoke it every day for about two or three months and then one of us'll quit for a while and find out for ourselves what happens."

That's exactly what we did. I was the first one to stop for a trial, and I have yet to find any bad after-effects, outside of a twenty-month jail sentence.

(Before I go any further I want to make one thing clear: I never advocated that anybody should use marihuana, and I sure don't mean to start now. Even during the years when I sold the stuff I never "pushed" it like a salesman pushes vacuum cleaners or Fuller brushes. I had it for anybody who came asking, if he was a friend of mine. I didn't promote it anywhere, and I never gave it to kids, not even to little Frankie Walker. I sold it to grown-up friends of mine who had got to using it on their own, just like I did; it was a family affair, not any high-pressure business. Sort of everybody to their own notion, that was the whole spirit. I laid off five years ago, and if anybody asks my advice today, I tell them straight to steer clear of it because it carries a rap. That's my final word to all the cats: today I know of one very bad thing the tea can do to you—it can put you in jail. 'Nuff said.)

Most of us were getting our tea from some Spanish boys, and one day they showed up with a guy who pushed the stuff in Detroit when I was there. He wasn't selling it any more, but he put us in touch with another cat who kept coming up from Mexico with real golden-leaf, the best that could be had. As soon as we got some of that Mexican bush we almost blew our tops. Poppa, you never smacked your chops on anything sweeter in all your days of viping. It had such a wonderful smell and the kick you got was really out of this world. Guys used to say it tasted like chocolate candy, a brand Hershey never even thought of. I laid it on the cats in the Barbeque, and pretty soon all Harlem was after me to light them up. I wasn't working then and didn't have much money left to gaycat with, but I couldn't refuse to light my friends up. Before I knew it I had to write to our connection for a large supply, because everybody I knew wanted some. "Man, you can be ridin' on rubber in no time with that stuff, and it ain't against the law neither," the cats told me. "Just think how many cats you can make happy," they kept saying. Before I knew it, I was standing on The Corner pushing gauge. Only I did no pushing. I just stood under the Tree of Hope, my pokes full up, and the cats came and went, and so did all my golden-leaf.

Overnight I was the most popular man in Harlem. New words came into being to meet the situation: *the mezz* and *the mighty mezz*, referring, I blush to say, to me and to the tea both; *mezzroll*, to describe the kind of fat, well-packed and clean cigarette I used to roll (this word later got corrupted to *meserole* and it's still used to mean a certain size and shape of reefer, which is different from the so-called panatella); *the hard-cuttin' mezz* and *the righteous bush*. Some of those phrases really found a permanent place in Harlemese, and even crept out to color American slang in general. I was knocked out the other day when I picked up a copy of Cab Calloway's *Hipster's Dictionary* and found *mezz* defined there as "anything supreme, genuine"; and in Dan Burley's *Original Handbook of Harlem Jive* the same word is defined as meaning "tops, sincere"!

Stuff Smith wrote a song, later recorded by Rosetta Howard for Decca under the name of *If You're a Viper*, that started out

> *Dreamed about a reefer five foot long*
> *The mighty mezz but not too strong,*
> *You'll be high but not for long*
> *If you're a viper.*

The words *lozies* and *lozeerose* were coined so guys could refer to my gauge without having anybody else dig it, and some of our musician pals used to stick these hip phrases into their songs when they broadcast over the radio, because they knew we'd be huddled around the radio in the Barbeque and that was their way of saying hello to me and all the vipers. That mellow Mexican leaf really started something in Harlem—a whole new language, almost a whole new culture. The hard-cuttin' mezz really cut a brand-new one in this old world, through no fault of mine.

TEA FOR A VIPER

Meyer Berger

It took weeks of dickering to get into a marijuana party, because I was not a viper, which is the Harlem word for a marijuana smoker, but at last it was arranged. Suspecting that I might find the evening a long one, I took an equally uninitiated friend with me. We got out of a cab in front of a gray-stone tenement in one of the darker spots on 140th Street at eleven o'clock on the appointed Saturday night and rang the bell of the right-hand apartment on the ground floor. When the door opened a few inches, escaping marijuana smoke, mixed with the fumes of cheap incense and stale steam heat, came at us like an oven blast. Chappy, the little saddle-colored man who runs the place, led us into the dark interior.

It was difficult at first to make out his friends and fellow-vipers in that fetid flat. Hashish smokers (marijuana and hashish, I had learned, are the same thing) dislike strong light. The only illumination in Chappy's place was a blue bulb glowing in the glass case of the slot-machine phonograph. All tea pads, or marijuana joints, use the blue lamps and nickel machines to induce and sustain the hashish mood. They play special recordings of viper, or weed, songs with weird ritualistic themes. One of these was playing when we came in. Big Boo, a long-armed blackamoor, sprawled on one of the four broken-down couches in the room and thumped the floor with a bony fist, in time with the rhythm. Boo was high. The others were silent.

"Meet the writin' man," Chappy said, introducing my companion at the same time. Vicki and Fruits, two slender wenches with high breasts, giggled and the blue light shone on their perfect teeth and on their oversized imitation-pearl earrings. Big Boo rolled his head to acknowledge the introduction but didn't interrupt his tom-tom beat. Steel-Haid, a gigantic Negro with bulging eyes, thrust out a big paw and mumbled something. Duke and Arthur, a couple of foppish sprigs in their early twenties, seemed friendly but suspicious. Chappy hurried down the long apartment corridor to answer the doorbell, while my friend and I sat in awkward silence, sharing the sofa with the girls.

I was fascinated by Boo. His eyes were shut tight now. His thick lips parted and he wailed a low accompaniment to the dragging tempo of the weed song. The girls swayed and hummed. The song ended and the record slid back into the stack. Boo's bullet head perked up as if someone had worked it with a string.

Vicki laughed. "Boo's high," she said.

"Yea, momma," chanted Boo. His eyes opened and a vapid grin creased his face.

"Boo goin' blow his top," sneered Arthur. " 'Tain't twelve an' Boo's sent."

"Nay, man," Boo bragged. "Sent, but not spent. Don' high-gyve Boo."

Viper vocabulary changes fast—perhaps to confuse the police. A smoker is high when contentment creeps over him. If he smokes to excess he blows his top; that is, he gets sick. When he reaches a stage of full contentment his body is "sent." "High-gyve" is conversational baiting, or teasing a smoker. Marijuana cigarettes have a dozen names. Right now they are sticks, reefers, Mary Anns, tea, gyves, gauge- or goofy-butts. A pinched-off smoke, or stub, is a roach. Tea pads where inferior cigarettes are sold are heat pads; these places add dry tea leaves or dry grass to supplement the marijuana supply. Pads where semiconscious smokers are robbed of their money are creeper joints. The automatic phonograph is the piccolo and a detective is The Man.

Chappy's pad is one of four in that particular gray-front tenement. There are hundreds of such places in Harlem—many more of them than there were speakeasies during prohibition. Chappy's suite is a middle-class pad—four rooms with nine couches set against the cracked, cream-colored walls, with a few limp easy chairs to handle the overflow. Some of the upperclass pads have as many as eight and nine rooms, elegant furniture, lots of decorative silk dolls, gaudy hangings, and artistic moonlight scenes painted on dark velvet. Wine is an aid to the hashish smoker and all the pads sell it—a cheap lo-cal"ink." A few sell shake-up, too, which is a fierce whiskey made by shaking up straight alcohol and a little coloring: a dangerous combination when mixed with hashish. Chappy won't handle it. "I don't pour no trouble" is the way he puts it.

Ground-floor pads keep their windows shut tight. This is an invitation to dioxide suffocation, but Chappy thinks that's better than letting the sickly-sweet odor of burning marijuana into the street for the first passing pounder, or patrol-man, to smell. "One whiff," said Chappy, "and we get a bust." ("Bust" is Harlem for a raid.) They burn cheap ten-cent-store incense to disguise the marijuana odor. Vipers don't seem to mind the damp warmth in the sealed pads. They get quicker action from the weed in that atmosphere. Some vipers get high on a single stick, but others need three or four. Chappy has one customer, a Harlem blues singer, who can inhale fifteen in four hours, but she's unusual. Many swing musicians and chorus girls are inveterate vipers. The drug acts quickly on the musical sensibilities and gives a weird, indefinable lag to their rhythm. It's a sexual excitant, too. Canary breeders learned that long ago. They feed the birds on marijuana seed in mating time by mixing it with the customary seed. In Harlem some of the tea pads are bed houses, but not Chappy's place. "I got my self-respec'," he says.

Fresh customers came dragging into Chappy's at midnight. They kept Chappy busy. Some took off their overcoats but most of them didn't bother. One group of well-dressed vipers retired to one of the back rooms. Chappy served them reefers and wine and closed the French door with the dirty-white curtains. By this time the main parlor held about twenty smokers, all sucking at reefers. The piccolo played without cease. Smoke and incense snaked through the room in visible layers.

Vicki's cigarette burned a ragged hole in the dark and her giggling increased. At each puff you could hear the peculiar hissing intake of breath that marks the smoking technique of the viper. Inhaling this way gets the smoke to the brain more quickly. Exhalation is slow and reluctant. The longer the smoke is retained, the greater the effect. The reefers are handmade, half as long as an ordinary cigarette, and thinner. They have double paper wrappers because the weed is coarse and apt to break through. Dry throat and hunger pangs mark the beginning of the high stage in a smoker. That's why vipers sometimes carry a little bag of peppermints or peanuts.

A new arrival called to Chappy across the room. "Deuce me, man," he said. "Deuce for Buck," chanted Chappy, bringing out two reefers and collecting a quarter. An ace is a single stick and sells for fifteen cents. Impoverished customers are served at the door. They pay only ten cents because they smoke "on the walk"—in their own homes or anywhere outside a regular pad. Chappy adds the extra tax on inside patrons to pay for wear and tear on his furniture and for atmosphere and rent. His rent is thirty dollars a month. He pays eighteen dollars a pound for cigarettes and makes about two-hundred-per-cent profit on them. When his stock runs low he calls a dealer at 110th Street and Lenox Avenue and an automobile brings a fresh supply.

Federal agents had told me that vipers are always dangerous; that an overdose of marijuana generates savage and sadistic traits likely to reach a climax in axe and icepick murders. They cited the case of a Florida cracker who killed his whole family—five or six people—with the woodshed axe. Robert Irwin, the artist who killed the Gedeons and their boarder with an icepick, had ten reefers in his room, which the police found when they searched the place. The hairy-chested gun girl who murdered a bus driver in New Jersey a short while ago testified that marijuana drove her to it. Detectives in Harlem suspect the marijuana defence may be the latest style with smart criminal lawyers. In their own dealings with hashish users taken in raids, the police uptown never had a tough one. "They just act restless when we get them to the station house," one cop explained. "They never fight."

Medical experts seem to agree that marijuana, while no more habit-forming than ordinary cigarette smoking, offers a shorter cut to complete madness than any other drug. They say it causes deterioration of the brain. Chappy's customers scoffed at this idea. They said reefers only make them happy. They didn't know a single viper who was vicious or mad. Once in a while some smoker gets a bit horsy and overplayful, but they "bring him down" just by talking to him. They say the marijuana makes the blood pound in their veins and gives them the sensation of suspension in mid-air. As they get high, the walls recede, lights back away, and their legs and fingers don't respond. Reflexes go haywire. They get to giggling. Time and sound and distance seem to stretch like a rubber band. It is easy, watching them, to understand why a smoker would feel that he was crawling when his car was doing eighty miles an hour. Chappy said that it was even dangerous for a viper to cross a street when he was high. "You hear a auto horn an' you see the lights," he explained. "You think they a mile away an' they right on top of you."

From the piccolo case, above the throb and beat, came the words of the viper song, low and soothing. The soloist was some husky-voiced woman.

> I dreamed about a reefer five feet long,
> Mighty, immense, but not too strong,

> You be high, but not for long,
> If you're a viper.

Boo was thumping the floor again, with his eyes shut tight. Vicki jumped up, and Steel-Haid caught her and crushed her against his body. They jerked to the music's beat, her slender form bending at sharp angles, in perfect rhythm with the tune. Her head shot back in an ecstatic fling. The blue bulb lighted their laughing faces.

"I'm the Queen of Ever'thing," Vicki shrilled. "I gotta be high before I swing."

The magnetic pull got Arthur and Fruits. They met in the centre of the dark room in violent contact, locked an amorous embrace, and went into a creepy dance. The recumbent vipers moaned in voodooistic chorus:

> Light yo' tea an' let it be,
> If you're a viper.
> When yo' throat get dry
> You know you're high.
> Ever'thing is dandy.
> Truck on down to the candy sto',
> Bust yo' conk on pep'min' candy,
> Then you know yo' body's sent,
> You don't care if you don't pay rent,
> Sky is high and so am I,
> If you're a viper.

Chappy's customers danced themselves breathless and rolled on the couches, convulsed with soft laughter. They didn't talk much. By three o'clock most of them were completely under, just able to moan and giggle with the music.

The smokers went through alternate periods of exaltation and exhaustion. They never stopped their silly laughter. Yet none of it was noisy; there was nothing, for example, to compare with the racket and hubbub that come in the latter hours of an ordinary cocktail party. As a rule, customers lie around until the stupor leaves them. That may be anywhere from an hour to five or six hours, depending on the individual. When a customer is ready to cut out—the term for departing—Chappy "brings him down" with milk. The milk seems to hasten clearing of the brain.

Marijuana is made from the flowering top and leaves of India hemp plant. It is one of the oldest drugs in the world and has a different name in every country. It is bhang, hashish or hasheesh, mazra, kef, reefer weed, or Cannabis sativa. In the *Pharmacopœia* it is cannabis indica. In medical practice it is used to induce sleep or hypnosis. Commercially it is used for rope, twine, bags, mats, and canary food. It grows anywhere.

Marijuana growing in and around Manhattan had the federal agents crazy for a long time. The stuff turned up in empty lots in the best neighborhoods as well as on the city dumps. They even found some under the Queensboro Bridge, near Sutton Place. Federal and city sleuths laid elaborate traps for the growers but never caught anyone. Recently someone in the federal service figured the thing out—the mysterious crops came from marijuana seed dumped from the trays of canary cages. That won't happen any more. Under a law passed last August all marijuana seed intended for birds must be sterilized in 220 degrees of oven heat before it goes on the market. Such seed will not germinate. Right now most of the smokers' supply comes from New Jersey, Staten Island, and Westchester.

The use of reefers has become so widespread that the federal government is preparing a concentrated drive on dealers. Since a federal law was passed last October rating marijuana with vicious narcotics—heroin, cocaine, and the rest— the agents' activity has been greatly increased. There are thousands of white vipers in the city, but nowhere are the pads as thick or popular as in upper Harlem and in the Spanish and Mexican quarter around 110th Street and Fifth Avenue. Down that way reefers are sold in candy stores, restaurants, and grocery stores. In Harlem, marijuana is taking the place of whiskey. A viper can get drunk on anywhere from one to four or five cigarettes—ten to fifty cents' worth— while it would cost him a dollar or two for a whiskey jag. No hangover, either.

By five o'clock the atmosphere in Chappy's place was that of a Turkish bath. The piccolo was grinding out the viper song for the hundredth time. Chappy was high, too. He grinned foolishly, left sentences in mid-air, and when he walked he used the gait that comes from the floating sensation—a slow-motion gliding walk called the seven-foot step. Vicki and Fruits and two new wenches—The Trush and Lili—kept at their primitive dancing in delirious spasms, occasionally dropping back on the sofas, doubled with hushed laughter. Boo thumped. Chappy floated as he served fresh sticks and wine. It was Sunday morning and no one had to go home. No one but my friend and myself. The door of the pad shut behind us. We swallowed the sharp, cold air in grateful gulps.

Chapter 66

The Government Response

The Federal Bureau of Narcotics (FBN) was founded in 1930. In the excerpts below from the FBN annual reports of 1931, 1933, and 1937, we can trace a striking change in the tone in which marijuana is discussed, from the matter-of-fact description in the first selection to the dramatic warnings in the last report.

Historical, as well as popular, accounts of drug use in the recent American past usually paint the longtime head of the Bureau of Narcotics, Harry J. Anslinger, as a fervent, even monomaniacal, warrior against all drugs. Anslinger, in this version of events, was ever eager to lead the charge of the FBN into the fray, In the case of marijuana, however, the image does not conform to reality.

Anslinger's goal was to avoid responsibility for control of the cannabis problem. The FBN's resources were fully absorbed in dealing with the opiates and cocaine, and much of its focus was on preventing cross-border trafficking, as the raw components for these drugs were grown, and most of their manufacturing took place, outside the United States. The success the bureau enjoyed would be compromised if it also had to take on the duty of eradicating a domestic plant that grew ubiquitously. For that reason, Anslinger urged the states to enact a uniform antidrug statue that included cannabis. Each state then would be obliged to decide how much of its resources to apply to the marijuana problem. As the 1937 report reveals, Anslinger also strongly encouraged the involvement of "worthy civic groups" in fighting marijuana abuse.

TRAFFIC IN OPIUM AND OTHER DANGEROUS DRUGS, 1931

Federal Bureau of Narcotics

Much of the general data given in the previous report with reference to the growth of Indian hemp in the United States remains applicable to the period covered by this report. Therefore, such general data is repeated with revision and amplification necessary to include developments during 1931.

Indian hemp (*Cannabis sativa*) is not indigenous. The early cultivation of hemp in the United States was of the small European variety, but this has been replaced since 1857 by the larger Chinese hemp. Practically all of the seed for present-day American hemp culture is grown in the Kentucky River valley. It was originally grown in the New England colonies for fiber used in making home-spun. It was also grown in the Virginia and Pennsylvania colonies and was cultivated at an early date in the settlements of Kentucky from whence it spread to Missouri. It has been grown at various times in Illinois, near Champaign; in the Kankakee River valley in Indiana; in southeastern Pennsylvania; and in Nebraska, Iowa, and California. At one time as much as 40,000 acres per annum were devoted in the United States to the cultivation of this plant for its fiber. The trend of production, however, is definitely downward due apparently to intensive competition with cheaper fiber crops. The commercial hemp production of the country is practically all in Wisconsin, Illinois, and Kentucky, the total area being approximately 750 acres in 1931. However, it is also abundant as a wild plant in many localities in western Missouri, Iowa, southern Minnesota, and in the Southwestern and Western States, where it is found as a roadside weed. A small amount of Indian hemp is imported for medical purposes, probably due to the fact that the imported variety is richer in cannabin, but during the calendar year 1931 the total quantity imported for these purposes amounted only to 74 pounds, of a total value of $636.

In the Southwest where there is a considerable element of Mexican population familiar with the use of the drug "marihuana" it is believed that there is some production of that drug from the female inflorescence of the plant. When the crop is grown for fiber, the harvest takes place when the male flowers are beginning to shed pollen. At this stage the female inflorescence, from which the drug is made, is too immature to possess narcotic properties, and in order to make use of the plant as a drug it is consequently necessary to permit it to remain in the field for several weeks longer. Unless the male plants are removed before the pollen is distributed, the female flowers will be pollinated and a large quantity of seed will develop. This is understood greatly to reduce the physiologically active substances in the inflorescence.

Traffic in Opium and Other Dangerous Drugs, 1933

Federal Bureau of Narcotics

The commercial hemp production of the country (which is used for the fiber) is now practically limited to Wisconsin and Kentucky, the total area being 190 acres in 1933. About 100 acres in Iowa were used for growing this plant, but it is believed that in Iowa not all was harvested or used for any purpose. Cannabis sativa, however, grows wild in almost every State in the Union. There is extensive wild growth of the plant in the States of Arizona, Colorado, New Mexico, Texas, Utah, and Wyoming. It is also clandestinely cultivated in these States and in a number of other States. In the States growing beets for the beet-sugar industry, the Mexican laborers in the fields clandestinely plant patches of this weed among the beet plants, and harvest it and sell the drug or use it personally for the gratification of personal desire.

The production and use of Indian hemp (cannabis sativa, hasheesh, mari-huana) within the United States are not prohibited by Federal law. The laws of some 34 States and of the Territory of Hawaii control either the cultivation, sale, or possession of marihuana, but these State laws are not uniform. All of the 34 States and the Territory of Hawaii govern the sale of this drug; 31 of them and Hawaii make its possession unlawful; while 13 of them and Hawaii control its cultivation.

As to importation, it may be said that, by regulation under the Food and Drugs Act, approved June 30, 1906, collectors of customs are directed to refuse delivery of all consignments of dried flowering tops of the pistillate plants of cannabis sativa, unless the importer shall first execute a penal bond conditioned that the drug referred to will not be sold or otherwise disposed of for any purpose other than in the preparation of medicine. No cannabis sativa was imported during 1933.

A disconcerting development in quite a number of States is found in the apparently increasing use of marihuana by the younger element in the larger cities.

The drug is most commonly used in the form of cigarettes, selling generally from 15 to 25 cents each, or from 3 for 25 cents to 3 for 50 cents, but it is also used mixed with beer or other alcoholic beverages, for its stimulating properties.

There is some smuggling of this drug to and from Mexico, also some interstate traffic in the States of the Rocky Mountain region, but not to a great extent. The Canadian authorities have advised of some smuggling of this drug into Canada, especially from Detroit and its vicinity. There has been some unlawful importation of this drug by ship, but since the hemp grows wild to such an extent, it is assumed that the total quantities of this drug clandestinely introduced into the United States from foreign countries cannot be very large.

On November 23, 1933, upon arrival of the steamship *Metapari* at Pier 7, North River, New York City, from Kingston, customs officers conducted a search of the vessel and found among other articles, a package containing marihuana, the drug being seized because it was not entered on the ship's manifest.

An increasing effort is noted by the various States in endeavoring to stamp out the growing evil of the use of marihuana, as shown by the increased number of arrests and prosecutions of violators of the various State laws controlling this drug.

TRAFFIC IN OPIUM AND OTHER DANGEROUS DRUGS, 1937

Federal Bureau of Narcotics

Illicit Traffic in Marihuana (Cannabis sativa L.)

The consumption of marihuana reached such serious proportions in the United States as to call for the enactment of national-control legislation during the year.

This gives the enforcement authorities a new weapon and enables the Federal Government to deal with the marihuana problem in the same realistic manner as it deals with other dangerous drugs. The traffic in marihuana, except in isolated instances, is separate and distinct from the traffic in other drugs, both as to sellers and users.

The (Federal) Marihuana Tax Act became effective October 1, 1937, and between that date and the close of the year Federal officers reported 250 violations of the act, involving 369 seizures of marihuana in various forms, and 223 arrests. The total number of seizures of marihuana reported by Federal and State officers during the year amount to 704. These involved 7,145 marihuana cigarettes, 345 kilos, 893 grams of dried bulk marihuana. 15 kilos, 146 grams of seeds, 70,280 growing plants 44.153 kilos of green marihuana, and growing marihuana scattered through 872 hectares of land, all of which were destroyed.

All of the 48 States of the Union and the Territory of Hawaii have control legislation of some nature on marihuana. Many State and city officers throughout the country have been quick to realize the dangers of the drug, and have taken hold of marihuana enforcement problems in a most commendable manner. Numerous police departments have been educating their forces in the recognition of the marihuana plant. There have also been initiated local campaigns to eradicate the plant from vacant lots and back yards in various localities where it has been found growing.

The widespread dissemination of educational material during the year is bringing forcibly before the notice of the people the extremely pernicious effects of marihuana smoking and the necessity for eradicating it.

Unquestionably these combined efforts have materially discouraged any attempt to organize the illicit traffic on a large scale. (Unlike other drugs, marihuana is not generally handled by well-organized distributing syndicates.) The authorities, however, feel obliged to pay special attention to marihuana law violations: One of the most disturbing elements in connection with the illegal use of this drug is its potential danger to a different group. Young people not previously contaminated with drugs appear to be especially susceptible to the marihuana smoking practice.

Few of the cases reported under the Marihuana Tax Act are of sufficient international interest to be set out in detail. A number of representative cases of major importance, involving violations of this act or the various state laws for the control of marihuana, are summarized in the succeeding paragraphs under headings indicating the localities in which they occurred.

Denver, Colo.

Among the first cases tried under the Marihuana Tax Act of 1937 were those against Samuel Richard Caldwell and Moses Baca, both of Denver, Colo. Caldwell, an ex-convict, was arrested for selling and smoking marihuana. He admitted possession and sale of the drug and stated that he had personally brought it from the State of Kansas, claiming to have harvested it from a patch growing wild outside of Kansas City. Caldwell had a criminal record showing 11 previous arrests on various charges dating from 1921. He was sentenced to serve 4 years in a Federal prison.

Moses Baca was arrested on a charge of assaulting his wife. Although only 23 years old, he had a long criminal record involving 12 previous arrests dating from 1931. He admitted being under the influence of marihuana at the time of the assault, and upon search of his residence one-fourth ounce of marihuana was found in a bureau drawer. He was then charged with a violation of the Marihuana Tax Act and was sentenced to serve 18 months in a Federal prison.

In Denver, Colo., Juan Moya, alias Juan Valley, was arrested while under the influence of marihuana and fought the officers so savagely that it took four 200-pound men almost 10 minutes to subdue him. At the time of arrest, the defendant attempted to eat the contents of a can of marihuana he was trying to dispose of. He succeeded in eating about one-half of the can before the others could take the balance away from him.

Moya was convicted and sentenced to 2 years' imprisonment and fined $500.

He has had numerous convictions for the use and sale of drugs, and is alleged to be a habitual user of marihuana. He usually resists violently when arrested, and on one occasion escaped from arresting Federal officers under gunfire after making three sales of drugs. Moya has also been arrested several times for forgery.

He is considered dangerous to society when at large.

State Highways, Iowa

Between August 1 and August 17, 1937, the Iowa Highway Commission destroyed approximately 1,000 acres of marihuana growing wild along highways in the State.

Detroit, Mich.

Between July 15 and August 9, 1937, the Detroit Police Department destroyed several tons of marihuana found growing partly wild and partly under cultivation in various vacant lots and back yards in the city of Detroit, the amounts in the several plots ranging from 20 to 3,360 pounds.

Chelsea, Mich.

On August 26, 1937, a narcotic officer and State officers destroyed approximately 25,000 marihuana plants from 6 to 12 feet in height growing on a farm near Chelsea, Mich. There was no evidence that any of the tenants of the farm recognized the weed until a guest identified it as marihuana. From the appearance of the patches the marihuana had evidently been planted by a former tenant.

Grand Rapids, Mich.

On September 23, 1937, narcotic and police officers destroyed about 2,000 marihuana plants growing on a vacant lot. It was alleged that a person whose name was unknown was obtaining the drug from this lot and selling cigarettes, but since the lot was being used as a playground by children of the neighborhood it was deemed advisable to destroy the plants immediately rather than leave them and attempt to apprehend the person responsible for their growth.

Coatesville, Pa.

Acting on information that Joe Gracia was selling marihuana in Contesville, Pa, narcotic officers assisted by local officers made purchases from him totalling approximately 2 pounds, then arrested Gracia and seized from the basement of his home one large trunk containing 487 ounces of marihuana and one small wooden drum containing 328 ounces of marihuana.

Gracia was tried, convicted, and sentenced to serve 3 years in a Federal penitentiary.

Philadelphia, Pa.

On October 22 and 23, 1937, two plots of marihuana were found in the heart of the city of Philadelphia. The marihuana—about 3,000 plants on one plot and 3,500 plants on the other—was cut and burned by Federal and State officers.

Everettville, W. Va.

Acting on information that Pete Lopez, alias Mexican Pete, was growing and selling marihuana in Everettville, W. Va., narcotic officers assisted by local officers made four purchases totalling 7 ounces 369 grains of marihuana from him and from a colored woman, Lucy Vaughn, then arrested Lopez and upon searching his house found and seized 15 pounds 8 ounces 120 grains of marihuana. It was found that he was growing the marihuana in a corn field near his cabin and 345 stalks bare of leaves and seeds, were cut and burned.

Lopez, 37 years old, claimed to have smoked marihuana since he was about 10 years old. Investigation disclosed that he was engaged in illicit traffic in marihuana on a large scale solely for monetary gain. He was tried, convicted, and sentenced to 10 years in a Federal prison. Lucy Vaughn was sentenced to 1 year in a county jail.

Miami, Fla.

A seizure of marihuana of international significance was effected near Miami, Fla., on October 9, 1937. An old oil drum containing 53½ pounds of the drug was found on the beach where it had been landed and buried in September by Capt. William Hood, British subject, resident of British Honduras, master of the Honduran schooner *Alert* and Octavio Carrillo, a Mexican, both of whom were arrested. The marihuana is alleged by the defendants to have come aboard the vessel at Baca La Chica, British Honduras, in two sacks which came from Xcalat, Mexico, and was removed from the vessel before it came through quarantine at Miami.

Hood was convicted and sentenced to serve 2 years in the penitentiary. Carillo was sentenced to serve 1 year and 1 day.

Educational Work

The Bureau of Narcotics believes that the efforts expended by it during the year on preventive educational work, and particularly regarding marihuana, have been fruitful of much good. There has been constant demand for speakers and for written information on the narcotic and marihuana problems, manifesting an active desire on the part of many worthy civic organizations to be assistance in stamping out the abuse of narcotic drugs. The Bureau is particularly gratified with the excellent work done by the General Federation of Women's Clubs, the National Congress of Parents and Teachers, and the National Woman's Christian Temperance Union in informing the public regarding the dangers attending the illicit use of narcotic drugs.

Over 100 addresses were delivered, on request, by various officials of the Bureau to organizations throughout the country such as the various medical associations, the American Pharmaceutical Manufacturers' Association, various police school and State police training schools, the Training School of the Federal Bureau of Investigation and the National Police Academy, the Woman's Christian Temperance Union, the American Legion, various churches, hospital groups, and lodges. The Institute of Government, Kiwanis, Rotary, and other clubs, colleges of pharmacy and science, parent-teacher associations, Associations of University Women, Peace Officers' Training Schools, the National Police Academy, Peace Officers Association, and other interested groups.

The Commissioner of Narcotics personally fulfilled a number of lecture engagements before national groups on the narcotic problem.

The Bureau of Narcotics has also furnished assistance to various States toward educating enforcement agencies and State and city chemists concerning the identification of marihuana.

Courts

In passing sentence in the Baca and Caldwell cases (reviewed elsewhere in this report), Judge J. Foster Symes, of Denver, Colo., made the following noteworthy statement in stressing the seriousness of the use of marihuana:

I consider marihuana the worst of all narcotics—far worse than the use of morphine or cocaine. Under its influence men become beasts, just as was the case with Baca. Marihuana destroys life itself. I have no sympathy with those who sell this weed.

In future I will impose the heaviest penalties. The Government is going to enforce this new law to the letter.

In sentencing one Wong Kop, cafe operator and prominent member of Memphis' Chinese colony, for conviction of a narcotic law violation, Federal Judge John D. Martin, Sr., of the Western District of Tennessee, made the following statements:

It is one of the most corrupt rackets in the United States today. From it come mind, body, and soul destroying habits that rob the victim of reason. There is no habit that can more encourage criminality in its worst form.

All this can be laid to the viper who puts narcotics into the hands of victims for the gain of money.

Sentences of imprisonment were imposed on a number of counts which will require Wong Kop to serve 10 years' imprisonment in a Federal institution, and to pay fines amounting to $3,000.

If this attitude prevailed in all districts of the United States, it would act as a strong deterrent to the illicit traffic in drugs.

Chapter 67

Marijuana Comes under Federal Control

Anslinger's superiors at the Treasury Department found a way to bring marijuana under federal control in 1937, when the Supreme Court upheld the National Firearms Act (1934). This act required anyone selling, loaning, or bartering for a machine-gun to pay a transfer tax and receive a transfer stamp. The catch was that the government would not print any stamps, and so no such sales, loans, and so forth could legally take place. The law was challenged on the grounds that a tax law that could not raise taxes was unconstitutional, but the Court rejected this argument.

By about a month after this decision, the Treasury Department had succeeded in having a bill introduced before Congress that called for receipt of a transfer stamp at any time that marijuana changed hands. In this case, some stamps were printed. They probably were intended for commercial sales of hemp, as the FBN opposed any medical use of cannabis.

THE MARIHUANA TAX ACT OF 1937

An act to impose an occupational excise tax upon certain dealers in marihuana, to impose a transfer tax upon certain dealings in marihuana, and to safeguard the revenue therefrom by registry and recording.

Be it enacted by the Senate and House of Representatives of the United States of America in Congress assembled, That when used in this Act—

(a) The term "person" means an individual, a partnership, trust, association, company, or corporation and includes an officer or employee of a trust, association, company, or corporation, or a member or employee of a partnership, who, as such officer, employee, or member, is under a duty to perform any act in respect of which any violation of this Act occurs.

(b) The term "marihuana" means all parts of the plant Cannabis sativa L., whether growing or not; the seeds thereof; the resin extracted from any part of such plant; and every compound, manufacture, salt, derivative, mixture, or preparation of such plant, its seeds, or resin; but shall not include the mature stalks of such plant, fiber produced from such stalks, oil or cake made from the seeds of such plant, any other compound, manufacture, salt, derivative, mixture, or preparation of such mature stalks (except the resin extracted therefrom), fiber, oil, or cake, or the sterilized seed of such plant which is incapable of germination.

(c) The term "producer" means any person who (1) plants, cultivates, or in any way facilitates the natural growth of marihuana; or (2) harvests and transfers or makes use of marihuana.

(d) The term "Secretary" means the Secretary of the Treasury and the term "collector" means collector of internal revenue.

(e) The term "transfer" or "transferred" means any type of disposition resulting in a change of possession but shall not include a transfer to a common carrier for the purpose of transporting marihuana.

SEC. 2. (a) Every person who imports, manufactures, produces, compounds, sells, deals in, dispenses, prescribes, administers, or gives away marihuana shall (1) within fifteen days after the effective date of this Act, or (2) before engaging after the expiration of such fifteen-day period in any of the above-mentioned activities, and (3) thereafter, on or before July 1 of each year, pay the following special taxes respectively:

(1) Importers, manufacturers, and compounders of marihuana, $24 per year.

(2) Producers of marihuana (except those included within subdivision (4) of this subsection), $1 per year, or fraction thereof, during which they engage in such activity.

(3) Physicians, dentists, veterinary surgeons, and other practitioners who distribute, dispense, give away, administer, or prescribe marihuana to patients upon whom they in the course of their professional practice are in attendance, $1 per year or fraction thereof during which they engage in any of such activities.

(4) Any person not registered as an importer, manufacturer, producer, or compounder who obtains and uses marihuana in a laboratory for the purpose of research, instruction, or analysis, or who produces marihuana for any such purpose, $1 per year, or fraction thereof, during which he engages in such activities.

(5) Any person who is not a physician, dentist, veterinary surgeon, or other practitioner and who deals in, dispenses, or gives away marihuana, $3 per year . . .

SEC. 4. (a) It shall be unlawful for any person required to register and pay the special tax under the provisions of section 2 to import, manufacture, produce, compound, sell, deal in, dispense, distribute, prescribe, administer, or give away marihuana without having so registered and paid such tax.

(b) In any suit or proceeding to enforce the liability imposed by this section or section 2, if proof is made that marihuana was at any time growing upon land under the control of the defendant, such proof shall be presumptive evidence that at such time the defendant was a producer and liable under this section as well as under section 2.

SEC. 5. It shall be unlawful for any person who shall not have paid the special tax and registered, as required by section 2, to send, ship, carry, transport, or deliver any marihuana within any Territory, the District of Columbia, or any insular possession, or from any State, Territory, the District of Columbia, any insular possession of the United States, or the Canal Zone, into any other State, Territory, the District of Columbia, or insular possession of the United States. . . .

SEC. 6. (a) It shall be unlawful for any person, whether or not required to pay a special tax and register under section 2, to transfer marihuana, except in pursuance of a written order of the person to whom such marihuana is transferred, on a form to be issued in blank for that purpose by the Secretary. . . .

SEC. 7. (a) There shall be levied, collected, and paid upon all transfers of marihuana which are required by section 6 to be carried out in pursuance of written order forms taxes at the following rates:

(1) Upon each transfer to any person who has paid the special tax and registered under section 2 of this Act, $1 per ounce of marihuana or fraction thereof.

(2) Upon each transfer to any person who has not paid the special tax and registered under section 2 of this Act, $100 per ounce of marihuana or fraction thereof.

(b) Such tax shall be paid by the transferee at the time of securing each order form and shall be in addition to the price of such form. Such transferee shall be liable for the tax imposed by this section but in the event that the transfer is made in violation of section 6 without an order form and without payment of the transfer tax imposed by this section, the transferor shall also be liable for such tax.

(c) Payment of the tax herein provided shall be represented by appropriate stamps to be provided by the Secretary and said stamps shall be affixed by the collector or his representative to the original order form. . . .

SEC. 8. (a) It shall be unlawful for any person who is a transferee required to pay the transfer tax imposed by section 7 to acquire or otherwise obtain any marihuana without having paid such tax; and proof that any person shall have had in his possession any marihuana and shall have failed, after reasonable notice and demand by the collector, to produce the order form required by section 6 to be retained by him, shall be presumptive evidence of guilt under this section and of liability for the tax imposed by section 7. . . .

SEC. 9. (a) Any marihuana which has been imported, manufactured, compounded, transferred, or produced in violation of any of the provisions of this Act shall be subject to seizure and forfeiture and, except as inconsistent with the provisions of this Act, all the provisions of internal-revenue laws relating to searches, seizures, and forfeitures are extended to include marihuana. . . .

(d) The Secretary is hereby directed to destroy any marihuana confiscated by and forfeited to the United States under this section or to deliver such marihuana to any department, bureau, or other agency of the United States Government, upon proper application therefor under such regulations as may be prescribed by the Secretary. . . .

SEC. 12. Any person who is convicted of a violation of any provision of this Act shall be fined not more than $2,000 or imprisoned not more than five years, or both, in the discretion of the court. . . .

SEC. 18. This Act may be cited as the "Marihuana Tax Act of 1937."

Chapter 68

The Danger of Marijuana

Following the passage of the Marihuana Tax Act of 1937, Commissioner Anslinger promulgated lurid tales of the dangers of marijuana use. Because the FBN had received no extra funds to deal with this new problem, the informational campaign he planned had to be inexpensive, as well as effective in discouraging the spread of the drug. This 1937 article appeared in a popular magazine with nationwide distribution. The extravagant style of warning aimed at preventing the possibly curious from trying marijuana even once.

MARIJUANA: ASSASSIN OF YOUTH

H. J. Anslinger with Courtney Ryley Cooper

The sprawled body of a young girl lay crushed on the sidewalk the other day after a plunge from the fifth story of a Chicago apartment house. Everyone called it suicide, but actually it was murder. The killer was a narcotic known to America as marijuana, and to history as hashish. It is a narcotic used in the form of cigarettes, comparatively new to the United States and as dangerous as a coiled rattlesnake.

How many murders, suicides, robberies, criminal assaults, holdups, burglaries, and deeds of maniacal insanity it causes each year, especially among the young, can be only conjectured. The sweeping march of its addiction has been so insidious that, in numerous communities, it thrives almost unmolested, largely because of official ignorance of its effects.

Here indeed is the unknown quantity among narcotics. No one can predict its effect. No one knows, when he places a marijuana cigarette to his lips, whether he will become a philosopher, a joyous reveler in a musical heaven, a mad insensate, a calm philosopher, or a murderer.

That youth has been selected by the peddlers of this poison as an especially fertile field makes it a problem of serious concern to every man and woman in America.

There was the young girl, for instance, who leaped to her death. Her story is typical. Some time before, this girl, like others of her age who attend our high schools, had heard the whispering of a secret which has gone the rounds of American youth. It promised a new thrill, the smoking of a type of cigarette which contained a "real kick." According to the whispers, this cigarette could accomplish wonderful reactions and with no harmful aftereffects. So the adventurous girl and a group of her friends gathered in an apartment, thrilled with the idea of doing "something different" in which there was "no harm." Then a friend produced a few cigarettes of the loosely rolled "homemade" type. They were passed from one to another of the young people, each taking a few puffs.

The results were weird. Some of the party went into paroxysms of laughter; every remark, no matter how silly, seemed excruciatingly funny. Others of mediocre musical ability became almost expert; the piano dinned constantly. Still others found themselves discussing weighty problems of youth with remarkable clarity. As one youngster expressed it, he "could see through stone walls." The girl danced without fatigue, and the night of unexplainable exhilaration seemed to stretch out as though it were a year long. Time, conscience, or consequences became too trivial for consideration.

Other parties followed, in which inhibitions vanished, conventional barriers departed, all at the command of this strange cigarette with its ropy, resinous odor. Finally there came a gathering at a time when the girl was behind in her studies and greatly worried. With every puff of the smoke the feeling of despondency lessened. Everything was going to be all right—at last. The girl was "floating" now, a term given to marijuana intoxication. Suddenly, in the midst of laughter and dancing, she thought of her school problems. Instantly they were solved. Without hesitancy she walked to a window and leaped to her death. Thus can marijuana "solve" one's difficulties.

The cigarettes may have been sold by a hot tamale vendor or by a street peddler or in a dance hall or over a lunch counter or even from sources much nearer to the customer. The police of a Midwestern city recently accused a school janitor of having conspired with four other men, not only to peddle cigarettes to children, but even to furnish apartments where smoking parties might be held.

A Chicago mother, watching her daughter die as an indirect result of marijuana addiction, told officers that at least fifty of the girl's young friends were slaves to the narcotic. This means fifty unpredictables. They may cease its use; that is not so difficult as with some narcotics. They may continue addiction until they deteriorate mentally and become insane. Or they may turn to violent forms of crime, to suicide or to murder. Marijuana gives few warnings of what it intends to do to the human brain.

The menace of marijuana addiction is comparatively new to America. In 1931, the marijuana file of the United States Narcotic Bureau was less than two inches thick, while today the reports crowd many large cabinets. Marijuana is a weed of the Indian hemp family, known in Asia as *Cannabis Indica* and in America as *Cannabis Sativa*. Almost everyone who has spent much time in rural communities has seen it, for it is cultivated in practically every state. Growing plants by the thousands were destroyed by law enforcement officers last year in Texas, New

York, New Jersey, Mississippi, Michigan, Maryland, Louisiana, Illinois, and the attack on the weed is only beginning.

It was an unprovoked crime some years ago which brought the first realization that the age-old drug had gained a foothold in America. An entire family was murdered by a youthful addict in Florida. When officers arrived at the home they found the youth staggering about in a human slaughterhouse. With an ax he had killed his father, his mother, two brothers, and a sister. He seemed to be in a daze.

"I've had a terrible dream," he said. "People tried to hack off my arms!"

"Who were they?" an officer asked.

"I don't know. Maybe one was my uncle. They slashed me with knives and I saw blood dripping from an ax."

He had no recollection of having committed the multiple crime. The officers knew him ordinarily as a sane, rather quiet young man; now he was pitifully crazed. They sought the reason. The boy said he had been in the habit of smoking something which youthful friends called "muggles," a childish name for marijuana.

Since that tragedy there has been a race between the spread of marijuana and its suppression. Unhappily, so far, marijuana has won by many lengths. The years 1935 and 1936 saw its most rapid growth in traffic. But at least we now know what we are facing. We know its history, its effects, and its potential victims. Perhaps with the spread of this knowledge the public may be aroused sufficiently to conquer the menace. Every parent owes it to his children to tell them of the terrible effects of marijuana to offset the enticing "private information" which these youths may have received. There must be constant enforcement and equally constant education against this enemy, which has a record of murder and terror running through the centuries.

The weed was known to the ancient Greeks and it is mentioned in Homer's *Odyssey*. Homer wrote that it made men forget their homes and turned them into swine. Ancient Egyptians used it. In the year 1090, there was founded in Persia the religious and military order of the Assassins, whose history is one of cruelty, barbarity, and murder, and for good reason. The members were confirmed users of hashish, or marijuana, and it is from the Arabic *"hashshashin"* that we have the English word "assassin." Even the term "running amok" relates to the drug, for the expression has been used to describe natives of the Malay Peninsula who, under the influence of hashish, engage in violent and bloody deeds.

Marijuana was introduced into the United States from Mexico, and swept across America with incredible speed.

It began with the whispering of vendors in the Southwest that marijuana would perform miracles for those who smoked it, giving them a feeling of physical strength and mental power, stimulation of the imagination, the ability to be"the life of the party." The peddlers preached also of the weed's capabilities as a "love potion." Youth, always adventurous, began to look into these claims and found some of them true, not knowing that this was only half the story.

They were not told that addicts may often develop a delirious rage during which they are temporarily and violently insane; that this insanity may take the form of a desire for self-destruction or a persecution complex to be satisfied only by the commission of some heinous crime.

It would be well for law-enforcement officers everywhere to search for marijuana behind cases of criminal and sex assault. During the last year a young male addict was hanged in Baltimore for criminal assault on a ten-year-old girl. His defense was that he was temporarily insane from smoking marijuana. In Alamosa, Colo., a degenerate brutally attacked a young girl while under the influence of the drug. In Chicago, two marijuana-smoking boys murdered a policeman.

In at least two dozen other comparatively recent cases of murder or degenerate sex attacks, many of them committed by youths, marijuana proved to be a contributing cause. Perhaps you remember the young desperado in Michigan who, a few months ago, caused a reign of terror by his career of burglaries and holdups, finally to be sent to prison for life after kidnapping a Michigan state policeman, killing him, then handcuffing him to the post of a rural mailbox. This young bandit was a marijuana fiend.

A sixteen-year-old boy was arrested in California for burglary. Under the influence of marijuana he had stolen a revolver and was on the way to stage a holdup when apprehended. Then there was the nineteen-year-old addict in Columbus, Ohio, who, when police responded to a disturbance complaint, opened fire upon an officer, wounding him three times, and was himself killed by the returning fire of the police. In Ohio a gang of seven young men, all less than twenty years old, had been caught after a series of 38 holdups. An officer asked them where they got their incentive.

"We only work when we're high on 'tea,' " one explained.

"On what?"

"On tea. Oh, there are lots of names for it. Some people call it 'mu' or 'muggles' or 'Mary Weaver' or 'moocah' or 'weed' or 'reefers'—there's a million names for it."

"All of which mean marijuana?"

"Sure. Us kids got on to it in high school three or four years ago; there must have been twenty-five or thirty of us who started smoking it. The stuff was cheaper then; you could buy a whole tobacco tin of it for fifty cents. Now these peddlers will charge you all they can get, depending on how shaky you are. Usually though, it's two cigarettes for a quarter."

This boy's casual story of procurement of the drug was typical of conditions in many cities in America. He told of buying the cigarettes in dance halls, from the owners of small hamburger joints, from peddlers who appeared near high schools at dismissal time. Then there were the "booth joints" or Bar-B-Q stands, where one might obtain a cigarette and a sandwich for a quarter, and there were the shabby apartments of women who provided not only the cigarettes but rooms in which girls and boys might smoke them.

"But after you get the habit," the boy added, "you don't bother much about finding a place to smoke. I've seen as many as three or four high-school kids jam into a telephone booth and take a few drags."

The officer questioned him about the gang's crimes: "Remember that filling station attendant you robbed—how you threatened to beat his brains out?"

The youth thought hard. "I've got a sort of hazy recollection," he answered. "I'm not trying to say I wasn't there, you understand. The trouble is, with all my gang, we can't remember exactly what we've done or said. When you get to 'floating,' it's hard to keep track of things."

From the other youthful members of the gang the officer could get little information. They confessed the robberies as one would vaguely remember bad dreams.

"If I had killed somebody on one of those jobs, I'd never have known it," explained one youth. "Sometimes it was over before I realized that I'd even been out of my room."

Therein lies much of the cruelty of marijuana, especially in its attack upon youth. The young, immature brain is a thing of impulses, upon which the "unknown quantity" of the drug acts as an almost overpowering stimulant. There are numerous cases on record like that of an Atlanta boy who robbed his father's safe of thousands of dollars in jewelry and cash. Of high-school age, this boy apparently had been headed for an honest, successful career. Gradually, however, his father noticed a change in him. Spells of shakiness and nervousness would be succeeded by periods when the boy would assume a grandiose manner and engage in excessive, senseless laughter, extravagant conversation, and wildly impulsive actions. When these actions finally resulted in robbery the father went at his son's problem in earnest—and found the cause of it a marijuana peddler who catered to school children. The peddler was arrested.

It is this useless destruction of youth which is so heartbreaking to all of us who labor in the field of narcotic suppression. No one can predict what may happen after the smoking of the weed. I am reminded of a Los Angeles case in which a boy of seventeen killed a policeman. They had been great friends. Patrolling his beat, the officer often stopped to talk to the young fellow, to advise him. But one day the boy surged toward the patrolman with a gun in his hand; there was a blaze of yellowish flame, and the officer fell dead.

"Why did you kill him?" the youth was asked.

"I don't know," he sobbed. "He was good to me. I was high on reefers. Suddenly I decided to shoot him."

In a small Ohio town, a few months ago, a fifteen-year-old boy was found wandering the streets, mentally deranged by marijuana. Officers learned that he had obtained the dope at a garage.

"Are any other school kids getting cigarettes there?" he was asked.

"Sure. I know fifteen or twenty, maybe more. I'm only counting my friends."

The garage was raided. Three men were arrested and 18 pounds of marijuana seized.

"We'd been figuring on quitting the racket," one of the dopesters told the arresting officer. "These kids had us scared. After we'd gotten 'em on the weed, it looked like easy money for a while. Then they kept wanting more and more of it, and if we didn't have it for 'em, they'd get tough. Along toward the last, we were scared that one of 'em would get high and kill us all. There wasn't any fun in it."

Not long ago a fifteen-year-old girl ran away from her home in Muskegon, Mich., to be arrested later in company with five young men in a Detroit marijuana den. A man and his wife ran the place. How many children had smoked there will never be known. There were 60 cigarettes on hand, enough fodder for 60 murders.

A newspaper in St. Louis reported after an investigation this year that it had discovered marijuana "dens," all frequented by children of high-school age. The same sort of story came from Missouri, Ohio, Louisiana, Colorado—in fact, from coast to coast.

In Birmingham, Ala., a hot-tamale salesman had pushed his cart about town for five years, and for a large part of that time he had been peddling marijuana cigarettes to students of a downtown high school. His stock of the weed, he said, came from Texas and consisted, when he was captured, of enough marijuana to manufacture hundreds of cigarettes.

In New Orleans, of 437 persons of varying ages arrested for a wide range of crimes, 125 were addicts. Of 37 murderers, 17 used marijuana, and of 193 convicted thieves, 34 were "on the weed."

One of the first places in which marijuana found a ready welcome was in a closely congested section of New York. Among those who first introduced it there were musicians, who had brought the habit northward with the surge of "hot" music demanding players of exceptional ability especially in improvisation. Along the Mexican border and in seaport cities it had been known for some time that the musician who desired to get the "hottest" effects from his playing often turned to marijuana for aid.

One reason was that marijuana has a strangely exhilarating effect upon the musical sensibilities (Indian hemp has long been used as a component of "singing seed" for canary birds). Another reason was that strange quality of marijuana which makes a rubber band out of time, stretching it to unbelievable lengths. The musician who uses "reefers" finds that the musical beat seemingly comes to him quite slowly, thus allowing him to interpolate any number of improvised notes with comparative ease. While under the influence of marijuana, he does not realize that he is tapping the keys with a furious speed impossible for one in a normal state of mind; marijuana has stretched out the time of the music until a dozen notes may be crowded into the space normally occupied by one. Or, to quote a young musician arrested by Kansas City officers as a "muggles smoker":

"Of course I use it—I've got to. I can't play any more without it, and I know a hundred other musicians who are in the same fix. You see, when I'm 'floating,' I own my saxophone. I mean I can do anything with it. The notes seem to dance out of it—no effort at all. I don't have to worry about reading the music—I'm music-crazy. Where do I get the stuff? In almost any low-class dance hall or night spot in the United States."

Soon a song was written about the drug. Perhaps you remember:

> Have you seen
> That funny reefer man?
> He says he swam to China;
> Any time he takes a notion,
> He can walk across the ocean."

It sounded funny. Dancing girls and boys pondered about "reefers" and learned through the whispers of other boys and girls that these cigarettes could make one accomplish the impossible. Sadly enough, they can—in the imagination. The boy who plans a holdup, the youth who seizes a gun and prepares for a murder, the girl who decides suddenly to elope with a boy she did not even know a few hours ago, does so with the confident belief that this is a thoroughly logical action without the slightest possibility of disastrous consequences. Command a person "high" on "mu" or "muggles" or "Mary Jane" to crawl on the floor and bark like a dog, and he will do it without a thought of the idiocy of the action. Everything, no matter how insane, becomes plausible. The underworld calls marijuana "that stuff that makes you able to jump off the tops of skyscrapers."

Reports from various sections of the country indicate that the control and sale of marijuana has not yet passed into the hands of the big gangster syndicates. The supply is so vast and grows in so many places that gangsters perhaps have found it difficult to dominate the source. A big, hardy weed, with serrated, swordlike leaves topped by bunchy small blooms supported upon a thick, stringy stalk, marijuana has been discovered in almost every state. New York police uprooted hundreds of plants growing in a vacant lot in Brooklyn. In New York State alone last year 200 tons of the growing weed were destroyed. Acres of it have been found in various communities. Patches have been revealed in back yards, behind signboards, in gardens. In many places in the West it grows wild. Wandering dopesters gather the tops from along the right of way of railroads.

An evidence of how large the traffic may be came to light last year near La Fitte, La. Neighbors of an Italian family had become amazed by wild stories told by the children of the family. They, it seemed, had suddenly become millionaires. They talked of owning inconceivable amounts of money, of automobiles they did not possess, of living in a palatial home. At last their absurd lies were reported to the police, who discovered that their parents were allowing them to smoke something that came from the tops of tall plants which their father grew on his farm. There was a raid, in which more than 500,000 marijuana plants were destroyed. This discovery led next day to another raid on a farm at Bourg, La. Here a crop of some 2,000 plants was found to be growing between rows of vegetables. The eight persons arrested confessed that their main source of income from this crop was in sales to boys and girls of high-school age.

With possibilities for such tremendous crops, grown secretly, gangdom has been hampered in its efforts to corner the profits of what has now become an enormous business. It is to be hoped that the menace of marijuana can be wiped out before it falls into the vicious protectorate of powerful members of the underworld.

But to crush this traffic we must first squarely face the facts. Unfortunately, while every state except one has laws to cope with the traffic, the powerful right arm which could support these states has been all but impotent. I refer to the United States government. There has been no national law against the growing, sale, or possession of marijuana.

As this is written a bill to give the federal government control over marijuana has been introduced in Congress by Representative Robert L. Doughton of North Carolina, Chairman of the House Ways and Means Committee. It has the backing of Secretary of the Treasury Morgenthau, who has under his supervision the various agencies of the United States Treasury Department, including the Bureau of Narcotics, through which Uncle Sam fights the dope evil. It is a revenue bill, modeled after other narcotic laws which make use of the taxing power to bring about regulation and control.

The passage of such a law, however, should not be the signal for the public to lean back, fold its hands, and decide that all danger is over. America now faces a condition in which a new, although ancient, narcotic has come to live next door to us, a narcotic that does not have to be smuggled into the country. This means a job of unceasing watchfulness by every police department and by every public-spirited civic organization. It calls for campaigns of education in every school, so that children will not be deceived by the wiles of peddlers, but will know of the insanity, the disgrace, the horror which marijuana can bring to its victim. And, above all, every citizen should keep constantly before him the real picture of the "reefer man"—not some funny fellow who, should he take the notion, could walk across the ocean, but—

In Los Angeles, Calif., a youth was walking along a downtown street after inhaling a marijuana cigarette. For many addicts, merely a portion of a "reefer" is enough to induce intoxication. Suddenly, for no reason, he decided that someone had threatened to kill him and that his life at that very moment was in danger. Wildly he looked about him. The only person in sight was an aged bootblack. Drug-crazed nerve centers conjured the innocent old shoe-shiner into a destroying monster. Mad with fright, the addict hurried to his room and got a gun. He killed the old man, and then, later, babbled his grief over what had been wanton, uncontrolled murder.

"I thought someone was after me," he said. "That's the only reason I did it. I had never seen the old fellow before. Something just told me to kill him!"

That's marijuana!

Chapter 69

Clinical Observations of Marijuana Users

In 1939 Dr. Walter Bromberg was in charge of a court psychiatric clinic in New York City. His research reports contain fewer fearful accounts of drug use than does most of the contemporary medical literature. In particular, he refuted the claim that marijuana use incited criminal behavior, a view widely held in the 1930s. Nevertheless, what Bromberg did assert about marijuana was disturbing enough. He concluded that the drug released inhibitions and stimulated impulsive actions, drawing a more aggressive image of the marijuana user than the one familiar to observers in the 1960s and later. These contrasting views provide an insight into the ability of prevailing cultural attitudes and concerns to affect the perception of drugs and drug users and, at times, to influence the direction of research and its interpretation.

Marihuana

A Psychiatric Study

Walter Bromberg

For almost ten years, marihuana smoking in the United States has engaged the attention of police officials, narcotic officers, prosecutors, judges and physicians. With its spread, the attention given marihuana in the press has increased. It is frequently a theme in contemporary literature; even the stage and screen have exploited its theatrical possibilities. It has been blamed in the press and by responsible officials for insanity, suicide and crime, especially among the youth of the country, and is fast attaining the position of a public enemy. In 1931 the International Narcotic Education Association in its Geneva convention acted to include marihuana (hashish) in an international treaty for the limitation of the distribution of narcotic drugs. The marihuana excise tax law was enacted by Congress and made effective Oct. 1, 1937. It makes the use of marihuana, except by qualified persons, illegal. The penal code, based on the uniform narcotic drug act in the public health law in New York, as in other states, classes marihuana (cannabis) with opium derivatives and cocaine, and its use or sale constitutes a crime.

In 1934 I reported eleven cases from the Bellevue Hospital of mental reactions induced by smoking marihuana and reviewed the literature on the subject. The present paper brings that material together and includes subsequent study of the problem and observations made since 1934.

The drug is a product of the flowering tops of the hemp plant (Cannabis americana or Cannabis sativa). In America the name marihuana, which is said to be a corruption of the Portuguese "maraguango," meaning intoxicant, is used. It has numerous picturesque names, such as muggles, reefers, Mary Warner, Indian hay, the weed and tea. The hemp plant, a tall bush with long green leaves, is cultivated for hemp fiber in the midwest and also grows wild throughout the nation. The method is to roll the dried flowering tops into cigarets. The leaves and flowering tops of the plant are covered by a resin whose composition is unknown. Government chemists, especially Blatt, Wollner and Matchett, found five fractions in cannabinol, the alleged active principle. The Beam test, hitherto regarded as specific in detecting the active principle chemically, has been found of no value. The chemistry of the drug needs and is undergoing thorough revision. However, for practical purposes, marihuana, hashish and cannabis may be considered synonymous.

Legend envelops the origin of the use of cannabis, and Walton has recently described its fascinating history. In the latter part of the nineteenth century and the decade beginning the twentieth century, there was a revival of interest in hashish as a substance for studying sense perception in laboratories of experimental psychology. S. Weir Mitchell, William James and others worked with it.

Recently marihuana has been alleged to be the frequent cause of crime, such as assault, murder, rape and robbery, and of suicides especially among young people. The Foreign Policy Association listed ten cases of atrocious crimes committed by persons under its influence. Frequent reference is made to a report by Eugene Stanley, district attorney of New Orleans, a hotbed of marihuana usage, in which he stated that, among 450 men indicated for major crime in New Orleans during 1930, 125 were marihuana addicts, slightly less than half the total number of murderers were addicts and from 18 to 20 per cent of all persons tried for larceny, robbery and assault were users of marihuana. The League of Nations subcommittee received a report from Dr. J. Bouquet, acknowledged to be a world expert on cannabis, in which he stated that "the use of cannabis, whether smoked or ingested in its various forms, undoubtedly gives rise to a form of addiction which has serious social consequences (abandonment of work, propensity to theft and crime, disappearance of reproductive power)."

The experience which forms the basis of this paper was gathered in the Bellevue Hospital and the Psychiatric Clinic of the Court of General Sessions (having jurisdiction over felonies in New York County) over a period of six years. Persons brought to the hospital are those showing overt mental symptoms; hence the vast proportion of marihuana smokers in New York City probably do not reach medical hands.

Psychiatric Observations

There has been considerable literature on the intoxication and insanity-producing effect of cannabis in papers from Asia, Europe and the United States. To sum up this material, it can be said that the syndromes are of three types: (*a*) intoxication, (*b*) toxic psychosis, with or without an admixture of other types of mental reactions (schizophrenic, manic-depressive), and, according to Eastern European and Asiatic observers, (*c*) chronic dementia and deterioration following prolonged use. Apparently the third type, a deteriorating process, has not been observed in American clinics.

My experiences with mental conditions following the use of marihuana indicate that there are two categories of mental reaction: (1) acute intoxication (marihuana psychosis), containing sensory, motor and subjective elements, lasting from several hours to several days, often with anxiety or hysterical reactions and transient panic states or depressions, and (2) toxic psychoses, including (*a*) those in which there are many admixtures of a disturbed sensorium with delusional and emotional reactions amounting to a psychosis, but with the common characteristic toxic signs, and (*b*) atypical functional psychoses which are initiated by marihuana or colored by marihuana in their symptoms but continue in the form of the underlying psychosis, the marihuana-induced state apparently representing an incipient stage in the psychosis. There were fourteen cases of acute intoxication and seventeen of toxic psychosis in our series.

1. *Acute Intoxication* (*Marihuana Psychosis*).—The distinction between acute intoxication due to marihuana and psychosis due to marihuana depends on the severity of the symptoms. Acute intoxication, induced by smoking from one to four cigarets, brings about after an interval varying from one half to five hours one or all of the following symptoms: an increase in motor activity, a feeling of excitement, mental confusion, disorientation, crowding of perception, elementary visual illusions and hallucinations, euphoria and talkativeness. In addition, numerous subjective experiences occur, such as increased speed of thought processes, a feeling of intellectual brilliance, change in time perception, various somatic feelings, hunger, dizziness, a feeling of swelling of the head, lightness of the extremities, a sensation of walking on air, lengthening of the limbs and sexual illusions. Usually the sexual excitement is caused by the fact that the possible sexual objects become extraordinarily desirable. It is not so much a matter of increased potency as of increased reaction to sexual fantasies and illusions. One patient said "I saw black and white women lying in bed with legs separated, as if expecting men . . . some women in the park with nothing on, doing nasty dances, moving their hips. I chased after them." Others stated that women appeared amazingly beautiful. One patient said "In the subway I felt very sexy. I wanted to touch every woman who passed."

The speeded-up physical motility has its counterpart in rapid speech. There is a feeling on the part of the subject that he is witty, even brilliant; his ideas flow quickly and words come readily to his tongue. Conclusions and answers seem to come to mind ready formed and surprisingly clear, without the effort of thinking.

This feeling of clarity is of course spurious. Actually the productions of the intoxicant are hard to follow, for when the subject wishes to explain what he has thought there is only confusion. The rapid flow of ideas gives a subjective impression of brilliance of thought and observation. The sense of increased speed of thinking apparently has an effect on memory; hence the confusion that appears when the subject tries to recall what was thought during the intoxication.

The smoker finds it pleasant to be with others and to impart his experiences to them. This is reflected in the fact that marihuana is ordinarily smoked at parties or in groups. It is felt that this need for a social setting is a reaction to an inner anxiety arising from the threat of bodily destruction implied in somatic illusions induced by marihuana. In the ordinary case of marihuana smoking, especially when the subject is used to the drug, this threat becomes converted to euphoria, which develops to uncontrollable fits of laughter. Nevertheless inquiry shows that almost every smoker is aware of definite uneasiness at the outset of the intoxication. The descriptions from smokers in Harlem and from experimental subjects agree on this point. In the words of a user of two years' standing, initiates "shrink together, feel tight inside and get frightened." After they smoke it more than once, the reality of these frightening somatic illusions becomes less. In occasional instances, and these are the cases which are apt to come to medical attention, the anxiety with regard to death, insanity, bodily deformity and bodily dissolution is startling. The patient is tense, nervous, frightened; a state of panic may develop. Often suicide or assaultive acts are the result. The anxiety state is so common in patients admitted to the hospital for uncomplicated marihuana psychosis that it can be considered part of the intoxication syndrome.

Notes taken on experimental subjects who were psychologically trained illustrate these points:

> The first subject smoked two cigarets within forty minutes. Immediately after the second a feeling of lightness in the vertex of the head was felt. The head was expanding; there was a feeling of mild excitement. Now the head felt heavy and there was a definite feeling of lengthening in the legs and a tension in the back muscles of the thigh. The head felt alternately light and heavy. There was a sensation as though the top of the head were lifted, with about a 4 inch increase in height, accompanied by optic images of skulls and skeletons. There was a feeling as of the arms rising up in the air. The subject was aware of a feeling of confusion. Suddenly he saw terrifying images of legs and arms in a dissecting room.

> The second subject smoked two cigarets. He said: "I feel a little euphoric at first, but with the first draw my heart feels faster and my eyes a little heavier. I feel myself perspiring all over and shaking. I can feel a slight dizziness. I feel weak; the dizziness has left and I am perspiring." (He was asked to walk around the room. He refused to do so and became negativistic.) "On looking back I remembered that I had sexual thoughts during the time of the experiment. Time seemed to pass in a peculiar way, there being a combination of fastness and slowness. I took my first inhalation a few minutes after 9, and when I looked at the clock and saw that it was 10 after 9 I was very much surprised because it seemed like hours. The whole experiment seems now as if it lasted much longer than it did. Walking home I

walked slowly in front of oncoming cars and felt a sense of recklessness connected with not being able to walk faster and not caring."

It is remarkable how much anxiety appears when one looks for experimental subjects among the public. The drug is popularly supposed to release aggressive and sexual impulses beyond the point of control; it is also regarded as being habit forming. The history and social connotation of hashish smoking strongly aids in the development of anxieties masking sexual fantasies and aggressive impulses of those who have not taken the drug. This has gone on almost to the point of mass hysteria. Walton has collected a great number of experiences of hashish users among literary and scientific men for the past century. The connotations regarding hashish have been absorbed by both the public and medical observers from these detailed reports, which feature voluptuous, languorous, supernatural and semi-delirious elements following the use of hashish. While such experiences are authentic, it is important for public officials and medically trained observers to realize the literary background from which earlier reports of hashish usage sprang.

In clinical material, as indicated, the effects of marihuana range from mild intoxications to transitory psychoses which require psychiatric aid. The effects vary and not all the symptoms occur in every case. . . .

The personality factor is of undoubted importance in such cases. After the toxic state passed off in those cases in which the intoxication reached deeply enough into the personality, a basic psychotic state developed. At times the toxic features are in the background, the personality reactions being predominant. The inner relationship between cannabis and the onset of a functional psychotic state is not always clear. The inner reaction to somatic sensation seems to be vital. Such reactions consisted of panic states which disappeared as soon as the stimulus (effects of the drug) faded. It's generally known in psychopathology that when the perception of one's own bodily sensations is disturbed or is liable to be profoundly affected psychologically. Disturbances in perception of the body model (körperscema), which is built up of kinesthetic, tactile, visual and other stimuli and integrated into the core of the personality, elicit some type of reaction. Such disturbances act as a blow to the ego, invoking defensive reactions of anxiety, apprehension and projection, which approach schizophrenia or are schizophrenic in their clinical manifestations. . . .

In some cases the drug makes relatively little difference in the content of the psychosis. It is for the clinician to determine how much marihuana influences the clinical picture. In South Africa, where dagga (the equivalent of marihuana) smoking is very widespread, a diagnosis of marihuana psychosis is made in the case of any "toxic psychosis in which there are very good grounds for assuming addiction to dagga smoking." It is felt that there should be more exact criteria, such as that outlined for a diagnosis of marihuana psychosis, by which I mean disorder sensorium, characteristic colored visual hallucinations, time changes and subjective and somatic feelings. One is apt to overestimate the place of marihuana in the causation of a psychotic picture. . . .

With psychopathic personalities, those with deep inferiorities, the use of drugs is a method of supporting the ego. Marihuana does not always produce the desirable effect. Apparently it is not strong enough to affect the problems which have involved the deeper layers of the personality. Such persons adopt heroin or morphine very soon after a short experience with marihuana. The experience of drug addicts seen at the Court of General Sessions confirms this. Persons addicted to heroin, morphine, cocaine or opium never return to cannabis. Such persons are admittedly psychopathic, in that they need an increment of drug to make their lives tolerable. . . .

Criminologic Aspects

The history of the use of cannabis, especially in the Old World, indicates the relation between the drug and violent crime. The English writer Peebles noted the high incidence in India of the use of hashish among the criminal insane. Of 652 cases studied, in 24.6 per cent the cause was found to be hashish. In Asia Minor and in northern Africa, among the Arabs, where the use of cannabis is high, it is conceded by officials that there is a direct relation between the drug and crime. Officials state that dagga (hemp) smokers in South Africa, predominantly natives, steal, lie and tend to moral deterioration. Of the dagga users, 37 per cent were dangerous and 13 per cent destructive to property, according to the history. In the south of this country (New Orleans) the incidence of marihuana addicts among major criminals is admittedly high. Sporadic reports from elsewhere in the country of murders and assaults due to marihuana appear in the press frequently. It is difficult to evaluate these statements, because of their uncritical nature. The bulletin prepared by the Foreign Policy Association lists ten cases "culled at random from the files of the U.S. Bureau of Narcotics" of murder and atrocious assault in which marihuana was directly responsible for the crime. Among the ten patients, the second, J. O., was described as having confessed how he murdered a friend and put his body in a trunk while under the influence of marihuana.

J. O. was examined in this clinic; although he was a psychopathic liar and possibly homosexual, there was no indication in the examination or history of the use of any drug. The investigation by the probation department failed to indicate use of the drug marihuana. The deceased, however, was addicted to heroin.

Our observations with respect to marihuana and crime were made in the Court of General Sessions over a period of five and a half years. The material in that court is limited as to residence to New York County, although it must be remembered that the offenders come from many sections of the country and are of many racial types. This is important, because the British investigators have noted in India that cannabis does not bring out the motor excitement or hysterical symptoms in Anglo-Saxon users that occur in natives. There are several other difficulties in collecting reliable material, on being the complete dependence on the history and statements of the prisoners without an opportunity for objective tests or other corroborative check, as in the case of other drugs, e.g. heroin or morphine. During routine interviews of some 17,000 offenders in six and a half years, several hundred have been found who had direct experience with marihuana. Their testimony checks with experimental results and clinical experiences with regard to the symptoms of intoxication, the absence of true addiction and the negative connection with major crime. Especially is this noteworthy among sexual offenders and in cases of assault or murder. The extravagant claims of defense attorneys and the press that crime is caused by addiction to marihuana demands careful scrutiny, at least in this jurisdiction. . . .

Of more than 16,000 prisoners, 200 were convicted on drug charges and found to be users of drugs although convicted of other charges. Cases of possession for sale are handled in the Court of General Sessions, which has jurisdiction over felonies.

Of this group of 200, sixty-seven were users of marihuana in some degree whether convicted of the crime of selling marihuana or of another crime. The remaining 133 offenders were users of morphine or heroin. It is vital to note again that the only measure of the use of marihuana is the statement of the offender. Selling or possession does not establish usage or its extent if present. On this score one naturally meets evasion and denial fairly consistently. The most reliable source of information is the persons arrested for other crimes and questioned in the routine course of psychiatric study, who have contact with the underworld.

Of the sixty-seven studied, forty-six were convicted of possession and sale of drugs and twenty-one on other charges. Of the twenty-one convicted of crimes other than the possession and sale of drugs, eight were convicted of burglary, five of grand larceny, three of robbery, two of assault, one each of petit larceny, forgery and first degree murder and none of sexual offenses. Burglary, grand larceny and robbery, then, account for sixteen of the twenty-one. There were but two sex cases involving sexual offenses among the marihuana cases, in both of which sodomy had occurred as a previous offense. In three cases the prisoners were what might be called constant users of marihuana. One had commenced the use of marihuana three years before; another, with a sixteen year record, indicated that marihuana had been used for fifteen years; the third referred to his use of marihuana as of "several years' duration." None of the offenders reported any lasting effects from marihuana. Questions as to the habit-forming nature of the drug were all answered in the negative.

In only nine cases of the sixty-seven was the criminal record found to commence with a drug charge, indicating that there was not in those cases a close relationship between drugs and the beginning of a career of crime. One must bear in mind that this can be only a presumptive conclusion, in that the offenders may have used drugs without being arrested and thus coming into official statistics.

Most of the narcotic cases in New York County are heard in the Court of Special Sessions, where misdemeanants are handled and where indictments on charges of the possession of drugs for use are returned. In the Court of Special Sessions in the same six year period, of approximately 75,000 indictments for all crimes, 6,000 resulted in convictions for the possession and use of drugs. Since neither the law, the district attorney nor the police department makes any distinction between the several kinds of narcotics in arraignments or indictments, there were no figures from which to estimate the number of users of marihuana as distinguished from the number of users of other drugs. A system of sampling the 6,000 cases was therefore adopted in order to furnish an approximate estimate of the total number of marihuana users who came into conflict with the law.

In this sampling the records of 1,500 offenders, or 25 per cent of the 6,000, were examined. Of these, 135 were charged in connection with marihuana. From this fact it was estimated that about 540 offenders, or 9 per cent of all drug offenders coming to the Court of Special Sessions in six years, were users of marihuana. In analyzing this sample of 135 cases, it was found that ninety-three offenders had no previous record, the previous charge or charges of eight concerned only drugs, five had records including drug charges and twenty-nine had records not including drug charges. Among those with longer records, that is, from four to seven previous arrests, none showed progression from the use of drugs to other crimes.

As measured by the succession of arrests and convictions in the Court of General Sessions (the only method of estimation), it can be said that drugs generally do not initiate criminal careers. Similarly, in the Court of Special Sessions, only 8 per cent of the offenders had previous charges of using drugs and 3.7 per cent had previous charges of drugs and other petty crimes. In the vast majority of cases in this group of 135, then, the earlier use of marihuana apparently did not predispose to crime, even that of using other drugs. Whether the first offenders charged with the use of marihuana go on to major crime is a matter of speculation. The expectancy of major crimes following the use of cannabis in New York County is small, according to these experiences.

Habituation

The problem of habituation to cannabis is of grave importance. It should be remembered that marihuana has been used in conjunction with morphine, heroin or cocaine. Occasionally an astute drug pedler will adulterate marihuana cigarets with morphine or heroin in order to retain his clientele. Such a situation came to notice at Bellevue Hospital, where a youth was admitted for addiction to heroin acquired in this manner. Hence care must be exercised in evaluating the question of habituation to marihuana to determine whether one is not dealing with adulterated cannabis.

The medical diagnosis of habituation can depend only on the accepted criteria of acquired tolerance and after-effects on withdrawal of the drug. Users of marihuana examined in the clinic invariably state that an increase in dosage is not necessary to achieve the desired effect as time goes on. The increase in cigaret consumption, if it occurs, is apparently related to how often the smoker wishes to experience the sensations produced. To my knowledge, the effects of withdrawal have never been systematically observed in a controlled environment. It has not been possible to observe satisfactorily marihuana users on their entrance into custody to establish their behavior after cessation of usage. For one thing, the law does not allow questioning of a defendant regarding his charge prior to trial. The fact that offenders brought up on marihuana charges do not request medical treatment on their incarceration (with its cessation of drug supply) argues for the absence of withdrawal symptoms. As is well known, users of morphine and opium become violently ill on being taken into custody and away from the source of their drug and are vociferous in their demands for treatment.

Nevertheless, the wide discrepancies between the reports of some jurisdictions and some physicians and those of the New York jurisdiction in the question of addiction to cannabis deserves thought. In the main, American authorities support the view that marihuana is not a habit-forming drug. Asiatic and European writers are not in accord with this opinion. It is worth recording that, because of difficulty in this court in proving marihuana to be a habit-forming drug (*People v. Williams*), the Law Revision Commission, appointed by the New York State Legislature, was requested to amend the Penal Code, section 1751, to read "narcotic" rather than "habit-forming" drug (March 26, 1938). The most that one can say on the basis of ascertainable facts is that prolonged use of marihuana constitutes a "sensual" addiction, in that the user wishes to experience again and again the ecstatic sensations and feelings which the drug produces. Unlike addiction to morphine, which is biochemically as well as psychologically determined, prolonged use of marihuana is essentially in the service of the hedonistic elements of the personality.

Psychiatry of Offenders

It would be worth while to study the individual personalities of those offenders who had used the drug. All were given psychiatric examinations; of the sixty-seven, none were found to be psychotic. Three were said to have a neurosis, by which is meant a definite clinical neurosis or underlying anxiety, inferiority reactions and character defects clinically demonstrable. The diagnosis for twelve was psychopathic personality with drug addiction involving use of other drugs, and for one was psychopathic personality of the paranoid type.

The others presented personality difficulties of varying types, being recognized as the aggressive type, emotionally unstable type, maladjusted adolescent type, immature type, egocentric type, submissive type and adynamic type. The remainder showed no personality defects other than the remote effects of a low cultural environment. None were considered mentally defective. The main group were within the limits of average intelligence. The psychologic status of the group was high average intelligence one, average intelligence forty-one, dull normal intelligence twenty-one and borderline intelligence four.

Comment

... The marihuana psychoses reported in the American literature vary only quantitatively from those reported elsewhere, except that cases have not been reported of dementia as described in the Orient. When the intoxication initiates a functional psychosis or is part of an incipient psychosis, obviously the personality factors and the emotional reaction of the patient to the symptoms are more important than the purely physiologic cerebral effects of cannabis. In other words, every case of marihuana intoxication presents a complex picture which must be studied in the light of the individual case. The important problem of suicidal attempts following the use of marihuana has been indicated in the cases reported to represent the response to attacks of anxiety and panic reaction induced by the drug. Unquestionably marihuana is a dangerous drug from this point of view.

The physiologic psychology involved in use of the drug is of deep interest but will not be entered into here. I have discussed this elsewhere.

Summary

1. The rise of popular interest in the influence of marihuana on insanity, crime and addiction to drugs during the last ten years in many quarters of America points to the usefulness of a psychiatric review of the problem.

2. In thirty-one cases of insanity following the use of marihuana (marihuana psychosis) observed at the Bellevue Hospital, including eleven reported in 1934, the condition was classified as (1) acute intoxication, lasting from hours to days (fourteen cases), and (2) toxic psychoses, lasting from weeks to months (seventeen cases); often the toxic picture was superimposed on a basic functional mental disturbance, such as schizophrenia.

3. Marihuana is a contraband preparation of the hemp plant (Cannabis sativa) which contains the active principle cannabis. The common use is in cigarets. Smoking produces characteristic symptoms. It affects the emotional sphere, inducing euphoria and less commonly anxiety and apprehension, and the subjective world, involving feelings of unreality and aberration of the time sense. It induces feelings of bodily change, such as lengthening of the limbs and swelling of the head; it influences the motility, causing restlessness and excitement in varying degrees in different persons, and it produces mental confusion with possible visual illusions and hallucinations.

The basic personality of the smoker appears to be a vital factor in the development of a marihuana psychosis. Countless persons use marihuana without the development of an observable mental condition. Occasionally use of the drug represents the incipient stage of a functional psychosis. In such cases there appears to be an intimate relation between the dissociation in the patient's personality and the subjective effects of the drug, which tend to when the dissociation and produce a psychosis. In the acute intoxication, no permanent effect is observable by psychiatric examination after the effects wear off in from one to three days.

5. In sixty-seven cases involving marihuana from the Court of General Sessions, New York County, it was found in general that early use of the drug apparently did not predispose to crime. No positive relation could be found between violent crime and the use of marihuana in the cases observed in the Psychiatric Clinic. No cases of murder or sexual crimes due to marihuana were established.

6. The reported lack of increased tolerance and the absence of demonstrable withdrawal symptoms argues against the theory that marihuana is habit forming. The final solution of the problem of addiction waits on further experience and controlled experiment. The present study allows at this time only the statement that the use of marihuana is a "sensual addiction" in the service of the hedonistic elements of the personality.

The La Guardia Report

A year after the passage of the Marihuana Tax Act of 1937, Mayor Fiorello La Guardia of New York City invited the New York Academy of Medicine to organize a study of marijuana. The academy was asked to sort through the many claims about the drug and provide a scientific basis for warning about the dangers of use. The FBN provided marijuana for the study, which explored several areas of concern about marijuana, including the extent of use in the city, presence among schoolchildren, relationship with criminals and criminal behavior, effect on mental and physical functioning and physiology, effect on behavior, and addictiveness.

When it became clear that the study, completed in 1941, would conclude that marijuana was much less dangerous than the FBN asserted, the bureau did what it could to minimize its impact. Obviously, the La Guardia Report, as it was called, struck at the core of the FBN's strategy: to paint marijuana in such obnoxious terms that no one would even try it once. Publication of the report did not take place until 1944 and the media gave it little notice, so public awareness of the conclusions of this study was quite limited.

The report was attacked by the Journal of the American Medical Association *in a 1945 editorial. The style of the editorial reads like an Anslinger essay, but it is unsigned, so we cannot be sure of the author. In any case, for the highly regarded* JAMA *to counter the La Guardia Report was a great boost to the FBN cause. Little more was heard of the La Guardia Report until marijuana returned in the 1960s, and supporters used the 1944 report to argue for lowering or eliminating penalties for use.*

THE MARIHUANA PROBLEM IN THE CITY OF NEW YORK

Mayor's Committee on Marihuana

The widespread publicity describing the dangerous effects of marihuana usage in New Orleans and other southern cities, especially among school children, had its repercussion in the city of New York, and some anxiety was experienced as to the possibility that similar conditions were present or might develop here. Because of this, Mayor La Guardia asked The New York Academy of Medicine for an opinion as to the advisability of studying the whole marihuana problem. The Academy recommended that such a study be made and outlined its scope in general terms. Following this, the Mayor appointed a committee empowered to make the study. This committee consisted of two internists, three psychiatrists, two pharmacologists, and one public health expert, and the Commissioners of Correction, of Health, and of Hospitals, and the Director of the Division of Psychiatry of the Department of Hospitals, ex officio.

The Committee formulated a plan for the study, and the expenses were arranged for through grants by the New York Foundation, the Friedsam Foundation and the Commonwealth Fund. The study was begun in April 1940.

The first phase of the study concerned the extent of marihuana smoking in New York City, its incidence among school children, its relation to crime, and its effects on individuals using it. For obtaining this information, the Commissioner of Police assigned to the Committee six police officers, four men and two women, who served as "plain clothes" investigators. These investigators circulated in the districts in which marihuana appeared to be most widely used, particularly Harlem, associated with marihuana users, and found out as much as possible about sources of supply, means of distribution, and effects of marihuana on users. Included in this survey were a careful watch on school children in both grade and high schools and interviews with school principals.

As a result of this investigation the Committee came to the conclusion that marihuana distribution and usage is found mainly in Harlem, the population of which is predominately Negro and Latin-American, and to a less extent in the Broadway area extending from 42nd to 59th Streets. The local supply comes from individual peddlers and from "tea-pads," which are establishments for marihuana smoking. There are no figures available as to the number of marihuana users in New York City, but a conservative estimate is that there are some 500 peddlers and 500 "tea-pads" in Harlem.

The marihuana users with whom contact was made in this study were persons without steady employment. The majority fall in the age group of 20 to 30 years. Idle and lacking initiative, they suffer boredom and seek distraction. Smoking is indulged in for the sake of conviviality and sociability and because it affords a temporary feeling of adequacy in meeting disturbing situations.

The confirmed user smokes from 6 to 10 cigarettes a day. The effects are easily recognized by the smoker, the desirable stage being what is known as "high." When this is reached, the smoking is stopped. If a "too high" state is reached, the taking of beverages such as beer or sweet soda pop, or a cold bath are considered effective countermeasures.

In most instances, the behavior of the smoker is of a friendly, sociable character. Aggressiveness and belligerency are not commonly seen, and those showing such traits are not allowed to remain in "tea-pads."

The marihuana user does not come from the hardened criminal class and there was found no direct relationship between the commission of crimes of violence and marihuana. "Tea-pads" have no direct association with houses of prostitution, and marihuana itself has no specific stimulant effect in regard to sexual desires.

There is no organized traffic in marihuana among New York City school children, and any smoking that occurs in this group is limited to isolated instances.

Smoking marihuana can be stopped abruptly with no resulting mental or physical distress comparable to that of morphine withdrawal in morphine addicts.

The second division of the study was the clinical one, the purpose of which was to ascertain the effects of marihuana on the individual user. There were two phases of this work, the general medical study and the psychological study. Wards in the municipal hospital on Welfare Island (now known as Goldwater Memorial Hospital) were made available by the Commissioner of Hospitals. The subjects for the study were drawn from the prison population at the Penitentiary on Riker's Island, as arranged by the Commissioner of Correction. They were under sentence for terms varying from three months to three years, most of them for what would be called minor criminal offenses. They volunteered for the study, the purpose and procedure of which had been fully explained to them. They were kept in the hospital in groups of 6 to 10, for a period of study of approximately a month. The subjects afforded the sample especially desired, for over half of them were marihuana smokers and the others of the class from which marihuana smokers come. The personnel conducting the study consisted of a physician in charge, with an assistant physician, three psychologists, and a secretary. The subjects were under the constant supervision of the medical staff, nurses and attendants.

In studying the effects of marihuana on the 77 subjects selected for the study, the drug was given either in the form of an extract taken by mouth, or was smoked in cigarettes. The dose given to produce definite systemic reactions ranged from a minimal one of 1 cc. to a maximum of 22 cc. of the extract, and from 1 to 10 cigarettes. The effects of smoking appeared immediately and usually passed off in from one to three or four hours. Those from the extract came on more gradually and persisted for a longer time, in some instances for twenty-four hours or more. As the dose for any individual was increased, the effects usually were more marked and of longer duration, but the effect of any given dose varied with the individual subjects.

Although some of the subjects became restless and talkative under marihuana influence, a mental state characterized by a sense of well-being, relaxation and unawareness of surroundings, followed by drowsiness, was present in most instances when the subject was left undisturbed. Generally, there was observed a difficulty in focusing and sustaining mental attention. In company, the subjects were lively and given to talkativeness, fits of laughter and good-natured joking. The pleasurable effects, classed as euphoric, were frequently interrupted or re-placed by a state of apprehension of varying degree.

In a limited number of the subjects there were alterations in behavior giving rise to antisocial expression. This was shown by unconventional acts not permit-ted in public, anxiety reactions, opposition and antagonism, and eroticism. Ef-fects such as these would be considered conducive to acts of violence. However, any tendency toward violence was expressed verbally and not by physical actions, and in no case was restraint by force needed.

In addition to its effect on mental states, physical symptoms resulting from the administration of marihuana were recorded. Of these, tremor, ataxia, dizziness, a sensation of floating in space, dilation of the pupils, dryness of the throat, nausea and vomiting, an urge to urinate, hunger, and a desire for sweets were the most striking. Tremor and ataxia and dizziness were of the greatest frequency. These symptoms may be disturbing to the subject, and if marked enough, cause anxiety and interrupt the euphoric state.

On some occasions, instead of the marihuana concentrate, preparations supplied by Dr. Roger Adams were given. These were tetrahydrocannabinol, made from cannabidiol, corresponding to a principle found in the plant, a synthetic tetrahydrocannabinol, an isomer of the natural one, and a synthetic hexyl-hydrocannabinol. They all produced effects similar in character to those from the concentrate. Their relative potency could be determined only approximately. The rough estimate was that 1 cc. of the concentrate had as its equivalent 15 mg. of the natural tetrahydrocannabinol, 60 mg. of the hexyl-hydrocannabinol, and 120 mg. of the synthetic tetrahydrocannabinol.

In the total group studied, what are known as psychotic episodes occurred in 9 of the subjects. In 6 instances, they were of short duration, persisting for from three to ten hours, and were characterized by mental confusion and excitement of a delirious nature with periods of laughter and of anxiety. These effects correspond to those often reported in marihuana literature and are examples of acute marihuana intoxication which in many ways is similar to acute alcoholic intoxication. In the other 3 cases, one subject had a mild psychotic reaction after smoking one cigarette. Later, a typical psychotic state came on four hours after the subject had taken tetrahydrocannabinol and persisted for six days. This subject subsequently was found to have a history of epileptic attacks so that the psychotic episode was probably related to epilepsy. The second subject had previously been a drug addict. She was given marihuana on several occasions, at times showing only euphoric effects and other times confusion and worriment. She left the hospital depressed and moody, and a week later was committed to a State hospital with the diagnosis of psychosis. After six months, she was discharged as cured. The third subject showed no unusual effects of marihuana which was given on several occasions during his stay at the hospital. Some days after his return to the penitentiary he developed a psychotic state diagnosed "Psychosis with psychopathic personality." This was considered an example of what is known as "prison psychosis," a condition which has been noted in persons emotionally unstable subjected to the depressing atmosphere of prison incarceration. The precise role of marihuana in the psychotic states in the three unstable subjects is not clear. In the case of the second and third subject, the fact that they were sent back to prison to complete their sentences must be considered an important if not the main factor in bringing on the psychosis.

In the clinical study of the effect of marihuana on functions of various organs of the body, there were found an increase in pulse rate and blood pressure and an increase in blood sugar and metabolic rate. No changes were found in the circulation rate and vital capacity. Tests on renal and liver function were negative. No changes were found in blood counts and hemoglobin, or blood nitrogen, calcium and phosphorus concentrations. The electrocardiogram showed no abnormalities which could be attributed to direct action on the heart, and from a few observations made, marihuana appeared to be without effect on gastric motility and secretion. The positive results found, as well as the occurrence of nausea and vomiting, an increase in the frequency of urination, and the sensation of hunger and an increase in appetite, may be considered results of central nervous excitation, producing peripheral effects through the autonomic nervous system.

The psychological study, planned and carried out by experienced psychologists, was concomitant with the general medical one and was devoted to determining the effects of marihuana on psychomotor responses and certain special abilities, on intellectual functioning, and on emotional reactions and personality structure.

For psychomotor effects, procedures were followed which gave records affording quantitative measurement. Static equilibrium and hand steadiness were the functions most strongly affected by marihuana. The body swaying was general in direction and not greater in one axis than in others. These effects came on during the first hour after the extract was given, reached a peak in about four hours, and persisted for some eight hours. After smoking, the effects came on much sooner—within a few minutes—and were of shorter duration, about three hours. Complex hand and foot reactions showed impairment, but simple reaction time, the strength of grip, speed of tapping, auditory acuity and musical ability, and estimation of short time intervals and small linear distances were unchanged. The findings in the women corresponded to those in the male subjects. In both groups there was marked individual variability, irrespective of dosage.

It was found that marihuana in an effective dose impairs intellectual functioning in general. Included under this heading are adverse effects on speed and accuracy in performance, on the application of acquired knowledge, on carrying out routine tasks, on memory, and on capacity for learning.

Marihuana does not change the basic personality structure of the individual. It lessens inhibition and this brings out what is latent in his thoughts and emotions but it does not evoke responses which would otherwise be totally alien to him. It induces a feeling of self-confidence, but this is expressed in thought rather than in performance. There is, in fact, evidence of a diminution in physical activity. While suggestibility may be increased by small doses, larger ones tend to induce a negativistic attitude.

From the study as a whole, it is concluded that marihuana is not a drug of addiction, comparable to morphine, and that if tolerance is acquired, this is of a very limited degree. Furthermore those who have been smoking marihuana for a period of years showed no mental or physical deterioration which may be attributed to the drug.

The lessening of inhibitions and repression, the euphoric state, the feeling of adequacy, the freer expression of thoughts and ideas, and the increase in appetite for food brought about by marihuana suggest therapeutic possibilities. From limited observations on addicts undergoing morphine withdrawal and on certain types of psychopathic disturbances, the impression was gained that marihuana had beneficial effects, but much more extensive and controlled study is required for definite conclusions to be drawn concerning therapeutic usage. It should be borne in mind that the effects of marihuana, more than in the case of other drugs, are quite variable in different individuals and in the same one at different times.

The chapter on the pharmacology of marihuana, prepared by Dr. Loewe, reviews the results of collaborative work of three laboratories (The Pharmacological Laboratory at the Cornell Medical College, the William Albert Noyes Laboratory at the University of Illinois, and the Laboratory of the Bureau of Narcotics at Washington, D.C.) which led to the discovery of the active principles, the elucidation of their origin, and the assembling of data on the relationship between chemical structure and biological activity. The chapter is introduced by a survey of the geographical distribution and botanical relationships of plants with marihuana activity.

The principles involved in bioassay are discussed and a method for marihuana assay described. The synthetic tetrahydrocannabinol of Adams was taken as the standard of reference and the characteristic reaction of ataxia in dogs measured quantitatively for the degree of activity. By this method the potency of samples and preparations of marihuana and of natural and synthetic principles has been determined and relationships between chemical structure and pharmacological activity elucidated.

The main components which have been isolated from marihuana oil containing the active principles are cannabidiol, cannabinol and isomeric tetrahydrocannabinols. The first two, but not the last, have been obtained as crystalline substances. The chemical structure and synthesis of these compounds have been described by Adams.

The typical effects of marihuana on man are ascribed to actions on the central nervous system. In dogs, the characteristic effect is ataxia. A delayed increase in pulse rate, a decrease in respiratory rate and blood pressure, and retching and vomiting were also observed. These effects are produced by tetrahydrocannabinol, but not by cannabinol or cannabidiol. A derivative of the latter, tetrahydrocannabidiol, after a latent period of from thirty to seventy minutes following intravenous injection, had a specific convulsant action on the dog.

In rabbits a characteristic effect of marihuana extracts is corneal areflexia. This is also not produced by cannabidiol or cannobinol but does occur after tetrahydrocannabinol. However, impure oil mixtures have this action to a greater extent, from which it is suggested that a third unknown principle is present in the plant.

Cannabidiol has a synergistic hypnotic action with pernoston in mice. Neither cannabinol nor the synthetic tetrahydrocannabidiols had this effect.

The ataxia action of marihuana was considerably increased by a central stimulant, benzedrine.

No evidence was found of an acquired tolerance for the drug.

In examination of the data presented in the detailed clinical study it is seen that the effects reported were in the main those produced by the extract of marihuana taken by mouth. With the extract, the absorption is gradual and the action persists as long as the active principles are circulating throughout the body. The doses given were fixed ones and once taken the effects were beyond the subjects' control. Giving the extract thus afforded a longer period for study and insured greater accuracy in dosage. In New York, as far as is known, marihuana is rarely if ever taken in this form but is smoked in cigarettes. However, it is shown in the study that the effects from smoking correspond in kind to those from the extract. The difference is that, in smoking, the effects come on promptly and are of much shorter duration. How marked the reaction becomes depends on the number of cigarettes smoked and this is entirely under the subjects' control. The sensations desired are pleasurable ones—a feeling of contentment, inner satisfaction, free play of imagination. Once this stage is reached, the experienced user realizes that with further smoking the pleasurable sensations will be changed to unpleasant ones and so takes care to avoid this.

THE JOURNAL OF THE AMERICAN MEDICAL ASSOCIATION ATTACKS THE LA GUARDIA REPORT

For many years medical scientists have considered cannabis a dangerous drug. Nevertheless, a book called "Marihuana Problems" by the New York City Mayor's Committee on Marihuana submits an analysis by seventeen doctors of tests on 77 prisoners and, on this narrow and thoroughly unscientific foundation, draws sweeping and inadequate conclusions which minimize the harmfulness of marihuana. Already the book has done harm. One investigator has described some tearful parents who brought their 16 year old son to a physician after he had been detected in the act of smoking marihuana. A noticeable mental deterioration had been evident for some time even to their lay minds. The boy said he had read an account of the La Guardia Committee report and that this was his justification for using marihuana. He read in *Down Beat*, a musical journal, an analysis of this report under the caption "Light Up Gates, Report Finds 'Tea' a Good Kick."

A criminal lawyer for marihuana drug pedlers has already used the La Guardia report as a basis to have defendants set free by the court.

The value of the conclusions is destroyed by the fact that the experiments were conducted on 77 confined criminals. Prisoners were obliged to be content with the quantities of drug administered. Antisocial behavior could not have been noticed, as they were prisoners. At liberty some of them would have given free rein to their inclinations and would probably not have stopped at the dose producing "the pleasurable principle." A recent tragedy, the case of the hotel bell boy who killed a federal guard in Oklahoma City while under the influence of marihuana, is more eloquent testimony concerning the dangers of the drug.

The report states that the relation between marihuana and crime is unfounded. This opinion, based on tests of 77 prisoners, denies much available evidence. Kolb, nationally known addiction expert, after reading the report stated "one may say of such a drug that, if it were abused as alcohol is abused, it might be an important cause of crimes and other misdemeanors." The annual reports of the League of Nations are filled with cases on the relation between marihuana and crime. Likewise the recent article which appeared in the December 1944 issue of *War Medicine* entitled "The Marihuana Addict in the Army," by Capt. Eli Marcovitz and Capt. Henry J. Meyers, is a devastating refutation of the information contained in the La Guardia report.

The report proposes the use of marihuana in the treatment of drug addiction and chronic alcoholism. Bouquet, the League of Nations expert, and others agree with Kolb that this proposal enters dangerous territory and that the result can only be the substitution of one addiction for another.

The book states unqualifiedly to the public that the use of this narcotic does not lead to physical, mental or moral degeneration and that permanent deleterious effects from its continued use were not observed on 77 prisoners. This statement has already done great damage to the cause of law enforcement. Public officials will do well to disregard this unscientific, uncritical study, and continue to regard marihuana as a menace wherever it is purveyed.

Chapter 71

Recommending a "Discouragement Policy"

Marijuana use seemed to explode in the 1960s. One of the goals of the Comprehensive Drug Abuse Prevention and Control Act of 1970 was to require a reevaluation of marijuana from the ground up — its nature as a mood-altering substance, the demography of its use, and what should be done about it. In part for that purpose, Congress and the president established a National Commission on Marihuana and Drug Abuse.

The first report of the commission, issued in March 1972, dealt with marijuana. Its most noteworthy conclusion was that marijuana use should be "decriminalized," that is, the individual user should not be criminally liable, although sellers, those growing the plant for sale, and any others in the chain of sales still would be subject to criminal punishment. This recommendation so angered President Nixon that he refused to receive the report publicly, in spite of the fact that the chair of the commission was a Republican governor, Raymond P. Shafer. The president vowed that marijuana use would not become legal during his tenure. The commission also instituted a national survey of drug use, which would become institutionalized and which still continues.

Marijuana: A Signal of Misunderstanding

National Commission on Marihuana and Drug Abuse

Implementing the Discouragement Policy

Choice of this social control policy does not automatically dictate any particular legal implementation. . . . there is a disturbing tendency among participants in the marihuana debate to assume that a given statement of the drug's effects, its number of users or its social impact compels a particular statutory scheme.

Law does not operate in a social vacuum, and it is only *one* of the institutional mechanisms which society can utilize to implement its policies. Consequently, the evaluation of alternative legal approaches demands not only logic but also a delicate assessment of the mutual relationship between the law and other institutions of social control, such as the church, the family and the school.

The Role of Law in Effective Social Control

... A preference for individual productivity underlies this society's opposition to indiscriminate drug use; the fact that so few of the 24 million Americans who have tried marihuana use it, or have used it, irresponsibly, testifies to the extent to which they have internalized that value.

The hypothesis that widespread irresponsibility would attend freer availability of marihuana suggests not that a restrictive policy is in order but rather that a basic premise of our free society is in doubt. We note that the escalation thesis, used as an argument *against* marihuana rather than as a tool for understanding individual behavior, is really a manifestation of skepticism about individual vulnerabilities. For example, one-half of the public agreed with the statement that "if marihauna were made legal, it would make drug addicts out of ordinary people."

At the same time, we do feel that the threat of excessive use is most potent with the young. In fact, we think *all* drug use should continue to be discouraged among the young, because of possible adverse effects on psychological development and because of the lesser ability of this part of the population to discriminate between limited and excessive use. . . .

The inclination of so many young people to experiment with drugs is a reflection of a so-called successful socialization process on one hand, and of society's ambivalence to the use of drugs on the other. . . .

This nation tries very hard to instill in its children independence, curiosity and a healthy self-assurance. These qualities guarantee a dynamic, progressive society. Where drugs are concerned, however, we have relied generally on authoritarianism and on obedience. Drug education has generally been characterized by overemphasis of scare tactics. Some segments of the population have been reluctant to inform for fear of arousing curiosity in young minds. Where drugs are concerned, young people are simply supposed to nod and obey.

This society has always been and continues to be ambivalent about the non-medical (in the strict sense) use of drugs. And this ambivalence does not escape our children. If we can come to grips with this issue, we might convince our youth that the curiosity that is encouraged in other aspects of our culture is undesirable where drugs are concerned.

The law is at best a highly imperfect reflection of drug policy. The laws proscribing sale of tobacco to minors are largely ignored. Prohibitions of sale of alcohol to minors are enforced sporadically. As to marihuana, there are areas throughout this nation where possession laws are not enforced at all. In other sections, such proscriptions are strictly enforced, with no apparent decrease in marihuana use.

As a guiding doctrine for parents and children, the law is certainly confusing when it imposes widely varying punishments in different states, and even in different courts of the same state, all for use of the same substance, marihuana. That marihuana use can be treated as a petty offense in one state and a felony in another is illogical and confusing to even the most sincere of parents.

The law is simply too blunt an instrument to manifest the subtle distinctions we draw between the motivations and the circumstances of use. At the same time, legal status carries a certain weight of its own, and other institutions must take account of the law in performing their functions.

In legally implementing our recommended social policy, we seek to maximize the ability of our schools, churches and families to be open and honest in discussing all drugs, including marihuana. The law must assist, not impede. In this respect, we note with concern the counterproductive tendency in our society to seek simple solutions to complex problems. Since the statutory law is a simple tool, the tendency in our society to look to the law for social control is particularly strong.

We have discussed the four basic social policy objectives of elimination, discouragement, neutrality and approval of marihuana use and have selected discouragement of use, with emphasis on prevention of heavy and very heavy use, as our generalized aim. We have considered three legal responses, each with a wide range of alternatives:

1. Total Prohibition
2. Partial Prohibition
3. Regulation.

Total Prohibition

The distinctive feature of a total prohibition scheme is that all marihuana-related behavior is prohibited by law. Under the total prohibition response now in force in every state and at the federal level, cultivation, importation, sale, gift or other transfer, and possession are all prohibited acts. In 11 states and the District of Columbia, simply being present knowingly in a place where marihuana is present is also prohibited; and many states prohibit the possession of pipes or other smoking paraphernalia. For our purposes, the key feature of the total prohibition approach is that even possession of a small amount in the home for personal use is prohibited by criminal law.

From the very inception of marihuana control legislation, this nation has utilized a policy of a total prohibition, far more comprehensive than the restrictions established during the prohibition of alcohol.

Until recent years, society was operating under an eliminationist policy. The exaggerated beliefs about the drug's effects, social impact, and user population virtually dictated this legal approach. During this entire period, total prohibition was sought through the use of heavier and heavier penalties until even first-time possession was a felony in every jurisdiction, and second possession offenses generally received a mandatory minimum sentence without parole or probation. Yet the last few years have seen society little by little abandoning the eliminationist policy in favor of a containment policy.

Under the total prohibition umbrella, this containment policy has been implemented by a unique patchwork of legislation, informal prosecutorial policy and judicial practice. Possession is now almost everywhere a misdemeanor. Although some term of incarceration remains as a penalty for possessors, it is generally not meted out to young first offenders or to possessors of small amounts. Instead, most such offenders are dismissed or informally diverted to agencies outside the criminal system by those within the system who are trying to help them avoid the stigma of a criminal record.

Offenders who are processed within the criminal justice system generally receive fines and/or probation. In many jurisdictions, enforcement officials make little or no effort to enforce possession proscriptions, concentrating instead on major trafficking. Possessors are generally arrested only when they are indiscreet or when marihuana is found incident to questioning or apprehension resulting from some other violation. From our surveys, state and federal, we have found that only minimal effort is made to investigate marihuana possession cases.

Such a tendency is a reflection of the adoption of a containment policy. By acting only when marihuana appears above ground, enforcement officials are helping to keep its use underground. The shift away from the elimination policy has been matched by a similar shift in legal implementation, but the distinctive feature of the total prohibition scheme still remains: all marihuana-related behavior, including possession for personal use within the home, is prohibited by criminal law.

Is such a response an appropriate technique for achieving the social control policy we outlined above? The key question for our purposes is whether total criminal prohibition is the most suitable or effective way to discourage use and whether it facilitates or inhibits a concentration on the reduction and treatment of irresponsible use. We are convinced that total prohibition frustrates both of these objectives for the following reasons.

1. Application of the Criminal Law to Private Possession Is Philosophically Inappropriate

With possession and use of marihuana, we are dealing with a form of behavior which occurs generally in private where a person possesses the drug for his own use. The social impact of this conduct is indirect, arising primarily in cases of heavy or otherwise irresponsible use and from the drug's symbolic aspects. We do not take the absolutist position that society is philosophically forbidden from criminalizing any kind of "private" behavior. The phrase "victimless crimes," like "public health hazard," has become a rhetorical excuse for avoiding basic social policy issues. We have chosen a discouragement policy on the basis of our evaluation of the actual and potential individual and social impact of marihuana use. Only now that we have done so can we accord appropriate weight to the nation's philosophical preference for individual privacy.

On the basis of this evaluation we believe that the criminal law is too harsh a tool to apply to personal possession even in the effort to discourage use. It implies an overwhelming indictment of the behavior which we believe is not appropriate. The actual and potential harm of use of the drug is not great enough to justify intrusion by the criminal law into private behavior, a step which our society takes only with the greatest reluctance.

2. Application of the Criminal Law Is Constitutionally Suspect

... While the judiciary is the governmental institution most directly concerned with the protection of individual liberties, all policy-makers have a responsibility to consider our constitutional heritage when framing public policy. Regardless of whether or not the courts would overturn a prohibition of possession of marihuana for personal use in the home, we are necessarily influenced by the high place traditionally occupied by the value of privacy in our constitutional scheme.

Accordingly, we believe that government must show a compelling reason to justify invasion of the home in order to prevent personal use of marihuana. We find little in marihuana's effects or in its social impact to support such a determination. Legislators enacting Prohibition did not find such a compelling reason 40 years ago; and we do not find the situation any more compelling for marihuana today.

3. Total Prohibition Is Functionally Inappropriate

Apart from the philosophical and constitutional constraints outlined above, a total prohibition scheme carries with it significant institutional costs. Yet it contributes very little to the achievement of our social policy. In some ways it actually inhibits the success of that policy.

The primary goals of a prudent marihuana social control policy include preventing irresponsible use of the drug, attending to the consequences of such use, and deemphasizing use in general. Yet an absolute prohibition of possession and use inhibits the ability of other institutions to contribute actively to these objectives. For example, the possibility of criminal prosecution deters users who are experiencing medical problems from seeking assistance for fear of bringing attention to themselves. In addition, the illegality of possession and use creates difficulties in achieving an open, honest educational program, both in the schools and in the home.

In terms of the social policy objective of discouraging use of the drug, the legal system can assist that objective in three ways: first, by deterring people from use; second, by symbolizing social opposition to use; and finally, by cutting off supply of the drug.

The present illegal status of possession has not discouraged an estimated 24 million people from trying marihuana or an estimated eight million from continuing to use it. Our survey of the country's state prosecuting attorneys shows that 53% of them do not believe that the law has more than a minimal deterrent effect in this regard. Moreover, if the present trend toward passive enforcement of the marihuana law continues, the law ultimately will deter only indiscreet use, a result achieved as well by a partial prohibition scheme and with a great deal more honesty and fairness.

A major attraction of the law has been its symbolic value. Yet, society can symbolize its desire to discourage marihuana use in many other, less restrictive ways. The warning labels on cigarette packages serve this purpose, illustrating that even a regulatory scheme could serve a discouragement policy. During Prohibition, the chosen statutory implementation symbolized society's opposition to the use of intoxicating beverages; yet, most jurisdictions did not think it necessary to superimpose a proscription of possession for personal use in the home.

Finally, prohibiting possession for personal use has no substantive relation to interdicting supply. A possession penalty may make enforcement of proscriptions against sale a little easier, but we believe this benefit is of minimal importance in light of its costs. . . .

In addition to the misallocation of enforcement resources, another consequence of prohibition against possession for personal use is the social cost of criminalizing large numbers of users. Our empirical study of enforcement of state and federal marihuana laws indicates that almost all of those arrested are between the ages of 18 and 25, most have jobs or are in school, and most have had no prior contact with the criminal justice system. The high social cost of stigmatizing such persons as criminals is now generally acknowledged by the public at large as well as by those in the criminal justice system. . . .

A final cost of the possession laws is the disrespect which the laws and their enforcement engender in the young. Our youth cannot understand why society chooses to criminalize a behavior with so little visible ill-effect or adverse social impact, particularly when so many members of the law enforcement community also question the same laws. These young people have jumped the fence and found no cliff. And the disrespect for the possession laws fosters a disrespect for all law and the system in general.

On top of all this is the distinct impression among the youth that some police may use the marihuana laws to arrest people they don't like for other reasons, whether it be their politics, their hair style of their ethnic background. Whether or not such selectivity actually exists, it is perceived to exist.

For all these reasons, we believe that the possession offense is of little functional benefit to the discouragement policy and carries heavy social costs, not the least of which is disrespect and cynicism among some of the young. Accordingly, even under our policy of discouraging marihuana use, the better method is persuasion rather than prosecution. Additionally, with the sale and use of more hazardous drugs on the increase, and crimes of violence escalating, we do not believe that the criminal justice system can afford the time and the costs of implementing the marihuana possession laws. Since these laws are not mandatory in terms of achieving the discouragement policy, law enforcement should be allowed to do the job it is best able to do: handling supply and distribution.

A criminal fine or similar penalty for possession has been suggested as a means of alleviating some of the more glaring costs of a total prohibitory approach yet still retaining the symbolic disapproval of the criminal law. However, most of the objections raised above would still pertain: the possibilities of invasion of personal privacy and selective enforcement of the law would continue; possessors would still be stigmatized as criminals, incurring the economic and social consequences of involvement with the criminal law; the symbolic status of marihuana smoking as an anti-establishment act would be perpetuated.

On the other hand, a fine most likely would deter use no more than does the present possibility of incarceration. It would continue to impede treatment for heavy and very heavy use and would persist in directing law enforcement away from the policy's essential aim which is to halt illegal traffic in the drug.

For all these reasons, we reject the total prohibition approach and its variations.

Regulation

Another general technique for implementing the recommended social policy is regulation. The distinguishing feature of this technique is that it institutionalizes the availability of the drug. By establishing a legitimate channel of supply and distribution, society can theoretically control the quality and potency of the product. The major alternatives within this approach lie in the variety of restraints which can be imposed on consumption of the drug and on the informational requirements to which its distribution can be subject.

We have given serious consideration to this set of alternatives; however, we are unanimously of the opinion that such a scheme, no matter how tightly it might restrict consumption, is presently unacceptable.

1. Adoption of a Regulatory Scheme at This Time Would Inevitably Signify Approval of Use

In rejecting the total prohibition approach, we emphasized the symbolic aspects. In essence, we do not believe prohibition of possession for personal use is necessary to symbolize a social policy disapproving the use. Theoretically, a tightly controlled regulatory scheme, with limited distribution outlets, significant restraints on consumption, prohibition of advertising and compulsory labeling, could possibly symbolize such disapproval. Our regulatory policy toward tobacco is beginning slowly to reflect a disapproval policy toward cigarette smoking. Nonetheless, given the social and historical context of such a major shift in legal policy toward marihuana, we are certain that such a change would instead symbolize approval of use, or at least a position of neutrality. . . .

2. Adoption of a Regulatory Scheme Might Generate a Significant Public Health Problem

We noted above that institutionalizing availability of the drug would inevitably increase the incidence of use, even though that incidence might otherwise decrease. Of greater concern is the prospect that a larger incidence of use would result in a larger incidence of long-term heavy and very heavy use of potent preparations.

There are now approximately 500,000 heavy users of less potent preparations in this country, representing about 2% of those who ever tried the drug. Even if the prevalence of heavy use remained the same in relation to those who ever used, this at-risk population would inevitably increase under a regulatory scheme. If the emotional disturbances found in very heavy hashish users in other countries were to occur in this country, the adverse social impact of marihuana use, now slight, would increase substantially.

We have acknowledged that society, nonetheless, chose to run such a risk in 1933, when Prohibition was repealed. But alcohol use was already well-established in this society, and no alternative remained other than a regulatory approach. In light of our suspicion that interest in marihuana is largely transient, it would be imprudent to run that risk for marihuana today.

3. Adoption of a Regulatory Scheme Would Exacerbate Social Conflict and Frustrate a Deemphasis Policy

A significant segment of the public on both sides of the issue views marihuana and its "legalization" in a highly symbolic way. Any attempt to adopt a regulatory approach now would be counterproductive in this respect. The collision of values resulting from such a dramatic shift of policy would maintain the debate at a highly emotional level and would perpetuate the tendency to perceive marihuana use as a symbol of the struggle between two conflicting philosophies.

4. Not Enough Is Known about Regulatory Models in This Area

Advocates of legalization of marihuana are often inclined to propose a licensing scheme or an "alcohol model" without offering a specific program of regulation taking all the variables into account. Responsible policy planning cannot be so cursory. Consequently, we have given serious study to the many issues presented by such a scheme and to the nation's experience with other drug licensing schemes. On the basis of our inquiry, we are convinced that such a step should not be taken unless a realistic assessment of the efficacy of existing schemes and their potential application to marihuana indicates it would be successful. Such an assessment raises a number of disturbing questions.

The regulatory approaches which this nation has used in the cases of alcohol and tobacco have failed to accomplish two of their most important objectives: the minimization of excessive use and the limitation of accessibility to the young. Despite the warning and restraints on distribution and consumption, more than 50 million Americans smoke cigarettes regularly, and more than nine million Americans are "problem" drinkers. We have previously cited data indicating how many of our children begin habits which have been legally forbidden to them. Since the young user and the chronic user of marihuana are of primary concern to our public health officials, the lack of success with alcohol and tobacco discourages an assumption that the regulation of supply would minimize use by the younger generation.

Another important purpose of a regulatory scheme is to channel the product through a controlled system of supply and distribution. In that way the quality and quantity of the substance can be regulated. The efficacy of such a scheme as applied to marihuana is questionable. . . .

Another disturbing question is raised by the issue of potency regulation. Most advocates of legalization stipulate potency limitations as one feature of their scheme. Presumably they would limit the THC content of the regulated product. This is not an easy undertaking. Especially when cannabis is so easily grown and a black market is so easily created, we are dubious about the success of a regulatory scheme distributing only a product with low THC content. Again, attention must be paid the prospect of increased hashish use under a regulatory scheme; merely stipulating potency control is not sufficient. . . . The heavy, long-term use of hashish is a source of major concern to the Commission from both private and public health standpoints.

These are a few of the problems confronting the policy-maker if he seeks to devise an effective regulatory system of distribution for what is, in fact, a universally common plant. Our doubts about the efficacy of existing regulatory schemes, together with an uncertainty about the permanence of social interest in marihuana and the approval inevitably implied by adoption of such a scheme, all impel us to reject the regulatory approach as an appropriate implementation of a discouragement policy at the present time.

Future policy planners might well come to a different conclusion if further study of existing schemes suggests a feasible model; if responsible use of the drug does indeed take root in our society; if continuing scientific and medical research uncovers no long-term ill-effects; if potency control appears feasible; and if the passage of time and the adoption of a rational social policy sufficiently desymbolizes marihuana so that availability is not equated in the public mind with approval.

Partial Prohibition

The total prohibition scheme was rejected primarily because no sufficiently compelling social reason, predicated on existing knowledge, justifies intrusion by the criminal justice system into the private lives of individuals who use marihuana. The Commission is of the unanimous opinion that marihuana use is not such a grave problem that individuals who smoke marihuana, and possess it for that purpose, should be subject to criminal procedures. On the other hand, we have also rejected the regulatory or legalization scheme because it would institutionalize availability of a drug which has uncertain long-term effects and which may be of transient social interest.

Instead we recommend a partial prohibition scheme which we feel has the following benefits:

- Symbolizing a continuing societal discouragement of use;
- Facilitating the deemphasis of marihuana essential to answering dispassionately so many of the unanswered questions;
- Permitting a simultaneous medical, educational, religious, and parental effort to concentrate on reducing irresponsible use and remedying its consequences;
- Removing the criminal stigma and the threat of incarceration from a widespread behavior (possession for personal use) which does not warrant such treatment;
- Relieving the law enforcement community of the responsibility for enforcing a law of questionable utility, and one which they cannot fully enforce, thereby allowing concentration on drug trafficking and crimes against persons and property;
- Relieving the judicial calendar of a large volume of marihuana possession cases which delay the processing of more serious cases; and
- Maximizing the flexibility of future public responses as new information comes to light.

No major change is required in existing law to achieve all of these benefits. In general, we recommend only a decriminalization of possession of marihuana for personal use on both the state and federal levels. The major features of the recommended scheme are that: production and distribution of the drug would remain criminal activities as would possession with intent to distribute commercially; marihuana would be contraband subject to confiscation in public places; and criminal sanctions would be withdrawn from private use and possession incident to such use, but, at the state level, fines would be imposed for use in public.

Specifically, we recommend the following statutory schemes.

Recommendations for Federal Law

Under the Comprehensive Drug Abuse Prevention and Control Act of 1970, Congress provided the following scheme with respect to marihuana, by which was meant only the natural plant and its various parts, not the synthetic tetrahydrocannabinol (THC):

- Cultivation, importation and exportation, and sale or distribution for profit of marihuana are all felonies punishable by imprisonment for up to five years for a first offense and by up to 10 years for a second offense (the available penalty is doubled for sale to a minor).
- Possession of marihuana with intent to distribute is a felony punishable by imprisonment for up to five years for the first offense and by up to 10 years for a second offense.

- Possession of marihuana for personal use is a misdemeanor punishable by up to one year in jail and a $1,000 fine for first offense and by up to two years in jail and a $2,000 fine for second offense (expungement of criminal record is available for first offenders).
- Transfer of a small amount of marihuana for no remuneration is a misdemeanor punishable by up to one year in jail and a $1,000 fine for first offense and by up to two years in jail and a $2,000 fine for second offense (Congress singled out marihuana in this way to allow misdemeanor treatment of casual transfers and permitted first offender treatment, as allowed for possession for personal use).

The Commission recommends *only* the following changes in federal law:

- POSSESSION OF MARIHUANA FOR PERSONAL USE WOULD NO LONGER BE AN OFFENSE, BUT MARIHUANA POSSESSED IN PUBLIC WOULD REMAIN CONTRABAND SUBJECT TO SUMMARY SEIZURE AND FORFEITURE.
- CASUAL DISTRIBUTION OF SMALL AMOUNTS OF MARIHUANA FOR NO REMUNERATION, OR INSIGNIFICANT REMUNERATION NOT INVOLVING PROFIT WOULD NO LONGER BE AN OFFENSE.

The Commission further recommends that federal law be supplemented to provide:

- A PLEA OF MARIHUANA INTOXICATION SHALL NOT BE A DEFENSE TO ANY CRIMINAL ACT COMMITTED UNDER ITS INFLUENCE, NOR SHALL PROOF OF SUCH INTOXICATION CONSTITUTE A NEGATION OF SPECIFIC INTENT.

Recommendations for State Law

Under existing state marihuana laws, cultivation, distribution and possession with intent to distribute are generally felonies and in most states possession for personal use is a misdemeanor. The Commission strongly recommends uniformity of state laws and, in this regard, endorses the basic premise of the Uniform Controlled Substances Act, drafted by the National Conference of Commissioners on Uniform State Laws. The following are our recommendations for a uniform statutory scheme for marihuana, by which we mean, as under existing federal law, only the natural cannabis plant and its various parts, not the synthetic tetrahydrocannabinol (THC):

Existing Law

- CULTIVATION, SALE OR DISTRIBUTION FOR PROFIT AND POSSESSION WITH INTENT TO SELL WOULD REMAIN FELONIES (ALTHOUGH WE DO RECOMMEND UNIFORM PENALTIES).

Private Activities

- POSSESSION IN PRIVATE OF MARIHUANA FOR PERSONAL USE WOULD NO LONGER BE AN OFFENSE.

- DISTRIBUTION IN PRIVATE OF SMALL AMOUNTS OF MARIHUANA FOR NO RE-
  MUNERATION OR INSIGNIFICANT REMUNERATION NOT INVOLVING A PROFIT
  WOULD NO LONGER BE AN OFFENSE.

Public Activities

- POSSESSION IN PUBLIC OF ONE OUNCE OR UNDER OF MARIHUANA WOULD NOT
  BE AN OFFENSE, BUT THE MARIHUANA WOULD BE CONTRABAND SUBJECT TO
  SUMMARY SEIZURE AND FORFEITURE.
- POSSESSION IN PUBLIC OF MORE THAN ONE OUNCE OF MARIHUANA WOULD BE
  A CRIMINAL OFFENSE PUNISHABLE BY A FINE OF $100.
- DISTRIBUTION IN PUBLIC OF SMALL AMOUNTS OF MARIHUANA FOR NO REMU-
  NERATION OR INSIGNIFICANT REMUNERATION NOT INVOLVING A PROFIT
  WOULD BE A CRIMINAL OFFENSE PUNISHABLE BY A FINE OF $100.
- PUBLIC USE OF MARIHUANA WOULD BE A CRIMINAL OFFENSE PUNISHABLE BY
  A FINE OF $100.
- DISORDERLY CONDUCT ASSOCIATED WITH PUBLIC USE OF OR INTOXICATION BY
  MARIHUANA WOULD BE A MISDEMEANOR PUNISHABLE BY UP TO DAYS IN JAIL,
  A FINE OF $100, OR BOTH.
- OPERATING A VEHICLE OR DANGEROUS INSTRUMENT WHILE UNDER THE INFLU-
  ENCE OF MARIHUANA WOULD BE A MISDEMEANOR PUNISHABLE BY UP TO ONE
  YEAR IN JAIL, A FINE OF UP TO $100, OR BOTH, AND SUSPENSION OF A PERMIT
  TO OPERATE SUCH A VEHICLE OR INSTRUMENT FOR UP TO DAYS.
- A PLEA OF MARIHUANA INTOXICATION SHALL NOT BE A DEFENSE TO ANY
  CRIMINAL ACT COMMITTED UNDER ITS INFLUENCE NOR SHALL PROOF OF SUCH
  INTOXICATION CONSTITUTE A NEGATION OF SPECIFIC INTENT.
- A PERSON WOULD BE ABSOLUTELY LIABLE IN CIVIL COURT FOR ANY DAMAGE
  TO PERSON OR PROPERTY WHICH HE CAUSED WHILE UNDER THE INFLUENCE OF
  THE DRUG. . . .

Discussion of Potential Objections

Having discussed our recommended scheme at the federal and state levels, we think it useful to answer some objections we anticipate will be raised. Possible objections are:

1. Partial prohibition is not a sufficient reflection of the discouragement policy.
2. Partial prohibition is logically inconsistent.
3. A possession penalty is necessary for effective enforcement of sale proscriptions.
4. Partial prohibition won't "work" for marihuana any more than it did for alcohol.
5. A possession offense is essential as a device for detecting problem users.
6. Retention of a possession offense is required by our international obligations.

7. A firm distinction should be drawn between less potent and more potent preparations.

1. The Partial Prohibition Approach Is a Sufficient Reflection of the Discouragement Policy

To those who would argue that a criminal sanction against use is a necessary implementation of an abstentionist policy, we need only respond that this country has not generally operated on that assumption. We would be astounded if any person who lived during the 1920's was not aware of a definite governmental policy opposed to the use of alcohol. Yet, *only five states prohibited possession for personal use during Prohibition.* The failure of the 18th Amendment, the Volstead Act and 43 state prohibition acts to criminalize private possession certainly did not signify official approval of or neutrality toward alcohol use. . . .

Our nation has not generally seen fit to criminalize private drug-related behavior; only in the narcotics area was possession made a crime and marihuana was brought within the narcotics framework because of unfounded assumption about its ill effects. We think it is time to correct that mistaken departure from tradition with respect to marihuana. As during Prohibition, the drug will remain contraband, and its distribution will be prohibited.

Even as late as 1965, an abstentionist drug policy was not thought to require prohibition for personal use. At that time, Congress enacted the Drug Abuse Control Amendments, bringing LSD, amphetamines and barbiturates under federal control. National policy was clearly opposed to use of the hallucinogens and the non-prescription use of amphetamines and barbiturates, yet Congress did not impose a penalty for possession. Whether or not Congress' subsequent decision in 1968, to impose such a penalty was appropriate is an issue we will cover in our next Report after analyzing the individual drugs controlled. The important point now is that such a penalty is not a necessary feature of a discouragement policy for marihuana, regardless of its propriety for other drugs.

2. The Partial Prohibition Approach Is Not Logically Inconsistent

It will be argued that a law which permits a person to acquire and use marihuana but does not permit anyone to sell it to him for profit is logically unsound. We do not agree. If we had recommended a social policy of approval or neutrality toward use, partial prohibition would indeed have been illogical. However, under a discouragement policy, such a scheme is perfectly consistent.

Under partial prohibition, use is discouraged in three main ways. First, law enforcement authorities will make a concerted effort to reduce the supply of the drug. If a person wishes to use marihuana, he will have to seek out a person to sell it to him; and if his seller is in the business of distributing marihuana for profit, the seller is violating the law.

Second, the user will have to confine his disapproved behavior to the home. If he uses the drug in public, he has committed an offense; if he possesses it in public, it may be made summarily seized as contraband.

Third, continuing efforts will be made by educators, public health officials, and official government spokesmen to discourage use. Realizing that educational efforts are not always successful, we would hope for a sound program. In any event, the law should be an ancillary rather than a focal consideration.

There is nothing theoretically inconsistent about a scheme which merely withdraws the criminal sanction from a behavior which is not immoral but which is disapproved. The individual is being allowed to make his own choice. Hopefully, he will choose not to use marihuana. If he chooses to do so, however, he will have to do so discreetly and in private. Apart from its ultimate possession by the user, however, all marihuana-related activity is prohibited. The drug is contraband from its initial growth, through its harvest and distribution. It ceases to be contraband only when possessed and used in the home.

3. Prohibition of All Possession Is Not Essential to Prohibition of Sale

The other side of the "inconsistency" objection is the argument by law enforcement officials that they cannot adequately enforce proscriptions against sale without a possession penalty. We disagree. We have already explained that enforcement of a possession offense to some extent *impedes* the effort to reduce supply. Possession cases are generally regarded in the law enforcement community and by judges and prosecutors as "cheap" cases. Few seriously contend that prosecution of possessors reduces supply.

Some persons argue in response that the law should remain on the books as a tool not against the possessor but against the seller. They say that a possession offense is helpful in three ways. First, a prosecution can be used as a bargaining tool to encourage the possessor to reveal his source; this is called "turning an informant." Second, the police may know that a person is a seller, but may not be able to prove either sale or intent to sell, so they can at least charge such suspected sellers with simple possession.

Third, a corollary of the second argument is that the possession offense provides a useful tool in the "plea bargaining" process. That is, a seller may plead guilty to the lesser offense of possession, now generally a misdemeanor, instead of running the risk of trial and conviction of the more serious offense of sale, generally a felony. The prosecution may accept such a "bargain" if it is uncertain of the strength of the case, to avoid delay in sentencing, to reduce judicial backlog or in return for information from the defendant.

From an institutional standpoint, we do not find these arguments persuasive. First, if a possession offense is on the books, possession is a criminal activity. We oppose criminalizing conduct when its purpose and intent is directed not toward that conduct but toward another behavior.

In answer to the informant argument, the marihuana user (and this may not be true of other drugs) is simply too low in the distributional chain to help very much. . . . The National Survey shows most users receive their marihuana from their friends or acquaintances either as a gift or at cost. Rarely is the time spent on him or on his "source" a fruitful allocation of the law enforcement official's time. Also, it is institutionally improper to hold the criminal sanction over a person to force him to talk, when we otherwise would be unwilling to use that sanction.

As to the "lack of proof" and "plea bargaining" arguments, we believe they challenge a fundamental tenet of our criminal justice system. That is, under our law, a person is not guilty just because the police think he is guilty; his offense must be proven beyond a reasonable doubt to a judge or jury. If a possession offense were not on the books, the police would have to gather enough evidence to convict the seller of sale or of possession with intent to sell, and the prosecution would have to convince the judge beyond a reasonable doubt. The defendant, suspected seller or not, is entitled to due process of law.

The "lack of proof" argument is nothing more than a plea for an "easy out" when the police do not have enough evidence. This simply represents an admission that law enforcement officials want a possession offense which they can apply selectively, to people whom they think, but cannot prove, are sellers. Such a notion is inconsistent with the basic premise of our system of equal treatment under the law. If "simple" possession is not an offense for some, it is not an offense for all. A "known seller" is entitled to the same rights as anyone else: criminal conduct must be proved beyond a reasonable doubt. We do not favor coddling criminals. We do insist, as did the framers of the Constitution, that suspected criminal behavior be proved.

4. That Partial Prohibition Did Not "Work" for Alcohol Doesn't Mean It Won't for Marihuana

Prohibition failed to achieve its avowed purpose of eliminating the use of intoxicating liquors from American life. Risking an over-simplification, we think two reasons were essentially responsible for this failure: the unwillingness of a substantial minority, and probably a majority, of the American public to discard a habit deeply ingrained in their lives; and the inability of the law enforcement community to eliminate the bootlegging traffic which catered to this continuing demand.

As we have repeatedly noted, one of the reasons for adoption of a partial prohibition approach is uncertainty about the extent to which marihuana use is ingrained in American culture. Indeed, adoption of partial prohibition is the best way to find out for sure. If the social interest turns out to be only transient, this policy will prove particularly appropriate.

Similarly, an increase in marihuana use may be prevented by a concerted effort to eliminate major trafficking, the scope of which is presently only a small fraction of Prohibition bootlegging. We do not pretend that supply of a plant so easily grown can be eliminated. However, an intensive effort to eliminate commercial criminal enterprise should have some impact on the extent of use.

5. The Possession Offense Is Not Required as a Detection Device

In addition to their deterrent and symbolic functions, the drug possession laws serve a third function not shared by most other criminal laws. Like laws against public drunkenness, they facilitate societal detection of drug-dependent persons. Ideally, such persons, although apprehended by law enforcement authorities, may be detained for purposes of treatment and rehabilitation.

Whatever the merits of such an argument for the opiates and alcohol, such an argument does not apply to marihuana. Only a very small percentage of marihuana users are drug-dependent or are in need of treatment. Their dependence is generally upon multiple drug use, not on marihuana. In any event, the existence of such a small population does not justify retention of the possession offense as a detection device.

6. International Obligations Do Not Require Maintenance of a Possession Penalty

Some have raised the possibility that removal of simple possession criminal penalties would contravene this country's obligations under the Single Convention on Narcotic Drugs (1961), to which it became a signatory in March, 1967. We do not believe the provisions of that Convention compel the criminalization of possession for personal use.

Nowhere in the Convention are its Parties expressly required to impose criminal sanctions on possession for personal use. Article 4 requires Parties to "take such legislative and administrative measures as may be necessary. . . . to limit exclusively to medical and scientific purposes the production, manufacture, export, import, distribution of, trade in, use and possession of drugs." Penal sanctions are not necessarily included in this formulation.

Article 36, which deals specifically with penal provisions, requires each party to adopt "such measures as will ensure" that the listed activities, including possession, "shall be punishable offenses." Some have argued that this provision requires prohibition of personal use.

However, from a comprehensive study of the history of the Convention, the Commission has concluded that the word "possession" in Article 36 refers not to possession for personal use, but to possession as a link in illicit trafficking. This interpretation is bolstered also by the failure to include "use" in Article 36 even though it has been included in Article 4.

Finally, we must consider Article 33, which provides that "the Parties shall not permit the possession of drugs except under legal authority." This Article also does not require the imposition of any sanctions on possession for personal use. Experts consulted by the Commission have indicated that this Article may, nevertheless, require that the Parties limit possession and use to medical and scientific purposes. To affirmatively allow drugs to remain in the possession of persons for non-medical use would in this view contravene Articles 4 and 33 to read together. From this perspective our international obligations may require the classification of marihuana as contraband. For this reason, together with a desire to symbolize our discouragement policy in a clear way, we have included the contraband feature in our legal implementation scheme.

In conclusion, our reading of the Convention is that a Party may legitimately decide to deal with non-medical use and possession of marihuana through an educational program and similar approaches designed to discourage use.

7. No Potency Distinction Is Necessary at the Present Time

Following the approach taken in the Comprehensive Drug Abuse Prevention and Control Act of 1970, we have drawn a line between the natural cannabis plant and the synthetic tetrahydrocannabinols. "Marihuana" is defined as any and all parts of the natural plant. That we choose this approach for purposes of statutory implementation does not mean that we are unaware of the difference between the less potent and more potent preparations of the natural plant. . . .

The highest risk of cannabis use to the individual and society arises from the very long-term, very heavy use of potent preparations commonly called hashish. No such pattern of use is known to exist in the United States today.

The predominant pattern of use in the United States is experimental or intermittent use of less potent preparations of the drug. Even when hashish is used, the predominant pattern remains the same. In addition, whatever the potency of the drug used, individuals tend to smoke only the amount necessary to achieve the desired drug effect.

Given the prevailing patterns of use, the Commission does not believe it is essential to distinguish by statute between less potent and more potent forms of the natural plant. Reinforcing this judgment are the procedural and practical problems attending an effort to do so.

If the criminal liability of an individual user is dependent on the THC content of the substance, neither he nor the arresting officer will know whether he has committed a crime until an accurate scientific determination is made. Even if such accurate determinations were feasible on a large scale, which is not now the case, such after-the-fact liability is foreign to our criminal laws.

Under present circumstances, then, a statutory line based on potency is neither necessary nor feasible. We emphasize also that any legal distinction is an artificial reflection of the Commission's major concern: the heavy use of the drug over a long term. The most emphatic element of official policy should be to discourage such use, especially of the more potent preparations. Unfortunately precise legislative formulations regarding the amount of the drug presumed to be for personal use do not assist this effort at all. Whether it is lawful to possess one ounce of hashish or a proportionate amount based on potency (for example, one-fourth ounce), an individual prone to use the drug heavily will do so. Society's resources should be committed to the task of reducing supply of the drug and persuading our citizens not to use it. Expenditure of police time and financial resources in an attempt to ascertain the THC content of every seized substance would make little, if any, contribution to this effort.

A Final Comment

. . . In this Chapter, we have carefully considered the spectrum of social and legal policy alternatives. On the basis of our findings, . . . discussed in previous Chapters, we have concluded that society should seek to discourage use, while concentrating its attention on the prevention and treatment of heavy and very heavy use. The Commission feels that the criminalization of possession of marihuana for personal use is socially self-defeating as a means of achieving this objective. We have attempted to balance individual freedom on one hand and the obligation of the state to consider the wider social good on the other. We believe our recommended scheme will permit society to exercise its control and influence in ways most useful and efficient, meanwhile reserving to the individual American his sense of privacy, his sense of individuality, and, within the context of an interacting and interdependent society, his options to select his own life style, values, goals and opportunities.

The Commission sincerely hopes that the tone of cautious restraint sounded in this Report will be perpetuated in the debate which will follow it. For those who feel we have not proceeded far enough, we are reminded of Thomas Jefferson's advice to George Washington that "Delay is preferable to error." For those who argue we have gone too far, we note Roscoe Pound's statement, "The law must be stable, but it must not stand still."

We have carefully analyzed the interrelationship between marihuana the drug, marihuana use as a behavior, and marihuana as a social problem. Recognizing the extensive degree of misinformation about marihuana as a drug, we have tried to *demythologize* it. Viewing the use of marihuana in its wider social context, we have tried to *desymbolize* it.

Considering the range of social concerns in contemporary America, marihuana does not, in our considered judgment, rank very high. We would *deemphasize* marihuana as a problem.

The existing social and legal policy is out of proportion to the individual and social harm engendered by the use of the drug. To replace it, we have attempted to design a suitable social policy, which we believe is fair, cautious and attuned to the social realities of our time.

Chapter 72

Long-Term Effects Uncertain

A decade after the Marihuana Commission report, the National Institutes of Health asked the Institute of Medicine (IOM) of the National Academy of Sciences to study the hazards and the possible therapeutic value of marijuana and to suggest research needs. The institute was not to concern itself with the legal aspects of the question.

The report that resulted straddled the issues. For example, the authors expressed alarm at finding long-term storage of marijuana metabolites in the fatty tissues of the body but were unable to specify what damage this might cause. Dr. Arnold S. Relman, editor of the New England Journal of Medicine *and the chair of the study committee, commented, "We give no comfort to those with strong positions on either side of the argument."*

REPORT ON THE HEALTH-RELATED EFFECTS OF MARIJUANA

Institute of Medicine

The Institute of Medicine (IOM) of the National Academy of Sciences has conducted a 15-month study of the health-related effects of marijuana, at the request of the Secretary of Health and Human Services and the Director of the National Institutes of Health. The IOM appointed a 22-member committee to:

- analyze existing scientific evidence bearing on the possible hazards to the health and safety of users of marijuana;
- analyze data concerning the possible therapeutic value and health benefits of marijuana;
- assess federal research programs in marijuana;
- identify promising new research directions, and make suggestions to improve the quality and usefulness of future research; and
- draw conclusions from this review that would accurately assess the limits of present knowledge and thereby provide a factual, scientific basis for the development of future government policy.

This assessment of knowledge of the health-related effects of marijuana is important and timely because marijuana is now the most widely used of all the illicit drugs available in the United States. In 1979, more than 50 million persons had tried it at least once. There has been a steep rise in its use during the past decade, particularly among adolescents and young adults, although there has been a leveling-off in its overall use among high school seniors in the past 2 or 3 years and a small decline in the percentage of seniors who use it frequently. Although substantially more high school students have used alcohol than have ever used marijuana, more high school seniors use marijuana on a daily or near-daily basis (9 percent) than alcohol (6 percent). Much of the heavy use of marijuana, unlike alcohol, takes place in school, where effects on behavior, cognition, and psychomotor performance can be particularly disturbing. Unlike alcohol, which is rapidly metabolized and eliminated from the body, the psychoactive components of marijuana persist in the body for a long time. Similar to alcohol, continued use of marijuana may cause tolerance and dependence. For all these reasons, it is imperative that we have reliable and detailed information about the effects of marijuana use on health, both in the long and short term.

What, then, did we learn from our review of the published scientific literature? Numerous acute effects have been described in animals, in isolated cells and tissues, and in studies of human volunteers; clinical and epidemiological observations also have been reported. This information is briefly summarized in the following paragraphs.

Effects on the Nervous System and on Behavior

We can say with confidence that marijuana produces acute effects on the brain, including chemical and electrophysiological changes. Its most clearly established acute effects are on mental functions and behavior. With a severity directly related to dose, marijuana impairs motor coordination and affects tracking ability and sensory and perceptual functions important for safe driving and the operation of other machines; it also impairs short-term memory and slows learning. Other acute effects include feelings of euphoria and other mood changes, but there also are disturbing mental phenomena, such as brief periods of anxiety, confusion, or psychosis.

There is not yet any conclusive evidence as to whether prolonged use of marijuana causes permanent changes in the nervous system or sustained impairment of brain function and behavior in human beings. In a few unconfirmed studies in experimental animals, impairment of learning and changes in electrical brain-wave recordings have been observed several months after the cessation of chronic administration of marijuana. In the judgment of the committee, widely cited studies purporting to demonstrate that marijuana affects the gross and microscopic structure of the human or monkey brain are not convincing; much more work is needed to settle this important point.

Chronic relatively heavy use of marijuana is associated with behavioral dysfunction and mental disorders in human beings, but available evidence does not establish if marijuana use under these circumstances is a cause or a result of the mental condition. There are similar problems in interpreting the evidence linking the use of marijuana to subsequent use of other illicit drugs, such as heroin or cocaine. Association does not prove a causal relation, and the use of marijuana may merely be symptomatic of an underlying disposition to use psychoactive drugs rater than a "stepping stone" to involvement with more dangerous substances. It is also difficult to sort out the relationship between use of marijuana and the complex symptoms known as the amotivational syndrome. Self-selection and effects of the drug are probably both contributing to the motivational problems seen in some chronic users of marijuana.

Thus, the long-term effects of marijuana on the human brain and on human behavior remain to be defined. Although we have no convincing evidence thus far of any effects persisting in human beings after cessation of drug use, there may well be subtle but important physical and psychological consequences that have not been recognized.

Effects on the Cardiovascular and Respiratory Systems

There is good evidence that the smoking of marijuana usually causes acute changes in the heart and circulation that are characteristic of stress, but there is no evidence to indicate that a permanently deleterious effect on the normal cardiovascular system occurs. There is good evidence to show that marijuana increases the work of the heart, usually by raising heart rate and, in some persons, by raising blood pressure. This rise in workload poses a threat to patients with hypertension, cerebrovascular disease, and coronary atherosclerosis.

Acute exposure to marijuana smoke generally elicits broncho-dilation; chronic heavy smoking of marijuana causes inflammation and pre-neoplastic changes in the airways, similar to those produced by smoking of tobacco. Marijuana smoke is a complex mixture that not only has many chemical components (including carbon monoxide and "tar") and biological effects similar to those of tobacco smoke, but also some unique ingredients. This suggests the strong possibility that prolonged heavy smoking of marijuana, like tobacco, will lead to cancer of the respiratory tract and to serious impairment of lung function. Although there is evidence of impaired lung function in chronic smokers, no direct confirmation of the likelihood of cancer has yet been provided, possibly because marijuana has been widely smoked in this country for only about 20 years, and data have not been collected systematically in other countries with a much longer history of heavy marijuana use.

Effects on the Reproductive System and on Chromosomes

Although studies in animals have shown that Δ-9-THC (the major psychoactive constituent of marijuana) lowers the concentration in blood serum of pituitary hormones (gonadotropins) that control reproductive functions, it is not known if there is a direct effect on reproductive tissues. Delta-9-THC appears to have a modest reversible suppressive effect on sperm production in men, but there is no proof that it has a deleterious effect on male fertility. Effects on human female hormonal function have been reported, but the evidence is not convincing. However, there is convincing evidence that marijuana interferes with ovulation in female monkeys. No satisfactory studies of the relation between use of marijuana and female fertility and child-bearing have been carried out. Although Δ-9-THC is known to cross the placenta readily and to cause birth defects when administered in large doses to experimental animals, no adequate clinical studies have been carried out to determine if marijuana use can harm the human fetus. There is no conclusive evidence of teratogenicity in human offspring, but a slowly developing or low-level effect might be undetected by the studies done so far. The effects of marijuana on reproductive function and on the fetus are unclear; they may prove to be negligible, but further research to establish or rule out such effects would be of great importance.

Extracts from marijuana smoke particulates ("tar") have been found to produce dose-related mutations in bacteria; however, Δ-9-THC, by itself, is not mutagenic. Marijuana and Δ-9-THC do not appear to break chromosomes, but marijuana may affect chromosome segregation during cell division, resulting in an abnormal number of chromosomes in daughter cells. Although these results are of concern, their clinical significance is unknown.

The Immune System

Similar limitations exist in our understanding of the effects of marijuana on other body systems. For example, some studies of the immune system demonstrate a mild, immunosuppressant effect on human beings, but other studies show no effect.

Therapeutic Potential

The committee also has examined the evidence on the therapeutic effects of marijuana in a variety of medical disorders. Preliminary studies suggest that marijuana and its derivatives or analogues might be useful in the treatment of the raised intraocular pressure of glaucoma, in the control of the severe nausea and vomiting caused by cancer chemotherapy, and in the treatment of asthma. There also is some preliminary evidence that a marijuana constituent (cannabidiol) might be helpful in the treatment of certain types of epileptic seizures, as well as for spastic disorders and other nervous system diseases. But, in these and all other conditions, much more work is needed. Because marijuana and Δ-9-THC often produce troublesome psychotropic or cardiovascular side-effects that limit their therapeutic usefulness, particularly in older patients, the greatest therapeutic potential probably lies in the use of synthetic analogues of marijuana derivatives with higher ratios of therapeutic to undesirable effects.

The Need for More Research on Marijuana

The explanation for all of these unanswered questions is insufficient research. We need to know much more about the metabolism of the various marijuana chemical compounds and their biologic effects. This will require many more studies in animals, with particular emphasis on subhuman primates. Basic pharmacologic information obtained in animal experiments will ultimately have to be tested in clinical studies on human beings.

Until 10 or 15 years ago, there was virtually no systematic, rigorously controlled research on the human health-related effects of marijuana and its major constituents. Even now, when standardized marijuana and pure synthetic cannabinoids are available for experimental studies, and good qualitative methods exist for the measurement of Δ-9-THC and its metabolites in body fluids, well-designed studies on human beings are relatively few. There are difficulties in studying the clinical effects of marijuana in human beings, particularly the effects of long-term use. And yet, without such studies the debate about the safety or hazard of marijuana will remain unresolved. Prospective cohort studies, as well as retrospective case-control studies, would be useful in identifying long-term behavioral and biological consequences of marijuana use.

The federal investment in research on the health-related effects of marijuana has been small, both in relation to the expenditure on other illicit drugs and in absolute terms. The committee considers the research particularly inadequate when viewed in light of the extent of marijuana use in this country, especially by young people. We believe there should be a greater investment in research on marijuana, and that investigator-initiated research grants should be the primary vehicle of support.

The committee considers all of the areas of research on marijuana that are supported by the National Institute on Drug Abuse to be important, but we did not judge the appropriateness of the allocation of resources among those areas, other than to conclude that there should be increased emphasis on studies in human beings and other primates. . . .

Conclusions

The scientific evidence published to date indicates that marijuana has a broad range of psychological and biological effects, some of which, at least under certain conditions, are harmful to human health. Unfortunately, the available information does not tell us how serious this risk may be.

Our major conclusion is that what little we know for certain about the effects of marijuana on human health—and all that we have reason to suspect—justifies serious national concern. Of no less concern is the extent of our ignorance about many of the most basic and important questions about the drug. Our major recommendation is that there be a greatly intensified and more comprehensive program of research into the effects of marijuana on the health of the American people.

Chapter 73

The Legalization of Marijuana: Hearings

*In 1972 the National Organization for the Reform of Marijuana Laws (NORML) peti-
tioned the Bureau of Narcotics and Dangerous Drugs (the predecessor of the Drug
Enforcement Administration [DEA]) to transfer marijuana from a position on the drug
schedule as a Class I drug (categorizing it as legal only for approved research) to a Class
V drug (a category with few mandated controls), or to a designation with no controls
whatsoever. A lengthy legal odyssey led to a formal hearing before the administrative law
judge of the agency, now called the DEA, in 1987 and 1988. By this time, NORML had
reduced its request to a rescheduling from Class I to Class II (a category in which drugs
are strictly controlled, on the model of morphine, but are available for most physicians to
prescribe).*

*The hearings brought together experts on both sides. They testified and also were
subject to cross-examination. On September 6, 1988, the decision of the judge, Francis L.
Young, was released. Surprisingly, the DEA administrative law judge had concluded
that marijuana should be reclassified as a Class II drug. The DEA, which had the power
to accept or reject this decision, reacted with astonishment. It stated its reasons for
rejecting the judge's recommendation in an account published in 1989 in the* Federal
Register.

*Excerpts are given here from Judge Young's discussion of the main therapeutic claims
for marijuana: its usefulness in treatment with chemotherapy and for glaucoma, multiple
sclerosis, spasticity, and hyperthyroidism, and its relative safety under medical supervision. The response of the DEA Administrator follows. Full testimony and rebuttals
appear in the original documents.*

Opinion and Recommended Ruling on the
Marijuana Rescheduling Petition

U.S. Department of Justice, Drug Enforcement Administration

I. Introduction

This is a rulemaking pursuant to the Administrative Procedure Act, 5 U.S. § 551,
et seq., to determine whether the marijuana plant (Cannabis sativa L) considered
as a whole may lawfully be transferred from Schedule I to Schedule II of the

schedules established by the Controlled Substances Act (the Act), 21 U.S.C. § 801, *et seq*. None of the parties is seeking to "legalize" marijuana generally or for recreational purposes. Placement in Schedule II would mean, essentially, that physicians in the United States would not violate Federal law by prescribing marijuana for their patients for legitimate therapeutic purposes. It is contrary to Federal law for physicians to do this as long as marijuana remains in Schedule I.

This proceeding had its origins on May 18, 1972 when the National Organization for the Reform of Marijuana Laws (NORML) and two other groups submitted a petition to the Bureau of Narcotics and Dangerous Drugs (BNDD). . . .

II. *Recommended Ruling*

It is recommended that the proposed findings and conclusions submitted by the parties to the administrative law judge be rejected by the Administrator except to the extent they are included in those hereinafter set forth, for the reason that they are irrelevant or unduly repetitious or not supported by a preponderance of the evidence. 21 C.F.R. § 1316.65(a)(1).

III. *Issues*

As noted above, the agreed issues are as follows:

Principal issue:

Whether the marijuana plant, considered as a whole, may lawfully be transferred from Schedule I to Schedule II of the schedules established by the Controlled Substances Act.

Subsidiary issues:

1. Whether the marijuana plant has a currently accepted medical use in treatment in the United States, or a currently accepted medical use with severe restrictions.
2. Whether there is a lack of accepted safety for use of the marijuana plant under medical supervision.

IV. *Statutory Requirements for Scheduling*

The Act provides (21 U.S.C. § 812(b)) that a drug or other substance may not be placed in any schedule unless certain specified findings are made with respect to it. The findings required for Schedule I and Schedule II are as follows:

Schedule I.—

(A) The drug or other substance has a high potential for abuse.
(B) The drug or other substance has no currently accepted medical use in treatment in the United States.
(C) There is a lack of accepted safety for use of the drug or other substance under medical supervision.

Schedule II.—

(A) The drug or other substance has a high potential for abuse.
(B) The drug or other substance has a currently accepted medical use in treatment in the United States or a currently accepted medical use with severe restrictions.
(C) Abuse of the drug or other substances [*sic*] may lead to severe psychological or physical dependence.

As noted above the parties have stipulated, for the purpose of this proceeding, that marijuana has a high potential for abuse and that abuse of it may lead to severe psychological or physical dependence. Thus the dispute between the two sides in this proceeding is narrowed to whether or not marijuana has a currently accepted medical use in treatment in the United States, and whether or not there is a lack of accepted safety for use of marijuana under medical supervision.

The issues as framed here contemplate marijuana's being placed only in Schedule I or Schedule II. The criteria for placement in any of the other three schedules established by the Act are irrelevant to this proceeding. . . .

V. Accepted Medical Use in Treatment — Chemotherapy

Discussion

. . . It is clear beyond any question that many people find marijuana to have, in the words of the Act, an "accepted medical use in treatment in the United States" in effecting relief for cancer patients. Oncologists, physicians treating cancer patients, accept this. Other medical practitioners and researchers accept this. Medical faculty professors accept it. Nurses performing hands-on patient care accept it.

Patients accept it. As counsel for CCA perceptively pointed out at oral argument, acceptance by the patient is of vital importance. Doctors accept a therapeutic agent or process only if it "works" for the patient. If the patient does not accept, the doctor cannot administer the treatment. The patient's informed consent is vital. The doctor ascertains the patient's acceptance by observing and listening to the patient. Acceptance by the doctor depends on what he sees in the patient and hears from the patient. Unquestionably, patients in large numbers have accepted marijuana as useful in treating their emesis. They have found that it "works". Doctors, evaluating their patients, can have no basis more sound than that for their own acceptance.

Of relevance, also, is the acceptance of marijuana by state attorneys-general, officials whose primary concern is law enforcement. A large number of them have no fear that placing marijuana in Schedule II, thus making it available for legitimate therapy, will in any way impede existing efforts of law enforcement authorities to crack down on illegal drug trafficking.

The Act does not specify by whom a drug or substance must be "accepted [for] medical use in treatment" in order to meet the Act's "accepted" requirement for placement in Schedule II. Department of Justice witnesses told the Congress during hearings in 1970 preceeding passage of the Act that "the medical profession" would make this determination, that the matter would be "determined by the medical community." The Deputy Chief Counsel of BNDD, whose office had written the bill with this language in it, told the House subcommittee that "this basic determination . . . is not made by any part of the federal government. It is made by the medical community as to whether or not the drug has medical use or doesn't".

No one would seriously contend that these Justice Department witnesses meant that the *entire* medical community would have to be in agreement on the usefulness of a drug or substance. Seldom, if ever, do *all* lawyers agree on a point of law. Seldom, if ever, do *all* doctors agree on a medical question. How many are required here? A majority of 51%? It would be unrealistic to attempt a plebiscite of all doctors in the country on such a question every time it arises, to obtain a majority vote.

In determining whether a medical procedure utilized by a doctor is actionable as malpractice the courts have adopted the rule that it is acceptable for a doctor to employ a method of treatment supported by a respectable minority of physicians.

In *Hood* v. *Phillips*, 537 S.W. 2d 291 (1976) the Texas Court of Civil Appeals was dealing with a claim of medical malpractice resulting from a surgical procedure claimed to have been unnecessary. The court quoted from an Arizona court decision holding that

> a method of treatment, as espoused and used by . . . a respectable minority of physicians in the United States, cannot be said to be an inappropriate method of treatment or to be malpractice as a matter of law even though it has not been accepted as a proper method of treatment by the medical profession generally.

Ibid. at 294. Noting that the Federal District court in the Arizona case found a "respectable minority" composed of sixty-five physicians throughout the United States, the Texas court adopted as "the better rule" to apply in its case, that

> a physician is not guilty of malpractice where the method of treatment used is supported by a respectable minority of physicians.

Ibid.

In *Chumbler* v. *McClure*, 505 F.2d 489 (6th Cir. 1974) the Federal courts were dealing with a medical malpractice case under their diversity jurisdiction, applying Tennessee law. The Court of Appeals said:

. . . The most favorable interpretation that may be placed on the testimony adduced at trial below is that there is a division of opinion in the medical profession regarding the use of Premarin in the Treatment of cerebral vascular insufficiency, and that Dr. McClure was alone among neurosurgeons in Nashville in using such therapy. The test for malpractice and for community standards is not to be determined solely by a plebiscite. Where two or more schools of thought exist among competent members of the medical profession concerning proper medical treatment for a given ailment, each of which is *supported by responsible medical authority*, it is not malpractice to be among the minority in a given city who follow one of the *accepted* schools.

505 F.2d at 492 (Emphasis added). See, also, *Leech v. Bralliar*, 275 F.Supp. 897 (D.Ariz., 1967).

How do we ascertain whether there exists a school of thought supported by responsible medical authority, and thus "accepted"? We listen to the physicians.

The court and jury must have a standard measure which they are to use in measuring the acts of a doctor to determine whether he exercised a reasonable degree of care and skill; they are not permitted to set up and use any arbitrary or artificial standard of measurement that the jury may wish to apply. The proper standard of measurement is to be established by testimony of physicians, for it is a medical question.

Hayes v. Brown, 133 S.E. 2d. 102 (Ga., 1963) at 105.

As noted above, there is no question but that this record shows a great many physicians, and others, to have "accepted" marijuana as having a medical use in the treatment of cancer patients' emesis. True, *all* physicians have not "accepted" it. But to require universal, 100% acceptance would be unreasonable. Acceptance by "a respectable minority" of physicians is all that can reasonably be required. The record here establishes conclusively that at least "a respectable minority" of physicians has "accepted" marijuana as having a "medical use in treatment in the United States." That others may not makes no difference.

The administrative law judge recommended this same approach for determining whether a drug has an "accepted medical use in treatment" in *The Matter Of MDMA Scheduling*, Docket No. 84–48. The Administrator, in his first final rule in that proceeding, issued on October 8, 1986, declined to adopt this approach. He ruled, instead, that DEA's decision on whether or not a drug or other substance had an accepted medical use in treatment in the United States would be determined simply by ascertaining whether or not "the drug or other substance is lawfully marketed in the United States pursuant to the Federal Food, Drug and Cosmetic Act of 1938. . . ."

The United States Court of Appeals for the First Circuit held that the Administrator erred in so ruling. That court vacated the final order of October 8, 1986 and remanded the matter of MDMA's scheduling for further consideration. The court directed that, on remand, the Administrator would not be permitted to treat the absence of interstate marketing approval by FDA as conclusive evidence on the question of accepted medical use under the Act.

In his third final rule on the matter of the scheduling of MDMA the Administrator made a series of findings of fact as to MDMA, the drug there under consideration, with respect to the evidence in that record. On those findings he based his last final rule in the case.

That third final rule dealing with MDMA is dealing with a synthetic, "simple", "single-action" drug. What might be appropriate criteria for a "simple" drug like MDMA may not be appropriate for a "complex" substance with a number of active components. The criteria applied to MDMA, a synthetic drug, are not appropriate for application to marijuana, which is a natural plant substance.

The First Circuit Court of Appeals in the MDMA case told the Administrator that he should not treat the absence of FDA interstate marketing approval as conclusive evidence of lack of currently accepted medical use. The court did not forbid the Administrator from considering the absence of FDA approval as *a* factor when determining the existence of accepted medical use. Yet on remand, in his third final order, the Administrator adopted by reference 18 of the numbered findings he had made in the first final order. Each of these findings had to do with requirements imposed by FDA for approval of a new drug application (NDA) or of an investigational new drug exemption (IND). These requirements deal with data resulting from controlled studies and scientifically conducted investigations and tests.

Among those findings incorporated into the third final MDMA order from the first, and relied on by the Administrator, was the determination and recommendation of the FDA that the drug there in question was not "accepted". In relying on the FDA's action the Administrator apparently overlooked the fact that the FDA clearly stated that it was interpreting "accepted medical use" in the Act as being equivalent to receiving FDA approval for lawful marketing under the FDCA. Thus the Administrator accepted as a basis for his MDMA third final rule the FDA recommendation which was based upon a statutory interpretation which the Court of Appeals had condemned.

The Administrator in that third final rule made a series of further findings. Again, the central concern in these findings was the content of test results and the sufficiency or adequacy of studies and scientific reports. A careful reading of the criteria considered in the MDMA third final order reveals that the Administrator was really considering the question: *Should* the drug be accepted for medical use?; rather than the question: *Has* the drug *been accepted* for medical use? By considering little else but scientific test results and reports the Administrator was making a determination as to whether or not, in his opinion, MDMA *ought* to be accepted for medical use in treatment.

The Agency's arguments in the present case are to the same effect. In a word, they address the wrong question. It is not for this Agency to tell doctors whether they should or should not accept a drug or substance for medical use. The statute directs the Administrator merely to ascertain whether, in fact, doctors have done so.

The MDMA third final order mistakenly looks to FDA criteria for guidance in choosing criteria for DEA to apply. Under the Food, Drug and Cosmetic Act the FDA is deciding—properly, under that statute—whether a new drug *should be* introduced into interstate commerce. Thus it is appropriate for the FDA to rely heavily on test results and scientific inquiry to ascertain whether a drug is effective and whether it is safe. The FDA must look at a drug and pass judgement on its intrinsic qualities. The DEA, on the other hand, is charged by 21 U.S.C. § 812(b)(1)(B) and (2)(B) with ascertaining what it is that other people have done with respect to a drug or substance: *"Have they accepted* it?;" not *"Should they accept* it?"

In the MDMA third final order DEA is actually making the decision that doctors have to make, rather than trying to ascertain the decision which doctors have made. Consciously or not, the Agency is undertaking to tell doctors what they should or should not accept. In so doing the Agency is acting beyond the authority granted in the Act.

It is entirely proper for the Administrator to consider the pharmacology of a drug and scientific test results in connection with determining abuse potential. But abuse potential is not in issue in this marijuana proceeding.

There is another reason why DEA should not be guided by FDA criteria in ascertaining whether or not marijuana has an accepted medical use in treatment. These criteria are applied by FDA pursuant to Section 505 of the Federal Food, Drug and Cosmetic Act (FDCA), as amended. When the FDA is making an inquiry pursuant to that legislation it is looking at a synthetically formed *new drug*. The marijuana plant is anything *but* a new drug. Uncontroverted evidence in this record indicates that marijuana was being used therapeutically by mankind 2000 years before the Birth of Christ.

Uncontroverted evidence further establishes that in this country today "new drugs" are developed by pharmaceutical companies possessing resources sufficient to bear the enormous expense of testing a new drug, obtaining FDA approval of its efficacy and safety, and marketing it successfully. No company undertakes the investment required unless it has a patent on the drug, so it can recoup its development costs and make a profit. At oral argument Government counsel conceded that "the FDA system is constructed for pharmaceutical companies. I won't deny that."

Since the substance being considered in this case is a natural plant rather than a synthetic new drug, it is unreasonable to make FDA-type criteria determinative of the issue in this case, particularly so when such criteria are irrelevant to the question posed by the Act: Does the substance have an accepted medical use in treatment?

Finally, the Agency in this proceeding relies in part on the FDA's recommendation that the Administrator retain marijuana in Schedule I. But, as in the MDMA case, that recommendation is based upon FDA's equating "accepted medical use" under the Act with being approved for marketing by FDA under the Food, Drug and Cosmetic Act, the interpretation condemned by the First Circuit in the MDMA case. . . .

The overwhelming preponderance of the evidence in this record establishes that marijuana has a currently accepted medical use in treatment in the United States for nausea and vomiting resulting from chemotherapy treatments in some cancer patients. To conclude otherwise, on this record, would be unreasonable, arbitrary and capricious. . . .

VI. Accepted Medical Use in Treatment — Glaucoma

Discussion

Petitioners' briefs fail to show that the preponderance of the evidence in the record with respect to marijuana and glaucoma establishes that a respectable minority of physicians accepts marijuana as being useful in the treatment of glaucoma in the United States.

This conclusion is not to be taken in any way as criticism of the opinions of the ophthalmologists who testified that they accept marijuana for this purpose. The failure lies with petitioners. In their briefs they do not point out hard, specific evidence in this record sufficient to establish that a respectable minority of physicians has accepted their position.

There is a great volume of evidence here, and much discussion in the briefs, about the protracted case of Robert Randall. But when all is said and done, his experience presents but one case. The record contains sworn testimony of three ophthalmologists who have treated Mr. Randall. One of them tells us of a relatively small number of other glaucoma patients whom he has treated with marijuana and whom he knows to have responded favorably. Another of these three doctors has successfully treated only Randall with marijuana. The third testifies, despite his successful experience in treating Randall, that marijuana does not have an accepted use in such treatment.

In addition to Robert Randall, Petitioners point to the testimony of three other glaucoma patients. Their case histories are impressive, but they contribute little to the carrying of Petitioner's burden of showing that marijuana is accepted for medical treatment of glaucoma by a respectable minority of physicians. . . .

Petitioners have placed in evidence copies of a number of newspaper clippings reporting statements by persons claiming that marijuana has helped their glaucoma. The administrative law judge is unable to give significant weight to this evidence. Had these persons testified so as to have been subject to cross-examination, a different situation would be presented. But these newspaper reports of extra-judicial statements, neither tested by informed inquiry nor supported by a doctor's opinion, are not entitled to much weight. They are of little, if any, materiality.

Beyond the evidence referred to above there is little other "hard" evidence, pointed out by petitioners, of physicans accepting marijuana for treatment of glaucoma. Such evidence as that concerning a survey of a group of San Francisco ophthalmologists is ambiguous, at best. The revelant document establishes merely that most of the doctors on the grand rounds, who responded to an inquiry, believed that the *THC capsules or marijuana* ought to be available.

In sum, the evidence here tending to show that marijuana is accepted for treatment of glaucoma falls far, far short of the quantum of evidence tending to show that marijuana is accepted for treatment of emesis in cancer patients. The preponderance of the evidence here, identified by petitioners in their briefs, does not establish that a respectable minority of physicians has accepted marijuana for glaucoma treatment. . . .

VII. Accepted Medical Use in Treatment — Multiple Sclerosis, Spasticity and Hyperparathyroidism

Discussion

. . . The administrative law judge concludes that, within the meaning of the Act, 21 U.S.C. § 812(b)(2)(8), marijuana "has a currently accepted medical use in treatment in the United States" for spasticity resulting from multiple sclerosis and other causes. It would be unreasonable, arbitrary and capricious to find otherwise. The facts set out above, controverted by the Agency, establish beyond question that some doctors in the United States accept marijuana as helpful in such treatment for some patients. The record here shows that they constitute a significant minority of physicians. Nothing more can reasonably be required. That some doctors would have more studies and test results in hand before accepting marijuana's usefulness here is irrelevant.

The same is true with respect to the hyperparathyroidism from which Irvin Rosenfeld suffers. His disease is so rare, and so few physicians appear to be familiar with it, that acceptance by one doctor of marijuana as being useful in treating it ought to satisfy the requirement for a significant minority. The Agency points to no evidence of record tending to establish that marijuana is not accepted by doctors in connection with this most unusual ailment. Refusal to acknowledge acceptance by a significant minority, in light of the case history detailed in this record, would be unreasonable, arbitrary and capricious. . . .

VIII. Accepted Safety for Use under Medical Supervision

Discussion

The Act, at 21 U.S.C § 812(b)(1)(C), requires that marijuana be retained in Schedule I if "[t]here is a lack of accepted safety for use of [it] under medical supervision." If there is no lack of such safety, if it is accepted that this substance can be used with safety under medical supervision, then it is unreasonable to keep it in Schedule I.

Again we must ask—"accepted" by whom? In the MDMA proceeding the Agency's first Final Rule decided that "accepted" here meant, as in the phrase "accepted medical use in treatment", that the FDA had accepted the substance pursuant to the provisions of the Food, Drug and Cosmetic Act. 51 Fed. Reg.

36555 (1986). The Court of Appeals held that this was error. On remand, in its third Final Rule on MDMA, the Agency made the same ruling as before, relying essentially on the same findings, and on others of similar nature, just as it did with respect to "accepted medical use." 53 Fed. Reg. 5156 (1988).

The administrative law judge finds himself constrained not to follow the rationale in that MDMA third Final Order for the same reasons as set out above in Section V with respect to "accepted medical use" in oncology. . . . Briefly, the Agency was looking primarily at the results of scientific tests and studies rather than at what physicians had, in fact, accepted. The Agency was wrongly basing its decision on a judgment as to whether or not doctors *ought to have* accepted the substance in question as safe for use under medical supervision. The criteria the Agency applied in the MDMA third Final Rule are inappropriate. The only proper question for the Agency here is: *Have* a significant minority of *physicians accepted* marijuana as safe for use under medical supervision?

The gist of the Agency's case against recognizing marijuana's acceptance as safe is to assert that more studies, more tests are needed. The Agency has presented highly qualified and respected experts, researchers and others, who hold that view. But . . . it is unrealistic and unreasonable to require unanimity of opinion on the question confronting us. . . . Acceptance by a significant minority of doctors is all that can reasonably be required. This record makes it abundantly clear that such acceptance exists in the United States.

Findings are made above with respect to the safety of medically supervised use of marijuana by glaucoma patients. Those findings are relevant to the safety issue even though the administrative law judge does not find accepted use in treatment of glaucoma to have been shown.

Based upon the facts established in this record and set out above one must reasonably conclude that there is accepted safety for use of marijuana under medical supervision. To conclude otherwise, on this record, would be unreasonable, arbitrary and capricious.

IX. Conclusion and Recommended Decision

Based upon the foregoing facts and reasoning, the administrative law judge concludes that the provisions of the Act permit and require the transfer of marijuana from Schedule I to Schedule II. The judge realizes that strong emotions are aroused on both sides of any discussion concerning the use of marijuana. Nonetheless it is essential for this Agency, and its Administrator, calmly and dispassionately to review the evidence of record, correctly apply the law, and act accordingly.

Marijuana can be harmful. Marijuana is abused. But the same is true of dozens of drugs or substances which are listed in Schedule II so that they can be employed in treatment by physicians in proper cases, despite their abuse potential.

Transferring marijuana from Schedule I to Schedule II will not, of course, make it immediately available in pharmacies throughout the country for legitimate use in treatment. Other government authorities, Federal and State, will doubtless have to act before that might occur. But this Agency is not charged with responsibility, or given authority, over the myriad other regulatory decisions that may be required before marijuana can actually be legally available. This Agency is charged merely with determining the placement of marijuana pursuant to the provisions of the Act. Under our system of laws the responsibilities of other regulatory bodies are the concerns of those bodies, not of this Agency.

There are those who, in all sincerity, argue that the transfer of marijuana to Schedule II will "send a signal" that marijuana is "OK" generally for recreational use. This argument is specious. It presents no valid reason for refraining from taking an action required by law in light of the evidence. If marijuana should be placed in Schedule II, in obedience to the law, then that is where marijuana should be placed, regardless of misinterpretation of the placement by some. The reasons for the placement can, and should, be clearly explained at the time the action is taken. The fear of sending such a signal cannot be permitted to override the legitimate need, amply demonstrated in this record, of countless sufferers for the relief marijuana can provide when prescribed by a physician in a legitimate case.

The evidence in this record clearly shows that marijuana has been accepted as capable of relieving the distress of great numbers of very ill people, and doing so with safety under medical supervision. It would be unreasonable, arbitrary and capricious for DEA to continue to stand between those sufferers and the benefits of this substance in light of the evidence in this record.

The administrative law judge recommends that the Administrator conclude that the marijuana plant considered as a whole has a currently accepted medical use in treatment in the United States, that there is no lack of accepted safety for use of it under medical supervision and that it may lawfully be transferred from Schedule I to Schedule II. The judge recommends that the Administrator transfer marijuana from Schedule I to Schedule II.

DENIAL OF MARIJUANA SCHEDULING PETITION

U.S. Department of Justice, Drug Enforcement Administration

This is a final order of the Administrator of the Drug Enforcement Administration (DEA) denying the petition of the National Organization for Reform of Marijuana Laws (NORML) to reschedule the plant material marijuana from Schedule I to Schedule II of the Controlled Substances Act. This order follows a rulemaking on the record as prescribed by the Controlled Substances Act, 21 U.S.C. 801, *et seq.*, and the Administrative Procedures Act, 5 U.S.C. 551, *et seq.*

There are seven parties in the rulemaking proceeding. Four parties, NORML, the Alliance for Cannabis Therapeutics (ACT), the Cannabis Corporation of America (CCA), and Carl Eric Olsen, comprised the pro-marijuana parties, those advocating the rescheduling of marijuana from Schedule I to Schedule II. The three remaining parties, who advocated that marijuana remain in Schedule I, were DEA, the National Federation of Parents for a Drug-Free Youth, and the International Association of Chiefs of Police (IACP).

The two issues involved in a determination of whether marijuana should be rescheduled from Schedule I to Schedule II are whether marijuana plant material has a currently accepted medical use in treatment in the United States, or a currently accepted medical use with severe restrictions; and whether there is a lack of accepted safety for use of marijuana plant material under medical supervision. After a thorough review of the record in this matter, the Administrator rejects the recommendation of the administrative law judge to reschedule marijuana into Schedule II and finds that the evidence in the record mandates a finding that the marijuana plant material remain in Schedule I of the Controlled Substances Act.

The pro-marijuana parties advocate the placement of marijuana plant material into Schedule II for medical use in the treatment of a wide variety of ailments, including nausea and vomiting associated with chemotherapy, glaucoma, spasticity in amputees and those with multiple sclerosis, epilepsy, poor appetite, addiction to drugs and alcohol, pain, and asthma. The evidence presented by the pro-marijuana parties includes outdated and limited scientific studies; chronicles of individuals, their families and friends who have used marijuana; opinions from over a dozen psychiatrists and physicians; court opinions involving medical necessity as a defense to criminal charges for illegal possession of marijuana; state statutes which made marijuana available for research; newspaper articles; and the opinions of laypersons, including lawyers and associations of lawyers. The Administrator does not find such evidence convincing in light of the lack of reliable, credible, and relevant scientific studies documenting marijuana's medical utility; the opinions of highly respected, credentialed experts that marijuana does not have an accepted medical use; and statements from the American Medical Association, the American Cancer Society, the American Academy of Ophthalmology, the National Multiple Sclerosis Society, and the Federal Food and Drug Administration that marijuana has not been demonstrated as suitable for use as a medicine. Each of these areas will be discussed separately.

The record contains many research studies which have been published in scientific journals and many unpublished studies conducted by individual states. In order to evaluate the validity of any research study many factors must be considered. Certain scientific practices have been generally accepted by the scientific community which are designed to increase the validity of experimental studies. Studies or research projects which do not follow these accepted scientific practices have very limited, if any, credibility. A review of such studies must first examine the degree to which researchers control, or hold constant, all the variables which could affect the results, except the variable being studied. For example, if you wish to evaluate the effectiveness of marijuana on a group of glaucoma patients, you must control any other medication which the patient is taking. Otherwise, it is impossible to conclude that the results are attributable to the marijuana.

The second factor, or aspect of the design of a research project which must be evaluated, is the placebo effect. This is the tendency of research subjects to act and respond in a manner they believe is expected of them. To eliminate this factor, research subjects are usually "blinded," or not informed, of what drug they are receiving. Results of non-blind studies are questionable since they could be attributable, in large part, to psychological reactions of subjects rather than any real effects from the experimental drug. The next factor which must be minimized or eliminated for a research study to be valid is the expectation of the researcher. This is especially true where the effect being measured is subjective and not objective. For example, if the researcher is evaluating if the patient is nauseated, that is very subjective. If the researcher knows which patients are receiving the experimental drug, his perception of the results could be significantly altered.

Other factors to be considered when evaluating the validity of research include the number of subjects in the study, how the subjects are selected for the study, the length of the study, or how many times the experimental drug is administered, and the measurement of results in quantifiable, objective terms. The fewer the subjects in a research study, the less valid the results. If the sample of subjects is not statistically significant, the chances of the same results being duplicated in other individuals is reduced. Subjects for a research study should be randomly selected and representative of the population that is targeted to use the drug. Testing of marijuana in cancer patients for relief of nausea and vomiting should not be limited to those who have previously used marijuana recreationally and request its use in the study. The length of a study is particularly significant when the drug is to be used to treat a chronic condition such as glaucoma or spasticity. Studies based upon acute or one-time administration of the drug must be viewed with caution when the goal is treatment of a chronic condition. The effectiveness of the drug for long-time administration and the existence of side effects resulting from chronic use will not be revealed in acute studies.

In addition to factors related to the design and execution of a research study, there are two other factors which must be reviewed in evaluation of a research study. Research results are always considered tentative or preliminary until they have been replicated or confirmed by another researcher. The research study must be reported in sufficient detail to permit others to repeat it. Finally, publication of a study in a scientific journal, especially a journal which subjects an article to review prior to publication, adds validity to a study. Journal publication subjects a study to review and scrutiny by the scientific community and opens the door to replication of the studies. Unpublished studies are inherently suspect.

While research studies with the limitations mentioned above may provide useful and preliminary data which will be valuable in designing further studies, research studies with substantial limitations are not sufficient to support a determination that a drug has an accepted medical use. Both the published and unpublished research studies submitted by the pro-marijuana parties in this proceeding to support marijuana's medical use suffer from many deficiencies. They are, in essence, preliminary studies. None of these studies has risen to the level of demonstrating that marijuana has an accepted medical use for treatment of any medical condition. The three medical conditions for which the majority of evidence in the record was presented are: (1) Nausea and vomiting associated with chemotherapy. (2) glaucoma, and (3) spasticity associated with amputation or multiple sclerosis. Evidence presented in each area will be discussed separately.

Nausea and Vomiting

Five studies were presented by the pro-marijuana parties to support the medical use of marijuana as an antiemetic. The first study by Sallan, et al., *Antiemetic Effect of Delta-9-Tetrahydrocannabinol in Patients Receiving Cancer Chemotherapy*, 293 New England Journal of Medicine, 795–797 (1975), utilized synthetic tetrahydrocannabinol (THC) and not the plant material marijuana. Although delta-9-THC is an active ingredient in the marijuana plant material, marijuana contains over 400 other chemicals. At least 61 of these chemicals are cannabinoids. All these chemicals could have some effect on the human body. Since THC is only one of many active ingredients in marijuana, THC studies are of very limited value in evaluating the therapeutic utility of marijuana. The route of administration, smoking versus oral injection, is a significant difference between use of marijuana and THC. Therefore, the results of the Sallan study are of little or no benefit in evaluating the medical utility of marijuana for treatment of nausea and vomiting associated with chemotherapy.

The second study compared a combination of pure THC and marijuana to placebo cigarettes. This study by Chang, et al., *Delta-9-Tetrahydrocannabinol as an Antiemetic in Cancer Patients Receiving High-Dose Methotrexate*, 91 Annals of Internal Medicine, 819–824 (1979), was randomized, double-blind, and placebo controlled. The study concluded, "that a combination of oral and smoked THC is a highly effective antiemetic compared to placebo . . ." This study was limited to 15 subjects, some of whom received both marijuana and THC at the same time. The validity of the results of this study is severely limited by its small size and administration of the mixture of the two drugs, THC and marijuana. The study is not helpful in determining the therapeutic utility of marijuana alone in treating nausea and vomiting.

The third study conducted by Dr. Thomas J. Ungerleider, a psychiatrist, involved the administration of marijuana to 16 bone marrow transplant patients suffering from severe nausea and vomiting from radiation therapy. The results of this study are of little value due to the limited number of patients, the subjective nature of the data, and the fact that the results of the study were never published. The conclusion that there was less nausea and vomiting with use of marijuana was based upon the subjects' and researcher's subjective determination. There were no objective measurements, such as number of incidents or frequency of vomiting. During cross-examination, Dr. Ungerleider indicated that the results of the study were not published because there was not enough hard data.

The fourth study compared marijuana to THC as an antiemetic. Levitt, et al., *Pandomized Double Blind Comparison of Delta-9-Tetrahydrocannobinol (THC) and Marijuana As Chemotherapy Antiemetics.* (Meeting Abstract), 3 Proc. Annu. Meet. Am. Soc. Clin. Oncol. 91 (1984). It concluded that THC is superior to marijuana in controlling nausea and vomiting. A specific formulation of synthetic THC has been approved for marketing and is available as a prescription drug for treatment of nausea and vomiting associated with cancer chemotherapy.

The fifth study presented by the pro-marijuana parties is actually a group of programs, collectively labeled "Controlled Substances Therapeutic Research Programs," conducted by six states in the 1970's and 1980's. These programs involved the use of both marijuana cigarettes and synthetic THC capsules. The programs were given Investigational New Drug (IND) approval by the Food and Drug Administration (FDA) and the marijuana and THC were supplied by the Federal Government. The protocols of these programs were very loosely constructed. There were no controls. That is, there were no individuals who did not take the experimental drugs to compare with those who did. The studies were not blind or double-blind. Every research subject knew what drug they were receiving and, in many cases, were permitted to request either marijuana or THC. The studies were not randomized. In most instances, the results were measured by the subject's subjective evaluation of the drug's effectiveness. This is even more of a problem where the drug in question is a psychotropic or mind-altering substance like marijuana, which by its very nature makes some individuals feel "high," and may distort their perception of physical symptoms. There were no objectively measured results. The results were not published in scientific journals and, in some cases, data were lost or not recorded. The number of individuals who actually smoked marijuana in these studies was relatively small. These state studies were born of compassion and frustration. They abandoned traditional scientific methods in favor of dispensing marijuana to as many individuals as possible on the chance that it might help them. Though well-intentioned, these studies have little scientific value.

The research studies presented by the pro-marijuana parties in this proceeding do not support a conclusion that marijuana has a therapeutic use for treatment of nausea and vomiting associated with chemotherapy.

The pro-marijuana parties presented many testimonials from cancer patients, their families, and friends about the use of marijuana to alleviate nausea and vomiting associated with chemotherapy. These stories of individuals who treat themselves with a mind-altering drug, such as marijuana, must be viewed with great skepticism. There is no scientific merit to any of these accounts. In many cases the individuals were taking a variety of other medications and were using anything which might help treat the cancer as well as the nausea. They were using marijuana purchased on the street, and were unaware of the strength of the drug. They were not using the drug under medical supervision. Many of these individuals had been recreational users of marijuana prior to becoming ill. These individuals' desire for the drug to relieve their symptoms, as well as a desire to rationalize their marijuana use, removes any scientific value from their accounts of marijuana use. There is no doubt that these individuals and their loved-ones believed that marijuana was beneficial. The accounts of these individuals' suffering and illnesses are very moving and tragic; they are not, however, reliable scientific evidence, nor do they provide a basis to conclude that marijuana has an accepted medical use as an antiemetic.

There were many physicians and other medical experts who testified in this proceeding. In reviewing the weight to be given to an expert's opinion, the facts relied upon to reach that opinion and the credentials and experience of the expert must be carefully examined. The experts presented by the pro-marijuana parties were unable to provide a strong scientific or factual basis to support their opinions. In addition, many of the experts presented by the pro-marijuana parties did not have any expertise in the area of research in the specific medical area being addressed. The pro-marijuana parties presented the testimony of five psychiatrists to support the use of marijuana as an antiemetic. None of these individuals is an oncologist, nor have they treated cancer patients. Three of the psychiatrists, Drs. Grinspoon, Ungerleider and Zinberg are current or former board members of NORML or ACT. All these physicians indicated that they relied on scientific studies which they had read, their experience with cancer patients, or stories from others, to reach their conclusions. When questioned on cross-examination as to which studies they relied upon, most were unable to list one study. A review of the available literature has already demonstrated the unreliability of the studies that exist. The testimonials upon which these psychiatrists relied are also scientifically suspect. The opinions of these psychiatrists are, therefore, of little value in determining whether marijuana is therapeutically useful as an antiemetic.

Two pharmacologists, Drs. Morgan and Jobe, presented testimony on behalf of the pro-marijuana parties. Dr. Morgan is a professor at the City College of New York. He does not treat patients, nor is he an oncologist. His opinions are based upon a review of scientific studies and stories told to him by others. He has ties to NORML and is in favor of legalizing marijuana. Dr. Jobe is a pharmacologist and psychiatrist. He testified that his knowledge of marijuana's effects as a drug are based upon a review of the literature and stories from individuals undergoing chemotherapy. On cross-examination, Dr. Jobe indicated that this anecdotal information came from approximately four or five individuals. He also indicated that his knowledge of the scientific studies conducted with marijuana was not current. The opinions of Drs. Morgan and Jobe are of little value in determining whether marijuana has a medical use.

Two general practitioners, Drs. Weil and Kaufman, also provided testimony on behalf of the pro-marijuana parties. Neither are oncologists, nor do they treat cancer patients. Dr. Weil is a wellness counselor at a health spa, and Dr. Kaufman is an officer of a company that audits hospital quality control programs. Dr. Weil has written a number of books on drugs and admitted that he has personally used every mind-altering, illicit drug he has written about. Dr. Kaufman stopped practicing medicine in 1974, and was unable to provide any information on cross-examination regarding the basis for his opinion that marijuana has an accepted medical use. Neither Dr. Weil nor Dr. Kaufman has a credible basis for their opinions regarding marijuana, and, therefore, their testimony will be disregarded.

Four oncologists presented testimony on behalf of the pro-marijuana parties. They were Drs. Goldberg, Silverberg, Bickers, and Stephens. Dr. Goldberg is a board certified oncologist, but practices primarily internal medicine. She only administers chemotherapy to one or two patients a year. In her career, she has administered chemotherapy to no more than ten patients whom she believed to be using marijuana. On cross-examination, she could not recall any studies regarding marijuana. Dr. Goldberg was a member and financial contributor to NORML. Dr. Silverberg has practiced oncology for 20 years. He is a Professor of Clinical Oncology at the University of California at San Francisco, but is not a board certified oncologist. In his testimony, Dr. Silverberg indicated that there was voluminous medical research regarding marijuana's effectiveness in treating nausea and vomiting. On cross-examination. Dr. Silverberg could not identify any studies, and was forced to admit that he had been incorrect and that there were, in fact, very few studies conducted using marijuana as an antiemetic. Although Dr. Silverberg has advised patients to use marijuana to control nausea and vomiting associated with chemotherapy, he has never been involved in any research nor has he documented any of his observations. Dr. Bickers is an oncologist in New Orleans and is a Professor of Medicine at the Louisiana University School of Medicine. Although Dr. Bickers claims that young patients have better control over nausea and vomiting after using marijuana, he has never documented this claim. Dr. Bickers was unable to identify any scientific information which he relied upon in reaching his conclusion regarding marijuana. Dr. Stephens, an oncologist, Professor of Medicine and Director of Clinical Oncology at the University of Kansas, characterized marijuana as a "highly effective, and in some cases, critical drug in the reduction of chemotherapeutically-induced emesis." During cross-examination, Dr. Stephens stated that he was unaware of any scientific studies which had been done with marijuana, and that he had never done research or treated patients with marijuana. He indicated that he received his information about the patient's use of marijuana from the nursing staff or the patient's family. None of these oncologists based their opinions about marijuana on scientific studies or their own research. Most did not base their opinions on their direct observations, but on the opinions of others. In light of lack of scientific basis for these opinions, they will be given little regard.

The agency presented the testimony of nationally recognized experts in oncology. Dr. Ettinger, a Professor of Oncology at Johns Hopkins School of Medicine, is the author of over 100 published articles on cancer treatment. Dr. Ettinger testified:

There is no indication that marijuana is effective in treating nausea and vomiting resulting from radiation treatment or other causes. No legitimate studies have been conducted which make such conclusions.

He continued by stating that:

Although extensive research has been conducted using . . . (THC) . . . as antiemetic treatment for cancer chemotherapy patients, very little research has actually been conducted using marijuana . . . for the same purpose. Most of the information concerning marijuana's effectiveness is anecdotal or comes from uncontrolled studies.

Dr. Gralla, a Professor of Medicine at Cornell University Medical College, and an Associate Attending Physician at Sloan-Kettering Memorial Cancer Center, is an oncologist who has spent his entire professional career devoted to cancer research and treatment. Dr. Gralla has conducted extensive research with antiemetic drugs and testified that there are currently many new medicines that control nausea and vomiting associated with chemotherapy more effectively than marijuana. He also stated that most physicians and oncologists have little interest in marijuana because of its negative side effects and other problems associated with its use. In conclusion Dr. Gralla stated that he and his fellow cancer specialists at Sloan-Kettering do not accept marijuana as being medically useful to treat nausea and vomiting associated with chemotherapy.

Dr. Laszlo, currently Vice President of Research for the American Cancer Society, is an expert who has devoted the majority of his over 30 years in medicine to the treatment of cancer. During his career, he spent eleven years as the Director of Clinical Programs at the Duke University Comprehensive Cancer Center. Dr. Laszlo has authored numerous scientific articles about cancer research and treatment and has written a book titled, *Antiemetics and Cancer Chemotherapy*. In his testimony for this proceeding, Dr. Laszlo stated that he does not advocate the use of marijuana as an antiemetic, in part, because there has not been sufficient testing of marijuana to show that it is a safe and effective drug. He also indicated that because there are other available, highly effective antiemetics, a physician does not need to resort to a crude drug such as marijuana. Dr. Laszlo concluded that marijuana does not have a currently accepted medical use in the United States for treatment of nausea and vomiting resulting from cancer chemotherapy.

The American Cancer Society provided DEA with its policy statements regarding medical use of marijuana. The administrative law judge refused to admit this document into evidence in this proceeding, relegating it to the "public comment" section of the record. The Administrator, however, considers this document to be extremely relevant and, indeed, of substantial importance in this matter. The American Cancer Society has, and continues to support research with substances which may provide relief to cancer patients, including marijuana. It states, however, that the results of clinical investigations are insufficient to warrant the decontrol of marijuana for medical use. The American Medical Association has expressed a similar opinion.

The Food and Drug Administration has provided DEA with a scientific and medical evaluation of marijuana, as well as testimony from one of its leading pharmacologists. Evaluating marijuana against its criteria for safety and effectiveness, FDA has concluded that there is inadequate scientific evidence to support a finding that marijuana is safe and effective for treating nausea and vomiting experienced by patients undergoing chemotherapy.

The pro-marijuana parties presented cases in which courts did not convict individuals of a crime associated with possession and use of marijuana based upon a legal defense of "medical necessity." These cases have no relevance to this proceeding which relates to marijuana's possible medical use. The courts found only that these individuals, who were seriously ill and believed that marijuana would help them, did not have criminal intent in possessing or using marijuana. The judges and juries in these proceedings were not deciding medical and scientific facts, but legal issues. These decisions do not provide scientific evidence that marijuana has a medical use.

The pro-marijuana parties also presented evidence that 34 states passed laws permitting marijuana's use for medical purposes in those states. These laws provided that marijuana should be available for medical research. The term "research" is essential to a reading of these statutes. These laws made marijuana available for research and, in some states, set up research programs to study marijuana's safety and effectiveness as a medicine. These statutes are read for what they are, encouraging research involving marijuana. They are not an endorsement by state legislatures that marijuana has an accepted medical use in treatment.

The numerous testimonials and opinions of lay persons which were presented in this proceeding by the pro-marijuana parties are not useful in determining whether marijuana has a medical use. While experiences of individuals with medical conditions who use marijuana may provide a basis for research, they cannot be substituted for reliable scientific evidence. For the many reasons stated in the previous discussion of scientific evidence, these statements can be given little weight. Similarly, endorsements by such organizations as the National Association of Attorneys General, that marijuana has a medical use as an antiemetic, are of little persuasive value when compared with statements from the American Cancer Society and the American Medical Association.

Glaucoma

The pro-marijuana parties presented several studies to support their contention that marijuana has a medical use for treatment of glaucoma. In order for a drug to be effective in treating glaucoma it must lower the pressure within the eye for prolonged periods of time and actually preserve sight or visual fields. The studies relied upon by the pro-marijuana parties do not scientifically support a finding that marijuana has a medical use for treatment of glaucoma. Five of the studies presented by the pro-marijuana parties are pure THC studies. As previously noted, THC is only one constituent among hundreds found in marijuana.

Therefore, the consequences of an individual ingesting pure THC as compared to smoking marijuana are vastly different. A few of the studies presented do document that heavy doses of marijuana over a short time period reduce eye pressure in most individuals. However, there are no studies which document that marijuana can sustain reduced eye pressure for extended time periods. The acute, or short-term, studies also show various side effects from marijuana use, including lowered blood pressure, rapid heart beat, and heart palpitations. In a 1979 study conducted by Drs. Merritt, Crawford, Alexander, Anduze, and Gelbart, the conclusions included a statement: "It is because of the frequency and severity with which untoward events occurred that marijuana inhalation is not an ideal therapeutic modality for glaucoma patients."

The pro-marijuana parties presented testimonials of individuals who suffer from glaucoma and believe their condition has benefited from the use of marijuana. Most of these individuals used marijuana recreationally prior to discovery of their illness. Chief among the individuals presenting statements was Robert Randall. Mr. Randall is president of ACT, and has been on NORML's Board of Directors since 1976. He had been a strong advocate for medical use of marijuana. Mr. Randall also has glaucoma. Mr. Randall began smoking marijuana as a college student in 1963, long before he was diagnosed in 1972 as having glaucoma. At that time Mr. Randall was treated with standard glaucoma medications. In the mid 1970's Mr. Randall was involved in a preliminary research study conducted by Dr. Robert Hepler. Dr. Hepler conducted some of the first published short-term marijuana studies relating to glaucoma. Dr. Hepler told Mr. Randall that he believed that marijuana in combination with other standard glaucoma medications would be helpful in reducing his eye pressure. In 1975, Mr. Randall was arrested for growing and possessing marijuana. His defense was medical necessity. Subsequently, he began receiving marijuana under an Investigational New Drug (IND) protocol sponsored by his physician. He also continued to receive standard glaucoma medications. Since 1978, Mr. Randall has been treated by Dr. North. Mr. Randall receives marijuana from the Federal Government and continues to take standard glaucoma medications. Two physicians who treated Mr. Randall, including Dr. North, testified that Mr. Randall's eye pressure appears to have been controlled and his vision kept stable for the last several years.

Mr. Randall smokes approximately 8 to 10 marijuana cigarettes a day. Since Mr. Randall continues to take other glaucoma medications, his controlled eye pressure cannot be attributable solely to marijuana use. In fact, Dr. North testified that Mr. Randall needs the standard medications as well as marijuana, and that the marijuana itself is not totally effective in decreasing Mr. Randall's eye pressure. Mr. Randall's experience with marijuana, although utilized under a physician's directions, is not scientific evidence that marijuana has an accepted medical use in treatment of glaucoma. Dr. Merritt, one of Mr. Randall's physicians, responded to the question of why he did not publish the results of Mr. Randall's treatment by saying, "A single isolated incident of one person smoking marijuana is not evidence for other ophthalmologists who may want to use the drug."

Dr. Hepler, the physician who conducted preliminary studies with marijuana and initially advised Mr. Randall to use marijuana with his other medications, now states that there is insufficient scientific evidence to conclude that marijuana is effective in treating glaucoma. The pro-marijuana parties rely primarily on the opinions of two of Mr. Randall's physicians. Drs. North and Merritt, in supporting their contention that marijuana has a medical use in treatment of glaucoma. Dr. North indicated that his conclusion that marijuana has a medical use in treatment of glaucoma is based solely on his observations of Mr. Randall. Dr. Merritt is a board certified ophthalmologist and researcher who has authored many articles on the use of marijuana and cannabinoids to reduce eye pressure. Dr. Merritt based his opinion that marijuana has a medical use in treatment of glaucoma on published scientific studies, treatment of Mr. Randall, and treatment of other glaucoma patients. As previously stated, all the available studies concern high doses of marijuana taken over short periods of time. Even Dr. Merritt admitted that there are no studies to show that marijuana repeatedly lowers eye pressure over long time periods. The maintenance of lowered eye pressure is crucial in treating individuals with glaucoma. On cross-examination, Dr. Merritt was unable to provide either the specific number of individual patients he had observed or any scientific data relating to those patients. Although Dr. Merritt is a well-known ophthalmologist, the basis for his opinion that marijuana has a medical use in the treatment of glaucoma is not scientifically sound.

The agency presented several experts who testified that there is insufficient scientific evidence to support a conclusion that marijuana has a medical use in treatment of glaucoma. In addition to Dr. Hepler, they include Dr. George Spaeth, Professor of Ophthalmology, Director of the Glaucoma Service at Will's Eye Hospital in Philadelphia and President of the American Glaucoma Society; and Dr. Keith Green, Professor of Ophthalmology, pharmacologist and researcher who has conducted research with both marijuana and THC. Perhaps the most persuasive evidence concerning the use of marijuana in treating glaucoma is the opinion of the American Academy of Ophthalmology, an organization representing 12,000 physician members and 6,000 other medical professionals who specialize in the treatment of ophthalmology. The Academy has concluded that insufficient data exists to demonstrate the safety and efficacy of using smoked marijuana in the treatment of glaucoma. FDA has also determined that there is insufficient evidence to conclude that marijuana has a medical use in treatment of glaucoma.

Spasticity

In support of their contention that marijuana has a medical use in treatment of spasticity in amputees and those with multiple sclerosis, the pro-marijuana parties presented three studies involving THC, testimonials of individuals with spasticity who use marijuana, medical opinions, and state court decisions on the medical necessity defense. The three studies presented by the pro-marijuana parties were very small studies. All three totalled 17 patients, and used THC, not marijuana, to treat spasticity. There are no studies using marijuana to treat spasticity. These studies do not provide a scientific basis to conclude that marijuana has a medical use in treating spasticity.

Dr. Denis Petro, a board certified neurologist, testified on behalf of the pro-marijuana parties that he believes that marijuana has a currently accepted medical use in treating spasticity. He testified that his opinion is based on the THC studies, experiences and observations of patients, and historical accounts of marijuana use. Dr. Petro knew of no studies in which marijuana was used to treat spasticity. He testified that his information from patients consisted of them telling him how the street marijuana these patients used at home affected their spasticity. He did not conduct any clinical studies or make objective measurements. Dr. Petro's opinion is not based upon any reliable scientific evidence. The same psychiatrists and general practitioners who reported marijuana had a medical use in treating nausea and vomiting and glaucoma also stated that marijuana had a medical use in treating spasticity. None of these physicians based their opinions on reliable scientific evidence.

The agency presented the testimony of national experts in the area of multiple sclerosis and spasticity. Dr. Kenneth Johnson is the Chairman of the Department of Neurology at the University of Maryland School of Medicine and manages the Maryland Center for Multiple Sclerosis (MS). He is the author of over 100 scientific and medical articles on MS. Dr. Johnson has spent most of his medical career researching MS and has diagnosed and treated more than 6,000 patients with the disease. He testified that he is unaware of any legitimate research involving marijuana to treat symptoms of MS. He further stated that, "[t]o conclude that marijuana is therapeutically effective without conducting vigorous testing would be professionally irresponsible." Dr. Donald Silberberg, Chairman of the Department of Neurology at the University of Pennsylvania School of Medicine and Chief of Neurology Service at the Hospital of Pennsylvania, has been actively researching and treating MS for most of his career. He has written over 130 medical articles on MS. He concluded that not only is there no legitimate medical or scientific evidence to support a conclusion that marijuana is effective in treating MS or spasticity, but that long-term treatment of MS patients with marijuana could be worse than the original disease. Dr. Silberberg placed no value on the reports of patients who claimed relief of their symptoms with marijuana because of the sporadic and episodic nature of MS attacks.

The National Multiple Sclerosis Society has concluded that marijuana is not an accepted medical treatment for spasticity. Dr. Stephen Reingold, Assistant Vice President for Research of the National Multiple Sclerosis Society, indicated in his testimony that because there are no well-designed, well-controlled research studies using marijuana to treat spasticity, the society does not endorse or advocate the use of marijuana for such a purpose.

The evidence presented by the pro-marijuana parties regarding use of marijuana to treat various other ailments such as pain, decreased appetite, alcohol and drug addiction, epilepsy, atopic neurodermatitis, scleroderma and asthma was limited to testimony of individuals who had used marijuana for those conditions and the testimony of the psychiatrists or general practice physicians mentioned earlier. There is not a shred of credible scientific evidence to support any of their claims.

With regard to marijuana's safety for use under medical supervision, the Administrator must again rely on the scientific evidence. While the pro-marijuana parties argue that no one has died from marijuana use, and the individuals who use it have testified that they have not experienced adverse effects, there is little or no scientific evidence to support their claims. For example, while Robert Randall claims marijuana smoking has had no adverse effect on his health or respiratory system, he has not had a physical examination or pulmonary function test in over ten years.

In order to be effective, a drug's therapeutic benefits must be balanced against, and outweigh, its negative or adverse effects. This had not been established with marijuana. As the previously discussed evidence has demonstrated, there is as yet no reliable scientific evidence to support marijuana's therapeutic benefit. It is, therefore, impossible to balance the benefit against the negative effects. The negative effects of marijuana use are well-documented in the record. Marijuana smoking, the route of administration advocated by many witnesses presented by the pro-marijuana parties, causes many well-known and scientifically documented side effects. These include decreased blood pressure, rapid heart rate, drowsiness, euphoria, disphoria and impairment of motor function, not to mention various negative effects on the respiratory and pulmonary systems. Therefore, the only conclusion is that marijuana is not safe for use under medical supervision, because its safety has not been established by reliable scientific evidence.

In summary, the Administrator finds that there is insufficient, and in many instances no, reliable, credible, scientific evidence, supported by properly conducted scientific research, to support a conclusion that marijuana has a medical use to treat any ailment or disease. In addition, there is a lack of scientific evidence to support a conclusion that marijuana is safe for use under medical supervision. This agency, and the Government as a whole, would be doing the public a disservice by concluding that this complex psychoactive drug with serious adverse effects has a medical use based upon anecdotal and unreliable evidence. The evidence presented by the promarijuana parties in this proceeding consisted of a few published scientific studies involving marijuana and THC, testimony of general practice physicians and psychiatrists, and testimony of individuals who have used marijuana for various medical conditions. The majority of these individuals did not use marijuana under medical supervision and used "street" marijuana. In contrast, recognized, credentialed specialists in the fields of oncology, glaucoma and multiple sclerosis, and organizations involved in medical research in these areas, have concluded that marijuana does not have an accepted medical use in treatment in the United States. The Administrator would be abdicating his responsibility to the public if he concluded that marijuana has a medical use and is safe for use under medical supervision.

The preceding discussion is based upon the Administrator's review of the entire record in this matter. This record contains volumes of documents and testimony. The procedural history of this scheduling has extended for many years. The procedural history and the findings of fact and conclusions of law upon which the Administrator's decision is based are set forth below.

Procedure

This rulemaking proceeding was originally initiated by a petition filed by NORML on May 18, 1972, with the Bureau of Narcotics and Dangerous Drugs (BNDD). This petition requested that marijuana be removed from the Controlled Substances Act, or in the alternative, be moved to Schedule V of the Act. After a series of proceedings, including bearings before BNDD and DEA and remands by the United States Court of Appeals for the District of Columbia Circuit, the matter was again the subject of a DEA hearing. This hearing followed a 1980 remand by the United States Court of Appeals for the District of Columbia Circuit, *NORML* v. *DEA and HEW*, No. 79–1660 (D.C. Cir. Oct. 16, 1980), in which the Court ordered DEA to refer all matters to the Department of Health and Human Services (HHS) for a scientific and medical evaluation and recommendation for scheduling. The matter was forwarded to HHS by DEA, and the Food and Drug Administration (FDA) published "Proposed Recommendations to the Drug Enforcement Administration Regarding the Scheduling Status of Marijuana and Its Components and Notice of Public Hearing," in the Federal Register, 47 FR 28141 (1982). On September 16, 1982, FDA conducted a legislative-type hearing at which it received written and oral testimony. On May 13, 1983, the Assistant Secretary for Health forwarded his department's scientific and medical findings and scheduling recommendation regarding marijuana plant material to the Administrator of DEA. In this document the Assistant Secretary recommended that marijuana plant material continue to be controlled in Schedule I. On July 2, 1987, the Assistant Secretary for Health submitted a letter to the DEA Deputy Administrator in which he stated that it continued to be the position of the Department of Health and Human Services that marijuana continue to be controlled in Schedule I based upon its lack of accepted medical use in treatment in the United States.

This current proceeding was initiated by publication of a notice of hearing in the Federal Register on June 24, 1986, which advised any individual interested in participating in the proceedings to file a written notice of such intent. Seven organizations or individuals participated in the proceeding. Four prehearing conferences were held in late 1986 and 1987. Direct and rebuttal testimony were filed in written affidavit form. Fourteen days of hearings, for the purpose of cross-examination of witnesses, were held in three cities. All parties were permitted to file proposed findings of fact, conclusions of law and argument with Administrative Law Judge Francis L. Young. The pro-marijuana parties, as petitioners, filed their proposed findings on April 15, 1988. The Government filed its proposed findings on May 16, 1988. The pro-marijuana parties then filed rebuttal on June 3, 1988. The administrative law judge issued his opinion and recommended ruling, findings of fact, conclusions of law and decision on September 6, 1988. Exceptions to the administrative law judge's recommended decision were filed by NORML, ACT, and the Government. By letter dated December 9, 1988, the administrative law judge forwarded the entire record to the Administrator of DEA.

The Administrator has carefully reviewed the entire record in this matter and hereby issues this final order as prescribed by 21 CFR 1316.67. The Administrator does not accept the recommendation of the administrative law judge that marijuana has an accepted medical use in treatment of some medical conditions, that marijuana has accepted safety for use under medical supervision, and that marijuana should be rescheduled into Schedule II of the Controlled Substances Act. The Administrator finds that marijuana must remain in Schedule I of the Controlled Substances Act because it has no accepted medical use in treatment of any condition in the United States and it is not safe for use under medical supervision. The Administrator has reviewed the proposed findings of fact submitted by all parties and those formulated by the administrative law judge. The Administrator adopts the findings of fact submitted by the Government as his own and in their entirety. They are as follows:

Findings of Fact

1. The cannabis plant (*Cannabis sativa L.*) is an annual weed which belongs to the plant family Cannabaceae. This family has only one genus, the genus *Cannabis* which consists of one highly variable species, *sativa*. Many varieties of this species are known to exist.

2. Over 400 different chemicals have been identified in the extracts of the plant *Cannabis sativa*. They belong to 18 chemical classes of organic compounds. There are at least 61 different cannabinoids. The proportions and concentrations of these cannabinoids, including THC, differ from plant to plant depending on growing conditions, age of the plant, and factors surrounding harvest. THC levels found in cannabis may vary-from less than 0.2% in some plants to greater than 10% in high quality plants.

3. Cannabis or marijuana cannot be defined chemically, nor can it be easily standardized. No totally reliable classification system based on a single chemical analysis exists. Twenty-one (21) cannabinoids have been clinically evaluated. Most of this testing centered on the psychotropic effects of the compounds, and only eight or nine of the cannabinoids have been tested for therapeutic utility. These studies have only been cursory except for the testing of synthetic THC Cannabigerol (CBG) cannabinoids show antibacterial activity against gram positive bacteria, and have been shown to effect basic cell metabolism. Cannabinol (CBN) type compounds have exhibited anticonvulsant, anti-inflammatory, immunological, and behavioral effects. CBN has also exhibited possible potentiation of THC effects in man. Cannabidiol (CBD) has exhibited anticonvulsant activity.

4. As well as significant variations in naturally occurring active substances in natural cannabis, there are variations in the active substances based on conditions

under which the plant material has been maintained or stored. THC is labile to air oxidation forming cannabinol (CBN). Cannabidiol (CBD), in the presence of oxygen and light and upon heating, is converted to cannabielsoic acids.

5. It is not known how smoking or burning marijuana plant material affects the chemical composition of cannabinoids and their products. A large number of pyrolytic products is produced by burning that have not been identified for most of the constituents in *Cannabis*. Smoking as a dosage form to deliver marijuana to the human body is unsuitable for medical treatment due to: (1) Lack of standardization of the marijuana, (2) lack of knowledge of the amounts of each constituent available, (3) lack of knowledge of the activity of the chemicals while burning, (4) amount of product ingested being dependent on the individual's smoking technique, and (5) possible carcinogenic effect of smoking. There are no drugs which are delivered by smoking which are medically used in the United States.

6. *Cannabis sativa L.* was one of the first plants to be used by man for fiber, food, medicine, and in social and religious rituals. There were approximately 20 traditional medicinal uses of cannabis preparations in the 19th century. These included those recognized in 19th century medicine as well as folkloric use. These uses were based upon tradition and experience rather than scientific proof. Early literature is replete with reports of the inconsistent or contradictory effects of marijuana preparations. The cannabis used for medical purposes in the United States and in Western medicine from the mid-19th to the early 20th century was cannabis extract which was orally administered as tinctures and pills. By 1938, marijuana preparations were seldom used in medical practice, and the American Medical Association stated that, "Cannabis at the present time is slightly used for medicinal purposes . . ." In 1941, marijuana passed out of the *National Formulary* and *The United States Pharmacopeia*.

7. Historically, man used natural plants to treat various ailments. With the advent of science, man began to use plant extracts to determine their effects. These extracts were crude drugs. Fifty years ago *The United States Pharmacopeia* listed many crude drugs. In recent times, scientists discovered that crude extracts owed their activity to chemical compounds and began isolating the chemical compounds from the plants and their extracts. Current technology emphasizes the development of synthetics of natural drugs by using the natural drugs as models.

8. Currently, there are only four plants used in their natural states for medical purposes in the United States. Three others are utilized in crude extract form. These include ipecac and opium extracts, which must meet standards for potency and purity established in *The United States Pharmacopeia* before they can be used for medical purposes. In contrast to variations in cannabinoid content evident in cannabis, naturally occurring opium derivatives remain quantitatively stable and the potency can be chemically standardized.

9. Modern drug research is based on the use of well-defined preparations of pure compounds which, when administered to patients, allow reproducible results. The problems associated with using natural substances as drugs include

the inability to regulate the doses of active constituents, and the interaction of the active constituents with other potentially active compounds in the natural substance. The presence of active constituents in most natural drugs may vary based on genetic factors, country of origin and growing conditions. As a result, most natural drugs cannot meet established quality control standards in the United States. Before a drug substance may be used in the practice of medicine, it must have a composition of active ingredients that has been established and accepted as standard. Such standardization, which includes identity, purity, potency, and quality, is specified in either a New Drug Application (NDA) or an official compendium such as *The United States Pharmacopeia* or *National Formulary*.

10. There is no difference in the pharmacological effect between the THC isolated from cannabis and the synthetically produced THC which is now marketed in the United States.

11. In the late 1960's, the Department of Health, Education and Welfare (DHEW) initiated a process to facilitate research with marijuana and THC. The FDA reviewed Investigational New Drug (IND) applications for marijuana and THC, assisted researchers and physicians in preparing IND protocols, and sent out information packets and model protocols.

12. The IND procedure is the process by which drugs are introduced into man and their safety and effectiveness is evaluated over a period of years. The stated objectives of the FDA in regulating the clinical testing of new drugs are to "protect the rights and safety of human subjects of such testing while, at the same time, facilitating the development and marketing of beneficial drug therapies." The Food, Drug, and Cosmetic Act emphasizes the need to carry out scientifically valid studies as well as the need to control the investigational drug supply and obtain informed consent of the subject or patient. The drug used in the study must be able to be traced to the patient, and the investigator must submit annual reports to FDA and report adverse reactions.

13. The protocols for the INDs with marijuana, especially the state protocols and the protocols for individual patients did not describe controlled studies. Controlled studies are necessary as the basis of a New Drug Application (NDA). No NDA for marijuana has been submitted to FDA for approval. Thus, marijuana remains an investigational drug subject to IND requirements. Due to the lack of an approved NDA, marijuana is not available by prescription in the United States.

14. As of January 6, 1987, there were 30 active INDs for marijuana; 82 INDs for marijuana have been discontinued.

15. The National Institute on Drug Abuse (NIDA) has shipped a total of 160,700 marijuana cigarettes for human studies from 1976 to 1986. Fifty-nine thousand (59,000) cigarettes were shipped to eight sponsors for human use outside state-sponsored programs. More than half of those, 30,900 cigarettes, were shipped to one sponsor during that period.

16. Thirty-four states have passed legislation concerning the use of cannabis (marijuana) and THC by physicians. Of these states, at least 24 define this use of marijuana and THC as research. Of these 34 states, only 17 states (New Mexico,

Illinois, Louisiana, Washington, Florida, Michigan, Oregon, Colorado, California, Nevada, Ohio, West Virginia, Georgia, Arizona, New York, Vermont and Tennessee) had approved INDs for marijuana or marijuana/THC as of March 1, 1984. Ten state-sponsored programs received marijuana cigarettes from the NIDA during the period 1978 to 1986. During this period 101,700 cigarettes were distributed to those states; California received 38,700 cigarettes, the most of any state. New Mexico received 8,700 cigarettes in the period from 1978 to 1986. In 1986, four state programs received a total of 1,860 cigarettes. In March 1982, a National Conference on the Therapeutic Application of Cannabinoids was held. The report of that conference indicates that "state programs in general had a small volume of participation and a high loss of data." The report also concluded that the designs of the state programs varied widely.

17. The California Research Advisory Panel, a California government agency, sponsored the California Cannabis Therapeutic Research Program. After six years of operation, from 1979 to 1986, the Research Advisory Panel found that only 101 patients received 210 treatments with marijuana cigarettes. Slightly more than one-third of the patients received a second treatment of marijuana cigarettes. Approximately 20 percent of the patients stopped using the cigarettes either because the cigarettes were ineffective, or the side effects were too severe.

18. Approximately 250 individuals received marijuana and/or THC capsules under the New Mexico Controlled Substances Therapeutic Research Program from February 1979 to June 1980 for control of nausea and vomiting associated with cancer chemotherapy. For admission to the program, patients must have experienced nausea and vomiting in previous chemotherapy. An average of four to six individuals a month participated in the program, Approximately 20 New Mexico physicians participated in the state-wide program. There was no randomization in the study; the patients themselves chose to use either marijuana or THC. They were also free to switch from one drug to the other once they began treatment. Under the program, 16 individuals switched from one drug to the other, 13 switched from cigarettes to capsules, the others from capsules to cigarettes. Of the patients selected for evaluation, 94 used THC capsules and 75 used marijuana cigarettes. There was no objective measurement of success or failure. The patients evaluated themselves based upon the degree of nausea and vomiting in previous chemotherapy sessions as compared with the degree of nausea and vomiting when marijuana or THC was used.

19. One hundred-five patients enrolled in the State of Georgia marijuana and THC research study which was designed to evaluate the efficacy and toxicity of marijuana and THC as an antiemetic in cancer patients undergoing chemotherapy treatment. Emory University enrolled 85 patients in their marijuana and THC research study. Thirty-eight patients from the State of Georgia study, and 81 patients from the Emory University study were evaluated. Of the 119 patients evaluated in the combined studies, 44 smoked marijuana; the other 75 used THC capsules. The success rate for use of THC capsules was 76 percent, and the success rate for smoking marijuana was 68.2 percent. Success was measured by patient self-assessment or satisfaction. The primary reason for marijuana's failure

as a treatment was the patients' intolerance of the cigarettes, or its failure to improve nausea and vomiting.

20. Of the 165 individuals evaluated in the Michigan Therapeutic Research Project for the years 1980–1982, 83 received only marijuana. Another 31 received marijuana after receiving Toracan (a phenothiazine in the same family as Compazine) during the same trial. The purpose of the trial (Trial A) was to evaluate the efficacy of marijuana to control nausea and vomiting induced by cancer chemotherapeutic agents. Thirty-four (34) of the patients discontinued the study because they did not like smoking marijuana. Twenty-one (21) patients reported the adverse effect of sleepiness/fatigue, 13 reported sore throat, 7 reported headache, and 4 reported being light-headed after smoking marijuana. Of 93 individuals who smoked marijuana at the first patient session, 14 reported no nausea, 31 reported mild nausea, 22 reported moderate nausea, and 19 reported severe nausea. Of the 93 patients who smoked marijuana in the initial session, 63 percent reported they felt "high" and 58 percent reported no increased appetite stimulation.

21. The State of New York Controlled Substances Therapeutic Research Program Report for 1982 indicates that by the end of July 1982, 840 marijuana cigarettes had been distributed to 45 patients under the New York program. These 45 patients had 99 treatment episodes. The treatment of 18 patients was evaluated, and 15 found that they benefited from smoked marijuana in some manner. For the period from November 1981 to May 1986, 199 patients received marijuana cigarettes under the New York program. During that period, 6,044 marijuana cigarettes were distributed. Of the 199 patients who received marijuana, only 90 were evaluated. The evaluations were based solely on patient self-assessments of nausea and vomiting, appetite, physical status, mood, "high" feeling, and a record of the amount of drug taken. The program was also plagued by lack of compliance with reporting procedures. The results of the evaluations indicated that large percentages of the individuals who received chemotherapeutic agents which are known to produce moderate to severe emesis failed to respond to the smoked marijuana. The New York Summary Report concluded that while preliminary results of the "Inhalation Marijuana Research Project" were encouraging, further analysis, more data, and more research are needed.

22. The July 1983 Report of the State of Tennessee program to evaluate marijuana and THC in treatment of nausea and/or vomiting associated with cancer therapy indicates that 43 patients have been enrolled in the program. Of these, 27 were evaluated. The patients enrolled in the program self-evaluated their nausea and vomiting, appetite and food intake, physical state, mood, high, and dosages of the drugs they received. Twenty-one (21) of the 27 patients used marijuana cigarettes. Nineteen (19) of the 21 evaluated the cigarettes as successful, success being defined as partially, moderately or very effective. The major reason for failure of marijuana cigarettes was smoking intolerance.

23. Nausea and vomiting (emesis) are common side effects of cancer chemotherapy. Vomiting is controlled by two distinct areas in the brain, the vomiting center and the chemoreceptor trigger zone (CTZ). Various cancer chemothera-

peutic agents can trigger the vomiting center and the CTZ, thus causing nausea and vomiting. The incidence of emesis resulting from cancer chemotherapy often depends upon the type of agent used for the chemotherapy treatment. Chemotherapeutic agents most often associated with emesis also induce emesis of the greatest severity. Cisplatin causes the highest incidence of emesis, whereas methotrexate causes only a moderate incidence of emesis. Other factors not specifically related to chemotherapy can also influence a patient's emesis, such as emotional status, alcohol consumption, age, and past chemotherapy experience.

24. Prior to 1930, little research was conducted regarding antiemetics used to treat nausea and vomiting related to cancer chemotherapy. At that time, the most commonly used antiemetic was Compazine (prochlorperazine). Compazine was largely ineffective in treating emesis caused by most cancer chemotherapy regimens. Since 1980, research with new antiemetics has proliferated. As a result of this additional research, several new and highly effective antiemetics and their combinations are now available including: metoclopramide, thiethylperazine malate, baloperidol, dexamethasone, diphenhydramine, droperidol, fluphenazine hydrochloride, perphenazine, lorazepam, dronabinol (synthetic THC) in sesame oil in a soft gelatin capsule, and nabilone (a synthetic substance chemically and pharmacologically similar to THC).

25. To properly evaluate the effectiveness of a new antiemetic drug, researchers must perform carefully conducted randomized, double-blind testing of the drug against either a placebo or an established antiemetic, using a statistically significant patient population. Several factors are important when planning or evaluating an antiemetic study; these include: (a) Standardization of the emetic stimulus, (b) accuracy in data collection, with the use of objective parameters, such as the number of emetic episodes and the volume and duration of emesis, (c) standardization of patient population, with an indication of whether or not patients had previously received chemotherapy, and (d) proper selection of route of administration, and drug schedule and dosage, based upon proper trials with the agent. In addition, it is important to determine quantitatively the efficacy of antiemetic agents used singularly, so that results can be compared and further trials, including combination studies, can be planned appropriately.

26. For a new antiemetic drug to be considered effective, it must be as effective or more effective in controlling emesis than the currently-available antiemetics.

27. Relatively few scientific or medical studies have been conducted to evaluate marijuana's effectiveness as an antiemetic. Information concerning marijuana's antiemetic properties is primarily anecdotal. The research that has been conducted with marijuana has been primarily in the form of loose, uncontrolled studies which provide little valuable information as to the drug's effectiveness. Most research with marijuana has been conducted under state protocols. The state sponsored research conducted thus far has not employed carefully controlled double-blind, randomized testing of marijuana, nor has it involved large patient populations. As a result, little reliable information can be gleaned from these types of studies.

28. Based upon the lack of quality testing, marijuana's antiemetic activity is

not as established as that of THC or other available antiemetics. There are no double-blind randomized studies which have concluded that marijuana is as effective or more effective than synthetic THC, or any of the other currently available antiemetics. In fact, in 1984, the only controlled, randomized, double-blind, crossover study comparing the antiemetic effectiveness of smoked marijuana to orally ingested synthetic THC involved 20 patients and concluded that orally ingested THC was superior to smoked marijuana.

29. Although THC is usually a constituent present in marijuana, since marijuana also contains at least 60 other active cannabinoids in varying quantities, the results of antiemetic trials using THC cannot be extrapolated in evaluating marijuana's antiemetic properties. For example, cannabidiol, a constituent present in marijuana, can potentiate some effects of THC, while suppressing other effects, including the antiemetic effect.

30. No formal, well-controlled studies have been conducted which compare marijuana's effectiveness as an antiemetic against any of the currently available antiemetics such as metoclopramide, haloperidol, dexamethasone, prochlorperazine, nabilone, lorazepam, or any of the highly effective combinations of available antiemetics.

31. The only studies which have been conducted using marijuana as an antiemetic include the following: (1) The state programs (discussed previously): (2) the study mentioned above which compared smoked marijuana to oral synthetic THC and concluded that THC was more effective: (3) a "compassionate" study conducted by Thomas J. Ungerleider involving 16 bone marrow transplant patients. In that study, the efficacy of the drug was measured only by subjective testing techniques; and (4) a study conducted by Alfred E. Chang which involved 15 patients receiving methotrexate chemotherapy.

32. The purpose of the Chang study was to compare the antiemetic effectiveness of THC to a placebo. Initially in the study, patients randomly received either an oral THC capsule or placebo capsule prior to chemotherapy. Neither the patients nor the researchers were aware of which drug they received. Three separate chemotherapy trials were conducted during the study. Only if the patient vomited during a trial would he or she receive a marijuana cigarette for the remaining doses of that chemotherapy trial. All patients who received marijuana cigarettes were experienced smokers. The study does not indicate how many patients resorted to smoking marijuana during each trial. Since six patients did not vomit at all on the THC, they did not receive marijuana cigarettes. The purpose of the study was not to compare the effectiveness of oral THC to marijuana but, rather, to compare THC's effectiveness against a placebo. Dr. Chang concluded that the combination of oral THC and smoked marijuana is a highly effective antiemetic in patients receiving methotrexate chemotherapy. Although Dr. Chang found that smoked marijuana was more reliable than oral THC in achieving therapeutic blood levels, he also found that it had drawbacks in patient acceptability: patients complained of its adverse taste, which induced nausea and vomiting in some instances. He also surmised that patients who are

nonsmokers may not be willing and/or able to smoke marijuana. Based upon these drawbacks, Dr. Chang concluded that "an alternative parenteral drug route needs to be established if THC [or marijuana] is to have wide clinical acceptability." In addition, he determined that additional studies relating to drug tolerance, effectiveness against nausea and vomiting produced by other chemotherapy regimens, and comparisons with conventional antiemetics needed to be conducted.

33. A study conducted by Stephen E. Sallan, M.D., which is cited by both NORML and ACT, involved a double-blind, randomized evaluation of the antiemetic effect of synthetic THC capsules in 16 patients receiving chemotherapy (although 22 patients participated in the study, only 16 received oral THC). There is no indication as to what types of chemotherapeutic agents were administered to the patients during the study. Dr. Sallan concluded that THC had antiemetic effects. In addition, he made some "preliminary observations" comparing the antiemetic effect of smoked marijuana and oral THC capsules, based upon some patients' illicit use of marijuana which was neither qualitatively nor quantitatively controlled. He found that "[f] or most patients, both smoked and oral routes had identical effects." This study was not a scientific comparative study of smoked marijuana and oral THC, but rather a formal comparison between oral synthetic THC and placebo.

34. Even in its limited use, marijuana has not been shown to be very effective in reducing nausea and vomiting when used with chemotherapeutic agents which produce severe emesis.

35. In contrast to marijuana, synthetic oral THC (dronabinol), nabilone, metoclopramide, and other currently available antiemetics have been tested extensively through well-designed, controlled double-blind studies for both safety and efficacy. For example, more than 1,300 patients were tested with synthetic THC before it was made available as a Schedule II drug. Marijuana, on the other hand, has only been tested in 20 patients in a formal comparative study, and roughly less than 500 patients in loosely controlled state studies.

36. Neither marijuana nor oral THC has been demonstrated to be an effective antiemetic for patients receiving radiation therapy. In a THC study conducted at UCLA, Dr. Ungerleider concluded that oral THC was only slightly more effective than Compazine in controlling emesis caused by radiation therapy. No studies evaluating marijuana's effectiveness in this area were introduced during this proceeding.

37. Since the advent of the new, highly effective antiemetics, few cancer chemotherapy patients discontinue treatment as a result of nausea and vomiting.

38. Although the newer antiemetics and their combinations have been shown to be highly effective in treating emesis, even in conjunction with chemotherapy treatments known to produce severe nausea and vomiting in most patients, a small number of patients are refractory to all antiemetic treatment. There is no scientific or medical reason to believe that patients who do not respond well to currently-available antiemetics would respond any better after smoking mari-

juana. The only method to determine marijuana's effectiveness for that purpose would be to conduct controlled double-blind trials with the drug in that group of patients.

39. There is no scientific or medical support for the hypothesis that marijuana or any of the cannabinoids are effective in treating emesis in children receiving chemotherapy. Again, only controlled trials comparing marijuana to other available antiemetics could support that contention. No such trials have been conducted as of this time.

40. Smoking as a route of administration for antiemetics has not been demonstrated to be more advantageous than intravenous or oral administration. The claimed advantage of self-titration through smoking is only a hypothesis and has not been scientifically proven. In fact, oral administration of antiemetics is highly effective if effective antiemetics are given. Intravenous administration also is highly effective, especially since most chemotherapy agents are intravenously administered as well.

41. Currently available antiemetics are also highly effective in outpatient care. Most patients can receive the newer antiemetics on an outpatient basis. There is no scientific or medical reason to conclude that marijuana is better-suited than currently available antiemetics in the treatment of emesis of outpatients. Carefully conducted clinical trials would be needed to demonstrate otherwise.

42. In addition to not being as effective or more effective than currently-available antiemetics, the use of smoked marijuana in the treatment of emesis in cancer patients has significant drawbacks. As a psychoactive substance, marijuana causes anxiety and panic in inexperienced users. Marijuana smoking also caused nausea and vomiting in some patients, and left an unpleasant residual taste. Because tachycardia and orthostatic hypotension are negative side effects of marijuana smoking, it should not be administered to patients with heart problems such as arteriosclerotic heart disease and angina. Marijuana smoking can also lead to pulmonary problems including bronchitis and emphysema. Marijuana is a crude plant material which contains pathogenic bacteria that could prove harmful to immuno-compromised patients with various cancers or leukemias. The cannabinoids present in marijuana can further suppress the immune functions of individuals whose immune systems are already severely compromised by chemotherapeutic agents. Also, few patients can tolerate marijuana smoking. In fact, in the state programs employing marijuana, significant numbers of patients either switched from smoking to oral THC capsules or withdrew from research because they could not tolerate smoking marijuana. In Dr. Ungerleider's study involving 16 bone marrow transplant patients, three dropped out of the study because they found marijuana smoking to be undesirable, even though at the time of the study, no other antiemetics were available to them. In addition, because of the lack of standardization of the drug and varying smoking techniques, there is a problem with bioavailability and reproducibility of an administered dose of the drug. If the dose is not constant from treatment to treatment, the patient may go unprotected.

43. The combination of currently available antiemetics produce less side ef-

fects than do each of the drugs given individually. These combinations produce less side effects than the cannabinoids, including marijuana. There is no scientific or medical evidence which demonstrates that marijuana produces fewer and less severe side effects than the currently-available antiemetics.

44. Patient satisfaction with the combination antiemetic therapy is greater than that seen with marijuana.

45. Interest in research using marijuana to treat emesis in cancer chemotherapy patients has waned as the availability of new, highly-effective antiemetics has increased.

46. Patient interest in using marijuana to treat emesis caused by chemotherapy has also declined in recent years.

47. The oncological community does not consider marijuana to have currently accepted medical use in the United States for the treatment of emesis caused by cancer chemotherapy. In addition, David Ettinger, M.D., Richard Cralla, M.D., and John Laszlo, M.D., each a highly respected oncologist and antiemetic researcher who has treated numerous patients and conducted extensive research with various cannabinoids and highly effective antiemetics, have concluded that based upon their research and knowledge of the field, marijuana does not have a currently accepted medical use in the United States for the treatment of emesis caused by cancer chemotherapy, nor has it been proven safe for use under medical supervision.

48. The American Cancer Society has concluded that insufficient research has been conducted to advocate that marijuana be used as an antiemetic for chemotherapy patients.

49. In its 1984 report, the National Academy of Sciences did not make any conclusions regarding marijuana's accepted medical use in the treatment of emesis in cancer chemotherapy patients. The only conclusion made in the report was that marijuana's antiemetic properties were less established than those of synthetic THC.

50. The American Medical Association has concluded that marijuana does not have a currently accepted medical use in the United States for the treatment of emesis caused by cancer chemotherapy, nor has it been proven to be safe for use under medical supervision.

51. Glaucoma is a term which describes a group of chronic ocular diseases which cause an increase in intraocular pressure that damages the retina and optic nerve and can lead to an eventual loss of vision. The most common form of glaucoma is primary open-angle glaucoma (POAG). This form of glaucoma is caused by an obstruction in the pathways for fluid exit from the eye while fluid inflow continues unabated. As a result, the pressure within the eye (intraocular pressure) increases beyond a level tolerated by the eye and can cause damage to the retina and optic nerve.

52. Persons suffering from glaucoma have intraocular pressures which are higher than their eyes can tolerate. Traditionally, glaucoma was measured by a statistical measure of intraocular pressure (a norm), meaning that if an individual's pressure was higher than the average, he was thought to have glaucoma; if

the pressure was below the norm, he was thought not to have glaucoma. It is now known that this is not the proper method for diagnosing glaucoma. Ninety-five percent of individuals with statistically-elevated intraocular pressure are never afflicted with glaucoma, while one-third of glaucomatose individuals have intraocular pressures in the statistically normal range.

53. Effective treatment for glaucoma involves the use of pharmaceutical agents or surgical procedures that prevent progressive optic nerve damage. If intraocular pressure can be lowered sufficiently, it can usually alter the course of the glaucoma. But, merely reducing intraocular pressure is not necessarily beneficial to the eye, and pressure reduction does not necessarily prevent glaucomatose optic nerve damage. For a treatment to be effective, it must lower intraocular pressure sufficiently to prevent additional damage to the optic nerve and retina, and also not cause unacceptable damage to the eye or to other parts of the body. In addition, it must be able to sustain the lowered pressure and preserve visual function for the patient's lifetime.

54. When new glaucoma treatments are tested for efficacy, they are evaluated for their ability to sufficiently lower intraocular pressure and to maintain visual fields. To properly measure the treatment's effect on both, it must be used in long-term testing. Timolol, a drug currently used to treat glaucoma, has been tested in this manner. Before it was approved for use in treating glaucoma, timolol was rigorously tested in 300 to 400 persons through controlled, double-masked clinical trials. These studies involved treating patients with the drug for a minimum of three months, with a majority of the studies lasting for six months or more, during which time, the patients' visual fields were measured to determine whether there had been any progression of the disease. In addition, other conventional glaucoma medications have proven their efficacy through years of clinical experience. The miotics, epinephrine compounds and carbonic anhydrase inhibitors have been proven effective in lowering intraocular pressure and preserving visual function.

55. The most efficacious way of delivering any drug to the eye is through a topical drop, rather than by systemic application. Topical application reduces the possibility of systemic adverse effects from a drug since the total amount of the drug being delivered to the body is considerably less.

56. In 1971, Robert S. Hepler, M.D. and Ira R. Frank, M.D. published preliminary results of one of the first experiments which measured the effect of smoked marijuana on intraocular pressures of, normal, healthy males. The study involved acute administration of smoked marijuana through an ice-cooled water pipe to eleven youthful men who did not suffer from glaucoma. After the one-time administration of the marijuana, nine subjects experienced decreases in intraocular pressure which ranged from 16 percent to 45 percent, one subject experienced a 4 percent increase in intraocular pressure, and one subject experienced no change following smoking. These results were later published in 1974 as part of a larger study in which Thomas J. Ungerleider, M.D. participated, aimed at measuring pupillary constriction, intraocular pressure, tear production, and conjunctival hyperemia (redness and irritation of the eye). The overall study in-

volved 21 healthy subjects who smoked marijuana in an ice-cooled water pipe. Only the 11 subjects described in the earlier publication were tested for changes in intraocular pressures. In addition to the results of changes in intraocular pressures, the authors also noted that smoking marijuana was associated with minor decreases in pupillary size, decrease in tear production, and conjunctival hyperemia. Central visual acuity, refraction, peripheral visual fields, binocular fusion and color vision were not altered by the single-dose administration of the marijuana. In addition, the authors noted that fatigue and sleepiness occurred several hours following the marijuana-induced "high".

57. There are no published scientific reports or studies which demonstrate marijuana's ability to lower intraocular pressures in long-term chronic testing of glaucomatose research subjects. The only long-term study reported was one conducted by Dr. Hepler at U.C.L.A. The study evaluated responses of 19 normal, non-glaucomatose patients for a period of 94 days. The results of the 94-day study were not available at the time Dr. Hepler's paper was published. The only conclusions made were that in the normal research subjects, intraocular pressure showed a prompt drop as soon as the subjects began to smoke, and that there were no indications of cumulative effects upon the intraocular pressure response.

58. There are few published scientific reports or studies which evaluate marijuana's effect on lowering intraocular pressure in glaucomatose individuals. All of the studies involve acute administration of the drug and each involve relatively small numbers of research subjects. In 1976, Drs. Hepler and Petrus reported the results of their study which involved 12 research subjects who suffered from glaucoma. Each subject was seen on four occasions. On one occasion, the subjects were given a placebo in a smokable form: on the other occasions, the subjects were either given oral (synthetic) THC or smoked marijuana. Some of the research subjects continued their usual courses of medication during the testing. The published study only reported the results of four of the research subjects. Two subjects failed to achieve a reduction in intraocular pressure. Also, the study did not indicate which of the four subjects, if any, had continued their conventional medication during the study. The study did not differentiate between the effectiveness of marijuana or oral THC. The researchers concluded that "patients with proven glaucoma frequently, although not invariably, demonstrate substantial decrease in intraocular pressure following smoking of marijuana or ingestion of THC." In 1976, Drs. Hepler, Frank and Petrus reported on the results of another small study involving 11 glaucomatose individuals who were observed after acute administration of marijuana. Of the 11 patients studied, seven demonstrated drops in intraocular pressure averaging 30 percent. The remaining four did not experience any drop in intraocular pressure.

In 1979, Drs. Merritt and Crawford published results of an acute study of the effects of marijuana and placebo on 16 glaucomatose research subjects. They concluded that "inhaled tetrahydrocannabinol (delta-9-tetrahydrocannabinol) lowers blood pressure and intraocular pressure, commensurately with tachycardia [rapid heart rate], in systemic normotensive and hypertensive glaucoma patients." In 1980, Drs. Merritt, Crawford, Alexander, Anduze, and Gelbart reported the results of a study which observed the effect of acute administration of marijuana and placebo to 18 glaucoma patients. They concluded that acute administration of marijuana lowered both intraocular pressure and blood pressure in a heterogenous glaucoma population. They also noted that eight of the patients suffered from anxiety with tachycardia and palpitations: five suffered from postural hypotension (reduction in blood pressure upon standing); 18 suffered from sensory alterations including hunger, thirst, euphoria, drowsiness and chills: and nine suffered from conjunctival hyperemia and ptosis (drooping upper eyelid). Based on the side effects, the researchers concluded that "it is because of the frequency and severity with which untoward events occurred that marijuana inhalation is not an ideal therapeutic modality for glaucoma patients." A total of no more than 50 glaucomatose individuals have been administered smoked marijuana in a research setting.

Approximately 40 of these individuals received marijuana during limited acute trials of the drug. The progress of the other individuals, who included Robert Randall and other individuals who used marijuana in conjunction with their conventional glaucoma medications, were never published since they only involved anecdotal observations, providing insufficient data to report which would be useful for other ophthalmologists in treating patients with glaucoma.

59. In 1976, Dr. Mario Perez-Reyes reported the results of his preliminary study of acute intravenous administration of various cannabinoids on intraocular pressure. Twelve normal, nonglaucomatose patients were injected with a variety of cannabinoids which are present in marijuana; the cannabinoids were administered individually so that the effects could be evaluated separately. He concluded that several of the cannabinoids had intraocular pressure lowering qualities, including delta-8-tetrahydrocannabinol, which is less psychoactive than THC. THC appears to be the most effective cannabinoid for acutely reducing intraocular pressure, but is also the most psychoactive. Although marijuana, which consists of various cannabinoids, would have a different effect on eye pressure than one of its single constituents, the literature indicates that the effect would either be the same or less.

60. There are no published scientific or medical reports which evaluate marijuana's ability to preserve the visual function of glaucomatose individuals.

61. None of the IND reports or studies submitted in this processing have compared marijuana's effectiveness in lowering intraocular pressure and preserving visual function to any of the currently accepted glaucoma medications. Although not proven through comparative studies, it is accepted that reductions in intraocular pressure continue for longer periods of time following administration of either timolol, pilocarpine, or phospholine iodide, than following administration of smoked marijuana.

62. No evidence was introduced in this proceeding from states which have scientific protocols for researching marijuana's effect in the treatment of glaucoma. In 1986, the California Research Advisory Committee reported the results of its research protocol in this area which covered only the use of THC. Only one individual received marijuana cigarettes for glaucoma. This was after the Re-

search Advisory Panel mailed information about the program to ophthalmologists throughout the State of California. Rhode Island reported that 28 ophthalmologists in that state were contacted to determine if they had any interest in conducting research with marijuana. None of the ophthalmologists contacted responded affirmatively. Those who responded to the inquiry claimed that the drugs which were currently available sufficiently controlled glaucoma.

63. Acute administration of marijuana has demonstrated unacceptable negative side effects in research subjects participating in glaucoma studies. These side effects include orthostatic hypotension, tachycardia, conjunctival hyperemia, euphoria, dysphoria, drowsiness, depersonalization, difficulty in concentrating and thinking, impairment of motor coordination. Since the drop in intraocular pressure after smoking marijuana noted in acute studies lasts for approximately four to five hours, with the maximal fall occurring about one to two hours after administration, to be considered in treating glaucoma, marijuana would have to be administered six to eight times per day for the duration of disease. Such use constitutes chronic administration of the drug. The negative effects of chronic administration of marijuana have not been adequately tested. Yet, specific unacceptable negative effects can be attributed to chronic administration of marijuana. These include: possible brain damage, sore throat, rhinitis, bronchitis and emphysema; suppression of luteinizing hormone secretion in women (which affects the production of progesterone): abnormalities in DNA synthesis, mitosis and growth; carcinogenicity; and genetic mutations.

64. While marijuana plant material and some cannabinoids have been shown to lower intraocular pressure in acutely-treated normal human volunteers and glaucoma patients, it may lower intraocular pressure without preventing visual impairment in glaucoma patients. As noted above, there has been no documentation that marijuana use preserves the visual function of glaucomatose individuals. Because acute studies have shown that marijuana appears to act by lowering intraocular pressure and blood pressure concomitantly, there is some concern that lowering the blood pressure limits the blood supply to the optic nerve. Since the optic nerve relies on a constant supply of blood to function adequately, there is a concern that by reducing its blood supply by lowering systemic blood pressure, visual function will be further impaired in glaucomatose individuals.

65. Based on the lack of documented evidence showing its utility in lowering introacular pressure in the long-term and maintaining visual function, coupled with the adverse side effects associated with its use, most experts agree that smoked marijuana has not been proven to be a viable drug for the treatment of glaucoma. These medical and scientific experts include: Mario Perez-Reyes, M.D. (a source often cited by NORML and ACT); Robert Hepler. M.D.; Keith Green, Ph.D.; George Spaeth, M.D.; Leo Hollister, M.D.; Reese Jones, M.D.; and Raphael Mechoulam, Ph.D. In addition, in previously published articles, John Merritt, M.D., a witness for ACT, has taken the position that marijuana's use in treating glaucoma is unacceptable because of the frequent and untoward side effects associated with its use. Also, the American Academy of Ophthalmology, an organization which represents more than 12,000 physician members and approx-

imately 6,000 other medical professionals who specialize in the field of ophthalmology, has taken the position that insufficient data exists to demonstrate the safety and efficacy of using smoked marijuana in the treatment of glaucoma. The National Academy of Sciences, another source frequently cited by NORML and ACT, also concluded that smoking marijuana is not suitable for the treatment of glaucoma.

66. Multiple Sclerosis (MS) is the major cause of neurological disability among young and middle-aged adults. It is a life-long disease which attacks the myelin sheath (the coating surrounding the message-carrying nerve fibers in the brain and spinal cord). Once the myelin sheath is destroyed, it is replaced by plaques of hardened tissue known as sclerosis. The plaques can obstruct impulses along the nerve systems which will produce malfunctions in the body parts affected by the damaged nervous system. The symptoms can include one or a combination of the following; weakness, tingling, numbness, impaired sensation, lack of coordination, disturbances in equilibrium, double vision, loss of vision, involuntary rapid eye movement, slurred speech, tremors, stiffness, spasticity (involuntary and abnormal contractions of muscle or muscle fibers), weakness of limbs, sexual dysfunction, paralysis, and impaired bladder and bowel functions. Spasticity can also result from serious injuries to the spinal cord, not related to MS. The effects of MS are sporadic in most individuals, and the symptoms occur episodically, either triggered by the malfunction of the nerve impulses or by external factors. Because of the variability of symptoms of the disease, MS is difficult to detect and diagnose. There is no known prevention or cure for MS; instead, there are only treatments for the symptoms.

67. There are no published scientific reports or studies which evaluate marijuana's effectiveness in treating spasticity. The only existing information regarding the use of marijuana to treat the effects of MS or spasticity is primarily anecdotal. Anecdotal information is only useful for providing a basis for conducting controlled research with the drug to evaluate its effectiveness. In order to sufficiently verify that a drug is effective for treating MS or spasticity, double-blind, controlled studies must be conducted on large groups of persons.

68. The only studies evaluating the effect of cannabinoids on MS and spasticity employed synthetic THC or cannabidiol. These studies have been uniformly small, and the data presented are insufficient to evaluate the nature and quality of controls used. In 1981, Drs. Denis J. Petro and Carl Ellenberger published the results of a limited acute study using synthetic THC. That study involved the acute administration of oral synthetic THC to nine MS patients. The researchers noted that the spasticity scores of four of the nine patients improved significantly after the administration of the synthetic THC; one patient improved after receiving the placebo; only two of three patients who felt improved actually demonstrated improvement by objective criteria. The EMG index of spasticity (electromyography—a method of measuring reflex responses, neuromuscular function and condition, and extent of nerve lesion) was impractical in five of the nine patients. The researchers concluded that further study should be conducted to determine the effectiveness of THC or one of its derivatives in treating spastic-

ity. In a 1988 abstract, W. C. Hanigan, R. Destree, and X. T. Troung reported the results of a 20-day study in which they administered oral synthetic THC to five spastic patients. They concluded that two patients experienced significant reductions in stretch resistance and reflex activity; and one patient withdrew from the study because of negative emotional side effects. In another abstract, R. Sandyk, P. Consroe, L. Stern and S. R. Snider, evaluated the effects of cannabidiol (a major non-psychoactive cannabinoid of marijuana) on three patients suffering from Huntington's Disease (a progressive central nervous system disease characterized by muscular twitching of the limbs or facial muscles). The first week they noted mild improvement in choreic movements. Further improvement was noted the second week and remained stable for another two weeks. The only side effects observed were cases of transient, mild hypotension.

69. There are no reported scientific or medical studies which have compared the effectiveness of marijuana, or its derivatives, with conventional treatments for MS and spasticity. There is no indication that marijuana would be more effective or safer than currently available treatments. In addition, conventional drugs may reduce spasticity with fewer side effects than marijuana.

70. No long-term clinical studies employing marijuana, or any of its derivatives, have been conducted with respect to treating MS or spasticity.

71. The long-term safety of using marijuana to treat MS and spasticity has yet to be established. Marijuana's long-term effects on memory and intellect, its pulmonary effects, risks in pregnancy, and tolerance to the drug, are unresolved. Since marijuana may have undesirable side effects at doses necessary to reduce spasticity, the use of marijuana for long-term treatment such as is needed to treat MS and spasticity would be worse than the disease itself.

72. None of the state reports submitted in this proceeding indicate that any state research with marijuana was conducted with respect to spasticity. The National Multiple Sclerosis Society does not advocate the use of marijuana to treat spasticity associated with MS. In addition, the International Federation of Multiple Sclerosis Societies does not recommend marijuana's use in treating spasticity. Also, noted neurologists who specialize in treating and conducting spasticity research, including Drs. Silberberg and Johnson, concluded that marijuana has not been proven to have an accepted medical use in the treatment of spasticity, nor has it been proven to be safe under medical supervision. Dr. Denis Petro, a witness for ACT, concluded in his synthetic THC study that "research needs to cover a larger and better controlled sample before any definitive statement would be possible."

73. Epilepsy involves the progressive recruitment of normal brain neurons into rhythmic and then high frequency bursting. With the overwhelming of inhibitory restraints, the pauses between bursts disappear and are replaced by tonic high frequency firing and the seizure appears. A prominent feature of epilepsy is its episodic nature.

74. There are no studies of the effects of crude marijuana on existing epileptic symptoms in man. Only survey and case report data are available. In 1976, Dennis M. Feenely reported the results of his survey among young epileptics in

the Journal of the American Medical Association. In that survey, young epileptics were questioned about their illicit use of marijuana, amphetamine. LSD, barbiturate, cocaine and heroin. Most of the subjects reported that marijuana had no effect on their seizures. In addition, one subject reported that his marijuana use reduced the frequency of seizures, while another subject claimed that marijuana caused him to have seizures. Also, published case reports indicate marijuana's conflicting properties of both reducing and causing seizures. Although case reports and surveys of this type are not highly reliable sources of scientific information, they follow the conflicting pattern suggested in animal studies employing synthetic THC.

75. Smoked marijuana has only been tested on experimental epilepsy in one study. That study evaluated marijuana's effect on seizures in five mongrel dogs. After chronic administration of marijuana smoke, two of the five dogs exhibited grand mal convulsions. In a study involving the administration of marijuana smoke to normal rats, "popcorn convulsions" (involuntary vertical jumping) were observed in 50 percent of the animals after 6 to 9 exposures to the drug.

76. Because of its potential to induce convulsant seizures, marijuana should not be used by epileptics.

77. Cannabidiol (CBD) has also been studied for its anticonvulsant effects in animals. CBD is neither psychoactive nor convulsant. Conclusions drawn from animal testing of this drug suggest that CBD shows promise as an anticonvulsant, and that its use should be clinically investigated in human epilepsy to determine its therapeutic utility.

78. Marijuana has not been proven to be an effective appetite stimulant, or antianorectic drug. Most studies have involved oral THC rather than marijuana. In a doubleblind study employing smoked marijuana, normal patients using marijuana increased their caloric intake more than those using the placebo, but the variability was too great to draw any conclusions. Studies employing THC have failed to demonstrate an appreciable appetite stimulating or antianorectic effect. State reports of cancer chemotherapy patients receiving either synthetic THC or marijuana have failed to support any claims of marijuana's appetite stimulating properties. Several of the currently available antiemetics have appetite-stimulating properties. With patients undergoing cancer chemotherapy, controlling emesis generally eliminates problems with anorexia or appetite loss. Marijuana has not been compared with currently available antiemetics to evaluate its appetite stimulating properties.

79. There is no scientific or medical indication that marijuana is effective in the treatment of either alcoholism or drug addiction. Recent studies now demonstrate that abuse of marijuana and alcohol are frequently combined. In addition, animal studies present no evidence that marijuana is more effective than currently available treatments for opiate withdrawal.

80. Marijuana has not been demonstrated to be an effective analgesic. Studies have demonstrated that marijuana and THC both increase and decrease pain. In addition, there is no indication that marijuana or synthetic THC are as effective or more effective than currently available analgesics.

81. Marijuana has not been shown to be effective in the treatment of asthma and bronchial spasms. Although smoked marijuana and THC were found to have bronchodilating effects following acute and short-term administration, smoke, even if it provides relief, is not desirable for asthmatics. Also, long-term smoking of marijuana reduces bronchodilation and causes significant airway obstruction.

82. Although marijuana has also been suggested for several other medical problems, there is insufficient scientific data to support its use for these purposes. Although marijuana and some of the cannabinoids have sedative or hypnotic effects, their activity is not constant, nor is there any indication that marijuana is even comparable to currently-available antianxiety and insomnia medications. There also is no support for marijuana's use as an antidepressant drug. Nor is there sufficient indication that marijuana, or its constituents, would be a useful medical alternative in the treatment of hypertension, neoplasms (tumors).

83. One of the primary methods for determining whether a particular drug is safe for use under medical supervision is to weigh its actual therapeutic benefit against its negative or unintended side effects. A side effect is a pharmacologic activity other than the desired effect. If the measurable therapeutic benefits of the drug outweigh its negative effects, the drug is generally considered safe for use; if the negative effects outweigh the therapeutic benefits, the drug is not considered safe for its intended use.

84. In evaluating the negative side effects of a drug, several factors are taken into consideration. Generally, initial animal studies are conducted to determine the drug's toxicity. An LD-50 is established (the dose which causes death in 50 percent of the animals tested). Factors other than the LD-50 are also considered in determining safety and toxicity. Additional pharmacological data is also needed, including the drug's bioavailability, metabolic pathways and pharmacokinetics. Acute and chronic testing must be conducted; first in animals, then in humans.

85. Most pharmacological research with cannabis or its constituents has actually been conducted with orally ingested THC, rather than smoked marijuana. Although the pharmacologic effects are presumed to be similar, the studies with oral THC do not provide a complete picture of marijuana's effects. Few of the other cannabinoids have been pharmacologically evaluated. The health consequences from smoking marijuana are likely to be quite different than those of orally ingested THC. Yet most of the chronic animal studies have been conducted with oral or intravenous THC.

86. There is a need for more information about the metabolism of the various marijuana constituents and their biologic effects. This requires many more animal studies. Then the pharmacologic information obtained from the animal studies must be tested in clinical studies involving humans. The pharmacologic testing of cannabinoids in animals thus far has shown that while they do not appear to be highly toxic, they exert some alteration in almost every biological system that has been studied.

87. Well-designed studies on the health effects of marijuana are relatively few.

This is especially true with respect to chronic studies. Field studies in this area are deficient. Most are too small to detect unusual or rare consequences which could be of great importance. In addition, only modest research has been conducted using healthy male volunteers; very limited studies have been conducted using females, older individuals, or persons in poor health. The studies using marijuana on healthy male volunteers lead to a biased conclusion that the drug is safe without properly evaluating the populations at risk. To eliminate any such bias and to expand our knowledge of the chronic, long-term effects of marijuana use, sophisticated epidemiological studies of large populations, similar to those conducted for alcohol and tobacco use, must be done. It may take years of extensive research before all of marijuana's deleterious effects become apparent.

88. The acute effects of marijuana use are fairly well established. Marijuana smoking usually causes acute changes in the heart and circulation which are characteristic of stress, including rapid heart rate (tachycardia), orthostatic hypotension, and increased blood concentrations of carboxyhemoglobin (hemoglobin combined with carbon monoxide). Therefore, the drug is not indicated for persons who suffer from cardiovascular problems including angina, congestive heart failure, and arteriosclerosis. In addition, acute marijuana use also causes euphoria: dysphoria; anxiety; confusion: psychosis; drowsiness; convulsions; and impairment of motor coordination, tracking ability and sensory and perceptual functions. Based upon these effects, marijuana should not be used by anxious or depressed, or unrecognized psychotic individuals, and epileptics.

89. Many persons who have smoked marijuana in a research setting could not tolerate its harshness and complained of throat soreness and other problems associated with smoking as a route of administration. In addition, many patients cannot, and will not, smoke a substance like marijuana for therapeutic purposes.

90. Even though inadequate studies have been conducted concerning the effects of long-term chronic use of marijuana, certain detrimental effects on respiratory and pulmonary functions are well-established. Marijuana smoke inhibits pulmonary antibacterial defense systems, possibly making marijuana users more susceptible to bacterial infections of the lung. One chronic smoking experiment tested pulmonary functions of healthy volunteer subjects before and after 47 to 59 days of daily smoking of approximately five cigarettes per day. The study concluded that very heavy smoking for only six to eight weeks caused mild but significant airway obstruction. In addition, a study of heavy hashish (a crude smokable preparation of cannabis resin) users revealed a high incidence of bronchopulmonary consequences, including chronic bronchitis, chronic cough, and mucosal changes of squamous metaplasia (a precancerous change). Chronic smoking can also result in emphysema.

91. Regular and frequent marijuana smoking causes preneoplastic changes in airways similar to those produced by smoking tobacco. Marijuana smoke does not contain nicotine; but like tobacco, it does have an equally complex aerosol of particles in a vapor phase that form a tar mixture. The mixture contains many of the same hydrocarbons contained in tobacco tars which are thought to be associated with cancer causation. Marijuana also contains more tar than tobacco

cigarettes. Animal studies using smoked marijuana have documented the growth of precancerous cells after 30 months. Dr. C. Leuchtenberger, a professor at the Swiss Institute for Experimental Cancer Research, noted that exposure of human lung explants to fresh marijuana or tobacco cigarette smoke evoked abnormalities in DNA synthesis, mitosis, and growth with consequent genetic disturbances that may lead to malignant transformation. The abnormalities were more pronounced following exposure to marijuana than to tobacco smoke. These findings were later confirmed in a similar study. Marijuana smoke also contains benzene, a substance associated with leukemia, and 2-aminonapthalene, which causes bladder cancer.

92. Recent evidence also indicates that marijuana can depress an individual's immune function. The immune system's sensitivity to marijuana depends on the cannabinoid compound and varies among immune cell types. In addition to the various cannabinoids, bacteria present in the plant material can further affect the immune function. A number of microbial contaminants have been isolated from marijuana samples, including pathogenic aspergillus, *Klebsiella pneumoniae*, *Enterbacter agglomerans*, group D streptococcus, *Enterbacter cloace*, *Bacillus* sp. and salmonella enteritis. The bacteria were found in both licit and illicit supplies of marijuana. At the Memorial Sloan-Kettering Cancer Center, it is estimated that 60 patients die each year from invasive aspergillus. Aspergillus was cultured from samples of marijuana from patients who developed invasive pulmonary and allergic bronchopulmonary aspergillus. The data supports the theory that marijuana smoking during periods of immunosuppression (as during cancer chemotherapy), may lead to infection. Therefore, because of its own immunosuppression properties, and its propensity for causing infections in immunosuppressed individuals, marijuana smoking may be contraindicated in cancer chemotherapy patients.

93. Studies conducted with respect to passive inhalation of heavy marijuana smoke demonstrate that passive inhalation of a substantial amount of sidestream marijuana can produce subjective effects, plasma levels of THC and urinary cannabinoid metabolites, in subjects similar to those found after the smoking of marijuana. The researchers concluded that with sufficient time and high marijuana smoke conditions, it becomes difficult to distinguish between active smoking and passive inhalation.

94. Marijuana has also produced genetic and non-genetic birth defects in many animal species. Pure THC is not thought to produce permanent alterations of genes in cells studied to date, but other components of cannabis smoke can cause such mutations. When animals of one generation were exposed to cannabis smoke during pregnancy, birth defects were found in the third generation, suggesting that a gene change had been transmitted through second generation animals which were only exposed to cannabis smoke prior to birth. Cannabis smoke has been related to the increased numbers of early fetal deaths, decreased fetal weight, and an increased death rate at birth in study animals. Although there have been some cases reported of deformed babies being born to marijuana smoking mothers, no causal links can be made based upon the limited evidence.

Further human research is necessary to establish or rule out such effects. Based upon the insufficient and inconclusive research in this area, pregnant women and those with marginal fertility may be at risk in smoking marijuana, even at moderate levels.

95. Chronic marijuana use may also have a toxic effect on the human brain. Preliminary studies indicate that THC changes the way sensory information gets into and is acted on by the hippocampus. Chronic exposure damages and destroys nerve cells and causes other changes which are identical to normal aging and may be additive to the aging process. Therefore, chronic marijuana use could result in serious or premature memory disorders. The results of these studies are now being confirmed.

96. Animal studies and some human studies have found that in males, sperm count and motility are decreased during cannabis use. In female animals. THC suppresses the secretion of luteinizing hormone. Prolonged suppression would eventually lower gonadal steroid levels. Whether these changes have any effect on human sexual function and fertility is not yet known.

97. In addition to the known and suspected health risks associated with marijuana use, there is also evidence to suggest that tolerance to its therapeutic effects also develops.

98. The National Academy of Sciences found that the dose of marijuana necessary to produce a therapeutic benefit is often close to one that produces an unacceptable frequency of toxic side effects.

99. The severity and frequency of negative side effects experienced from marijuana smoking exceed those caused by accepted medications used to treat glaucoma, emesis and Multiple Sclerosis and spasticity.

100. Because of its unacceptable side effects and undetermined therapeutic utility, smoked marijuana is not recommended for the treatment of glaucoma, emesis, Multiple Sclerosis and spasticity, epileptic seizures and convulsions, asthma, appetite loss or anorexia, alcoholism and drug abuse, pain and inflammation, anxiety, insomnia, migraine headaches, hypertension, depression, infections or tumors.

Conclusion

The Administrator finds that the administrative law judge failed to act as an impartial judge in this matter. He appears to have ignored the scientific evidence, ignored the testimony of highly-credible and recognized medical experts and, instead, relied on the testimony of psychiatrists and individuals who used marijuana. The administrative law judge relied heavily on anecdotal accounts of marijuana use by both physicians and seriously ill persons. The administrative law judge's findings of fact ignored any evidence presented by the Government. For example, in his findings regarding marijuana and nausea and vomiting associated with chemotherapy. Judge Young cites many of the physicians presented by the pro-marijuana parties by name as accepting marijuana as "medically useful." Not once in his findings or discussion does the judge acknowledge or mention the Government's experts. Not once does the judge mention why he chose to find the pro-marijuana parties' evidence more credible. The administrative law judge failed to acknowledge the position of a major organization of physicians, the American Medical Association; and those of organizations whose existence is dedicated to the treatment and study of the diseases at issue such as the American Cancer Society, the National Academy of Ophthalmology and the National Multiple Sclerosis Society. He chose instead to rely on the testimony of a very small number of physicians. Most significantly, the administrative law judge did not follow the standard for "accepted medical use in treatment in the United States," and "accepted safety for use . . . under medical supervision" established by the Administrator in previous scheduling proceedings. The administrative law judge chose, instead, to develop his own standard for both accepted medical use and accepted safety; standards which were specifically rejected by the Administrator in the scheduling of 3.4-methylenedioxymethamphetamine (MDMA).

The administrative law judge did not even apply his own standard consistently. While the administrative law judge found that marijuana had an accepted medical use in treatment of nausea and vomiting associated with chemotherapy; of spasticity associated with multiple sclerosis and amputation: and of pain associated with hyperparathyroidism; he concluded that it did not have accepted medical use in treatment of glaucoma. His rationale was that in applying his standard of accepted medical use, which is that a "significant minority" of physicians accept marijuana as medically useful, there were not enough physicians to establish such a "significant minority" with respect to glaucoma. In contrast, he found that one physician's opinion was sufficient to establish an accepted medical use of marijuana with regard to hyperparathyroidism, because that was a rare disease.

The Administrator rejects the administrative law judge's findings and conclusions. They were erroneous; they were not based upon credible evidence; nor were they based upon evidence in the record as a whole. Therefore, in this case, they carry no weight and do not represent the position of the agency or its Administrator. The inadequacy of Judge Young's analysis of the case is exemplified by his acceptance of, and reliance upon, irresponsible and irrational statements propounded by the pro-marijuana parties. Such statements include the following: "marijuana is far safer than many of the foods we commonly consume. For example, eating ten raw potatoes can result in a toxic response. By comparison, it is physically impossible to eat enough marijuana to induce death." That such a statement would come from the proponents of marijuana is understandable. To give it the weight of an administrative law judge's finding is appalling.

The administrator has accepted the agency's findings of fact as his own. In order to conclude that these facts support a conclusion that marijuana remain in Schedule I, they must be applied to the criteria set forth in the Controlled Substances Act for substances in Schedule I.

The three criteria are found at 21 U.S.C. 812(b)(1) and are as follows:

(a) The drug or other substance has a high potential for abuse.
(b) The drug or other substance has no currently accepted medical use in treatment in the United States.
(c) There is lack of accepted safety for use of the drug or other substance under medical supervision.

For purposes of this proceeding, the parties stipulated that marijuana has a high potential for abuse. The criteria for substances listed in Schedule II also includes that the drug has a high potential for abuse.

The issue of what "currently accepted medical use in treatment in the United States," and "accepted safety for use ... under medical supervision" mean, has been the subject of a previous scheduling proceeding involving the drug MDMA. In that proceeding, the Administrator did not adopt Judge Young's recommendation and defined both phrases to mean approved for marketing as safe and effective pursuant to the Food, Drug, and Cosmetic Act 51 FR 36552, October 8, 1986. The Administrator's decision was reviewed by the United States Court of Appeals for the First Circuit in *Grinspoon* v. *DEA*, 828 F.2d 881 (1987). The Court remanded the matter to the Administrator finding that his standard was too restrictive. The Court did not suggest a standard to be adopted and, instead, stated that "Congress has implicitly delegated to the Administrator the authority to interpret these portions of the CSA ..." *Grinspoon*, p. 892. The Administrator then published a revised final rule in which he listed several characteristics of a drug or other substance which has an "accepted medical use in treatment in the United States." 53 FR 5150, February 22, 1988. These characteristics are:

1. Scientifically determined and accepted knowledge of its chemistry;
2. The toxicology and pharmacology of the substance in animals;
3. Establishment of its effectiveness in humans through scientifically designed clinical trials;
4. General availability of the substance and information regarding the substance and its use;
5. Recognition of its clinical use in generally accepted pharmacopeia, medical references, journals or textbooks;
6. Specific indications for the treatment of recognized disorders;
7. Recognition of the use of the substance by organizations or associations of physicians; and
8. Recognition and use of the substance by a substantial segment of the medical practitioners in the United States.

These characteristics rely heavily on verifiable scientific data and acceptance by the medical community. These two areas go hand-in-hand, as aptly demonstrated by the record in this proceeding. Most physicians and organizations of physicians rely on scientific data in formulating their opinions regarding the safety and effectiveness of a drug and whether they will provide it for their patients. Many of the experts and organizations who concluded that marijuana did not have an "accepted medical use in treatment in the United States," stated that they reached this conclusion because of the lack of adequate scientific data to support the safety and efficacy of marijuana. The Administrator also notes that the Controlled Substances Act and its legislative history require him to consider scientific evidence in determining the schedule in which a drug should be placed. For example, the Controlled Substances Act at 21 U.S.C. 811(c) lists eight factors to be considered in evaluating the three scheduling criteria. Included among those factors are "scientific evidence of its pharmacological effect, if known" and "the state of current scientific knowledge regarding the drug or other substance." In addition, the Controlled Substances Act requires the Administrator to request a scientific and medical evaluation from the Secretary of Health and Human Services. The Administrator is then bound by the Secretary's recommendation as to scientific and medical matters. 21 U.S.C. 811(b). In this proceeding, the Assistant Secretary for Health has provided the Administrator with an extensive scientific and medical evaluation in which it was recommended that marijuana remain in Schedule I because there is insufficient scientific and medical evidence to conclude that marijuana is a safe and effective drug.

It is clear from the evidence presented in this proceeding that marijuana does not have the characteristics of a drug which has an "accepted medical use in treatment in the United States." Because of the complex composition of marijuana, containing over 400 separate constituents (many of which have not been tested) varying from plant to plant, the chemistry, toxicology and pharmacology of marijuana is not established. As discussed previously, the effectiveness of marijuana has not been documented in humans with scientifically-designed clinical trials. While many individuals have used marijuana and claim that it is effective in treating their ailments, these testimonials do not rise to the level of scientific evidence. Marijuana is available from the Federal Government to those researchers who obtain proper licensure. However, the evidence suggests that only small numbers of researchers and physicians have obtained marijuana for this purpose, and that some research programs sponsored by states had trouble getting physicians to participate. The vast majority of physicians do not accept marijuana as having a medical use. Marijuana is not recognized as medicine in generally accepted pharmacopeia, medical references, journals or textbooks. As evidenced by expert physician testimony and the statements of many professional medical and research organizations, marijuana is not accepted by organized medicine or a substantial segment of the physician population. The administrative law judge's conclusion that a "respectable minority" of physicians is all that is necessary to establish accepted medical use in treatment in the United States is preposterous. By placing a substance in Schedule II, the Administrator, and through him, the Federal Government, establishes a national standard for drug use. Using the same criteria as medical malpractice cases to determine a national standard of medical acceptance is untenable. It must be recognized that in every profession, including the medical and scientific community, there are those that deviate from the accepted practices of the profession. These deviations may be the beginning of new revolutionary treatments or they may be rejected as quackery. The opinions of those few physicians and scientists are not sufficient to create a finding of national acceptance. The Administrator feels that, in light of the potential risks of declaring a drug has an accepted medical use in treatment in the United States, he must adhere to the strict standard that was established in the MDMA proceeding. It is clear that the evidence conclusively demonstrates that marijuana does not have an accepted medical use in treatment in the United States or an accepted medical use with severe restrictions.

The Administrator's standard for "accepted safety for use . . . under medical supervision" was also stated in the second MDMA final rule published on February 22, 1988. 53 FR 5156. The tests for determining accepted safety of a drug were stated as follows:

> The first requirement in determining safety of a substance is that the chemistry of the substance must be known and reproducible. The next step is to conduct animal toxicity studies to show that the substance will not produce irreversible harm to organs at proposed human doses. Limited clinical trials may then be initiated, but they must be carefully controlled so that adverse effects can be monitored and studies terminated if necessary . . . safety in humans is evaluated as a risk/benefit ratio for a specific use. 53 FR 5158.

It is clear that marijuana cannot meet the criteria set forth above for safety under medical supervision. The chemistry of marijuana is not known and reproducible. The record supports a finding that marijuana plant material is variable from plant to plant. The quantities of the active constituents, the cannabinoids, vary considerably. In addition, the actions and potential risks of several of the cannabinoids have not been studied. Animal toxicity studies with marijuana show several potential risks or hazards of marijuana use, especially when the marijuana is smoked. These hazards have not been evaluated against the benefit or effectiveness of the drug. This is due, in great part, to the fact that marijuana's effectiveness in treating specific medical conditions has not been established by reliable scientific studies. Since a proper risk/benefit ratio cannot be made, the safety of marijuana for medical use cannot be demonstrated. Such lack of information is the basis for the majority of the medical and scientific community, and the Food and Drug Administration, concluding that marijuana does not have "accepted safety for use . . . under medical supervision." The Administrator, therefore, concludes that marijuana lacks "accepted safety for use . . . under medical supervision."

As a final note, the Administrator expresses his displeasure at the misleading accusations and conclusions leveled at the Government and communicated to the public by the pro-marijuana parties, specifically NORML and ACT. These two organizations have falsely raised the expectations of many seriously ill persons by claiming that marijuana has medical usefulness in treating emesis, glaucoma, spasticity and other illnesses. These statements have probably caused many people with serious diseases to experiment with marijuana to the detriment of their own health, without proper medical supervision, and without knowing about the serious side effects which smoking or ingesting marijuana may cause. These are not the Dark Ages. The Congress, as well as the medical community, has accepted that drugs should not be available to the public unless they are found by scientific studies to be effective and safe. To do otherwise is to jeopardize the American public, and take advantage of desperately ill people who will try anything to alleviate their suffering. The Administrator strongly urges the American public not to experiment with a potentially dangerous, mind-altering drug such as marijuana in an attempt to treat a serious illness or condition. Scientific and medical researchers are working tirelessly to develop treatments and drugs to treat these diseases and conditions. As expressed in the record, treatments for emesis (nausea and vomiting) associated with cancer chemotherapy have advanced significantly in the last ten years. Recent studies have shown an over 90 percent rate of effectiveness for the new antiemetic drugs and therapies. NORML and ACT have attempted to perpetrate a dangerous and cruel hoax on the American public by claiming marijuana has currently accepted medical uses. The Administrator again emphasizes that there is insufficient medical and scientific evidence to support a conclusion that marijuana has an accepted medical use for treatment of any condition, or that it is safe for use, even under medical supervision.

Based upon the evidence in the record and the conclusions discussed previously, the Administrator, under the authority vested in the Attorney General by section 201(a) of the Controlled Substances Act (21 U.S.C. 811(a)) and delegated to the Administrator of the Drug Enforcement Administration by regulations of the Department of Justice, 28 CFR 0.100(b), hereby orders that marijuana remain a Schedule I controlled substance as listed in 21 CFR 1308.11(d)(14).

This order is effective December 29, 1989.

Chapter 74

Medical Legalization of Marijuana

In the 1990s proponents of the medical use of marijuana raised the issue to a new intensity by successfully pursuing initiatives in several states to allow marijuana to be prescribed to patients. Of course, federal laws take precedence over state laws, and therefore these initiatives have little legal significance. Nevertheless, supporters hoped that federal enforcement officials would overlook the attempts to change marijuana policy.

Barry R. McCaffrey, director of the Office of National Drug Control Policy (ONDCP), took the position that if some medical value could be firmly established for cannabis, it ought to be made available to patients. However, he specifically excluded as a delivery method for the drug smoking marijuana cigarettes and pointed out that a prescribable form of tetrahydrocannabiniol (THC), the primary active ingredient of cannabis, had been available for some years. Clearly, McCaffrey was extremely concerned that the claimed medical benefit of cannabis was being used as a wedge to open the door to full legalization. In this 1996 statement he reiterates his opposition to the state initiatives and to a change in the Schedule I status of marijuana, and calls on the National Academy of Sciences for an up-to-date statement on the medical value of cannabis.

STATEMENT BY THE DIRECTOR OF THE OFFICE OF NATIONAL DRUG CONTROL POLICY

Barry R. McCaffrey

All of us in the Office of National Drug Control Policy thank the [Senate Judiciary] Committee for the opportunity to testify today about the dangerous implications of two ballot initiatives approved last month—Arizona's Proposition 200 and California's Proposition 215—on our national drug control policy. Having worked with the Congress and members of this committee for nine months to reduce drug use and its consequences in America, I share your concern that these two measures threaten to undermine our efforts to protect our children from dangerous psychoactive drugs. It would not be an exaggeration to say that the very essence of our National Drug Control Strategy—our resolve to prevent the 68 million Americans under the age of 18 from becoming a new generation of drug addicts—could be undone by these imprudent, unscientific, and flawed initiatives.

These drug legalizing initiatives are dangerous.

They make drug abuse more likely. Marijuana is a "gateway" drug. Perhaps the most definitive study about the relationship between smoking marijuana, "harder" drugs and subsequent substance abuse and dependency problems is the 1994 report *Cigarettes, Alcohol, Marijuana: Gateways to Illicit Drug Use* prepared by the Center on Addiction and Substance Abuse (CASA) at Columbia University. This report found that smoking, drinking and using marijuana lead a large number of children and adults to experimentation, regular use and addiction involving substances like cocaine. Some of the key findings of the 1994 report include:

Children who have used marijuana are more than 85 times likelier to use cocaine than children who have never used marijuana.

The younger an individual uses any gateway drug, the more often an individual uses any gateway drug, the more gateway drugs an individual uses, the likelier that individual is to experiment with cocaine, heroin, and other illicit drugs and the likelier that individual is to become a regular adult drug user and addict.

Sixty percent of children who smoke marijuana before age 15 move on to cocaine; only one-fifth of those who smoke marijuana after age 17 use cocaine.

They undermine safe medical procedures. The regulatory procedures overseen by the Food and Drug Administration have made the United States one of the safest countries in the world with regard to medications. A rigorous process of scientific testing is required before any drug is authorized for use by the public. Both the California and Arizona measures would bypass this proven approval process and set dangerous precedents. Scientific method, not electoral ploys, should be the basis by which we decide what is good public health policy.

They send the wrong message to our children. Coming at a time that marijuana use has doubled among our youth, these initiatives threaten to undermine our efforts to prevent drug use by our children. Labeling marijuana as "medicine" sends the wrong message to children that it is a safe substance. Drug use by youngsters is even more dangerous than adult drug abuse not only because of youthful immaturity but because of ongoing physical development. Growing children may be more susceptible to neurological damage from drugs than adults because their central nervous system is still developing. Our vulnerable youth should be receiving the undiluted message that marijuana is a dangerous drug; that using it is both detrimental to one's physical and mental health.

They threaten the national effort to protect our children from dangerous drugs.

Arizona's Proposition 200 seeks to okay medical use of heroin, LSD, and marijuana. Despite useful provisions such as creating a parents' commission on drug education and prevention, requiring persons who commit a violent crime while under the influence of drugs to serve 100% of their sentence, and providing for court-supervised treatment programs, the central purpose of the Arizona initiative is to strike at the very core of the system that protects all Americans from bogus medications and our children from dangerous drugs. Proposition 200 would allow doctors to prescribe drugs such as LSD, heroin, and marijuana in violation of federal law.

California's Proposition 215 would allow marijuana to be smoked without a prescription and without any age limits. This loosely-worded initiative would allow Californians to obtain and use marijuana with just a physician's recommendation for any illness for which marijuana ostensibly provides relief. It also seeks to exempt those who do so from criminal prosecution or sanction. It too is in violation of federal law.

They are part of a wider effort to undermine our National Drug Control Strategy. These ballot initiatives are not representative of Arizonan or Californian aspirations. They came about in large part because of the efforts of out-of-state legalizers who spent over $2 million in Arizona and California in support of both propositions. By comparison, in-state anti-drug organizations raised less than $100,000 to oppose these drug legalization initiatives. Pro-drug organizations see Arizona and California as the start of what will be a state-by-state effort to overturn the policies we have developed to turn back the tide of drugs and protect our children.

The initiatives are wrong: marijuana is not medicine.

No clinical evidence demonstrates that smoked marijuana is good medicine. The National Institutes of Health (NIH) has examined all existing clinical evidence from both animal and human research in order to determine the efficacy of smoked marijuana. It has concluded that there is no clinical evidence to suggest that smoked marijuana is superior to currently available therapies for glaucoma, weight loss and wasting associated with AIDS, nausea and vomiting associated with cancer chemotherapy, muscle spasticity associated with multiple sclerosis or intractable pain. Health and Human Services Secretary Donna E. Shalala recently reiterated this conclusion in her statement that:

> "There is no scientifically sound evidence that smoked marijuana is medically superior to currently available therapies, including an oral prescription medication containing the active ingredient in marijuana."

Marijuana as medicine has been widely rejected. Serious medical organizations as the American Medical Association, the American Cancer Society, the American Academy of Ophthalmology, the National Multiple Sclerosis Association oppose "medical marijuana" initiatives. The National Institutes of Health, i.e. the National Eye Institute, the National Cancer Institute, the National Institute for

Neurological Disorders and Stroke, the National Institute of Dental Research, and the National Institute on Allergy and Infectious Diseases concur that there is no scientific evidence to support the use of marijuana as a medicine. National leaders such as former Surgeon General C. Everett Koop condemned the Arizona and California propositions as did former Presidents Gerald Ford, Jimmy Carter, and George Bush. President Clinton and Vice President Gore are firm in their opposition to these legalization initiatives. The anecdotal information about the supposed medicinal benefits of marijuana offered by the backers of these proposals has not convinced those who base their conclusions on scientific fact.

Smoked marijuana is harmful. NIH scientists are also concerned that smoked marijuana could be harmful to people with impaired immune systems, particularly AIDS patients, who are susceptible to lung infections such as pneumocystis pneumonia. NIH is further concerned that smoking marijuana is significantly associated with bacterial pneumonia among HIV-infected individuals. Secretary Shalala shares these concerns. She has stated that:

> "There is clear scientific evidence that marijuana is harmful to one's brain, heart, and lungs. It limits learning, memory, perception, judgment, and complex motor skills like those needed to drive a vehicle. It has been shown to damage motivation and interest in one's goals and activities. It can cause chronic coughing and bronchitis. In short, it is a very dangerous drug."

Alternative therapies are adequate. The principal active ingredient in marijuana is delta-9-Tetrahydrocannabinol (THC). Purified, synthetic THC is known as dronabinol and is marketed under the trade name Marinol. Marinol is commercially available as an antiemetic for cancer patients and to treat anorexia associated with weight loss in patients with AIDS. Other drugs and treatments are available for the conditions smoked marijuana would ostensibly ameliorate, including 24 drugs approved by the FDA for glaucoma and many for nausea associated with cancer chemotherapy and chronic pain. Many of these drugs are considered superior to marijuana in effectiveness and safety. Because these oral medications are free of the contaminants found in smoked marijuana, they do not harm the lungs, heart, and immune system the way that smoked marijuana does.

It would be wrong to liberalize our drug control policies.

Marijuana remains the most commonly used illegal drug. Last August's National Household Survey on Drug Abuse (NHSDA), which measures drug use among the general population, found that marijuana remains the most common illicit drug in America. It was used by 77 percent of current drug users (9.8 million of the estimated 12.8 million Americans who used an illicit drug during the past month from the date of questioning). The NHSDA survey found that cocaine, the second most prevalent illegal drug, was used by 1.5 million Americans (or 0.7 percent of the population). The number of "past-month" drug users in America has declined by more than 10 million from a high of 23.3. million in 1985—

an extraordinary change in behavior. Since 1991 for example, there has been a 28 percent decline in the number of cocaine users.

More children are smoking marijuana at earlier ages. According to NHSDA, the rate of marijuana use by 12–17 year olds doubled between 1992 and 1995, going from 3.4 percent to 8.2 percent. The number of new marijuana users has been increasing since 1991, after a long-term decrease since 1975. The 1995 survey estimated that 2.3 million individuals used marijuana for the first time in 1994 (compare to 530,000 first-time cocaine users). The survey also found a steady decline in the mean age of first use of marijuana since 1987. The mean age of first use dropped from 17.8 years in 1987 to 16.3 years in 1994.

Increased prevalence of marijuana is showing up in our emergency rooms. The national Drug Abuse Warning Network (DAWN) survey which provides estimates of the number of drug-related hospital emergencies also reflected the increased prevalence of marijuana. The 1995 DAWN survey, which records information about drug users who go for treatment at hospital emergency rooms, showed that marijuana continued to be mentioned more often than any other substance in drug-related hospital emergencies. It also found that it was almost always mentioned in combination with some other substance. Between 1994 and 1995, marijuana-related episodes rose 17 percent from 40,183 episodes in 1994 to 47,069 in 1995. The 12 to 17-year-old cohort had the fewest number of marijuana-related episodes in 1995 but the highest growth in such episodes (increasing from 6,539 incidents in 1994 to 8,230 in 1995).

We cannot afford to send wrong messages to our children. The University of Michigan's excellent *Monitoring the Future* (MTF) annual survey of drug use among secondary school students suggests that today's youth have become more accepting of drug use. Recent surveys have demonstrated that our children's disapproval of drugs and perception of the risks associated with drug use have declined throughout this decade, beginning in 1990. As a result, our children are using alcohol, tobacco, and illegal drugs in greater numbers. We cannot afford to further erode youth attitudes towards drugs by allowing marijuana to be falsely depicted as a safe drug and as effective medicine. Indeed, we must act immediately to correct erroneous attitudes held by our youngsters so that fewer will use drugs. We cannot afford to return to the tragic levels of drug use among American youth that were prevalent in our recent past. ONDCP looks forward to the release of the 1996 *Monitoring the Future* survey. For the past 22 years this survey has been one of the most useful barometers of youth attitudes towards drugs.

How to respond to the challenge to the National Drug Control Strategy.

We all have a stake in this debate. What is at risk is not just the public health of Arizona and California, it is the well-being of our nation's youth. No American should stand idly by while a pro-drug minority systematically attacks the drug control system we have in place to protect our children and our citizens. More than 50 million Americans who used drugs in their youth subsequently rejected them. They understand the dangers marijuana and other illegal drugs pose. California, by virtue of its size and the energy and creativity of its citizens, has been a national trendsetter in many fields. We cannot afford to allow the Arizona and California mistake to become a drug-legalizing step to be repeated in the other 48 states of the union.

All Americans must know the truth about marijuana. The American people make the right decisions when they have accurate information. We must make the case against marijuana scientifically and dispassionately. Scare tactics will not work. We will need the active support and attention of the news media to educate all Americans about the nature of the drug abuse threat we face.

We should consider previous failed efforts to legalize marijuana. It's been tried before and it doesn't work. In 1975, the Alaska Supreme Court invalidated a portion of the state's criminal statute that prohibited the possession of marijuana. The court held in Ravin v. State that possession of marijuana by adults at home for personal use is constitutionally protected because Article I, section 22 of the Alaska constitution expressly guaranteed the people's "right to privacy." Between 1975 and 1991, possession of up to four ounces of marijuana by an adult was lawful in Alaska. However, the purchase, sale, and distribution of marijuana continued to be illegal. As a result of this de facto decriminalization, marijuana use among Alaskan teenagers doubled. In response, concerned citizens, especially the National Federation of Parents for Drug-Free Youth, sponsored an anti-drug referendum that was approved by voters in 1990. We should all learn from Alaska's experience: when drugs become more acceptable, as reflected in law, their use and abuse will increase—especially among our youth.

Marijuana should remain a "Schedule I" drug. Congress has prohibited the general availability of marijuana for use as medicine by placing it in Schedule I of the federal Controlled Substances Act. This federal law of 1970 schedules drugs according to their effects, medical use, and potential for abuse. Schedule I drugs are those defined as having "a high potential for abuse . . . no currently accepted medical use in treatment in the United States. . . . [and] a lack of accepted safety for use of the drug or other substance under medical supervision." Other Schedule I drugs include heroin, LSD, hashish, methaqualone, and designer drugs. The law further provides that, to place marijuana in Schedule II (as cocaine is) or in a lower schedule, there must be a finding that it has a "currently accepted medical use in treatment in the United States. . . ." The Department of Health and Human Services knows of no medical or scientific evidence that suggests a re-evaluation of the scheduling of marijuana under federal law. Drug Enforcement Administrator Thomas A. Constantine firmly opposes a rescheduling of marijuana "because there is no evidence that marijuana is an effective medical treatment." He also asks "at a time when our nation is looking for solutions to the problem of teenage drug use, how can we justify giving a stamp of approval to an illegal substance which has no legitimate medical use?"

Further research should be considered. Established federal policy is to treat research on the therapeutic use of marijuana the same as research on any other drug of abuse potential. Neither the FDA nor the National Institutes of Health are opposed to controlled and well-conducted clinical trials or studies for any drug including marijuana. The FDA would of course follow regulations governing the use in humans of investigational new drug substances and the requirements for approval of a new medication. As with all controlled substances, therapeutic marijuana would be subject to all of the stipulations of the U.S. Controlled Substance Act. This act requires an application be registered with the Drug Enforcement Administration. This is a process independent from FDA's review and would be required in order for clinical studies to proceed. There is presently no clinical evidence to suggest that marijuana leaf should be permitted to become the first U.S. Food and Drug Administration–approved medicine in the form of a cigarette.

We must continue to uphold our federal laws. Drug use and its consequences have gone down in large part because of the efforts of federal, state, and local law enforcement agencies. Upholding our laws has been and must continue to be an essential component of our drug control strategy. Deputy Assistant Attorney General Mary Lee Warren affirmed this principle to Los Angeles county Sheriff Brad Gates . . . "it should be clear, however, that, whatever the applicable state law, those who distribute or use marijuana act in violation of federal law and are therefore subject to federal prosecution."

ONDCP will continue to oppose drug legalizing initiatives. ONDCP was honored to support the efforts of concerned Arizonans and Californians in the months preceding the November election. Subsequent to the passage of both initiatives, ONDCP continues to energetically coordinate the federal, state and local responses to this threat to our National Drug Control Strategy. We appreciated the leadership of Senator Dianne Feinstein in California and Senator John Kyl in Arizona and the efforts of police chiefs, educators, and other public officials who stood for our children.

But Washington alone can't make a difference. Drug use and its consequences are reduced when the entire nation mobilizes not when hearings are held in Washington. Individual Americans, communities, and organizations concerned with our children's well-being have already reduced the number of drug users by some 10 million in the past decade. Treatment and prevention efforts by groups such as ASPIRA, Boys' and Girls' Clubs, D.A.R.E., P.R.I.D.E., Community Anti-Drug Coalitions of America, Lions, Elks, Kiwanis, Rotary, and other civic organizations, National Crime Prevention Council, National Family Partnership, National Family in Actions, National Association of State Alcohol and Drug Abuse

Directors, TASC, and the Partnership for a Drug-Free America have been critical components of this national drug control effort. Nevertheless, the attitudes and statements of national leaders are important. They set the tenor of the debate. They can also underscore to all Americans our collective seriousness about this problem.

Parents must constitute the first line of defense. Ultimately, America's drug abuse problem will only be minimized if parents, teachers, coaches, ministers, and counselors running youth-oriented organizations motivate young Americans to reject drugs. Youngsters and adolescents listen most to those they know, love and respect. The best weapons in the struggle against drugs may well be the kitchen table and the discussions about drugs that take place in our homes. We must ensure that parents are aware of the dangers drugs pose so that they can speak knowledgeably to their children about drugs. We should arm parents with the information they need. Children can be misled easily by myth, rumor, and the false notion that drugs are glamorous. For our children's sake, we need to act today. By doing so, we can reduce the number of addicted adults who will cause enormous damage to themselves and our society tomorrow.

Conclusion.

The Office of National Drug Control Policy strongly opposes Arizona's Proposition 200 and California's Proposition 215. The President has approved the coordinated opposition to these drug legalization measures by the Department of Justice and the DEA, the Department of Health and Human Services, and the Department of Education. The two measures are in contradiction of federal law. They both violate the medical-scientific process by which safe and effective medicines are evaluated for use by the medical community. Both measures are actually a quasi-legalization of dangerous drugs. We believe these two measures are unwise and represent a threat to our congressionally approved National Drug Control policy.

Chapter 75

Therapeutic Benefits and Health Risks of Marijuana

This 1999 Institute of Medicine report recommends more research on the cannabinoids, while noting the harmfulness of certain aspects of marijuana use.

MARIJUANA AND MEDICINE: ASSESSING THE SCIENCE BASE

Janet E. Joy, Stanley J. Watson, and John A. Benson

Public opinion on the medical value of marijuana has been sharply divided. Some dismiss medical marijuana as a hoax that exploits our natural compassion for the sick; others claim it is a uniquely soothing medicine that has been withheld from patients through regulations based on false claims. Proponents of both views cite "scientific evidence" to support their views and have expressed those views at the ballot box in recent state elections. In January 1997, the White House Office of National Drug Control Policy (ONDCP) asked the Institute of Medicine (IOM) to conduct a review of the scientific evidence to assess the potential health benefits and risks of marijuana and its constituent cannabinoids (see the Statement of Task [below]). That review began in August 1997 and culminates with this report.

The ONDCP request came in the wake of state "medical marijuana" initiatives. In November 1996, voters in California and Arizona passed referenda designed to permit the use of marijuana as medicine. Although Arizona's referendum was invalidated five months later, the referenda galvanized a national response. In November 1998, voters in six states (Alaska, Arizona, Colorado, Nevada, Oregon, and Washington) passed ballot initiatives in support of medical marijuana. (The Colorado vote will not count, however, because after the vote was taken a court ruling determined there had not been enough valid signatures to place the initiative on the ballot.)

Can marijuana relieve health problems? Is it safe for medical use? Those straightforward questions are embedded in a web of social concerns, most of which lie outside the scope of this report. Controversies concerning the nonmedical use of marijuana spill over into the medical marijuana debate and obscure the real state of scientific knowledge. In contrast with the many disagreements bearing on social issues, the study team found substantial consensus among experts in the relevant disciplines on the scientific evidence about potential medical uses of marijuana.

This report summarizes and analyzes what is known about the medical use of marijuana; it emphasizes evidence-based medicine (derived from knowledge and experience informed by rigorous scientific analysis), as opposed to belief-based medicine (derived from judgment, intuition, and beliefs untested by rigorous science).

Throughout this report, *marijuana* refers to unpurified plant substances, including leaves or flower tops whether consumed by ingestion or smoking. References to the "effects of marijuana" should be understood to include the composite effects of its various components; that is, the effects of tetrahydrocannabinol (THC), which is the primary psychoactive ingredient in marijuana, are included among its effects, but not all the effects of marijuana are necessarily due to THC. *Cannabinoids* are the group of compounds related to THC, whether found in the marijuana plant, in animals, or synthesized in chemistry laboratories.

Three focal concerns in evaluating the medical use of marijuana are:

1. Evaluation of the effects of isolated cannabinoids;
2. Evaluation of the risks associated with the medical use of marijuana; and
3. Evaluation of the use of smoked marijuana.

Effects of Isolated Cannabinoids

Cannabinoid Biology

Much has been learned since the 1982 IOM report *Marijuana and Health*. Although it was clear then that most of the effects of marijuana were due to its actions on the brain, there was little information about how THC acted on brain cells (neurons), which cells were affected by THC, or even what general areas of the brain were most affected by THC. In addition, too little was known about cannabinoid physiology to offer any scientific insights into the harmful or therapeutic effects of marijuana. That all changed with the identification and characterization of cannabinoid receptors in the 1980s and 1990s. During the past 16 years, science has advanced greatly and can tell us much more about the potential medical benefits of cannabinoids.

Conclusion: At this point, our knowledge about the biology of marijuana and cannabinoids allows us to make some general conclusions:

- Cannabinoids likely have a natural role in pain modulation, control of movement, and memory.

- The natural role of cannabinoids in immune systems is likely multi-faceted and remains unclear.
- The brain develops tolerance to cannabinoids.
- Animal research demonstrates the potential for dependence, but this potential is observed under a narrower range of conditions than with benzodiazepines, opiates, cocaine, or nicotine.
- Withdrawal symptoms can be observed in animals but appear to be mild compared to opiates or benzodiazepines, such as diazepam (Valium).

Conclusion: The different cannabinoid receptor types found in the body appear to play different roles in normal human physiology. In addition, some effects of cannabinoids appear to be independent of those receptors. The variety of mechanisms through which cannabinoids can influence human physiology underlies the variety of potential therapeutic uses for drugs that might act selectively on different cannabinoid systems.

Recommendation 1: Research should continue into the physiological effects of synthetic and plant-derived cannabinoids and the natural function of cannabinoids found in the body. Because different cannabinoids appear to have different effects, cannabinoid research should include, but not be restricted to, effects attributable to THC alone.

Efficacy of Cannabinoid Drugs

The accumulated data indicate a potential therapeutic value for cannabinoid drugs, particularly for symptoms such as pain relief, control of nausea and vomiting, and appetite stimulation. The therapeutic effects of cannabinoids are best established for THC, which is generally one of the two most abundant of the cannabinoids in marijuana. (Cannabidiol is generally the other most abundant cannabinoid.)

The effects of cannabinoids on the symptoms studied are generally modest, and in most cases there are more effective medications. However, people vary in their responses to medications, and there will likely always be a subpopulation of patients who do not respond well to other medications. The combination of cannabinoid drug effects (anxiety reduction, appetite stimulation, nausea reduction, and pain relief) suggests that cannabinoids would be moderately well suited for particular conditions, such as chemotherapy-induced nausea and vomiting and AIDS wasting.

Defined substances, such as purified cannabinoid compounds, are preferable to plant products, which are of variable and uncertain composition. Use of defined cannabinoids permits a more precise evaluation of their effects, whether in combination or alone. Medications that can maximize the desired effects of cannabinoids and minimize the undesired effects can very likely be identified.

Although most scientists who study cannabinoids agree that the pathways to cannabinoid drug development are clearly marked, there is no guarantee that the fruits of scientific research will be made available to the public for medical use. Cannabinoid-based drugs will only become available if public investment in cannabinoid drug research is sustained and if there is enough incentive for private enterprise to develop and market such drugs.

Conclusion: Scientific data indicate the potential therapeutic value of cannabinoid drugs, primarily THC, for pain relief, control of nausea and vomiting, and appetite stimulation; smoked marijuana, however, is a crude THC delivery system that also delivers harmful substances.

Recommendation 2: Clinical trials of cannabinoid drugs for symptom management should be conducted with the goal of developing rapid-onset, reliable, and safe delivery systems.

Influence of Psychological Effects on Therapeutic Effects

The psychological effects of THC and similar cannabinoids pose three issues for the therapeutic use of cannabinoid drugs. First, for some patients—particularly older patients with no previous marijuana experience—the psychological effects are disturbing. Those patients report experiencing unpleasant feelings and disorientation after being treated with THC, generally more severe for oral THC than for smoked marijuana. Second, for conditions such as movement disorders or nausea, in which anxiety exacerbates the symptoms, the antianxiety effects of cannabinoid drugs can influence symptoms indirectly. This can be beneficial or can create false impressions of the drug effect. Third, for cases in which symptoms are multifaceted, the combination of THC effects might provide a form of adjunctive therapy; for example, AIDS wasting patients would likely benefit from a medication that simultaneously reduces anxiety, pain, and nausea while stimulating appetite.

Conclusion: The psychological effects of cannabinoids, such as anxiety reduction, sedation, and euphoria can influence their potential therapeutic value. Those effects are potentially undesirable for certain patients and situations and beneficial for others. In addition, psychological effects can complicate the interpretation of other aspects of the drug's effect.

Recommendation 3: Psychological effects of cannabinoids such as anxiety reduction and sedation, which can influence medical benefits, should be evaluated in clinical trials.

Risks Associated with Medical Use of Marijuana

Psychological Risks

Marijuana is not a completely benign substance. It is a powerful drug with a variety of effects. However, except for the harms associated with smoking, the adverse effects of marijuana use are within the range of effects tolerated for other medications. The harmful effects to individuals from the perspective of possible medical use of marijuana are not necessarily the same as the harmful physical effects of drug abuse. When interpreting studies purporting to show the harmful effects of marijuana, it is important to keep in mind that the majority of those studies are based on *smoked* marijuana, and cannabinoid effects cannot be separated from the effects of inhaling smoke from burning plant material and contaminants.

For most people the primary adverse effect of *acute* marijuana use is diminished psychomotor performance. It is, therefore, inadvisable to operate any vehicle or potentially dangerous equipment while under the influence of marijuana, THC, or any cannabinoid drug with comparable effects. In addition, a minority of marijuana users experience dysphoria, or unpleasant feelings. Finally, the short-term immunosuppressive effects are not well established but, if they exist, are not likely great enough to preclude a legitimate medical use.

The *chronic* effects of marijuana are of greater concern for medical use and fall into two categories: the effects of chronic smoking and the effects of THC. Marijuana smoking is associated with abnormalities of cells lining the human respiratory tract. Marijuana smoke, like tobacco smoke, is associated with increased risk of cancer, lung damage, and poor pregnancy outcomes. Although cellular, genetic, and human studies all suggest that marijuana smoke is an important risk factor for the development of respiratory cancer, proof that habitual marijuana smoking does or does not cause cancer awaits the results of well-designed studies.

Conclusion: Numerous studies suggest that marijuana smoke is an important risk factor in the development of respiratory disease.

Recommendation 4: Studies to define the individual health risks of smoking marijuana should be conducted, particularly among populations in which marijuana use is prevalent.

Marijuana Dependence and Withdrawal

A second concern associated with chronic marijuana use is dependence on the psychoactive effects of THC. Although few marijuana users develop dependence, some do. Risk factors for marijuana dependence are similar to those for other forms of substance abuse. In particular, anti-social personality and conduct disorders are closely associated with substance abuse.

Conclusion: A distinctive marijuana withdrawal syndrome has been identified, but it is mild and short lived. The syndrome includes restlessness, irritability, mild agitation, insomnia, sleep disturbance, nausea, and cramping.

Marijuana as a "Gateway" Drug

Patterns in progression of drug use from adolescence to adulthood are strikingly regular. Because it is the most widely used illicit drug, marijuana is predictably the first illicit drug most people encounter. Not surprisingly, most users of other illicit drugs have used marijuana first. In fact, most drug users begin with alcohol and nicotine before marijuana—usually before they are of legal age.

In the sense that marijuana use typically precedes rather than follows initiation of other illicit drug use, it is indeed a "gateway" drug. But because underage smoking and alcohol use typically precede marijuana use, marijuana is not the most common, and is rarely the first, "gateway" to illicit drug use. There is no conclusive evidence that the drug effects of marijuana are causally linked to the subsequent abuse of other illicit drugs. An important caution is that data on drug use progression cannot be assumed to apply to the use of drugs for medical purposes. It does not follow from those data that if marijuana were available by prescription for medical use, the pattern of drug use would remain the same as seen in illicit use.

Finally, there is a broad social concern that sanctioning the medical use of marijuana might increase its use among the general population. At this point there are no convincing data to support this concern. The existing data are consistent with the idea that this would not be a problem if the medical use of marijuana were as closely regulated as other medications with abuse potential.

Conclusion: Present data on drug use progression neither support nor refute the suggestion that medical availability would increase drug abuse. However, this question is beyond the issues normally considered for medical uses of drugs and should not be a factor in evaluating the therapeutic potential of marijuana or cannabinoids.

Use of Smoked Marijuana

Because of the health risks associated with smoking, smoked marijuana should generally not be recommended for long-term medical use. Nonetheless, for certain patients, such as the terminally ill or those with debilitating symptoms, the long-term risks are not of great concern. Further, despite the legal, social, and health problems associated with smoking marijuana, it is widely used by certain patient groups.

Recommendation 5: Clinical trials of marijuana use for medical purposes should be conducted under the following limited circumstances: trials should involve only short-term marijuana use (less than six months), should be conducted in patients with conditions for which there is reasonable expectation of efficacy, should be approved by institutional review boards, and should collect data about efficacy.

The goal of clinical trials of smoked marijuana would not be to develop marijuana as a licensed drug but rather to serve as a first step toward the possible development of nonsmoked rapid-onset cannabinoid delivery systems. However, it will likely be many years before a safe and effective cannabinoid delivery system, such as an inhaler, is available for patients. In the meantime there are patients with debilitating symptoms for whom smoked marijuana might provide relief. The use of smoked marijuana for those patients should weigh both the expected efficacy of marijuana and ethical issues in patient care, including providing information about the known and suspected risks of smoked marijuana use.

Recommendation 6: Short-term use of smoked marijuana (less than six months) for patients with debilitating symptoms (such as intractable pain or vomiting) must meet the following conditions:

- failure of all approved medications to provide relief has been documented,
- the symptoms can reasonably be expected to be relieved by rapid-onset cannabinoid drugs,
- such treatment is administered under medical supervision in a manner that allows for assessment of treatment effectiveness, and
- involves an oversight strategy comparable to an institutional review board process that could provide guidance within 24 hours of a submission by a physician to provide marijuana to a patient for a specified use.

Until a nonsmoked rapid-onset cannabinoid drug delivery system becomes available, we acknowledge that there is no clear alternative for people suffering from *chronic* conditions that might be relieved by smoking marijuana, such as pain or AIDS wasting. One possible approach is to treat patients as *n*-of-1 clinical trials (single-patient trials), in which patients are fully informed of their status as experimental subjects using a harmful drug delivery system and in which their condition is closely monitored and documented under medical supervision, thereby increasing the knowledge base of the risks and benefits of marijuana use under such conditions.

Statement of Task

The study will assess what is currently known and not known about the medical use of marijuana. It will include a review of the science base regarding the mechanism of action of marijuana, an examination of the peer-reviewed scientific literature on the efficacy of therapeutic uses of marijuana, and the costs of using various forms of marijuana versus approved drugs for specific medical conditions (e.g., glaucoma, multiple sclerosis, wasting diseases, nausea, and pain).

The study will also include an evaluation of the acute and chronic effects of marijuana on health and behavior; a consideration of the adverse effects of marijuana use compared with approved drugs; an evaluation of the efficacy of different delivery systems for marijuana (e.g., inhalation vs. oral); an analysis of the data concerning marijuana as a gateway drug; and an examination of the possible differences in the effects of marijuana due to age and type of medical condition.

Specific issues

Specific issues to be addressed fall under three broad categories: science base, therapeutic use, and economics.

Science Base

- Review of the neuroscience related to marijuana, particularly the relevance of new studies on addiction and craving
- Review of the behavioral and social science base of marijuana use, particularly an assessment of the relative risk of progression to other drugs following marijuana use
- Review of the literature determining which chemical components of crude marijuana are responsible for possible therapeutic effects and for side effects

Therapeutic Use

- Evaluation of any conclusions on the medical use of marijuana drawn by other groups
- Efficacy and side effects of various delivery systems for marijuana compared to existing medications for glaucoma, wasting syndrome, pain, nausea, or other symptoms
- Differential effects of various forms of marijuana that relate to age or type of disease

Economics

- Costs of various forms of marijuana compared with costs of existing medications for glaucoma, wasting syndrome, pain, nausea, or other symptoms
- Assessment of differences between marijuana and existing medications in terms of access and availability

Recommendations

Recommendation 1: Research should continue into the physiological effects of synthetic and plant-derived cannabinoids and the natural function of cannabinoids found in the body. Because different cannabinoids appear to have different effects, cannabinoid research should include, but not be restricted to, effects attributable to THC alone.

Scientific data indicate the potential therapeutic value of cannabinoid drugs for pain relief, control of nausea and vomiting, and appetite stimulation. This value would be enhanced by a rapid onset of drug effect.

Recommendation 2: Clinical trials of cannabinoid drugs for symptom management should be conducted with the goal of developing rapid-onset, reliable, and safe delivery systems.

The psychological effects of cannabinoids are probably important determinants of their potential therapeutic value. They can influence symptoms indirectly which could create false impressions of the drug effect or be beneficial as a form of adjunctive therapy.

Recommendation 3: Psychological effects of cannabinoids such as anxiety reduction and sedation, which can influence medical benefits, should be evaluated in clinical trials.

Numerous studies suggest that marijuana smoke is an important risk factor in the development of respiratory diseases, but the data that could conclusively establish or refute this suspected link have not been collected.

Recommendation 4: Studies to define the individual health risks of smoking marijuana should be conducted, particularly among populations in which marijuana use is prevalent.

Because marijuana is a crude THC delivery system that also delivers harmful substances, smoked marijuana should generally not be recommended for medical use. Nonetheless, marijuana is widely used by certain patient groups, which raises both safety and efficacy issues.

Recommendation 5: Clinical trials of marijuana use for medical purposes should be conducted under the following limited circumstances: trials should involve only short-term marijuana use (less than six months), should be conducted in patients with conditions for which there is reasonable expectation of efficacy, should be approved by institutional review boards, and should collect data about efficacy.

If there is any future for marijuana as a medicine, it lies in its isolated components, the cannabinoids and their synthetic derivatives, isolated cannabinoids will provide more reliable effects than crude plant mixtures. Therefore, the purpose of clinical trials of smoked marijuana would not be to develop marijuana as a licensed drug but rather to serve as a first step toward the development of nonsmoked rapid-onset cannabinoid delivery systems.

Recommendation 6: Short-term use of smoked marijuana (less than six months) for patients with debilitating symptoms (such as intractable pain or vomiting) must meet the following conditions:

- failure of all approved medications to provide relief has been documented,
- the symptoms can reasonably be expected to be relieved by rapid-onset cannabinoid drugs,
- such treatment is administered under medical supervision in a manner that allows for assessment of treatment effectiveness, and
- involves an oversight strategy comparable to an institutional review board process that could provide guidance within 24 hours of a submission by a physician to provide marijuana to a patient for a specified use.

Scientific Research on Marijuana

The importance of the ONDCP's reply to the 1999 Institute of Medicine report is the implication that research support is likely to result from the exchange. Critics of the government's policies on marijuana often have said that the National Institutes of Health do little research on the drug, regardless of how often and for how long research has been recommended as the way to settle disagreements about its safety. Now it seems likely that intensive research will be conducted.

WHITE HOUSE DRUG POLICY OFFICE ISSUES STATEMENT ON INSTITUTE OF MEDICINE'S REPORT ON MARIJUANA AND MEDICINE

The White House Office of National Drug Policy (ONDCP) issued the following statement today following the release of the Institute of Medicine's report, *Marijuana and Medicine: Assessing the Science Base*:

We are delighted that science is the basis of the discussion of this issue, as it must be. In January 1997, ONDCP asked the Institute of Medicine to conduct a review of the scientific evidence for assessing the potential health benefits and risks of marijuana and its constituent cannabinoids. ONDCP believed that an objective and independent evaluation of research regarding the use of marijuana for medicinal purposes was appropriate given the ongoing debate about cannabis and its health effects.

The report released today by the Institute of Medicine represents the most thorough analysis to date of the relevant scientific literature. It summarizes recent advances in molecular and behavioral neuroscience, in particular newly elaborated systems of transmitters, receptors, and antagonists—all illuminating the physiological effects of cannabinoids. The Institute of Medicine has addressed all issues that ONDCP requested be examined, including: the science base and gaps in scientific knowledge regarding use of marijuana for medicinal purposes; scientific information about marijuana's mechanism of action; peer-reviewed literature on the uses of marijuana; and costs associated with various forms of the component chemical compounds in marijuana and other pharmacotherapies for special medical conditions. We thank the principal investigators, members of the advisory panel, biomedical and social scientists, patients, advocates, report reviewers, and all who supported the Institute of Medicine in developing this comprehensive report.

The report contains six specific recommendations that address:

1. Continued research into the physiological effects of cannabinoids.
2. Clinical trials of cannabinoid drugs for symptom management.
3. Evaluation of psychological effects of cannabinoids in clinical trials.
4. Studies of individual health risks in smoking marijuana.
5. Clinical trials of marijuana use under limited circumstances for medical purposes.
6. Short-term use of smoked marijuana under strict conditions for patients with debilitating symptoms.

These recommendations are supported by the following observations:

- Scientific data indicate the potential therapeutic value of cannabinoids for pain relief, control of nausea and vomiting, and appetite stimulation. This value would be enhanced by a rapid onset of drug effect.
- The psychological effects of cannabinoids are probably important determinants of their potential therapeutic value. They can influence symptoms indirectly, which could create false impressions of the drug effect or be beneficial as a form of adjunctive therapy.
- Numerous studies suggest that marijuana smoke is an important risk factor in the development of respiratory diseases, but the data that could conclusively establish or refute this suspected link have not been collected.
- Because marijuana is a crude THC delivery system that also delivers harmful substances, smoked marijuana generally should not be recommended for medical use. Nonetheless, marijuana is widely used by certain patient groups, which raises both safety and efficacy issues.
- If there is any future for marijuana as medicine, it lies in its isolated components—the cannabinoids and their synthetic derivatives. Isolated cannabinoids will provide more reliable effects than crude plant mixtures. Therefore, the purpose of clinical trials of smoked marijuana would not be to develop marijuana as a licensed drug, but such trials could be a first step towards the development of rapid-onset, nonsmoked cannabinoid delivery systems.

The Office of National Drug Control Policy appreciates the contributions made by the Institute of Medicine to the debate on the medical efficacy and safety of cannabinoids. We will carefully study the recommendations and conclusions contained in this report. We will continue to rely on the professional judgement of the Secretary of Health and Human Services, the Director of the National Institutes of Health, and the Surgeon General on all issues related to the medical value of marijuana and its constituent cannabinoids. We note in the report's conclusion that "the future of cannabinoid drugs lies not in smoked marijuana, but in chemically-defined drugs that act on the cannabinoid systems that are a natural component of human physiology." We look forward to the considered responses from our nation's public health officials to the interim solutions recommended by the report.

Sources and Permissions

Documents listed here are in the public domain unless otherwise specified. For permission to reprint selections from copyrighted works, the editor gratefully acknowledges the copyright holders.

Part I: Alcohol

E. H. Cherrington, *The Evolution of Prohibition in the United States of America: A Chronological History of the Liquor Problem and the Temperance Reform in the United States from the Earliest Settlements to the Consummation of National Prohibition* (Montclair, NJ, 1920), 16–17.

Stephen Hales, *A Friendly Admonition to the Drinkers of Brandy and other Distilled Spirituous Liquors* (1730), 3–23.

College of Physicians, London, Petition to the House of Commons, in *The Roll of the College of Physicians of London*, ed. William Munk, 2d ed., vol. 2., *1701–1800* (London: College of Physicians of London, 1878), 53.

College of Physicians, Philadelphia, "Deleterious Effects of Distilled Spirits on the Human System," in *American State Papers, Miscellaneous*, vol. 1 (Washington, D.C.: Gales and Seaton, 1832), 20–21.

Benjamin Rush, *An Inquiry into the Effects of Ardent Spirits upon the Human Body and Mind, with an Account of the Means of Preventing, and of the Remedies for Curing Them* (1785), reprinted in *Medical Inquiries and Observations* (New York: Arno, 1972), 153–76.

Lyman Beecher, *Six Sermons on the Nature, Occasions, Signs, Evils and Remedy of Intemperance*, 4th ed. (1828).

Eliza Jane Trimble Thompson, Her Two Daughters, and Frances E. Willard, *Hillsboro Crusade Sketches and Family Records* (Chicago: Woman's Temperance Publishing Association, 1896), 57–66, 73–80.

C. H. Mead, G. E. Chambers, and W. A. Williams, *Silver Tones: A New Temperance and Prohibition Song Book* (Warnock, OH: W. A. Williams, 1892), 17, 24.

W.C.T.U. Songs (Evanston, IL: National Woman's Christian Temperance Union Publishing House, 1928), 2–3.

William Thayer Smith, *Primer of Physiology and Hygiene: A Textbook for Primary Classes, with Special Reference to the Effects of Stimulants and Narcotics on the Human System* (New York: Ivison, Blakeman, Taylor, 1885), 72–73, 90–92, 124–27.

Katherine Lent Stevenson, "Frances E. Willard (February 17, 1903)," *Temperance Educational Quarterly* 1, no. 1 (January 1910).

Frances E. Willard, "Scientific Temperance Instruction in Public Schools: A Message of Fifteen Years Ago," *Temperance Educational Quarterly* 1, no. 2 (April 1910): 5–8.

Proceedings: Fifteenth National Convention of the Anti-Saloon League of America (Westerville, OH: American Issue Publishing, 1913), 14–17, vol. 15 (1912–13) of a series, Proceedings of the Annual Conventions of the Anti-Saloon League of America.

Testimony by Representatives Hobson and Mann in Debate over House Joint Resolution No. 168, *Congressional Record*, 63d Cong., 1914, 52, pt. 1:513–14, 530–31.

Richmond Pearson Hobson, *Alcohol and the Human Race* (New York: Fleming H. Revell, 1919), 7–10.

Charles R. Stockard, "The Influence of Alcoholism on the Offspring," *Proceedings of the Society for Experimental Biology and Medicine* 9 (1911–12): 71–72.

U.S. Constitution, amendment 18.

National Prohibition Act, 66th Cong., 1st sess., H.R. 6810, October 28, 1919.

Irving Fisher, *Prohibition at Its Worst* (New York: Macmillan, 1926), 1–14, 70–77, 82.

Charles S. Wood, ed., *A Criticism of National Prohibition* (Washington, D.C.: Association against the Prohibition Amendment, 1926), foreword, 9–15.

Pierre S. du Pont, Transcript of a speech given over the CBS radio network on June 9, 1932. Eleutherian Mills Historical Library, Hagley Museum and Library, Wilmington, Delaware. Reprinted by permission.

Franklin D. Roosevelt, "Campaign Address on Prohibition," Sea Girt, N.J., August 27, 1932, *Public Papers and Addresses of Franklin Delano Roosevelt*, comp. Samuel I. Rosenman, 13 vols. (New York: Random House 1938–50), vol. 1, *The Genesis of the New Deal, 1928–32*, pp. 684–91.

Franklin D. Roosevelt, "Campaign Address on the Federal Budget," Pittsburgh, October 19, 1932, *Public Papers and Addresses of Franklin Delano Roosevelt*, comp. Samuel I. Rosenman, 13 vols. (New York: Random House, 1938–50), vol. 1, *The Genesis of the New Deal, 1928–32*, pp. 810–11.

"Roosevelt Proclaims Repeal; Urges Temperance in Nation," *New York Times*, December 6, 1933, 1–2.

"The Twelve Steps of Alcoholics Anonymous," www.alcoholics-anonymous.org/english/E_FactFile/M-24_d6.html. The Twelve Steps are also reprinted in *Alcoholics Anonymous Comes of Age: A Brief History of A.A.* (New York: Alcoholics Anonymous Publishing, 1957), 50.

Howard W. Haggard and E. M. Jellinek, *Alcohol Explored* (Garden City, NY: Doubleday, Doran, 1942), 204–9. © 1942 by Doubleday and Co., a division of Random House, Inc. Reprinted by permission of Doubleday, a division of Random House, Inc.

Letter to the editor with response, *Journal of the American Medical Association* 120, no. 1 (September 5, 1942): 88. © 1942 by the American Medical Association.

E. M. Jellinek, *The Disease Concept of Alcoholism* (New Haven: College and University Press, 1960), 33–41. © 1960 by Alcohol Research Documentation, Inc., Rutgers Center of Alcohol Studies, Piscataway, NJ, 08854. Reprinted by permission.

Health Caution on Fetal Alcohol Syndrome, statement from HEW News Conference, June 1, 1977.

Anti-Drug Abuse Act of 1988, P.L. 100–690, 100th Cong., November 18, 1988.

Office for Substance Abuse Prevention, *Message and Material Review Process* (1989), 1, 9–13, and Editorial Guidelines.

Part II: Drugs

Section I: Opiates

Thomas De Quincey, *Confessions of an English Opium-Eater* (1822), 187–89, 191–93.

Rudolf Schmitz, "Friedrich Wilhelm Sertürner, and the Discovery of Morphine," *Pharmacy in History* 27, no. 2 (1985): 62. Reprinted by permission of Pharmacy in History, quarterly journal of the American Institute of the History of Pharmacy.

Norman Howard-Jones, "A Critical Study of the Origins and Early Development of Hypodermic Medication," *Journal of the History of Medicine and Allied Sciences* 2 (spring 1947): 201–2, 208–14, 232–34, 244–45. Reprinted by permission of Oxford University Press.

The Medical and Surgical History of the Civil War (Wilmington, NJ: Broadfoot, 1991), vol. 6, 547–48. © 1991 by Broadfoot Publishing. Reprinted by permission.

F. E. Oliver, "The Use and Abuse of Opium," in Massachusetts State Board of Health, *Third Annual Report* (Boston: Wright and Potter State Printer, 1872), 162–77.

George Wood, *A Treatise on Therapeutics and Pharmacology or Materia Medica*, 3d ed., 2 vols. (Philadelphia: Lippincott, 1868), 711–14, 725–28.

Letter, *Journal of Mental Science* (London), January 1889, 546–50.

Clifford Allbutt, "On the Abuse of Hypodermic Injections of Morphia," *Practitioner* 3 (1870): 327–30.

Alonzo Calkins, *Opium and the Opium-Appetite* (Philadelphia: Lippincott, 1871), 54–55.

Edward Levinstein, *Morbid Craving for Morphia*, trans. C. Harrer (London: Smith, Elder, 1878), 3–5.

Norman Kerr, *Inebriety, or Narcomania: Its Etiology, Pathology, Treatment and Jurisprudence* (London: Lewis, 1894), 111–17.

Charles W. Carter, "What Is the Morphine Disease?" *Journal of Inebriety* 30 (spring 1908): 28–33.

William Osler, *The Principles and Practices of Medicine* (Edinburgh: Young J. Pentland, 1894), 1005–7.

Alexander Lambert, "The Obliteration of the Craving for Narcotics," *Journal of the American Medical Association*, 53, no. 13 (September 25, 1909): 985–89.

Eugene O'Neill, *Long Day's Journey into Night* (New Haven: Yale University Press, 1955), 138–41. © 1955 by Yale University Press. Reprinted by permission of Yale University, owner of literary rights.

Harrison Act, P.L. 223, 63rd Cong., December 17, 1914.

United States v. Doremus, 249 U.S. 86 (1919).

Webb et al. v. United States, 249 U.S. 96 (1919).

Sara Graham-Mulhall, *Opium: The Demon Flower* (New York: Montrose, 1926), 162–65.

Ernest Bishop, *The Narcotic Drug Problem* (New York: Macmillan, 1920), 1–10.

Richmond P. Hobson, *Mankind's Greatest Affliction and Gravest Menace* (Los Angeles: International Narcotic Education Association, 1928): pamphlet. Reprinted in *Narcotic Education* 1 (April 1928): 51–54.

Boggs Act, P.L. 255, 82nd Cong., November 2, 1951.

Narcotic Control Act of 1956, P.L. 728, 84th Cong., July 18, 1956.

Drug Addiction: Crime or Disease? Interim and Final Reports of the Joint Committee of the American Bar Association and the American Medical Association on Narcotic Drugs (Bloomington: Indiana University Press, 1961), 159–66.

Task Force on Narcotics and Drug Abuse, President's Commission on Law Enforcement and Administration of Justice, *Task Force Report: Narcotics and Drug Abuse* (Washington, D.C.: GPO, 1967), 1, 6, 8, 9–20.

National Commission on Marihuana and Drug Abuse, *Drug Use in America: Problem in Perspective* (Washington, D.C.: GPO, 1973), 1–5.

Drug Abuse Control Amendments of 1965, P.L. 89–74, 89th Cong., July 15, 1965.

Comprehensive Drug Abuse Prevention and Control Act of 1970, P.L. 91–513, 91st Cong., October 27, 1970.

Anti–Drug Abuse Act of 1986, P.L. 99–570, 99th Cong., October 27, 1986.
Anti–Drug Abuse Act of 1988, P.L. 100–690, 100th Cong., November 18, 1988.

Section II: Cocaine

"A New Alkaloid in Coca," *American Journal of Pharmacy* 32 (September 1860): 450–51.

G. Archie Stockwell, "Erythroxylon Coca," *Boston Medical and Surgical Journal* 96 (1877): 399, 401–4.

William A. Hammond, "Coca—Its Preparations and Their Therapeutical Qualities, with Some Remarks on the So-Called Cocaine Habit," *Virginia Medical Monthly*, November 1887, 598–610.

Sigmund Freud, "Über Coca," in *Cocaine Papers by Sigmund Freud*, ed. Robert Byck (New York: Stonehill, 1974), 54–56, 58–59, 61, 63–65, 69–73. Translated by Steven A. Edminster, additions to the translation by Frederick C. Redlich. © 1963 by Sigmund Freud Copyrights, Ltd., London. Reprinted by permission.

J. B. Mattison, "Cocaine Dosage and Cocaine Addiction," *Lancet*, May 21, 1887, 1024–26.

"The Treatment of Chronic Cocaine Poisoning, or Cocaino-Mania," *Journal of Inebriety* 21 (1898): 195–98.

Connecticut State Medical Society, "Report of the Committee on Matters of Professional Interest in the State," *Proceedings of the Connecticut Medical Society*, 1894, 254–57, 259–60, 263–64.

"The Cocain Habit," *Journal of the American Medical Association* 34 (June 1900): 1637.

"The Cocain Habit," *Journal of the American Medical Association* 36 (February 1901): 330.

Edward Huntington Williams, "The Drug-Habit Menace in the South," *Medical Record*, February 7, 1914, 247–49.

Hamilton Wright, "Report on the International Opium Commission and on the Opium Problem as Seen within the United States and Its Possessions," Senate Doc. no. 377, 61st Cong., 2d sess., Feb. 21, 1910, 11, 32–33, 48–51, 58–62.

"Report of the Mayor's Committee on Drug Addiction," *American Journal of Psychiatry* 10 (1930): 438, 470, 453–54.

Domestic Council on Drug Abuse Task Force, *White Paper on Drug Abuse* (Washington, D.C.: GPO, 1975), 24–25.

Richard Steele et al., "The Cocaine Scene," *Newsweek*, May 30, 1977, 20–22, 25. © Newsweek Inc., all rights reserved. Reprinted by permission.

"Coke Kills," *Newsweek*, December 29, 1986, 52. © Newsweek, Inc., all rights reserved. Reprinted by permission.

Larry Martz et al., "Trying to Say 'No,'" *Newsweek*, August 11, 1986, 14–18. © Newsweek, Inc., all rights reserved. Reprinted by permission.

"Reagan: Drugs Are the 'No. 1' Problem," *Newsweek*, August 11, 1986, 18. © Newsweek, Inc., all rights reserved. Reprinted by permission.

Testimony of Dr. Robert Byck, in *Cocaine: A Major Drug Issue of the Seventies, Hearings before the Select Committee on Narcotics Abuse and Control*, 96th Cong., 1st sess., July 24, 26, October 10, 1979.

Section III: Cannabis

Fitz Hugh Ludlow, *The Hasheesh Eater: Being Passages from the Life of a Pythagorean* (New York, 1857), 18–28.

Victor Robinson, *An Essay on Hasheesh* (New York: Medical Review of Reviews, 1912), 34–35, 40–41, 29–31.

Committee of Revision, *The Pharmacopoeia of the United States of America*, 11th ed. (Easton, PA: Mack, 1936), 104.

U.S. Department of Agriculture, *Drug Plants under Cultivation: Drug Bulletin 663* (Washington, D.C.: Bureau of Plant Industry, 1920), 24–25.

Milton "Mezz" Mezzrow and Bernard Wolfe, *Really the Blues* (New York: Citadel, 1946), 71–77, 213–16. © 1946 by Citadel Press, all rights reserved. Reprinted by permission of Citadel Press/Kensington Publishing Corp., www.kensingtonbooks.com.

Meyer Berger, "Tea for a Viper," *New Yorker*, March 12, 1938, 36–41.

Federal Bureau of Narcotics, *Report by the Government of the United States of America for the Calendar Year Ended December 31, 1931: On the Traffic in Opium and Other Dangerous Drugs* (Washington, D.C.: GPO, 1932), 49–50.

Federal Bureau of Narcotics, *Report by the Government of the United States of America for the Calendar Year Ended December 31, 1933: On the Traffic in Opium and Other Dangerous Drugs* (Washington, D.C.: GPO, 1934), 35–36.

Federal Bureau of Narcotics, *Report by the Government of the United States of America for the Calendar Year Ended December 31, 1937: On the Traffic in Opium and Other Dangerous Drugs* (Washington, D.C.: GPO), 53–58.

Marihuana Tax Act of 1937, P.L. 238, 75th Cong., August 2, 1937.

H. J. Anslinger with Courtney Ryley Cooper, "Marihuana: Assassin of Youth," *American Magazine*, July 1937, 18–19, 150–53.

Walter Bromberg, "Marihuana: A Psychiatric Study," *Journal of the American Medical Association* 113, no. 1 (July 1, 1939): 4–5, 7–12.

Mayor's Committee on Marihuana, *The Marihuana Problem in the City of New York: Sociological, Medical, Psychological and Pharmacological Studies* (Metuchen, NJ: Scarecrow Reprint Co., 1973 [1944]), 213–20.

"Marihuana Problems," *Journal of the American Medical Association* 127, no. 17 (April 28, 1945): 1129. © 1945 by the American Medical Association. Reprinted by permission.

National Commission on Marihuana and Drug Abuse, *Marijuana: A Signal of Misunderstanding* (Washington, D.C.: GPO, 1972), 135–40, 142–55, 161–67.

Institute of Medicine. *Report on the Health-Related Effects of Marijuana* (Washington, D.C.: GPO, 1982).

U.S. Department of Justice, Drug Enforcement Administration, In the Matter of Marijuana Rescheduling Petition (Docket no. 86–22), *Opinion and Recommended Ruling, Findings of Fact, Conclusions of Law and Decision of Administrative Law Judge*, September 6, 1988.

U.S. Department of Justice, Drug Enforcement Administration, "Marijuana Scheduling Petition; Denial of Petition," *Federal Register* 54, no. 249 (December 29, 1989): 53767–84.

Statement by General Barry R. McCaffrey, Director, Office of National Drug Control Policy, submitted for the record to the Senate Committee on the Judiciary, December 2, 1996. Available at www.whitehousedrugpolicy.gov/news/testimony/dope.html.

Janet E. Joy, Stanley J. Watson, and John A. Benson, eds., *Marijuana and Medicine: Assessing the Science Base* (Washington, D.C.: Institute of Medicine, 1999), 1–11.

"White House Drug Policy Office Issues Statement on Institute of Medicine's Report on Marijuana and Medicine," March 17, 1999. Available at www.whitehousedrugpolicy.gov/news/press/1999/031799.html.

Index

About the Editor

David F. Musto, M.D., is a professor of the history of medicine and professor of child psychiatry at the Yale School of Medicine and lecturer in history and American studies at Yale University. He is the author of *The American Disease: Origins of Narcotic Control.*

Printed in the USA
CPSIA information can be obtained
at www.ICGtesting.com
JSHW051118191223
53978JS00008B/16

9 780814 756638